THE

PARISH REGISTER

OF

Christ Church, Middlesex County, Va.

FROM

1653 to 1812

CLEARFIELD

Originally Published by
The National Society of the Colonial Dames of America
in the State of Virginia
Richmond, 1897

Reprinted
Genealogical Publishing Co., Inc.
Baltimore, 1964

Baltimore, 1975

Reprinted for
Clearfield Company, Inc. by
Genealogical Publishing Co., Inc.
Baltimore, Maryland
1990, 1997

Library of Congress Catalogue Card Number 64-20864
International Standard Book Number 0-8063-0073-6

Made in the United States of America

INTRODUCTION.

The section in Virginia comprised within the present county of Middlesex, was at first included in Lancaster county and parish. Some time before 1666 that parish was divided into two portions, separated by the Rappahanhock river, and the new parishes were named Lancaster and Pyanketank. In 1666 they were reunited under the name of Lancaster, but a few years later again was separated and acquired the organization which they retained through the Colonial period, as Christ Church, Lancaster, and Christ Church, Middlesex. The register of the latter is printed in this book.

The vestry-book of Christ Church, Middlesex, beginning in 1663 and ending in 1767, which is now preserved at the Episcopal Theological Seminary, Alexander county, Va., shows that a Mr. Morris was minister from 1663 to 1666. He was succeeded in 1668 by Rev. John Shepherd, who at the time of his death in 1683, is described by his vestry as "our late worthy minister." In November of that year Major-General Robert Smith, one of the vestry, who had been commissioned to procure a minister, returned from England, bringing with him Rev. Duell Pead. This clergyman served the parish acceptably for seven years and then returned to England, where, it is believed, he became rector of Newland, St. Lawrence, Essex. Rev. Mathew Lidford, Mr. Pead's successor in 1692, only lived about a year, and was in turn followed by Rev. Samuel Gray, a most unworthy minister, who was tried for his life, for causing the death of one of his slaves by a severe whipping. This, it is presumed, caused his resignation or expulsion, as in 1699 the minister was Rev. Robert Yates, who continued until 1703 or 1704, when he returned to England in ill health. He appears to have been esteemed by his vestry, who continued his salary for some time in hope of his return. In 1704 he was succeeded by his son Bartholomew Yates, B. A., Brasenose College, Oxford, 1698, who continued to be the much loved and trusted incumbent, until his death on July 26, 1734. He was also a visitor and professor of William and Mary College. A tomb erected by his parishioners at Christ Church, bears testimony to the high regard in which he was held. Rev. John Klug succeeded to Mr. Yates in 1767, and, it is believed, continued until his death in 1795. He is represented to have been a pious and efficient minister.

The church now standing in the parish was built in 1712, and succeeded one, on the same spot, which was ordered to be built in 1666.

Bishop Meade says of the parish: "This being an early settlement, lying on one of the finest rivers in Virginia, and near the bay, we might expect to find here many of the ancestors of some of the most respectable families of Virginia. As the vestrymen were chosen from the leading citizens of each parish, we shall give, in the order in which they appear on the vestry-book for more than a hundred years, a full list of all who served the parish in that capacity. Those who have any acquaintance with the Virginia families, and with many who have dispersed themselves throughout the West and South, will readily trace great numbers to the parish of which we are treating. For the sake of brevity, we shall only mention the surnames. Corbin, Perrott, Chewning, Potter, Vause, Weeks, Willis, Cock, Curtis, Smith, Dudley, Thacker, Skipwith, Beverley, Wormeley, Jones, Miller, Scarborough, Woodley, Whitaker, Robinson, Warwick, Gordon, Chichester, Midge, Churchill, Burnham, Wormeley, 2d; Kemp, Smith, 2d; Cary, Dudley, 2d; Smith, 3d; Daniel, Price, Mann, Seager, Vause, 2d; Cock, 2d; Cant, Skipwith, 2d; Wormeley, 3d; Thacker, 2d; Grymes, Beverley, 2d; Kilbee, Kemp, 2d; Corbin, 2d; Robinson, 2d; Walker, Jones, 2d; Wormeley, 4th, Stanard, Churchill, 2d; Robinson, 3d; Walker, 2d; Robinson, 4th; Harden, Wormeley, 5th; Corbin, 3d; Smith, 4th; Grymes, 2d; Stanard, 2d; Reid, Carter, 2d; Elliott, Miles, Montague, Grymes, 3d; Nelson, Smith, 4th."

The register here printed was, together with the vestry-book, among those collected by Bishop Meade, and deposited in the Episcopal Theological Seminary, where it now is. The Virginia Society of Colonial Dames is indebted to the trustees of the Seminary for permission to bring the register to Richmond for the purpose of copying.

The copy here printed was made by one of the Virginia Dames, Mrs. Sally Nelson Robins, of Richmond, and compared with the original, and verified by Messrs. Edward W. James and William G. Stanard.

PARISH REGISTER,

MIDDLESEX COUNTY, VIRGINIA.

Novemb^r: the 19th. 1663.

At a Vestry held for the parish of Lancaster at the House of Mr Henry Corbin &c.

Whereas it doth appeare that there is an Act of Assembly Injoyning all Parishes to keep a perfect Register of all Christenings, Burialls and marriages, as by the said act will more at large appeare, In obedience whereunto we the Vestry of Lancaster parish being the Major part of us now mett together Doe hereby Authorize and appoint Mr Henry Corbin to keepe a true Register of Every thing Required by the Said Act for this Ensuing yeare and it is further agreed that Every Vestry man shall take the Charge of the said Register for a whole yeare, if a Clerk be not provided in the Interim.

CUTHBERT POTTER
ABRAHAM WEEKES
THOMAS WILLIS
ROBERT CHOWNING
JOHN VAUSE
HENRY CORBIN
RICHARD PERROTT.

Register of Christ Church Parish.

BURIALLS 1685.

Madam ffrances Wormeley the wife of Coll° Christop' Wormeley Esq', Departed this Life on the 25th of May 1685 & was buried at home. In theire Garden the next Day following being 26th of May 1685.

Mrs Martha Boodle Departed this Life 10th and was buried 12th July 1685.

Thomas Allen (Smith of this County) Departed this Life 10th of Augt 1685 being the same Day whereon he was Married to Lucy Blake & Dyed before night and was buried ye next day following.

Mr John Batcheldor Departed this Life 4th Xemb & was Buried at home the 7th Xemb 1685.

Anthony Barlow Departed this Life 12th Xemb. and was buried at home ye 15th Xemb. 1685.

Matthew Bentley Departed this Life 8th of January & was buried 11th of January 1685.

Mrs Agatha Robinson wife of Mr Christop^r Robinson Departed this Life 25th of January 168⅚ & was buried 27th January 168⅚.

John Dawd, Cooper & Servant to Majo^r Robert Beverley Departed this Life 17th of Septemb 1686.

Thomas Beverley the Sone of Majo^r Robert Beverley and Madam Katherine his Wife Departed this Life 20th of September 1686 and was buried at the Lower Chap^{ll} In the Ile 22th September 1686.

Rachell Dewd the Wife of Richard Dewd Departed this Life ye 29th of July 1681. and was buried in the Church Yard of our Lower Chap^{ll} ye 30th July 1681.

Elizabeth Poticarie Servt Tho Dudley died ye po Sep^t & was buried 2th 1681.

William Allen Departed this Life 4th of Septemb 1681 & was buried in ye Lower Chap^{ll} Church yard ye next day following being 5th 9^{br} 1681.

William Watson Departed this Life 6th Xemb. & was buried in the Church yard of the great Church 8th of Xemb. — 1681.

Henry Stalker Departed this Life 12th Xemb. 1681 & was buried next day.

Robert Stephens Departed this Life 21th of Jan'y 1682 & buried 23th following.

Henry Chichley Kt. & his Maj^{ts} Deputy Governor of Virginia Departed this Life on Munday morning Early being 5th of ffebuary 168¾ & was Buried in Christ Church Chancell Middlesex County neare the Comunion Table 9th of ffebuary 168¾ following &c.

John Hunten Dyed at Majo' Beverley's & was buried there 23th of febr. 168¾.

M' John Sheppard, Minister of this parish Departed this Life 30th of June 1683 about 5 or 6 of ye Clock afternoone & was buried in ye Great Church at y⁰ head of ye Ile on ye Second day of July following &c.

Elizabeth Stamper y⁰ Wife of Jno. Stamper depar^{ td} this Life 29th Aprill 1683.

Thomas Williams y⁰ husband of Bridg^t depar^{ td} this Life 20th Xemb 1683 and was buried in ye Great Churchyard 23th Xemb. 1683.

John Smith Servant to Coll⁰ Ch^r Wormeley Esqr Departed this Life 10th March & was buried the 11th of March 168¾.

Capt Henry Creyke Departed this Life p⁰ June & buried at home 6th June 1684.

Christopher . . . . er Departed this Life 26th June & was buried yt very night.

Amie Orphan Departed this Life 26th June & was buried y⁰ p⁰ July 1684.

John Slanter Departed this Life y⁰ 18th & was buried 19th of August 1684.

William Young Departed this Life 26th & was buried 28th of Sept at Ed. Dockey.

Mrs Mary Bentley the wife of Mr Matthew Bentley Departed this Life ye 27th of Septemb. & was buried 29th of Septemb. 1684.

Mr Humphrey Jones Departed this Life 16th & was buried 20th of Octob. 1684.

Margaret Ashton Departed this Life 24th & was Buried 28th of March 1684.

The Honerable Lady Madam Katherine Wormeley Wife to the Honble Ralph Wormley Esqr Departed this Life 17th of May 1685 & was buried in the Chancell of the Great Church betweene ye Honble * * * * * Chickley & * * *

CHRISTENINGS &c.

Mary Daughter of John and Mary Batcheldor bap^{ts} Sept. 12th 1653.
Sarah Daught^r of Jno. and Mary Batcheldor born
Rebecca Daughter of Jno. & Mary Batcheld^r was borne Octo^{br} 2th 1658.
William Sone of Jno. & Mary Batcheld^r was Born July 22th 1667 of a Munday betweene one and two of Clock.
Thomas Sone of Richard & Marg^t Williams Bap^{ts} Sept 22th 1670.
Sarah Daughter of Jno. & Jane Watts was Bap^{ts} Octob^r 30th 1670.
Sarah Daughter of James & Mary Hopkins bap^{ts} October 30th 1670.
Ann Daughter of Rich^d and Anne Robinson bap^{ts} No^{vr} 20th 1670.
William Sone of W^m and Eliz^a Wood was bap^{ts} July 17th 1670.
Sarah Williams was Baptized the 5th of March 1670.
Alice the Daughter of Tho. and Marg^t Weatherby bap^{ts} March 20th 1670.
Clem^t the Sone of Mary Sanders was Christened the 16th of Ap^{rll} 1671.
Aliz^a Daughter of Daniell & Mary Banbry was Christ^d Ap^{rll} 16th 1671.

William the Sone ffrances Porter and Lucy the Daughter of John and Jone Blake was Christened the 7th of May 1671.
Ann the Daughter of Tho. and Eliz^a Conaway Christn^d May 20th 1671.
Micoll the Daught^r of Jno. and Jone Blake was born Sept. 13th 1658.
Sarah Daughter of the above said was born Aprill 8th 1660.
George the sone of the ab. sd. the 8th of March, 1661.
Dianah Daughter of the ab. sd. borne 11th January 1663.
Eliz^a Daughter of ye ab. sd. was born 19th Sept. 1664.
Jone the Da^{tr} of the ab. sd. was born 10th of No^{br} 1664.
Lucy the D^r of the ab. sd. was Christn^d the 7th of May 16**.
Being the age of seven Children of John and Jone Blake above said &c.

1671 &c. CHRISTININGS &c.

Jone the Daughter of Thomas and Grace Shoare and Amey the Daughter of Ralph and Marg^t Smith were bap^{tz} Augt 20th 1671.
Andrew the Sone of William and Presilla Watson born ffeb^r 23th 1669.
Erasmus the son of John and Barbara Allin Christn^d Sept 10th 1671.
Sarah Daughter of Richard and Marg^t Williams Christn^d Octo^{br} 22th 1671.
Mary Daughter of David and Joane Allinson Christn^d Octo^{br} 29th 1671.
Bryan the son of Bryan and Hannah Harkins born ffeb^r 20th 1663.
Cornelius the sone of ye afores'd Bryan & Hannah Harkins was born August the 25th 1666.
William the sone of Wm. and Presilla Watson was born Jan^r 17th 1671.
Cussandra ye Daughter of Jno. Sutton & Eliz^a Ellis Christn^d Decem^{br} 25th 1671.
ffrances Daughter of ffrances and Erasmus Withers Chr^d March 17th 1671.
Edward the sone of Edward Michaell Christened April 28th 1672.
Edward the son of Thomas Williams and Bridg^t Catt May 19th 1672.

BURIALLS Vizt.

Richard Rumiger Servant to Mr. Robert Chowning Drowned in his Creek Decemb^r the 12th 1660.
Alice Daughter of Tho. and Mary Tugwell Dyed & was buried November the 22th 1660.
John Wilch dyed and was Buried 30th 1660.
Thomas Butterfield M^r. Boswel's Servant Dyed Decemb^r 5th 1660.
Arthur   M^r. Vaus man Dyed Jan^r 1st 166$^?_?$.
William Owen Servt to Henry Corbin Dyed July 13th 1661.
Matthew Booker Servant to Mr Jno. Vause was drowned May 26th 1661.
James Poynter Serv't to Mr Perrott Dyed Augst 28th 1661.
William Green Servant to Mr Perrott Dyed Augst 25th 1661.
Richard Travars Servant to Mr Perrott Dyed Augst 30th 1661.
Rich'd Woodcock Servant to Mr Boswell Dyed Octo^{br} 10th 1661.
Alice Ripinge Servant to M^r. Boswell Dyed July 20th 1661.

Mr Shereefes Servant to Mr Corbin Dyed Octo^{br} 11th 1661.
John Gibbor Servant to Mr Corbin Dyed Decemb^{br} 2th 1661.
John Ballard Servant to Mr Christo^r Withnell Dyed ffeb^r 20th 1661.
John Crispe Servant to Mr Batcheldor Dyed Septemb^r 30th 1661.
John Thomas Servant to Mr Thacker, Dyed March 5th, 1662.
Hugh Williams Servant to Mr Curtis Dyed July   th
Dorcas Stamper the wife of John Stamper Dyed July 16th 1667.
John Smyth Husband to Marg^t Smyth Dyed Decem^{br} 16th 1669.
Capt. Wormely's Wife's Son Aylmer Dyed the 16th and was Buried the 18th of January In the Chancell near the South end of ye Communion Table 1669.
Mary wife to Tho. Reenes and her Sone were Buried in ye Alley Novemb^r 27th (neare her Pew) 1669.
William Hill was Buried in the Church Yard ffebruary 12th 1669.
Edward Thompson was Buried in the Entering into ye Chancell May 21th 167 .

CHRISTENINGS Viz^t.

Lettice Corbin the Daughter of Henry Corbin Esqr was born and Christened the 25th Day of   1657.
Alice Corbin Daughter of Henry Corbin Esqr was borne halfe an houre after five o'clock in the evening Feby 14th 1660.
Robert Chowning Sone of Robert and Jone Chowning was Christened ffebruary 23th 1660.   Born 4th of May 1659.
Mary Willis Daughter of Tho. and Mary Willis Christened ffeb^r 23th 1660.
Thomas Willis Sone of Tho. and Mary Willis was born Sept. 8th 1660.
Ellianor Willis Daughter of Tho. & Mary Willis borne Aprill 18th 1655.
Richard Willis Sone of Tho. & Mary Willis borne Augst 29th 1656.
John Willis Sone of Tho. and Mary Willis borne Novem^{br} 24th 1658.
Elizabeth Daughter of Tho. and Marg^t Williams Christ^{ed} Ap^{rll} 4th 1661.
Katherine Daughter of Abraham and Millicent Weekes christened the 15th of December 166 .
Winifrid Corbin daughter of Henry and Alice Corbin was borne the 3^d Day of Novemb^r at 12 a Clock at night, and Christn^d the 12th of Aprill 1662.
George the Sone of Jno. and ffrances Hazlewood borne   25th 1661.
Diana Vause Daughter of Jno. and Ann Vause Christened Aprill 9th 1662.
Henry the Sone of Henry and Eltonhead Thacker was borne the 9th Day of August 1663.
Ann Daughter of Henry and Alice Corbin was borne ffeb^r 9th and was Christened the 29th of the same Month 1664.
Henry Sone of Henry and Alice Corbin ffeb^r 12th At one a Clock in the Morning and was Christened on Easter Tuesday March 22th, 1667.
Mary the Daughter of Andrew and Sarah Williamson was Borne the ffirst Day of Novemb^r about 3 a Clock in the After Noone 1669.
Ann Daughter of David and Jone Allinson was borne March 12th 1665.

Catherine the Daughter of David and Jone Allinson borne March 18th 1667.
David Sone of David and Jone Allinson was borne the 18th Day of August about one of Clock in the after Noone 1669.
Margaret Daughter to William and Eliz^a Loyall was borne the 18th Day of August ab^t one of the Clock in ye afternoone 1669.
William Son of William and Eliz^a Downing was borne Novem^{br} 17th 1665.
Elizabeth Daughter of W^m & Eliz^a Downing was borne Sept. 23th 1670.
Thomas the Sone of Edward and Ann Bateman was Christned Sept. 1st 1672.
Ralph the Son of Jane Watts was Christned Septem^{br} the 22th 1672.
Edward Thacker the Sone of Henry and Eltonhead Thacker was Borne the 7th of January An. 1665.
Martha the Daughter of the above Named Thacker borne Decem^{br} 5th 1667.
Alice the Daughter of the above Named Thacker borne Decem^{br} 30th 1671.
Lettice the Daughter of the above Named Thacker borne ffebry 27th 1669.
Marke the Sone of Matthew Gibson and Eliz^a Lawright was borne the 29th of January 1667.
William and Ann Hares Childe, Named Ann was Christned March 30th 1673.

The Age of Severall Negroes of Mr Richd Perrott.

Thomas Mack Sone of Richard and Tugg borne 15th of July 1663.
ffrank Sone of Sampson and Kate borne the 12th of Aprill 1668.
Hannah Daughter of W^m and Kate borne Octo^{br} the 1st 1672.
Toney Sone of Toney and Sarah Borne 10th of Aprill 1672.
These negroes above were Entered Aprill 30th 1673.

July 22th 1673 Doodis Minor's Negros Entred.

Mary Daughter of Deco and Phelis Borne July 1663.
Nann Daughter of the above Negro, was borne July 1666.
James Sone of the above Negro, was borne January 1669.
Betty Daughter of the above Negro, was borne March 1672.
Pallas Daughter of the abovs^d Negro, borne March 1672.

Mr Reeves three negros were Entered July 6th 1672.

James aged Nine yeares Octo^{br} next.
Tom aged Two yeares and a halfe.
Benn aged Two yeares and a halfe

MARRIAGES Viz^t.

William Baldwin and Magret Cook married Dec^{br} 19th 1660.
Robert Thompson and Marg^t Welch widow of Jno. Welch ffebruary 19th 1660.
Richard Howell and Ann Wilberton April 12th 1662.
Thomas Cordwell and Elizabeth Collyer
Robert Taylor and Elizabeth Welch Aprill 11th 1662.
John Blewford and Elizabeth Parrat.

CHRISTENINGS.

Ann Daughter of Allexand^r and Mary Murra Christen^d Augst 24th.
Ann Daughter of Rich^d and Margaret Williams Christn^d Jan^r 18th 1673.
Ann Daughter of Tho. and Grace Shore Christened ffebry 8th 1673.
Mary Daughter of Tho. and Mary Tugwell born The Last Octo^{br} 1661.
Thomas Sone of ye above named Tugwell born June 16th 1664.
Ann Daughter of ye above named Tugwell born March 15th 1666.
Henry Sone of ye above named Tugwell borne Octo^{br} 7th 1670.
Marg^t Daughter of Ellianor and Jno^o Carryer Christn^d Ap^{rll} 20th 1673.
William Son of W^m and Grace Copeland borne March 26th 1667.
John Sone of the above named Copeland borne March 21th 1669.
Mary Daughter of Allexand^r and Mary Murra Chrs^{td} Dec^{br} 20th 1674.
William Poole the Sone of W^m and Sarah Poole born March 7th 1668.
Maxamilian Petty the Sone of Maxamilian and Christian Petty was born 28th Novemb 1677.
Sarah Daughter of Jno. and Mary Wortham borne Novem^{br} 12th 1663 Between 11 and 12 a Clock at night, Sarah Departed this Life the 16th of January 1670.
Mary Daughter of the aboves^d Wortham borne the 11th ffeb^r 1665 about 8 a Clock at night, and Departed this Life the 21th of Decemb^{br} 1676.
John Sone of the aboves^d Wortham Borne September 27th 1669 about 4 a Clock after noone.
Margaret Daughter of the aboves^d Wortham borne ffeb^r 20th and Christened 26th of March 1671.
Margaret departed this Life the 9th of Aprill 1676.
Joseph Son of the aboves^d Wortham borne the 2th of July 1676 And Dyed the 9th of June the same yeare.
George Sone of the aboves^d Wortham was borne 20th of Aprill and Christened the 19th of May 1673.
Oswald Sone of Jno. and Eliz^a Wortham borne the first day of Ap^{rll} 1685.
Elizabeth Daughter of the above^{sd} Wortham borne ffebruary 20th 1686.
Chichley Corbin Thacker The Sone of Henry and Eltonhead Thacker was borne 4th January Ann^o 1673.
Jno Stamper the Sone of Jno. and Elizabeth Stamper was borne the 29th of August 1677 and was baptized at the house of the said Jno Stamper p. Mr Sheppard, 8th of Octo^{br} 1677.
Thomas Ross the Sone of Andrew and Mary Ross borne the 22th of May and Baptized 22th of June ffollowing 1677.
Sarah Poole the Daughter of William and Sarah Poole was borne the 3th of Septemb. 1671.
The age of 3 children of David and Mary George Viz^t
Alice George was borne the 4th Xamb^r 1671.
David George was Borne the 12th of ffebruary 1673.
John George was Borne the 6th of July 1675.

The age of 4 children of Thomas & Jane Kidd Vizt.
Elizabeth Kidd was borne the ffirst of Septemb. 1672.
William Kidd was borne the 22 of March 1675.
Jane Kidd was borne the 12 of January 1677.
Mary Kidd was baptiz^d the　　　Day of August
　The age of 3 children of John and Sarah Davis vizt
Alice Davis was borne the 30th of June 1676.
Sarah Davis was borne the 31th of January 1678.
John Davis was borne the 7th of July 1681.

Robert and Jane Price theire children Viz^t
Margaret Price was Borne the 14th of August 1670 about 12 a Clock and Baptized 12th of Septemb following.
John Price was Borne 29th of January about 5 afternoone and Baptized 2th of March 1672.
Robert Price was borne 19th of Novemb. and baptized 22th of the same 1674.
Jane Price was borne 10th of July 1676 about 4 afternoone and was bap^{ts} 14th of August.
Elizabeth Price was borne ye 7th of Novemb. 1681 and bap^{ts} at home 13th of Novemb. 1681.
Mary Price was Borne 3th of May 1679 and baptized at home the 25th Ditto 1679.
Katherine Price was borne 6th of January and baptized at home 13th January, 168$\frac{2}{3}$.
Elizabeth the Daughter of Mary Stradford was borne 3th of May and baptized the 24th of August 1679.
Hannah Daughter of Ann Nunnam was bap^{ts} 9th of ffebruary 167$\frac{8}{9}$.
Ann the Daughter of Mary Green was bap^{ts} at Lower Chap^{ll} May 9th 1680.
William the Sone of Susanna Jaxon baptized at ye Gr^t Church Jan^r 18th 167$\frac{9}{80}$.
Katherine Daughter of Ann Corell bap^{ts} at Maj^r Generall Smith's Octo^{br} 17th 1680.
Sarah the Daughter of William Hughs by Baptized Jan^r 16th 1680.
Elizabeth the Daughter of Wm Waller by Kath. Lestridge bap^{ts} feb^r 20th 1680.
Elizabeth Daughter of Phillip Torksey by Mary ffrench bap^{ts} Aprill 10th 1681.
Ann King Daughter of Julian & Rebeca King was borne 25th Novemb^r 1676.
Elizabeth Daughter of Edm^d Sanders by ffrances was bap^{ts} 17th Novemb^r 1681.
William the Illegitimate Sone of Hannah Majo^r Beverlys maid Jan^r 8th 168$\frac{1}{2}$.
Ann the Illegitimate Daughter of Tho. Thompson by Jane Burk bap^{ts} June 4th 1682.
Rich'd Robinson Sone of Rich'd and Ann Robinson was borne 12th of March 1674.

　The age of 3 children of John & Eliz^a Riseing:
William Riseing was borne the last Day of Aprill 1669.
Elizabeth Riseing was borne the 15^d of September 1672.
John Riseing was borne the 28th of March 1676.

The age of 3 children of William & Eltonhead Stanard:
Eltonhead Stanard was borne 2th of Septemb' 1678.
Sarah Yates by marriage Sarah Stanard was borne 12th of July 1680.
William Stanard was borne 15th of ffebruary 1682.
Ann the Illegitimate Daughter of George Anderton by Sarah was baptized p. M' Pead 7th of March 168¾.
Walter the Illegitimate Son of Walter Lewis by Jane Burk baptized p. M' Pead 6th of Aprill 1684.

The age of 4 children of Alexand' & Mary Murrey:
Ann Murrey was borne the 12th of Aprill 1673.
Mary Murrey was borne the 22th of Novemb. 1674.
Rebeca Murrey was borne the 28th of Octo^{br} 1676.
John Murrey was borne the 20th of January 1678.
Francis the sone of ffrancis & Eliz^a Dodson borne 15th of July 1684.
Ann Smith Daughter of Anthony Smith & Ann his wife borne the 10 day of July, and baptized 11th of August 1678.
Elizabeth Lee Daughter of Tho. and Eliz^a Lee baptised 11th of Augst 1678.
John Atwood Sone of James and Mary Atwood was borne the 14th of July 1678, and was baptised 22th of Sep^t 1678.
Thomas Jones Sone of Tho. & Mary Jones bap^{te} 3th of Novemb. 1678.
Richard Daniell sone of William & Jochebed Daniell was borne Sept. 30th 1678.
John Lee Sone of Majo' Richard Lee and Mad^m Lettice Lee his wife was baptized 3th of Xember 1678.
George Davis the Sone of George & Susanna Davis bap^{te} 22th Xemb 1678.
Sarah Clay Daughter of George and Sarah Clay borne 4th Xemb and was baptized 2th of ffebruary 1678.
Margret Askew Daughter of Rich^d and Eliz^a Askew bap^{te} 2th Jan^{ry} 1678.
Christopher Sutton Son of Jno and Eliz^a Sutton borne ffeb^{ry} 27th 1678.
Mary Hill Daughter of Tho. & Ann Hill was borne the 14th of ffebruary and baptized the 6 of Aprill 1678.
Dianah Young the Daughter of William and Johan' Young borne the 19th of ffebruary 1678 and was baptised 6th of Aprill 1678.
Richard Allen the Sone of Rich^d and Ann Allen borne 17th Jan^{ry} 1678 and Baptized 13th of Aprill 1679.
Gerrat Minor the Sone of Doodis and Eliz^a Minor was Baptized 13th of Aprill 1679.
Elizabeth Mins the Daughter of Thomas and Ann Mins borne the 29th of March, and baptized 11th May 1679.
Mary Colless the Daughter of Ambr's and Elizabeth Colless was borne the 25th of Aprill and baptized 18th of May 1679.
John Burk the Sone of Jno & Jane Burk borne 16th of Augst 1678 and baptized 18th of May 1679.
Elizabeth Tuydey Daughter of Eliz. Tudey borne March 24th 1678 bap^{te} Ap^r 20th 1679.
Elizabeth Norman Daughter of Henry & Ann Norman borne 29th May 1679 and baptized 15th June Ditto yeare.

Jane Burnet Daughter of W^m & Loretta Burnet borne 14th May bap^{ts} 15th June 1679.

Susanna Gess Daughter of William and Eliz^a Guess borne 7th Ap^r bap^{ts} 13th July 1679.

Robena Hughs Daughter of Jno & Eliz^a Hughes borne 30th July bap^{ts} 31th August 1679.

Sarah the Daughter of Peter & Ellinor Brunwell was baptized 2th of November 1679.

Joseph Micham Sone of John & Micall Micham borne 17th Octo^{br} bap^{ts} 23th Novr 1679.

John & Elizabeth Patre the Sone and Daughter of Matthew & Eliz^a Patre bap^{ts} 7th Xmb. 1679.

Ann Thomas Daughter of Robert and Ancoretta Thomas baptized 21th Xemb. 1679.

Margaret the Daughter of Andrew and Sarah Williamson borne 16th of August 1679 and baptized 25th Xemb. 1679.

Robert Smith Sone of Tho. & Eliz. Smith bap^{ts} 18 Jan^{ry} 1679.

Thomas Stacey Sone of Tho. & Eliz^a Stacey bap^{ts} ffeb^r 18th 1679.

Mary Daughter of W^m & Eliz^a Wood bap^{ts} 22th ffeb^r 1679.

Katherine Wormeley Daughter of Capt. Ralph Wormeley Esqr was Bap^{ts} 4th March 1679.

Winifrid Seager Daughter of Randolph & Mary Seager bap^{ts} Ma^r 14th 1679.

Elizabeth Basket Dau^{tr} Jno. & Eliz^a Basket bap^{ts} 14th March 1679.

Jno. Charles Richman Son of Tho. and Eliz^a Richman borne 30th Jan^r 1679.

Winifrid Nichols Da^r of Henry & Alice Nichols bap^{ts} 14 feb.

An acco^t of Christenings and ages of Children for the yeare 1680 &c.

Elizabeth Weatherston the Daughter of Thomas & Elizabeth Weatherstone was baptised at the Lower Chappell p Mr Sheppard the 28th of March.

Mary Slanter the Daughter of John and Sarah Slanter was borne 4th of March 1679, and baptized 28th of March 1680.

Dorothy Long the Wife of Daniel Long aged   yeares was Baptized at the Upper Chappell p. Mr Shepard 4th of Aprill, the above yeare.

Ann Petty the Daughter of Maxamilian and Christian Petty was borne the 25th of March and was Baptized at home p. Mr Sheppard 11th of Aprill.

Elizabeth Jones the Daughter of Thomas and Mary Jones was bap^{ts} 2th of May.

Mary Slanter the Daughter of Anthony and Dorothy Slanter was bap^{ts} 25th Ap^{rll}.

Joseph Humphrys the Sone of John and Ann Humphrys bap^{ts} 9th of May.

Johannah Bristow the Daughter of Jno and Michall Bristow bap^{ts} 9th May.

Ann Mason the Daughter of Josiah and Eliz^a Mason Baptized 30th of May.

James Williams the Sone of John and Mary Williams baptized 6th of June.

Thomas Brookes the Sone of Richard and Mary Brooks bap^{ts} 27th of June.

Catherine Maynell the Daughter of Robert and Dorothy Maynell bap^{ts} 27th June.

Nicholas House the Sone of Nich° and Eliz^a House baptized 8th of August.

Joseph Orphin the Sone of Henry and Anne Orphin was borne 11th of July. and was baptized at the Lower Chap^{ll} p. Mr Sheppard 22th of August.

John Brent the Sone of Jn° and Jane Brent was bap^{ts} 22th of August.

Charles Brookes the Sone of Jonathan and Sarah Brookes was borne 12th Augt and baptized 29th Ditto.

Sarah Wilson the Daughter of Thomas and Mary Wilson bap^{ts} 12th of Septemb.

Ann Roberts the Daughter of Griffuth and Ann Roberts bap^{ts} 19th of Sept.

Benjamine Davis ye Sone of George & Susannah Davis baptiz^d 26th of 7temb.

John Gibbs the Sone of Grigory and Mary Gibbs was bap^{ts} p. Mr Shep^d 10th Octo^{br}.

William Burnett ye Sone of William & Loretta Burnett bap^{ts} 24th of Octob.

Peter Gates the Sone of Thomas and Roseamond Gates bap^{ts} 12th of Xemb.

William Parker Reymey Sone of Barnard and Ann Reymey bap^{ts} 2th of Jan^{ry}.

Elizabeth Summers Daughter of Jn° and Eliz^a Summers bap^{ts} 2th of of Jan^{ry}.

William Beverley Sone of Majo^r Robert Beverley & Katherine Beverley was Baptized 4th of January.

William & Ellianor Doss the Sone and Daughter of John and Ann Doss bap^{ts} 16th of Jan^{ry}.

Thomas Allen the Sone of Richard & Ann Allen borne 23th No^{br} bap^{ts} 23th Jan^{ry}.

Richard Atwood the Sone of James and Mary Atwood was bap^{ts} 30th of Jan^{ry}.

An Accompt of Christenings & Ages of Children For the Yeare 1681.

Ann Wooley Daughter of George & Sarah Wolley was baptized 10th of Aprill.

Mary Gardner the Daughter of Thomas and Diana Gardner was bap^{ts} 10th of Aprill.

Sarah Dudley the Daughter of James and Eliz^a Dudley Was bap^{ts} 27th ffebry.

William Baldwin the Sone of Tho. and Mary Baldwin borne 14th ffeb^r bap^{ts} 18th ditto.

Thomas Mins ye Sone of Tho. & Ann Mins baptized at ye Great Church 24th Aprill.

Elizabeth Tosely Daughter of Tho. & Eliz^a Tosely was bap^{ts} 29th of May.

Robert Murrey Sone of Alexd^r Murrey was borne 7th of Ap^{rll} & baptiz^d 4th of June.

William Gess the Sone of William & Eliz⁸ Guess was baptized 4th of June.
John Man ye Sone of Jno. Man & Dorothy his wife bap^{ts} at home 8th of June.
Elizabeth Webb Daughter of James & ffrancis Webb bap^{ts} 21st of Augst.
Jane Alldin the Daughter of Robert and Ellianor Alldin bap^{ts} Ditto Day.
John Vivion the Sone of Jno. and Marg^t Vivion baptized 28th of August.
Christian Worsdale Daughter of Richard & Martha Worsdale bap^{ts} 20th of August.
John Chayney the Sone of William and Penelope Chaney was borne 8th of August, and baptized p. Mr John Sheppard at the Upper Chap^{ll} 11th of Septemb.
Robert Guilliams Sone of Robert & Ann Guilliams borne 22th Augst bap^{ts} 18 7temb.
Thomas Davis Sone of Jno. & Sarah Davis bap^{ts} at ye Upper Chap^{ll} 16th of Octob.
Katherine Allen Daughter of W^m & Kath. Allen borne 2th Sep^t bap^{ts} 16th of October.
John Jones Sone of Rice & Jane Jones borne 31th Aug^t & bap^{ts} 3th of Octob. following.
Ann Goodlow the Daughter of George & Mary Goodlow bap^{ts} 23th of October.
Mary Carter ye Daughter of Wm. and Pen^o Carter was bap^{ts} 23th of October.
Richard Perrott Sone of Richd Perrott Junr by Sarah his wife borne 5th Octo^{br} bap^{ts} 17th Sep^t.
ffrances Weathers ye Daughter of John and Marg^t Weathers bap^{ts} 27th Novemb.
John Williams the Sone of Tho. & Mary Williams bap^{ts} 4th of September.
Mary Middleton Daughter of William & Mary Middleton bap^{ts} 4th Septmb.
Rice Curtis the Sone of Giles & Mary Curtis borne 4th No^{vr} bap^{ts} 15th January.

Christenings ffor the Year 1681—&c.

Katherine Seager the Daughter of Randolph & Mary Seager bap^{ts} 5th feb^r.
Thomas Smith Sone of Tho. & Eliz^a Smith was Baptized 5th of ffeb^{ry}.
Henry Ryder the Sone of John & Grace Rydr bap^{ts} 26th of ffebruary.
Robert & Ann The sone and Daughter of Eliz^a Wood was bap^{ts} 19th of March.
Alice Davis Daughter of Henry and Ann Davis bap^{ts} 19th of March.

MARRIAGES, &c.

Edward Ellis & Susannah Hill both of this pish was Married 7th July 1678.
William Loyall and Margaret Thompson was Married the 17th of Septemb. 1678

Joseph Mason and Elizabeth Burton was Married the 11th of July 1678.

Thomas Hedgcock & Margery Simmons was Married the 23th Xemb. 1678.

Richard Arrow and Ann Suckling was Married the 24th of Xemb. 1678.

Nicholas House and Elizabeth Hall Married the 20th of January 1678.

William Burnett & Loretta Pannell was Married 20th of January 1678.

Ambros Collis and Elizabeth Lawrence was Married 26th of January 1678.

William Cotterell and Rose Hollyday was Married p. License 2th ffebry 1678.

James Parker & Elizabeth Dudley Married p. Lycence the 21th of ffebruary 1678.

* * * gyn & Margaret Bridger was married p. Lycence the 27th of ffebruary 1678.

* * * Patris & Eliza Mayo was married the 4th of March 1678.

Majo' Robert Beverley & M'" Katherine Hone was Married in Gloster 28th March 1679.

Thomas Wilson & Mary Seers both of this p'ish was Married 27th of Aprill 1679.

Robert Thomas & Ancoretta Wells was married y" 10th of June 1679.

John Vause and Elizabeth Calloway were Married p. Lycence 14th of June 1679.

Henry Davis and Ann West were Married the 29th of June 1679.

James Dudley & Mary Welch was Married in Gloster p. Lycence 18th of July 1679.

William King & Martha Richardson was Married 28th of July 1679.

Peter Brumwell & Ellianor Edwards was Married 10th of August 1679.

Thomas Smith and Elizabeth Clabor were Married 17th of August 1679.

Thomas Gates & Rose Stake was Married the 27th of August 1679.

Richard Hogans & Katherine Clarke was Married 9th of Septemb. 1679.

Majo' Phillip Lightfoot & M'" Alice Corbin was Married p. Lycence 23 Sep'"" 1679.

Jonathan Stanly & Barbary Weybole was married the 28th of Septemb. 1679.

John Davis & Sarah Watts was Married the 26th of January 1679.

John Doss and Ann Taylor was Married the 26th of January 1679.

ffrancis Dodson & Eliz" Harrelson was Married the 5th of ffebruary 1679.

Rice Jones & Jane Cock was Married p Lycence the 10th of ffebruary 1679.

Robert Deputy & Ann Wright was Married the 23th of ffebruary 1679.

Here Endeth the Acco' of Marriages for y" Yeare 1679.

CHRISTENINGS &c.

An Accompt of Christenings ffor the Yeare 1682.

ffrances the Daughter of Robert and Katherine Williamson was borne the 21th of Decemb 1682.

Thomas Basket sone of John and Eliz⁴ Basket was bap⁽ᵗ 16th of Aprill.

Mary Brim Daughter of Jno. & Mary Brim was borne 7th of Jan'ʸ last and baptized the 16th of Aprill.

Elizabeth Douton the Daughter of Anthony & Eliz⁴ Douton was borne the 31th of Xemb'ʳ 1681 and bap⁽ᵗ ye 16th of Aprill ye Above Yeare.

Elizabeth Brim Daughter of Jno. & Mary Brim was borne 7th of Jan'ʸ and baptized 16th of Aprill.

Hance Erixson the sone of Hance and Judith Erixson was bap⁽ᵗ 16th Aprill.

William Hughes sone of Wᵐ and Eliz⁴ Hughes borne 17th March & bap⁽ˢ 14th of May.

John Mountague the sone of Peter and Mary Mountague was bap⁽ᵗ 21th May.

Marvill Moseley the Sone of Marvill and Sarah Moseley bap⁽ᵗ 21th May.

Thomas Blewford the Sone of Tho. & Mary Blewford bap⁽ᵗ 21th of May.

John Ingram the Sone of James and Sarah Ingram bap⁽ᵗ 21th of May.

Mary Jones the Daughter of Tho. & Mary Jones was bap⁽ᵗ the 2ᵈ of July.

Elizabeth Brumwell Daughter of Peter & Eliz⁴ Brumwell bap⁽ᵗ 18th of July.

Ann Docker Daughter of Edward & ffrances Docker borne 3th of July and Baptized the 13th of August 82.

John West Sone of Nich⁰ and Hannah West was borne 5th of August and Baptized yᵉ 3ᵈ of September.

Thomas Brookes the sone of Richard and Eliz⁴ Brookes was borne the 22th of July and baptized the 3ᵈ of September.

Rebecca Hill the Daughter of Tho. & Ann Hill borne 30th of August and Baptized 17th of September.

William Bristow Sone of Jno. & Michall Bristow was baptzᵈ 29th of October.

Robert Maynell the Sone of Robert & Dorothy Maynell borne 28th Septmb.

ffrances Hancock Daughter of Tho. & Eliz⁴ Hancock was borne 5th of Novemb.

Elizabeth Musgrane Daughter of Michⁿ Musgrane was baptizᵈ 19th November.

Sarah Burnett the Daughter of Wᵐ & Coretta Burnett was bap⁽ᵗ 19th November.

MARRIAGES. 1681.

Edward Clark & Ann Allison was Married yᵉ 13th of April 1681.

Benjamine Pickworth & Eliz⁴ Cooper was Married p Lycence 14th Aprill 1681.

Hance Erickson & Judith Hayden was Married upon 17th of Aprill 1681.
Edward Docker & ffrances Dalley was Married 18th of Aprill 1681.
John Sheeres & Mary Osbondistall was Married 17th of May 1681.
Francis Frygore & Katherine Weaver was Married 8th of June 1681.
William Carter & Penelope Pew was Married upon 31th of August 1681.
John Weathers & Margaret Powell was Married at my Lady Skipwiths 3th Octo^{br} 81.
John Needles & Eliz^a Man was Married 24th of Octob. 1681.
John Lewis of New Kent County & Eliz^a O. Brissell of this prsh 24th Octob 1681.
William Hughs & Mary Drue was Married 28th of Novemb. 1681.
James Dyer & Ann Ashwin was Married the ffirst of Xemb. 1681.
William Thompson & Grace Elwood was Married 24th of ffebruary 1681-2.
Robert Williamson & Katherine Lewis were Married 27th of ffebruary 168½.
Michaell Musgrane & Elizabeth Ball were Married 12th of April 1680.
Robert Munday & Sarah Sackerman was Married the   of Aprill 1680.
Thomas Gardner & Diana Blake was Married the   of April 1680.
Samuell Onely & Jane Parkes was Married the 25th of Aprill 1680.
John Payne & Ann Enos was Married the 9th of May 1680.
Joshua Lanson & Ann Smith was Married p. Lycence 17th of May 1680.
John Lanson & Mary Kilbey was Married p. Lycence 19th of August 1680.
Phillip Hunnings & Eliz^a Parris was Married 12th of Septemb 1680.
Richard Worsdall & Martha Woodgar was Married 26th Septemb. 1680.
David Nichols & Jone Barnett was Married 11th of November 1680.
John Johnson & Mary Broadbent Married 22th of November 1680.
William Allen & Katherine Smith were Marryed 2th Decemb. 1680.
Oswald Cary & Ann Jaxon Marryed p. Lycence 19th December 1680.
James Webb & ffrances Herbert was Married 19th December 1680.
John Brookes & Mary Hutchings were Marryed 23th of January 1680.
James Bendall & Eliz^a Blake was Marryed 30th January 1680.
John Ryder & Grace ffoster was Married the first Day of ffeb^{ry} 1680.
John Brewer & Mary English was Married upon 7th of ffebruary 1680.
Henry Bray & Ann Hodgekings was Married upon 12th ffeb^{ry} 1680.
Richard Dues & Rachell Norris was Married upon 14th ffebruary 1680.

Here Endeth ye Accompt of Marriages for the yeare.

MARRIAGES &c., 1682.

John Ross & Ann Humphreys was Married the 4th of June 1682.
George Guest & Mary Jones was Marryed the 2th of July 1682.

John Walcom of this parish & Eliz⁂ Coventry of Petso parish in Gloster Mar⁴ 10th July, 1682.
William Tignor Jun⁣ʳ of ffairefield parish in the County of Northumberland and Dorothy Hill of this parish was Married the 18th of July 1682.
William ffitz Jeffreys & Ann Dudenfield were Married 3th of August 1682.
John Elee & Margaret Loyall of this parish was Married 2th of Aug° 1682.
William Wakefield & Mary Barnes of this pish was Married 2th of Aug⁣ᵗ 1682.
David Barwick and Mary Michener of this psh Married 31st of Agust 1682.
Thomas Thompson & Eliza Hill of this parish was Married 17th of Septemb 1682.
Augustine Scarbrough & Dorothy Eddington was Married 6th of Octob⁣ʳ 1682.
John Deverdall & Jone Blake of this pish. was Married yᵉ 9th of Octob⁣ʳ 1682.
Roger Prichard & Rebecca Yates of this parish Married 23th of Octob⁣ʳ 1682.
Thomas Paine & Mary Mountague was Married 24th of October 1682.
Isaac Saserson & Mary Cooper both of this pish. Married 21th of November 1682.
Richard Gabriell & Johannah Buttersby were Married 31th of Xemb 1682.
Edmund Owen & Margᵗ Thomas both of this pish. Married 5th of January 1682.
William Smith & Sissely Jones both of this pish. was Married 18th January 1682.

BURIALLS—1678.

Michaell Nickingson Departed this Life the 29th of July & was buried the 30th of July 1678.
Mary Daniel ye Daughter of William Daniel & Jochebed his Wife departed this Life upon 12th of September & was buried 13th Ditto 1678.
Ann Smith being the Second Daughter of that Name to Anthony & Ann Smith departed this Life 16th of Septemb. 1678.
Elizabeth Mins the Daughter of Thomas & Ann Mins Departed this Life 19th of October & was buried 20th Ditto 1678.
Elizabeth Boulton yᵉ Wife of Daniell Boulton Departed this Life the 24th and was buried 25th of Octob. 1678.
Joseph Hill Servant to Joseph Harvey was found Dead in the Woods the 24th of January 1678.
Ellianor Jones the Wife of Humphry Jones departed this Life 9th Janʳʸ 1678 and was buried in the Ile of the Upper Chap⁣ˡˡ 12th Ditto.
Daniell Boulton Departed this Life 11th Janʳ 1678 & was buried by his wife.
Edward Matthews departed this Life 25th & was burried 26th of ffebruary 1678.

Richard Collins Serv't to Jno Dudley departed this Life 4th August 1678 and was buried the same day in the Lower Chap[ll] Church Yard.

ffrancis Bridge the Sone of ffrancis & Marg[t] Bridge departed this Life 15th of Aug[t] 1679 and was buried in the Ile of Lower Chap[ll] the next day following &c.

Coll[o] Giles Brent of Potomac Departed this Life 2th of September 1679 and was buried in the Great Church Yard y[e] next day following &c.

John Pickworth Carpenter departed this Life 11th of Septemb 1679 & was buried in the great Church Yard ye day following.

John Comby departed this Life 26th of Septemb 1679 & was buried In the great Church Yard the next day following &c.

John Vause Departed this Life 26th of February 1679 & was buried In M[r] Christop[r] Robinsons orchard &c.

Elizabeth Vause the Wife of M[r] Jno. Vause Dec'd was buried 25th Xbr.

Coll[o] John Burnham Departed this Life y[e] 4th of January 1680 & was buried in the Chancell of ye Upper Chap[ll] 11th of Jan[ry] 1680.

ffrances Wormeley Daughter of Coll[o] Christop[r] & ffrances Wormely was Buried at home in theire Garden the 14th of January 1680.

William Sheffield depart[d] this Life 7th of ffebruary and was buried In the Lower Chap[ll] Yard 8th of Ditto.

1682 WEDDINGS OR MARRIAGES &c 1683.

John Tidbury & Eliz[a] Ball both of this parish was Married 25th Jan[ry] 1682.

Robert Roberts & Isabella Baker both of this parish was Married 13th ffebruary 1682.

Aron Williamson & Eliz[a] Waterton of this parish was Married 7th of June 1683.

Phillip Torksey & Mary ffrench y[e] 31th of July 1683.

Richard Reynolds and Margaret Smith was married y[e] 5th Aug[st] 1683.

John Pound and Elizabeth Joy was Married y[e] 28th of Octob 1683.

William Laurence and Johannah Sydnor both of Lancaster County was Married p. M[r] Duell Pead 16th Xemb 1683 p. Lycence.

Thomas Hickman & Martha Thacker was Married ye 18th Xemb. 1683 p Lycence.

John Dearclone & Katherine Clarke was Married 19th of Xemb. 1683.

Samuell Sharpe & Mary Simpson was Married 23th of Xemb. 1683.

John Cocking & Hannah Hollinsworth was Married 28th Xemb. 1683.

William Holley & Sarah Chaseman was Married 9th of January 1683.

Thomas Vahane & Mary Thompson was Married 10th of January 1683.

Robert Blackley & Jane Kidd was married 29th of January 1683.

Hugh Watts & Johnna Marye was married p p'son Carr in New Kent 29th Jan[ry] 1683.

John Collins & Marg[t] Weekes was married at M[r] Abra. Weekes ye po Aprill 1684.

Richard ffarrell & Winifrid Watts was married ye 27th of Aprill 1684.
John Stamper and   was married p Mr Pead 8th of May 1684.
Richard Gabriell & Ann Taylor was married p Mr Pead po August 1684.
Henry Osbond and Mary Simpson was married p Mr Pead ye * *
William Woodard of Ware River & Bridg^{t} Williams of this p'ish was married 14th Ag^{t}–84.
Zachariah Mullins & Mary Mabraine of ye p'ish was married 7th of Septemb. 1684.
Nicholas Love & Eliz^{a} Thackston both of this p'ish was married 18th Septemb 1684.
Ezechias Rhodes & Eliz^{a} Nicholls both of this p'ish was married 22th Octob. 1684.
John Pitts & Mary Goodin both of this parish was married y^{e} 26th of Octob. 1684.
John Nicholls & Mary Lewis both of this p'ish was married 20th Novemb. 1684.
Tobias Mickleburrough & Eliz^{a} Minor both of this p'ish married 21th Xemb. 1684.
George Priestnall & Eliz^{a} Williams both of this p'ish was married po Jan^{ry} 168$\frac{4}{5}$.
Thomas Stiff & Sarah Salter both of this p'ish was married 8th of ffebry 1684.
David Berwick Junr &   both of this p'ish was married 16th ffebruary 1684.
Ralph Cole & Eliz^{a} Hopkins both of this p'ish was marryed the
William Bennett & Mary Smith both of this p'ish marryed 18th ffebruary 1684.

WEDDINGS OR MARRIAGES 1685 &c.

George Haslewood & Ann Robinson both of this parish was marryed the 28th of ffebruary 168$\frac{4}{5}$.
Peter Chilton and Susan Jaxon was marryed y^{e} 2th of March 168$\frac{4}{5}$.
William Carter and Elizabeth Russell was marryed 18th of June 1685.
John Gordon and Mary Gordon was marryed y^{e} 17th of June 1685.
Edward Sanders and Elizabeth Teel was marryed y^{e} 6th of January 1685.
Humphry ffloyd & Marg^{t} King was marryed ye 19th of Octob^{r} 1685.
Robert Boodle and Elizabeth Best was married 19th of Octob^{r} 1685.
William Willis & Bridg^{t} Robinson was marryed 23th of June 1685.
William Loyal & Mary Masey was marryed August 6th 1685.
Thomas Allen & Lucey Blake was marryed 10th Augt 1685 & he dyed yt very Day.
Martin Masey & Elizabeth Kidd was married 17th of Septemb 1685.
John Bodgam of Gloster County & Mary Wallas of this parish was marry'd the 30th of Xemb 168$\frac{5}{6}$.
Thomas Williams & Isabella Roberts both of this pish marryed 19th January 168$\frac{5}{6}$.

Thomas Wadding & Mary Vuite both of this pish were marryed 19th January 168⅔.
Thomas Benson & Dorothy Sutton both of this pish was marryed 11th ffebry 168¾.

CHRISTENINGS 1682 &c.

. . . . Clerk the . . . . of Richard & . . . . Clarke was baptized 12 Novemb. 1682.
Elizabeth Musgrane ye Daughter of Michall & Eliza Musgrane was Baptized 19th of November 1682.
Sarah Burnett ye Daughter of Wm & Loretta Burnett bap{tz} 19th Novemb. 1682.
Lettice Shippey ye Daughter of Richd & Mary Shippey was bap{tz} 19th Xemb. 1682.
William ye Illegitimate Sone of Walter by Katherin Lestridge bap{tz} 25th Xemb. 1682.
Mary Wilson ye Daughter of Thomas & Mary Wilson was bap{tz} ye 31th Xemb. 1682.
Sarah Bendall Daughter of James & Eliza Bendall was borne ye 26th Xemb and baptized 11th of ffebruary 168¾.
Margaret Orphin ye Daughter of Henry & Amey Orphin borne 11th Xemb. bap{tz} 4. Ma{r} 1682.
Elizabeth Sandford ye Daughter of John & Sarah Sandford borne 17th January and baptized 4th of March following &c 168¾.
Tobias Allen ye Sone of Richard & Anne Allen borne ye 30th of January and Baptized 11th of March following &c 168¾.
Humphry Jones ye Sone of Humphry & ———— Jones borne in Lancaster County & bap{tz} in Middlesex County at Mr Jones his house p. Mr Shepard 11th march 168¾
Ann Clay ye Daughter of George & Sarah Clay was baptized 25th of march 1683.
John Alldin ye Sone of Robert & Ellianor Alldin borne po march 168¾ (1683) and was Baptized ye 8th of Aprill 1683 &c.
John Summers ye Sone of John & Eliza Summers was baptized ye 8th Aprill 1683.
Margaret Weatherstone ye Daughter of Tho. & Margt Weatherstone bap{tz} 6th May 1683.
Michall Micham ye Daughter of John & Michall Micham was borne 7th ap{rl} and Baptized ye 27th of May 1683.
Judith Wormeley ye Daughter of Collo Christop{r} Wormeley & ffrances Wormeley his wife was borne ye 25th of May & baptized At home 7th of June 1683.
Sarah Murrey ye Daughter of Alexand{r} & Mary Murrey borne 10th of May & Baptized 15th of July 1683.
William Dudley ye Sone of William & Mary Dudley borne ye po Aprill and baptized ye 29th of July 1683.
Katherine Wallis ye Daughter of Vallentine & ——— Wallis baptized 29th July 1683.
Thomas Patris ye Sone of Matthew & Eliza Patris baptized 5th of Augt 1683.
Thomas Clincker ye sone of Tho. Clincker by Ginney Bess (a ffree negro woman) was baptized 5th of Aug{o} 1683. mr. John Cocking Godfather &c.

Margaret ye Daughter of John Pound by Eliz. Joy bap^tu 5th of Augt 1683.
Thomas Weekes ye sone of ffrancis & Eliz^a Weekes baptized 5th August 1683.
Rose Gates Daughter of Tho & Rose Gates was baptized 5th of August 1683.
James Ross sone of Andrew & Mary Ross was baptized 5th of August 1683.

CHRISTENINGS—1683 & 1684.

John Stapleton ye sone of Tho. & ffrances Stapleton was borne 10th of August 1683.
Thomas Carter ye sone of William & Penelope Carter bap^tu 5th of Augt 1683.
Henry Guthridge ye sone of John & Rebe^a Guthridge bap^tu 5 of August 1683.
John Mynor ye sone of Doodis & Eliz^a Mynor was bap^tu 6th of Septemb. 1683.
Efforella Perrott ye Daughter of Rich^d & Sarah Perrott bap^tu 28th Septemb 1683.
Sarah Davis ye Daughter of John & Sarah Davis was bap^tu 4th of Novemb. 1683.
Phillip Phillips Jane Phillips sone and Daughter of Thomas & Eliz^a Phillips (both Capt Creeks Negroes) was baptized 2th of Xemb. 1683.
Elizabeth Butcher ye Daughter of Richard & Mary Bucher bap^tu 16th Xemb. 1683.
Moses Norman ye sone of Tho. & Mary Norman was bap^tu 19th Xemb. 1683.
ffrances Gilliams ye Daughter of Robt. & Ann Gilliams bap^tu 26th Xemb. 1683.
Katherine Price ye Daughter of Robert & Jane Price was bap^tu 13th Janry. 168¾.
Agatha Daniell ye Daughter of W^m & Jochabed Daniel bap^tu 6th of March 168¾.
Henry Basket ye sone of Jno. & Eliz^a Baskett bap^tu p. Mr Pead 23th of March, 168¾.
Barnett ffreeman ye sone of Barnett & Ann ffreeman was bap^tu 23th March, 168¾.
Charles Lee ye sone of Tho. & Eliz^a Lee was baptized p Mr Pead 23th of March, 168¾.
Olliver Seager ye sone of Randolph & Mary Seagur bap^tu 23th March 168¾.
Margarett Dearelone ye Daughter of Jno. & Katherine Dearelone bap^tu 30th Ma^r 1684.
Winifrid Williamson ye Daught^r of Henry &   Williamson bap^tu po. Aprill 1684.
John Burk ye sone of Jno. & Mary Burk was bap^tu p. Mr Pead 2th of Aprill 1684.
Margarett Vivion ye Daughter of Jno. & Marg^t Vivion bap^tu 2th of Aprill 1684.
Thomas Thompson ye sone of Tho. & Eliz^a Thompson bap^tu 6th of Aprill 1684.

John Sutton y⁰ sone of   & Eliz* Sutton was bap^ts p. Mr Pead 6th of Aprill 1684.
Thomas Roberts y⁰ sone of Robert & Isabell Roberts bap^ts 6th of Aprill 1684.
Joane Salter ye Daughter of Jno & Sarah Salter was bap^ts p. Mr Pead 6th Apr^ll 1684.
Sarah Sadler ye Daughter of Samll & Eliz* Sadler bap^ts 6th of Aprill 1684.
Elizabeth Guest y⁰ Daughter of George and Mary Guest bap^ts 13th Aprill 1684.
John Smith y⁰ sone of Tho. & Eliz* Smith was bab^ts 13th of Aprill 1684.
Abraham Trigg ye sone of Daniell and   Trigg baptiz^d 4th of May 1684.
Mary Ryder ye Daughter of Jn⁰ & Grace Ryder was bap^ts 4th of May 1684.
Humphrey Dudding y⁰ sone of Humphrey & Sarah Dudding bap^ts 4th May 1684.
Phillip Torkes ye sone of Phill & Mary Torkes was bap^ts 8th of June 1684.
Mary Scarbrough y⁰ Daughter of Augustine & Dorothy Scarbrough was Baptized the 8th of June 1684.
Mary Atwood y⁰ Daughter of James & Mary Atwood bap^ts 5th of July 1684.
William Hill y⁰ Sone of Tho. & Ann Hill was baptized 20th of July 1684.

CHRISTENINGS.—1684 &c.

Thomas Chayney y⁰ Sone of William & Penelope Chayney borne June 11th and Baptized 27th of July 1684.
Thomas Chowning y⁰ Sone of Robert & Ann Chowning was baptized 27th of July 1684.
Mary Breame ye Daughter of John & Mary Braeme was Bap^ts 27th of July 1684.
Efferydytus Lawson ye Sone of John & Mary Lawson was bap^ts 10th of August, 1684.
Charles Gibson Sone of Mary Gibson y⁰ widow of Gregory Gibson bap^ts 7th Septemb 1684.
John Gabriell y⁰ Sone of Richard & Ann Gabriell was bap^ts ye 7th of Septemb 1684.
Thomas Sharpe the Sone of Sam^ll & Mary Sharpe was bap^ts 4th of Septemb 1684.
James Webb the Sone of James & ffrances Webb baptized 28th of Septemb 1684.
Robert Blackley y⁰ Sone of Robert & Jane Blackley was bap^ts 20th of Octob. 1684.
Mary Watts y⁰ Daughter of Hugh & Johannae Watts was bap^ts 9th of Novemb. 1684.
John Williams y⁰ Sone of Tho. & Eliz* Williams was baptized 18th of Novemb. 1684.
John Guy the Sone of Tho. & Mary Guy was baptized 30th of Novemb. 1684.
Mary Tignor ye Daughter of William & Dorothy Tignor bap^ts 4th Xemb. 1684.

Jonathan Brookes y⁰ Sone of Jon. & Sarah Brookes was borne 4th Xemb. 1684.
Charles Stacy y⁰ Sone of Thomas & Eliz^a Stacy baptized 11th of January 168$\frac{4}{5}$.
Ann Breame the Daughter of John & Mary Breame bap^{tz} 11th January 168$\frac{4}{5}$
Thomas White the Sone of James & Eliz^a White of New Kent bap^{tz} 11th Jan^{ry} 168$\frac{4}{5}$.
Presilla Whealer y⁰ Daughter of Tho. & Ellianor Whealer bap^{tz} y⁰ po ffebruary 168$\frac{4}{5}$.
John Larking aged about   yeares was bap^{tz} at y^e Great Church p. Mr Duell Pead In the face of the Whole Congregation 8th of ffebruary 168$\frac{4}{5}$.
John Williams y⁰ Sone of Aron & Eliz^a Williams Bap^{tz} 18th of Novemb 168$\frac{4}{5}$.
William Vaughan y⁰ Sone of Tho. & Mary Vaughan bap^{tz} 15th of february 168$\frac{4}{5}$.
Michall Bristow y⁰ Daughter of Jno. & Michall Bristow bap^{tz} 15th ffebry 168$\frac{4}{5}$.
Mary Rhodes y⁰ Daughter Ezehias & Eliz^a Rhodes was bap^{tz} 15th ffeb^{ry} 168$\frac{4}{5}$.
Elizabeth Roe y⁰ Daughter of Thomas & Mary Roe was bap^{tz} 15th ffebruary. 168$\frac{4}{5}$.
Katherine Collins y⁰ Daughter of Jno. & Marg^t Collins bap^{tz} 22th ffebruary 168$\frac{4}{5}$.
Hannah ffletcher y⁰ Daughter of Edward & Mary ffletcher bap^{tz} po. March 168$\frac{4}{5}$.
William King y⁰ Sone of William & Martha King bap^{tz} y^e 15th of March 168$\frac{4}{5}$.
Henry Blewford y⁰ Sone of Tho. &   Blewford was bap^{tz} 15th of March 168$\frac{4}{5}$.
Ann Ingram y⁰ Daughter of James & Sarah Ingram bap^{tz} 15th March 168$\frac{4}{5}$.
Katherine ffarrell y⁰ Daughter of Rich^d & Winifrid ffarrell bap^{tz} 12th Aprill 1685.
Arthur Bendall y⁰ Sone of James & Eliz^a Bendall borne 14th of Jan'y 168$\frac{4}{5}$ & Baptized 12th of Aprill 1685.
Hannah Barbee y⁰ Daughter of W^m & Eliz^a Barbee bap^{tz} 12th of Aprill 1685.

CHRISTENINGS—1685 &c.

Margaret Brumwell ye Daughter of Peter & Ellinor Brumwell bap^{tz} 12th Aprill 1685.
Nicholas Jones y⁰ sone of Rice & Jane Jones was bap^{tz} at ye upper Chap^{ll} 3th May 1685.
Prissilla Middleton y⁰ Daughter of William & Mary Middleton bap^{tz} 3th of May 1685.
Margarett Slawter y⁰ Daughter of Jn⁰ & Eliz. Slawter was bap^{tz} 10th of May 1685.
James Micham y⁰ sone of Jn⁰ & Michall Micham was bap^{tz} 17th of May 1685.
Thomas Hancock y⁰ sone of Tho. & Eliz^a Hancock was bap^{tz} 24th of May 1685.

Phillip Brooks y⁰ sone of Rich⁴ & Eliza Brooks was bap⁵ y⁰ 24th of May 1685.
Katherine Aldin ye Daughter of Robert & Ellianor Aldin bap⁵ y⁰ 24th of May 1685.
John Seager ye sone of Randolph & Mary Seager bap⁵ 29th of May 1685.
James ye Illigitimate sone of Jno. Haddley by Mary Steeres bap⁵ 17th of June 1685.
Edward James y⁰ sone of Robert & Dorothy James bap⁵ 16th of August 1685.
Elizabeth Prichett y⁰ Daughter of Roger & Rebecca Prichett bap⁵ 16th August 1685.
Richard Buttler y⁰ sone of Rich'd & Mary Buttler bap⁵ 30 of August 1685.
Katherine Williamson y⁰ Daughter of Robert & Kath. Williamson bap⁵ 6th Septemb. 1685.
Mary Dudding y⁰ Daughter of Humphrey & Sarah Dudding bap⁵ 6th Septemb. 1685.
John Walters ye sone of William & Katherine Walters was bap⁵ 20th Septemb 1685.
Nathaniell Guess y⁰ sone of William & Eliz⁰ Guess was bap⁵ 4th of Octob. 1685.
Thomas Haslewood ye sone of Tho. & Mary Hazlewood bap⁵ 18th of Octob. 1685.
Ann Dowlin ye Daughter of Antho. & Eliza Dowlin bap⁵ 18th of Octob. 1685.
Oswald Wortham y⁰ sone of John & Eliz⁰ Wortham bap⁵ 4th of Aprill 1685.
John Sandersee y⁰ sone of Edward & Eliza Sandersee bap⁵ y⁰ po. June 1685.
Robert Thackston y⁰ sone of Rich⁴ & Eliza Thackston borne 2th Octob. bap⁵ 22th Novemb 1685.
Robert Perrott y⁰ sone of Rich⁴ & Sarah Perrott Jun' bap⁵ 26th of Novemb. 1685.
Rose Curtis y⁰ Daughter of Charles & Rose Curtis bap⁵ 26th of November 1685.
George-Stapleton y⁰ sone of Tho. & ffrances Stapleton was borne 26th of Novemb. and Baptized at y⁰ great Church 10th of January 168⅚.
William Sandford y⁰ sone of Jno. & Sarah Sandford bap⁵ 7th of ffebruary 168⅚.
Mary Scarbrough y⁰ Daughter of Augustine & Dorothy Scarbrough bap⁵ 7th feb. 168⅚.
Richard Allen y⁰ sone of Richd & Ann Allen was bap⁵ 14th of ffebruary 168⅚.
John Brim y⁰ sone of John & Mary Brim was bap⁵ 14th of ffebruary 168⅚.
Elizabeth Mickleburrough y⁰ Daughter of Tobias & Eliz⁰ Mickleburrough bap⁵ 14th feb. 168⅚.
Robert Benson ye Sone of Tho. & Dorothy Benson bap⁵ 11th of ffebruary 168⅚.

WEDDINGS OR MARRIAGES 1686.

John Johnson & Lucina Blake both of this p'ish was married ye 6th of Aprill 1686.
Lewis Gasking & Ann Chambers both of this parish was marryed 6th of Aprill 1686.
Ralph Parr & Pheby Matthews both of this parish was married ye 1686.
William Sheppard & Sarah Edey both of this parish was married y® 20th May 1686.
Thomas Blackby & Margarett Jones both of this parish marryed 4th Octob. 1686.
William Humphreys & Sarah Davis both of this parish was maried 28th Nov. 1686.
William Nicholson & Grace Lewis both of this parish was married 2th Novemb 1686.
Richard Greenstead & Katherine Nicholls both of this parish was maried p. Mr. Pead y® 30th of Decemb. 1686.
Edward Canadey & Alice Nicholls both of this parish was married 30th Xemb. 1686.
Nicholas Rice & Ann Tugwell both of this parish was married 6th ffeb. 1686.
John Guthry & Eliz⁂ Basket both of this parish was marryed 6th ffeb. 1686.
William Jones of new Kent County & Alice Lee of this pish mary'ed 8th July 1686.
William Daniell Jun' & Constance Vause both of this pish was married 24 July 1686.
William Williamson & Sarah Danger both of this pish marrid 23th August 1686.
John Perrin & Judith Spencer both of this parish was marryed 2th Sept. 1686.
John Williams & Mary Cordwell both of y⁑ parish married 10th of Octob. 1686.
George Johnston & Eliz⁂ White both of this pish marrid the 1686.

BURIALLS.—1686 &c.

Richard Dews Departed this Life 9th of Novemb. & was buried at M' William Pooles 11th of Novemb. 1686.
M' Richard Perrott Sen' & president of Middlesex County Court departed this Life 11th and was buried 15th of November 1686.
Thomas Radley Departed this Life 13th & was buried 18th of January 1686.
M" Mabell Harvie wife of Joseph Harvie depart⁴ this Life 26th of Jan'⁷ & was buryed y® po. ffebruary 1686.
Theophylas Hone of this parish Departed this Life 3th & was buryd 5th of ffeb. 1686.
The Lady Ann Skipwith of this parish Departed this Life 5th of March and was Buryed 6th of March 1686.
Majo' Robert Beverley of this parish Departed this Life 15th of March and was buryed 19th of March 1686.
M" Jane Price Departed this Life 27th of March and was Buryed at home the 29th of March 1687.

CHRISTENINGS—1685 1686 & 1687.

Peter Mynor the Sone of Doodis & Elizᵃ Mynor was Baptized 7th of March 168⅜.
Jacob Stiff the Sone of Tho. & Sarah Stiff borne 11th of Janʳ bapᵗˢ 21th March 168⅜.
Robert Dudley the Sone of William & Mary Dudley baptized 21th March 168⅜.
Henry yᵉ Illegitimate Sone of Tho. Ballard was baptized 21th of March 168⅜.
Issabella Willis yᵉ Daughter of William & Bridgᵗ Willis bapᵗˢ 21th of March 168⅜.
Elizabeth Murrey Daughter Allˣ & Mary Murrey bapᵗˢ 4th of Aprill 1686.
Ann Brewer yᵉ Daughter of Jno. & Mary Brewer was bapᵗˢ 18th Aprill 1686.
Mary Standly yᵉ Daughter of Tho. & Rebecca Standly bapᵗˢ 18th Aprill 1686.
Thomasin Gates yᵉ Daughter of Tho. & Rose Gates was bapᵗˢ 9th of May 1686.
Thomas Musgrane yᵉ Sone of Michaell & Elizᵃ Musgrane bapᵗˢ 23th May 1686.
Elizabeth Carter yᵉ Daughter of Wᵐ & _____ Carter borne 6th of June 1686.
Theophilus Man ye Sone of John & Dorothy Man borne . . . bapᵗˢ 5th Xemb. 1686.
Henry yᵉ Sone of Henry & Ann Davis of Montagues Island bapᵗˢ 19th of Septemb. 1686.
Thomas ffitz Jeffryes yᵉ Sone of Wᵐ ffitz Jeffreys & Ann his wife borne 23th Augᵒ 1686.
William ffitz Jefferyes Sone of Wᵐ ffitz Jeffreys & Ann his wife borne 24th May 1682.
John Jefferyes yᵉ Sone of Wᵐ & ffrances Jefferyes borne 30th of Augᵗ 1686.
Sarah Cocking yᵉ Daughter of Jno. & Hannah Cocking borne 6th Augᵒ bapᵗˢ 7th Noᵇʳ 1686.
Ellianor yᵉ Illegitimate Daughter of Samˡˡ Banks by Mary Brown born 16th May and baptized 7th of Novemb. 1686.
John Summers the Sone of Jno. & Elizᵃ Summers bapᵗˢ at yᵉ Uper Capˡˡ 14th Noᵇʳ 1686.
Charles Mullens yᵉ Sone of Zacheriah & Mary Mullens bapᵗˢ 14th Novemb. 1686.
George yᵉ Illegitimate Sone of Tho. Hucklescot by Elizᵃ Ward borne 19th May and baptizᵈ 28th of Novembʳ 1686.
Rebecca Hill yᵉ Daughter of Tho. & Ann Hill bapᵗˢ at yᵉ lower Chapˡˡ 28th 9ᵇʳ 1686.
Sarah ffarrell yᵉ Daughter of Richᵈ & Winifrid ffarrell bapᵗˢ 19th Xemb. 1686.
Sarah Trigg yᵉ Dauʳ of Daniell & Susannah Trigg bapᵗˢ 26th of Xemb. 1686.
Thomas Doss yᵉ Sone of Jno. & Ann Doss bapᵗˢ at yᵉ lower Chapˡˡ 9th January 1686.
ffrances Dudley yᵉ Daughter of Tho. & ffrances Dudley baptized 9th January 1686.

Eliz. Barwick ye Daught^r of Geo. & Mary Barwick bap^ts at ye Low^r Chap^ll 20th ffeb. 1686.
Mary Elliott ye Daughter of Tho. & Sarah Elliott bap^ts at ye Upper Chap^ll 27th ffeb^ry 1686.
Eliz^a Gellett ye Daught^r of Tho. & Ann Gellett baptized 27th of ffebruary 1686.
Christop^r Beverly ye Sone of Robt. & Katherine Beverly bap^tz at home 19th March 1686.
Habias Mugguire ye Dat^r of Jno. & Eliz^a Mugguire bap^ts at Mr Prices 29th March 1687.
Peter Guillams Sone of Ann & Robt Guillams bap^ts at home 29th of March 1687.
James Curtis Sone of James & Eliz^a Curtis bap^ts at home 12th of Aprill 1687.
Deuell Pead sone of Mr Deuel Pead & Mad^m Sarah Pead borne 14th Xemb & bap^ts 21th Xemb 1687.

An Acco^t of ye Register of Middlesex County Giving into the Secretaries office Beginning III. 78^r 1686.

BURIED VIZ^t.

11th Septemb. Mary the widow of James Hopkings.
17. Ditto. John Davis Servt to Majo^r Robt. Beverly.
22. Ditto. Tho. the Sone of Robert & Kath. Beverley.
10. Octob. William Rogers of Worchestershire Servt to Alexd^r Murrey.
11. Novemb. Richd Dews of Yorkshire overseere to Majo^r Beverley.
15. Ditto Mr Richd Perrott Senr Presid^t of Midd^x County Court.
20. Xemb. Daniell Long &c.
— Ditto. John sone of William & Jochebed Daniell.
9 January Mrs Mary Mynor Widow of Mountagues Island.
— Ditto. Peter an negro of Mr John Worthams.
16 Ditto. Ann ye Wife of Richard Allen.
18 Ditto. Thomas Radley of London.
— Ditto. Mary ye Wife of John Bourk.
22 Ditto. John sone of Jno. & Mary Purvis.
— Ditto. Thomas sone of Thomas & Mary Williams.
— Ditto. Hannah Cock Servt to Mr Jno. Nicholls.
— Ditto. Thomas Williams of Hartford Shire.

BURIED.

po ffebry Mrs Mabell Harvey ye wife of Joseph Harvie.
5 Ditto Theophilus Hone native.
8 Ditto Richd Bishop Souldier buried at Mr Richd Robinsons.
10 Ditto Jonathan Brookes.
12 Ditto Samuell Simpson native.
15 Ditto Negro Harry Servt to Mr Richd Robinson.
17 Ditto Mary Payne.
— Ditto Jonathan Whitehead of Southworth London.
23 Ditto James Nicholson of Ixby in Cumberland In England.
27 Ditto William Thompson.
— Ditto Thomas Browne an Indian.

28 Ditto Mary Daughter to Tho. & Mary Haslewood.
4 March. Thomas Elliott of Chipping Orgur in Essex.
6 Ditto The Lady Ann Skipwith &c.
7 Ditto Thomas Chowning Native.
— Ditto Hannah Daughter to Christop' & Katherine *Kilbee*.
— Ditto Hester Daughter to Timothy Davis native.
12 Ditto George ye Illigitimate sone of Nurse Dawny at Brandon.
19 Ditto Maj' Robert Beverley of Yorkshire.
20 Ditto George Williams of Kent In England.
— Ditto Humphry Dudding &c.
23 Ditto Peter an Negro of Alice Thackers.
24 Ditto Richard Ellis.
25 Ditto 1687 Thomas Tugwell native.
26 Ditto John Davis of Bristow.
— Ditto Job. Gibson.
27 Ditto James Atwood a Yorkshire man.
28 March 1687 Susan wife to Daniell Trigg native.
— Ditto Israell Gray &c.
29 Ditto Jane wife to Robert Price.
— Ditto Vallentine Vallis Cooper.
— Ditto John sone to David George.
30 Ditto George Hanson.
  ffoure negros of Mr Chr. Robinson.
po. Aprill Alice Wife to William Jones native.
4 Ditto Mary Widow of Jno. Davis, whose mayden name was Mary Greene.
7 Ditto James Webb.
— Ditto William Olliver of ye Ile of Ely neare Cambridge.
— Ditto Thomas Standly.
11th April Mary the Ellegitimate Daughter of Owen Fox and Mary Hudson native.
13 Ditto Henry Ballard ye Illegitimate son of Ballard.
— Ditto Eliz Wife to Tho. Stacy native.
16 Ditto Mary wife to Allexand^r Murrey She was of London.
18 Ditto Betty an negro of William Daniells.
— Ditto Betty an negro of Mr Robert Smiths at Brandon.
  65 in this acco^t Buried &c.

1686 CHRISTENED &c.

Septemb. Theophilus the sone of John & Dorothy Man.
9 Ditto Henry ye sone of Henry & Ann Davis of Mountagus Islad.
Octob Thomas ye Sone of William & Ann ffitz Jeffereys of Rappahannock.
— Ditto John sone to William & ffrances Jefferys.
No^{br} 9 Nov^{br} Sarah Daughter to Jno & Hannah Cocking.

— Ditto Ellianor ye Illegetimate Daughter of Sam^{ll} Banks. By Henry Browne &c.
14 Ditto John sone to Jno & Eliz. Summers.
— Ditto Charles sone to Zachariah & Mary Mullens.
20 Ditto. John ye Sone of W^m & Jochebed Daniell.
28 Ditto George ye Illegitimate sone of Tho. Hacklefoot by Eliz^a Ward.

— Ditto Rebecca Daughter of Tho. and Ann Hill.
19. Xemb. Sarah Daughter to Rich^d & Winifrid ffarrell.
— ditto. Sarah Daughter to Daniell & Susannah Trigg.
9 Jan^{ry} Thomas sone to John & Ann Doss.
— Ditto ffrances Daughter to Thomas and ffrances Dudley.
14 Ditto. John sone of George & Eliz^a Johnston.
10 ffeb^{ry} William sone to William & Grace Thompson.
14 Ditto William Sone to Nicholas & Rose Coleby.
20 Ditto Elizabeth Daughter to Geo. and Mary Barwick.
27 Ditto. Mary Daughter to Thomas & Sarah Elliott.
— Ditto Elizabeth daughter to Thomas & Ann Jellett of Rappahannock.
10 March Elizabeth daughter to John & Eliz^a Wortham.
19 Ditto Christopher sone to Robert & Katherine Beverley.
21 Ditto . Hobbs sone to ffrancis & Eliz^a Weekes.
29 Ditto Peter sone to Robert & Ann Guillams.
— Ditto Phebias Daughter to John & Eliz^a Mackguire.
12 Aprill James sone to James & Eliz^a Curtis.
27 In this Acco^t Christened &c.

1686 MARRIED.

2 Septemb. John Perin of Sussex in England & Judith Spencer Widow of Kent in England.
21 Ditto. John Davis of Bristow and Mary Greene &c.
4 Octob. Thomas Blackey of Cumberland in England & Marg^t Jones of Clamorganshire in Wales.
10 Ditto John Williams of Oxfordshire & Mary Cordwell of Shropshire In England.
2 Novemb. William Nicholson & Grace Lewis &c.
20 Xemb. John Macguire and Elizabeth Dourey.
27 ditto John Purvis and Mary Shippey.
30 Novemb. Edward Canaday and Alice Nicholls.
— Ditto. Richard Greensted and Catherine Nicholls.
4 Jan^{ry}. Pythagorus Powell of Katesby in Northamptonshire & Ann Reynor of Hartfordshire &c.
24 Ditto. William Daniell Junr & Constance Vause both Natives.
6 ffeb^r. John Guttery of Scotland & Eliz. Baskett &c.

65 Buried
27 Christened
12 Cupple Married

104 In all.

M^o
  Whereas Mr Richard Perrott hath built a Pew in the Chancell on the further side opposite to the Pulpitt in ye Upper Chappell of the County of Middlesex, and a Stable also, which Pew and Stable Is for the Use of Henry Corbin Esqr properly belonging to him and to those that Shall have and Enjoy the house and Land Whereon he now Liveth, on and for ever. It appeareth that ye Said Mr Richard Perrott hath Received full Sattisfaction of Coll^o Henry Corbin Esqr for building the abovesaid, by Virtue of a Receipt given Under his hand which beareth Date from September the 29th 1669.

CHRISTENED—1687.

John Masey the Sone of Ralph & Margaret Masey bap^{tz} ye po. May 1687.
Mary ye Daughter of Sarah, widow of Jonathan Brookes bap^{tz} po. May 1687.
William Barbee Sone of W^m & Eliz^a Barbee bap^{tz} 15th of May 1687.
Avarilla Curtis ye Daughter of Charles & Rose Curtis bap^{tz} 15th May 1687.
Charles Grasson Sone of Tho. and Mary Grasson Baptized 15th May 1687.
William Watts ye Sone of Hugh & Johannah Watts bap^{tz} 22th of May 1687.
Thomas Bristow Sone of Jno. & Michall Bristow bap^{tz} 12th of June 1687.
Elizabeth ye Daughter of Patrick & Marg^t Goodridge bap^{tz} 12th June 1687.
John Blackley ye Sone of Robt. & Jane Blackley bap^{tz} 24th of Julye 1687.
Jane Curtis ye Daughter of Giles & Mary Curtis bap^{tz} 24th of Julye 1687.
Thomas the Sone of Ellianor Wheler Widow of Tho. Wheeler 31th of Julye 1687.
Alice Rhodes y^e Daugh^r of Ezekiah & Rhodes bap^{tz} 7th of Aug^o 1687.
John y^e Illegitimate Sone of Eliz^a Servt to Mad^m Beverly bap^{tz} 28th Augt 1687.
Sarah King y^e Daughter of W^m & Martha King baptiz^d 25th of Septemb. 168$\frac{7}{8}$.
Ann Guttrey y^e Daugh^r of Jno. & Eliz^a Guttrey was bap^{tz} 16th of Octob. 1687.
Thomas ffearne y^e Sone of Jno. & Mary ffee alias ffearne bap^{tz} po No^{br} 1687.
William Tignor Son of W^m & Dorothy Tignor bap^{tz} 30th of Octob. 1687.
William Carter y^e Sone of William & Penlopec Carter bap^{tz} 6th No^{br} 1687.
John ffearman sone of Jno. & Ursula ffearman bap^{tz} 6th of Novem^{br} 1687.
Peter ye sone of Peter & Susanna Shelton bap^{tz} y^t 15th Novem^{br} 1687.
James the sone of James & Eliz^a Bendall bap^{tz} 20th of November 1687.
William ye sone of John & Mary Bodgam bap^{tz} 7th Xemb 1687.
William the sone of William & Mary Loyall bap^{tz} 11th of January 1687.
Thomas the sone of George and Ann Clark baptized 4th of ffebruary 1687.
Eliz^a Daughter of James & Eliz^a Dudley bap^{tz} 12th of ffebruary 1687.
Sarah ye Daughter of Mr Deuell Pead & Madam Sarah Pead his wife was borne 7th of ffebruary 1687 and bap^{tz} 26th of ffeb^{ry} 1687.
John ye Sone of John & Sarah Hipkings baptized 20th of ffebruary 1687.

Ann y* Daughter of Samuell & Ann Ingram bap^{ts} 26th ffebruary 1687.
Judith y* Daughter of Robert and Sarah Clark bap^{ts} 11th of March 1687.
Here Ends the Acco^t of this Register The 10th of Aprill 1688.

WEDDINGS OR MARRIAGES 1687.

Edward Sanders & Mary Browne both of this parish was marryed 6th May 1687.
Thomas Chrisp & Dorothy Long both of this parish was marryed 18th of May 1687.
Martin Masey & Eliz^a Slanter both of this parish was marryed the—
Thomas Robey & Ann Wallis both of this pish was marryed 27th of June 1687.
James Pate & Eliz^a Eddington both of this pish marryed 27th of June 1687.
Abraham Depree & Rebecca Smith both of Rappahannock marryed 3^d July 1687.
Robert George & Sarah Elliott both of this parish was marryed 6th of July 1687.
Benjamin Marsh of New England & Katherine Allison of this pish was Marryed at Mr Robinsons house p Mr Pead 10th of July 1687.
James Shackleford was marryed 14th of July 1687.
Nicholas ffowle & ffrances Webb both of this pish marryed 24th July 1687.
Joseph Carter & Mary Grant both of this parrish was marryed 4th Septemb 1687.
Joseph Smith & Eliza Rammage was marryed 22th of September 1687.
John ffearman & Ursula Roberts both of this pish mar^d 25th Septemb. 1687.
William Beamont & Eliz^a Hughs both of this pish marryed 10th October 1687.
Samuell Ingram & Ann Hartley both of this pish marryed 17th Octob. 1687.
Henry Emmerson & Eliz^a ffree both of this prish was marryed 17th Octob. 1687.
James Parker of New Kent of Southwell In Notinghamshire & Ellinor Abbott widow of Piscataway was married 18th of October 1687.
John ffearne of Gloster & Mary Lee of this pish Married ye po. November 1687.
William Brooks & Ann Cardwell both of this pish marryed 8th of Novemb. 1687.
John Littlefield & Susannah Sandeford was marryed 17th of Novemb. 1687.
Mr Christopher Robinson & Mad^m Katherine Beverly were mar^d 17th of 9^{br} 1687.
John Stone of Ridgely in Staffordshire & Mary O. Brissell native were Marryed ye 10th of November 1687.
Nicholas Payne of London & Mary Hackney Native Marryed 17th Xemb 1687.

Edward Sitterne of London & Jane Jones of this pish was marryed p^o Jan^r 1687.
Mr John Vause & Eliz. Weekes both natives was married 19th of January 1687.
Robert Daniell & Marg^t Price both natives of this pish mari^d 7th ffeb^{ry} 1687.
The Hon^{rble} Ralph Wormeley Esqr And Madam Eliz Armisted of Gloster was married at Coll^o Armsteds in Gloster 16th of ffebruary 1687.
William Anderson & Ann Clever both of this pish was m^d 23th of ffeb^r 1687.
Thom^s Stacy of Coulchester in Essex & Rebecca Standly was married 27th ffeb^r 1687.
Mr John Wortham & Mrs Prudence Needham was married 26th of ffebruary 1687.
Jno Bloss of Coulchest^r & Ann Ball Native was married 27th of ffeb^r 1687.

Here ended the Acco^t of this Register 10th Aprill 1688.

BURIALLS. V$_{IZ}^t$:

———— Curtis the Daughter of Charles & Rose Curtis Departed this Life the 18th of September 1687.
Samuell Smith y^e sone of Mr Alexd^r Smith Departed this Life 5th of May 1687.
Jeremy Vynn of Norwidge departed this Life 17th of July 1687.
Nicholas Cock of this parish departed this Life 25th of Octob 1687.
Mr Robert Smith of this parish Departed this Life 27th of Octob 1687.
George Watson of the Barbadoes Servant to Mr Robert Smith Departed this Life 5th of December 1687.
Max Petty of this parish departed this Life 12th of Xember 1687.
Mary Bodgham of this parish (native) Departed this Life 12th Xemb. 1687.
Elizabeth Wortham of this parish Departed this Life 16th of Jan^r 1687.
John Loyall Sone of Jno Loyall Departed this Life 20th of January 1687.
Mrs Marg^t Perrott ye Wife of Mr Richd Perrott Senr departed 30th of Jan^r 1687.
Jane Sitterne of this parish departed this Life 4th of ffebruary 1687.
Nicholas Colbee of this p^{r}ish Departed this Life 17th of ffebruary 1687.
Mary Athy of this parish departed this Life 23th of ffebruary 1687.
Sarah Martin of this pish hired Servt to Tho. Norman departed 25th ffeb^r 1687.
Doctor William Poole of this parish departed this Life 29th ffeb^{ry} Leap yeare 1687.
Thomas Purify Gardener to Ralph Wormely Esqr Departed 28th of ffeb^r 1687.

Here endeth The acco^t of this Register ye 10th of Aprill 1688.

BURIALLS—1687—Viz^t.

Samuell Smith Son of Allexand^r Smith Departed this Life 5th May 1687.
Mr Jeremy Vynn of Norwich Departed this Life 17th of July 1687.
Mr Nicholas Cock the 25th October 1687.
Mr Robert Smith 27th Octob^r 1687.
George Walton of ye Barbados 5th Xemb. 1687.
Max Petty the 12th Xembr 1687.
Mary Bodgham the 12th Xemb^r 1687.
Elizabeth Wortham the 16th January 1687.
John Loyall the 21th January 1687.
Jane Sitterne the 4th ffebruary 1687.
Nich^o Coleby the 17th ffebruary 1687.
Mary Athy the 23th ffebruary 1687.
Sarah Martin the 25th ffebruary 1687.
Do^r William Poole the 29th ffeb^r 1687.
Thomas Purify Gardener 28th ffeb^r 1687.

HERE WE BEGIN. WEDDINGS &c. AN NEW ACCO^t 1688.

Henry Osborne & Alice George both of this parish was Married p Mt Pead 15th of May 1688.
William Gough of New Kent & Alice Thacker of this parish were Marryed at Thackers 31th of May 1688.
William Southward & Marg^t Lewis both of this p^{r}ish were mar^d 17th Ap^{rll} 1688.
Samuell Acton & Honour Berry both of this psh. were married at Mountagues 12th of July 1688.
Thomas Beamont & Mary Coster both of this pish marry^{e}d p. Lycence the 28th of June 1688.
Thomas Winger & Ann Doss of this parish were Marryed 15th of July 1688.
William Hobbs ye Shoemaker at Willis was marryed.
Edward Pierce & Katherine Humphryes of this pish was marryed 2th Sep^t 1688.
William Needler & Mrs Dorothy Man both of this pish was married 1688.
John Chedle & Millicent Hughs both of this pish was marryed 9th Octob. 1688.
Richard Bennett & Sarah Harrison both of this p. was maried 28th Octob. 1688.
William Johnson of Norwich & Mary Bennett of West Chester was Marryed 10th of ffebruary 168$\frac{8}{9}$.

Joyned together in y^e State of Holy Matrimony by Mr. Deuel Pead;
David Davis & Martha King of this parish the . . . of . . . 168$\frac{8}{9}$.
Thomas Guy & Susannah Burford the 14th of Octob. 1689.
Paul Thilman & Mrs Margaret Price widow of Mr Robt Price Jan^r 27th 1689.
William Terrey & Elizabeth Cooper Aprill 21th 1689.
John Nash (Native) and Mary Jenkinson of Cumberland in England were Marryed p. Lycence p. Mr Duel Pead the 12th of July 1690.
Ralph Wilkeson & the Widow Richans 25th of July 1690.
John Swift & Elizabeth Lone August 6th 1690.

Richard Davison and Katherine Downe the   of   1690.
Mr Randolph Seager and Madam Ann Cary were marryed 2th July 1691.
William Scarbrough and ffrances Macrory the —— —— 1691.
Here Endeth the acco^t of Marriages Given Into the Secretarys Office the 15th Day of October 1692.
Here we begin an New acco^t of

CHRISTENINGS—1688 &c.

Elizabeth ye Daughter of Nicholas & Mabell Paine borne 3th of March 1688 and baptized 3th of June 1688.
Alice ye Daughter of Jno & Mary Brim borne 10th ffeb^r bap^{ts} 16th June 1688.
George ye sone of Robert & Ann Chowning was borne 16th of ffeb^r 1688, and was baptized the 10th of June 1688.
Mary Daughter of Tho. & Mary Blewford borne 18th March bap^{ts} 10th of June 1688.
Thomas the sone of Anthony & Eliz^a Dowtin borne 9th May bap^{ts} 3th of June 1688.
Thomas the sone of W^m & Mary Dudley borne 31th of May bap^{ts} 24th of June 1688.
John the sone of Jno & Eliz^a Lane borne 10th of Aprill bap^{ts} ye po. May 1688.
Elizabeth Robinson y^e Daughter of Mr Chr. Robinson and Mad^m Kath Robinson borne 18th of Augt Just at night & bap^{ts} at home 20th Augt 1688.
Robert the son of Mr Robert Boodle & Mary his wife borne 15th Novemb. 1688. ffebruary the 17th 168$\frac{8}{9}$. Baptized at ye Upper Chappell.
Richard sone to William and Ellinor Sadler.
Martha Daughter to Robert and Katherine Williamson.
Ralph ye Son of William and Mary Loyall.
Elizabeth Daughter to Robert and Dorothy James.
James sone to Jno. and Bloss.
Lettice Daughter to Nicholas & Eliz^a Lee.
Thomas Sone to John and Millicent Chedle.

March the 10th 168$\frac{8}{9}$ Baptized at ye Upper Chappell.

John ye Sone to Hugh and Johannah Watts.
Milliner Daughter to John & Ann Massey.

Aprill the 14th 1689 Baptised at Christ Church.

Elizabeth Daughter to Robert and Ann Gilliam.

Baptized at ye Upper Chappell the 7th of Aprill 1689.

William y^e sone of John ffearman and Ursula his Wife.
Thomas Sone of Thomas Gates and Rose his wife.
Sarah Daughter to John Alford and Lettice his Wife.

Baptized at the Upper Chappell 28th of Aprill 1689.

Ann Daughter to Henry Osborne and Alice his wife.
Mary Daughter to John Macguire and Eliz. his wife.
Katherine Daughter to Edward Berry and Sarah his wife.
Edward Sone to William Chayney and Pen his wife.

Agatha Daugh. to Mr Jno. Vause & Mrs Eliz^{a} Vause bap^{ts} 28th of ffeb^{r} 168$\frac{8}{9}$.

Agatha Daughter of Deuel & Sarah Pead born 20th of Octob. ab^{t} 10 morning & bap^{ts} 27th ditto—1689.

BURIALLS—1688.

Mary the Daughter of Hugh & Johannah Watts Departed this Life 3th May 1688.

John Willis Departed this Life 4th and was Buried the 6th of May 1688.

Christopher ffisher of Ireland departed this Life y^{e} — June was bur^{d} 30th June 1688.

Walter Cane of Slaigh in Ireland Servt to Wm Tignor depart^{d} this Life p^{o} July. and was bury^{ed} 3th of July 1688.

Richard Askall Servt to James Dudley Departed this Life 6th of July 1688.

Eliz^{a} Dudley wife of James Dudley Departed this Life 8th of July 1688.

John Simpson of Barkin in Essex departed this Life 11th of July 1688.

Prudence Wortham ye Wife of Jno Wortham departed this Life 25th 7^{br} 1688.

Thomas Naylor serv^{t} to Mr Chr. Robinson Dyed the 23th of Nemb. 1688.

Mrs Ann Robinson Wife to Mr Richd Robinson Dyed 8^{br} 5th 1688.

John Cutter departed this Life the 11th of Octob 1688.

Elizabeth Atwood Departed this Life the 15th of Aprill 1689.

Mr Thomas Heyward Clerk of ye great Church Departed this Life 1689.

Mrs Eltonhead Stanard departed this Life October 28th 1689.

Two Servants belonging to Mr Robert Price (a man & a woman) Departed this Life in August—1689.

Thomas Pullen departed this Life 20th of December 1689.

Mr Robert Price Departed this Life the 11th of January 168$\frac{9}{9}$.

Robert Porter Departed this Life the 27th of January 168$\frac{9}{9}$.

Richard Thaxton departed this Life 2th of March 168$\frac{9}{9}$.

Eusebias O.Bressell was buried the 7th of March 168$\frac{9}{9}$.

Nicholas Lone Departed this Life the 7th of June 1690.

William Nicholson Dyed 19th & was buried the 21th of August 1690.

Edmund Mickleburrough Sen. departed this Life 27th of August 1690.

Honour Acton Dyed 3th and was buried 4th of Octob 1690.

Mary Wife of Mr Randolph Seager Departed this Life 8th of No^{br} 1690. and was buried in the Upper Chappell &c.

Richard the Son of Samuell Acton Dyed 9th of ffebruary 169$\frac{0}{1}$.

Capt Oswald Cary Dyed the 17th of ffebruary 169$\frac{0}{1}$.

Mr John Vause Dyed the 9th of September 1691.

John y^{e} Son of Do^{r} Robert Boodle was buried the 21th of Decemb 1691.

Mr John Wortham Departed this Life the 8th of June 1692.

Capt Walter Whittaker Dyed 27th of July 1692.

Here Endeth the Accot of Burialls Given into the Secretarys office the 15th of Octob. 1692.

CHRISTENINGS—1689 & 1690.

Elizabeth Daughter to Anthony & Ann Ridgaway borne 8th June 1689.
John ye Sone of John & Eliz^a Guthrey bapt^z 28th July 1689.
William sone of Mr Randolph Seagur and Mary his wife was borne 28th of August and baptized 8th of Septemb 1689.
John Sone to Richard & Eliz^a Brookes baptized 8th Septemb 1689.
William Sone to Mr William & Constance Daniell bap^{ts} at home the 8th of September 1689.

Christened at the Upper Chappell ye 1th day Xember 1689.

Mary Daughter to John Barlow and Pheby his wife.
Elizabeth Daughter to Zachariah Mullens & Mary his Wife.
Catherine Daughter to Robert George & Sarah his Wife.
Thomas Sone of Mr Thomas Stapleton & ffrancis his Wife.
Richans y^e Sone of John & Mary Brim bap^{ts} 23th ffeb^r 168$\frac{8}{9}$.
John y^e Sone of Jno & Jane Smith bap^{ts} at home 23th ffeb^r 168$\frac{8}{9}$.
Elizabeth Daughter to J^{no} & Eliz. Summers bap^{ts} 16th March 168$\frac{8}{9}$.

Baptized at y^e Upper Chappell the 6th of Aprill 1690.

Thomas the Sone of Humphrey and Jane Salt.
Samuell y^e Sone of Robert and Ann Chowning was Borne the 27th of ffebruary 1690, Baptized y^e 6th of Aprill.
Jane y^e Daughter of Patrick & Margaret Michaell y^e Same day.
Jeremiah ye Sone of Peter & Eliz^a Rawlings of New Kent County bap^{ts} p. Mr Pead 6th of Aprill 1690.
John the Sone of William & Marg^t Southward bap^{ts} at ye Great Church the 13th of August 1690.
John ye Sone of John & Pen. Evans was bap^{ts} at Upper Chap^{ll} 4th May 1690.
William ye Sone of W^m & Ann Brookes baptized 25th of May 1690.
Mayo & Sarah The sone and Daughter of John & Sarah Bourk borne 22th of May and baptized 15th of June 1690.
William ye Sone of Joseph and Mary Carter bap^{ts} 15th of June 1690.
Andrew the Sone of Jno & Sarah Hipkings was bore 11th of May and baptized 22th of June at ye Great Church 1690.

1690 1691 & 1692 &c.

Elizabeth ye Daughter of John & Michall Bristow bap^{ts} 6th of July 1690.
Rebecca y^o Daughter of George & Eliz. Johnston bap^{ts} 6th of July 1690.
Thomas Sone of Robert & Sarah Clark bap^{ts} 6th of July 1690.
Sarah Daughter of Roger & Rebecca Prichard bap^{ts} 6th of July 1690.
Elizabeth Daughter of James & Sarah Ingram bap^{ts} 6th of July 1690.
Elizabeth Daughter of Anthony & Eliz. Dowlin bap^{ts} 21th of Augt 1690.
Katherine Vallott ye Daughter of Claud & Ann Vallott was borne the 2th of September 1690 and bap^{ts} 28th of the Same month 1690.
Ann y^e Daughter of George and Ann Haslewood borne the last day of November and baptized 28th of December 1690.
Theophilus y^e Sone of Mr Christop^r Robinson & Katherine his wife was baptized the ffirst day of January 169$\frac{0}{1}$.

Mary the Daughter of Mʳ Randolph & Mʳˢ Mary Seager borne the 9th of Novemb. and baptized 11th of Ditto 1690.
William Sone of Tho. & Elizᵃ Hancock bapᵗˢ 20th of ffebruary 169⅔.
Clara the Daughter of Mʳ Christʳ & Mʳˢ Kath. Robinson was borne the 11th day of October 1689.
John the Son of Mʳ Robert & Mʳˢ Mary Boodle was borne 24th of January and bapᵗˢ 19th of ffebruary 169⅔.
John Nash the Son of John & Mary Nash was borne 22th of Octob. between Sun Sett and Darke and was bapᵗˢ 13th of Novemb. 1691.
Henry the Sone of Ann Jones was baptized the 7th of Septemb 1689.
James the Sone of James & Jone Lewis baptized 30th of Novemb. 1690.
John the Sone of Robert & Kath Williamson bapᵗˢ 30th of August 1691.
Henry the Sone of Peter & Abigall Chilton bapᵗˢ 20th of Septemb. 1691.
Lucas the Sone of Robert & Ann Gilham bapᵗˢ 27th of March 1692.
Rebecca the Daughter of James & Ann Cooper bapᵗˢ 2th of Augᵗ 1692.
Joseph the Sone of Robert & Elizᵃ Humphreys bapᵗˢ 11th Septemb. 1692.
William Hackney the Sone of Wᵐ Hackney Junʳ borne 22th Janʳʸ 1691.
George the Sone of William & Mary ffreeston borne yᵉ 1st of Octoᵇʳ 1690.
William the Sone of Tho. & ffrances Dudley bapᵗˢ 8th of October 1693.
John the Son of Jno. & Sarach Sandefford was Born the tenth of October 1691.

Here Endeth the accoᵗ of Christenings Given Into the Secretarys office the 15th of Octob. 1692.

The Age of Mʳ Richard Perrott & Sarah his wife.

Richard Perrott the Sone of Mʳ Richard Perrott Dec'd was Borne the 24th of ffebruary 1650 Being the first Man Child that was gott and borne In Rappahannock River of English parents &c.
Sarah Perrott was borne In Ware Parish in Gloster County on a Sunday about 2 a clock afternoone the 16th of Augᵗ 1657 being the Daughter of Majoʳ Tho. Curtis by Averilla his Wife, and was marryed to the said Perrott 11th of ffebʳ 1672. Being then the widow of one Mʳ Wᵐ Halfhide &c.

The names of what children (& the Times When) have been born to the abovesaid Mʳ Richard Perrott, and Sarah Perrott of Middlesex County.

Henry Perrott the Sone of the abovesaid Perrott was borne the 25th of January—1657.
ffrank the Daughter of the above said was borne 28th of Augᵗ 1677.
Sarah the Daughter of ye abovesaid was borne 21th of Sepʳ 1679.
Richard the Sone of the abovesaid Perrott was borne 5th of Octob 1681.

Averilla the Daughter of the abovesaid was borne 3th of Augt 1683.
Robert the Sone of the abovesaid was borne 25th of Octo{sup}br{/sup} 1685.
Curtis the Sone of the abovesaid was borne 19th of Augt 1688.
Mary the Daughter of the abovesaid was borne 19th of Jan'y 1690.
Churchhill Blake the Sone of Thomas & Margaret Blake was borne 30th of November 1690.
John Sandeford the Sone of Jno & Mary Sandeford was born the 17th of Octob 1691.
Elizabeth Musgrane the Dauter of Michaell & Elizabeth Musgrane was borne 18th of August 1693.
ffrances Needles ye Daughter of W^m & Dorothy Needles was borne 19th of March 1690.

CHRISTENINGS—1693 & 1694.

William ffurnelt ye Sone of Jno & Alice ffurnett bap^{ts} 16th of ffeb^{ry} 1693.
John ye Sone of George & Eliz. Blake bap^{ts} 7th of Aprill 1693.
William & Roger begotten of Two Servant Wenches belonging to Coll^o Christopher Wormeley baptized the first of them on the 30th of March the other on the 7th of Aprill 1693.
Edward Sone of Charles & Marg^t Whittaker bap^{ts} 18th of June 1693.
Sarah the Daughter of Tho. & Marg^t Chilton bap^{ts} 16th of July 1693.
Elizabeth Needles Daug^{tr} of W^m & Dorothy Needles borne 20th of March 169$\frac{2}{3}$ and baptized 16th of July 1693.
Andrew y^e Sone of Augustine & Eliz. Williamson bap^{ts} 30th of July 1693.
Elizabeth the Daughter of Ezekias & Eliz^a Rhodes bap^{ts} 27th of Augt 1693.
Elizabeth y^e Daughter of Ambros & Eliz^a Burfutt bap^{ts} 10th Sept. 1693.
Thomas the Sone of Peter & Abig^{ll} Chilton bap^{ts} 20th of Septemb 1693.
Katherine ye Daughter of W^m & Eliz^a Priest bap^{ts} 20th of Septemb. 1693.
Elizabeth the Daughter of Hugh & Hannah Watts bap^{ts} 20th of Septemb. 1693.
Elizabeth ye Daughter of Anthony & Isabella Banks bap^{ts} 5th Novemb. 1693.
Thomas the Sone of James & Jone Lewis bap^{ts} 5th of Novemb. 1693.
Mary the Daughter of James & Ann Dudley bap^{ts} 24th of ffebruary 1693.
Mary the Daughter of Jno & Sarah Sandeford bap^{ts} 24th of March 1693.
George the Sone of Edmund & Mary Sanders bap^{ts} 24th of March 169$\frac{3}{4}$.
Thomas the Sone of Peter & Ellianor Brumwell bap^{ts} 15th of Aprill 1694.
Nicholas the Sone of Jno & Michall Bristow bap^{ts} 17th of June 1694.
Nicholas the Sone of Tho. & Eliz^a Stiff bap^{ts} 8th of July 1694.
John the Sone of Robert & Ann Gilham bap^{tr} 19th of July 1694.
ffrances the Daughter of Tho. & Cassandra Townsand bap^{ts} 9th Sept. 1694.

Daniell the Sone of Jno & Susannah Ress bap^{tz} 24th of Septemb. 1694.

Katherine a Mulatto Woman was baptized the 11th of Novemb. 1694.

Robert Wortham the Sone of George Wortham & Sarah his Wife was borne 4th of October & baptized 16th of Ditto 1694.

Margaret the Daughter of Joshua & Mary Gore borne ye 1st Octob. 1694 and was baptized the 2th of Xemb. following.

Here we begin—BURIALLS &c.

Mr Matthew Lidford (our late Minister) Departed this life the 22th of March Anno Domo. 169$\frac{3}{4}$.

Mr Richard Robinson Senr was buried 19th of Xemb. 1693.

Mrs Ann Gray the Wife of Mr Samuell Gray (our minister) Departed this life the 8th of August 1696.

Sarah y^{e} Wife of John Sandeford departed this Life May ye 8th & Buried ye 9th 1706.

Mary ye Wife of Richard Alford departed this Life May ye 18th & Buried ye 20th 1706.

Mary ye Wife of Robert Bigge departed this Life June ye 4th and Buried ye 5th 1706.

Elizabeth ye Daughter of Mr Robert Dudley & Mrs Elizabeth his Wife departed this Life June ye 20th and was Buried June ye 21st Anno Domi 1706.

Elizabeth ye Daughter of Ezekias Rhodes & Elizabeth his Wife departed this Life July ye 20th and was Buried July ye 22nd Anno Domi^{o} 1706.

Elizabeth Sutton departed this Life Octob ye 27th & was Buried Novemb^{r} ye 1st 1706.

Thomas Thompson Was Buried December ye 16th Anno Domi 1706.

Amy ye Wife of George Barack was Buried Decemb ye 25th Anno Domi 1706.

George Dudly ye Son of Maj^{or} Robert Dudly departed this Life April y^{e} 12th And was Interred April y^{e} 15th Anno Domini 1707.

John y^{e} Son of John & Mary Gibbs departed this Life March y^{e} 31st and was Interred April y^{e} 1st Anno Domin 1708.

Edyth ye Wife of John Dudly departed this Life March y^{e} 4th and was Interred March y^{e} 6th Anno Domi. 170$\frac{8}{9}$.

Margaret Goar y^{e} Daughter of Joseph Goar departed this Life May y^{e} 1st and was Interred May y^{e} 2nd Anno Domi 1709.

Elizabeth Clifton departed this life febuary y^{e} 11th and was Interred february y^{e} 12th: Anno Domi 170$\frac{8}{9}$.

Coll^{nl} John Grimes departed this Life August y^{e} 28th and was Interred August ye 31st A. D. 1709.

CHRISTENINGS.—1694 & 1695.

Dorothy Wallis y^{e} Daughter of William & Ann Wallis was borne the 11th of November 1694.

Maccrora Scarbrough Sone of William & ffrances Scarbrough was baptized the 3d of ffebruary 169$\frac{4}{5}$

Ann Hames the Daughter of Charles & Eliz^{a} Hames bap^{tz} 3th of ffeb^{r} 169$\frac{4}{5}$.

Mary the Daug^{r} of Susannah & Edward Gough bap^{tz} 5th of ffeb^{ry} 169$\frac{4}{5}$.

Rebecca Hackney Daughter of W^m & Mary Hackney bap^ts 3th ffeb^ry 169$\frac{4}{5}$.
Elizabeth the Daughter of Allexand^r & Eliz^a Mesan was borne the 11th of Xemb and bap^ts 10th of March 169$\frac{4}{5}$.
John the Sone of John J. Johnson and Lucy his wife was borne the 6th of January and baptized 24th of March 169$\frac{4}{5}$.
Rachell the Daughter of ffrancis and Mabell Dodson was born the 20th of ffebruary 169$\frac{4}{5}$ and bap^ts 5th of May 1695.
George Gray the sone of Mr Samuell Gray and Mrs Ann Gray his wife was borne 23th of Aprill being St. George's Day and was baptized the 5th of May at his owne house, Mr William Churchhill and Capt William Daniell being God Fathers, and Mrs Ann Grimes God Mother 1695.
Joyce Bodgham the Daughter of John & Hannah Bodgham was baptized the 12th of May—1695.
Sarah Toxell the Daughter of Phillip and Mary Toxell was Baptized 12th of May 1695.
John Dudley the Sone of John & Eliz^a Dudley bap^ts 23th June 1695.
Elizabeth Gilley ye Da^tr of Tho. & Jane Gilley bap^ts 23th of June 1695.
ffrances Gressam ye Daughter of Tho. & Eliz^a Gresham was Borne 26th of March and baptized the 23th of June 1695.
Charles the Son of Tho. & Mary Williamson was Borne 15th of July and baptized the 4th of August 1695.
John the sone of Jno & Michall Miller bap^ts 4th of August 1695.
Elizabeth the Dau^tr of George & Eliz^a Blake bap^ts 18th of August 1695.

CHRISTENINGS—1695 &c.

Ann the Daughter of Jno & Mary Aston baptized 10th of Augt 1695.
Uriah the sone of Jno and Ann Boulton bap^ts 27th of Octob 1695.
Ann the Daughter of Samuell & Ann Ingram bap^ts 19th Novemb. 1695.
Susannah Jones Daughter of Roger & Mary Jones was borne the 19th of November and was Christened the same day at Mr Churchhills house p. Mr Samuell Gray 1695.
Christopher Kilbee the Sone of William & Johannah Kilbee was borne the   of Jan^r and bap^ts the 9th of ffeb^ry 169$\frac{5}{6}$.
Robert Williamson the Sone of Robert & Katherine Williamson was Borne 19th of Jan^r and baptized 23th of ffeb^r 169$\frac{5}{6}$.
William Newton the sone of William &   Newton was Borne 3th of January and Baptized the 2th of March 169$\frac{5}{6}$.
Dorothy Dudley Daughter of Thomas & ffrances Dudley was Borne the   and baptized 10th of May 1696.
John Needles the sone of William and Dorothy Needles was Baptized the 10th of May 1696.
Sarah Sandeford the Daughter of John & Sarah Sandeford was bap^ts the 10th of May 1696.
Catherine Workley the Daughter of Benjamine & Elizabeth Workley was bap^d 10th of May 1696.
Ezechias Rhodes the Sone of Ezechias & Elizabeth Rhodes was Baptized 10th of May 1696.

44

Katherine Baldwin Daughter of Edward & Keziah Baldwin was Baptized 5th of July 1696.

CHRISTENINGS.

William Dudley the Son of James & Ann Dudley bap^{tz} 2th of Augt 1696.

Benjamine Gray the Sone of Mr Samuell Gray Minister & Madam Ann Gray his wife was baptized at his house parson Vicaris and Mr John Grimes being God ffathers and Madam Elizabeth Wormeley God Mother. The 10th of August 1696.

The names and Ages of the Children of William and Grace Thompson.

Sarah the Daughter of the above said Thompson was borne the 13th of March 168¾.

William the Sone of ye abovesaid Thompson was borne the 10th of Octob 1685.

Mary the Daughter of the abovesaid was borne 2th of Sept. 1689.

Samuell the Sone of ye abovesaid was Borne 11th Novemb. 1691.

Elizabeth Smith ye Daughter of Robert & Elizabeth Smith was Bap^{tz} the 8th of November 1696.

Sarah Lawson the Daughter of Rowland & Ann Lawson was baptized 15th of November 1696.

Sarah Gore Daughter of Joshua Gore and Mary his wife was Borne 6th of Novemb. and baptized 6th Decemb 1696.

The Names and Ages of Two Children of Mr Henry Thacker & Elizabeth his wife &c.

Elizabeth Thacker was borne the 3th of December being Monday 1694.

ffrances Thacker was Borne the 19th Decemb^r being Satterday 1696.

CHRISTENINGS &c.

The Names and Ages of 3 Negros of Mr Henry Thacker's.

Dick the Sone of Nick and Jenney was borne 10th of March 1690.

Billey the Sone of Sampson & Nell was born 20th of ffeb^{ry} 1691.

Ned the Sone of Nick and Jeney was borne 20th of April 1694.

Sarah Haines the Daughter of Charles & Eliz^a Haines bap^{tz} 7th No^{br} 1697.

Aimey Gresham ye Daughter of Tho. & Mary Gresham bap^{tz} 9th Nov. 1697.

Elizabeth Beverley the Daughter of Capt Henry Beverley & Mrs Elizabeth Beverley his wife was baptized p. Mr Gray at Esq. Wormeleys the 9th of Novemb 1697.

Richard Burnett the Sone of Jone Burnett was borne 16th Xemb. and baptized the ——— ——— 1697.

Churchhill Jones the Sone of Roger & Mary Jones was borne 15th of Jan^r and bap^{tz} 13th of March 169⅞.

William the Sone of William & Johannah Kilbee bap^{tz} 13th of March 169⅞.

James Duglas the Sone of James & Ann Duglas bap^{tz} 13th March 169⅞.

John ffurnett y^{e} Sone of Jno & Alice ffurnett bap^{tz} 13th of March 169$\frac{7}{8}$.
Ellianor Duglas the Daughter of James & Ann Dudlass was borne the 9th of June 1691.
Johannah Hackney the Daughter of William & Eliz^{a} Hackney was borne 8th of March & baptized 3th of Aprill 1698.
Isabella Hill the Daughter of William & Ann Hill was borne the ffirst of May 1698.
Arthur Nash The Sone of John & Mary Nash was Borne y^{e} 16th of November 1696 & was Bap^{tz} the 14th of ffebruary 169$\frac{6}{7}$.
The ages of two Children of Richard & Sarah Winn.
Mary Winn was borne 16th of Xember 169$\frac{6}{7}$.
Sarah Winn was borne 17th of January 169$\frac{8}{9}$.

CHRISTENINGS.—&c.

John Blake the Sone of George & Eliz^{a} Blake was bap^{tz} 1th May 1698.
Thomas Marston the Sone of Jno & Ann Marston was borne the 30th of August about 10 aClock & was bap^{tz} 15th Sept 1698.
William Roe y^{e} Sone of Jno & Katherine Roe bap^{tz} y^{e} 1st May 1698.
William Needles y^{e} Sone of W^{m} & Dorothy Needles bap^{tz} 22th June 1698.
Patrick Miller y^{e} Sone of Jno & Michall Miller bap^{tz} 22th of Jan^{r} 169$\frac{8}{9}$ and was borne the 29th of December 169$\frac{8}{9}$.
Mary Gore y^{e} Daughter of Joshua & Mary Gore was borne the 2th of Decemb. & baptized 22th of January 169$\frac{8}{9}$.
Elizabeth Gibbs y^{e} Daughter of Jno & Mary Gibbs bap^{tz} 22th Jan^{r} 169$\frac{8}{9}$.
James Cooper ye Sone of James & Ann Cooper was bap^{tz} 22th of Jan^{r} 169$\frac{8}{9}$.
Ambros Dudley the Sone of ffrancis & Dudley bap^{tz} 17th No^{br} 1698.
Elizabeth Ashton y^{e} Daughter of Tho. & Eliz. Ashton was baptized the 8th of ffebruary 169$\frac{8}{9}$.
Vallentine Wallis y^{e} Sone of William and Ann Wallis was Baptized 27th of March 1699.
Richard Phiney the Sone of Jno & Marg^{t} Phiney bap^{tz} 28th May 1699.
William Rhodes the Sone of Ezechias and Eliza Rhodes was baptized 28th of May 1699.
Sarah Daughter to John & Ann Boulton bap^{tz} 25th of June 1699.
Mary the Daughter of Capt Kemps Maide bap^{tz} 25th of June. 1699.
Richard the Sone of Jno Sandefords Maid bap^{tz} 25th of June 1699.
Rebecca Dennis the Daughter of Jno & Catherine Dennis was baptized the 22th of Septemb. 1699.
William Dunston the Sone of Thomas & Eliz^{a} Dunston was Baptized the 26th of July 1699.
Grace Sibley the Daughter of John Sibley was bap^{tz} 26th July 1699.
Zebulun the Sone of James & Jone Lewis bap^{tz} 22th of Octob 1699.

CHRISTENINGS &c.

Judith Cardis the Daughter of Uriah Cardis was borne 28th Sept. and baptized the 29th of Octob. 1699.
Ellianor the Daughter of Arthur & Mary Smith bap^{tz} 31th X^{br} 169$\frac{9}{700}$.

The names & Ages of Six Children of Ezechias and Elizabeth Rhodes &c.

Mary Rhodes was borne the 5th of January 1684.
Alice Rhodes was borne 18th of July 1687.
John Rhodes was borne the 12th of ffebruary 1689.
Elizabeth Rhodes was borne 7th of July 1693.
Ezechias Rhodes was borne the 6th of Aprill 1696.
William Rhodes was borne the 23th of Aprill 1698.
Thomas Berry son of Gerrat Berry was Born In January & Bap'^r 23th ffeb'^r 1699.
Mary Beverley the Daughter of M'^r Henry Beverley and M'^rs Eliz'^a Beverley was borne 11th of Novemb. 1699.
William Porter Sone of W'^m & Jane Porter bap'^t 4th March 1690.
John Hackney Dodson the sone of ffrancis Dodson was Baptized the 4th of March 1690.
Margaret Martin the Daughter of M'^rs Eliz'^a Martin was Baptized 7th of March 1690.

CHRISTENINGS 1700.

William Scarbrough the Son of William & ffrances Scarbrough was Baptized 9th of May 1700.
Elizabeth Humphreys the Daughter of Robert & Rebecca Humphreys was baptized 19th of May 1700.
William Austine the Sone of John Austine bap'^t 19th of May 1700.
Sarah Blake the Daughter of John & Eliz'^a Blake bap'^t 19th May 1700.
Margarett Cooper y'^e Daughter of James Cooper bap'^t 19th of May 1700.
Mary Chilton the Daughter of ———— Chilton baptized 9th of June 1700.
Mary Almond was bap'^t the 9th of June 1700.
Mussella a Negro Boy of Majo'^r Dudleys bap'^t 9th of June 1700.
Lettice an Negro gile of Majo'^r Dudleys bap'^t 9th of June 1700.
Clemence y'^e Daughter of Augustine & Jane Owen was borne the 4th of June and bap'^t 21th of July 1700.
Stephen Gibbs the Sone of Jn'^o & Mary Gibbs bap'^t 21th of July 1700.
William Gardner the Sone of William & Mary Gardner was borne 2th of July and baptized 21th of July 1700.
John Marston the Sone of Jn'^o & Ann Marston was borne the 13th of July and baptized 14th of August 1700.
Susannah Churchhill Jones the Daughter of Roger & Mary Jones was baptized the 14th of August 1700.
Mary Portwood the Daughter of Tho. & Barbary Portwood was borne 19th of ffebruary & baptized 24th of Xember 1699.
Charles Baker the Sone of William & Susannah Baker bap'^t 14th July 1700.
Zebulun Chilton the Sone of Peter & Abigall Chilton bap'^t 4th Aug'^o 1700.
Ann Kemp the Daughter of Coll'^o Matthew Kemp & Madam Ann Kemp his Wife was borne 12th of Sept. & bap'^t 22th Sept. 1700.

The ages of 5 Children of Tho. & Mary Gresham.
Charles Gresham was Borne the 10th of March 1687.
Thomas Gresham was borne the 9th of June 1689.
John Gresham was borne the 5th of January 1692.
Ffrancis Gresham was borne the 26th of March 1695.
Amey Gresham was borne the 12th of July 1700.
The Said Amey was by her first husband Gardner &c.

Hannah the Daughter of William &   Beamont was baptised the 13th of October 1700.
Elizabeth Miller the Daughter of John and Michall Miller was borne 26th of Sep' and baptised 8th Novemb. 1700.
John Marchum the Sone of William & Eliz: Marchum was borne 6th of xember & bap" 9th of February 1700.
Elizabeth the Daughter of Tho. & Eliz: Still bap" 16th Feb' 1700.
Joseph the Sone of Tho. & Barbary Portwood bap" 9th March 170½.
Mary the Daughter of Valentine & Ann Wallas was borne the 26th of February & baptized the 30th of March 1701.
Ann Newton the Daughter of William and Amey Newton, was baptized 30th of March 1701.
Ann Hill the daughter of W^m & Ann Hill bapt^{ed} 30th March 1701.
Elizabeth Gilley the Daughter of Tho. & Jane Gilley was baptised the 13th of June 1701.
Foure Negroes of the Widow Briscoe Baptized—Viz' Frances, Sarah, Katherine, Phelis; all baptized the 6th of June 1701.

CHRISTENINGS.

Betty an Negro of Cap' Smiths was borne 13th of July and was baptized the 13th of July 1701.
Thomas the Sone of Edward Williams was borne 7th of July and was baptized the 3^d of August 1701.
Robert an Illegitimate of a woman belonging to Do' Stapleton was baptized the 3^d of August 1701.
John the Sone of Tho. & Eliz^a Baker borne 22th of Aug' and baptized 14th of Septemb. 1701.
Susannah the Daught' of Jn° & Mary Michener was borne 19th of August and baptized 21th Septemb 1701.
Elizabeth Simms the Daughter of Tho. & Ann Simms was borne 21th of September & baptized &c 1699.
Ann the Daughter of the aforesaid Simms was borne the 19th of August and baptized 16th of Septemb 1701.
Robert the Sone of Cap' Henry Beverley and Madam Elizabeth Beverley his Wife was borne 6th of No^{vr} 1701.
Arthur the Sone of Edward & Keziah Ball born 14th March 1697.
Johannah the Daughter of the said Ball borne 14th Ap^{rll} 1699.
An the Daughter of Jn° & Marg' Phiney bap" 16th No^{vr} 1701.
Mary Godbee the Daughter of Edward & ffrances Godbee was borne the 13th of Octob. & bap" 23th of Ditto 1701.
Thompson the Sone of Patrick Quidley bap" 25th of Jan^{ry} 1701.
Marg' the Daughter of Charles & Eliz^a Haines bap" 25th Jan' 1701.
Edward the Sone of Ed. & Keziah Ball was bap" 1th of March 1701.
William the Sone of Augustine & Jone Dews was borne the 17th of December 1701.

Here ends the accot of Register Transcribed out of the Old Booke In the Yeare 1702 &c.   p. John Nash.

The Birth of Negro Children.

Belonging to Mr Francis Weeks Junr. Negro Peter was Born Anno Dom. 1694.
Negro Jinny was Born Anno Dom 1696. Negro Ben Was Born An. Do. 1697.
Negro Dick was Born Anno Domi 1702. Negro Numer was Born An. Do. 1705.
Negro Milly Belonging to Mrs Milicent Weeks Was Born Anno. Dom. 1695.
Negroes Belonging to John Bristow. Negro Betty was Born in July 1696.
Negro Dy was Born in April, Anno Domini 1702.
Negroes Belonging to Mr Garrett Minor. Palles was Born 8. Feb^{r}y Year 1700.
Hannah a Negro was Born In April Anno Dom 1702.
Nan was Born In March Anno Domini 170⅔.
Negroes Belonging to Thomas Warrick were Born as followeth.
Frank was Born June Ye 14th 1699: Peter was Born June Ye 14th 1701.
Negroe Cate Belonging to Mr Robert Daniel was Born May Ye 3d. 1704.
Negroes Belonging to Mr John Meacham. Peter was Born Aug. Ye 8th 1702.
Moll was Born february Ye 13th Anno Domi. 170⅔.
Negroe Richard belonging to Mrs Pennellope Chainy was Born May Ye 1st 1696.
Negroe Mat a Boy Belonging to Mr William Montague was Born In Apr. 1695.
Negroes Belonging to Mr Thomas Montague were Born as followeth.
Negroe Moll was Born In feb^r 1692 & Ben was Born In May 1694.
Sam: A Negroe was Born in Jan: 1699. Sara was Born May ye 2d 1704.
Lily a Negro Girl Belonging to John Hadly was Born february ye 15th 170⅝.
Ye Birth of Negro Children Belonging Collo^{nl} William Churchhill Esq Were Born as followeth; Betty a Negro Girl was Born June ye 21st 1705.
Sarah a Negro Girl was Born August ye 27th Anno Domini 1705.
Sue a Negro Girl was Born Septemb ye 29th Anno Domini 1705.
Nell a Negro Girl Belonging to Samuel Hoyl was Born in March Anno Domi 170⅔.
Robbin a Negro Boy belonging to John Hipkings was Born In May: 1706.
Thamer a Negro Girl belonging to Mr Roger Jones was Born September the 7th Anno Domini 1707.
Will a Negroe Boy belonging to John Vivion born 8^{br} ye 8th 1707.
Cate a Negroe Girl belonging to William Barbee Born Jan^r ye 28th Anno Domi 170⅔.
Jack a Negroe Boy belonging to John Adley was Born february ye 27th 170⅝.

Robina Negroe Boy belonging to Matthew Hunt was Born April y[e] 8th 1708.
Negroes belonging to M[r] George Wortham Born as followeth
Gill Born In March 169½. Sue Born December 1703.
Cate Born Novemb[r] Anno Domini 1706.

Here begins a Short Acco[t] of Christenings Marriages & Burialls Transcribed out of a Book Kept at the Upper Chappell from ye 7th of Aprill Anno 1689 &c. Some of it being Record[d] before.

CHRISTENINGS—1690.

Richard the Sone of Samuell & Honour Acton was bap[tz] at M[r] Seagers p. M[r] Sam[ll] Gray the 10th of November 1690.
John the Sone of David and Martha Davis was bap[tz] 10th of Novemb. 1690.
Sarah the Daughter of Jn[o] & Ursula ffearman bap[tz] 10th of Novemb. 1690.
Richard the Sone of Jn[o] & Eliz[a] Guttrey was bap[tz] the 3d of Aprill 1691.
Benjamine the Sone of Jn[o] & Mary Bowman bap[tz] the 3th of Aprill 1691.
Randolph the Sone of Joseph & Eliz[a] Smith was borne 2th of Aprill and was bap[tz] the 14th of June 1691.
Mary the Daughter of Martin Masey was baptized the 14th of June 1691.
Katherine the Illegitimate Daughter of Mary Nash, late servant to M[r] Randolph Seager was baptized the 5th of July 1691.
Mary the Daughter of Richard & Katherine Davidson bap[tz] 3th of Aprill 1691.
Mary the Daughter of Robert & Dorothy James baptized 5th of July 1691.
William the Sone of William & Sarah Batchelder bap[tz] 26th of July 1691.
Thomas the Sone of Jn[o] & Eliz[a] Lewis was baptized the 26th of July 1691.
Henry the Sone of Henry & Eliz[a] Emmerson bap[tz] 18th of October 1691.
William the Sone of William & Ellianor Sadler borne 19th of October. 1691.
Robert the Sone of Robert & Margaret Daniell was borne 21th Septmb. 1691.
John the Sone of Anthony & Ann Ridgaway was bap[tz] 16th of January 169½.
Elizabeth the Daughter of M[r] William Chayney & Penellope his wife was baptized 31th of January 169½.
John the Sone of John & Millicent Chedle was bap[tz] 31th of Jan[r] 169½.
Alice Davis the Illegitimate Daughter of ——— Davis by Mary Care was baptized the 31th of January 169½.
Paul the Sone of Jn[o] & Eliz[a] Swift was baptized 21th of ffebruary 169½.
John the Sone of William & Ann Brookes was bap[tz] 21th of ffebruary 169½.

Martha the Daughter of David Davis was baptized 13th of March 169½.
Sarah the Daughter of Jn⁰ & Michall Bristow bap^ts 13th of March 169½.

CHRISTENINGS.

John the Sone of Mr William Daniell & Constance his Wife was borne the ffirst Day of ffebruary & bap^ts 10th of March 169½.
Elizabeth Daughter of Thomas & Hannah Haines bap^ts 24th of Aprill 1692.
George the Sone of William & Mary Carter was borne 22th of Aprill and was baptized the 22th of May 1692.
Johannah the Daughter of John & Mary Brim baptized 12th of June 1692.
Ann the Daughter of Robert and Ann Chowning bap^ts 12th of June 1692.
Rebecca the Daughter of Roger and Rebecca Prichard bap^ts 12th June 1692.
Edward the Sone of William and Rebecca Hutson of Rappahannock County was baptized the 3d of July 1692.
William the Sone of William and Eliz^a Marsh borne 5th July bap^ts 24th Ditto 1692.
Agatha the Dau^tr of Mr James Curtis & Eliz^a his wife bap^ts 25th of July 1692.
John the Sone of George and Rebecca Duffe borne 27th July bap^ts 2th Augt 1692.
Masey the Sone of Jn⁰ and Eliz^a Guthery was bap^ts 4th of Septemb 1692.
James the Sone of John & Penelope Evans of Rapp^a bap^ts 16th of Octob 1692.
Charles the Sone of Edward & Katherine Pierce was borne 1st of Augt 1692.
George the Sone of George & Eliz^a Johnston baptized 27th of Novemb 1692.
Elianor the Daughter of Jn⁰ & Eliz^a Kersey bap^ts 27th of November 1692.
Ann the Daughter of Nicholas & Mabell Paine bap^tr 27th of November 1692.
Ann the Daughter of Nicholas & Ann Rice was bap^ts 27th of November 1692.
Penelope the Daughter of Anthony & Eliz^a Dowlin borne 12th of Octob. 1692 and Baptized the 26th of November 1692.
Pead the Sone of Jn⁰ & Michall Micham bap^ts 8th of Jan^ry 169¾.
John the Sone of Andrew & Isabella Wilson bap^ts 12th of March 169¾.
Sarah Daughter of Robert and Sarah George bap^ts 12th of March 169¾.
Ann the Daughter of Claud Vallott & Ann his Wife was borne the 31th of July, and was baptized the 14th of August 1693.
Elizabeth ye Daughter of Martin & Eliz^a Masey was borne 20th of Sep^t and was baptized 29th of Octob. 1693.
Lettice ye Daughter of Jn⁰ and Mary Burk borne 24th Sep^t bap^ts 29th Octob. 1693.

Mary Tugwell the Daughter of Henry & Mary Tugwell borne 20th of Sept. and baptized the 29th of October 1693.
Ann the Daughter of Barnard & Eliz^a Paine was borne 22th of Septemb and was baptized 29th of October 1693.

CHRISTENINGS.

Mary the Daughter of Charles Walker was baptized 29th of Octob 1693.
Ann the Daughter of Mr Thomas Stapleton by ffrances his Wife was borne the 14th of September 1693.
Jane the Daughter of ffrancis Taylor & Eliz^a his Wife was borne the 15th of November and baptized 31th of December 1693.
Phillip the Sone of William and Mary Carter borne 10th X^{br} bap^{tz} 4th Jan^r 169¾.
William the Sone of William & Bridget Willis baptized 4th of Jan^r 169¾.
Ann the Daughter of William and Ann Brookes bap^{tz} 21th of Jan^{ry} 169¾.
Hannah the Daughter of Jno & Millicent Chedle baptized 21th of Jan^{ry} 169¾.
Richard the Sone of Peter and Cary Tindall baptized 11th of ffebr. 169¾.
Eusebias the Sone of Jno & Eliz^a Lewis borne 22th Jan^r bap^{tz} 4th of March 169¾.
Sarah the Daughter of John and Eliz^a Pace was baptized 22th of Aprill 1694.
Jane the Daughter of Robert & Dorothy James bap^{tz} 22th of Aprill 1694.
Mary the Daughter of Michaell & Mercy Curtis bap^{tz} 3th of June 1694.
John ye Sone of Jno and Mary Bowmon bap^{tz} 15th of July 1694.
John the Sone of George &   Cummings bap^{tz} 15th of July 1694.
Penelope Daughter of William &   Carter bap^{tz} 15th of July 1694.
John the Sone of George & Mary Guest bap^{tz} 5th of August 1694.
Margaret ye Daughter of Robert & Katherine Williamson bap^{tz} 5th Augt 1694.
Hannah the Daughter of Jacob & Eliz^a Booseley bap^{tz} 5th of August 1694.
William Meacham the Sone of Jno & Michaell Meacham was Borne the 25th of ffebruary 1694.
John Lantor the Sone of Thomas Lantor was Borne the 30th Day of July and Baptized the 1st of Octo^{br} In the Yeare 1698.
Peter Lantor the Son of Thomas Lantor was born 25th Jan^{ry} and Baptized 18th of ffebruary In the yeare 167⁸⁄₈.
Simon Son of William and Hannah Poobert was born ye 22nd Septemb. 1699.
Mary Gardiner daughter of W^m & Ann Gardiner was born ye 22nd day of September 1699.

WEDDINGS OR MARRIAGES.

Thomas Kidd and Alice Trigg were Marryed 18th of Septemb. 1690.
Jacob Booseley and Elizabeth Nash were Marryed 15th of June 1691.
Henry ffreeman and Ann Porter were Marryed the   1691.
William Carter and Mary Goodlow were Marryed 2th of July 1691.
George Duff and Rebecca Nash were Marryed 4th of July 1691.
Tobias Mickleburrough & Grace Nicholson were mar^d 17th Sept. 1691.
Mr Matthew Lidford & Mrs Lettice Weekes were Marryed 6th Jan^r 169½.
John Kersey and Elizabeth Priestnall were Marryed 2th of June 1692.
Henry Tugwell and Mary Baskett were Marryed 26th of Augt 1692.
Joseph Harrison and ffrances Haslewood Marryed 11th No^{vr} 1692.
John Waycomb and Eliz^a Micham were Marryed 31th Xm^{br} 169¾.
Timothy Tracy and Rebecca Goodrich marry^d 19th ffeb. 169¾.
Henry Meeres and Dorothy Hunt were married 22th of May 1693.
Thomas Spencer of King & Q^n County & Eliz^a Whelling of this parrish were Marryed 14th Xemb. 1693.
Angell Jacobus of ffarnum parish in Richmond County And Ann Vallott of this parish Widow were Marryed p Lycence the 12th of July Ann° 1694.

BURIALLS &c.

Frances the Daughter of M^r Jn° Sheppard Dec'd by ffrances his Wife Dyed the 24th of March 169⅘.
Theophylus the Sone of Mr Chr. Robinson and Mrs Katherine Robinson his wife was buried 14th of Aprill 1691.
Griffin the Sone of Jn° & Eliz^a Lewis was buried 28th of Sep^t 1691.
Amey a Servant Wench of Mr Chr. Robinson's buried 22th Octob. 1691.
Henry Nicholls Senr was buried the 9th of Aprill 1692.
Mary the Daughter of Mr Randolph Seager by Mary his Wife was buried in the Upper Chappell 17th of Aprill 1692.
Madam Katherine Robinson the wife of Mr Chr. Robinson Departed this Life 23th of Aprill 1692.
William Craine Dyed the 13th of August 1692.
Elizabeth Waycomb Dyed the 13th of August 1692.
Ann Jones Dyed the 14th of August 1692.
Elizabeth Willis Dyed the 17th of August 1692.
Elizabeth Swift Dyed 24th of August 1692.
Caleb Whelling Dyed the 3d of Septemb 1692.
George the Sone of Mr Geo. Haslewood Dyed 13th of Septemb. 1692.
John Guy the Sone of Tho. & Mary Guy Dyed 3th of Octo^{br} 1692.
Mr George Haslewood Departed this Life 10th of November 1692.
Mary Thompson Dyed the 5th of Decemb 1692.
Claud Vallott 29th and was buryed 31th of January 169¾.
Ralph Wilkeson Dyed the 2d of ffebruary 169¾.
Rebecca Duff Dyed the 15th of December 1693.
Mrs Sarah Perrott the Wife of Mr Richd Perrott Departed this Life the 26th of December 169¾.

Margaret Masey Dyed the 21th of December 169^{3}_{4}.

BURIALLS &c.

Mr William Chayney Dyed In January 169^{3}_{4}.
Richard Parry Dyed in January 169^{3}_{4}.
John Elec Dyed In January 169^{3}_{4}.
John Brewer Dyed the 5th of ffebruary 169^{3}_{4}.
Thomas Mins Dyed In ffebruary 169^{3}_{4}.
ffrances Docker was buried the 3d of March 169^{3}_{4}.
John Duff the Sone of George & Rebecca Duff Dyed 5th June 1694.
Thomas Marston Dyed the 24 Day of October In the year 1704.
Thomas Smith departed this life the 21st of May 1705.
Mary Ye Wife of Theophilus Stanton departed this Life September Ye 27th And was Interred September Ye 29th Anno Domi. 1705.
Charls Williams was Interred July Ye 27th Anno Domi 1706.
John Ye Son of Nathan Underwood & Diana his wife departed this life October Ye 24th And was Buried Ye 25th of Ye Same Anno Domini 1706.
Hannah Jones Ye Wife of John Jones dyed 8br Ye 25th & Buried Ye 27th of Ye Same 1706.
John Nickols departed this Life Novemr Ye 27th & Buried Novembr Ye 30th 1705.
Frances Ye Wife of William Serdsborow Departed this Life Janry Ye 17th & Buried Ye 19th 170^{5}_{6}.
Mrs William Kilby departed this Life Febry Ye 3d & was Buried febry Ye 5th Anno Domi 170^{5}_{6}.
William Porter departed this Life febry Ye 17th & was Buried febry Ye 20th Anno Dom. 170^{5}_{6}.
William Hartford departed this Life february Ye 8th Anno Domini 170^{5}_{6}.
Sarah Ye Wife of Richard Stevens departed this Life March Ye 19th & Buried March Ye 22nd 170^{5}_{6}.
John Sibley deceased April Ye 7th & was Buried April Ye 10th Anno Domi 1706.
Thomas Roberts departed this Life April Ye 16th & was Buried April Ye 18th 1706.
Henry Gale departed this Life May Ye 2d & was Buried May Ye 3d Anno Domini 1706.
Richard Stevens Departed this Life Decembr Ye 18th & Buried Ye 20th 170^{5}_{6}.

CHRISTENINGS.

Abraham Mountague the Sone of William & Lettice Mountague was baptized 28th of September 1701.
Richard Win the Sone of Richd & Sarah Win was baptizd Ditto day 1701.
Mary the Daughter of Jno & Mary Guthery baptz 23th of January 170^{1}_{2}.
Ann the Daughter of William & Mary Carter baptz 23th of January 170^{1}_{2}.
George the sone of Henry & Eliza Goodlow baptz 23th of Janry 170^{1}_{2}.
Margaret the Daughter of Jno & Eliza Pace baptz 15th of March 170^{1}_{2}.

Jane the Daughter of Robert & Ann Blackley
Ann the Daughter of Rich^d & Eliz^a Allin
Elizabeth the Daughter of Michaell & Mercy Curtis
Sarah the Daughter of Ralph & Alice Masey
John the Sone of Edmund & Jane Mickleburrough
Thomas the Sone of Nicholas & Dorothy Newton
Richard the Illegitimate Sone of Ann Hughs
Daniell the Sone of John & Michaell Micham
John the Sone of Joseph & Jane Micham
Henry the Sone of Robert & Marg^t Daniell
} were all 10 of them Baptiz^d the 15th Day of March 170½.

Margaret Murrow the Daughter of Ann Murrow, Bastard was born ye 1 Day of Aprill 1701.
Jane the Daughter of Robert & Sarah George bap^ts 19th of Aprill 1702.
Katherine ye Daughter of George & Katherine Twyman bap^ts Ditto day 1702.
Elizabeth the Daughter of William & Mary Danill was baptized 15th of March 170½.
Peter Brim the Sone of Jno & Mary Brim was borne 6th of Aprill and Baptized the 12th of May 1702.
William the Sone of William & Hannah Proverb was bap^ts the 12th of May 1702.
Margaret the Dau^tr of W^m and Marg^t Kidd was bap^ts 12th of May 1702.
Charles the Sone of Charles & Mary Maderions was borne the 10th of ffebruary and bap^ts on Whit Sunday 1702.

CHRISTENINGS.

William Mountague the Sone of Tho & Katherine Mountague was Baptized 14th of June 1702.
ffrances the Sone of Jno & Eliz^a Summers bap^ts 14th of June 1702.
Ann the Daughter of William & Ann Gardner bap^ts Ditto Day 1702.
Jacob the Sone of Robert & Katherine Williamson was borne the 12th of June & was Baptized 22th of July 1702.
Thomas the Sone of Henry & Eliz^a Smith was borne 16th July And Baptized 22th of the Same 1702.

Here endeth the Acco^t of the Whole Register Transcribed out of Both ye old Register Books of Christ Church parish In Midd^x County.
Being Transcribed by order of Vestry held the 20th of Novemb. An. 1701.

p. Jno Nash.

Robert ye Son of Major Robert Dudley & Mrs Elizabeth his Wife was Born february ye 14th Anno Domini 1691.
Elizabeth ye Daughter of Mary Canidy was Born April ye 4th. Anno Domi 1704. An Illegitimate.

Att a generall Assembly begun at James Citty 8th of June 1680.

An Act for preventing Insurrections of Negros &c.

Whereas the ffrequent meeting of considerable Numbers of Negro Slaves under pretence of Feasts and Burialls, is Judged & Deemed of Dangerous Consequences, for prevention whereof for ye ffuture, Be it Enacted by the Kings most Excellent Majesty, by and with the Consent of this gen'rll Assembly, and it is hereby Enacted by the Authority aforesaid, that from and after the publication of this Law, it shall not be Lawfull for any Negro or other Slave, to carry or arme himselfe with any Club, Staff, Gun, Sword, or any other Weapon of Defence or offence, nor to goe nor Depart from his Masters Ground without a Citifficate from his Master, Mistris or Overseere, and Such permission not to be granted but upon particular and necessary occasions, and every Negro or Slave so offending not haveing a Certifficate as aforesaid, Shal be Sent to the next Constable who is hereby Impowered and Required to give the Said Negro Twenty Lashes on the bare back well laid on and So Sent home to his said Master, Mistriss or Overseer.

And it is further Enacted by the Authority aforesaid that if any Negro or other Slave Shall presume to lift up his hand in opposition against any Christian, Shall for every Such offence upon due proofe made thereof by the Oath of the party before a Majistrate have and receive Thirty Lashes on the bare back well laid on, And it is hereby further Enacted by the Authority aforesaid, that if any Negro or other Slave Shall absent himselfe from his Masters Service and ley hid and Lurking in obscure places, Committing Injuries to ye Inhabitents, and Shall Resist any pson or p'sons that shall by any Lawfull Authority be Imployed to apprehend and take the Said Negro, that then in case of such Resistance, It shalbe Lawfull for such p'son of p'sons to Kill the Said Negro or Slave so lying out and Resisting, and this Law to be once every Six months published at the Respective County Courts and Parish Churches within this Collony.

CHRISTENINGS.

Anne daughter of Sr Wm Skipwith & Lady Sarah his Wife born July 31 1703.
Jonas Whitlock the Son of James & Margaret Whitlock his Wife was Baptized March y^e 18th Anno Domini 170$\frac{4}{5}$
Ann Matthews the Daughter of William & Mary Matthews his Wife was born March y^r 23d And Baptized April y^e 6th Anno Domini 1705.
William Watliss the Son of Elizabeth Watliss was Baptized April y^e 29th 1705.
Ann Dunkington y^r Daughter of Elizabeth Dunkington was Bap. April y^e 29th 1705.
James Townsend ye Son of John Townsend and Damaris his Wife was Born April ye 20th Anno Domini 1705.
John Smith Son of Thomas and Ruth Smith his Wife was Born January ye 24th Anno Domini 1704.

The Births of three children of James Smith and his Wife Ann Smith:

Elizabeth Smith was Born September ye 1st Anno Domini 1699.
James Smith was Born ye 25th of June Anno Domini 1702.
Ann Smith was Born ye 27th of October Anno Domini 1704.
Thomas Jones y^e Son of Roger Jones & Mary his Wife was Born the 23rd of August Anno Domini 1704.

Benjamin Williamson y⁰ Son of Robert Williamson and Catherine his Wife was Born April y⁰ 21st & Baptized July y⁰ 1st 1704.

Ann Smith y⁰ Daughter of Thomas & Ann Smith his Wife was Born January y⁰ 10th Anno Domini $\frac{1699}{1700}$.

Ann Shepherd an Illegitimate the Daughter of Mary Shepherd was Baptized September y⁰ 2nd Anno Domini 1705.

John Finney y⁰ Son of John & Margaret Finney his Wife was Born March y⁰ 1st Ano. Domi 1697.

William Finney y⁰ Son of John & Margaret Finney his Second Wife was Baptized March y⁰ 10th Anno Domi 1706.

Francis y⁰ Son of Samuel & Ann Loe his Wife was Born July y⁰ 10th Anno Domini 1704.

Elizabeth Maxum y⁰ Daughter of Thomas & Elizabeth Maxum his Wife was Baptized March y⁰ 10th Anno Domi 1706.

William Gilley y⁰ Son of Thomas Gilley and Jane his wife was Baptized March y⁰ 22d Anno Domini 1706.

At a Gen^{rll} Assembly begun at James Citty November the 10th 1682. An additional Act for the better preventing Insurrections by Negros.

Whereas a certaine Act of Assembly held at James Citty y⁰ Eight day of June In the Yeare of our Lord 1680 Intitaled an Act preventing Negros Irsurrections hath not had its Intended Effect for want of due Notice thereof being Taken, It is enacted by the Govern^r Councill and Burgisses of this p'sent Grand Assembly and by the Authority thereof that for the better putting y⁰ said Act in Due Execution the Church Wardens of Each parish in this Cuntry at the Charge of the parish by the first Day of January next, provide true Coppies of this and the aforesaid Act, and make or Cause Entry to be made thereof in the Register booke of the said parish and that ye minister or Reader of Each parish shall twice Every yeare vizt Some one Sunday or Lords day in Each of the Months of September and March in Each parish Church or Chappell of Ease in Each parish in the time of Divine Service after the Reading of the Second lesson, Reade and Publish both this p'sent and the aforesaid Recited Act, under paine such Church Warden Minister or Reader Makeing Default to forfeit Each of them Six hundred pounds of Tobacco, one halfe to the Informer, and y⁰ other halfe to the use of the poore of the said parrish and for the further better preventing Such Insurrections by Negros or Slaves Be it likewise Enacted and it is hereby Enacted by the Authority aforesaid, that noe Master or Overseer Shall at any time after the 20th Day of January next Knowingly permitt or suffer without the leave or Lycence of his or theire Master or overseere, any Negro or Slave not properly belonging to him or them, to Remaine or be upon his or theire Plantation above the space of ffoure hours at any one time. Contrary to the Intent of the before recited act, upon Paine to fforfeit being thereof Lawfully convicted before Some one Justice of the peace within the County where the ffact shall be comitted by the Oath of two Witnesses at the least, The Sume of Two hundred pounds of Tobacco in Caske for Each time so offending, to him or them that will sue for the same for which the Said Justice is hereby Impowered to award Judgment and Execution.

Transcribed out of the Register Booke at ye Upper Chappell &c.

John Nash and Ann Brewer both of Christ Church Parish in Middlesex County were Married ye 28th day of October, In the Yeare of our Lord 1703.

The Births of Negro Children.
The Birth of Negro Children belong to Captn John Smith.
Negro Judith was Born ye 21st day of November Anno Domini 1702.
Negro Mulatto Charls was Born ye 8th day of April Anno Domini 1704.
Negro Cesar Belonging to Mr Roger Jones was Born 8^{br} ye 6th 1704.
The Birth of Three Negro Children belonging to James Curtis Senr:
Negro Harry was Born In May 1698. Negro Frank was Born february 1699. Negro Tony was Born In february 1701.
Degal Negro belonging to Minor Minor was Born Octob^r ye 5th 1692.
Sue a Negro Girl belonging to James Smith was Born In May 1705.
The Ages of Negro Children Belonging to Mr Bartholomew Yates: Alice Born Octo^{br} y^e 15th 1694. Katey Born Novemb^r y^e 1st 1695; Gresham Born May the 28th 1700; Sue Born Octob^r y^e 1st 1702. Toney born Octob^r the 25th 1702; Harry born March y^e 10th 170$\frac{3}{4}$. Sarah Born June y^e 14th 1705; Molly Born March 4th 1696.
Mary a Negro Belonging to Thomas Hipkins was Born July 1694.
Negro Will Belonging to Mr Roger Jones was Born June y^e 16th 1706.
The Birth of Negro Children Belonging to Capt. John Smith:
Negro Anthony was Born July y^e 21st Anno Domi 1705.
Negro Frank a Boy was Born february y^e 9th 170$\frac{3}{4}$.
Negro Tom was Born June y^e 21st Anno Domi 1706.
Rose a Negro Girl Belonging to Mrs Elizabeth Dudley was Born A. D. 1702.
Robbin Mingoll A Negro Belonging to Robert Dudley was Born An. Dom. 1706.
The Birth of Negroes belonging to Mr Frances Weeks Senr:
Negro Letty was Born March y^e 17th Anno Domini 1701.
James Morris Son of Elizabeth A Mulatto Woman was Baptized by Mr Andrew Jackson March y^e 15th Anno Domi 170$\frac{3}{4}$.
Negroe Major a Boy Belonging to John Bristow was Born July y^e 31st 1706.
Negroe Frank a Girl belonging to Mrs Penelope Parrott was Born Aug. y^e 24th 1706.
Phillis Daughter of Nanney belonging to James Curtis Sen. born June y^e 1706.

CHRISTENINGS—1702.

James Smith the Sone of James and Ann Smith was borne the 5th Day of June in the yeare of our Lord 1702.
John Man the Sone of John Man and Jane his wife was borne the ffirst Day of May 1702.

Catherine Kilbie the Daughter of William and Johannah Kilbee was baptized the 9th of September 1702.
Robert Davis the Sone of Elisha and Elizabeth Davis was borne the 14th of October 1702.
John Gibbs the Sone of John and Mary Gibbs was Borne the 9th Day of October 1702.
Benjamine Gore the Sone of Joshua &   Gore was Baptized the 9th Day of December 1702.
James Rhodes the Sone of Ezechias and Elizabeth Rhodes was Baptized the 9th Day of December 1702.
Martha the Daughter of John and Ann Marston was borne the 7 Day of December 1702.
Judah the Daughter of Roger and Mary Jones was born the 26th Day of December 1702.
James Stiffe the Sone of Thomas and Elizabeth Stiffe was Baptized the 13th of January 170¾.
George Blake the Sone of George and Elizabeth Blake was Baptized the 13th Day of January 170¾
Francis Porter the Sone of William and Jane Porter was Borne the 9th of January 170¾.
John the Sone of Uriah Cardis was Borne the 3th Day of January 170¾.

This is Reserved for Registering the Birth of Negro Children in particular &c.

Nedd a Negro Boy Slave Belonging to Mr Edwin Thacker was Borne the 7th Day of January 1698.
Nanney a Negro Girle Slave belonging to Mr Edwin Thacker was borne the 15th Day of March in the Yeare 1698.
Moll a Negro Girle Slave belonging to Mr Richard Kemp was borne the 5th Day of August in the yeare 1700.
Cress a Negro Girle Slave belonging to Mr Richd Kemp was born the 3th Day July in the yeare 1700.
Juda a Negro Slave of Mr Richard Kemp was borne the 7th Day of September In the Yeare 1697.
Nora a Negro Girle Slave belonging to Mr Richard Kemp was Borne the ffirst of October In the Yeare 1703.
Dinah a Negro Girle Slave belonging to Mr Richd Kemp was Borne the 13th of November in the Yeare 1694.
Nedd a Negro Boy Slave belonging to Mr Richard Kemp was borne the 12th of August In the Yeare 1694.
Alice a Negro Girle Slave belong to Capt Robert Daniell was borne the 2th Day of Septemb^r In the Yeare 1698.
Ben a Negro boy Slave belonging to the Said Capt Robert Daniel borne the 4th Day of Aprill In the Yeare 1700.
Captain a Negro boy Slave of ye Said Daniell was borne the ffirst Day of Aprill 1702.
Franck a Negro Girl Slave belonging to Mr Edwin Thacker Borne on the 15th Day of ffebruary In the Yeare 1702.
Billey a negro boy slave belonging to Mr Edwin Thacker Borne on the 27 day of March In ye Yeare 1703.

Mingo a Negro boy Slave, son of Nan belonging to Mr Rice Curtis was born ye 15 Day of May 1704) Registered the 20th of July 1714.

CHRISTENINGS.

Joshua Lewis the Sone of James Lewis and Jone his wife was Borne the 27th Day of Decemb^r Anno Domini 1702.

Frances Berry the Daughter of Garrett Berry and Eliza his Wife was borne the 5th Day of ffebruary 170⅔.

Theophilus the Sone of Nicholas Branch and Mary his Wife was Baptized the 30th of March 1703.

Rebecca Godbee the Daughter of Edward Godbee & Frances his Wife was baptized ye 2th of June 1703.

William Bennett the Sone of William and Sarah Bennett was baptized the 2th of June 1703.

Abigall Smith the Daughter of Arthur and Mary Smith was Borne the 4th of August 1702.

Thomas the Sone of Henry Meacham and Mary his Wife was baptized the 26th of June 1703.

Christopher Robinson the Sone of Mr John Robinson and Maddam Catherine Robinson his Wife was borne 1th of July 1703.

Mabell Dodson the Daughter of Francis and Mabell Dodson was Baptized the ffirst Day of September 1703.

James Black the Sone of James and Ann Black was baptz^d the 26th Day of August In the Yeare 1702.

Frances the Daughter of Henry Tuggle and Mary his Wife was baptized the 26 Day of August 1702.

Sarah Preston the Daughter of Jacob and Mary Preston was Baptized the 23 Day of September 1702.

Jacob Brooks the Sone of William and Sarah Brooks Baptiz^d the 21 of Novemb^r In the Yeare 1702.

CHRISTENINGS.

Henry Johnston the Sone of George Johnston and Elizabeth his Wife was Baptized the 21 Day of Novemb^r In the Yeare 1702.

Margarett Lantor the Daughter of Thomas and Isabella Lantor was Baptized the 21th Day of Novemb^r In the Yeare 1702.

Winifrid Kidd the Daughter of Thomas and Alice Kidd was Baptized the 21th Day of Novemb^r In the Yeare 1702.

Ann Crank the Daughter of Matthew and Elizabeth Crank was Borne the 22th Day of August In the Yeare 1702.

Thomas Norman the Sone of Robert and Elizabeth Norman was borne the 9th Day of January and baptized 11th of March 170⅔.

Mary Hall the Daughter of Martin and Mary Hall was born the 2 Day of February And was baptized the 11th of March A^{nno} 170⅔.

Sarah Bird the Daughter of John and Elizabth Bird was Baptized the 24th Day of March In the Yeare 170⅔.

Sarah Siddon the Daughter of Edward & Ann Siddon was Baptized the 24 Day of March In the Yeare 170⅔.

Sarah the Daughter of Hermon and Elizabeth Church Yard was baptized the 24th Day of March In the Yeare 170⅔.

John George the Sone of David and Catherine George was Baptized the 18th Day of Aprill In the Yeare 1703.

Elizabeth Winn, the Daughter of Richard and Sarah Winn was Baptized the 18th Day of Aprill In the Yeare 1703.
Edward Suthern the Sone of John and Catherin Suthern was Baptized the 23th Day of May In the Yeare 1703.
John Wood the Son of Thomas and Elizabeth Wood was Baptized the 23 Day of June In the Yeare 1703.
Robert Kidd the Son of William and Marg^t Kidd was Baptized the 20th Day of July In the Yeare 1703.

CHRISTENINGS.

The Ages of thre Children of Mr Richard Kemp and Mrs Ellianor Kemp his Wife.
Ann Kemp was Borne the 13th Day of August In ye Yeare 1694.
Rachell Kemp was Borne the 3th Day of April In ye Yeare 1696.
Richard Kemp was Born the 6th Day of Aprill In ye Yeare 1698.

The Ages of Three Children of Edmund Mickleburrough and Jane his Wife.
Edmund Mickleburrough was Born the 22th Day of Decemb^r 1696.
Robert Mickleburrough was Born the 24th Day of October 1698.
John Mickleburrough was Born the 15th Day of Decemb^r 1701.

The Ages of Four Children of Michael & Mercy Curtis.
Mary Curtis was Born the 7th Day of March In ye Yeare 169?.
Thomas Curtis was Born the 27th Day of Decemb^r In the Yeare 1695.
Michall Curtis was Born the 1st Day of Septemb^r In ye Yeare 1698.
Elizabeth Curtis was Borne the 25th of October In the Yeare 1701.

The Ages of Four Children of Richard and Ann Shurley.
Abraham Duff the Sone of George Duff Dec^d by Ann his Wife (the now Wife of the Said Richd Shurley was borne the 15th of December 1696.
Ann Shurley was borne the 12th Day of Decemb^r In ye Year 1698.
Thomas Shurley was borne the 19th of Decemb^r In the Yeare 1700.
Richard Shurley was borne the 8th Day of August In ye Year 1703.

CHRISTENINGS.

Edwin Thacker the Son of Mr Edwin Thacker and Mrs Frances Thacker his Wife borne on the Third Day of July at Twelve A Clock in ye Day In the Yeare of our Lord 1695.
Ann Thacker the Daughter of Mr Edwin Thacker and Mrs Frances Thacker his Wife Borne on the 27th Day of Septemb^r att Six a Clock in the Morning In the Yeare 1696.
John Thacker the Son of Mr Edwin Thacker and Mrs Frances Thacker his Wife Borne on ye 15th Day of January att Twelve a Clock in ye Day In the Yeare 1697.
Sarah Meacham ye Daughter of Joseph Meacham and Jane his wife was born ye 17 day of November 1703.
Elizabeth Hore ye Daughter of John & Jane Hore Baptized ye 22 Day of December 1703.
William Courlles ye Son of Michaell and Mercy Curlls his Wife was borne ye 26 day of January 170?.

Michaell Attwood ye Daughter of Richard & Sarah Attwood was baptized yn 26 Day of January 170¾.
David Davis ye Son of David & Mary Davis his Wife was Baptized ye 26 day of January 170¾.
Peter Chisman ye Son of George & Catherine his Wife was borne ye 29 day of August 1703.
Sarah ye Daughter of William & Mary Daniell was Baptized ye 23 day of Febuary 170¾.
Mary Mountague yn Daughter of William & Leette his Wife was Baptized ye 23 day of Febuary 170¾.
John Medderus ye Son of Charles & Mary Medderus his Wife was borne ye 21 day of ffebuary 170¾.
Paul Thilman ye Son of Paul & Sarah his Wife was Baptized ye 23 day of ffebuary 170¾.

CHRISTNINGS.

Richard Blackle ye Son of Robert and Ann Blackle his wife was Baptized ye 2 day of Aprill 1704.
Henry Goodlow ye Son of Henry & Elizabeth Goodlow his wife was baptized ye 2 day of Aprill 1704.
John Manuell ye Son of Edmun & Ann Manuell his wife was bapts ye 2 day of Aprill 1704.
Joseph Cartter ye Son of William & Mary Carter was Baptized ye 30 day of Aprill 1704.
John Maze ye Son of Ralph & Alice Maze was Baptizd ye 21 day of May 1704.
Thomas Emerson ye Son of Henry & mary his wife was baptized ye 21 day of May 1704.
Mary Pearce ye Daughter of John & Elizabeth Pearce was Baptized ye 23 day of July 1704.
Elizabeth Cranke ye Daughter of Mathew & Elizabeth Cranke was Baptized ye 23 day of July 1704.
Rite Curtis ye Son of Rite and Elizabeth Curtis was Baptized ye 3 day of September 1704.
Margrett Shurle ye Daughter of Richd & Ann Shurlle was Baptized ye 3 day of September 1704.
John George ye Son of Robert & Sarah George was Baptized ye 3d day of September 1704.
John George ye Son of Robert & Smith George was Baptized ye 24 day of September 1704.

Negro Children belonging to Mr William Churchhill Born as ffolloweth.

Major a Boy born July 1694.
Joan a Girl borne ye 2 day of September 1696.
Cott a Boy borne September 1697.
Tomboy a Boy borne August 1698.
Saturday a Boy borne June ye 1 day 1700.
May a Boy borne May ye 1 day 1701.
Mary a Girle borne ye 3 day of May 1701.
Sunday a Boy borne in Aprill 1703.
Thursday a boy Borne November 1703.

WEDDINGS OR MARRIAGES.

Hugh Finley & Mary Picket were Married Jan Ye 8th 1703.
Thomas Kingsley & Mary Ockoldham were Married ⎱ April y° 14th
Robert Biggs & Mary Armistead were Married ⎰ 1703.
William Chelton & Margaret Wheatherstone were Married May y° 18th 1703.
M' John Lomax & M" Elizabeth Wormley were Married June Y° 1st 1703.
Theophilus Staunton & Mary Percifull were Married June y° 2nd
William Harfoot & Mary Caree were Married July y° 14th 1703.
William Barber & Mary Gray were Married July y° 22nd 1703.
Gabriel Roberts & Sarah Bendall were Married July y° 26th
M' William Churchhill & M" Elizabeth Wormley were Married Octob, y° 5th.
William Hamock & Elizabeth Tight were Married Octob' y° 6th.
John Davis & Elizabeth Crank were Married Octob' y° 28th 1703.
Christopher Robinson & Judith Beverley were Married Octob' ye 12th.
John Nash & Ann Brider were Married Octob' y° 28th 1703.
Christopher Sutton & Hope Branmount were Married Novembr' ye 3d.
John Dangerfield & Mary Conway were Married Novemb' y" 11th.
Thomas Roberts & Mary Stevens were Married Novemb' y° 26th 1703.
Richard Straughan & Catherine Murrell were Married Decemb' y° 1st.
George Clay & Elizabeth Thompson were Married Decemb' y° 30th
Nicholas Harvey & Mary Norwood were Married Jan. ye 15th 1704.
James Daniel & Margaret Vivion were Married Jan y° 27th 1704.
John Curles & Rebecca King were Married Feb. y° 2d 1704.
Richard Rennall & Honnor Carvenoth were Married Feb. y° 23d 1704.
James Jordan & Ann Burk Feb. y° 23rd were Married 1704.
John Vivion & Christian Briscoe were Married Feb. y° 23d 1704.
Walter Roberts & Jone Bocker were Married Apr. y° 16th 1704.
Thomas Crank & Ann Goodlow were Married June y° 22nd 1704.
Jeptha Edmunds & Ellener Doss were Married August y° 18th 1704.
Thomas Pateman & Lettice Shippey were Married Aug. y° 16th 1704.
Marvill Mosely & Aggatha Daniell were Married Aug y° 31st 1704.
John Parson & Mary Osborn were Married Septem'' y° 28th 1704.
John Gallifor & Mary Hues were Married Octob' y° 5th 1704.
Richard Moor & Alice Holly were Married Octob' y° 26th 1704.
Thomas Arle & Elizabeth Johnson were Married Octob' y° 26th 1704.
John Carbett & Catherine Alden were Married Novemb' y° 9th 1704.
William Bristow & Margaret Stark were Married Decemb' y° 7th 1704.
Bartholomew Yates & Sarah Mickleburrough Married Sept 14 1704.

CHRISTENINGS.

Armistead Churchhill ye Son of Mr William Churchhill and Elizabeth his Wife Was Borne att Rosegill in Christ Church parish In Middlesex County in Virginia ye 25 day of July 1704 being of a Tuesday about 5 or 6 a Clock in ye Afternoon and was Baptized ye 1 day of August following by Mr Bartholomew Yeats Minister

Margrett Haynes ye Daughter of Charles & Elizabeth Haynes was Borne ye 24 day of January 1705.

Mary Hunphrys ye Daughter of Joseph & Elizabeth Humphrys Was Borne ye 24 day of January 170⅘.

George Wortham the Son of Mr George & Mrs Mary Wortham his Wife was Born Feb ye 5th Anno Domini 1699.

Sarah Wortham was Born Decemb^r ye 26th 1701.

John Wortham was Born Decemb^r ye 22d 1703.

Christopher Robinson ye Son of Mr John & Catherine Robinson his Wife was Born July ye 1st about six of the Clock In the Afternoon Anno Domini 1703.

John Robinson was Born feb: ye 3d About 10 of the Clock In the Afternoon his father and Mother Above Named Ann Dom 1704.

John Barnatt ye Son of John and Ann Barnatt his wife was Baptized Decemb^r ye 3d Anno Domini 1704.

Rachel Daniel ye Daughter of James and Margoret Daniel his Wife was Born Octob^r ye 14th and was Baptized Novemb^r ye 15th Anno Domini 1704.

Zacharias Gibbs the Son of John and Mary Gibbs his Wife was Baptized feb. ye 1st Anno Domini 1704.

Thomas Straughan the Son of Richard and Katherine Strauhan his Wife was Baptized feb. ye 1st Anno Domini 1705.

Edward Williams ye Son of Edward and Catherine Williams his Wife was Baptized feb. ye 4th Anno Domini 1705.

Howard Williams the Son of Charls and Ann Williams his Wife was Baptized Jan ye 3d Anno Domini 1705.

John a Negro of Mr Henry Thackers was Baptised feb ye 25th Anno Domini 1704.

CHRISTENINGS.

Richard Reynald Y^e son of Richard & Honor his Wife was Baptized Octob^r Y^e 15th Anno Domi 1704.

Ann Y^e Daughter of James Jordan & Ann his Wife Was Baptized Octob^r Y^e 15th Anno Domi 1704.

Jane Y^e Daughter of Thomas Stapleton and Mary his Wife was Baptized Octob^r Y^e 1st Anno Domi 1704.

John Y^e Son of Henry Tuggle & Mary his Wife was Baptized Novemb^r Y^e 5th Anno Domi 1704.

Thomas Y^e Son of Thomas Lanton and Ezebella his Wife was Baptized Novemb^r Y^e 5th Anno Domi 1704.

Abraham Y^e Son of James Baskett and Honor his Wife was Baptized January Y^e 7th Anno Domi 170⅘.

John Y^e Son of John Zachary And Eleanor his Wife was Baptized, Born January Y^e 7th Anno Domi. 170⅘.

Francis Thilman Y^e Son of Paul Thilman And Sarah his Wife was Born february Y^e 1st And Baptized Y^e 29th 1700.

Thomas Y⁰ Son of Thomas Williams and Elizabeth his Wife was Baptized february Y⁰ 18th Anno Domi 170⅘.
Henry Y⁰ Son of Edmund Mickleberry And Jane his Wife was Baptized February Y⁰ 18th Anno Domi 170⅘.
Peter Benet Y⁰ Son of William and Sarah Benet was Born November the Y⁰ 7th and was Baptized December Y⁰ 10th 1704.
Robert Y⁰ Son of Averila And Edward Couch was Born November Y⁰ 27th And was Baptized December Y⁰ 31st Anno Domi 1704.
John Y⁰ son of John and Jane Man his Wife was Born December Y⁰ 25th And was Baptized January y⁰ 21st Anno Domi 170⅘.
Elizabeth Y⁰ Daughter of Christopher And Hope Sutton his Wife was Born December Y⁰ 17th and Baptized January Y⁰ 21st 170⅘.
Elizabeth Y⁰ Daughter of Mʳ William and Killbee Namely Hannah Killbee his wife was Born January Y⁰ 13th And Baptized Y⁰ 11th of February Anno Domini 170⅘.

CHRISTENINGS.

Mary Y⁰ Daughter of Thomas and Mary Goddin his wife was Born December Y⁰ 19th And was Baptized february Y⁰ 11th Anno Domi 170⅘.
Robert Y⁰ Son of Robert and Judith Johnson his Wife was Born february Y⁰ 4th And Baptized, March Y⁰ 4th Anno Domi 170⅘.
John Y⁰ Son of Thomas And Mary Roberts was Born february Y⁰ 24th And Was Baptized March Y⁰ 25th Anno Domi 1705.
Elizabeth Y⁰ Daughter of Samuell and Margarett Philips was Born february Y⁰ 12th And was Baptized March Y⁰ 25th 1705.
John Y⁰ Son of John and Ann Morgan was Born March Y⁰ 17th And was Baptized April Y⁰ 15th Anno Domi 1705.
Hannah Y⁰ Daughter of John and Michal Miller his Wife was Born March Y⁰ 6th and was Baptized April Y⁰ 15th Anno Domi 1705.
John Y⁰ Son of John and Mary Millener was Born April Y⁰ 12th And Baptized May Y⁰ 6th Anno Domi 1705.
Sith Y⁰ Daughter of Hezekiah And Elizabeth Roads was Born June Y⁰ 2d And Baptized June Y⁰ 17th Anno Domi 1705.
William Y⁰ Son of Locklin and Ann Cannedy was Born february Y⁰ 1st And Baptized March Y⁰ 4th Anno Domi 1705.
Ann Y⁰ Daughter of Uriah and Sarah Carder was Born May Y⁰ 5th And Baptized June Y⁰ 17th Anno Domi 1705.
William Y⁰ Son of John and Rebecca Hughs was Born May Y⁰ 21st and Baptized July Y⁰ 1st Anno Domi 1705.
John Y⁰ Son of John and Rebecca Hughs was Born May Y⁰ 21st And Baptized July Y⁰ 1st Anno Domi 1705.
Thomas Y⁰ Son of William and Margaret Chelton was Born June Y⁰ 26th And Baptized July Y⁰ 29th 1705.
Ann Y⁰ Daughter of John and Ann Marston was Born * * Baptized August Y⁰ 19th.
Theodoret Y⁰ Son of Theophilus and Mary Stanton was * * And Baptized August Y⁰ 19th * *
Ann daughter of Wᵐ & Hannah Probent born 22d Decem * *

CHRISTENINGS.

Gray Skipwith Y^e Son of Sr William and Sarah Skipwith Lady his Wife was Born August Y^e 25th and Baptized Septem^{br} Y^e 20th 1705.
James Y^e Son of William and Mary Barley was Born August Y^e 16th and Baptized September Y^e 30th 1705.
John Y^e Son of Edward and Frances Godbee his Wife was Baptized April Y^e 1st 1705.
John Y^e Son of Patrick and Ann Manuel his Wife was Baptized April Y^e 1st 1705.
James Y^e Son of William and Mary Jones his Wife was Baptized April Y^e 1st 1705.
Aggatha Y^e Daughter of William & Margarett Kidd his Wife was Bap. April Y^e 1st 1705.
Elizabeth Y^e Daughter of John & Elizabeth Hickey his Wife was Bap. April Y^e 1st 1705.
Frances Y^e Daughter of Thomas & Alice Kidd his Wife was Baptized April Y^e 22nd 1705.
Averila Y^e Daughter of Joseph & Averila Hardee his Wife was Baptized April Y^e 22nd 1705.
Henry Y^e Son of John & Elizabeth Bird his Wife was Baptized May Y^e 13th 1705.
Robert Y^e Son of Robert & Mary Turrell his Wife was Baptized May Y^e 13th 1705.
Catherine Y^e Daughter of William & Ann Gardener his Wife was Bap. May Y^e 13th 1705.
Mary Y^e Daughter of David & Mary Davis his Wife was Baptized May Y^e 13th 1705.
Marvell Y^e Son of Marvell & Agatha Mosely his Wife was Bap. June Y^e 3d 1705.
John Y^e Son of John & Catherine Southern his Wife was Bap. August Y^e 12th 1705.
Joseph Y^e Son of Joseph & Jane Meacham his Wife was Baptized Y^e 7th of October and Born Y^e 15th Day of September Anno Domi 1705.
Mary Y^e Daughter of Jacob & Mary Preston his Wife was Bap. October Y^e 7th 1705.
Penelope Chany Y^e Daughter of Thomas & Mary Warwick his Wife was Bap. 9^{br} Y^e 7th 1705.
Edward Y^e Son of Edward & Ann Sidorn his Wife was Born October Y^e 1st And Baptized November Y^e 11th Anno Domi 1705.
Edward Wortham Y^e Son of Mr George & Mary Wortham his Wife was Born December Y^e 24th Anno Domini 1705.
John Nash Y^e Son of John and Ann Nash his Wife was Born November Y^n 19th & Baptized Y^n 20th of Y^e Same the Reverend Bartholomew Yates And Y^e Said John Nash Standing as Godfathers And Mercy Curtis as Godmother Anno Domini 1704.
John Jones Y^e Son of John & Hannah Jones his Wife was Baptized February Y^n 24th Anno Domi 170$\frac{5}{6}$
Richard Straughan Y^e Son of Richard & Catherine Straughan his Wife * * * May Y^e 12th Anno Domini 1706.

* * * Daughter of Edward & Kezia Ball his Wife Was Born March Y^e 31st * * * * * Y^e 26th Anno Domini 1706.
* * * * * * * of Augustine & Jane Owen his Wife was Baptized * * * * Anno Domini 1706.

CHRISTENINGS.

Catherine Y^e Daughter of Edward & Keziah Ball was Born January Y^e 25th Anno Domini 1696.

Elizabeth Daughter of Y^e above Ball was Born May Y^o 1st 1704.

Thomas Y^e Son of Richard & Martha Basford his Wife was Baptized Septemb^r Y^e 8th Anno Domi 1706.

Illegitimate—Joanna Y^e Daughter of   a Servant to Mr Thomas Kemp In Gloucester County was Baptized Septemb^r Y^e 8th Anno Domi 1706.

Elizabeth Y^e Daughter of Nathan & Diana Underwood his Wife was Born Y^e 22nd Day of Novemb^r & Baptized Y^e 22d of Decemb^r it being Y^e Lords day In Stratton Major Parrish in King & Queen County, By Emmanuel Jones Minister of Petsoe Parish in Gloucester County her Sureties being James Overstreet & Elizabeth Potter, Derby Cauniff & Hannah his Wife Y^e day & time of her Nativity being Wednesday About Y^e dawning of Y^e day Anno Domini 1700.

John Y^e Son of Nathan & Diana Underwood his Wife was Born Y^e 24th Day of August About Y^e dawning of Y^e day it being Saturday & S^{nt} Bartholomew day, And was Baptized Septemb^r Y^e 29th being the lord's day, by ye Reverend Bartholomew Yates In Christ Church his Sureties being John Townsend Robert Johnson & Mrs Elizabeth Dudley Anno Domini 17 Peter Y^e Son of James & Margaret Daniel his Wife was Baptized Septemb Y^e 29th.

Hanna Y^e daughter of Thomas & Ann Symes his Wife was Baptized Sep. Y^e 29th Anno Domini.

William Y^e Son of John & Margaret Davis his Wife was Baptized Sep. Y^e 29th Anno Domini.

William Y^e Son of Matthew & Mary Hunt was Bap. 8^{br} Y^e 20th.

Mary Y^e Daughter of Thomas & Ezabella Lantor his Wife was Born about 12 of Y^e Clock Sept. Y^e 9th 1700.

Jeremiah Y^e Son of Thomas Early and Elizabeth his Wife was Bap. Dec Y^e 9th 1705.

Humphrey Y^r Son of Humphrey Jones & Jane his Wife was Born Nov. Y^e 25th and Bap. Y^e 20th of Jan. Anno Dom 1705.

John Y^e Son of Richard Win & Sarah his Wife was Bap Y^r Same day.

Anne ye Daughter William Probert & Hannah his wife was Bap. *

Elizabeth Y^e Daughter of John Aldin & Frances his Wife was Bap. Feb Y^e 10th 1704.

Anne Y^e Daughter of Robert Blackley & Ann his Wife was Bap Y^e same Day 17—

Matthew Y^e Son of Sara Brooks an Illegitimate was Bap: Y^e same day 170—

Catherine Daughter of Bartholomew & Sarah Yates Borne 24th of June 17—

CHRISTENINGS.

Aggatha ye Daughter of Thomas Buford & Elizabeth his wife was Born August ye 13th Anno Domini 1705.
Garrett ye Son of Mr Robert Daniel & Mrs Margaret his wife was Born July ye 7th Anno Domini 1705.
John ye Son of John Goodwin & Mary his Wife was Bap Aprill ye 7th 1706.
Joanna ye Daughter of David George & Catherine his wife was Bap ye same day 1706.
Joanna ye Daughter of Henry Emmerson & Mary his wife was Bap ye same day 1706.
Susanna ye Daughter of John Hore & Jane his wife was Bap ye same day 1706.
Margaret ye Daughter of William Simmons & Margaret his wife was Bap ye same day 1706.
Thomas ye Son of Philip Warrick & Catherine his wife was Bap. Ap^r ye 18th 1706.
Mary ye Daughter of James Brown & Elizabeth his Wife was Bap. ye Same day 1706.
John ye Son of William Balding & Sarah his Wife was Baptized May ye 9th 1706.
Mary ye Daughter of Abraham Trigg & Elizabeth his wife was Bap. ye Same day 1706.
Robert ye Son of William Carter & Mary his wife was Bap. June ye 30th 1706.
Henry ye Son of Richard Perrot & Sara his wife was Born ye 25th of feb^{ry} 1706.
Jane ye Daughter of John Pace & Elizabeth his wife Bap. Sep^{tr} ye 22nd 1706.
Elizabeth ye Daughter of Henry Goodlow & Elizabeth his wife was Bap. ye same day 1706.
Susanna ye Daughter of Mr. Harry Beverley & Mme Elizabeth his wife was Bapt. Novemb^r ye 17th Anno Domini 1706.
Ann ye Daughter of Thomas Sibley & Eleaner his wife was Born Novemb ye 3d and Baptized Decemb^r ye 23d Anno Domi 1705.
Jacob ye Son of Georg Blake & Elizabeth his wife was Born Decemb^r ye 8th and Baptized January ye 13th Anno Domi 170⅝.
Dorothy ye Daughter of Henry Mitcham & Mary his wife was Born Decemb^r ye 12th & Baptized ye Same Day Anno Domini 170⅝.
Averilla ye Daughter of Robert Dudley & Elizabeth his wife was Born March * * & Baptized March ye 31st Anno Domi 1706.
* * * ye Daughter of Robert Humphreys & Rebecca his wife was Born february 6th * * & Baptized february ye 18th Anno Domi 170⅝.
William ye Son of William Downing & Elizabeth his wife was Born June ye 3d and Baptized July ye 14th Anno Domini 1706.
Daniel ye son of Daniel Holland & Jane his wife was Born July ye 15th and Baptized August ye 4th Anno Domi 1706.
Robert ye Son of Richard Wait & Anne his wife was Born July ye 4th and Baptized August ye 4th Anno Domi 1706.
Catherine ye Daughter of John Phillips & Jane his wife was Born June ye 27th and Baptized ye Same day Anno Domini 1706.

Charles ye Son of Owen Selaman & Esther his wife was Born Septemb^r ye 14th & Baptized Octob^r ye 6th Anno Domini 1706.

CHRISTENINGS.

Jane ye Daughter of Francis Dodson & Mable his wife was Baptized May ye 12th & Born April ye 13th Anno Domi 1706.

Edy ye Daughter of John Dudley & Edy his wife was Born April ye 12th & Baptized May ye 12th Anno Domi 1706.

Catherine ye Daughter of William Hamat & Elizabeth his wife was Born June ye 5th & Baptized July ye 14th Anno Domi 1706.

William ye son of Jonathan Herrin & Ann his wife was Born August ye 18th & Baptized Octob^r ye 6th Anno Domi 1706.

Ann ye Daughter of Joseph Humphreys & Elizabeth his wife was Born Septemb^r ye 3d & Baptized Octob^r ye 6th Anno Domi 1706.

Jane ye Daughter of William Wallis & Ann his wife was Baptized 8^{br} ye 21st and Born Octob^r ye 2d Anno Domini 1706.

John ye Son of Joseph Hutchinson & Mary his Wife was Baptized Novemb^r ye 17th 1706.

Hope ye Daughter of Christopher Sutton & Hope his wife was Bapt: ye Same Day 1706.

Mary Loe ye Daughter of Samuel Loe & Ann his Wife was Bap: Decemb^r ye 1st 1706.

Ann ye Daughter of Samuel Hoyl & Elizabeth his wife was Bap: December 22nd 1706.

Elizabeth ye Daughter of Edward & Aventa Couch his wife was Bap. Decemb^r 29th 1706.

Priscilla Churchhill y^e Daughter of Collo^{nl} William Churchhill Esqr & Mme Elizabeth Churchhill his wife was Born of a friday Night about Nine or ten A Clock Being y^e 21st of Decemb^r Anno Domi 1705, And was Baptized y^e first day of January following Anno Domi 170$\frac{5}{6}$ By y^e Reverend Mr Bartholomew Yates our present Minister.

Sarah y^e Daughter of James Smith & Ann his wife was Baptized Jan^{ry} y^e 12th 170$\frac{6}{7}$.

Judith y^e Daughter of Edward & Catherine Williams was Bap: Jan^{ry} y^e 12th 170$\frac{6}{7}$

Agatha y^e Daughter of Hugh Watts & Hannah his wife Bap. Jan^{ry} y^e 12th 170$\frac{6}{7}$.

Diana y^e Daughter of John Ashur & Susanna his wife was Bap. March y^e 2d 170$\frac{6}{7}$.

Elizabeth Y^e Daughter of William hill & Ann his Wife Was Bap. Y^e Same day 170$\frac{6}{7}$.

Elizabeth Y^e Daughter of William Bennett & Sarah his Wife was Bap Y^e same day 17—.

Jacob Y^e Son of Georg Blake & Elizabeth his Wife was Bap. March Y^e 16th 1706.

Richard Y^e Son of John Barnett & Ann his Wife was Bap. March Y^e 16th 1706.

Catherine Y^e Daughter of Mr Bartholomew Yates Minister And M^{dm} Sarah Yates his Wife was Born June Y^e 24th & Baptized July Y^e 4th Anno Domi 1706.

Mary Y^e Daughter of Mr Roger Jones & M^{dm} Mary his Wife was Bap. March Y^e 23d 170$\frac{6}{7}$.

Mary Y^e Daughter of Mr John Robinson & M^{dm} Catherine Robinson his Wife was Born January Y^e 3d Anno Domini 170⅔.

John Y^e Son of Edward Clark & Ann his Wife was Born March Y^e 31st And Baptized April Y^e 7th Anno Domini 1707.

Mary Y^e Daughter of Francis Coffly & Mary his Wife was Bap Apr^l Y^e 20th 1707.

Marrin Y^e Daughter of John Gibbs & Mary his Wife was Bap. Apr^l Y^e 20th 1707.

Sarah Daughter of Bartholomew & Sarah Yates Borne March 3d 1707.

CHRISTENINGS.

Elizabeth Y^e Daughter of Gabriel Roberts & Sarah his Wife was Baptized May Y^e 25th Anno Domini 1707.

Ruth Y^e Daughter of Thomas Maxum his Wife Baptized May Y^e 25th Anno Domini 1707.

Joice Y^e Daughter of Robert Johnson & Judith his Wife was Baptized June Y^e 22nd Anno Domini 1707.

Matthew an Illegitimate Born of an Irish Woman was Baptized Y^e Same Day Anno Domi 1707.

Mary Y^e Daughter of Robert Biggs & Elizabeth his Wife was Baptized August Y^e 3d Anno Domini 1707.

Christian Y^e Daughter of John Austin & Mary his Wife livers in Gloucester Was Baptized August Y^e 24th Anno Domi 1707.

Elizabeth Y^e Daughter of John Hughs And Rebecca his Wife was Baptized September Y^e 14th Anno Domi 1707.

Elizabeth Y^e Daughter of John Townsend & Damaris his Wife was Baptized September Y^e 28th Anno Domi 1707.

Benjamin Y^e Son of William Barbee & Mary his Wife Was Baptized October the 5th Anno Domini 1707.

Matthew Y^e Son of Matthew Evans & Elizabeth his Wife was Bap. Y^e Same day.

Catherine Y^e Daughter of William Southwort & Margaret his Wife Was Baptized Octob^r Y^e 19th Anno Domi 1707.

John & Jane being Twins Y^e Son & Daughter of Theophilus Staunton And Jane his Wife Were Baptized Octob^r Y^e 26th Anno Domi 1707.

Sara Carder Y^e Daughter of Uriah Carder & Sarah his Wife was Baptized Y^e same Day 1707.

William Y^e Son of Henry Brown & Elizabeth his Wife was Bap. Y^e Same day.

Ann Y^e Daughter of Benjamin Davis and Ann his Wife was Baptized November Y^e 6th Anno Domi 1707.

Susanna Y^e Daughter of William Matthews & Mary his Wife was Born July Y^e 4th Anno Domi 1706.

Samuel Y^e Son of William Matthews & Mary his Wife was Born Novemb^r Y^e 30th & Baptized Decemb^r Y^e 1st Anno Domi 1707.

Mary Y^e Daughter of Richard Straughan & Catherine his Wife was Baptized Decemb^r Y^e 7th Anno Domi 1707.

Michal Y^e Daughter of John Miller & Michal his Wife was Born Octob^r Y^e 31st & Baptized Decemb^r Y^e 7th 1707.

William Son of George & Mary Wortham borne 28th December 1707.

CHRISTENINGS.

Robert Y^e Son of James Dudley & Mary his Wife was Baptized January Y^e 18th Anno Domini 170$\frac{5}{6}$.
Susanna Y^e Daughter of John Davis & Margaret his Wife was Baptized Octob^r Y^e 1st Anno Domi 1707.
Nathan Underwood Y^e Son of Nathan Underwood & Diana his Wife was Born Y^e 9th being friday about nine of Y^e Clock in Y^e Morning & Was Baptized february Y^e 1st being Septuagesima Sunday. In christ Church by Y^e Reverend Mr Bartholomew Yates Minister of Y^e Same; his Sureties being Joseph Goear John Gibbs & Elizabeth Murry; Anno Domi 170$\frac{7}{8}$.
Simon Y^e Son of William & Anne Howard his Wife was Born January Y^e 11th & Baptized february Y^e 1st Anno Domi 170$\frac{7}{8}$.
William Y^e Son of Mr George Wortham & Mrs Mary his Wife was Born Decemb^r Y^e 28th & Baptized february Y^e 2d 170$\frac{7}{8}$.
Catherine Y^e Daughter of Thomas Robbason & Ann his Wife Was Baptized february Y^e 29th Anno Domi 170$\frac{7}{8}$.
Sarah Y^e Daughter of Thomas Davis & Mary his Wife Was Baptized Y^e Same Day Anno Domi 170$\frac{7}{8}$.
Abigail Y^e Daughter of John Marston & Ann his Wife Was Born January Y^e 25th & Baptized Y^e Same Day 170$\frac{7}{8}$.
John Y^e Son of John Burk & Michal his Wife Was Baptized Y^e Same Day 170$\frac{7}{8}$.
John Y^e Son of Willett Roberts & Mary .... his Wife B. Y^e Same Day Anno Domini Was Baptized 170$\frac{7}{8}$.
Judith & Elizabeth Daughters of Edward Williams & Catherine his Wife were Born March Y^e 4th & Baptized March Y^e 14th being Twins Anno Domini 170$\frac{7}{8}$.
Agnis Y^e Daughter of William Newberry & Agnis his Wife was Baptized April Y^e 2d Anno Domi 1708.
Mary Hoyt Y^e Daughter of Samuel Hoyt & Elizabeth his Wife was Baptized April Y^e 7th Anno Domi 1708.
Mary Y^e Daughter of Edward Ball & Kezia his Wife was Baptized April Y^e 26th Anno Domi 1708.
Rebecca Y^e Daughter of Francis Dodson & Mabel his Wife was Baptized May Y^e 2d Anno Domi 1708.
Edward Y^e Son of Edward Couch and Averilla his Wife was Baptized the Same Day Anno Domi 1708.

CHRISTENINGS.

Rebecca Y^e Daughter of John Jones & Parnell his Wife was Baptized May Y^e 16th Anno Domi 1708.
John Y^e Son of John & Mary Mitchener his Wife was Born April Y^e 4th Anno Domi 1705.
Alice Y^e Daughter of Charles Hayns & Ann his Wife was born Jan^r Y^e 21st 1704.
William & John Y^e Sons of Patrick Owen & Emary his Wife being Twins were Baptized May Y^e 23rd Anno Domi 1708.
Mary Y^e Daughter of John Mitchiner & Mary his Wife was Born June Y^e 16th Anno Domi 1699.
Averila Y^e Daughter of John Mundin & Frances his Wife Was Baptized June Y^e 13th 1708.

Anne Y^e Daughter of Thomas Chelton & Mary his Wife was Baptized Y^e Same Day 1708.
Samuel Y^e Son of William Marcum & Elizabeth his Wife was Baptized July Y^e 4th Anno Domini 1708.
James Y^e Son of Garrett Berry & Elizabeth his Wife Was Baptized August Y^e 8th Anno Domi 1708.
Richard Curtis Y^e Son of John Curtis Junr & Rebecca his Wife Born December Y^e 29th Anno Domi 1704.
John Y^e Son of Joseph Humphreys & Elizabeth his Wife Baptized Septemb^r Y^e 26th 1708.
Joanna Y^e Daughter of Robert Humphreys & Rebecca his Wife Was Baptized Octob^r Y^e 17th 1708.
Richard Wyett Y^e Son of Richard Wyett & Anne his Wife Was Baptized Novemb^r Y^e 7th Anno Domi 1708.
Christopher Y^e Son of Augustine Owen & Jone his Wife was Baptized Novemb^r Y^e 21st Anno Domi 1708.
Samuel Y^e Son of Samuel Loe & Ann his Wife Was Bap. this Day.
Thomas Y^e Son of Edmund Sanders & Mary his Wife was Bap. this Day.
Ann Y^e Daughter of Richard Daniel & Elizabeth his Wife was likewise Baptized this Day Anno Domi 1708.

CHRISTENINGS.

William Y^e Son of Joseph Hutchinson & Mary his Wife was Baptized Novemb^r Y^e 28th Anno Domi 1708.
John Ye Son of Thomas Symes & Ann his Wife was Baptized January Y^e 5th Anno Domi 170$\frac{8}{9}$.
Mary Y^e Daughter of Christopher Cutton & Hope his Wife was Baptized January Y^e 9th Anno Domi 170$\frac{8}{9}$.
Richard Y^e Son of John Dudley & Edith his Wife was Baptized the Same day Anno Domi 170$\frac{8}{9}$.
Nicholas Y^e Son of Jephtha Edmunds & Mary his Wife was Baptized Y^e Same Day Anno Domini 170$\frac{8}{9}$.
Mary an Illegitimate Y^e Daughter of Mary Rhodes was Baptized Y^e Same Day Anno Domi 170$\frac{8}{9}$.
Ruth Y^e Daughter of Edward Clark & Ann his Wife was Baptiz January Y^e 23d Anno Domi 170$\frac{8}{9}$
Marran Y^e Daughter of John Gibbs & Mary his Wife Baptized January Y^e 30th Anno Domi 170$\frac{8}{9}$
Sarah Y^e Daughter of John Barnatt & Ann his Wife was Baptized February Y^e 13th Anno Domi 170$\frac{8}{9}$.
Charles Y^e Son of James Daniel & Margaret his Wife Baptized 170$\frac{8}{9}$.
William an Illegitimate Son of Mary Canady was Born Octob^r Y^e 4th 1708 And Baptized March Y^e 13th A. D. 170$\frac{8}{9}$.
Elizabeth Y^e Daughter of Abraham Trigg & Elizabeth his Wife was Baptized March Y^e 27th Anno Domi 1709.
Christian Y^e Daughter of Benjamin Davis & Ann his Wife Was Baptized April Y^e 24th being Easter Day A. D. 1709.
Richard Y^e Son of William Bennet &   his Wife was Baptized May Y^e 1st A. D. 1709.
Mary Y^e Daughter of Thomas Lantor & Ezabella his Wife was Baptized May Y^e 22nd Anno Domi 1709.

Elizabeth Y^e Daughter of Lacklin Cannedy & Ann his Wife was Baptized the Same day Anno Domi 1709.
Edward Y^e Son of William Bristow & Margaret his Wife was Baptized July Y^e 6th Anno Domi 1709.
Elther Y^e Daughter of Thomas Maxum & Elizabeth his Wife was Baptized August Y^e 7th A. D. 1709.

CHRISTENINGS.

Sarah Y^e Daughter of Jonathan Herrin & Anne his Wife Was Baptized August Y^e 14th Anno Domi 1709.
William Y^e Son of Mr John Robinson & M^{dm} Catherine his Wife was Born March Y^e 25th Anno Domi 1709.
Gaffield Y^e Son of Henry Brown & Elizabeth his Wife was Born August Y^e 21st & Baptized Y^e 22d Anno Domi 17
William Y^e Son of John Ashur & Susanna his Wife was Baptized September Y^e 18th Anno Domi 1709.
Willet Y^e Son of Willett Roberts & Mary his Wife was Born August Y^e 11th & Baptized Septemb Y^e 25th 1709.
Roger Y^e Son of Mr Roger Jones & Mrs Mary his Wife was Baptized Decemb^r Y^e 18th Anno Domi 1709 Borne Y^e 18th October 1709.
Payton Y^e Son of Thomas Dudley Junr & Elizabeth his Wife Baptized January Y^e 22nd Anno Domi 170$\frac{9}{10}$.
Jane an Illegitimate Y^e Daughter of Ann an Irish Woman Servant to William Churchhill Esq. Baptized Y^e Same Day 170$\frac{9}{10}$.
Sarah Y^e Daughter of Francis Coffley & Mary his Wife was Baptized february Y^e 12th Anno Domi 170$\frac{9}{10}$.
Mary Y^e Daughter of Joseph Orphan & Constancy his Wife Was Baptized March Y^e 5th Anno Domi 170$\frac{9}{10}$.
Anne Y^e Daughter of John Owen & Michal his Wife Baptized Y^e Same Day Anno Domini 170$\frac{9}{10}$.

The Births of 5 Children of Henery & Eliz^a Thacker.
Henery Thacker borne Sunday Y^e 9th October 1698.
Martha Thacker borne Satturnday y^e 27th December 1701.
Chichely Thacker borne Sunday y^e 26th March 1704.
Lettice Thacker borne Satturnday y^e 26th ffebruary 1704.
Anne Thacker borne Wensday y^e 5th October 1709.
Peter Harding Son of Nicholas and Elizabeth Harding borne 27th Aprill 1709.

The Births of six Negro Children belonging to Mr Henery Thacker.
Toney ye Son of Sambo & Jenny borne October ye 14th 1698.
Judith ye Daughter of Ditt^o borne September ye 6th 1701.
Sam the Son of Jack & Becka borne ffebruary ye 8th 1701.
Winey the Daughter of Cesar & Joane borne June ye 7th 1705.
Nanny the Daughter of Sambo & Jenny borne March 2d 1705.
Molley the Daughter of Jack & Beck borne June ye 28th 1706.
John a Negro belonging to Mr Jno Vivion borne December ye 19th 1709.

The Births of Seven Negroes belonging to Mr John Smith Senior (vizt).

Negro Hally borne 18th November 1704. Negro Moll borne 16th ffebruary 1705. Negro Judy borne 15th June 1707. Negro Sanco borne 12th May 1708. Negro Hannah borne 26th September 1708. Negro Dinah borne 6th March 1709. Negro ffranke borne 31th May 1710.

Negro Ben Jeney's Son belonging to Captn John Smyth borne July ye 31th 1710.

Negro Molly belonging to Mr Bartholomew Yates born May ye 27th 1709.

Negro Willm baptized was borne (belonging to Ditto) July ye 13th 1709.

The Births of Ten Negro Children belonging to Captn Henery Armistead Registred ye 26th day of June 1711.

Emmanuell borne 13th December 1700. Bess borne ye 12th ffebruary 1701. Rose borne 3d May 1702. Mingo borne 9th October 1703. George borne 10th Aprill 1707. Hannah borne ye 6th October 1707. Gabriell borne 29th ffebruary 1708. Sue borne ye 10th May 1708. Tom borne ye 29th Aprill 1709. Jacob borne 10th May 1709.

Ned a Negro belonging to Hen. Tuggell borne 7th ffeb^ry 1709. Dick A Negro belonging to Mr Jno. Hipkins borne ye 27th March 1708.

The Births of three Negroes belonging to Mr Roger Jones Registred the 7th day of Aprill 1712.

Toney A Negro borne y^e 18th May 1711. Negro ffrank borne y^e 29th June 1711. Negroe Sarah borne y^e 11th Aprill 1711.

The Births of Three Negroes Belonging to Mr Rice Curtis Registered June ye 5th 17$\frac{1}{8}$.

ffrank borne y^e 20th of July 1708. Sarah borne y^e 25th of Aprill 1710. Judith borne y^e 2d of July 1711.

The Births of Sixteene Negroes Belonging to Mr Harry Beverley Registred Octob^r y^e 6th 171.

ffrank Daughter of Judith borne 15th July 1701. Maria Daughter of Judith borne 13th Octobo 1703. Sarah daughter of Judith borne 3d August 1705. Billy son of Phillis borne 15 November 1705. Bess daughter of Kate borne 26th August 1705. Moll daughter of Indian Fanny borne 2d May 1705. Moll daughter of Jenney borne 17th May 1706. Sarah daughter of Kate borne ye 25th September 1707. Ralph Son of Judith borne 10th August 1708. Harry Son of Jenney borne 15th of August 1708. Nanny daughter of Phillis borne 3d day of October 1709. Bob son of Kate borne 10th of October 1709. Anthony Son of Jenny borne 4th Aprill 1710. Beck daughter of Judith borne 5th March 1711. Peter son of Jenny borne 16th July 1712. Charles Son of Kate borne 2d day of October 1712.

The following Negroes Registred the 11th day of October 1712.

Charles A Negro belonging to Geo. Berwick borne y^e 20th day of June 1707. Robin A Negro belonging to Do. borne August y^e 4th day 1710.

Mingo A negro belonging to Oliver Seagar borne y\ue 26th day of May 1706.
Megg A negro belonging to Humphrey Jones borne y\ue 15th day of October 1706.
Peter a negro belonging to Garrett Minor borne y\ue 9th day of May 1707.
Winnie A negro belonging to Cap. Rob\ut Daniell borne y\ue 5th day of Aprill 1707.
Jack A negro belonging to Phillip Warwick borne y\ue 9th day of May 1707.
Ned A negro belonging to John Aldin borne 10th day of October 1707.
Winifred Morris a Molatto belonging to Francis Weekes Jun\ur baptized 25th day of Jan\ury 1707.
Tenny A negro belonging to Garrett Minor borne y\ue 20th day ffeb\ury 1709.
Cate A negro belonging to ffran. Weekes Jun\ur borne y\ue 25th day of December 1709.
Mingo A negro belonging to Cap. Robert Daniell borne 10th day of Aprill 1710.
Jack A negro belonging to Thomas Hazlewood borne y\ue 23th day of ffeb\ury 1709.
Cate A negro belonging to Thomas Mountague borne y\ue 21th day of July 1710.

CHRISTENINGS.

Marvell Son of Samuell and Anne Loe was baptized 24th of September 1710.
Julian Son of John & Hannah King baptized 5th November borne 1st October 1710.
Mary Daughter of Garrett & Elizabeth Berry baptized 5th of November 1710.
Mary Daughter of Thomas and Elizabeth Golder baptized 5th of November 1710.
Samuell the Son of George & Mary Wortham was borne 28th January 1709.
Mary Daughter of J\uno and Elizabeth Lewis baptized 3d January 1710.
John the Son of Augustine and Joane Owen baptized 22d Aprill 1711.
Mary Daughter of John & Mary Gibbs baptized 22d Aprill 1711.
Judith Daughter of Richard & Elizabeth Daniell baptized 22d Aprill 1711.
Thomas Son of Thomas & Eliza Maxum baptized 13th May 1711.
Stokeley Son of Henery & Hannah Toles baptized 3d June 1711.
Mary Daughter of Thomas & Mary Yarrow baptized 3d June 1711.
Mary Daughter of Edw\ud & Anne Clark baptized 3d June 1711.
John Son of John & Elizabeth ffoster baptized 3d June 1711.
Esther Daughter of Henery & Elizabeth Johnson baptized 3d June 1711.
Thomas Son of Sarah Palmer an Illegitimate baptized 7th September 1711.
Charles son of George & Mary Wortham borne 28th December 1711.

Ann Daughter of Edd^d &   Ball baptized 30th Aprill 1710.
Wm Son of J$^no}$ & Hannah Owen borne 15th of October 1711.
Mary Daughter of John & Elizabeth Saunders baptized 18th of November 1711.
Mary Daughter of William & Sarah Baldin baptized 9th December 1711.
Phebe Daughter of Edward & Keziah Ball baptized 2d March 1711.

Lower Chappel { Margarett Daughter of James Smyth & Ann his wife borne 11th March 1708. Robert an Illegittimate Son of Marg^tt Child. David Son of Robert & Eliza Mackey & Dorothy Daughter of Robert & Avarilla Couch all baptized the 16th Aprill 1710.

John Son of Thomas & Mary Davis baptized 30th June 1710.
John son of Robert & Judith Johnson baptized 20th August 1710.
Thomas Son of John & Michall Burk. Susanna daughter of Peter Chelton Juni^{or} & Eliza his wife were all baptized 20th August 1710.
John Son of W^m & Ann Hill baptized October 1st 1710.
Eliz^a Daughter of W^m & Mary Barbee born 1st Septr baptized 1st October 1710.
Ruth daughter of Nathan & Diana Underwood born 13th Septr baptiz^d October 22d 1710.
Ann daughter of Joseph & Lucretia Gore baptized 4th ffebruary 1710.
John Son of Joseph & Mary Hutchinson baptized 25th ffebruary 1710.
Thomas Son of Thomas & Mary Chelton. Ezekiah Son of John & Ann Rhodes were all baptized ye 25th ffebruary 1710.
Sarah daughter of Geo. & Eliza Blake borne 14th January 1710.
Eliza daughter of Joseph & Eliza Humfreys baptized 8th Aprill 1711.
Joseph Son of John & Katherine Rowe baptizd 29th Aprill 1711.
William Son of John & Ann Barbee, Ann daughter of John & Rebecca Hughes were all baptized 29th Aprill 1711.
David Son of Geo. & Eliz^a Berick baptizd 20th May 1711.
William Son of Thomas & Ann Godwin baptizd July 1st 1711.
Eliz^a daughter of Robert & Eliz^a Biggs baptizd 1st July 1711.
Mary daughter of Ed^{wd} & Eliza Saunders baptizd 14th October 1711.

CHRISTENINGS.

John Son of Robert & Rebecca Humphreys. Mary Daughter of William & ffrances Sandiford. Eliz^a daughter of Hugh & Rebecca Roach. and Ezabell daughter of Willett & Mary Roberts baptized att home 25th November 1711.
Joseph Son of William & Elizabeth Marcum borne 18th November & baptized 16th December 1711.
Robert Son of John & Catherine Robinson born Octo: ye 20. baptizd Nov. 5: 1711.

The Births of Six Children of Mr Harry Beverley and Elizabeth his wife.

Robert Son of Harry & Elizabeth Beverley was borne 6th day of November 27th day of March 1701.
Margarett Daughter of Ditto borne 27th day of March 1704.
Sussanna Daughter of Ditto borne 15th day of November 1706.
Katherine Daughter of Ditto borne 7th day of December 1708.

Judith Daughter of Ditto borne 25th day of October 1710.
Peter Son of Ditto borne 2d day of July 1712.
   Son of Henery & Eliz⁎ Browne borne 15th day of Aprill 1712.
Midle P'c'ncts { Benjamin Son of John & Margarett Davies baptized 3d day of August 1712.
Mary Daughter of W^m & Agnis Newbery baptized 3d day of August 1712.
Mary Daughter of Jon⁎ & Ann Henning D⁰ 17th of ffeb^ry 1711.
Ann Daughter of Jn⁰ & Alice Church D⁰ 9th of March 1711.
John Son of Jos. & Constance Orphan Baptized 18th of May 1712.
James Son of Charles & Eliza Richardson Do 18th of May 1712.
John Son of Jos. & Mary Hutchinson Do 25th of ffeb^ry 1710.
Tho⁎ Son of Geo. & Eliz⁎ Hardin Borne 3d of May 1712.
ffrances daughter of Francis & Mary Coffley baptized 10th of August 1712.
John Son of Xtopher & Hope Sutton. Sarah daughter of John & Mary Dayly. John Son of W^m & Hannah Cane borne August 5th. All three baptized Aug. 31th 1712.
Robert Son of Sr Wm Skipwith & Lady Sarah his wife. Ezekiah & W^m being twin Sons of J^no & Mary Bradley were all baptized 21th day of September 1712.
George Son of Geo. & Eliz⁎ Berwick borne 26th day of 7^br 1712.
Katherine daughter of Patrick & Ann Mannell baptized ye 9th day of ffebruary 1706.

Upper Chappell { Moses Son of W^m & Marg^tt Kidd baptized ye 30th day of March 1707.
Robert Son of John & Margarett Hardee baptized ye 30th day of March 1707.

Elizabeth daughter of Thomas & Elizabeth Hardy Warrwick baptized ye 30th day of March 1707.
Robert son of Robert & Kattherine Perrott. Katherine daughter of Henery & Eliz⁎ Smith both baptized this 27th day of Aprill 1707.
Agatha daughter of Matthew & Elizabeth Cranck baptized the 18th day of May 1707.
Mary daughter of Charles & Mary Maderas baptized ye 24th Day of Aprill 1707.
Judith daughter of Richard & Ann Shurly baptized ye 29th day of June 1707.
Robt. Son of Thomas & Elizabeth Williams baptized ye 10th day of August 1707.
Joannah daughter of Joseph & Avarilla Hardy baptized ye 3d day of August 1707.
Elizabeth daughter of Rich^d & Honour Reynalds baptized ye 3d day of August 1707.
John Son of Thomas & Elizabeth Bewford. Jonathan Son of David & Mary Davids. Elizabeth daughter of James & Elizabeth Browne were all three baptized 21th day of 7^br 1707.
William son of W^m & Ann Gardiner baptized born ye 6th day of 7^br 1707.
William son of Sr Wm Skipwith & Lady Sarah his Wife was born September ye 15 1707.

CHRISTENINGS.

John Son of John & Johanna Degge born October y⁰ 17. baptized 1707.
Thomas Son of Ralph & Mary Shelton baptized 9th day of November 1707.
John Son of Garrett & Diana Minor borne 29th day of June 1707.
Henery Son of Thomas & Alice Kid baptized 23th day of November 1707.
Thomas Son of Thomas & Lettice Bateman baptized 23th day of November 1707.
Philemon Son of James & Ann Black baptized 23th November 1707.
James Son of Robert & Marg⁴ Daniell borne 5th November 1709.
George Son of Robert & Anne Blacklee baptized 14th day December 1707.
Alexander Son of Alexander & Mary Graves borne 8th day of Jan'y 1707.
John Son of Richard & Martha Willis borne 1st day of Jan'y 1707.
James Son of Joseph & Jane Meecham baptized 15th day of ffebruary 1707.
John Son of Henery & Mary Emmerson baptized Do. day &c 1707.
Jⁿᵒ Son of Wᵐ & Mary Daniell baptized Do. day &c.
Jane daughter of Richard & Sarah Winn baptized Do. day &c.
ffrances daughter of ffrances & John Aldin baptized Do. day &c.
Richard Son of Richard & Sarah Perrott baptized 18th day of March 1708.
Mary daughter of Geo. & Hannah Guess baptized Do. day &c.
Elizabeth daughter of Wᵐ & Mary Jones born yᵉ 7th day of March 1708.
James Son of Jacob & Mary Pressnall baptized yᵉ 9th day of March 1708.
Elizabeth daughter of Ralph & Alice Mazy baptized Do. day &c.
John Son of Thomas & Sarah Chowning borne 27th day of August 1707.
Charles son of Charles & Dorothy Lee baptized 30th day of May 1708.
Mary daughter of Willᵐ & Mary Carter baptized 20th day of June 1708.
John Son of John & Jane Hoard baptized 1st day of August 1708.
Wᵐ Son of Henery & Mary Bewford borne yᵉ 17th day of June 1708.
Tobias Son of Edmond & Jane Mickleborough baptized yᵉ 17th day of June 1708.
Elizabeth daughter of Thomas & Anne Crank baptized Do. day &c.
Ann daughter of Matthew & Elizabeth Cap baptized Do. day &c.
Hally son of David & Kattherine George baptized 3d day of October 1708.
Thomas son of William & Joannah Semour baptized Do. day &c.
Elizabeth daughter of Hobbs & Mary Weekes baptized Do. day &c.
Joseph Son of Robert & Anne Homes baptized yᵉ 14th day of November 1708.
Macktyre Son of Thomas & Prudence Morris baptized Do. day &c.
Wᵐ Son of Jⁿᵒ & Michaell Owen borne yᵉ 4th day of November 1708.
Nickolas Son of Thomas & Mary Burk borne yᵉ 29th day of November 1708.

Mary daughter of W^m & Hannah Probent borne 16th day of November 1708.
Newsome Son of John & Eliz^a Pace baptized 6th day of ffebry 1708.
William Son of W^m & Marg^{tt} Simonds baptized Do. day &c.
Sarah daughter of Robert & Katherine Perrott baptized Do. day &c.
Jane daughter of John & Marg^{tt} Hardee baptized Do. day &c.
John Son of W^m & Marg^{tt} Kidd baptized 27th day of ffeb^{ry} 1708.
Charles Son of John & Elizabeth Hickee baptized ye 10th day of Aprill 1708.
John Son of Richard & Sarah Attwood borne ye 3d day of March 1708.
John Son of James & Anne Jordan baptized the 8th day of May 1709.
Jane daughter of Henery & Eliz^a Goodloe baptized Do. day &c.
Mary daughter of W^m & Elizabeth Mullings baptized Do. day &c.
Richard Son of Robert & Sarah George baptized ye 29th day of May 1709.
Michall daughter of James & Mary Meecham baptized the 10th day of July 1709.
Edward Son of W^m & Marg^{tt} Bristoll borne ye 4th day of June 1709.
Barker daughter of Humphrey & Elizabeth Jones baptized ye 31th day of July 1709.
Henery Son of John & Mary Meecham borne ye 25th day of July 1709.
Wm Son of W^m & Sarah Rattenig baptized the 21th day of August 1709.
Eliz^a daughter of Richard & Martha Willes baptized Do. day &c.
Anne daughter of W^m & Elizabeth Brooks baptized 2d day of October 1709.
Joseph Son of Joseph & Avarilla Hardy baptized y^e 23th day of October 1709.
Ralph Son of Ralph & Mary Shelton baptized Do day &c.
Martha daughter of Paile & Mary Cooper baptized Do. day &c.
Eliz^a daughter of Joseph & Mary Seares baptized y^e 13th day of November 1709.

MARRIAGES D C^a 1-1704.1—V$_{IZ}$^{t}.

John Hughes and Rebecca Hill married y^e 31th of December 1704.
Thos. Warwick & Eliz^a Goodrich y^e 23d January 1704.
John Alding & ffrances Williamson y^e 16th ffebruary 1704.
Humphrey Jones & Jane Hazlewood y^e 18th ffebruary 1704.
Joseph Andrews & Eliz^a Terrill y^e 20th of Aprill 1705.
John ffiney & Marg^{tt} Upton ye 12th of Aprill 1705.
John Goodwin & Mary Elliott ye 22nd of Aprill 1705.
John Price & Jane Smith ye 1st of May 1705.
Harman Churchyard and Eliza Perkins ye 26th of August 1705.
Phillipp Warwick & Catherine Twyman ye 5th of September 1705.
Robert Whitteker & Esther ffrancis ye 1st of October 1705.
Thos Maxam & Eliza Cooke ye 2nd of October 1705.
Sam^{ll} Hoyle & Eliza Elliott ye 23rd of October 1705.
John Maxkemett & Margarett Williams ye 28th of October 1705.
Dudley Jelley & Eliza Shelling ye 31th of October 1705.
Henery Ball & Alice Brookes ye 2nd of November 1705.

Patrick Owen & Mary Chills y° 23th of November 1705.
James Browne & Eliza Baldin ye 5th of December 1705.
Abraham Trigg & Eliza Guess y° 14th of December 1705.
Jeptha Edmunds & Mary Pain y" 24th of December 1705.
Joseph Hutchinson & Mary Needles ye 2nd of January 1705.
Richard Perrott & Sarah Pitts ye 15th of January 1775.
William Baldin & Sarah Lewis ye 17th of January 1705.
Richard Wait & Ann Dugless y° 3rd of ffebruary 1705.
Robert Perrott & Catherine Daniell y° 25th of March 1706.
Matthew Hunt & Mary Loyall y° 26th of March 1706.
Edward Parke & Anne fferne ye 26th of March 1706.
William Ryon & Elianour Jackson y° 18th of Aprill 1706.
Jonathan Horne & Anne Clay y" 14th of May 1706.
Henery Bailey & Catherine Denison y° 27th of May 1706.
ffrancis Coffley & Mary Wallis ye 24th of June 1706.
Thomas Davis & Mary Roberts y° 4th of August 1706.
Robert Biggs & Eliza Pate y° 2nd of September 1706.
John Austain & Anne Bolton y° 2nd of September 1706.
William Johnson & Eliza Paine y" 8th of September 1706.
Garrett Minor & Diana Vivion ye 17th of October 1706.
Thomas Dudley & Eliza Meecham y° 22nd of October 1706.
Theophilus Stanton & Jane Porter y° 28th of November 1706.
Thomas Chowning & Sarah Davis y° 20th of December 1706.
Thomas Smyth & Jane Annis y° 26th of December 1706.
Benj" Davis & Anne Williams y° 27th of December 1706.
John Custis & Avarilla Curtis y° 16th of January 1706.
John Degge & Johanna Killbee y° 21th of January 1706.
George Coleman & Martha Pressnall y° 27th of January 1706.
John Sandeford & Mary Walkell y° 13th of ffebruary 1706.
Edward Harrell & Margarett Brumwell y° 20th of Aprill 1707.
William ffiney & Honour Reardon y° 8th of May 1707.
James Walker & Clara Robinson y° 20th of May 1707.
Richard Attford & Mary Williams y° 29th of May 1707.
Henery Bewford & Mary Parsons y° 12th of September 1707.
Robert Deputy & Mary Huddle y° 9th of October 1707.
John Owen & Michaell Bristow y° 23th of October 1707.
James Areley & Jennett Ryell y° 18th of November 1707.
Samuell Samford & Isabella Langhee y° 21th of November 1707.
John Jones & Patrick Okendime y° 10th of ffebruary 1707.
Alexander Graves & Mary Stapleton y° 6th of Aprill 1708.
John Munday & ffrances Dudley y° 6th of Aprill 1708.
John Newton & Mary Michiner y° 6th of Aprill 1708.
Matthew Bowen & Eliz" Wood y° 6th of May 1708.
John Whately & Mary Hurford y° 23th of May 1708.

MARRIAGES &c. 1708. Viz'.

James Meecham & Mary fferne married y° 8th of July 1708.
Henery Bassett & Sarah Trigg y° 15th of July 1708.
Matthew Laundress & Eliz" Jenkins y° 26th of July 1708.
John Meechan & Mary Atwood y° 27th of July 1708.
William Brookes & Eliz" Cardwell y° 2d of September 1708.
John ffoster & Eliz" Bailey y° 14th of September 1708.
Hobbs Weekes & Mary Perrott y° 16th of September 1708.

Stokeley Gales & Anne Velott y" 21th of October 1708.
John Owen & Sarah King y" 31th of October 1708.
William ffaulkener & Mary Weekes y" 3d of November 1708.
John Gibson & Eliz" Willcocks y" 28th of November 1708.
Jonathan Brookes & Mary Tugell y" 27th of December 1708.
James Curtis & Agatha Vans y" 27th of December 1708.
Julian King & Sarah Snelling y" 30th of December 1708.
John Williams & Anne Shurley y" 17th of ffebruary 1708.
Thomas Olliver & Sarah Howes y" 21th of ffebruary 1708.
Michaell Smyth & Sarah Brookes y" 28th of Aprill 1708.
Joseph Alphin & Constantine Stiff y" 28th of Aprill 1708.
Matthew Perry & Sarah Murrey y" 28th of April 1708.
Peter Chelton & Eliz" Downing y" 1st of May 1708.
William Allford & Herodias Shibley y" 1st of May 1708.
William Stannard & Anne Hazlewood (Daughter of George Hazlewood Son & Heire of Capt" John Hazlewood late of Lond" Marriner deced) and Anne daughter of Richard and Anne Robinson (the Widdow & Heire of Abraham Moore deced married y" 3d of May 1708.
Daniell Downing & Lettice Love y" 27th of May 1708.
John Saunders & Eliz" Sibley y" 12th of June 1708.
William Hunt & Eliz" Holland y" 13th of June 1708.
James Mackey & Eliz" Brock y" 12th July 1708.
Isaack Hill & Marg" Jenings y" 28th of July 1708.
John Rhodes & Anne Paine y" 18th of August 1708.
Rinwing Gardiner & Anne Black y" 18th of August 1708.
Matthew Cock & Catherine Priest y" 12th of September 1708.
John Church & Alice Key y" 16th of October 1708.
ffrancis Parke & Anne Williams y" 18th of December 1708.
W" Dess & Katherine Woodyard y" 18th of December 1708.
John King & Hannah Adams y" 23rd of December 1708.
John Barbee & Ann Miller y" 25th of December 1708.
John Gutterie & Sarah Stiff y" 5th of January 1708.
James M"tyre & Hannah Boseley y" 5th of January 1708.
Hugh M"tyre & Catherine George y" 5th of January 1708.
Thomas Golden & Eliz" Goare y" 12th of January 1708.
Joseph Goare & Lucretia Tugwell y" 16th of ffebruary 1708.
Thomas Gilley & Mary Shephard y" 17th of ffebruary 1708.
John Owen & Hannah Probest y" 10th of Aprill 1708.
Powell Stampar & Mary Brookes y" 10th of Aprill 1708.
Edward Wallford & Rebecca Mason y" 10th of Aprill 1708.
Nicholas Jones & Anne Hoyle ye 11th of Aprill 1708.
William Tigwell & Priscella Snelling y" 20th of Aprill 1708.
William Elliott & Mary Neale y" 20th of Aprill 1708.
Edward Cambridge & Anne Nixson y" 1st of May 1708.
Thomas Clarke & Eliz" Toseley y" 22th of May 1708.
George Barwick & Elizabeth Bristow ye 7th of June 1708.
Jacob Stiff & Eliz" Clarke ye 5th of July 1708.
William Bushnell & Honour Reynalls y' 20th of July 1708.
Thomas Thornton & Agatha Curtis y" 25th of July 1708.
Thomas Cheedle & ffrances Godby y" 26th of July 1708.

MARRIAGES &c 1710—Viz^t.

Hugh Roach & Rebecca Bremont married ye 27th of July 1710.
John Gutterie & Jane Mitcham 4th of August 1710.
Minor Minor & Eliz^n Norman 22th of August 1710.
Edward Saunders & Eliz^a Austin 3d of August 1710.
William Hill & ffrances Needles 7th of September 1710.
Thomas Elliott & Eliz^a Dudley 21th of September 1710.
William Daniell & ffrances Boseley 24th of October 1710.
Henery Tugell & Eliz^a Browne 31th of October 1710.
Valentine Mayo & Anne Jordan 14th of November 1710.
Isaack Webb & Winifrid Hipkins 14th of November 1710.
Churchill Blakey & Sarah George 30th of November 1710.
William Sandeford & ffrances Townsend 25th of December 1710.
Arthur Donnelly & Lettice Downing 2d of January 1710.
Abraham Trigg & Judith Clarke 11th of January 1710.
John Mitcham & Mary Brame 1st of ffebruary 1710.
John Pinnell & Eliz^a Ingram 4th of Aprill 1710.
James Monnoughon & Elianor Martin 5th of April 1711.
Thomas Godin & Anne Webb 7th of April 1711.
John Bell & Mary Key 20th of Aprill 1711.
William Wheeler & Eliz^a Begerley 9th of May 1711.
Charles Richardson & Eliz^a Carter 2d of June 1711.
Thomas Cheny & Jane Swepstone 16th of June 1711.
William Cain & Hannah King 4th of July 1711.
Thomas Salt & Anne Gabriell 3d of August 1711.
Thomas Warrick & Mary Jones 4th of August 1711.
Thomas Machen & Mary Chelton 8th of August 1711.
Hen: Ware & Marg^tt Daniell 15th of August 1711.
Edward Radford & Mary Canady 23d of August 1711.
John Purvis & Winifred Nicholls 5th of September 1711.
John Johnson & Anne Stevens 21th of September 1711.
Arthur Thomas & Mary Saunders 26th of October 1711.
John Bradley & Mary Rhodes 2d of November 1711.
William Hackney & Alice Rhodes 2d of November 1711.
Richd Gibbs & Penelope Dewton 16th of November 1711.
Joseph Timberlin & Eliz^a Gray 11th of December 1711.
Daniell Hughes & ffrances Gresham 19th of December 1711.
Patrick Deacon & Rebecca Cooper 12th of January 1711.
Samuell Dagnell & Margarett Child 24th of January 1711.
Ralph Watts & Eliz^a Mullins 5th of february 1711.
John Berry & Mary Dudley 17th of ffebruary 1711.
Edward Couch & Sarah Thomson 26th of ffebruary 1711.
Edward Prendergast & Elizabeth Hickey 26th of ffebruary 1711.
William Blazedon & Sarah Palmer 3d of March 1711.
Thomas Bristow & Catherine Wortley 1st of May 1711.
Robert Brine & Mary Matthew 25 May 1711.
John Hughes & Jayne Calaham 27 May 1711.
Richard Winn & Anne Cocke 28 May 1711.
John Vivion & Eliz^a Thacker 19 June 1711.
Man Page & Judith Wormley 10 July 1711.
J^no Marston & Mary Terrill 31 July 1711.
Henery ffollwell & Katharine Williamson 4 September 1711.

Augale Cummins & Ellianor Williamson 18 September 1711.
James Crosswell & Anne Brooke 22 October 1711.
John Nash & Mary Curlis 22 December 1711.
John South & Elizabeth Smith 7 Jan'y 1711.
John Bristow & Mary Carter 8 Jan'y 1711.

MARRIAGES.

Edward Moor & Margrett Symons married Feb'y ye 13 1712.
James Bowman & Margrett Dearlow married Feb'y ye 14 1712.
John Ingram & Mary Croony married Feb'y ye 16 1712.
William Cheshire & Anne Davis married Aprill ye 12 1713.
Richard Wiat & Charity Beamont married Aprill ye 16 1713.
Peter Ballad & Mary Dabidie married June ye 2 1713.
John Cheedle & Lettice Southern married Sept. ye 14 1713.
James Riske & Anne Calvert married Sept. ye 24 1713.
Benjamine Woods & Elizabeth Wheeler married Novem' ye 16 1713.
Gabriell Ray & Elizabeth Gibbs married Novem' ye 22 1713.
Richard Allen & Mary Roebottom married Decem' ye 27 1713.
Moses Norman & Alice Canady married Jan'y ye 15 1713.
Samuell Batchelder & Catherine Vallott married Jan'y ye 21 1713.
Robert Dudley & Elizabeth Curtis married Feb'y ye 9 1713.
John Miller & Jane Hill married March ye 28 1714.
John Gresham & Anne Carnen married March ye 30 1714.
Thomas Hazlewood & Jane May married May ye 7 1714.
George Saunders & Anne Clark married May ye 9 1714.
Henry Ball & Sarah Bristow married May ye 12 1714.
John Watts & Elizabeth Worsell married June ye 17 1714.
Henry Barns & Johanna Lawrance married July ye 6 1714.
Ralph Lyall & Amy Mazey married August ye 19 1714.
Richard Steevens & Sarah Sandiford married Septemb^r ye 2 1714.
Curtis Perrott & Anne Daniell married Septemb' ye 3 1714.
George Bonden & Sarah Bennett married Septemb^r ye 8 1714.
Thomas Keiling & Catherine Ball married Septemb^r ye 30 1714.
Aquilla Snelling & Mary Goar married Novem^r ye 24 1714.
John Smith & Anne Smith married Novem^r ye 24 1714.
Thomas Hackett & Mary Jarrett married Novem^r ye 28 1714.
Andrew Terry & Elizabeth Moxam married Decem' ye 14 1714.
Jeffery Burk & Mary Ashton married Decem^r ye 19 1714.
William Markham & Elizabeth Wharton married Jan'y ye 9 1714.
George Chowning & Elizabeth Daniell married Feb'y ye 4 1714.
Edmond Hamerton & Sarah Thilman married Feb'y ye 10 1714.
Henry Bridgforth & Mary Chelton married April ye 18 1715.
Thomas Paine & Catherine Lydford married May ye 26 1715.
John Hatton & Anne Godin married July ye 11 1715.
Thomas Blakey & Mary Meacham married Decemb^r ye 5 1715.
William Seagur & Anne Scinco married Decem^r ye 15 1715.
William Vanhan & Mary Wake married Decem^r ye 25 1715.
John Brame & Elizabeth Beamon married Jan'y ye 24 1715.
James Hipkins & Mary Warner married Feb'y ye 9 1715.
William Davis & Elizabeth Allen married Feb'y ye 12 1715.
Eusebias Lewis & Mary Loyall married Ap. ye 5 1716.
John Watts & Elizabeth Foster married Ap. ye 12 1716.
John Pendergrass & Mary Alford married May ye 2 1716.

BURIALLS.

John Sadler buried the 31th day of October 1710.
John Meecham Dyed the 20th day of May 1712.
Phillipp Callvert dyed the 26th day of June 1712.
Elizabeth Sharlott dyed the 22th day of July 1712.
Ann daughter of Edward & Mary Radford buried 31th day of August 1712.
Jane daughter of Phillipp & Kath Warwick died ye 13th day of September 1712.
Mrs Ann Stannard wife Mr Wm Stannard departed this life on ffriday ye 5th day of X^{ber} 1712 about 12 of Clock att night aged twenty and two yeares and five days and having liv'd a married life three yeares Seven months and two days being great with child and near Eight months gone. Buried the 10th of December 1712.
William Son of Ralph and Alice Mazy buried ye 15th day of March 1712.
George Blake dyed ye 17th and was buried ye 19th day of July 1713.
Ralph Wormley Esqr dyed the 5th and was buried the 9th day of December 1713.
Mr William Mountague dyed the 7th and was buried the 10th day of X^{ber} 1713.
Mary Davies Widow dyed ye 7th and was buried the 9th day of March 1713.
Paul Thillman dyed the 14th and was buried the 17th day of March 1713.
Mrs Elizabeth Thacker Widow dyed the 22nd and was Interred the 25th May 1714.
Rebecca Johnson dyed ye 19th day of May & was buried ye 21th of May 1714.
Ben a negro belonging to Capt John Smith buried ye 7th of May 1714.
Elizabeth Marcum dyed ye 9th & was buried ye 11th of October 1713.
Thomas Tegnall dyed ye 10th & was buried ye 12th of October 1713.
John Okill dyed ye 25th of October & was buried 27th Ditto 1713.
Edmund Saunders dyed ye 1st and was buried ye 3d of November 1713.
John Curtis dyed November ye 8 & was buried 9^{ber} ye 10 1714.
Margrett Blakey dyed November ye 14 & was buried November ye 16 1714.
John Wacham dyed November ye 21 & was buried November ye 23 1714.
John Sandiford dyed Jan^{ry} ye 3 & was buried Jan^{ry} ye 6 1714.
Sarah Wormley dyed Jan^{ry} ye 12 & was buried Jan^{ry} ye 14 1714.
Alice Silvester dyed Jan^{ry} ye 6 & was buried Jan^{ry} ye 8 1714.
John Davies dyed Jan^{ry} ye 30 & was buried Jan^{ry} ye 31 1714.
John Watts dyed Decem. ye 17 & was buried December ye 18 1714.
Jack a negro belonging to John Smith Senr buried Feb. ye 9 1714.
Richard Hill dyed Jan^{ry} ye 23 & was buried Jan^{ry} ye 24 1714.
John Burk dyed March ye 13 & was buried March ye 14 1714.
Frank a negro belonging to John Smith buried March ye 27 1715.
Peter a negro belonging to George Wortham buried Feb^{ry} ye 22 1714.
Miles a negro belonging to James Walker buried March ye 15 1714.
Rinning Gardner dyed Ap: ye 7th was buried Ap: ye 9 1715.

Richard Allen dyed April ye 27th & was buried Aprill ye 30 1715.
Absolom Chowning dyed November ye 29 & was buried November ye 30 1714.
Kate a negro belonging to John Hoar buried May 22 1715.
William Bushnell dyed May ye 19 & was buried May y^c 21 1715.
Edmund Saunders dyed July ye 31 & was buried Augs^t y^u 1715.
Charles Lee dyed August ye 20 & was buried August ye 23 1715.
Anne Thacker dyed August ye 26 & was buried August ye 28 1715.
Alice Purvis dyed Septem^r ye 5 & was buried Septem^1 ye 7 1715.
Griffin Nichols dyed Septem^r ye 14 & was buried Septem^r ye 15 1715.
Johanna Humpheries dyed Augst ye 29 & was buried August 31 1715.
Elizabeth Chelton dyed Septem^1 ye 7 & was buried Septem^r ye 9 1715.
Macham Moor dyed Septem^r ye 9 & was buried Septem^r ye 10 1715.

    Bar Yates Minister.

BURIALLS.

Thomas White dyed Septem^r ye 12 & was buried Septem^r ye 13 1715.
John Manuell dyed Octo: ye 3 & was burried October ye 4 1715.
Reuben Skelton dyed Octo. ye 8 & was buried October ye 10 1715.
Martin Gardner dyed Septem^r ye 12 & was buried Septem^r ye 14 1715.
Diana Gardner dyed Septem^r ye 21 & was buried Septem^r ye 23 1715.
Jane Lawson dyed Octo: ye 8 & was buried October ye 11 1715.
Clara Walker dyed Octo: ye 25 & was burid October ye 29 1715.
Mary Pendergrass dyed Septem^r ye 15 & was buried Septem^r ye 17 1715.
Johanna Barnes dyed October ye 16 & was buried October ye 18 1715.
Elizabeth Baldwin dyed October ye 16 & was buried October ye 18 1715.
William Southworth dyed Jan^ry ye 6 & was buried Jan^ry ye 7 1715.
Anne Marion dyed Jan'y ye 6 & was buried Jan'ry ye 7 1715.
Bridgett Marion dyed Jan'ry ye 8 & was buried Jan'ry ye 9 1715.
William Lyall dyed Jan'ry ye 19 & was buried Jan'ry ye 21 1715.
George Pace dyed Jan'y ye 19 & was buried Jan'ry ye 21 1715.
Dorothy Manuell dyed Jan'y ye 1 & was buried Jan'y ye 3 1715.
Richard Waitt dyed August ye 10 & was buried August ye 12 1715.
Francis Dodson dyed Jan^ry ye 8 & was buried Jan^ry ye 11 1715.
Elizabeth Curtis dyed Jan^ry ye 20 & was buried Jan'ry ye 24 1715.
George Bowden died Jan'y ye 28 & was buried Jan'ry ye 31 1715.
Thomas Volve dyed Jan'y ye 15 & was buried Jan'y ye 17 1715.
Anne Cheshire dyed March ye 17 & was buried March ye 19 1715.
Mary Clay dyed Decem^r ye 2 & was buried Decem^r ye 4 1715.
Henry Goodloe dyed March ye 13 & was buried March ye 15 1715.
Thomas Smith dyed Jan'ry ye 15 & was buried Jan'ry ye 18 1715.
Nathan Underwood dyed ye 22 March & was buried March 24 1715.
William Kilpin dyed Ap. ye 14 & was buried Aprill ye 17 1716.
Mary an Indian Woman dyed May 16 & was buried May ye 18 1716.
Elizabeth Lee dyed July ye 26 & was buried July ye 27 1716.
Elizabeth Earley dyed July ye 6 & was buried July ye 8 1716.
Mary Nash dyed May ye 5 & was buried May ye 7 1716.
Ralph Mazey dyed July ye 20 & was buried July ye 22 1716.
Lydia Hamerton dyed August ye 9 & was buried August ye 10 1716.
Sarah Chowning dyed August ye 2 & was buried August ye 3 1716.

Violetta Seares dyed August ye 11 & was buried August ye 12 1716.
Hope Sutton dyed August ye 21 & was buried August ye 23 1716.
Sarah Haines dyed Sept. ye 4 & was buried ye Same day 1716.
John Warwick dyed Sept. ye 2 & was buried Septem^r ye 4 1716.
Michal Owen dyed Sept. ye 10 & was buried Septem^r ye 11 1716.
William Walker dyed Sept. ye 22 & was buried Septemr ye 23 1716.
Judith Lucas dyed August ye 15 & was buried August ye 16 1716.
Daniell Trigg dyed August ye 13 & was buried August ye 15 1716.
Benjamine Sparkes dyed Septem^r 29 & was buried October ye 1 1716.
Valentine Mayo dyed Octo 5 & was buried October ye 7 1716.

  Bar Yates Min^r

CHRISTENINGS.

Thomas son of W^m & Frances Hill born May ye 20 1711.
W^m son of John & Hannah Owen was borne ye 15 October, baptized ye 2d December 1711.
Dianah daughter of John & Dianah Davies baptized 2d day of March 1711.
Martha daughter of John & ffrancis Alding baptized 16th day of March 1711.
Susannah daughter of Abraham & Judith Trigg baptized Do. day &c. 1711.
William Son of W^m & Honour ffinny baptized 6th of Aprill 1712.
Thomas Son of Churchhill & Sarah Blacky baptized Do. day &c.
Sarah daughter of Thomas & Elizabeth Bewford baptized Do. day &c.
John son of Thomas & Mary Warwick borne 14th March 1711.
Mary daughter of Joseph & Avarilla Hardy borne 18th May 1712.
Henery Son of Jon^a & Mary Brooks borne 1st day of May 1712.
Jane daughter of Edmond & Jane Mickleborough borne 8th of Aprill 1712.
Direll Son of W^m & Marg^{tt} Kidd borne 16th of March 1711.
William Son of Robert & Katherine Perrott borne ye 20th of May 1712.
Cary daughter of Powell & Mary Stampar borne 23d June 1712.
William Son of William & Elizabeth Brooks borne 10th May 1712.
Mary daughter of Thomas & Lettice Bateman borne Do. day &c.
Joshabee daughter of Marvell & Agatha Moseley borne 29th day of May 1712.
Agatha daughter of Robert & Ann Blackly borne 9th May 1712,
Wm Son of Ralph & Alice Mazy borne 3d of August 1712.
Ann Daughter of James & Clara Walker borne 17th of January 1707.
John Son of James & Clara Walker borne 16th September 1709.
Katharine daughter of James & Clara Walker borne 3d November 1711.
Ann daughter of W^m & Ann Stannard born Satturn day August 26th 1710 about two of the Clock in the afternoon and Baptized by ye Revrd Mr Bartho: Yates ye 17th of ye same month 1710.
Marvell Son of Sam^{ll} & Ann Lee baptized ye 7th of December born ye 28th of October 1712.
Marg^{tt} daughter of Thomas & Eliz^a Elliott born ye 12th Jan^{ry} baptized 8th ffeb^{ry} 1712.

Ann daughter of Patrick & Rebecca Deagon born 30th Xber. baptize^d 8th ffeb^{ry} 1712.
Gregory Son of Thos & Ann Smyth born ye 31th Xber. baptized ye 8th ffebry 1712.
Bartho: Son of Bartho: & Sarah yates born ffeb^{ry} ye 9th baptiz^d ye 17th ffeb^{ry} 1712.
Robert Son of Thomas & Sarah Chowning born ye 20th day of March 1711.
John Son of Charles & Dorothy Lee born ye 28th August baptiz^d 5th day of October 1712.
Eliz^a daughter of Hugh & Catherine M^{cr}tyre born 28th Septr baptiz^d 19th October 1712.
Eliz^a daughter of Richard & Penelope Gibbs born 5th Septem^r baptized 19th October 1712.
Penelope daughter of Thom^s & Susanna Carter born 26th September baptized 19th October 1712.
William Son of Thomas & Jane Cheyny baptiz^d 19th October 1712.
John & Winifred (twins) Son & daughter of John & Winifred Purvis born 24th March 1711.
William Son of Richard and Sarah Perrott born 27th December baptized 22nd day of ffebruary 1712.
Joseph Son of Humphrey and Elizabeth Jones born 14th December baptized 22nd ffebry 1712.
Mary daughter of James and Mary Meecham born 30th Jan^{ry} baptiz^d 25th of ffeb^{ry} 1712.
Mary Daughter of Elizabeth Worsdell born 7^{ber} 11th 1708, baptized March 1st 1712.
Thomas Son of Jacob Stiff and Eliz^a his wife was baptized Aprill 12th 1712.
Robert Son of John & Mary Wake baptized April 12th 1713.
Mary daughter of William and Ann Hill baptized May 10th 1713.
Ann daughter of Sarah Bennett an Illegitimate baptized May 10th 1713.
Crisp Son of Ralph and Mary Shelton born Aprill 1st baptized May 17th 1713.
Mary daughter of Thomas and Katherine Bristow born May 1st baptized May 24th 1713.
William Son of William and Eliz^a Hammut baptized May 24th 1713.
John Son of Eliz^a Ballard Illegittimate baptized May 24th 1713.
Millicent daughter of Hobbs and Mary Weekes born 2d May baptized June 14th 1713.
Martha daughter of Henery and Sarah Baskett born May 15th baptized June 14th 1713.
Thomas Son of George and Eliz^a Blake baptized July 5th 1713.
Benjamine Son of John and Elianor Jones baptized August 2d 1713.
Thomas Son of Nathan and Diana Underwood born August 20th baptized Augt 24th 1713.
Jedidiah Son of John and Mary Bristow born August 10th baptized September 6th 1713.
George Son of George and Hannah Guest born August 3d baptized September 6th 1713.
Jane Daughter of Robert and Eliz^a Biggs baptized September 27th 1713.

Phillip Son of Phillipp and Katherine Warrick borne ye 20th of October 1713.
James Son of John & Elianor Medly was born ye 1st of August 1712.
Joseph Son of Mary and Joseph Seares baptized ye 15th of November 1713.
Judith daughter of David and Katherine George borne ye 2d of January. Alice daughter of John and Winifred Purvis borne ye 6th of December. Aaron Son of W^m and Marg^tt Kidd born ye 8th of December, Daniell Son of Abraham and Judith Trigg. All four baptized y^r 24th of Jan^{ry} 1713.
William Son of Angeto & Elianor Comings born ye 6th October & baptized y^r 6th November 1713.
Johanna Daughter of John & Johanna Degge born August ye 7. baptized 1711.

CHRISTENINGS.

William Son of William & Frances Hill born Novem^r ye 7 1712.
William Son of Mathew & Sarah Parry born March 27 baptized May ye 11 1712.
John Illegittimate Son of Martha Davies born ye 27th of ffebruary. Mary Daughter of W^m & Mary Daniell. Margarett daughter of Thomas and Marg^tt Croucher. Jane daughter of John & Jane Guttery. Jane daughter of James and Hannah Macktyre. Anne daughter of Henery & Eliz^a Goodloe. Elizabeth daughter of John & Elizabeth Lewis. Were all Seven baptized the 7th day of March 1713.
James Son of John & Jane Hord. Ann daughter of John & Mary Riley both baptized March 21th 1713.
Mary daughter of James & Ann Smyth borne the 10th day of December 1713.
David Son of J^{no} & Elianor Zachary. Elizabeth daughter of W^m & Sarah Baldin. Unity daughter of Henery & Rebecca Smyth. All three baptized the 4th day of April 1714.
Christopher Son of James & Agatha Curtis born the 11th baptized 19th of Aprill 1714.
Mary Daughter of Daniell & ffrances Hughes borne ye 21th August 1713.
Bartholomew Son of Edward and Ann Clark borne ye 5th October 1713.
Edward Son of Richard and Katherine Straughan borne ye 30th December 1713.
Daniell Son of Edward & Keziah Ball born ye 5th of Jan'y 1713.
John Illegittimate Son of Sarah Allcock borne 26th December 1713.
Isaack son of John & Margarett Hardy. John Son of John & Elianor Medley. Hannah daughter of Alexander & Mary Graves. & Margarett daughter of Churchill & Sarah Blakey all 4 baptized the 18th day of Aprill 1714.
Thomas Son of Thomas & Mary Warrick baptized ye 2d day of May 1714.
Mary daughter of Abell & ffaith Ducksworth. & Sarah daughter of Robert & Ann Blackly were both baptized the 13th day of June 1714.

Moses Son of Moses & Alice Norman baptized ye 27th day of June 1714.
Thomas Son of John & Alice Duggin. & Katherine daughter of W^m & Honour ffinney both baptized ye 8th day of August 1714.
Frances daughter of John & Ann Williams was borne ye 5th of August, Millicent daughter of John & Lettice Cheedle were both baptized ye 5th day of September 1714.
Ann daughter of George and Mary Wortham borne 28th May 1714.
Sarah daughter of Major Edmond Berkley and Lucia his wife was borne ye 9th of ffebruary 1713.
Judith daughter of Thomas & Mary Mitcham was borne ye 4th of November 1712.
Mary daughter of Augustine & Jone Owen baptized ye 25th of October 1713.
John Son of Powell and Mary Stampar baptized ye 17th of October 1714.
Elizabeth daughter of W^m and Elizabeth Brookes baptized ye 17th of October 1714.
William Son of John & Priscilla Brookes baptized ye 31th of October 1714.
Ann daughter of Richard and Mary Allen baptized ye 31th of October 1714.
Diana daughter Richard and Penelope Gibbs baptized ye 31th of October 1714.
Frances daughter of Christopher & Judith Robinson born ye 8 of Octo. baptized ye 17 of Octo. 1714.
Elizabeth & Martha daughters of W^m & Eliz^a Blackburn born Sept. 26th baptized Octo ye 24th 1714.
Sarah & Judith daughters of John & Eliz^a Wormley born June 20 baptized June ye 27 1714.
Henry Son of Sr Wm Skipwith & Lady Sarah his wife born Octo. 22 baptized Novem^r ye 21 1714.
Anthony Son of John & Johanna Degge born Novem^r ye 4 baptized Novem^r ye 22 1714.
Anne daughter of George & Eliz^a Barwich born May ye 30 baptized June ye 20 1714.
Absolom Son of Thomas & Sarah Chowning born Octo. ye 25 baptized Novem^r ye 28 1714.
William Son of William & Margrett Bristow born Feb. ye 2d baptized March ye 4 1713.
Betty daughter of Mathew & Sarah Parry born June 6 baptized July ye 10 1714.
William Son of William & Priscilla Tignor born Octo. 23 baptized Dec. ye 5 1714.
Mary daughter of John & Joice Tinny born Aug: 3 baptized Dec. ye 12 1714.
Betty daughter of Robert & Catherine Perrott born Dec. 3 baptized Dec. 25 1714.
Mary daughter of John & Rebecca Hues born   baptized Jan^{ry} 9 1714.
Richard Son of William & Frances Hill born Jan^{ry} 15 baptized Jan^{ry} ye 22 1714.

Parnell daughter of John & Parnell Jones born Decem^r 19 baptized Jan^{ry} ye 23 1714.
John son of Marvill & Agatha Mosely born Jan^{ry} 20 baptized Feb^{ry} ye 4 1714.

Bartho: Yates. Minis:

CHRISTENINGS.

Thomas Son of William & Mary Elliott born Dec. 19. baptized Feb. 6 1714.
Mary daughter of William & Alice Hackney born Jan^{ry} 14. baptized Feb. 6 1714.
John Stuart an illegitimate son of Frances Ingram born Feb. ye 1. baptized ye 13. 1714.
John Son of John & Elizabeth Vivion born August ye 10. baptized August ye 18. 1714.
Jane daughter of William & Jane Lawson born Feb^{ry} ye 12. baptized Febry ye 15. 1713.
Christopher Son of Christopher & Hope Sutton born Jan^{ry} ye 13. baptized Jan^{ry} ye 20. 1714.
Matthew Son of Thomas & Mary Yarrow born Feb'ry ye 4. baptized March 6. 1714.
Jane daughter of John & Elizabeth Watts born Feb'ry ye 6. baptized March 6. 1714.
John Son of Samuel & Catherine Batchelder born Feb'ry ye 5. baptized March 13. 1714.
Mary daughter of Thomas & Catherine Batts born Decem^r ye 12. baptized March 13. 1714.
Jacob Son of Jacob & Mary Presnall born Feb'ry ye 4. baptized March 13. 1714.
Thomas son of Thomas & Jane Cheny born Feb^{ry} ye 18. baptized March 13. 1714.
Thomas son of Thomas & Mary Machen born Feb. 22. baptized March ye 20. 1714.
Thomas son of Robert & Elizabeth Wilson born Feb. 24. baptized March ye 20. 1714.
Elizabeth daughter of Thomas & Elizabeth Elliott born March 5. baptized Ap. ye 3. 1715.
William son of Joseph & Lucretia Goare born March 8. baptized Ap. ye 3. 1715.
William son of Richard & Charity Waite born . . . . . . baptized Ap. ye 3. 1715.
Lodswick son of Humphery & Elizabeth Jones born Feb'ry ye 20. baptized Ap. ye 10. 1715.
Reuben son of Ralph & Mary Shelton born Febry ye 1. baptized April ye 10. 1715.
Thomas an illegitimate Son of Mary Deputy born Jan^{ry} 15. baptized April ye 10. 1715.
Anne daughter of Henry & Sarah Ball born March ye 3. baptized Aprill 10. 1715.
Sarah daughter of Mathew & Elizabeth Crank born Feb'ry ye 20. baptized Ap. 10. 1715.
Jane an illegitimate daughter of Anne Gerrard born Febry ye 14. baptized Ap. 10. 1715.

Mary daughter of Thomas & Anne Crank born baptized April 10. 1715.
Mary daughter of Joseph & Elizabeth Timberlin born March 28. baptized Ap. 24. 1715.
William son of William & Elizabeth Markham born March 29 baptized Ap. 24. 1715.
Henry son of Richard & Sarah Atwood born March 24. baptized May ye 1. 1715.
Elizabeth daughter of John & Hannah Owen born Ap. 2. baptized May ye 1. 1715.
Chichester son of Robert & Elizabeth Dudley born Ap: 8. baptized May ye 8. 1715.
John son of George & Sarah Bowden born Ap. 4. baptized May ye 15. 1715.
James son of Henry & Mary Bridgforth born May ye 12, baptized May 15. 1715.
George son of Charles & Dorothy Lee born Ap. 26. baptized May ye 22. 1715.
Sarah daughter of Hugh & Catherine Mactire born Ap. 10. baptized May 22. 1715.
Andrew son of John & Elizabeth South born Ap. ye 25. baptized May 29. 1715.
Ann daughter of John & Mary Murrey born Ap: 28 baptized May 29. 1715.
John son of John & Elizabeth Peniell born Ap. 27. baptized June ye 5 1715.
Elizabeth daughter of John & Mary Bradley born May 18. baptized June 5. 1715.
Anne daughter of Jacob & Elizabeth Stiff born May 15. baptized June ye 5. 1715.

Bar. Yates. Minis.

CHRISTENINGS.

James son of William & Frances Daniell born May ye 12. baptized June 12. 1715.
William son of Thomas & Elizabeth Baskitt born May 31. baptized June 26. 1715.
Sarah daughter of Samuel & Margret Dagnell born June 2. baptized July ye 3. 1715.
Edmund daughter of of George & Anne Saunders born July ye 2. baptized July 17. 1715.
Charles son of Charles & Mary Cooper born June 15. baptized July 24. 1715.
Thomas Hobs son of Hobs & Mary Weeks born June 11. baptized July 30. 1715.
Martin son of Thomas & Mary Hackett born July 15. baptized Augst 7. 1715.
Charles son of Joseph & Avarilla Hardee born July 19. baptized Augt 25. 1715.
John son of Richard & Sarah Steevens born May ye 31. baptized June 26. 1715.
William son of John & Anne Barnett born July 27. baptized Augst 28. 1715.

Rachell daughter of Henry & Elizabeth Tuggell born Augst 8. baptized Augst 28. 1715.
Mary daughter of John & Mary Bristow born Augst 15. baptized Septem^r 4. 1715.
Griffin son of Henry & Alice Nicholls born Augst 23. baptized Septem^r 9. 1715.
Lydia daughter of Thomas & Catherine Keiling born Augst 12. baptized Septem 11. 1715.
Dianah daughter of William & Anne Hill born Augst 25. baptized Septem^r 25. 1715.
Jane daughter of John & Anne Smith born Septem^r ye 8. baptized Septem^r 25. 1715.
William son of Ralph & Amey Lyall born Augst 24. baptized Octob^r 2. 1715.
John son of Daniell & Frances Hues born Septem^r 24. baptized Octob^r 3. 1715.
Thomas son of Thomas & Anne Smith born Septem^r 15. baptized October ye 6. 1715.
Mary an illegitimate daughter of Elizabeth Guttery born Augst 24. bapt. 8^{br} 16. 1715.
Sarah daughter of Thomas & Sarah Chowning born Septem^r ye 3. baptized Octo: 16. 1715.
Diana daughter of William & Anne Gardner born Augst 26. baptized Septem^r 18. 1715.
Richard son of Thomas & Mary Davis born Sept. 15. baptized Octo. 23. 1715.
John son of John & Elizabeth Saunders born Sept. 28. baptized Octo. 23. 1715.
Anne an illegitimate mulatto daughter of Mary Whistler born Ap. 12. baptized Nov^{em} 4. 1715.
Mary daughter of John & Jane Miller born Sept. 26. baptized Novem. 6. 1715.
Mary daughter of William & Mary Barbee born Sept. 30. baptized Novem. 6. 1715.
George son of John & Winifred Purvis born Octo: 17. baptized Novem. 13. 1715.
Ralph son of John & Elizabeth Wormley born Octo: 5. baptized Novem. 9. 1715.
Anne daughter of Arthur & Mary Thomas born Nov. 5. baptized Decem. 4. 1715.
John son of Thomas & Catherine Bristow born Nov. 9. baptized Decem. 4. 1715.
Robert son of John & Prudence Reagen born Octo: 6. baptized Novem. 25. 1715.
Amey daughter of John & Jane Stuart born Octo 24 baptized Decem. 11. 1715.
Rachell daughter of John & Elizabeth Davies born Novem 20. baptized Decem. 11 1715.
Thomas son of John & Anne Gresham born Novem. 23. baptized Decem 18. 1715.
William an illegitimate son of Susanna Dainly born Novem. 27 baptized Decem. 19. 1715.

James son of James & Mary Meecham born Decem'r 15. baptized Jan'ry 1. 1715.
Ellonar Daughter of William & Anne Cheshire born Novem. 24. baptized Decem. 18. 1715.
Mary daughter of Edward & Sarah Couch born Decemb'r 24. Baptized Jan. 2. 1715.
Judith daughter of John & Ethelred Lucas born Decem'r 24 baptized Jan'ry 2. 1715.
Bridgett daughter of Patrick & Anne Marion born Jan'ry y'e 7. baptized Jan'ry y'e 8. 1715.
Frances daughter of George & Elizabeth Carter born Novem'r 13. baptized Jan'ry y'e 15. 1715.
George son of John & Elizabeth Pace born Jan'ry y'e 8. baptized Jan'ry 16. 1715.
Robert son of Bartho: & Sarah Yates born Jan'ry y'e 8. baptized Jan'ry 20. 1715.

Bar. Yates. Minis.

CHRISTENINGS.

Thomas son of Peter & Elizabeth Chelton born Decem'r y'e 24. baptized Jan'ry 22. 1715.
Violetta daughter of Joseph & Mary Seares born Jan'ry ye 1 baptized Feb'ry 12 1715.
Lydia daughter of Edmund & Sarah Hamerton born Janry 4. baptized Febry 12. 1715.
William son of John & Mary Berry born Feb'ry ye 10. baptized Febry 25 1715.
Mary daughter of Henry & Sarah Basket born Novem. 15. baptized Decem. 18 1715.
Anne daughter of Ralph & Alice Mazey born Jan'ry y'e 25. baptized Feb'ry 26 1715.
Catherine daughter of John & Catherine Robinson born Feb'ry 23. baptized March 7 1715.
Sarah daughter of Valentine & Anne Mayo born Feb'ry y'e 10. baptized March 11. 1715.
William Son of Edward & Martha Brownley born Febry. y'e 3. baptized March 4 1715.
Catherine daughter of Edward & Rebecca Peirce born Jan'ry 10. baptized March 18. 1715.
Michal daughter of John & Michall Owen born Feb'ry ye 19. baptized March 18 1715.
John son of George & Elizabeth Barwick born Feb'ry 22. baptized March 18 1715.
Catherine daughter of John & Catherine Row born Feb'ry 16 baptized March 18. 1715.
Judith daughter of George & Elizabeth Chowning born March 21 baptized March 25. 1716.
Susanna daughter of Jonathan & Mary Brooks born March y'e 6 baptized Ap: y'e 8 1716.
Thomas son of Richard & Anne Winn born March y'e 5 baptized Ap: y'e 8. 1716.
Constant Daughter of John & Margrett Davies born March ye 10. baptized Ap: ye 15. 1716.

Sarah daughter of Michael & Sarah Smith born March ye 14. baptized Ap. ye 22. 1716.
William son of Thomas & Alice Kidd born Ap: ye 2d baptized Ap. ye 22. 1716.
James son of William & Margrett Kidd born March 27. baptized Ap. ye 22 1716.
Catherine daughter of Roger & Mary Jones born March ye 8. baptized Ap. ye 28 1716.
George son of George & Mary Roades born March 25. baptized Ap: ye 29. 1716.
Clara daughter of Curtis & Anne Perrott born Ap. 21 baptized Ap. ye 30. 1716.
John Son of John & Mary Gibbs born Ap. 5. baptized May 4 1716.
Elizabeth daughter of Gabriell & Elizabeth Ray born Ap. 3 baptized May 4. 1716.
George son of Churchhill & Sarah Blakey born Ap: 3. baptized May 6. 1716.
Thomas Son of Henry & Mary Beuford born Ap. 11. baptized May 6 1716.
John Son of Christopher & Sarah Chaffin born Ap. 1. baptized Ap. 29. 1716.
Martha daughter of John & Margrett Hardee born Feb^{ry} 12. baptized May 13. 1716.
Robert son of John & Elianor Medley born May 6. baptized June 3 1716.
William son of Edward & Anne Clarke born Ap. 26. baptized June 10 1716.
Anne daughter of Augustine & Joane Owen born May 6 baptized June 10. 1716.
Crispin son of Richard & Catherine Strauhan born May 10. baptized June 10. 1716.
Cary Son of James & Anne Smith born May 22 baptized June 10 1716.
William Son of Abraham & Judith Trigg born May 18 baptized June 17. 1716.
William son of Edward & Keziah Ball born May 25 baptized June 24 1716.
Avarilla daughter of Henry & Eliz^a Goodloe born June ye 20 baptized July 15 1716.
John Son of William & Bridget Gordon born July ye 12 baptized July 16 1716.
John Son of John & Frances Aldin born July ye 28, baptized August ye 26 1716.
John Son of John & Jane Guttery born August ye 16 baptized August ye 26 1716.
Sarah daughter of Jonathan & Mary Bell born July ye 3 baptized August ye 5. 1716.
George Son George & Anne Saunders born August ye 7 baptized August ye 31. 1716.

Bar. Yates Minis.

CHRISTENINGS.

John Son of Phillip & Catherine Warwick borne Augst 21, baptized Septem^r ye 1. 1716.
John son of Phillip & Catherine Warwick borne Augst 21. baptized Septem^r ye 1 1716.
James Son of George & Mary Wortham born Augst 17. baptized Septem^r ye 4 1716.
Lettice daughter of Thomas & Catherine Paine born Augst 8. baptized Septr 9 1716.
Alexander Son of Aquilla & Mary Snelling born July 23 baptized Septr ye 2 1716.
Anna daughter of Joseph & Elizabeth Humphries born Augst 18 baptized Sept. 16 1716.
Mary daughter of Thomas & Elizabeth Bewford born Augst 20 baptized Septr 23 1716.
Avarilla an illegitimate daughter of Alice Davis born   baptized Sept. ye 16. 1716.
Elizabeth daughter of Richard & Elizabeth Daniell born Sept. ye 5. baptized Sept. 30. 1716.
West an illegitimate Son of Sarah Jarvise born Sept. ye 6. baptized Sept. 30 1716.
Thomas Son of Jeffery & Mary Burk born September ye 9 baptized October ye 5. 1716.
Agatha daughter of Harry & Elizabeth Beverley born Septr 22. baptized October ye 12 1716.
Randolph Son of W^m & Anne Seagar born October 10. baptized octo^r ye 23. 1716.
John an illegitimate Son of Rebecca Hackney born Septr 13 baptized october 14 1716.
Anne daughter of Wm Daniell Senr & mary his Wife born Octo. 12. baptized Novem^r ye 4. 1716.
John Son of Patrick & Rebecca Deagle born October 30 baptized Novem^r 25 1716.
William Son of Usebius & Mary Lewis born Novem^r ye 26 baptized Decem^r ye 2 1716.
Benjamine Son of William & Sarah Baldin born Novem^r 11. baptized Decem^r ye 7 1716.
William Son of Robert & Elizabeth Daniell born Decem^r ye 3 baptized Decem^r ye 16. 1716.
John Son of Jonathan & Anne Herring born Octo. 8 baptized Novem^r ye 10 1716.
Elizabeth daughter of Robert & Elizabeth Dudley born Dec. 27. baptized Jan^r ye 7 1716.
Phillip Son of Thomas & Mary Warwick born Novem^r 27 baptized Jan^r 13 1716.
Billington Son of Joseph & Elizabeth Williams born Dec^{mr} 10. baptized Jan^r 13. 1716.
John Son of John & Anne Williams born Decem^r 20. baptized Jan^r 13 1716.
Elizabeth daughter of Stokely & Anne Toles born Decem^r 17 baptized Decem^r 30. 1716.
Mildred daughter of John & mary Rily born Decem^r 2. baptized Jan'y ye 27 1716.

Elizabeth daughter of Richard & mary Allen born Decem^r 24 baptized Jan'y ye 27 1716.
Susannah daughter of Powell & mary Stamper born Decem^r 19. baptized Jan^{ry} ye 27 1716.
Richard Son of Richard & Sarah Steevens born Jan'y 8. baptized Feb'y 3. 1716.
Sarah daughter of Edward & Elizabeth Sanders born Decem^r 28 baptized Jan^r 20. 1716.
John Son of John & Lettice Cheedle born Jan'y ye 5 baptized Feb'y ye 10 1716.
Anne daughter of George & Elizabeth Hardin born Dec. 21 baptized Feb'y ye 3. 1716.
Mary daughter of Ralph & Mary Shelton born Jan'y 21 baptized Feb'y ye 13 1716.
Anne daughter of Thomas & Jane Haslewood born Decem^r 30. baptized March ye 10. 1716.
James Son of Henry & Sarah Ball born Feb'y ye 16 baptized March ye 10 1716.
James Son of John & Jane Price born Feb'y ye 17 baptized March ye 10. 1716.
James Son of James & Margrett Daniell born Feb^{ry} ye 17 baptized March ye 17 1716.
William Son of Christopher & Judith Robinson born March ye 5 baptized March ye 17. 1716.
Roger Son of John & Anne Hatton born Decem^r ye 2d baptized Jan'y ye 20 1716.
William Son of Samuell & Catherine Batchelder born March 11 1716. baptized Ap. ye 7. 1717.
Beamont Son of Christopher & Hope Sutton born March ye 5. 1716. baptized March 31. 1717.
William Son of John & Mary Sparkes born march 6. 1716 & baptized Ap. ye 7 1717.
Mary daughter of David & Katherine George born March 12. 1716. baptized Ap. 7. 1717.
Mary & Jane daughters of George & Hannah Guest born March 24 1716 baptized Ap. 7. 1717.
Daniell Son of Daniell & Frances Hues born March 14 1716. baptized Ap. 14 1717.
William Son of Thomas & Catherine Keiling born March the 7. 1716. baptized Ap. 14. 1717.
Russell Son of William & Frances Hill born Feb'y ye 23. 1716 baptized Ap. 21. 1717.
Sarah daughter of Sr William Skipwith & Lady Sarah his wife born Ap. 11. baptized Ap. 25. 1717.
Bar. Yates. Minis.

CHRISTENINGS.

Elizabeth daughter of Humphery & Elizabeth Jones born March ye 19. 1716. baptized Ap. 28. 1717.
Elizabeth daughter of Thomas & Jane Cheney born March ye 19. 1716. baptized Ap. 28. 1717.
Elizabeth daughter of James & Hannah Mactire born March yc 23. 1716. baptized Ap. 28. 1717.

John son of Jacob & Elizabeth Stiff born April ye 2. baptized May ye 5. 1717.
Mary daughter of John & Mary Murray born Ap. 25. baptized May ye 17. 1717.
Susanna daughter of John & Elizabeth Lewis born Ap. 23. baptized May ye 26. 1717.
Agatha daughter of William & Anne Gardner born Ap. 21. baptized May ye 26. 1717.
Judith daughter of Edward & Margrett Farrell born Ap. 25 baptized June y^u 2. 1717.
Harry son of Joseph & Mary Seares born May ye 19. baptized June ye 23. 1717.
Frances daughter of Robert & Anne Blackley born May ye 29. baptized June ye 23. 1717.
William Son of William & Elizabeth Blackburne born June ye 12 baptized July ye 11. 1717.
Lucretia daughter of Hugh & Catherine Mactire born June ye 17. baptized July y^o 21. 1717.
John Son of John & Priscilla Brookes born June ye 20 baptized July ye 21. 1717.
John Son of William & Elizabeth Brookes born June ye 23 baptized July y^u 21 1717.
Sarah daughter of Thomas & Sarah Chowning born June ye 24. baptized July ye 21. 1717.
Judith daughter of Marvell & Agatha Moseley born July ye 12 baptized July ye 21. 1717.
William Son of Thomas & Mary Cardwell born July ye 7th baptized August ye 4 1717.
Elizabeth daughter of John & Micholl Owen born July ye 28 baptized August ye 18. 1717.
Anne daughter of Christopher & Mary Kelshaw born July y^u 31. baptized Sep^t ye 8. 1717.
William Son of William & Alice Hackney born August ye 13. baptized Sept. y^o 8. 1717.
John Son of Samuell & Anne Low born August ye 5 baptized Sept. ye 8 1717.
Elizabeth daughter of John & Elizabeth Vivion born August y^r 17. baptized Sept ye 9. 1717.
James Son of Robert & Elizabeth Biggs born August y^r 15 baptized Sept ye 15 1717.
Abel Son of Abel & Faith Ducksworth born Septem^r ye 13. baptized Sept. ye 29 1717.
Frances daughter of John & Prudence Reaguin born Sept. ye 8. baptized Sept y^u 29 1717.
Frances daughter of John & Anne Smith born Septem^r ye 16. baptized Sept ye 29 1717.
Joice daughter of Robert & Rebecca Humpheries born Sept. ye 5 baptized Octo. 20 1717.
Elizabeth daughter of John & Eleonour Pemberton born Sept. y^u 10 baptized Octo 20. 1717.
Abraham Son of Hobs & Mary Weekes born Septem^r 22. baptized October 27. 1717.

James Son of John & Elizabeth Batchelder born Octo: 22. baptized Novem' 5. 1717.
Catherine daughter of Ralph & Elizabeth Watts born Octo: 8 baptized Novem' 10. 1717.
Thomas Son of Thomas & Elizabeth Dudley born Sept. 18. baptized October 20 1717.
Mary daughter of John & Rebecca Hues born Sept: 28 baptized Novem' 17 1717.
Martha daughter of Thomas & Anne Smith born Octo: 31. baptized Novem' 21 1717.
—— an illegitimate daughter of Susanna Ward born Octo. 24 1717.
John Son of Thomas & Mary Hackett born Octo: ye 19. baptized Decem' ye 5 1717.
Joseph Son of Joseph & Lucretia Goar born Novem' ye 3. baptized Decem' ye 4 1717.
Josuah Son of John & Parnell Jones born Novem' 3. baptized Decem' ye 8 1717.
Sarah daughter of Hezekiah & Mary Ellis born Novem' 7. baptized Decem' 15. 1717.
John Son of William & Elizabeth Marcum born Decem' ye 1. baptized Decem' ye 15. 1717.
John Son of Eusebius & Mary Lewis born Decem' ye 8 baptized Jan' 19 1717.
Agatha daughter of John & Elizabeth Watts born Decem' ye 25. baptized Jan' 19. 1717.
Henry Son of Henry & Elizabeth Brown born August ye 26. baptized Novem' 17 1717.
Henry Son of Thomas & Mary Machen born Novem' 29. Baptized Jan'^{y} ye 5 1717.
William Son of Hugh & Rebecca Roach born Decem' 27. baptized Jan'^{y} ye 26 1717.
John Son of John & Sarah Fearn born Jan'^{y} ye 5 baptized Jan'y ye 26 1717.
Elizabeth an illegitimate daughter of Elizabeth Davis born Jan'y ye 16. baptized Jan'^{y} ye 26. 1717.

Bar. Yates: Min'

CHRISTENINGS.

Smith Son of John & Elizabeth South born Jan'y 24. baptized Jan'y 30 1717.
John Son of John & Frances Smith born Decem' 16. baptized Feb'y ye 5. 1717.
Gray Son of William & Mary Barbee born Jan'y 7 baptized Feb'y ye 16 1717.
John Son of Lawrance & Anne Collings born Feb'y ye 6 baptized Feb'y ye 16. 1717.
John Son of John & Elizabeth Nicholls born Jan'y 24 baptized Feb'^{y} 2 1717.
Jemima daughter of Richard & Hannah Brine born Jan'y 25 baptized Feb'^{y} 2 1717.
Thomas Son of Henry & Elizabeth Tugell born Jan'^{y} 26th baptized Feb'^{y} 23 1717.

Thomas Son of Thomas & Jane Grindee born Feb'y 4. baptized Feb'y 23 1717.
Anne daughter of David & Jane Murry born Jan'y 20. baptized Feb'y 23 1717.
Bridgett & Margrett daughters of William & Bridgett Gordon born & baptized March 5. 1717.
John Son of John & Anne Roades born Feb'y ye 1 baptized March ye 9 1717.
Mary daughter of John & Margrett Davies born Feb'y ye 11 baptized March ye 9. 1717.
Henry & Robert Sons of John & Winifred Purvis born March 11. baptized March 12. 1717.
Constant daughter of William & Frances Daniell born Feb'y ye 6 baptized March 16. 1717.
Sarah daughter of William & Sarah Baldin born Feb'y 22 baptized March 16 1717.
Thomas Son of Thomas & Mary Yarrow born Feb^{ry} 28. 1717. baptized March 30 1718.
Joseph Son of William & Margrett Kidd born March 1: 1717 baptized Aprill 6. 1718.
Sarah daughter of John & Elizabeth Wormley born March 23. 1717 baptized April 6. 1718.
Henry Son of John & Katherine Robinson born Ap. 7 baptized April 14 1718.
Henry Son of Mary Month a free Indian born Feb'y 24 1717 baptized April 14. 1718.
William Son of William & Hanah Cain born March 15 1717 baptized April 20 1718.
Dorothy daughter of William & Priscilla Tignor born March 25. baptized April 20 1718.
Peter Son of Thomas & Grace Mountague born March 28. baptized April 27 1718.
Perrott Son of Joseph & Avarilla Hardee born April 4 baptized April 27 1718.
Henry Son of George & Elizabeth Carter born May 13. baptized May 18 1718.
George Son of John & Anne Johnson born April 13. baptized May 18 1718.
John Son of John & Mary Pendergrass born April 25. baptized June 1 1718.
Elizabeth daughter of John & Elizabeth Pinion born April 27 baptized June 1 1718.
Mary daughter of Edward & Sarah Couch born April 20. baptized June 1 1718.
James Son of Edward & Anne Clarke born April 19. baptized May 25 1718.
Charles Son of William & Margrett Bristow born May 17. baptized July 13. 1718.
John Son of John & Jane Stuart born June 3. baptized July ye 20 1718.
Avarilla Curtis daughter of John & Etheldred Lucas born July 23. baptized Aug^n 3 1718.

Anne daughter of Thomas & Elizabeth Bewford born July 4. baptized August 10 1718.
Solomon Son of Matthew & Elizabeth Crank born July 17 baptized August 10 1718.
Thomas Son of Thomas Kidd jun' & Margrett his wife born July 22. baptized August 10. 1718.
James Son of John & Johanna Degge born July 14. baptized August y" 23 1718.
Priscilla daughter of John & Sarah Miller born July 24. baptized Aug'^{t} ye 24 1718.
William Son of Henry & Sarah Ball born August ye 7. baptized August ye 31 1718.
Robert Son of Robert & Elizabeth Dudley born August ye 23. baptized Septem' 14 1718.
Mary daughter of James & Anne Bristow born August ye 27 baptized Septem' 21 1718.
Elizabeth daughter of James & Rebecca Jemson born Sept 14 baptized Octo. 5 1718.
Priscilla daughter of William & Anne Hill born Sept. 17. baptized Octo. 5 1718.
Mary daughter of Arthur & Mary Thomas born   baptized Octo 5. 1718.

Bar. Yates Min'

CHRISTENINGS.

Anne daughter of Richard & Sarah Steevens born Novem' 3. baptized Decem' 7. 1718.
Mary daughter of William & Sarah Blazedon born Novem' 4. baptized Decem' 7 1718.
Christopher Son of Christopher & Sarah Chaffin born Novem' 11. baptized Decem' 7. 1718.
William Son of James & Mary Meacham born Septem' 23. baptized Octo. 12 1718.
Sarah daughter of John & Mary Moseley born Octo. 2 baptized Octo. 12 1718.
Mary daughter of John & Anne Conner born Sept. 26. baptized Octo. 26 1718.
Elizabeth daughter of Thomas & Frances Vivion born Octo. 14. baptized Octo. 27 1718.
Sarah daughter of Thomas & Mary Burk born Octo ye 1. baptized Novem' 2 1718.
Anne daughter of John & Margrett   born Septem' ye 24. baptized Novem' 16 1718.
Frances daughter of Bartho: & Sarah Yates born Novem' ye 15. baptized Novem' 17 1718.
John Son of John & Elizabeth Braine born Octo. 22. baptized Novem' 23 1718.
Hannah daughter of Jacob & Elizabeth Rice born Novem' 18. baptized Jan'y 7 1718.
Anne daughter of John & Mary Berry born Novem' ye 18 baptized ye 7 1718.
John Son of John & Mary Bradley born Octo. 28. baptized Decem' ye 7 1718.

Anny daughter of Alexander & Mary Graves born Novem' 16 baptized Decem' y' 14. 1718.
Frances daughter of Edwin & Elizabeth Thacker born Dec y' 3. baptized Decem' y' 19. 1718.
William Son of Ralph & Amey Lyall born Novem' 24 baptized Decem' y° 21 1718.
Edmund Son of John & Elizabeth Sanders born Decem' y' 2. baptized Jan'y y° 2 1718.
Robert Son of Edmund & Mary Pendergrass born Decem' y' 10. baptized Jan'' 4. 1718.
Elizabeth daughter of George & Elizabeth Guest born Decem' y' 15. baptized Jan'y 4. 1718.
John Son of John & Lucy Grymes born Jan'y y' 1st baptized Jan'y y' 15 1718.
Osborn Son of Thomas & Catherine Keiling born Decem' 4 baptized Jan'' y° 18 1718.
Samuel Son of John & Charity Ingram born Decem' y' 9. baptized Jan'' y' 18 1718.
Sarah daughter of Jacob & Elizabeth Stiff born Decem' y' 15. baptized Jan'' y' 18 1718.
John Son of Churchhill & Sarah Blakey born Decem' y' 14. baptized Jan'y 25. 1718.
Robert Son of Robert Daniell Jun' & Elizabeth his Wife born Jan'y 24. baptized Feb'y 15. 1718.
Agatha daughter of William Daniell Sen' & Mary his Wife born Jan'y 29. baptized Feb'y 15. 1718.
Grace daughter of William & Mary Tomson born Jan'y 23. baptized Feb'y y' 22 1718.
Benjamine Son of Jonathan & Ann Herring born Jan'' 22. baptized March y° 1. 1718.
Curtis Son of Curtis & Anne Perrott born Jan'' y' 30. baptized March y' 8 1718.
Nanny daughter of John & Jane Guttery born Jan'y y' 31. baptized March y' 8. 1718.
John Son of Henry & Mary Bewford born Feb'y y' 2. baptized March y° 8 1718.
Charles Son of Charles & Dorothy Lee born Feb'y y' 8 baptized March y' 8 1718.
Peter Son of Christopher & Judith Robinson born March y' 1. baptized March y' 11. 1718.
Christopher Son of Christopher & Mary Kelshaw born Feb. y' 11. baptized March y' 22. 1718.
Frances daughter of Robert & Elizabeth Williamson born Feb. 21. 1718. baptized March 25 1719.
Anne daughter of John & Anne Barnett born Feb'' 28. 1718. baptized March 27 1719.
Frances daughter of Daniel & Frances Hues born March 6. 1718 baptized April 3. 1719.
James Son of Augustine & Joan Owen born March 5. 1718. baptized Ap: 5. 1719.
Robert Son of Thomas & Susannah Clark born Jan'' 20. 1718. baptized April y' 12. 1719.

Catherine daughter of William & Anne Seagur born Feb'y 25 1718. baptized Aprill y° 12. 1719.
Frances daughter of Thomas & Catherine Paine born March 15. 1718 baptized Ap. y° 12. 1719.
Tobias Son of Richard & Mary Allen born March y° 30: baptized April y° 12. 1719.
John Son of John & Jane Price born March y° 29 baptized April y° 12. 1719.
John Son of John & Elizabeth Dobbs born April y° 3 baptized April y° 12. 1719.
Betty daughter of William & Lettice Guttery born March y° 20. 1718. baptized April 19. 1719.
Anne daughter of Stokely & Anne Towles born April 23. baptized May y° 3 1719.
John Son of John & Elizabeth Lewis born April y° 11. baptized May y° 3. 1719.
Mary daughter of Jonathan & Mary Brooks born Ap: y° 3. baptized May y° 3. 1719.
Bar Yates minis.

CHRISTENINGS.

John Son of John & Anne Gresham born August y° 6. baptized Sep' y° 13. 1719.
Joseph Son of Joseph & Elizabeth Humpheries born August y° 10. baptized Sep' y° 20. 1719.
Hannah daughter of William & Elizabeth Blackburne born August 30. baptized Sep' y° 29. 1719.
William Son of William & Catherine born Sep' y° 6. baptized Octo. 4 1719.
Mary daughter of John & Elizabeth Wormley born Sep' y° 21. baptized Octo. 6 1719.
Abraham Son of Abraham & Judith Trigg born Ap: 14. baptized May 10 1719.
Elizabeth daughter of John & Elizabeth Vivion born May 4. baptized May 19 1719.
Margrett daughter of Phillip & Margrett Brooks born Ap. 16. baptized May 24 1719.
Cassandra daughter of Thomas & Jane Cheney born Ap. 19. baptized May 24 1719.
Jonathan Son of Powell & Mary Stamper born April 21. baptized May 24 1719.
Anne daughter of Nicholas & Mary Bristow born April 26. baptized May 24 1719.
Henry Son of Joseph & Lucretia Goar born May y° 16. baptized June 7 1719.
William Son of William & Elizabeth Stanard born May y° 29 baptized June 8. 1719.
Rebecca daughter of Christopher & Rebecca Baines born Jan'y 20. 1718 baptized June 14. 1719.
Anne & Jane daughter of Thomas & Alice Kidd born May y° 7 baptized June 14. 1719.
John Son of James & Sarah Cole born May y° 16 baptized June y° 14 1719.

Thomas Son of Joseph & Mary Scares born May y⁣ᵉ 18 baptized June y⁣ᵉ 14 1719.
William Son of George & Elizabeth Chowning born June y⁣ᵉ 3d baptized June y⁣ᵉ 14 1719.
Judith daughter of William & Frances Hill born June y⁣ᵉ 2d baptized June y⁣ᵉ 28. 1719.
Judith daughter of Joseph & Elizabeth Williams born May y⁣ᵉ 3. baptized May y⁣ᵉ 30. 1719.
Frances daughter of Thomas & Mary Stapleton born June y⁣ᵉ 17. baptized July y⁣ᵉ 5. 1719.
Kesiah daughter of Richins & Hannah Brame born July y⁣ᵉ 2 baptized July y⁣ᵉ 26. 1719.
Catherine daughter of John & Prudence Reagin born July y⁣ᵉ 7. baptized July y⁣ᵉ 26. 1719.
Jane daughter of John & Mary Murry born July y⁣ᵉ 4. baptized Augst y⁣ᵉ 2 1719.
Jochebed daughter of Richard & Elizabeth Daniell born July y⁣ᵉ 14. baptized Aug⁣ᵗ y⁣ᵉ 4. 1719.
Keziah daughter of John & Johannah Blake born July y⁣ᵉ 12. baptized Augs⁣ᵗ y⁣ᵉ 9 1719.
Rachell daughter of John & Ann Smith born August y⁣ᵉ 17. baptized Aug⁣ˢᵗ y⁣ᵉ 23 1719.
Mary daughter of W⁣ᵐ Chancellor by Mary Cole born July y⁣ᵉ 10. baptized Aug⁣ˢᵗ y⁣ᵉ 30. 1719.
Anne daughter of Angello & Elionar Cummins born Augs⁣ᵗ y⁣ᵉ 29. baptized Octo. 4. 1719.
Francis Son of Francis & Anne Blunt born August y⁣ᵉ 29. baptized Octo. 11 1719.
William Son of James & Anne Smith born Septem⁣ʳ y⁣ᵉ 14. baptized Octo. 11. 1719.
William Son of Charles & Mary Gresham born August y⁣ᵉ 15: baptized Octo y⁣ᵉ 11. 1719.
Mary daughter of George & Sarah Freestone born Sept. 22. baptized Octo. 18. 1719.
John Son of Edward & Elizabeth Sanders born Octo. y⁣ᵉ 11. baptized Octo 25. 1719.
James Son of Benjamine & Mary Row born Octo. y⁣ᵉ 2. baptized Novem 1 1719.
William Son of Thomas & Mary Hackett born October y⁣ᵉ 17. baptized Novem⁣ʳ 8. 1719.
Harry Son of William & Sarah Anderson born Novem⁣ʳ y⁣ᵉ 5. baptized Novem⁣ʳ 19. 1719.
Joseph Son of Joseph & Joanna Timberlake born Octo. y⁣ᵉ 18. baptized Novem⁣ʳ 22. 1719.
Joanna daughter of Christopher & Catherine Kilbee born Octo y⁣ᵉ 27. baptized Novem⁣ʳ 22. 1719.
Benjamine Son of Edward & Keziah Ball born Novem⁣ʳ y⁣ᵉ 18. baptized Decem⁣ʳ 13. 1719.
Elizabeth daughter of William & Sarah Davis born Nov. 15. baptized Dec. 22. 1719.
Anne daughter of Thomas & Mary Cardwell born Novem⁣ʳ 20. baptized Dec. 20. 1719.

Thomas Son of John & Lettice Cheedle born Decem^r 10. baptized Decem^r 20. 1719.
Henry Son of William & Anne Fleet born Octo: ye 10. baptized Decem^r 30. 1719.
Sarah daughter of William & Alice Hackney born Novem^r ye 25. baptized Jan^{ry} ye 3. 1719.
Anne daughter of Thomas & Anne Smith born Decem^r ye 24. baptized Jan'y ye 17. 1719.
William Barbee Son of Christopher & Hope Sutton born Decem^r ye 9. baptized Jan'y ye 24. 1719.
William Son of William & Mary Webb born Jan^{ry} ye 5: baptized Jan^{ry} y^r 31. 1719.
Edwin Son of Edwin & Elizabeth Thacker born Jan^{ry} ye 17. baptized Feb^{ry} y^r 4. 1719.

Bar Yates. Min^r

CHRISTENINGS.

Elizabeth daughter of Francis & Sarah Timberlake born Septem^r ye 7. baptized Octo. 2. 1720.
Benjamine Son of John & Anne Roads born September ye 14. baptized Octo. ye 9. 1720.
Anne daughter of Thomas & Phrebe Tilley born September ye 16. baptized Octo. ye 9. 1720.
Sarah daughter of Matthew & Mary Kemp born Feb'y ye 2. baptized Feb'y 14 1719.
Samuel Son of Samuel & Katherine Batchelder born Jan'y ye 16. baptized Feb'y 21. 1719.
Willy Son of Robert & Anne Blackley born Jan'y ye 16. baptized Feb'y 21 1719.
Ambrose Son of Robert & Elizabeth Dudley born Feb'y ye 6 baptized Feb^{ry} ye 28 1719.
Thomas Son of Thomas & Grace Mountague born Feb'y ye 20. baptized Feb'y 28 1719.
George Son of John & Sarah Fearn born Feb'y ye 4. baptized march 6 1719.
Mary Daughter of Hugh & Rebecca Roach born Jan'y ye 23 baptized march ye 6. 1719.
Catherine daughter of Ralph & Mary Shelton born Jan'y 26. baptized march ye 13. 1719.
William Son of Benjamine & Elizabeth Beamon born Feb'y ye 9, baptized march ye 13. 1719.
William Son of Charles & Alice Cooper born Feb'y ye 16. baptized march ye 13 1719.
Jemima daughter of John & Elizabeth Batcheldor born Feb'y 24 baptized march 13. 1719.
Jane daughter of Thomas & Sarah Chowning born March ye 4. baptized March 13. 1719.
Mary daughter of John & Michal Williams born march ye 18. baptized march 21. 1719.
Edward Son of Edward & Margrett Farrell born Feb'y 27 1719 baptized March ye 27. 1720.

Fuller Son of Sr Wm Skipwith & Lady Sarah his Wife born March ye 2. 1719. baptized march 27. 1720.
Rachel a Mulatto daughter of Jane Tyre born Feb^{r}y 25. 1719. baptized April ye 3. 1720.
William Son of Mark & Sarah Wheeler born March ye 8. 1719. baptized Ap. ye 3. 1720.
John Son of John & Elizabeth Watts born March ye 4. 1719. baptized Ap: ye 10. 1720.
Anne daughter of John & Sarah Miller born March 31. baptized Ap. ye 24 1720.
Lucy daughter of John & Lucy Grymes born Ap. ye 18. baptized Ap. ye 24 1720.
Jane daughter of William & Catherine Wood born Mar. 24 1719. baptized Ap: ye 3. 1720.
Solomon Son of James & Margrett Ingram born April ye 5. baptized May 1. 1720.
Martha daughter of William & Sarah Balden born April ye 5. baptized May 1. 1720.
George Son of Thomas & Sarah Oldner born March ye 9. 1719. baptized Ap. ye 24. 1720.
Penelope a Slave belonging to James Walker baptized May ye 8 1720.
Anne daughter of Robert & Anne Spencer born Dec. 21. 1719. baptized May 15. 1720.
Joseph Son of Robert & Rebecca Humpheries born Ap: 8 baptized May 15. 1720.
Humphery Son of William & Elizabeth Brookes born May 3. baptized May 22. 1720.
Anne daughter of Usebius & Mary Lewis born May ye 4. baptized May 29 1720.
Catherine daughter of Henry & Elizabeth Goodloe born May 1 baptized June 12. 1720.
Samuell Son of William & Margrett Kidd born May ye 10 baptized June 12. 1720.
John Son of James & Margrett Bowman born June 3. baptized June 19 1720.
Thomas Son of John & Priscilla Brookes born May ye 11. baptized July ye 3 1720.
Anne daughter of Henry & Elizabeth Tugle born June ye 8. baptized July ye 3 1720.
John Son of Abell & Faith Ducksworth born June ye 10 baptized July ye 3 1720.
Lucy daughter of Harry & Elizabeth Beverly born July ye 3 baptized July ye 10 1720.
Richard Son of Richard & Honor Taylor born June 20. baptized July 24 1720.
Mary daughter of John & Frances Alldin born July ye 3. baptized August 14 1720.
Betty daughter of Hugh & Chathcrine Mactire born July ye 27. baptized Sep^t 4 1720.
Anne daughter of George & Elizabeth Carter born August ye 8 baptized Sep^t 4 1720.
Agatha daughter of John & Elizabeth Wormeley born Septem^r ye 10. baptized ye Same day 1720.

Ann daughter of Isaac & Elizabeth Allin born August ye 16. baptized Sep^t 11. 1720.
Samuell Son of Patrick & Rebecca Deagle born July ye 30. baptized Sept. 11 1720.
Joseph & Benjamine Sons of John & Parnell Jones born Septem^r 15. baptized Sep^t 18. 1720.
Ropert Son of Edmund & Elizabeth Mickleburrough born Sept. 11. baptized Sept. 25. 1720.
Elizabeth daughter of William & Elizabeth Stanard born Septem^r ye 18. baptized Sep^t 25. 1720.

CHRISTENINGS.

John Son of Ralph & Amy Lyall born Octo. 2. baptized Novem^r 13 1720.
Sarah daughter of William & Mary Tompson born Octo. ye 13 baptized Novem^r 13 1720.
Minor Son of Robert & Elizabeth Williamson born Octo ye 7. baptized Novemb^r 18 1720.
James Son of John & Margrett Davis born Octo. ye 17. baptized Novem^r 20 1720.
Lucy daughter of Thomas & Rose Wright born octo. ye 24. baptized Novem^r 20 1720.
Judith daughter of George & Anne Saunders born Octo: ye 27. baptized Novem^r 20 1720.
Sarah daughter of Joseph & Averella Hardee born Octo ye 19. baptized Novem^r 27 1720.
Jane Segar an illegitimate daughter of Elizabeth Nicholls born Octo. ye 19. baptized Novem^r 27. 1720.
John Son of Robert & Catherine Perrott born Novem^r ye 12. baptized Decem^r 7 1720.
Johannah daughter of William & Hannah Cain born Novem^r ye 15. baptized Dec. 11. 1720.
William Son of Bartholomew & Sarah Yates born Decem^r 10. baptized Dec. 14 1720.
Anne daughter of John & Lettice Cheadle born Decem^r ye 7 baptized Dec. 18. 1720.
Catherine daughter of Thomas & Catherine Keiling born Novem. 25. baptized Dec. 25. 1720.
Francis Son of Christopher & Mary Kelshaw born Decem^r ye 7. baptized Jan^ry 1. 1720.
Thomas Son of John & Elizabeth Lewis born Jan^ry ye 3. baptized Jan^ry ye 29 1720.
Anne daughter of Joseph & Jennett Jacobus born Jan^ry ye 15. baptized Jan^ry ye 29 1720.
Anne daughter of Daniell & Frances Hues born Jan^ry ye 15. baptized Feb^ry ye 5. 1720.
Aquilla Son of Aquilla & Mary Snelling born Feb^ry ye 4 baptized Feb^ry ye 10 1720.
Charles son of Charles & Dorothy Jones born Jan^ry ye 17. baptized Feb^ry ye 12 1720.
John Son of Paul & Susanna Philpots born March ye 4 baptized ye Same day 1720.

John Son of Henry & Judith Burk born Feb'y 27. baptized March ye 12 1720.
Kerenhappuch daughter of Richin & Hannah Brame born Feb'y 22. baptized March 12. 1720.
William Son of William & Mary Vaughan born Feb'y 3. 1720. baptized March 26 1721.
Sarah daughter of Thomas & Susannah Clarke born Feb'y 23. 1720. baptized Ap. ye 2 1721.
Robert Son of Churchhill & Sarah Blakey born March ye 7 1720. baptized Ap. ye 2. 1721.
John Son of George & Elizabeth Guess born March ye 24. 1720. baptized Ap. 2 1721.
William Son of John & Elizabeth Dobs born March ye 16. 1720 baptized Ap. 2 1721.
Jane a slave belonging to Capt John Smith baptized April ye 7 1721.
Catherine daughter of John & Jane Stuart born March ye 23. 1720. baptized Ap. 14. 1721.
Periot an illegitimate Son of Ann Pringle born March ye 1719 baptized Ap. 23. 1721.
Anne daughter of Thomas & Jane Haselwood born April 7. baptized May 4 1721.
Judith daughter of Samuel & Mary Spencer born March 22. 1720. baptized May 7 1721.
Susanna daughter of Henry & Elizabeth Blunt born March ye 31. baptized May 7. 1721.
Thomas Son of John & Elizabeth Peniell born April ye 8. baptized May ye 7 1721.
Elizabeth daughter of Henry & Sarah Emerson born April 10. baptized May 14 1721.
Sarah daughter of Ralph & Elizabeth Watts born April 11. baptized May 14 1721.
Ruben Son of Robert & Elizabeth Daniell born April 22. baptized May 14 1721.
Anna daughter of William & Anne Segar born May ye 15. baptized May 24 1721.
Thomas Son of Jacob & Elizabeth Stiff born Ap. ye 30. baptized May 28. 1721.
Morris Son of Richard & Sarah Steevens born May ye 6. baptized may 28. 1721.
Samuel Son of John & Jane Price born May ye 15. baptized May 30 1721.
Joseph Son of Joseph & Mary Seares born May ye 18. baptized June 4 1721.
William Son of John & Mary Sadler born June 5 baptized June 25 1721.
John Son of Henry & Sarah Ball born June ye 19 baptized July 11 1721.
Catherine daughter of Stokely & Anne Towles born July ye 5 baptized July 16 1721.
John Son of Nicholas & Mary Bristow born June ye 25 baptized July 16 1721.
James Son of James & Sarah Cole born June ye 24 baptized July 16 1721.

Avarilla daughter of Curtis & Anne Perrott born June y" 16. baptized July 16. 1721.

Bar. Yates Min'

CHRISTENINGS.

Anthony Son of Thomas & Anne Smith born July y" 8. baptized July 23 1721.

Ransom Son of Joseph & Constantine Alphin born June y" 27 baptized July 30 1721.

Thomas Son of William & Elizabeth Blackburne born July y" 3. baptized July 30 1721.

Catherine daughter of Christopher & Catherine Kilbee born July y" 5. baptized July 30 1721.

Alexander Son of John & Anne Smith born June 22. baptized July y" 4 1721.

John Son of John & Mary Murray born July y" 24 baptized August 2 1721.

Penelope daughter of Thomas & Jane Cheney born Aug. 6. baptized August 27 1721.

Agatha daughter of Marvell & Agatha Moseley born Aug. 12. baptized August 27 1721.

Mary daughter of Edwin & Elizabeth Thacker born Aug. 11. baptized Aug" 27 1721.

Alexander Son of Andrew & Sarah Murray born August y" 19. baptized Sept. 5. 1721.

Mary daughter of Christopher & Sarah Chaffin born Septem' 2. baptized Sept. 7 1721.

Jacob Son of Augustine & Joane Owen born August y" 12. baptized Sept y" 10 1721.

Agatha daughter of John & Elizabeth Wormley born Septem' 14. baptized Sept. 24 1721.

Elizabeth daughter of Henry & Mary Elizabeth Thacker born Sept. 22 baptized Octo. 2 1721.

Catharine daughter of Richard & Mary Allen born Septem' 16. baptized Octo 8. 1721.

Sarah daughter of Zebulon & Mary Chelton born Septem' 18. baptized Octo. 15 1721.

William Son of Richard & Anne Moulson born Octo. y" 10 baptized Octo. 20 1721.

John Son of Hezekiah & Anne Roades born Septem' 27. baptized Oct. 22 1721.

Margrett daughter of William & Sarah Blazeden born Septem' 27. baptized Oct° 22 1721.

Elizabeth daughter of Arthur & Mary Thomas born Septem' 21. baptized Octo. 22 1721.

Anne daughter of James & Mary Micham born Septem' 22. baptized Octo. 29 1721.

Jacob Son of Jacob & Elizabeth Rice born Septem' 17. baptized Novem' 4 1721.

Ruth daughter of Benjamine & Mary Row born Octo. 4. baptized Novem' 12 1721.

Thomas Son of Thomas & Catherine Pain born Octo. 22. baptized Novem' 19 1721.

Daniel & William Sons of Daniel & Frances Hues born Decem^r ye 3. baptized Dec. 5. 1721.
Mary daughter of William & Jane Cardwell born Octo. ye 4 baptized Decem^r 10 1721.
Catharine daughter of William & Margrett Kidd born Novem^r ye 5. baptized Decem^r 10 1721.
William Son of John & Mary Ryley born Novem^r ye 19: baptized Decem^r ye 10 1721.
John Son of James & Anne Jones born Novem^r ye 21. baptized Decem^r ye 10 1721.
John Son of Thomas & Grace Mountague born Novem^r 23. baptized Decem^r ye 14 1721.
Catherine daughter of James & Mary Bristow born Decem^r ye 15. baptized Dec. 28. 1721.
Rachell daughter of George & Mary Barwick born Decem^r 17. baptized Jan^{ry} 14 1721.
Benjamine Son of William & Alice Hackney born Decem^r 25 baptized Jan^{ry} 14 1721.
Anne daughter of Jonathan & Anne Herring born July 29. baptized August 20 1721.
Josiah Son of Oliver & Jane Segar born Dec. ye 16. baptized Jan^{ry} ye 17 1721.
Jane daughter of John & Catherine Tompson born Dec. ye 27. baptized Dec. ye 28 1721.
Christopher Son of Richard & Honor Tayloe born Dec. ye 25. baptized Jan'ry ye 21 1721.
Hannah daughter of William & Elizabeth Batchelder born Jan'ry ye 5. baptized Jan^{ry} ye 23. 1721.
Stephen Son of William & Mary Johnson born Decem^r ye 3. baptized Dec. ye 31 1721.
Thomas Son of Thomas & Mary Hackett born Jan'ry ye 9 baptized Feb'ry ye 11 1721.
Jedidah daughter of John & Elizabeth Bream born Jan'ry 18. baptized Feb'ry ye 11 1721.
Christian daughter of Angello & Elianor Cummins born Decem^r ye 27 baptized Jan'ry 28 1721.
John son of James & Margrett Daniel born Jan'ry ye 19. baptized Feb'ry 18 1721.
Lucretia daughter of Joseph & Lucretia Goar born Feb'ry ye 12. baptized Feb'ry 25 1721.
Robert Son of John & Mary Bradley born Jan^{ry} ye 21. baptized Feb'ry 25 1721.
John Son of William & Catherine Rice born Jan'ry ye 26. baptized March ye 4 1721.
Priscilla daughter of James & Margrett Ingram born Feb'ry ye 14. baptized March ye 4. 1721.
Beverley Son of William & Elizabeth Stanard born Feb^{ry} ye 24. baptized March ye 4 1721.
Edward Son of Edward & Elizabeth Saunders born Feb'ry ye 4 baptized March ye 11 1721.
Mary daughter of John & Anne Fearn born Feb'ry ye 20. baptized March ye 18. 1721.

    Bar. Yates Min^r.

CHRISTENINGS.

Philip Son of John & Lucy Grymes born March ye 11. baptized March 18. 1721.
John Son of William & Sarah Davis born Feb'y 26. baptized March ye 25 1722.
Augustine an illegitimate Son of Mary Hargrow born March ye 8. 1721. baptized March ye 31. 1722.
John Son of John & Sarah Miller born March ye 16. 1721 baptized April ye 1 1722.
John Son of Joseph & Anne Pace born March ye 14 1721 baptized April ye 8 1722.
Richard Son of Richard & Elizabeth Daniel born March 17. 1721 baptized Ap: ye 15 1722.
Benoni Son of John & Ruth Vickars born April ye 9 baptized Ap. y^n 18 1722.
Anne daughter of Henry & Anne Faulkner born March ye 20 1721, baptized Ap. ye 1. 1722.
John & Esther Son & daughter of Christopher & Mary Kelshaw born March ye 24. 1721, baptized Ap. ye 22. 1722.
John Son of Thomas & Elizabeth Dudley born Ap. ye 15. baptized April ye 22 1722.
Elizabeth daughter of Matthew & Mary Kemp born Ap. ye 28. baptized May ye 10 1722.
Benjamine Son of William & Sarah Anderson born Ap. ye 14 baptized May ye 13 1722.
Oswald Son of James & Anne Smith born May ye 1st baptized May ye 27 1722.
Jonathan Son of Jonathan & Mary Brooks born Ap. ye 6 baptized May ye 20 1722.
Margrett daughter of William & Anne Southworth born May ye 9. baptized June ye 10 1722.
William Son of Patrick & Rebecca Deagle born May ye 8. baptized June ye 10 1722.
Elizabeth daughter of Henry & Mary Tugle born June 22 baptized July ye 2 1722.
John Son of John & Anne Johnson born July ye 5 baptized July ye 9 1722.
Thomas Son of William & Frances Hill born June ye 17, baptized July ye 15 1722.
John Son of William & Elizabeth Gardner born August ye 1 baptized August ye 2 1722.
Elizabeth daughter of John & Johanna Blake born July ye 25. baptized August ye 5 1722.
John Son of Jonathan & Priscilla Johnson born July ye 31. baptized August ye 5. 1722.
Mary daughter of George & Elizabeth Guess born July ye 15. baptized August ye 12 1722.
John Son of Ralph & Mary Shelton born July ye 19 baptized August ye 12 1722.
Abraham Son of John & Margrett Hardee born July ye 5. baptized August ye 12 1722.
John Son of Thomas & Susanna Clark born July ye 5. baptized August ye 12 1722.

Michal daughter of William & Margrett Bristow born July ye 17. baptized August ye 19 1722.
Mary daughter of William & Mary Tomson born August ye 8. baptized Augst ye 21 1722.
William Son of Thomas & Susanna Oliver born July ye 27 baptized Augst ye 26 1722.
Robert Son of Robert & Elizabeth Williamson born July ye 31. baptized Septem^r 2 1722.
Elizabeth daughter of John & Anne Southworth born June ye 25. baptized July ye 29 1722.
Anne daughter of William & Lettice Guttery born Septem^r ye 12. baptized Sept. 22 1722.
Jacob Son of Jacob & Elizabeth Stiff born August ye 30 baptized Sept. ye 30 1722.
Anne daughter of William & Judith Dudley born Sept. ye 6. baptized October 7 1722.
Margrett daughter of William & Sarah Baldwin born Aug. ye 11. baptized Septr 23. 1722.
William Son of John & Margret Southern born August ye 16 baptized Septr 23 1722.
Benjamine Son of Henry & Elizabeth Tuggle born August ye 20. baptized Sept^{mr} 23 1722.
Jenny daughter of John & Mary Moseley born Octo. 1. baptized October ye 14 1722.
William Son of William & Margrett Johnson born Octo ye 8. baptized October ye 16. 1722.
James Son of Thomas & Elizabeth Greenwood born Octo. 12. baptized Octo. ye 16. 1722.
James Son of Samuel & Catherine Batchelder born Sept. ye 25. baptized Octo. ye 24. 1722.
Judith daughter of John & Rebecca Kidd born Octo. ye 8. baptized Novem^r 4. 1722.
Mary daughter of George & Elizabeth Harding born Novem^r 7. baptized Novem^r 9 1722.
Usebius Son of Usebius & Mary Lewis born Octo. ye 10 baptized Novem^r 11 1722.
Rowland Son of Christopher & Hope Sutton born Octo. ye 15. baptized Novem 18 1722.
Jane daughter of John & Micholl Williams born Octo. ye 27. baptized Novem^r 25 1722.
James Son of Robert & Chatherine Perrott born Novem^r ye 11. baptized Decem^r 18 1722.
Richins Son of Richins & Hannah Brame born Decem^r ye 3. baptized Decem^r 16 1722.
Betty daughter of Robert & Anne George born Decem^r ye 7 baptized Decem^r 16. 1722.
Anne daughter of Thomas & Mary Gibbs born Septem^r ye 30. baptized Novem^r 11. 1722.
Frances daughter of Edwin & Elizabeth Thacker born Octo. ye 2. baptized Octo. 28. 1722.
Anne daughter of George & Martha Chowning born Dec. 22. baptized Jan'y ye 6. 1722.

Elizabeth daughter of Hezekiah & Anne Roades born Dec. 23. baptized Jan'y ye 20 1722.

Bar. Yates. Min'

Mary daughter of Joseph & Mary Sears born Decem' ye 27, baptized Jan'y ye 27 1722.
Elizabeth daughter of Thomas & Jane Norman born Jan'y ye 17, baptized Jan'y ye 27 1722.
Beverley Son of John & Catherine Robinson born Jan'y 11. baptized Feb'y 1 1722.
Samuel Son of William & Jennet Chowning born Feb'y ye 11 baptized Same day 1722.
Margrett daughter of John & Elizabeth Lewis born Jan'y ye 25 baptized Feb'y 17 1722.
Jacob Son of James & Sarah Cole born Feb'y ye 5, baptized Feb'y ye 17 1722.
Susanna daughter of John & Mary Berry born Feb'y ye 17. baptized March 3. 1722.
Mary daughter of Thomas & Rose Wright born Feb'y ye 7 baptized March ye 17. 1722.
William Son of John & Mary Guttery born Feb'y ye 14 baptized March ye 10. 1722.
Anne daughter of Hugh & Catherine Mactyre born Feb'y y' 15. baptized March 10 1722.
Mary daughter of John & Priscilla Brookes born March ye 3. 1722 baptized March 31. 1723.
Mildred daughter of Richard & Anne Greenwood born March y^o 7 1722, baptized March 31. 1723.
Jane daughter of Oliver & Jane Segar born March ye 18. 1722 baptized March 31 1723.
George Son of George & Elizabeth Carter born Feb'y ye 27. 1722. baptized March 31 1723.
William Son of John & Jane Price born April ye 6 baptized April 28 1723.
Elizabeth daughter of Thomas & Anne Smith born Ap. ye 19. baptized May ye 5. 1723.
Daniel Son of William & Hannah Cain born March 10. 1722 baptized April ye 14 1723.
Isaack Son of John & Anne Rhodes born April ye 19. baptized May ye 12 1723.
Margret daughter of Robert & Elizabeth Daniell born Ap. ye 20. baptized May ye 19. 1723.
Judith daughter of Henry & Judith Burk born April 25. baptized May ye 19 1723.
Lucy daughter of William & Anne Daniel born April ye 21 baptized May ye 26 1723.
John Son of Henry & Sarah Putman born May ye 1. baptized June ye 2d 1723.
John Son of Patrick & Elizabeth Miller born June ye 4 baptized June ye 6 1723.
Charles Son of John & Lucy Grymes born May ye 31. baptized June ye 7 1723.

Mary daughter of Thomas & Jane Haslewood born May ye 16 baptized June ye 9 1723.
Anne daughter of Robert & Elizabeth Walker born May ye 17, baptized June ye 16. 1723.
Charles Son of Richard & Jane Moulson born June ye 9 baptized June ye 30. 1723.
James Son of John & Joyce Tiney born June ye 9 baptized June ye 30 1723.
Anne daughter of Henry & Elizabeth Ball born June ye 11. baptized June ye 30 1723.
Aquilla Son of Aquilla & Mary Snelling born June ye 28. baptized July ye 14 1723.
Thomas Son of John & Lettice Cheedle born July ye 6. baptized July ye 21 1723.
Elizabeth daughter of John & Anne Dudley born June ye 25. baptized July ye 28 1723.
Betty daughter of Henry & Sarah Emmerson born July ye 7. baptized August ye 11. 1723.
William Son of George & Anne Saunders born June ye 26 baptized August ye 4. 1723.
Sarah daughter of Francis & Sarah Timberlake born August ye 18. baptized August ye 21. 1723.
Clara daughter of John & Anne Smith born August ye 4 baptized Septem^r ye 8 1723.
Priscilla daughter of Rich^d & Sarah Steevens born August ye 11. baptized Septem^r ye 25 1723.
Charles Son of George & Amey Walker born Septem^r ye 3. baptized Septem^r ye 29 1723.
William Son of Jonathan & Mary Brooks born Septem^r ye 9. baptized Octo. ye 13 1723.
Thomas Son of Thomas & Susanna Clark born Septem^r ye 19. baptized Octo ye 13 1723.
Mary daughter of Richard & Mary Allen born Septem^r ye 23. baptized Novem^r ye 3. 1723.
Sarah daughter of Joseph & Elizabeth Smith born Septem^r ye 24. baptized Octo. ye 20. 1723.
Hezekiah Son of William & Hannah Roads born Octo. ye 8. baptized Octo ye 27. 1723.
Letitia daughter of Powel & Mary Stamper born Septem^r ye 22. baptized Novem^r ye 24. 1723.
Elizabeth daughter of John & Mary Saddler born Octo. ye 26. baptized Novem^r ye 24. 1723.
Mary daughter of Stockly & Anne Towles born Novem^r ye 1. baptized Novem^r ye 24. 1723.
Sarah daughter of William & Elizabeth Stanard born Novem^r ye 10. baptized Decem^r ye 2. 1723.
William Son of Arthur & Mary Thomas born Novem^r ye 15, baptized Decem^r ye 8. 1723.
William Still an illegitimate Son of   baptized Decem^r 15. 1723.
Betty daughter of Churchhill & Sarah Blakey born Novem^r ye 20. baptized Decem^r 15. 1723.

Elizabeth daughter of Jacob & Elizabeth Rice born Novem' ye 16. baptized Decem' 20. 1723.
Constant daughter of Augustine & Jone Owen born Novem' ye 16. baptized Decem' 22. 1723.
William Son of Christopher & Catherine Kilbee born Decem' ye 19. baptized Jan'y 12. 1723.
Anna daughter of William & Elizabeth Blackbourn born Jan'y ye 3. baptized Jan'y 19. 1723.

        Bar Yates Min'.

John Son of Thomas & Catherine Pain born Decem' ye 1. baptized Jan'y 22 1723.
Clement Son of Thomas & Grace Mountague born Decem' ye 29 baptized Jan'y 22. 1723.
William Son of Edward & Mary Clark born Jan'y ye 13. baptized Jan'y 22 1723.
Sarah daughter of Paul & Jane Thilman born Jan'y ye 5. baptized Jan'y ye 26 1723.
Thomas Son of John & Anne Southworth born Dec: ye 22 baptized Feb'y ye 2 1723.
John Son of William & Elizabeth Batchelder born Jan'y ye 3. baptized Feb'y ye 2. 1723.
Anne daughter of W^m & Alice Hackney born Decem' ye 18. baptized Jan'y 19. 1723.
Abby daughter of Zebulon & Mary Chelton born Jan'y ye 5. baptized Feb'y 9. 1723.
Samuel Son of William & Jennett Chowning born Jan'y ye 21 baptized Feb'y 16. 1723.
James Son of James & Margrett Ingram born Jan'y ye 14. baptized Feb'y 16. 1723.
John Son of John & Elizabeth Wormley born Jan'y ye 25. baptized Feb'y 13. 1723.
Charles Son of John & Jane Stuart born Jan'y ye 27 baptized Feb'y ye 23. 1723.
Mary daughter of Theophilus & Frances Branch born Jan'y 21. baptized March 15. 1723.
Robert Son of John & Mary Murray born Jan'y ye 28. baptized March ye 8 1723.
Jemima daughter of Nicholas & Mary Bristow born Jan'y ye 30. baptized March ye 8. 1723.
Anne daughter of William & Catherine Rice born Jan'y ye 30. baptized March ye 8 1723.
George Son of James & Mary Bristow born Feb'y ye 7 baptized March ye 8 1723.
Garritt Son of John & Mary Guttery born Feb'y ye 19. baptized March ye 8. 1723.
William Son of Henry & Elizabeth Blunt born Decem' 29 baptized March ye 22 1723.
Anne daughter of Curtis & Anne Perrott born Feb'y ye 20 baptized March y^r 24 1723.
John Son of John & Elizabeth Dobs born March ye 8, 1723. baptized March ye 29 1724.
Phebe daughter of James & Margrett Daniel born March ye 12 1723 baptized April ye 5. 1724.

Elizabeth daughter of Sr Wm Skipwith & Lady Sarah his Wife born March 22 1723. baptized Ap. 12. 1724.
William Son of William & Jane Cardwell born March ye 12. 1723, baptized April ye 29 1724.
Thomas Son of Daniel & Frances Hues born April ye 14 baptized May ye 3 1724.
William Son of William & Anne Segar born May ye 1. baptized May 9 1724.
Robert an illegitimate Son of Mary Mullens born baptized May 10 1724.
Elizabeth daughter of Robert & Elizabeth Williamson born April ye 6 baptized May 31. 1724.
Nevill Son of Joseph & Elizabeth Bohannon born June ye 1. baptized June 28 1724.
Josee Son of Joseph & Lucretia Goar born June ye 2. baptized July ye 5 1724.
Benjamine Son of Ralph & Mary Shelton born June ye 18. baptized July ye 12. 1724.
Peter Son of William & Mary Bennett born June ye 21. baptized July ye 19. 1724.
Anne an illegitimate daughter of Dorothy Row born July ye 17. baptized July ye 26. 1724.
Aquilla Son of Jonathan & Priscilla Johnson born July ye 19. baptized August ye 16. 1724.
James Son of Thomas & Elizabeth Greenwood born July ye 17 baptized August 2. 1724.
Catherine daughter of John & Catherine Tomson born July ye 16. baptized August 2. 1724.
Alice daughter of John & Lucy Grymes born August ye 10. baptized August 16. 1724.
Edwin Son of Edwin & Elizabeth Thacker born July ye 16. baptized July ye 25. 1724.
Anne daughter of John & Elizabeth Harris born July ye 28. baptized Augt ye 18 1724.
Judith daughter of Peter Johnson & Anna both slaves to Morrice Smith baptized Augt ye 18. 1724.
Henry Son of John & Elizabeth Shorter born August ye 8. baptized August ye 22 1724.
Elizabeth daughter of Rice & Martha Curtis born August ye 19. baptized Augt 26. 1724.
William Son of Christopher & Sarah Chafin born July ye 27 baptized Augt ye 29. 1724
John Son of Thomas & Rachel Amis born August ye 20. baptized Augt ye 30. 1724.
Mary daughter of Thomas & Ellis Faulkner born August ye 23 baptized Septem^r 27. 1724.
Lettice daughter of Peter Johnson & Anna both slaves to Morrice Smith baptized Augt ye 31. 1724.
Machen Son of John & Anne Fearn born August ye 16. baptized September ye 6 1724.
James Son of William & Anne Southworth born August 23. baptized Septem^r ye 13. 1724.

Samuel Son of William & Mary Tomson born Septem' ye 3. baptized Septem' ye 27 1724.
John Son of Jacob & Elizabeth Rice born October ye 16. baptized ye Same day 1724.
Anne daughter of John & Frances Heath born Septem' ye 15. baptized Octo' 25 1724.
Joannah daughter of John & Joannah Blake born Septem' 20. baptized Novem' ye 5. 1724.
John Son of Charles & Susanna Thomas born Octo. 13. baptized Novem' ye 8. 1724.
Nathan Son of Christopher & Hope Sutton born Novem' 22 baptized ye Same day 1724.
Thomas Son of John & Phobe Marston born Novem' ye 9 baptized Novem' ye 29 1724.
Diana daughter of James & Anne Smith born Novem' ye 8. baptized Novem' ye 29. 1724.

Bar. Yates Min'.

Richard Son of John & Elizabeth Lewis born Novem' ye 10. baptized Decem' ye 6. 1724.
Anne illegitimate daughter of Elizabeth Guttery born baptized Decem' ye 6. 1724.
Mary daughter of John & Elizabeth Brame born Novem' ye 5. baptized Decem' ye 6 1724.
Stephen Son of John & Mary Riley born Novem' ye 12. baptized Decem. 6. 1724.
Agnes daughter of Angello & Ellionar Commings born Novem' ye 11. baptized Dec. 13. 1724.
George Son of Jonathan & Anne Herring born Novem' ye 24. baptized Decem' ye 20. 1724.
Rachel daughter of William & Lettice Guttery born Novem' 29 baptized Jan'y 3 1724.
William Son of William & Hannah Roades born Dec. ye 3. baptized Jan'y 3. 1724.
Joyce daughter illegitimate of Elizabeth Stapleton born Dec. ye 3. baptized Jan'y 17. 1724.
Rachel daughter of John & Catherine Chowning born Decem: ye 26. baptized Jan'y 17. 1724.
John Son of Thomas & Rosannah Wright born Decem' ye 26. baptized Jan'y 24. 1724.
Melchisedek Son of Richins & Hannah Brame born Decem' ye 31, baptized Feb'y 7 1724.
Ralph Son of Ralph & Elizabeth Watts born Jan'y ye 1. baptized Feb'y 7. 1724.
Frances daughter of Joseph & Mary Seares born Jan'y ye 2. baptized Feb'y 7 1724.
Lewis Son of William & Sarah Baldwin born Jan'y ye 10. baptized Feb'y 7 1724.
Benjamine Son of Edward & Mary Clark born Feb'y ye 10. baptized March ye 7 1724.
John Son of Henry & Mary Tugle born Feb'y 12. baptized March ye 21. 1724.

John Son of Robert & Anne George born Feb'y 13. baptized March ye 21. 1724.
Elizabeth daughter of Robert & Jane Mash born Feb'y ye 20 baptized March 21. 1724.
Thomas Son of Jacob & Elizabeth Stiff born March 3. 1724 baptized April ye 4 1725.
William Son of John & Elizabeth Saunders born March ye 5. 1724. baptized April 4. 1725.
Mary daughter of John & Sarah Miller born March ye 19, 1724 baptized April 4 1725.
Anne daughter of Matthew & Mary Kemp born March ye 31. baptized April 9. 1725.
Agatha daughter of John & Anne Ridgway born March ye 5. 1724. baptized April 11. 1725.
Mary daughter of Robert & Eliza Daniel born March ye 22. 1724. baptized April 11 1725.
William Son of John & Elizabeth Peniel born March ye 16. 1724. baptized April 25. 1725.
Mary daughter of John & Mary Sadler born April ye 1st baptized May ye 2 1725.
Mary daughter of Usebius & Mary Lewis born April ye 10. baptized May ye 2. 1725.
Chickley Son of Thomas & Mary Hackett born April ye 21. baptized May ye 2. 1725.
Susanna daughter of Adam & Dorothea Cockborn born May 8. 1724. baptized May 13. 1725.
Jane daughter of Thomas & Jane Cheney born Ap. ye 28. baptized May ye 23 1725.
Henry Son of Oliver & Jane Segar born May ye 2 baptized May ye 23 1725.
James Son of Patrick & Rebeckah Deagle born April 23. baptized May ye 30 1725.
Anne daughter of W^m & Margrett Bristow born May ye 4. baptized May ye 30 1725.
Sarah daughter of Thomas & Mary Gibbs born April ye 30. baptized May ye 30 1725.
William Son of Henry & Elizabeth Tuggle born May ye 28 baptized July ye 4 1725.
George Son of Joseph & Anne Pace born June 10. baptized July ye 4 1725.
Robert Son of Thomas & Jane Norman born June ye 20. baptized July ye 4 1725.
Natty daughter of George & Elizabeth Guest born June ye 18. baptized July ye 4. 1725.
James Son of William & Hannah Cain born June ye 11. baptized July ye 18. 1725.
Elizabeth daughter of George & Agatha Twyman born June 28. baptized July ye 25. 1725.
Henry Son of Richard & Mary Allen born June ye 27 baptized July ye 25. 1725.
Elizabeth daughter of John & Mary Moseley born July ye 14. baptized July ye 25. 1725.

Henry Son of Samuel & Catherine Batchelder born July ye 3. baptized Augst 1. 1725.
Mary daughter of George & Mary Barwick born July ye 29. baptized Augst 5. 1725.
Jane daughter of Richard & Anne Jones born July ye 15. baptized Augst ye 8. 1725.
Anne daughter of James & Anne Russel born   baptized Augst 8. 1725.
Sarah daughter of Joseph & Elizabeth Humphris born July ye 18. baptized Augst 8. 1725.
Anne daughter of John & Mary Bradley born July ye 5. baptized Augst 8. 1725.
Susanna daughter of John & Margrett Southern born July ye 22. baptized Augst 15. 1725.
George Son of George & Martha Chowning born July ye 24 baptized Augst 15 1725.
Josiah Son of W^m & Anne Daniel born July ye 13. baptized Augst ye 22 1725.
Jane daughter of Patrick & Elizabeth Miller born August ye 2 baptized Augst ye 29. 1725.
Elizabeth daughter of John & Michal Williams born July ye 28 baptized Septem ye 5 1725.
James Son of Henry & Sarah Emerson born Augst ye 6 baptized September ye 5. 1725.
—ert Son of Randolph & Sarah Rodes born August ye 13. baptized September ye 5. 1725.

Bar. Yates Min^r

Betty daughter of Joseph & Elizabeth Smith born Augst ye 5. baptized Septem^r ye 12 1725.
Needles Son of William & Frances Hill born August ye 12 baptized Septem^r ye 19. 1725.
Elizabeth daughter of James & Mary Micham born Augst 27. baptized Septem^r ye 26. 1725.
Mary daughter of Joseph & Mary Holland born Augst 31. baptized Septem^r ye 26. 1725.
John Son of John & Anne Southworth born Septem^r ye 14. baptized October ye 3. 1725.
Sarah daughter of William & Elizabeth Batchelder born Augst 31. baptized October ye 4. 1725.
Anne daughter of John & Anne Roads born Septem^r ye 5. baptized October 10 1725.
Isaack Son of Thomas & Susanna Oliver born Octo. ye 2 baptized October ye 10. 1725.
Catherine daughter of Henry & Catherine Weight born Sept: ye 26 baptized Novem^r ye 21. 1725.
Anne daughter of John & Anne Smith born Septem^r ye 30. baptized October y 24 1725.
Armistead Son of Thomas & Margrett Alldin born Septem^r 23. baptized October ye 31. 1725.
Anne daughter of Patrick & Mary Knight born Octo. ye 7. baptized October ye 31. 1725.
Anne daughter of John & Sarah Fulsher born Octo. ye 26. baptized Novem^r ye 14 1725.

Ambrose Son of John & Anne Dudley born October ye 20. baptized Novem^r ye 21. 1725.
Rebecca daughter of Abraham & Mary Wharton born Octo. ye 29. baptized Novem^r: 21. 1725.
William Son of William & Sarah Anderson born Novem^r ye 5. baptized Novem^r: 21. 1725.
William Son of James & Agatha Jones born Octo^r ye 28. baptized Novem^r ye 28. 1725.
Elizabeth daughter of John & Anne Blake born Novem^r ye 5. baptized Novem^r ye 28. 1725.
Anne an illegitimate daughter of Mary Mullens born Octo. ye 24. baptized Decem^r: 19. 1725.
Thomas Son of John & Elizabeth Smith born Octo. ye 30. baptized Decem^r: ye 7. 1725.
John Son of John & Keziah Scanland born Novem^r: ye 30. baptized Decem^r 26 1725.
Elizabeth daughter of Edwin & Elizabeth Thacker born Novem^r 26. baptized Jan'y 5. 1725.
Anne daughter of Richard & Anne Greenwood born Jan'y 22. baptized Jan'y 30 1725.
Benjamine Son of John & Lucy Grymes born Jan'y ye 19. baptized Feb'y 6 1725.
Mary daughter of John & Elizabeth Wormley born Jan'y ye 23. baptized Feb'y 7. 1725.
George Son of Richard & Jane Moulson born Jan'y ye 17. baptized Feb'y 20 1725.
Jane daughter of Stokely & Anne Towles born Feb'y ye 10. baptized Feb'y 20 1725.
Edmund Son of William & Eleanor Crutchfeild born Feb'y 13. baptized March 8. 1725.
Avarilla daughter of John & Margrett Hardee born Jan'y 21. baptized March 13. 1725.
Rachel daughter of John & Mary Goar born Feb'y 21. baptized March 13 1725.
Priscilla daughter of Aquilla & Mary Snelling born Feb'y 18 1725. baptized March 27 1726.
Frances daughter of John & Rebecca Kidd born April ye 1 baptized April ye 2 1726.
Jane daughter of Churchhill & Sarah Blakey born Feb'y 24. 1725. baptized April ye 3. 1726.
Jennett daughter of William & Jennett Chowning born March ye 6. 1725. baptized April 3. 1726.
Joshua an illegitimate son of Mary Jones (alias) Haywood born Ap. ye 2. baptized April 5. 1726.
Conquest an illegitimate Son of Mary Jones alias Haywood born Ap. ye 2: baptized April 5. 1726.
Frances daughter of Richard & Susanna Curtis born March ye 25 baptized Ap: 10 1726.
Mary daughter of Rice & Martha Curtis born March 18. 1725 baptized Ap. 14. 1726.
Susanna daughter of Hezekiah & Anne Rodes born March ye 19. 1725. baptized Ap: 17 1726.

Kerah daughter of Powell & Mary Stamper born March 21 1725. baptized Ap: 24 1726.
Jonathan Son of Jonathan & Priscilla Johnson born April ye 28. 1726.
John Son of Robert & Priscilla James born April ye 7. baptized April ye 24 1726.
Robert Son of Robert & Bridgett Wilkings born May ye 18. baptized 1726.
John Son of William & Alice Hackney born May ye 30. baptized 1726.
Averilla daughter of James & Margrett Ingram born May 19. baptized June 12. 1726.
Elizabeth daughter of William & Margrett Johnson born May 28. baptized June 12. 1726.
Catherine daughter of John & Elizabeth Dobbs born July ye 1. baptized Augt 21 1726.
James Son of Arthur & Mary Thomas born August ye 22 baptized 1726.
Mary daughter of John & Catherine Tugle born August ye 13 baptized Septem^r y^r 4. 1726.
Hugh Son of Hugh & Catherine Mactire born July ye 19. baptized Septem^r y^r 4. 1726.
Thomas Son of William & Jane Cardwell born July ye 19. baptized Septem^r y^r 4. 1726.
James Son of Joshua & Martha Lewis born Septem^r ye 5. baptized 1726.
Mary daughter of Charles & Susanna Thomas born Septem^r ye 9. baptized 1726.
Benjamine Son of Christopher & Hope Sutton born August ye 27 baptized 1726.
Anne daughter of John & Elizabeth Weston born Octo: ye 10. baptized 1726.
John Son of John & Anne Johnson born October ye 24. baptized 1726.
Catherine daughter of John & Michall George born Octo ye 3. baptized October 16 1726.
Benjamine Son of Thomas & Elizabeth Greenwood born Octo ye 2. baptized October 16. 1726.
William Son of William & Sarah Cheseld born Octo ye 31. baptized Novem^r 27 1726.
Robert Son of William & Judith Dudley born Novem^r ye 10. baptized 1726.
Anna daughter of James & Mary Bristow born Octo ye 28 baptized Novem^r 12. 1726.
William Son of Nicholas & Mary Bristow born Novem^r ye 2. baptized Novem^r 12. 1726.
William Son of Thomas & Susanna Oliver born Novem^r ye 2 baptized 1726.
Mary daughter of William & Frances Mansfeild born Decem^r ye 12. baptized Jan^{ry} 8. 1726.
John Son of Christopher & Sarah Chaffin born Decem^r ye 20. baptized 1726.
Vivion Son of James & Margrett Daniel born July ye 1st baptized July 29 1726.

Richard Son of Francis & Sarah Timberlake born August ye 19. baptized 1726.
Elizabeth daughter of John & Mary Murrah born August 14 baptized 1726.
George Son of Joseph & Elizabeth Bohannan born August ye 20 baptized 1726.
Mary daughter of George & Hannah Nevill born Novem^r ye 20 baptized 1726.
William Son of Thomas & Rose Wright born Decem^r ye 8. baptized 1726.
Betty daughter of Joseph & Mary Seers born Jan^{ry} ye 1 baptized Jan'y ye 29 1726.
Catherine daughter of Thomas & Catherine Pain born Decem^r 19. baptized Jan'y ye 29. 1726.
Mary daughter of Oliver & Jane Segar born Decem^r ye 11. baptized Jan'y 29. 1726.
John Son of William & Anne Segar born Novem^r ye 9. baptized Novem^r 19. 1726.
Christopher Son of John & Sarah Miller born Jan'y ye 27. baptized Feb'y ye 2. 1726.
Mary daughter of John & Anne Southworth born Feb'y 2. baptized Feb'y ye 2 1726.
Clemence daughter of Edward & Sarah Ball born Jan'y ye 15. baptized Feby 5. 1726.
Elizabeth daughter of Henry & Elizabeth Ball born Decem^r 28. baptized Jan^{ry} 29 1726.
Henry Son of John & Mary Guttery born Jan'y 8. baptized Jan'y ye 29 1726.
Ellis daughter of Thomas & Ellis Faulkner born Jan^{ry} ye 30. baptized Feb'y 16. 1726.
James Son of John & Sarah Dazier born Feb'y ye 17 baptized March 3 1726.
Eliz^a ye daughter of W^m & Mary Bennett born December ye 1 1726.
Elizabeth daughter of Daniel & Frances Hughes born Jan^{ry} ye 19. baptized March 5. 1726.
Dorothy daughter of John & Anne Fearn born Feb'y ye 13. baptized March 5. 1726.
William Son of John & Elizabeth Thurston born Jan'y 2d baptized Feb'y 1 1726.
William Son of Armistead & Hannah Churchhill born Feb'y ye 24th baptized March ye 16. 1726.
William Son of John & Frances Heath born Jan'y ye 19 baptized Feb'y 19 1726.
Josias Son of John & Catherine Chowning born March ye 6. baptized March 24 1726.
James Son of Ralph & Mary Shetton born Feb'y 23. baptized March ye 23. 1726.
Francis a Slave belonging to ye Estate of James Walker dec'd baptized Ap. 23 1727.
Mary an illegitimate daughter of Jane Taylor born Feb'y 1726 baptized Ap. 26 1727.
George Son of John & Hannah Blake born April ye 6. baptized April ye 30. 1727.

Charles Son of Edward & Elizabeth Whittacre born Ap. ye 12. baptized April ye 21. 1727.
Frances daughter of Jonathan & Mary Brooks born April ye 19. baptized May ye 18. 1727.
Ruth daughter of Richard & Mary Allen born May ye 2. baptized May ye 28. 1727.
William son of Thomas & Anne Lee born May ye 6. baptized May ye 28 1727.
Josiah Son of Joseph & Anne Pace born May 31. baptized June ye 18. 1727.
Agatha daughter of Curtis & Anne Perrott born May 12. baptized June ye 18. 1727.
William Son of George & Agatha Twiman born May ye 20. baptized June ye 18. 1727.
John Son of William & Elizebeth Crowder born May 1 baptized May ye 28. 1727.
Elizabeth an illegitimate daughter of Mary Mullins born May ye 5. baptized July ye 9. 1727.
Elizabeth daughter of John & Elizabeth Braine born July ye 10. baptized July ye 30. 1727.
Frances daughter of John & Rebecca Kidd born baptized August ye 20 1727.
Edward Son of Edward & Mary Clark born August ye 17. baptized August ye 24 1727.
Ruth daughter of John & Elizabeth Smith born August ye 25. baptized ye Same day 1727.
Mary daughter of George & Amy Walker born July ye 30. baptized August ye 27 1727.
Millicent daughter of William & Elizabeth Blackburn born Sept. ye 7. baptized Sept. 24. 1727.
George Son of Robert & Elizabeth Daniel born Septem^r ye 13. baptized October ye 1. 1727.
Sarah daughter of Robert & Anne George born Septem^r ye 24. baptized October ye 1. 1727.
Thomas Son of Thomas & Anne Berry born Septem^r ye 5. baptized October ye 8. 1727.

Bar. Yates Min^r

Ruth daughter of Jacob & Elizabeth Stiff born Septem^r ye 6 baptized October ye 15 1727.
Anne daughter of John & Anne Ridgway born Septem^r ye 30 baptized October 22 1727.
Catherine daughter of Joseph & Elizabeth Smith born August ye 24 baptized Sept. 24 1727.
Benjamine Son of William & Rachel Baker born Octo. ye 28 baptized Novem^r 5 1727.
Rose daughter of Richard & Susanna Curtis born October ye 18, baptized Novem^r 5 1727.
Elizabeth daughter of John & Rebecca Arther born Septem^r ye 25. baptized Novem^r 19 1727.
Frances daughter of Theophilus & Frances Branch born Novr ye 17. baptized Decem^r 2 1727.

Robert Son of John & Mary George born Novem' ye 17. baptized Novem' 18 1727.
Benjamine Son of Robert & Elizabeth Williamson born Novem' 25. baptized Dec. 3 1727.
George Son of George & Martha Chowning was born Novem' 22. baptized Decem' 3 1727.
James Son of Robert & Bridgett Willkings was born Novem' 27. baptized Decem' 11 1727.
John Son of William & Hannah Roads was born Novem' ye 4 baptized Decem' 17 1727.
Lucy daughter of William & mary Gayer was born Decem' ye 17. baptized Jan'y 7 1727.
Anne daughter of Joshua & Martha Lewis was born Novem' ye 8. baptized Jan'y 7 1727.
Joseph Son of John & Margrett Southern was born baptized Jan'y 14 1727.
James Son of James & Rebecca Heptinstall was born Jan'y ye 4th baptized Jan'y ye 28. 1727.
Jane daughter of Francis & Elizabeth Porter was born Jan'y ye 15. baptized Feb'y 2 1727.
Jane daughter of John & Mary Sadler born Jan'y ye 15. baptized Feb'y ye 4 1727.
George son of George & Anne Wortham born Jan'y 19. baptized Feb'y 11 1727.
Phoebe daughter of John & Phoebe Marston born Jan'y 21. baptized Feb'y 18 1727.
Joseph Son of Stockley & Ann Towles born Feb'y ye 3. baptized Feb'y 25 1727.
Joseph Son of Samuel & Chatherine Batchelder born Feb'y ye 9. baptized Feb'y 25 1727.
Maurice Son of John & Anne Smith born Jan'y ye 12. baptized March 4 1727.
Frances daughter of William & Frances Hill born Jan'y ye 26. baptized March ye 10. 1727.
Meacham Son of John & Michal George born Feb'y ye 23. baptized March 17 1727.
William Son of William & Jennett Chowning born Feb'y ye 21. baptized March 17 1727.
Jacob Son of John & Anne Blake born Feb'y 28. baptized March ye 24 1727.
John Son of John & Michal Williams born March 19. 1727. baptized April ye 7 1728.
John Son of John & Mary Moseley born March 10. 1727 baptized April ye 7 1728.
Jane daughter of Henry & Sarah Emerson born March 10. 1727. baptized April ye 7 1728.
Henry Son of William & Margrett Johnson born March 2. 1727. baptized April ye 7 1728.
John Son of John & Elizabeth Weston born Feb'y ye 21. baptized March ye 24 1727.
Mary daughter of Henry & Anne Barnett born Ap: ye 3. baptized April 21 1728.

John Son of John & Frances Heath born April y" 14. baptized May y" 5 1728.
Michal daughter of George & Elizabeth Guess born April y" 5. baptized May y" 5 1728.
Thomas Son of Thomas & Sarah Older born baptized May y" 19 1728.
Elizabeth daughter of John & Lettice Burk born May y" 24 baptized May y" 26 1728.
Elizabeth daughter of William & Margrett Bristow born May y" 14 baptized June 9 1728.
William Son of James & Jane Dudley born May y" 27. baptized June y" 9 1728.
Sarah daughter of Paul & Clement Phillpotts born July y" 5 baptized July 11 1728.
John Son of Michael & Anne Arrowy born July y" 4. baptized July y" 28 1728.
Jane daughter of John & Anne Good born July y" 14. baptized July y" 28 1728.
Margrett daughter of James & Jenney Daniel born July 5. baptized July y" 28 1728.
Ruth daughter of Edward & Mary Clark born July y" 29. baptized August y" 11 1728.
Sarah daughter of Joseph & Eliz" Bohannan born August y" 5 baptized August y" 25 1728.
Anne daughter of Edwin & Elizabeth Thacker born August y" 3. baptized August y" 18 1728.
Mary daughter of John & Eliz" Ellerson born August y" 13. baptized Septem' 8. 1728.
Jane daughter of Henry & Frances Mickelburrough born August 19. baptized Septem' 8. 1728.
William Son of Usebius & Mary Lewis born July y" 3. baptized August y" 18 1728.
Elizabeth daughter of Thomas & Penelope Mountague born Septem' y" 10. baptized Septem' 29. 1728.
Ruth daughter of John & Eliz" Thurston born August y" 28. baptized Septem' y" 29. 1728.
John Son of Samuel & Susanna Fleming born Septem' y" 1 baptized Septem' y" 22. 1728.
John Son of Joseph & Mary Hardee born September y" 27. baptized Octo y" 20. 1728.
Anne daughter of William & Judith Gardner born Octo. y" 10. baptized Novem' 3. 1728.
Thomas Son of William & Anne Robinson born Octo. y" 7. baptized Novem' 3 1728.

Bar. Yates Min'.

Susanna daughter of John & Susanna Tomson born Octo. y" 21. baptized Novem' y" 10 1728.
Thomas Son of Peter & Elizabeth Mountague born Octo. y" 28. baptized Novem' y" 10 1728.
John Son of James & Margrett Ingram born Novem' y" 13. baptized Novem' 21 1728.
William an illegitimate Son of Susanna Williams born baptized Novem' 25 1728.

Mary daughter of John & Elizabeth Lewis born Novem^r ye 10 baptized Decem^r 1 1728.
Samuel Son of John & Elizabeth Dobbs born Novem^r ye 14. baptized Decem^r 1 1728.
Mary daughter of Matthew & Mary Kemp born Novem^r ye 25 baptized Decem^r 6 1728.
Betty daughter of George & Hannah Nevill born Decem^r ye 3. baptized Decem^r 14 1728.
Priscilla daughter of Jonathan & Priscilla Johnson born Novem^r ye 24 baptized Decem^r 15 1728.
Tabitha daughter of John & Catherine Tugell born Octo. ye 27. baptized Decem^r 22. 1728.
Elizabeth daughter of William & Catherine Southworth born Decem^r 5. baptized Decem^r 22. 1728.
Sarah daughter of Churchhill & Sarah Blakey born Novem^r 28. baptized Decem^r 22 1728.
John Son of Armistead & Hannah Churchhill born Decem^r ye 1 baptized Decem^r 23. 1728.
John Son of William & Elizabeth Long born Decem^r ye 1. baptized Decem^r ye 25. 1728.
Elizabeth daughter of Thomas & Rosamond Right born Decem^r ye 1 baptized Decem^r ye 29. 1728.
William Son of William & Mary Bennett born Decem^r ye 16. baptized Jan'y ye 5 1728.
Mary daughter of William & Betty Wallis born Decem^r ye 15 baptized Jan'y ye 12 1728.
Elizabeth daughter of Abraham & Mary Wharton born Decem^r ye 1. baptized Jan'y ye 5 1728.
Elizabeth daughter of James & Edy Stiff born Jan'y ye 14. baptized Jan'y ye 26 1728.
Esther daughter of Richard & Jane Moulson born Jan'y ye 2 baptized Jan'y ye 30. 1728.
Mary daughter of Richard & Anne Greenwood born Jan'y ye 5. baptized Feb'y ye 2. 1728.
Michal daughter of Christopher & Hope Sutton born Jan'y ye 11. baptized Feb'y ye 16. 1728.
Edmund Son of Joshua & Martha Lewis born Jan'y ye 20. baptized Feb'y ye 16. 1728.
Mildred Orrill an illegitimate daughter of Averilla Hardee born Feb'y 4. baptized Feb'y 23. 1728.
Alexander Son of John & Mary Murray born Jan'y ye 29. baptized March ye 2 1728.
Jacob Son of John & Anne Roads born Feb'y ye 20. baptized March ye 5 1728.
Henry Son of Aquilla & Mary Snelling born Feb'y 17 baptized March ye 9 1728.
John Son of John & Mary Rice born Feb'y ye 23 baptized March ye 11 1728.
William Son of William & Frances Mansfeild born Feb'y ye 11. baptized March ye 16. 1728.
Jane daughter of William & Jane Cardwell born Feb'y ye 12. baptized March ye 16. 1728.

Henry Son of Henry & Mary Tugel born Feb'y ye 24. baptized March ye 16 1728.
William Son of William & Hannah Cain born Feb'y ye 10. baptized march ye 9. 1728.
Sarah daughter of Thomas & Ellis Faulkner born March ye 8. baptized March ye 24 1728.
Mildred daughter of Thomas & Mary Furgoson born March ye 8. 1728 baptized April ye 4. 1729.
John Son of Thomas & Hannah Lee born March ye 28. baptized ye Same day 1729.
William an illegitimate Son of Mary Pace born March ye 28 baptized April ye 6. 1729.
John Son of Thomas & Anne Berry born March ye 22d 1728 baptized April ye 20. 1729.
William & James Sons of John & Mary Guttery born April 19. baptized May ye 11. 1729.
Judith daughter of Oliver & Jane Segar born April ye 20th baptized May ye 11. 1729.
Dianah daughter of William & Elizabeth Wood born May ye 10. baptized May ye 18. 1729.
Anne daughter of Edward & Elizabeth Whittaker born May ye 18. baptized May 25. 1729.
Thomas Son of James & Agatha Jones born April ye 28. baptized June ye 1. 1729.
Catherine daughter of John & Sarah Carrell born May ye 9. baptized June ye 1. 1729.
Lucy daughter of Edmund & Mary Berkley born June ye 5. baptized June ye 10. 1729.
Frances daughter of John & Elizabeth Smith born May ye 20. baptized June ye 22. 1729.
Daniel Son of Ralph & Mary Shelton born May ye 17. baptized June ye 22. 1729.
Samuel Son of Thomas & Elizabeth Greenwood born May ye 25. baptized June ye 22. 1729.
Richard Son of John & Mary Green born June ye 7. baptized June ye 22. 1729.
James an illegitimate Son of Mary Hamilton born June ye 7. baptized June ye 22. 1729.
Catherine daughter of George & Agatha Twyman born June ye 13. baptized June ye 22. 1729.
Elizabeth daughter of John & Elizabeth Weston born June ye 19. baptized July 1. 1729.
Joseph Son of Joseph & Elizabeth Smith born June ye 4. baptized June ye 29. 1729.
Benjamine Son of James & Mary Meacham born June ye 17. baptized July ye 13. 1729.
John Son of Jeremiah & Elizabeth Earley born July ye 3. baptized July ye 17. 1729.
James Son of Hugh & Catherine Mactire born July ye 14. baptized July ye 20. 1729.
James & John Sons of John & Sarah Miller born July ye 10. baptized July ye 27. 1729.

Bar Yates Min^r

Rice Son of Rice & Martha Curtis born July ye 30. baptized August ye 3. 1729.
Benjamine Son of John & Catherine Williams born July ye 5 baptized August ye 3. 1729.
Oliver Son of William & Anne Segar born June ye 15. baptized August ye 3. 1729.
Agatha daughter of William & Anne Daniel born July ye 5. baptized August ye 10. 1729.
Mary daughter of Francis & Elizabeth Porter born July y^c 24. baptized August ye 17 1729.
Joseph Son of William & Anne Anderson born July ye 26. baptized August y^c 17 1729.
Joseph Son of William & Jennett Chowning born August ye 8. baptized August ye 24. 1729.
Thomas Son of Thomas & Anne Lee born August ye 23. baptized August ye 25. 1729.
Aggy daughter of Marvel & Mary Moseley born July ye 21. baptized August ye 24. 1729.
Thomas Son of John & Anne Fearn born August ye 29. baptized Septem^r ye 2. 1729.
John Son of Edward & Sarah Ball born July ye 29. baptized August ye 31. 1729.
William Son of William & Elizabeth Davies born August ye 9. baptized September ye 14. 1729.
Judith daughter of John & Jane Day born Septem^r ye 21. baptized Septem^r ye 23. 1729.
Benjamine & Mary Son & daughter of Thomas & Christian Sanders born Sept. ye 10. baptized Sept 28. 1729.
Daniel Son of James & Rebecca Heptenstall born Septem^r y^c 14. baptized September ye 29 1729.
Moses Son of Richard & Mary Smither born August ye 2. baptized August ye 31 1729.
Bridgett daughter of Robert & Bridgett Wilkins born Septem^r ye 15 baptized Octo. 19. 1729.
Mary daughter of W^m & Elizabeth Crouders born September ye 26. baptized Octo. 26 1729.
John Son of William & Frances Thruston born Octo y^c 6. baptized Octo. 26 1729.
Catherine daughter of Phillip & Elizabeth Brooks born Septem^r 3. baptized Octo. 26 1729.
William Son of William & Eleonar Harbinson born October ye 27. baptized Novem^r 1. 1729.
John Son of John & Johanna Blake born October y^r 5. baptized October ye 19 1729.
Alexander Son of William & Susanna Saunders born Septem^r 19. baptized Octo. ye 19. 1729.
John Son of John & Anne Dudley born October ye 26. baptized Novem^r ye 9 1729.
Sarah daughter of John & Elizabeth Saunders born October ye 31. baptized Novem^r 9 1729.
Anne daughter of Henry & Sarah Putman born October ye 26. baptized Novem^r ye 9 1729.

William Son of Martin & Catherine Ferrell born Novem' y' 6. baptized Novem' 28. 1729.
Mary daughter of Joseph & Elizabeth Meacham born Novem' y° 11. baptized Decem' 7. 1729.
John Son of Zacharias & Mary Gibbs born Novem' y° 17. baptized Decem' 14. 1729.
Ellis daughter of Henry & Anne Jolly born Novem' y° 28. baptized Decem' 14. 1729.
William Son of Andrew & Elizabeth Davis born Octo y° 16. baptized Novem' y° 9. 1729.
James Son of John & Rebecca Bradley born Decem' y° 6. baptized Decem' 21. 1729.
Edward Son of William & Elizabeth Blackburne born Novem' 30. baptized Decem' 21. 1729.
Thomas Son of Patrick & Ellionar Boswell born Decem' y° 3. baptized Decem' 21. 1729.
John Son of George & Anne Wortham born Decem' y° 20. baptized Jan'y 6. 1729.
Paul & Richard Sons of Paul & Jane Thilman born Jan'y y° 17. baptized Jan'y 21 1729.
Frances daughter of Henry & Frances Mickleburrough born Novem' y° 30. baptized Decem' 28. 1729.
Daniel Son of W^m & Margret Johnson born Jan'y y° 11. baptized Jan'y y° 21 1729.
Sarah daughter of John & Lucy Grymes born Jan'y y° 29. baptized Feb'y y° 6 1729.
Charles Son of Curtis & Anne Perrott born Jan'y y° 22. baptized Feb'y y° 8 1729.
William Son of William & Elizabeth Kidd born Decem' y° 5. baptized Decem' y° 28. 1729.
Robert Son of Robert & Anne George born Decem' y° 15. baptized Decem' y° 28. 1729.
Elizabeth daughter of James & Mary Bristow born Decem' y° 18. baptized Feb'y y° 8. 1729.
Harding Son of James & Margret Ingram born Decem' y° 29. baptized Feb'y y° 8. 1729.
Anne daughter of John & Catherine Chowning born Jan'y y° 20. baptized Feb'y y° 8. 1729.
Sarah daughter of Edwin & Elizabeth Thacker born Jan'y y° 29. baptized Feb'y y° 11 1729.
Jane daughter of Richard & Mary Allen born Jan'y y° 7. baptized Feb'y y° 8 1729.
William Son of Jacob & Elizabeth Stiff born Jan'y y° 28. baptized Feb'y y° 1. 1729.
Stapleton Son of William & Jane Crutchfeild born Feb'y y° 14. baptized March 1. 1729.
Samuel Son of Robert & Elizabeth Daniel born Feb'y y° 7. baptized March 1. 1729.
Margret daughter of Roger & Frances Linn born Feb'y y° 9. baptized March 1. 1729.
Margret daughter of Henry & Mary Daniel born March y° 3. baptized March 22 1729.

Henry Son of John & Frances Heath born March ye 2. baptized March 22 1729.
Jemima daughter of John & Rebecca Kidd born March ye 6. baptized March 22. 1729.
John Son of John & Isabell Jones born Feb'y 26. 1729 baptized March 29 1730.
> Bar Yates. Min^r.

Daniel Son of Joseph & Anne Pace born Feb'y ye 26. baptized March ye 22 1729.
Caroline daughter of George & Amy Walker born March 13, 1729. baptized April ye 3 1730.
Avarilla daughter of Joseph & Elizabeth Humphries born Jan'y ye 24. baptized Feb. 22 1729.
Mary daughter of William & Frances Guttery born March ye 26. baptized April ye 3 1730.
Samuel Son of Nicholas & Mary Bristow born March ye 27 baptized April ye 12 1730.
Elizabeth daughter of George & Martha Chowning born March ye 20. 1729. baptized April ye 12. 1730.
John Son of Thomas & Elizabeth Marston born Ap: ye 3. baptized April ye 26. 1730.
Thomas Son of Joseph & Mary Seares born Ap. ye 9. baptized May ye 3 1730.
Williamson Son of John & Frances Bryant born April ye 21. baptized May ye 3. 1730.
Frances daughter of Stokeley & Anne Towles born May ye 8. baptized May ye 22 1730.
John Son of John & Mary Sadler born May ye 9. baptized May ye 24 1730.
John Son of Richard & Sarah Wate born April ye 14 baptized May ye 17 1730.
Dorothy daughter of Hugh & Anne Roach born May ye 14. baptized June ye 7 1730.
Catherine daughter of John & Anne Good born May ye 23 baptized June ye 14 1730.
Elizabeth daughter of Robert & Anne Beverley born June 10. baptized June ye 13 1730.
William Son of Thomas & Penelope Mountague born June ye 14. baptized June ye 23 1730.
Nathaniel Son of Armistead & Hannah Churchhill born June ye 16. baptized July 8. 1730.
Mary daughter of John Elizabeth Weston born June ye 30. baptized July 12 1730.
Elizabeth daughter of Charles & Johanna Curtis born June ye 30. baptized July 24 1730.
Robert Son of George & Jane Goodwin born July ye 23. baptized July ye 24. 1730.
Judith daughter of George & Elizabeth Guess born July 25. baptized August ye 16 1730.
Margret daughter of Henry & Sarah Emerson born August 19. baptized August 30. 1730.
Anna daughter of William & Frances Hill born July 25. baptized August 30. 1730.

William Son of John & Elizabeth Humphries born Septem' y' 1 baptized Septem 20. 1730.
Josias Son of John & Elizabeth Brim born Septem' ye 7. baptized September 27. 1730.
Josiah Son of Hugh & Catherine Martin born Septem' ye 9. baptized Octo. ye 18. 1730.
Judith daughter of Matthew & Mary Kemp born Octob' ye 21. baptized Novem' ye 4. 1730.
Elizabeth daughter of Aquilla & Margret Snelling born Octob' ye 8. baptized Nov: 4. 1730.
John Son of Henry & Jochebed Nash born Octo: ye 19. baptized Novem' ye 8. 1730.
Benjamine Son of John & Margret Southern born Octo: ye 29. baptized Novem' ye 8. 1730.
John Son of John & Phebe Marston born October ye 13. baptized Novem' 18 1730.
Sarah daughter of Jno & Mary Glen born October ye 30. baptized Novem' 23. 1730.
Elizabeth daughter of William & Judith Baldwin born October 28. baptized Novem' 29. 1730.
Elizabeth daughter of William & Elizabeth Wood born Novem' ye 9. baptized Novem' 29. 1730.
Jane daughter of John & Susanna Tomson born Novem' ye 1. baptized Novem' 29. 1730.
William Son of Joseph & Eliz^a Bohannan born Novem' ye 19. baptized Novem' ye 30. 1730.
William Son of Henry & Anne Barnet born Novem' ye 6. baptized Decem' ye 6 1730.
Christopher Son of William & Hannah Roads born Novem' ye 25. baptized Decem' ye 13. 1730.
Matthew Son of Usebius & Mary Lewis born Novem' ye 23. baptized Decem' ye 28. 1730.
Judith daughter of John & Anne Fearn born Decem' ye 30. baptized Jan'y ye 3. 1730.
William Son of James & Rebecca Heptinstall born Jan'y ye 12 baptized Jan'y ye 17 1730.
William Son of John & Agnes Bohannan born Jan'y ye 3. baptized Jan'y ye 17. 1730.
Edmund Son of Edmund & Mary Berkley born Decem' ye 5. baptized Jan'y 14. 1730.
James Son of Thomas & Mary Heath born Decem' ye 1. baptized Jan'y 10. 1730.
Mary daughter of Edward & Mary Clark born Decem' ye 31. baptized Jan'y 31. 1730.
John & William Sons of Oliver & Jane Segar born Jan'y ye 17. baptized Jan'y 19. 1730.
Chickeley Son of James & Jane Daniel born Jan'y ye 16. baptized Jan'y ye 31. 1730.
John Son of Eustace & Ruth Howard born Jan'y ye 16. baptized Feb'y ye 3. 1730.
Thomas Son of Thomas & Christian Saunders born Feb'y ye 5. baptized March ye 7. 1730.
Susanna daughter of Richard & Susanna Curtis born Feb'y ye 17. baptized March ye 7. 1730.

Elizabeth & Mary daughters of Thomas & Catherine Austin born March ye 10. baptized ye Same day 1730.
John Son of William & Betty Wallis born Jan'y ye 8. baptized Feb'y ye 21 1730.
Elizabeth daughter of Benjamine & Mary Pace born Jan'y ye 17. baptized Feb'y ye 21. 1730.
Anne daughter of Thomas & Mary French born Jan'y ye 25. baptized Feb'y ye 21. 1730.
Anne daughter of Michael & Anne Roan born Feb'y ye 14. baptized Feb'y ye 21. 1730.

Bar Yates Min^r

Charles Son of John & Lucy Grymes born March ye 11th baptized March ye 18 1730.
Caroline daughter of John & Anne Smith born Feb'y ye 17. baptized March ye 21 1730.
Catherine Randal a Slave belonging to ye estate of John Wormeley baptized March 21 1730.
John Son of John & Mary Goar born Feb'y ye 2. baptized march ye 14 1730.
Anna daughter of Marril & Mary Moseley born Feb'y ye 19. baptized March ye 14 1730.
Chicheley Corbin Son of Edwin & Eliz^a Thacker born March y^r 17. 1730 baptized March 25 1731.
George Son of Henry & Mary Daniel born March ye 17. 1730. baptized April ye 4 1731.
George Son of George & Agatha Twyman born March ye 29. baptized April ye 4 1731.
Stanton Son of James & Jane Dudley born March ye 17. 1730 baptized April ye 25 1731.
John Son of George & Margret Best born April ye 1. baptized April ye 12 1731.
Mary daughter of Thomas & Anne Berry born April ye 20. baptized May ye 9 1731.
William Son of Abraham & Mary Wharton born April ye 21. baptized May ye 16 1731.
John Son of John & Sarah Carrel born Ap: ye 10. baptized May y^r 2 1731.
John Son of William & Elizabeth Buford born Ap: ye 2. baptized may ye 2 1731.
Charles Son of Sampson & Elizabeth Darrill born May ye 8. baptized May 30 1731.
Joseph Son of William & Mary Bennet born May ye 2. baptized June ye 6 1731.
Richard Son of Richard & Mabel Steevens born may ye 3. baptized June ye 6 1731.
Jonathan Son of Jonathan & Mary Brooks born May ye 10. baptized June ye 13 1731.
Hannah daughter of William & Hannah Cain born May ye 8. baptized June ye 6 1731.
Hannah daughter of William & Anne Robinson born May ye 7. baptized June 20 1731.
Elizabeth daughter of Lunsford & Mary Lomax born June ye 10. baptized July ye 18 1731.

Reuben Son of John & Michal Williams born July ye 6. baptized July ye 15 1731.
Mary daughter of Wm & Rose Lewis born June ye 17. baptized August ye 1 1731.
William Son of Joseph & Elizabeth Smith born August ye 6. baptized August ye 8 1731.
James Son of Charles & Johanna Curtis born July ye 23. baptized August ye 14 1731.
Bartholomew Son of William & Jennet Chowning born July 2. baptized July 25 1731.
Garret Son of Edward & Agatha Southern born July ye 17. baptized July 25 1731.
Edmund Son of John & Rebecca Kidd born July ye 14. baptized August ye 15 1731.
Samuel Son of William & Margret Johnson born July ye 23. baptized August ye 15 1731.
Elizabeth daughter of Henry & Frances Mickleburrough born July ye 30. baptized August ye 15. 1731.
John Son of John & Elizabeth Smith born August ye 27. baptized Septr ye 5 1731.
Robert Son of Charles & Mary Carter born August ye 28. baptized Septem ye 6 1731.
Robert Son of William & Elizabeth Long born August ye 31. baptized Septemr ye 12 1731.
William Son of Richard & Anne Jones born August ye 16. baptized September ye 19 1731.
Anna daughter of Francis & Elizabeth Porter born Septemr ye 1. baptized Septemr ye 19. 1731.
Jacob & Benjamine Sons of Samuel & Catharine Batchelder born Septr ye 29 bapti{d} Sept 30. 1731.
Thomas Son of William & Jane Mountague born Sept. ye 9. baptized Octor ye 12 1731.
William Son of William & Frances Guttery born Sept. ye 7. baptized October ye 17 1731.
Mary daughter of Randolph & Sarah Rhodes born Augst 27. baptized Octobr ye 17 1731.
Mary daughter of John & Elizabeth Pace born Septemr 21. baptized October ye 17 1731.
Lettice daughter of Joseph & Anne Pace born Septemr 26. baptized October ye 17 1731.
Thomas Son of Richard & Anne Greenwood born Octo. 27. baptized October ye 30 1731.
Robert Son of Robert & Elizabeth Wilkings born Septemr ye 1. baptized October ye 10 1731.
Martha daughter of Hugh & Anne Roach born Septemr ye 8. baptized October ye 10 1731.
Jane daughter of Hugh & Judith Stewart born Octo: ye 15. baptized October ye 31 1731.
John Son of Paul & Susanna Philpotts born Octo ye 21. baptized October ye 31 1731.
Elizabeth daughter of Henry & Anne Jolly born Octo: ye 13. baptized October ye 31 1731.
Henry Son of John & Catherine Tugel born Septemr ye 27. baptized Novemr ye 7. 1731.

William Son of John & Elizabeth Elerson born October ye 1. baptized November ye 7. 1731.
William Son of William & Frances Thurston born Octo: ye 24. baptized November ye 7. 1731.
James Son of John & Mary Rice born October ye 31. baptized Novem^r ye 28. 1731.
Henry Son of William & Hannah Churchhill born Novem^r ye 16. baptized Decem^r ye 2. 1731.
Elizabeth daughter of Edward & Elizabeth Whittacer born Novem^r ye 12. baptized Decem^r ye 5. 1731.
Jane daughter of Hezekiah & Anne Rhoades born Novem^r ye 11. baptized Decem^r 12 1731.
William Son of Henry & Sarah Nixon born Novem^r ye 28. baptized Decem^r 19. 1731.
Pleasant Son of Thomas & Betty Wakefield born Novem^r ye 23. baptized Decem^r 19. 1731.
Sarah daughter of Alexander & Lucy Lister born Jan'y ye 9. baptized Jan'y ye 11 1731.

Bar. Yates Min^r.

John Son of William & Anne Anderson born Decem^r ye 4. baptized Decem^r ye 12. 1731.
William Son of John & Anne Dudley born Decem^r ye 26. baptized Jan'y ye 2 1731.
Judith daughter of Robert & Jane Dudley born Decem^r ye 26. baptized Jan'y ye 24 1731.
Sarah daughter of William & Anne Daniel born Jan'y ye 12. baptized Feb'y ye 4. 1731.
William Son of William & Susanna Saunders born Jan'y ye 12. baptized Feb'y ye 13. 1731.
William Son of Churchhill & Sarah Blakey born Jan'y ye 17. baptized Jan'y ye 30. 1731.
William Son of Robert & Elizabeth Daniel born Jan'y ye 22. baptized Jan'y ye 30. 1731.
Agatha daughter of William & Jane Cardwell born Decem^r ye 12. baptized Jan'y ye 30. 1731.
William Son of William & Mary Dawson born Jan'y ye 29. baptized Feb'y ye 3 1731.
Judith daughter of John & Johanna Blake born Feb'y ye 6. baptized March ye 5 1731.
John Son of Thomas & Anne Lee born Feb'y ye 26. baptized March ye 12 1731.
Richard Son of William & Anne Segar born Feb'y ye 21. baptized March ye 12 1731.
William Son of William & Elizabeth Thurston born March 13. 1731. baptized April ye 2. 1732.
William Son of John & Anne Johnston born April ye 17. baptized May ye 7 1732.
Mary daughter of John & Michel George born April ye 21. baptized May ye 14. 1732.
Elizabeth daughter of William & Elizabeth Crowdas born April ye 22. baptized May ye 14. 1732.
Mary daughter of W^m & Jane Crutchfield born April ye 25. baptized June ye 4. 1732.

Martha daughter of Moses & Dorothy Kidd born May ye 7. baptized June ye 4. 1732.
Thomas Son of W^m & mary Southern born June ye 6. baptized June ye 25 1732.
Anne daughter of Samuel & Mary Sorry born May ye 29. baptized June 25. 1732.
Alexander Son of Jonathan & Priscilla Johnson born July ye 4. baptized July ye 9. 1732.
Avarilla daughter of Jacob & Eliz^a Stiff born June ye 11. baptized July ye 9 1732.
Charles Son of Ignatius & Mary Tureman born July ye 26. baptized July ye 27. 1732.
George Son of George & Amey Walker born July ye 13. baptized August ye 9 1732.
Catherine daughter of Thomas & Catherine Price born August ye 4. baptized August 27. 1732.
Esther daughter of Robert & Mary Daniel born August ye 5. baptized August 27 1732.
Josiah Son of John & Elizabeth Dobbs born August ye 17. baptized August ye 28 1732.
William Son of William & Mary Gayer born July ye 16. baptized August ye 20 1732.
James Son of Richard & Sarah Waight born August ye 23. baptized Septem^r ye 3. 1732.
Lucy daughter of Aquilla & Margret Snelling born August ye 21. baptized Septem^r ye 10. 1732.
Catherine daughter of Thomas & Penelope Mountague born August ye 4. baptized Septem^r ye 11. 1732.
James Son of Henry & Mary Tugle born August ye 20. baptized Septem^r ye 17. 1732.
William Son of William & Judith Baldwin born Augst ye 27. baptized Septem^r ye 17. 1732.
Catherine daughter of William & Elizabeth Wood born Septem^r ye 6. baptized Septr ye 17. 1732.
Daniel Son of Curtis & Anne Perrott born August ye 10. baptized September ye 17. 1732.
Elizabeth daughter of Sampson & Elizabeth Dorrell born Augst 23. baptized Septem. ye 24. 1732.
Mary daughter of John & Rebecca Bradley born Septem^r ye 11. baptized Octo. ye 1 1732.
Elizabeth daughter of John & Anne Chowning born August ye 25. baptized Septem^r ye 17. 1732.
Susanna daughter of John & Sarah Carrell born Septem^r ye 29. baptized Octo: ye 8. 1732.
Judith daughter of Robert & Elizabeth Johnson born Octo: ye 8. baptized Octo: ye 16. 1732.
Phillip Son of James & Rebecca Heptinstall born Octo: ye 15. baptized Octo: ye 22. 1732.
Edward Son of Edward & Sarah Ball born October ye 7. baptized Novem^r ye 5 1732.
William Son of Thomas Marston & Eliz^a his Wife born Octo: ye 1. baptized Octo^r ye 22. 1732.
John Son of James & Ann Gibson born Novem^r ye 3d baptized Novem^r ye 12 1732.

Charles Son of Charles & Mary Carter born Octo: ye 15. baptized Novem^r ye 15 1732.
Lettice daughter of William & Frances Guttery born Novem^r 17. baptized Nov. 26. 1732.
John Son of Thomas & Lucy Naish born Octo: ye 6. baptized Decem^r ye 3. 1732.
Andrew Son of Andrew & Elizabeth Davis born Decem^r ye 30. baptized Jan'y ye 14. 1732.
Nathaniel Son of Christopher & Hope Sutton born Decem^r ye 20. baptized Jan'y ye 14. 1732.
Catherine daughter of Joseph & Mary Row born Decem^r ye 25. baptized Jan'y ye 14. 1732.
George Son of Thomas & Christian Sanders born Jan'y ye 11. baptized Jan'y ye 14. 1732.
Susanna daughter of Thomas & Christian Sanders born Jan'y ye 11. baptized Jan'y ye 14. 1732.
Elizabeth daughter of Richard & Mary Hearn born Decem^r ye 29. baptized Jan'y ye 14. 1732.

Bar Yates. Min^r.

Mary daughter of Eustace & Ruth Howard born Decem^r ye 25. baptized Feb'y ye 7. 1732.
Thomas Son of Richard & Catherine Greenwood born Jan'y ye 2. baptized Jan'y ye 21 1732.
Samuel Son of John & Margrett Southern born Jan'y ye 1. baptized Jan'y ye 21 1732.
William an illegitimate Son of Mary Hardee born Decem^r ye 15. baptized Jan'y ye 21. 1732.
John son of John & Susanna Tomson born Jan'y ye 27. baptized Feb'y ye 11 1732.
Anne an illegitimate daughter of Jane Tomson born   baptized Feb'y ye 18 1732.
Lucy daughter of John & Anne Roades born Feb'y ye 22 baptized Feb'y ye 25 1732.
Ruth daughter of James & Jenny Daniel born Jan'y ye 18. baptized Feb'y ye 11 1732.
Hannah daughter of Nicholas & Mary Bristow born Jan'y ye 9. baptized Feb'y ye 11 1732.
Joseph Son of Benjamine & Mary Pace born Jan'y ye 22. baptized Feb'y ye 11 1732.
Sarah daughter of Charles & Mary Wood born Feb'y ye 8. baptized March 4 1732.
James Son of Robert & Sarah Perrott born Jan'y ye 25. baptized March ye 4 1732.
Mary daughter of George & Anne Wortham born Feb'y ye 28. baptized March 6. 1732.
Thomas Son of John & Elizabeth Saunders born Jan'y ye 25 baptized Feb'y ye 4 1732.
Mary daughter of James & Jane Dudley born Feb'y ye 16. baptized March ye 18. 1732.
Ruth daughter of John & Mary Murrah born Feb'y ye 12. baptized March ye 11 1732.
Peter Son of Edward & Mary Clark born March ye 6. baptized March ye 23. 1732.

William Son of Marvel & Mary Moseley born March ye 29. baptized April ye 8. 1733.
Avarilla daughter of James & Mary Bristow born March ye 13. 1732. baptized April y^r 8. 1733.
William Son of Thomas & Anne Berry born March ye 27. baptized April ye 15 1733.
Ludwell Son of John & Lucy Grymes born April ye 26. baptized May y^r 6 1733.
Frances daughter of William & Betty Wallis born March ye 20. 1732 baptized April 29 1733.
Sarah daughter of James & Mary Meacham born March ye 29. baptized April y^r 29. 1733.
James Son of Michael & Anne Roan born April y^r 1. baptized April ye 29 1733.
Sarah daughter of Henry & Sarah Emerson born April ye 5. baptized April ye 29. 1733.
Elizabeth daughter of John & Mary Sadler born April ye 15. baptized April ye 29. 1733.
Jane daughter of William & Margrett Johnson born April ye 10. baptized April ye 29 1733.
William Son of Michal & Anne Rudd born April ye 18. baptized May ye 13 1733.
Jane daughter of James & Dianah Stuart born May ye 3. baptized May ye 27. 1733.
Sarah daughter of John & Sarah Owen born May ye 1. baptized May ye 27 1733.
Nelson Son of Edmund & Mary Berkeley born May ye 16. baptized June ye 3 1733.
Benjamine Son of Richard & Mabell Steevens born May ye 17. baptized June ye 3 1733.
Judith daughter of William & Jennet Chowning born April ye 22. baptized May ye 20. 1733.
Thomas Son of William & Mary Gardner born May ye 15. baptized May ye 20. 1733.
Reuben Son of Thomas & Mary Shelton born May ye 6. baptized June y^r 10. 1733.
Elizabeth daughter of Paul & Susanna Philpotts born May ye 24. baptized May y^r 27. 1733.
Mary daughter of John & Rebecca Arthur born May ye 6. baptized June y^r 17 1733.
William Son of John & Anne Lee born May ye 25. baptized June ye 22 1733.
William & John Sons of Caleb & Margrett Brooks born June ye 27. baptized June y^r 27. 1733.
Sarah daughter of Usebius & Mary Lewis born May ye 28. baptized July y^r 1 1733.
Arthur Son of Henry & Jochebed Nash born June ye 29. baptized July y^r 22 1733.
Sarah daughter of John & Agniss Bohannan born July ye 17. baptized July y^r 29. 1733.
Anne daughter of John & Anne Fearn born July ye 9. baptized July y^r 25 1733.
Abraham Son of John & Elizabeth Pace born July ye 23. baptized August y^r 17 1733.

Margret daughter of Oliver & Jane Seagar born July ye 7th baptized August ye 12. 1733.
William Son of Thomas & Mary French born August 2. baptized August 23. 1733.
Antony a Slave belonging to Bar. Yates baptized Septem^r ye 2. 1733.
Jane daughter of Charles & Jane Daniel born August ye 18. baptized Septem^r ye 9. 1733.
Susanna daughter of Christopher & Elizabeth Owen born August ye 24. baptized Septem^r 12. 1733.
George Son of William & Anne Anderson born Septem^r ye 13. baptized Septem^r 16 1733.
Mary daughter of Henry & Rachel Perrott born August ye 18. baptized Septem^r ye 23. 1733.
Harry Wood a Slave belonging to Bar Yates baptized Septem^r ye 30. 1733.

Bar Yates. Min^r

John Son of John & Elizabeth Humphries born Septem^r ye 24. baptized Octo. ye 7. 1733.
Hannah Jackson a Slave belonging to Christopher Robinson baptized October ye 7. 1733.
Edmund Son of Henry & Frances Mickleburrough born Septem^r ye 21. baptized Octo: ye 14. 1733.
Frances daughter of James & Catherine Gardner born Augst ye 5. baptized August ye 12 1733.
Thomas Son of Thomas & Catherine Price born Octo: ye 13. baptized Novem^r ye 4. 1733.
Elizabeth daughter of Nicolas & Anne Mealer born Novem^r 7. baptiz'd Novem^r 18 1733.
Mary a Slave belonging to Christopher Robinson baptized Novem^r ye 18 1733.
Mayo Son of Jonathan & Mary Brooks born Septem^r ye 17. baptized Novem^r ye 25. 1733.
John Son of William & Elizabeth Kidd born Novem^r ye 3. baptized Novem^r ye 25. 1733.
Frances daughter of George & Martha Chowning born Novem^r ye 6. baptized Novem^r ye 25. 1733.
Armistead Son of Armistead & Hannah Churchhill born Novem^r ye 25. baptized Decem^r 14. 1733.
Penelope daughter of Jno & Elizabeth Bream born Novem^r ye 8. baptized Decem^r 16 1733.
Mary daughter of Patrick & Anne Knight born Decem^r ye 7. baptized Decem^r 30 1733.
Elizabeth & Mildred daughters of Jacob & Mary Faulkner born Dec: 14. baptized Dec. 30 1733.
Sarah daughter of Matthew & Mary Crank born Decem^r ye 8. baptized Decem: 23 1733.
Keziah daughter of Joseph & Elizabeth Smith born Decem^r ye 16. baptized Jan'ry ye 13 1733.
Benjamine Son of Aquilla & Margrett Snelling born Decem^r ye 22. baptized Decem^r 30 1733.
Nicholas Son of Anthony & Mary Anne Collins born Feb'y ye 4. baptized Feb'y ye 10 1733.

Robert Son of John & Jane Goodwin born Decem' y' 30. baptized Jan'y y° 27 1733.
Betty daughter of Richard & Catherine Greenwood born Jan'y 15. baptized Jan'y y° 27. 1733.
Mary daughter of Jn° & Mary Henesey born Feb'y y° 12. baptized Feb'y y° 17 1733.
Mary daughter of George & Margrett Best born Jan'y y° 20. baptized Feb'y y° 17 1733.
John Son of Robert & Elizabeth Daniel born Feb'y y° 17. baptized March y° 10 1733.
John Son of Edward & Agnes Southern born Feb'y y° 13. baptized March y° 10 1733.
Mary daughter of Henry & Mary Daniel born Feb'y y° 12. baptized March y° 10 1733.
John Son of William & Jane Mountague born Feb'y y° 25. baptized March y° 10 1733.
Richard Son of William & Mary Bennet born Feb'y y° 6. baptized March y" 3. 1733.
Anne daughter of William & Anne Robinson born Feb'y y° 13. baptized March y" 3. 1733.
Benjamine Son of John Davis & Elizabeth his Wife born March y° 8. baptized March 24. 1733.
George Son of John & Judith Wortham born March y° 11. baptized March 24 1733.
John Son of John & Mary Crowdas born Feb'y 15. 1733. baptized March y° 31 1734.
William a Slave belonging to Edwin Thacker baptized March y° 31 1734.
Richard Cooper a Slave belonging to Edwin Thacker baptized March y° 31 1734.
Jane a slave belonging to John Walker baptized March y° 31 1734.
Mary daughter of Anthony & Mary Betson born March 28. baptized Ap: y° 10. 1734.
Sarah daughter of William & Judith Baldwin born March y° 31. baptized Ap. 28. 1734.
Lucy daughter of Charles & Frances Grymes born April y° 26. baptized May y° 6 1734.
Priscilla daughter of John & Susannah Boss born April y° 14. baptized May 4 1734.
Elizabeth daughter of John & Sarah Carrill born April y° 26. baptized May y° 19. 1734.
Jemima daughter of Randolph & Sarah Rhodes born May y° 1. baptized May y° 19. 1734.
William Son of Thomas & Mary Shaw born May y° 3. baptized May y° 26 1734.
Thomas Son of John & Johanna Blake born May y° 4. baptized May y° 12. 1734.
Elizabeth daughter of John & Mary Rice born May y° 7. baptized June y° 9 1734.
Frances daughter of Phillip & Elizabeth Brooks born May y° 20. baptized June y° 9. 1734.
Benjamine Son of Jonathan & Priscilla Johnson born June y° 1. baptized June y° 23. 1734.

Robert Wormeley Son of Landon & Elizabeth Carter born June ye 7. baptized June 27. 1734.
John Son of Charles & Mary Maderas born May ye 19. baptized June ye 10 1734.
Sabrina a Slave belonging to Edwin Thacker baptized June ye 30 1734.

Bar Yates Min^r.

Sarah daughter of John & Catherine Walker born June ye 30. baptized July ye 7th 1734.
Frances daughter of Edward & Martha Dillard born June ye 25. baptized July ye 10. 1734.
William Son of John & Catherine Macheal born June ye 15. baptized July ye 14. 1734.
William Son of Edward & Elizabeth Bristow born August 29 1734.
John Son of Jno & Mary Glen was born May 7th Baptiz'd June ye 30th. 1734.
Benjamin Son of Jno & Michal Williams born June 24th Baptiz'd June 30th 1734.
Elizabeth, Daughter of Charles & Elizth Fourget born June 23d. Baptiz'd August 16th 1734.
John Son of Jno & Rebeckah Kid, born August 2d. Baptiz'd August 16 1734.
Thomas Son of Jno & Rachel Chowning born July 13th Baptiz'd July 31st 1734.
Henry Son of William & Frances Thruston born July 22d. Baptiz'd August 3d. 1734.
Sarah Daughter of Willm & Judith Owen, born August 3d Baptiz'd Augst 3d. 1734.
Mary daughter of Henry & Sarah Brooks born Augst 10th Baptiz'd Augst 16th. 1734.
William Son of James & Chatharine Brown, Born Septem^r 23d. Baptiz'd Octr 13th 1734.
Susannah Daughter of Jno & Michal George Born Sepr 30th Baptiz'd Octr 13th 1734.
William Son of Willm & Elizth Wood, Born October 24th, Baptiz'd November 12th 1734.
George Son of George & Jane Goodwin Born Oct. 12th Baptiz'd Oct. 23d 1734.
Benjamin Son of   & Ann Jones Born Augst 25th 1734.
Paul Son of Paul & Susanna Phillpots born October 5th 1734.
John, Son of Abraham & Mary Wharton Born July 7th 1734.
Mical Daughter of Christopher & Ann Millar, Born Septr 19 1734.
Susannah, Daughter of Jno & Mary Berry, Born Octr 4th 1734.
Milecent, Daughter of Robt & Mary Daniel, Born Novr 18th Baptizd Decr 15th 1734.
Sarah, Daughter of George & Jane Blackley, Born Nov: 28th Baptiz'd Decr 15th 1734.
Ann, Daughter of Jno & Ann Dudley, Born Novr 4th Baptized Decr 1st 1734.
Rachel, Daughter of W^m and W^m and Ann Daniel born Nov. 9th Baptiz'd Dec. 22nd 1734.
Frances Daughter of Curtis & Ann Parrott born Decr 6th Baptiz'd Jan 5th 1734.

John Son of Robert & Mary Rogers born Decr 28th 1734.
Robert Son of John & Sarah Stamper born Decr 17th Baptiz'd Jan^ry 12th 1734.
Elizabeth, Daughter of W^m & Lucy Stapleton born Oct. 25th 1734.
Mary, Daughter of Jno & Ann Johnston born Nov. 5th 1734.
Catherine Daughter of Jno & Catherine Tuggle born Dec. 29. Baptiz'd Jan 26. 1734.
Lewis Son of Robt & Jane Dudley born Jan^ry 27th Baptiz'd Feb^ry 15th 1734.
Valentine Son of James & Ruth Mayo. born Feb^ry 2d Baptized Feb. 16th 1734.
William Son of W^m & Mary Southern born Decr 22d Baptiz'd Jan^ry 26th 1734.
Susanna Daughter of Churchhill and Sarah Blakey born Jan^ry 13th Baptiz'd Feb. 16 1734.
Mary Daughter of Andrew & Constant Hardee, born Jan^ry 19th Baptiz'd Jan: 26. 1734.
Abraham Son of James & Jane Daniel born Jan^ry 13th Baptiz'd Feb. 16th 1734.
Mary Daughter of Benjamine & Mary Pace born Jan^ry 20th Baptiz'd Feb. 16th 1734.
George a Slave belonging to Mrs Yates was Baptiz'd Feb^ry 16th 1734.
Elizabeth Daughter of James & Rebecka Hiptinstall born Ja'n^y 26th Baptiz'd Feb. 23rd 1734.
Peter Son of Charles & Jane Daniel Born January 30th Baptiz'd Feb: 23d 1734.
William Son of John & Sarah Owen Born January 25th Baptiz'd Feb. 23d 1734.
———— a Slave belonging to Mrs Wormley   Baptiz'd Feb. 23d 1734.

Jno Reade Min^r

Rebecka Daughter of Hugh & Ann Rouch Born Novem^r 25th 1734.
Susanna Daughter of William &   Goare Born feb. 2d Bapt. March 2d 1734.
Jeremiah Son of Robt & Eliz: Wilkins born Dec. 11th 1734.
Elizabeth Elizabeth Kate Sarah William Slaves belonging to Maj^r Edm^d Berkley, Baptiz'd March 2d 1734.
Joyce a Slave Belonging to Lewis Berkley Baptiz'd March 2d 1734.
Lucy Daughter of Christopher & Mary Robinson born Feb: 27th Baptiz'd March 5th 1734.
Lodowick Son of Robert & Sarah Parrott born Jan^ry 26th Baptiz'd feb^ry 16 1734.
James Son of W^m & Hannah Rhodes born Feb. 1st Baptiz'd March 2d 1734.
William Son of Crispin & Lettitia Shelton, born March 4th Bap. March 30th 1735.
Avarilla Daughter of W^m & Margrett Johnston born Mar. 7th Bap. March 30th 1735.
Barbee Son of Andrew & Elizabeth Davis born Feb: 2d Baptiz'd March 2 1734.
Charles Son of Charles & Mary Wood born March 24th Baptiz'd Ap: 20th 1735.

Ann daughter of Rich⁴ & Eliz^th George born March 18th Baptiz'd Ap: 20th 1735.
John Son of Edmund & Mary Day born March 10th Baptiz'd Ap: 13th 1735.
Judith Daughter of Stokely & Ann Towles born Ap 13. Baptized May 11th 1735.
Ann Daughter of Willm & Mary Gardiner born Ap: 8th Baptizd May 11th 1735.
Elizabeth Daughter of Willm & Hannah Pace born Ap. 18th Baptiz'd May 11th 1735.
John Son of Ignatius & Mary Tureman, born May 16th Baptiz'd June 1st 1735.
Samuel Son of Samuel & Mary Sorrow born May 5th Baptiz'd June 1th 1735.
Edmond Son of Tho' & Sarah Laughlin born June 21st Baptiz'd June 29th 1735.
Edward Son of Michael & Ann Reed born May 15th Baptiz'd June 8th 1735.
Benjamin Son of Jn° & Elizabeth Thruston born June 4th Baptiz'd July 13th 1735.
William Son of Jn° & Mary Lawsoe born May 21 1735.
William Son of Tho' & Lucretia Sanders born June 15th Baptiz'd July 27th 1735.
Andrew Son of W^m & Ann Anderson of Petsworth parish born July 4th Baptiz'd July 27th 1735.
Henry Son of Henry & Jone Snow born May 5th Baptiz'd May 25th 1735.
Elizabeth Daughter of Edward & Mary Clark born Aug^st 22d Baptiz'd Aug^st 31 1735.
Elizabeth Daughter of Caless & Marg^tt Brooks born Aug^st 10th Baptized August 31 1735.
James Son of John & Judith Wortham born Aug^st 23d 1735.
John Son of W^m & Frances Guttery born July 25th Baptiz'd Aug^st 24th 1735.
Rachel Daughter of Phillip & Eliz^th Brooks born July 26th Baptiz'd Aug^st 24th 1735.
Ann, Daughter of Duel & Judith Thurston born July 31. Baptiz'd Aug^st 24th 1735.
Charles Son of Tho' & Ann Lee Born Aug^st 10th Baptiz'd Aug^st 24 1735.
Henry Son of Rich⁴ & Catherine Greenwood born Aug^st 12th Baptiz'd Aug^st 24th 1735.
Thomas, Son of John & Amy Burck born Aug^st 11th Baptiz'd Sep^t 14th 1735.
Margarett, Daughter of Jn° & Margaret Southern Born Aug^st 18th Baptized Sep^t 14th 1735.
Jean, Daughter of James & Jean Dudley, Born July 10th 1735.
Oliver, Son of Willm & Eliz. Willis born Septr 2d Baptiz'd Octr 5th 1735.
Henry, Son of Henry & Frances Mickleburrough born Septr 9th Baptiz'd Oct. 5th 1735.
James Son of Thomas & Ann Berry born Septr 25th baptiz'd Octr 5th 1735.

John Son of W^m & Judith Owen born Octr 6th Baptiz'd Novr 13th 1735.
Ann, Daughter of Nicholas & Ann Meuler born Sept. 6th 1735.
Lewis, Son of Richard & Mabell Steevens born Sep^t 27th Baptiz'd Novr 9th 1735.
Leonard Son of Thos & Margrett Dawson born Octr 24th Baptiz'd Novr 2 1735.
Sarah, Daughter of Jno & Susanna Thomson born Novr 13th Baptiz'd Decr 7th 1735.
Mary Daughter of Willm & Jane Watts was born Sepr 14th Baptiz'd Novr 16th 1735.

   J. Reade Min^r.

Peter Rebeccah Alice Clara Slaves belonging to Christopher Robinson Baptiz'd Decr 26th 1735.
Sarah daughter of Jno & Johanna Blake born Novr 30th Baptiz'd Decr 21st 1735.
Eustace Son of Eustace & Ruth Howard born Decr 26th Baptiz'd Jan^ry 25th 1735.
Joseph Son of W^m & Judith Baldwin born Decr 21st Baptiz'd Jan^ry 18th 1735.
Sarah daughter of Henry & Rachel Parrett born Dec. 6th 1735.
Martha daughter of George & Martha Chowning born Jan^ry 17th 1735.
Penelope daughter of Jno & Eliz^th Brame born Novr 30th Baptiz'd Decr 28th 1735.
Thomas, Son of Henry & Frances Bueford born Novr 22d 1735.
Sarah, daughter of Jno & Ann Fearn born Jan^ry 28th Baptiz'd Feb. 1st 1735.
John, Son of Willm & Ann Yarrington born Feb. 22d 1735.
Thomas, Son of Thomas & Mary French born Jany 10th Baptiz'd Feb: 8th 1735.
William, Son of George & Eliz^th Gest born Jan^ry 11. Baptiz'd Feb. 8th 1735.
Thomas, illegitimate Son of Mercy Hornsby a Servt to James Crosbee born Feb: 14. Baptiz'd Feb 22nd 1735.
Thomas Son of Jno & Lucretia Greenwood, born Feb. 13. baptiz'd Feby 29th 1735.
Leonard, Son of Thos & Catherine Price born March 20th baptiz'd March 28th 1735.
Elizabeth, Daughter of Benjamine & Judith Davis born January 4th, baptiz'd 1735.
Ann Daughter of Geo. & Ann Wortham born Decr 22. Baptiz'd 1735.
Sarah Daughter of Grigg & Eliz^th Yarbrough born Feb. 20th Baptiz'd March 21 1735.
Jane, Daughter of Jno & Jane Goodwin born Feb. 27. Baptiz'd March 21 1735.
John Son of Patrick & Eliz^th Calliham born Jan^ry 1st. Baptiz'd March 21 1735.
Jane, Daughter of Willm & Frances Thurston born Feb. 20th Baptiz'd March 21 1735.

Elizabeth, Daughter of Daniel & Mary Moor, born March 21. Baptiz'd April 11 1736.

{ Given into the S. O. Ap 1736 } { Nicholas, Son of John & Catherine Tuggle born March 9th Baptiz'd april 11 1736.
Philip, Son of Thomas & Penelope Mountague born April 13th Baptiz'd Ap: 15 1736.
Willm Son of Henry a Slave belonging to Jn° Grimes Baptiz'd Ap: 25 1736. }

Sarah, Daughter of Chloe a Slave belonging to Jn° Grymes, Baptiz'd Ap: 25 1736.
Elizabeth, Daughter of Jn° & Elizth Humphries born Feb. 3d. Baptiz'd Feb. 22 1736.
Benjamine, Son of Randal & Sarah Rhodes born Ap: 8th Baptiz'd May 9th 1736.
Hester, Daughter of George & Jane Blackey, born Ap^l 6th. Baptiz'd May 9th 1736.
Judith, Daughter of Christopher & Mary Robinson born June 2. Baptiz'd June 10th 1736.
Ann, Daughter of Joseph & Elizth Smith born May 19th, Baptiz'd May 27th 1736.
Benjamine, Son of W^m & Ann Robinson born May 21st 1736.
George, Son of Samuel & Elizth Major born June 13th Baptiz'd July 11th 1736.
Paul Son of Henry & Sarah Brookes born June 14th Baptiz'd July 11th 1736.
Thomas, Son of John & Mary Hennesey, born July 9th. Baptiz'd July 11th 1736.
Betty, Daughter of William & Elizth Kidd, born June 5th Baptiz'd July 11th 1736.
William, Son of Charles & Judith Gunter, born Augst 5th Baptiz'd Augst 22d 1736.
Joseph, Son of Jn° & Elizth White, born July 18th Baptiz'd Augst 22nd 1736.
Jane, Daughter of James & Mary Bristow, born July 22d Baptiz'd Augst 1st 1736.
Judith, Daughter of Jn° & Ann Robinson born Sept. 8th Baptiz'd Sept. 14th 1736.
Henry Son of John & Mary Goare, born Sept. 10th Baptiz'd Sept. 26 1736.

{ Given into ye Secret: off Octr 1736 } { Christopher, Son of Robt & Eliz. Daniel, born Sept. 27. Baptiz'd Octo^r 8th 1736.
Oliver, Son of Jn° & Margrett Towles, born Sept. 1st. Baptiz'd 1736.
Sarah, Daughter of Jn° & Elizth Blake born Sept. 7th 1736. }

Mary, Daughter of Edwd & Martha Dillard born Sept: 28th. Baptiz'd Oct. 24, 1736.
Susanna, Daughter of Jn° & Elizth Davis born Oct. 17th Baptiz'd Oct. 30th 1736.
Ruth, Daughter of Robt & Betty Chowning, born Octr 9th Baptiz'd Oct: 21. 1736.
Willm Son of W^m & Mary Mullins born Octr 8th. Baptiz'd Novr 14th 1736.

Susanna, Daughter of Rich^d & Elizth George born Octr 28th. Baptiz'd Nov. 14th 1736.
Frances, Daughter of Christopher & Mary Ammon born Octr 28th Baptiz'd Nov^o 14th 1736.
Charles Thomas, a Slave belonging to Sarah Yates, Baptiz'd Novr 21 1736.
Lettice a Slave belonging to Sarah Yates Baptiz'd Novr 21 1736.
John Son of James & Martha Mayo born 9^{br} 14th & bapt. 9^{br} 14th 1736.
Hannah daughter of William & Elizabeth Backford born 9^{br} 9th & bapt. 10^{br} 10th 1736.
Henry Son of Joseph & Mary Tuggle born 9^{ber} 20th & bapt 10^{br} 10th.
Anny ye daughter of John Rachel Chowning born 10^{ber} 10th & bapt. 10^{br} 26th 1736.
Mary ye daughter of Charles & Mary Wood born born Jan 2d & bapt Feb. 4th 1736.
Benjamin ye Son of Robert & Mary Daniel born January 4th 1736.
Edwin ye Son of Daniel & Mary Basket born 10^{ber} 27th & bapt. Feb. 4th 1736.
Mary ye daughter of William & Elizabeth Wood born Jan. 29th bapt. 4th Feb. 1736.
Ruth ye daughter of Richard & Catharin Bushrod Wood born Jan. 2d & bapt. Feb. 11th 1736.
William ye Son of William & Mary Fretwell born January 31th 1736.
Thomas ye Son of Phillip & Cassandra Warwick born January 27th 1736.
James ye Son of Duel & Mary Kidd born Feb 10th & bapt. March 4th 1736.
Molly ye daughter of Ann Whistler a mulatto born 10^{ber} 18th 1736.
Catherine ye daughter of Robert & Sarah Parrott born March 23th & bapt. April 17th 1737.
Jane ye daughter of William & Jane Mountague born April 4th 1737.
Elizabeth daughter of Paul & Susanna Phillpots born May ye 27th 1737.
John ye Son of John & Sarah Stamper born April 14th & bapt. May 6th 1737.
Sarah ye daughter of William & Sarah Williams born May 5th & bapt. May 27th 1737.
George ye Son of Benjamine & Judith Kidd born May 3d & bapt. May 27th 1737.
William ye Son of Henry & Jochebed Nash born May 1st & bapt. May 27th 1736.
Edward ye Son of Robert & Elizabeth Bristow born August 13th 1736.
Martha ye daughter of Abraham & Elizabeth Wilson born Feb. 6th 1736.
Machen ye Son of John & Judith Wortham born February 25th 1736.
Charles ye Son of Charles & Jane Daniel was born Marth 2d 1736.
John ye Son of John & Mary Lawson was born March 4th 1736.
Mary ye daughter of William & Lucy Goar was born Feb: 1st 1736.

Judith daughter of Hugh & Ann Roach was born 9^{ber} 29th 1736.
Elizabeth daughter of John & Susannah Curtis was born March 18th 1736.
John ye Son of Christopher & Ann Miller was born Feb. 14th 1736.
Ann ye daughter of Aquilla & Margaret Snelling was born March 14th 1736.
Thomas & William twin Sons of Thomas & Hannah Lawson was born January 17th 1736.
Ann ye daughter of Edmund & Mary Day was born 10^{ber} 26th 1736.
Lewis ye Son of William & Elizabeth Hackney was born Feb. 4th 1736.
George ye Son of David & Diana Barrick was born March 4th 1736.
James ye Son of John & Ann Johnson was born March 28th 1737.
John ye Son of Benjamin & Judith Davis was born April 2d 1737.
Alford ye Son of John & Sarah Boss was born Jan. 1st & bapt. June 3rd 1737.
Mary ye daughter of John & Ann Dudley was born July 4th & bapt. July 31th 1737.
Ann ye daughter of John & Mary Matthews was born July 15th 1737.
Clara daughter of John & Catherine Walker was born 7^{ber} 7th & bapt 7^{ber} 9th 1737.
Charles ye Son of Charles & Mary Madarius was born May 9th & bapt. July 8th 1737.
Isaac ye Son of Peter & Elizabeth Hendson was born June 4th & bapt. July 8th 1737.
James ye Son of James & Catharine Brown was born June 13th & bapt. June 18th 1737.

Unto ye Secret: Office 1737.
{
Joseph ye Son of Andrew & Constance Hardee was born June 27th & bapt. July 8th 1737.
Agatha ye daughter of John & Agatha Hardee was born June 30th & bapt. July 8th 1737.
Griffin ye Son of John & Catherine Tuggle was born August 5th & bapt. August 28th 1737.
John ye Son of John & Michal George was born August 14th & bapt. August 25th 1737.
Ann ye daughter of Benjamin & Mary Pace was born August 20th & bapt 25th 1737.
John ye Son of Caleb & Margaret Brooks was born 7^{ber} 2d & bapt: 7^{ber} 9th 1738.
}

Elizabeth Daughter of Ralph & Sarah Wormley born Sepr ye 3d bapt ye 18th 1737.
Ann Daughter of Thomas & Christian Sanders born ye 25th of Sepr Baptized Novr ye 6th 1737.
Jane Daughter of William & Frances Thurston born ye 30th of Sepr Baptized Octo^r ye 23rd 1737.
Ratlif Son of Richard & Michal Jowel born ye 23d of Sepr 1737.
Ann Daughter of William & Ann Daniel born ye 18 of Octo^r Baptized Novr ye 20th 1737.
Sarah Daughter of Richard   Wright born ye 9th of Sepr 1737.
Frances Daughter of William & Frances Guthery born ye 21st of Sepr Baptized Octo^r ye 2d 1737.

James Son of Henry & Susanna Mickleburrough born y⁰ 18th of Octo^r
Ruth Daughter of Richard & Catharine Street born ye 26th of Octo^r
William Son of William & Judith Owen born y⁰ 4th of Nov^r
} Bap. Nov. 13th 1737.

Griffin Son of Grigg & Elizabeth Yarbrough born y⁰ 28th of Novr Baptized Dec. 4th 1737.
Ann Daughter of Thos & Mary Shaw born y⁰ 10th of March 1736.
James Son of Hugh & Elizabeth Martin born y⁰ 12th Jan^r 1736.
Frances Daughter of John & Ann Willcock born y⁰ 11. of March 1736.
John Son of Joseph & Mary Rowe born y⁰ 5th of Decem^r 1735.
George Son of Andrew & Elizabeth Davis born y⁰ 7th of March 1737.
Francis Son of Rich^d & Mabell Steevens born y⁰ 1st of Aug^st 1737.
John Son of John & Ann Humphris born y⁰ 11th of Decem^r 1737.
Richard Son of John & Mary Steevens born ye 6th of Decem^r 1737.
Humphry Son of Robert & Mary Rogers born ye 28th Nov. 1737.
Richard Son of Arthur & Jane Dye born y⁰ 5th of Decem^r baptized ye 5th of Feby 1737.
Elizabeth Daughter of Henry & Rachel George born Decem^r y⁰ 8th baptized Jan'y ye 8th 1737.
Anny Daughter of William & Ann Yarrington born Jan^ry y⁰ 11th baptized Jan^ry ye 29th 173⅞.
Jane Daughter of William & Margaret Johnston born Jan^ry y⁰ 21st bap^d ye 22 Died ye 22. 173⅞.
Mary Daughter of Edmund & Mary Berkeley born Jan^ry y⁰ 15th baptized Jan^ry ye 30th 173⅞.
Ann Daughter of Robert & Mary Williams born Jan^ry ye 21st baptized Feb^ry ye 19th 173⅞.
Lucy Daughter of Armistead & Hannah Churchhill born Jan^ry ye 17th baptized Feb^ry y⁰ 8th 173⅞.
Robert Son of George & Jane Blackley born Jan^ry ye 29th baptized Feb^ry ye 19th 173⅞.
John Son of Thomas & Catherine Price born Feb^ry ye 26th baptized March ye 22nd 173⅞.
John Son of John & Elizabeth Blake born Feb^ry ye 21st baptized March ye 19th 173⅞.
Charles Son of John & Ann Ginkins born Feb^ry ye 28th baptized March ye 26 1738.
Mary Daughter of Thomas & Mary Shelton bern Feb^ry ye 21st 173⅞.
William Son of Richard & Dorrity Gaines born March y⁰ 3d baptized March ye 19th 173⅞.
Christopher Son of Christopher & Mary Robinson born March ye 9th bap^e March ye 20th 173⅞.
Richard Son of Saml & Elizabeth Major born March ye 24th baptized April ye 2d 1738.
Thomas Son of John & Ann Price born March ye 13. baptized April ye 2d 1738.
Diana Daughter of John & Mary Crowdas born Feb^ry ye 25th baptized April ye 2 1738.

Tholomiah Son of Randal & Mary Rhodes born March yᵉ 15th baptized yᵉ 2d 1738.
Christopher Son of John & Anne Robinson born April yᵉ 2d baptized April yᵉ 10th 1738.
Judith Daughter of Edward & Mary Clark born March yᵉ 30th baptized April yᵉ 9th 1738.
William Son of Thoˢ & Sarah Tignor born March yᵉ 9th baptized 173⅛.
Jane Daughter of Henry & Jone Snow born March yᵉ 10th 1738.
William Son of William & Patience Colley born March yʳ 11th 1738.
James Son of John & Rebeckah Kidd born March yʳ 30th baptized April yᵉ 23d 1738.
Josiah Son of William & Elizabeth Wallis born March yʳ 31st baptized April yᵉ 23d 1738.
James Son of William & Mary Gardiner born April yʳ 27th baptized June yᵉ 4th 1738.
Henry Son of Richard & Elizabeth Allin born May yᵉ 28th baptized June yᵉ 4th 1738.
Abraham Son of John & Agatha Warwick born May yᵉ 19th baptized June yᵉ 4th 1738.
Ruthe Daughter of Edmund & Martha Ditton born May yᵉ 30th baptized June yᵉ 18th. 1738.
Frances Daughter of George & Mary Guest born Jane yᵉ 5th. baptized June 26th 1738.
Catherine Daughter of Churchhill & Sarah Blakey born July yʳ 2d. baptized July yᵉ 16. 1738.
James Son of James & Martha Mayo born Augˢᵗ 16th. baptized Augˢᵗ yᵉ 27th 1738.
Johannah Daughter of Thoˢ & Keziah Maxwell born Augˢᵗ yᵉ 29th. bapᵈ Sepʳ yᵉ 10th 1738.
Henry Son of John & Ann Hutson born Augˢᵗ yᵉ 13th baptized Sepʳ yᵉ 17th 1738.
Richard Son of John & Susannah Tomson born Sepʳ yᵉ 9th baptized Sepʳ yᵉ 17th. 1738.
Nathan Son of David & Elizabeth Snodgrass born April 28th 1738.
Hezekiah Son of Wᵐ & Hannah Rhods born June yᵉ 8th. baptized July 9th 1738.
Daniel Son of Seth & Mary Hunter born Sepʳ yᵉ 22. baptized 1738.
Sarah, Daughter of Wᵐ & anne Robinson born yᵉ Octoʳ 27th. 1738.
Benjamin Son of Joseph & Elizabeth Smith born 25th Octʳ 1738.
Benjamin Son of John & Mary Rhodes born March 18th. 1738.
Thomas Son of Wᵐ & Ann Segar born Augˢᵗ yᵉ 27. baptized Octoʳ yᵉ 8 1738.
Catherine Daughter of Thomas & Mary Trench born Sepʳ yᵉ 15th. bapᵈ Octoʳ 29. 1738.
Susana Daughter of Robᵗ & mary Trueman born 8ᵇʳ yᵉ 15th. bapᵈ Octoʳ 29 1738.
Ann Daughter of Patrick & Elizabeth Calcham born Octoʳ yᵉ 2d bapᵈ Octoʳ 19. 1738.
Mary Daughter of Alexander & Anna Snelling born Octoʳ 25th 1738.
Elizabeth Daughter of William & Mary Mullins born July 15th. bapᵈ Augˢᵗ 6. 1738.

John Son of Hugh & Elizabeth Martin born July y[e] 10th. bap[d] Aug[st] 6. 1738.
Margaret Daughter Benjamin & Judith Davis born Oct[r] 27th. 1738.
Robert Howrd born Novem[r] 15th 1738.
Ann Daughter of Tho[s] & Elizabeth Eliot born Oct[r] 25th. Bap[d] Nov[r] 19th 1738.
Elizabeth Camel daughter of Elizabeth Ammon born Oct[r] y[e] 2d. bap[d] Nov[r] 19th. 1738.
John Son of Augustine & Mary Owen born Novem[r] y[e] 20th bap[d] Decem[r] 31th. 1738.
Edward Son of John & Judith Wortham born Nov[r] y[e] 29th. 1738.
Cuffly Son of Henry & Sarah Brooks born Nov[r] y[e] 22. bap[d] Dec[r] 11th 1738.
Agatha Daughter of Ave Daniel born Decem[r] y[e] 22. bap[d] Jan[ry] y[e] 25th 173$\frac{8}{9}$.
William Son of John & Mary Brooks born Nov[r] y[e] 26th. 1738.
Mary Daughter of Edmund & Mary Day born Dec[r] 8th. bap[d] Dec[r] y[e] 25th 1738.
Mary Daughter of William & Rachel Griffin born Dec[r] 12th Bap[d] Jan[ry] 21th 1738.
Sarah Daughter of John & Agatha Hardee born Dec[r] y[e] 6th bap[d] Jan[ry] 5th. 173$\frac{8}{9}$.
Averilla Daughter of John & Margaret Southern born Dec[r] 25th. bap[d] Jan[ry] 21th 173$\frac{8}{9}$.
Catherine Daughter of Tho[s] & Penelope Mountague born Dec[r] 19th. bap[d] Jan[ry] 9th 173$\frac{8}{9}$.
George Son of Philip & Casandra Warwick born Dec[r] y[e] 13th. bap[d] Jan[ry] 9th 173$\frac{8}{9}$.
Marlow Son of Robert & Jane Dudley born Nov[r] y[e] 20th. bap[d] Jan[ry] 1st. 173$\frac{8}{9}$.
Richard Son of Edward & Elizabeth Bristow born Jan[ry] 7th bap[d] Jan[ry] 28. 173$\frac{8}{9}$.
Lucy daughter of Armistead & Hannah Churchhill born Jan[ry] 17th bap[d] Feb. 8. 173$\frac{8}{9}$.
Elizabeth daughter of Charles & Mary Wood born Feb[ry] 15. bap[d] March 4th. 173$\frac{8}{9}$.
Garret Son of Robert & Elizabeth Daniel born Jan[ry] 20th bap[d] Feb[ry] 19th. 173$\frac{8}{9}$.
John Son of William & Mary Fretwel born Feb[ry] 16th. bap[d] March 4th 173$\frac{8}{9}$.
Sarah Daughter of Tho[s] & Ann Lee born Feb[ry] 27th. bap[d] March 4th. 173$\frac{8}{9}$.
Powell Son of John & Sarah Stamper born March 20th bap[d] April 25th 173$\frac{8}{9}$.
Mary Daughter of Andrew & Elizabeth Davis born 11th of Feb[ry] 173$\frac{8}{9}$.
Elizabeth Daughter of Charles & Penelope Lee born Feb[ry] y[e] 12th. bap[d] March 4th 173$\frac{8}{9}$.
Elizabeth daughter of Harry & Jane Sears born Jan[ry] 8th bap[d] April 15th 1739.
John Son of John & Elizabeth Davis born Feb[ry] 26th bap[d] 18th March 173$\frac{8}{9}$.

Frances Daughter of Russel & Anne Hill born Feb^{ry} 25th bap 1738.
John Son of John & Mary Henesey born March 12th bap^d March 25th 1739.
William Son of George & Sarah Halcomb born March 27th 1739.
Charles Son of Robert & Betty Chowning born March 10th bap^d March 25th 1739.
John Son of Edward & Martha Dillard born March 30th bap'd May 5th 1739.
Sarah Daughter of John & Ann Johnson born April ye 21st 1739.
John Son of John & Rachel Chowning born April ye 1st bap^d April 15th 1739.
Leonard Son of Honnor Renand born April 30th 1739.
Henry Son of William & Elizabeth Beuford born April 17th bap^d May 6th 1739.
William Son of James & Elizabeth Dunlevy born April 29th 1739.
Elizabeth Daughter of Thos & Catherine Cheaney born May ye 1st bap^d May 4th 1739.
John Son of James & Isabel Gibson born May ye 11th 1739.
Benjamin Son of William & Margaret Johnson born May 3d bap^d May 27th 1739.
Catherine & Elizabeth Daughters of W^m & Jane Mountague born May 24th 1739.
Margaret Daughter of Duel & Mary Kid born May 16th bap^d June 17th 1739.
Samuel Son of James & Catherine Brown born May 28th bap^d June 17th 1739.
James Son of Charles & Jane Daniell born June 15th 1739.
Lucy Daughter of Patrick & Ann Knight born May 28th bap^d July 22d 1739.
Rhoda Daughter of Andrew & Constant Hardee born July 9th bap^d July 29th 1739.
Thomas Son of John & Ann Fearn born July ye 16th 1739.
Joseph Son of Joseph & Mary Tugle born July ye 2d bap^d July ye 29th 1739.
Samuel Son of William & Elizabeth Wood born July ye 24th, bap^d Augst ye 19th 1739.
James Son of James & Elizabeth Scrosby born Augst ye 13th bap^d Sepr ye 5th 1739.
James Son of Mary Ratford born Augst ye 13th 1739.
John Son of John & Susana Serd born Sepr ye 4th bap^d Sepr ye 9th 1739.
Lucy Daughter of John & Johanne Blakes born March 25th bap^d April 29th 1739.
John Son of John & Mary Matthews born Septr ye 19th 1739.
Benjamine Son of Paul & Margerret Phillpotts born Octo^r ye 13th 1739.
John Son of Rhodes & Elizabeth Geeenwood born Novr ye 19th Bap^d ye 12th of Decem^r 1739.
Benjamin Son of Benjamin & Judith Kidd born Novr 18th Bap^d 23d of Decem^r 1739.
Ann Daughter of Daniel & Sarah Guthrie born Novr 12th 1739.

Jane Daughter of Henry & Betty Daniel born Nov' ye 13th Bap^d Decr 5th 1739.
James Son of Christopher & Frances Curtis born Decem^r ye 6th Bap^d Decr ye 22d 1739.
Peter Son of Thomas & Judith Brumell born Decr ye 25th 1739.
Mary Daughter of William & Mary Mullens born Jan^ry 30th Bap^d Feb^ry 24th 1739.
Elias Son of Robt & Mary Williams born Feby 9th Bap^d Feby ye 24 173 9/10.
Peter Son of Robt & Eliz^a Daniel born Feby ye 6th 173 9/10.
Robert Son of John & Jane Aldin born Feb'y ye 17th 173 9/10.
Thos Son of George & Ann Wortham born Octo^r ye 27th 1739.
Randal Rodes Son of Randal & Mary Rodes was born Fe^bry ye 18th bap^d Feby ye 24 173 9/10.
Mary Shaw was born, Daughter of Thos & Mary Shaw January 13th 173 9/10.
Mary, Daughter of Charles & Mary Medarst was born Dec^nb 7th & Bap. Feb^ry ye 3d 173 9/10.
Mary, Daughter of John & Sarah Doss was born Jan^ry 3d 173 9/10.
Hugh Son Hugh & Ann Roach was born Feb^ry 6th 173 9/10.
Martha Daughter of John & Jane Blakey was born January 4th 173 9/10.
John Son of Henry & Jane Sears was born Dec^mbr 24th Bapt^d Jan^ry 25th 1740.
James Son of John & Ann Croffield was born Jan^ry 25th Bapt^d Feb^ry 15. 1740.
Martha, Daughter of Edward & Martha Dillard was born Jan^ry 8. Bapt^d Feb^ry 23rd 1740.
Leonard Son of John & Michal George was born Feb^ry 28. Bapt'd March 16 1740.
Thomas Son of Charles & Jane Daniel was born Decem^ber 11th & Bapt^d Feb^ry 3rd 1740.
William Son of Phillip & Cassandra Warwick was born March 6th Bapt^d March 8th 1740.
John Price Son of John & Ann Price was born March 11th Bapt^d April 6th 1740.
William Son of William & Frances Gutery was born March 16. Bapt^d April 6th 1740.
Ann Daughter of Richard & Elizabeth Allen was born March 28th Bapt^d May 18th 1740.
Martha Daughter of Edmund & Martha Dillon was born Aprill 14th 1740.
Jane Daughter of Thomas & Catharine Price was born April 11th Bapt^d May 2d 1740.
John Son of James & Martha Mayo was born April 29th Bapt^d May 18th 1740.
Sarah Daughter of John & Mary Breame was born April 9th 1740.
Elizabeth Daughter of William & Judith Owen was born April 6th 1740.
Oliver Son of Hugh & Elizabeth Martin was born April 7th 1740.
William Son of David & Dianah Berrick was born May 24th 1740.
Thomas Son of Thomas & Mary Shelton was born May 2nd 1740.

Charles Son of William & Patience Colley was born Nov^mb 11th 1739 Bapt^d May 14th 1740.
Ann Daughter of Jacob & Ann Acre was born May 20th Bapt^d June 8th 1740.
James Son of George & Elizabeth Gest was born May ye 9th 1740.
Catharine Daughter of Charles & Penelope Lee was born May 12th & Bapt^d June 8th 1740.
Thomas Son of Edward & Elizabeth Whitaker was born June 24 1740.
John Son of John & Susanna Williams was born June 7th Bapt^d June 8th 1740.
John Son of Thomas & Kezia Maxwell was born June 8th Bapt^d July 6th 1740.
John Son of Henry & Ann Bohannan was born Sep^mber 17th 1740.
William Son of William & Mary Gardiner was born July 30th Bapt^d August 10. 1740.
John Son of Edward & Mary Clarke was born July 6th 1740.
Richard Son of Andrew & Elizabeth Davis was born August 17th 1740.
Mary Daughter of Cary & Ann Smith was born Augt 8th Bapt^d Aug^st 24 1740.
Elizabeth Daughter of Richard & Sarah Wait was born Augt 15th 1740.
Elizabeth Daughter of John & Agatha Warwick was born Augt 6 1740.
Richard Son of Richard & Catharine Street was born Sep^mbr 22d Bapt^d Oc^ber 12th 1740.
Robert Son of Robert & Dorothea Brownley was born Sep^br 18th 1740.
Agnes daughter of John & Constance Uris was born Sep^ber 16th 1740.
George Son of Richard & Sarah English was born Sep^mber 26th 1740.
Judith Daughter of Joseph & Elizabeth Smith was born Sep^ber 18th 1740.
William Son of John & Lucretia Greenwood was born Sep^ber 28th Bap^t October 10. 1740.
Frances Daughter of William & Frances Thurston was born October 6th 1740.
Sarah Daughter of John & Rebekeh Kid was born Oct^ber 3d Bapt^d Nov^mber 2d 1740.
Martha Daughter of John & Mary Smith was born Nov^ber 12th 1740.
Samuel Son of John Judith Wortham born April ye 7th 1740.
Absolom Son of William & Elizabeth Hackney was born Oct^ber 7 1740.
Daniel Son of Daniel & Hannah Stringer was born Oct^ber 13th 1740.
Sarah Daughter William & Mary Southern was born Oct. 31st & Bapt. Nov^ber 23 1740.
John Son of William & Hannah Pace was born Oct^ber 31st & Bapt^d No^ber 23d 1740.
Augustine Son of Augustine & Mary Owen was born No^ber 1. & bapt. Nov^ber 23rd 1740.
Simon Son of Thomas & Sarah Laughlin was born Nov^ber 18th Bapt 24th 1740.

Frances Daughter of Will & Ann Daniel was born Nov^{ber} 9. Bapt Dec^{ber} 5th 1740.

Elizabeth Daughter of William & Betty Wallis was born Nov^{ber} 3. & Bapt Dec^{ber} 14th 1740.

Sarah Daughter of Samuel & Elizabeth Major was born Dec^{mber} 18th 1740.

George Son of George & Jane Blakley was born Dec^{ber} the 5th. Bapt. 14th 1740.

Robert Son of Robert & Jane Dudley was born Dec^{ber} the 6th 1740.

Mary Daughter of William & Elizabeth Davis was born Dec^{ber} 9th. Bapt Jan^{ry} 25 1740.

William Son of John & Martha Broocks was born Dec^{ber} 13th. & Bapt^d 21st 1740.

Stephen Son of William & Margeret Johnson was born Feb^{ry} y^e 1st Bapt^d March 14. 174$\frac{0}{1}$.

John Son of David & Ann Condon Ann Daughter of David & Ann Condon were born Feb^{ry} y^e 20th 174$\frac{0}{1}$.

John Son of Jonathan & Mary Hearin born Feb^{ry} 15th 174$\frac{0}{1}$.

Henry Son of Henry & Beatey Daniel born March 7th Bapt. March 29 174$\frac{0}{1}$.

James Son of W^m & Jane Mountague born Feb^{ry} 18th Bapt^d March 8th 174$\frac{0}{1}$.

& Susanna Daughter of Charles & Mary Wood born March y^e 15th Bap^t 29 174$\frac{0}{1}$.

Robert Chowning Son of Robert & Betty Chowning born March 2d Bapt March 29th 174$\frac{0}{1}$.

Ann Daughter of Eustace & Ruth Howard born March 8th Bapt. March 29 174$\frac{0}{1}$.

Hezekiah Son of John & Mary Rhodes born Jan^{ry} y^e 20th 174$\frac{0}{1}$.

Katherine Daughter of Robert & Mary Daniel born Feb^{ry} y^e 27th 174$\frac{0}{1}$.

Catherine Daughter of John & Catherine Tugle born Feb^{ry} 22nd Bap^d March 29th 1741.

Nathaniel Son of Rich^d & Elizabeth Steevens born Feb'y 28th Bap^d April 12th 1741.

Anne Daughter of John & Mary Cloudus born March 12th 174$\frac{0}{1}$.

Frankey Daughter of Constant Daniel born March 31st Bap^d April 19th 1741.

James Son of Patrick & Eliz^a Callaham born April 5th Bap^d April 19th 1741.

William Son of John & Eliz^a Davis born March 30th Bap^d April 12th 1741.

Benjamine Son of Edwd & Eliz. Bristow born April 15th Bap^d April 26th 1741.

Robert Son of Robert & Eliz. Daniel born May 2d. Bap^d May 10th 1741.

John Son of James & Mary Overstreet born April ye 4th Bap^d May 10th 1741.

Elizabeth Daughter of James & Agatha Jones born April 16th Bap^d May 10th 1741.

Mary Daughter of Thos & Dorothy Chilton born April 12th Bap^d 1741.

Anner Daughter of John & Susanna Thomson born April 14th 1741.

William Son of Henry & Eliz. Baden born April ye 27th Bap^d May 24th 1741.
John Son of John & Agatha Hardee born April ye 9th Bap^d May ye 10th 1741.
George Son of William & Mary Richeson born May ye 4th Bap^d May ye 31st 1741.
Rebecka Daughter of William & Mary Fretwell born May ye 23d. Bap^d May ye 31st 1741.
George Son of John & Ann Hudson born May ye 12th Bap^d June ye 21st 1741.
Henry Son of William & Eliz: Chowning born June 21st Bap^d July 12th 1741.
George Son of John & Ann Humphrys born May ye 19th 1741.
John Son of Jacob & Ann Acre born Augst ye 10th 1741.
William Son of John & Mary Matthews born Augst ye 21st 1741.
George Son of James & Ann Compton born Augst ye 21st 1741.
John Son of John & Sarah Stamper born Augst 17th Bap^d Sepr 13th 1741.
Lodowick Son of Thos & Sarah Tuggle born Sepr ye 14th. Bap^d Octo^r ye 4th 1741.
Sarah Daughter of John & Rachel Chowning born Augst ye 1st Bap^d Augst 23d 1741.
James Son of William & Eliz^a Wood born Augst ye 8th Bap^d Augst 23d 1741.
Henry Son of William & Mary Purcel born July ye 16th Bap^d Augst 23d 1741.
Mary Daughter of Obediah & Sarah Daniel born Sep^t 19th Bap^d Octo^r 4th 1741.
Jane Daughter of John & Mary Henesey born Sepr ye 23d Bap^d Octo^r ye 4 1741.
Luse Daughter of William & Eliz^a Hackney born Sepr ye 11th 1741.
Andrew Son of Andrew & Constance Hardee born Octo^r ye 10th Bap^d Octo^r 25th 1741.
Christopher Son of William & Ann Robinson born Novr ye 9th Bap^d 1741.
Sarah Daughter of John [&] Judith Wortham born Novr ye 14th 1741.
Elizabeth Daughter of William & Dorothy Parrott born Decr 13th Bap^d Decem^r 27th 1741.
Tomson Son of Jedediah & Catherine Bristow born Decr 14th 1741.
Thomas Son of Joseph & Mary Tugle born Decem^r 15th Bap^d Decr 17th 1741.
John Son of John & Mary Lawson born Jan^{ry} ye 3d Bap^d Jan^{ry} ye 31st 1741.
John & Sarah children of Thos & Lucretia Sanders born Jan^{ry} ye 18th Bap^d Jan^{ry} 31st 1741.
Elizabeth Daughter of John & Susanna Serd born Jan^{ry} ye 16th Bap^d Feb^{ry} 28th 174½.
Sarah Daughter of Edm^d & Mary Berkeley born Jan^{ry} ye 27th Bap^d 174½.
Mary Daughter of James & Elizabeth Dunlevy born March ye 11th 174½.

Sarah Daughter of Henry & Elizabeth Brooks born Feb^ry ye 9th 1741/2.
George Son of Edward & Mary Clark born Aug^st ye 11th 1742.
Catherine Daughter of John & Ann Prill born April ye 7th 1742.
Dorothy daughter of Richard & Phebe Jones born March 14th 1741/2.
Mary Daughter of John & Susanna Williams born May 6th Baptized May 23d 1742.
Catherine Daughter of Thos & Catherine Cheney born May 5th Bap^d May 23d 1742.
John Son of Edmund & Martha Ditton born May ye 21st 1742.
Elizabeth Daughter of John & Jane Alldin born May ye 23d 1742.
William Son of Thos & Ann Lee born May 16th Bap^d May ye 24th 1742.
Elizabeth & Sarah Daughters of Daniel & Hannah Stringer born July 5th Bap^d 1742.
William Son of William & Hannah Pace born August ye 6th 1742.
Jane Daughter of Samuel & Ann Wood born August ye 21st Bap^d Sepr 5th 1742.
Bernard or Barnit Son of James & Elizabeth Meacham born Aug^st 27th Bap^d Sep. 26th 1742.
Ann Daughter of William & Elizabeth Wood born Sepr ye 11th Bap^d Sepr 26th 1742.
Reuben Son of George & Jane Blackly born Sepr ye 6th Bap^d Sepr 26 1742.
Thomas Son of Thos & Kezia Maxwell born Septem^r ye 7th Bap^d Octo^r 1742.
William Son of Augustine & Mary Owen born Septem^r 20th Bap^d Novr 7th 1742.
Letice Daughter of Thos & Rachel Brooks born Octo^r 11th Bap^d Novr 7th 1742.
William Son of John & Mary Henesey born Octo^r 31st Bap^d Novr 7th 1742.
Henry Son of James & Isabell Gibson born Octr 9th Bap^d Octr 10th 1742.
Sarah Daughter of Bartho^o & Eliz^a Yates born Octo^r 29th bap^d Nov^ber 1742.
James Son of George & Mary Lee born Octr 6th bap^d Octr 8th 1742.
Sarah Daughter of Robert & Dorothea Bromley born Octr 11th 1742.
Elizabeth Daughter of Charles & Mary Medaris born Octo^br 17th Bap^d Dec 2nd 1742.
Sarah Daughter of Barth^o & Elizabeth Yates born Octo^br 29th Bap^d Novr 11th 1742.
Philiman Son of Joshua & Ann Jones born Novr 9th Bap^d 1742.
Benjamine Son of Daniel & Sarah Ball born Novr 22d 1742.
David Son of David & Dianna Berrick born Decem^r ye 1st 1742.
Elizabeth Daughter of William & Mary Jones born Decem^r 10th Bap^d 1742.
Jane Daughter of William & Mary Mullins born May ye 30th Bap^d June 13th 1742.
Micajah Son of Thos & Mary Shelton born June 20th Bap^d July 4th 1742.

Reuben Son of Rich^d & Elizabeth Allin born July ye 18th Bap^d Augst 15th 1742.
Francis Son of John & ——— White born Decem^r ye 5th 1742.
Jacob Son of William & Elizabeth Hackney born Decem^r 24th 1742.
Margaret Daughter of William & Frances Gutherie born Octo^r 9th. Bap^d Novr 7th 1742.
John Son of John & Mary Deagle born Jan^{ry} 11th 1742.
Mary Daughter of Edward & Eliz^a Sanders born Jan^{ry} 11th 1742.
Michal Son Robert & Eliz^a Wake born Jan^{ry} 7th 1742.
Lucy Daughter of Thomas & Joyce Dudley born Jan^{ry} 4th 1742.
John Son of John & Mary Saunders born Jan^{ry} 20th. Bap^d Jan^{ry} 30th 1742.
Benjamin Son of W^m & Mary Greenwood born Jan^{ry} 16th. Bap^d Jan^{ry} 30th 1742.
Ann Daughter of W^m & Frances Thurston born Jan^{ry} 14th. Bap^d Jan^{ry} 30th 1742.
Elizabeth Daughter of James & Catherine Brown born Jan^{ry} 4th. Bap^d Jan^{ry} 30th 1742.
William Son of William & Lucretia Cooper born Feb^{ry} 13th 1742.
William Son of John & Christian Boss born Febuary 7th 1742.
Ann Daughter of Garritt & Clary Daniel born Feb^{ry} 21st 1742.
George Son of Richard & Sarah Wait born Feb^{ry} 8th 1742.
Samuel Son of William & Margeret Johnson born Feb^{ry} 19th 174$\frac{2}{3}$.
John Son of William & Clare Marks born Feb^{ry} 16. Bap^d March 13th 174$\frac{2}{3}$.
Josiah Son of John & Mary Bream born Feb^{ry} 8th bap^d Feb^{ry} 20th 174$\frac{2}{3}$
Mary Daughter of James & Eliz^a Meacham born Feb^{ry} 12th 1743.
John Son of John & Jane Alldin born Jan^{ry} 10th 1743.
Milecent Daughter of Tabitha Shiprel born Jan^{ry} 9th. 1743.
Catherine & Elizabeth Daughters of John & Agatha Hardee born Decemb 15th 1743 baptized Jan^{ry} 14th 1743.
George Son of George & Ann Wortham born March ye 20th 1743.
Milecent Daughter of Ann Croffield born Jan^{ry} 20th 1743.
John Son of William & Eliz^a Davis Jan^{ry} 22nd 1743.
Mary Daughter of Robert & Eliz^a Daniel born Jan^{ry} 28th. Bap^d Feb^{ry} 12th 1743.
John Son of John & Mary Brooks born April 11th 1743.
Easter Daughter of Robert & Betty Chowning born March 25. bap^t Ap^{rl} 4 1743.
Solomon Son of William & Mary Gardner born May. 1st. bap^d May 3rd 1743.
Robert Son of John & Lucretia Greenwood born May 21th. 1743.
Elizabeth Daughter of Eustace & Ruth Howard born May 19th bap^d June 28th 1743.
Elizabeth Daughter of John & Mary Barruck born June 30th 1743.
Mary Daughter of Robert & Elizabeth Elliot born June 15th 1743.
Ann Daughter of Randal & Mary Rodes born June 16th 1743.
Catherine Daughter of Henry & Betty Daniel born June 25th 1743.
Jane Daughter of Charles & Penelope Lee born June 20th Bap^d July 17th 1743.
Robert Son of William & Jane Mountague born July 14th. Bap^d August 7th 1743.

Elizabeth Daughter of Edward & Elizabeth Whittakers born July 25 1743.

Mary Daughter of Charles & Ann Roane born August 20th Bap^d Sep^{ber} 18. 1743.

Susanna Daughter John & Susanna Williams born August 25 1743.

Sarah Daughter of Edward & Elizabeth Bristow born August 28th 1743.

Ann Daughter of William & Eliz^a Chowning born August 12. Bap^d Augt 18. 1743.

William Son of Patrick & Elizabeth Caleham born July 5th Bap^d August 17th 1743.

Caty Daughter of Thomas & Sarah Tugle born August 26th Bap^d Sep^{ber} 18 1743.

Susanna Daughter of Richard & Mary Paterson born August 24th Bap^d Sep^{ber} 18. 1743.

Salley Daughter of Jacob & Ann Acrey born September 15. 1743.

Judith Daughter of John & Judith Wortham born September 15th 1743.

William Son of John & Constance Urie born September 8th 1743.

Mary Daughter of Aaron & Johanna Hudging born September 13th 1743.

Lucy daughter of William & Betty Wollace born October 25th 1743.

John Warwick Son of Phillip & Cossandra Warwick born Oc^{ber} 26. bap^d Nov^{ber} 20. 1743.

Sarah Daughter of John & Sarah Stamper born Oc^{ber} 21th Bap^d Novem^{ber} 20. 1743.

Sarah Daughter of John & Rachel Chowning born Oc^{ber} 14. Bap^d Oc^{bei} 30. 1743.

Henry Son of Benjamine & Judith Kidd born Oc^{ber} 16th Bap^d Oc^{ber} 30. 1743.

Sarah Daughter of Peter & Elizabeth Hudson born October 3d 1743.

Elizabeth Daughter of Edward & Martha Dillard born October 20th Bap^d No^{ber} 13. 1743.

Rachel Daughter of Charles & Mary Wood born October 6th 1743.

Frances Daughter of John & Catherine Smith born November 17th 1743.

Judith Daughter of Armstead & Hannah Churchill born Nov^{ber} 21th Bap^d Dec^{ber} 4. 1743.

Elizabeth Daughter of Tobias & Margaret Allin born Dec^{ber} 1st Bap^d Jan^{ry} 1. 1743.

Peggy Daughter of Humphrey & Catherine Jones born Dec^{ber} 25. Bap^d Jan^{ry} 22 1743.

William Son of Harry & Mary Anderson born December 13th 1743.

Ann Daughter of John & Elizabeth Lyal born December 1st 1743.

Priscilla Daughter of William & Eliz^a Hackney born December 5th 1743.

Jane Jones Daughter of Sarah Clark born Feb^{ry} 16th Baptized March 4th 174$\frac{3}{4}$.

William Son of Richard & Ann Daniel born March 9th Bap^d March 18th 174$\frac{3}{4}$.

William an illegitimate Son of Eliz^a Davis born March 13th 174$\frac{3}{4}$.

Mary Daughter of Samuel & Ann Wood born March 27th Bap⁴ April yᵉ 15th 1744.
Sarah Daughter of James & Ave Cole born March yᵉ 25th Bap⁴ April yᵉ 20th 1744.
John Son of John & Frances Reade born June yᵉ 19th Bap⁴ yᵉ 20th 1744.
Mary Daughter of John & Mary Matthews born April yᵉ 6th 1744.
Ann Daughter of Jonathan Herring and Mary born Novʳ the 3d 1743.
Mary Daughter of Richard & Catherine Street born March yᵉ 25 bap⁴ April 15th 1744.
Jane Daughter of Harry & Jane Sears born April yᵉ 13th Bap⁴ May yᵉ 6th 1744.
    Daughter of Henry & Susannah Mickleburrough born Feb'ʸ yᵉ 25th 1744.
Sarah Daughter of Arthur & Ann Dye born Sepʳ 16th bap⁴ Novʳ 11th 1744.
Robert Son of Henry & Betty Daniel born Octoʳ yᵉ 18th 1744.
Absalom Son of Rich⁴ Eliz'ᵗʰ Steevens born May yᵉ 6th bap⁴ May yᵉ 20th 1744.
    Daughter of John & Loweresa Cooper born Sepʳ yᵉ 30th 1744.
Nathanell Son of Thoˢ & Christian Sanders born Sepʳ 14th 1744.
Lewis Son of John & Elizᵃ Davis born Jan'ʸ yᵉ 2d 1744.
Sarah Daughter of South & Rachel Smith born Sepʳ yᵉ 1th 1744.
Jemima Daughter of John & Mary Bream born Sepʳ yᵉ 13th bap⁴ Sepʳ 30th 1744.
William Son of John & Ann Hudson born Sepʳ yᵉ 18th bap⁴ Octoʳ yᵉ 21st 1744.
Anna Daughter of William & Rachell Brooks born Sepʳ 13th bap⁴ Octʳ yᵉ 21. 1744.
Jane Daughter of George & Jane Blackly born Sepʳ 29th bap⁴ Novʳ yᵉ 11th 1744.
Thomas Son of John & ——— Bowles born yᵉ 7th of Decem'ʳ 1744.
Elizᵃ Daughter of Wᵐ & Elizᵃ Chowning born Decem'ʳ 16th bap⁴ Jan'ʸ 13th 1744.
James Son of John & Mary Loson born Decem'ʳ 27th 1744.
Bartholomew Son of Barthᵒ & Elizᵃ Yates born Octoʳ 22nd Bap⁴ 1744.
Mathew Kemp Son of Robert & Elizᵃ Elliot born Jan'ʸ 10th 1744.
Mary Daughter of James & Mary Overstreet born Jan'ʸ 23d 1744.
Moseley Son of Obediah & Sarah Daniel born Jan'ʸ 13th bap⁴ Feb'ʸ 3d 1744.
Ann Daughter of William & Elizᵃ Bueford born Novʳ 6th Bap⁴ Decʳ 2d 1744.
Elizabeth Daughter of John & Sarah Sanders Junʳ born July yᵉ 2d 1744.
Elizabeth Daughter of John & Martha Brooks born Jan'ʸ 17th bap⁴ Feb'ʸ 24th 1744.
Jonathan Son of Henry & Elizᵃ Brooks born Jan'ʸ 19th bap⁴ Feb'ʸ 24th 1744.
Jane Daughter of John & Mary Guthrie born Feb'ʸ 3d bap⁴ Feb'ʸ 24th 1744.

Mary Daughter of James & Catherine Brown born April ye 6th bap^d ye 28th 1745.
Lucy Daughter of Daniel & Hannah Stringer born Feb^{ry} 8th 1744.
John Son of William & Mary Owen born April ye 18th 1744.
Margarett Daughter of Andrew & Constance Hardee born July 17th bap^d Augt 19th 1744.
Joanna Daughter of William & Eliz^a Healy born Feb^{ry} 22nd bap^d March 18th 1744.
Sally Porter Daughter of Janet Kelley born Decr 25th 1744.
Thomas Son of James & Catherine Parrott born Sepr ye 26th 1744.
Catherine Daughter of William & Eliz^a Cloudas born June 25th 1744.
Isaac Son of Charles [&] Penelope Lee born Octo^r 27th bap^d Decem^r 2d 1744.
John Hamment Son of John & Catherine Mack-Nell born Novr 13th 1744.
Prudence Daughter of Philip & Eliz^a Brooks born Feb^{ry} 28th Bap^d March 17th 174$\frac{4}{5}$.
Hannah Daughter of William & Hannah Pace born March y^e 9th 174$\frac{4}{5}$.
Son of Charles & Ann Roan born Jan^{ry} 7th 174$\frac{4}{5}$.
Elizabeth Daughter of George & Mary Lee born y^e 6th of April 1745.
Ame Daughter of John & Eliz^a Loyal born June y^e 3d 1745.
John Son of John & Mary Rhodes born March y^e 29th 1745.
Mary Daughter of John & Redith Wortham born May 2d 1745.
Samuel Son of Edward & Mary Clark born April 11th 1745.
Thomas Son of William & Elizabeth Jones born June 5th 1745.
Thomas Son of Charles & Mary Hodges born June 12th 1745.
Ann Daughter of Thomas & Ann Lee born July ye 1st Bap^d July ye 14 1745.
Benjamine Son of John & Catherine Tugle born July ye 10th Bap^d Augst 11th 1745.
Blackly Son of John & Mary Gardner born July ye 13th Bap^d Augst 11th 1745.
Samuel Son of William & Jane Mountague born July ye 27th Bap^d Augst 11th 1745.
Ann Daughter of William & Frances Gutherie born Augst ye 4th Bap^d Sepr 1st 1745.
Jane Daughter of Edward & Mary Southern born Augst ye 23d 1745.
John Son of John & Martha Stuard born Octo^r ye 15th 1745.
John Son of David & Diannah Berrick born Novr ye 17th 1745.
Frances Daughter of Robert & Lucy Daniel born Novr ye 25th 1745.
Lodowick Son of John & Lucretia Greenwood born June 25th Bap^d Augst 11th 1745.
Thomas Son of Thomas & Catharine Cheyney born Sepr 20th Bap^d Octo^r 13th 1745.
Elizabeth Daughter of William & Frances Thruston born Sepr 2d Bap^d Octo^r 13th 1745.
Chowning Son of Benjamine & Judith Kidd born Octo^r 9th Bap^d Octo^r 13th 1745.
Sarah & Jane Daughters of Thos & Sarah Tugle born Novr 13th Bap^d Novr 16th 1745.

Hannah Daughter of John & Elizabeth Cornelius born Octo' 20th Bap^d Decem' 15th 1745.
Mary Daughter of John & Sarah Stamper born Nov' 13th Bap^d Decem' 15th 1745.
Frances Daughter of John & Jane Aldin born Decem' 24th Bap^d Jan'y 9th 1745.
Elizabeth Daughter of John & Jane Beamen born Nov' 4th 1745.
William Son of James & Dorothy Davis born April 4th 1745.
Catherine Daughter of W^m & Mary Mullins born Sep' 29th Bap^d Nov' 3d 1745.
Daniel Son of Daniel & Sarah Ball born Octo' 30th 1745.
Benjamine Son of Charles & Mary Mederas born Sep' 4th Bap^d Octo' 13th 1745.
Benson Son of Thos & Elizabeth Siblee born Augst 16th 1745.
Mary Daughter of William & Mary Jones born Decem' y^e 10th 1745.
Jane Daughter of W^m & Elizabeth Wood born Sep' 8th Bap^d Sep' 22nd 1745.
John & Ann, Son & Daughter of George & Ann Wortham born Decem' 29th Bap^d 1745.
Elizabeth Daughter of Thos & Christian Sanders born Feb'y y^e 26th 174$\frac{5}{6}$.
Abraham Son of William & Mary Cloudas born March y^e 6th Bap^d March 30th 1746.
Mary Daughter of William & Anne Sadler born March 3d Bap^d March y^e 30th 1746.
Elizabeth Daughter of W^m & Mary Greenwood born Feb'y 11th Bap^d March 30th 1746.
Sarah Daughter of Charles & Ann Roane born March 17th Bap^d April 20th 1746.
Ann Daughter of John & Constance Uric born March y^e 2d 174$\frac{5}{6}$.
Bernard Son of John & Susana Seward born March y^e 8th Bap^d March 30th 1746.
Martin Son of W^m & Mary Gardner born Feb'y 14th Bap^d March 30th 1746.
Ann Daughter of W^m & Clare Marks born March 24th Bap^d April 20th 1746.
John Son of W^m & Sarah Robinson born Feb'y y^e 15th 174$\frac{5}{6}$.
Elizabeth Daughter of Stephen & Anne Tenor born March y^e 30th Bap^d 1746.
Thomas Son of Humphrey & Amy Garret born Jan'y 10th Bap^d Jan'y 26th 174$\frac{5}{6}$.
Robert Son of John & Catharine Smith born Feb'y 24th 174$\frac{5}{6}$.
Benjamine Son of W^m & Elizabeth Hackney born May 14th 1746.
Sarah Daughter of Harry & Mary Anderson born April y^e 19th 1746.
Elizabeth Daughter of Thos & Rose Blake born May y^e 19th 1746.
James Son of James & Cassandra Mackan born April 14th Bap^d Jan'y 1st 1746.
Lewis Son of John & Christian Boss born May 2d 1746.
Elizabeth Daughter of Edward & Elizabeth Bristow born May 7th 1746.
Daniel Son of David & Joshebed Jefferson born April 21st 1746.
Mary Daughter of Joathan & Mary Haren born July ye 6th 1746.

William Son of Jacob & Ann Acree born April 25th Bap⁴ June 22nd 1746.
Anne Daughter of Peter & Mary Hudson born June 17th Bap⁴ July 13th 1746.
William Son of John & Agatha Hardee born May 26th Bap⁴ June 22d 1746.
Lewis Son of Wᵐ & Agatha Cardwell born June 8th Bap⁴ June 22d 1746.
John Son of Andrew & Rachel South born May 25th Bap⁴ June 22d 1746.
Sarah daughter of Edward & Mary Clark born May yᵉ 2d 1746.
Ann Daughter of John & Ann Barrick born June yᵉ 2d 1746.
Henry Son of Tobias & Margaret Allin born July 28th Bap⁴ Augˢᵗ 24th 1746.
Elizabeth Daughter of John & Mary Matthews born July yᵉ 20th 1746.
Elizabeth Daughter of James & Ave Cole born Sepʳ 26th Bap⁴ 1746.
Sarah Daughter of John & Mary Patison born Augˢᵗ 5th 1746.
William Son of Samuel & Ann Wood born July 23d Bap⁴ Augˢᵗ 3d 1746.
Nanny Daughter of Henry & Tabitha Shepherd born Augˢᵗ 28th Bap⁴ Sepʳ 14th 1746.
Lucy Daughter of Philip & Mary Grymes born Augˢᵗ 24th Bap⁴ Augˢᵗ 26th 1743.
John Son of Philip & Mary Grymes born March yᵉ 28th Bap⁴ April 5th 1745.
Philip Ludwell Son of Philip & Mary Grymes born April 5th Bap⁴ May 9th 1746.
John Son of Robert & Elizabeth Elliot born Sepʳ 20th. Bap⁴ 1746.
John Son of Richard & Ann Daniel born Sepʳ 23d 1746.
John Son of John & Mary Bream born Septʳ 22d. Bap⁴ Octoʳ 26th. 1746.
Rachel Daughter of John & Rachel Chowning born Sepʳ 18th. Bap⁴ Octᵉ 5th. 1746.
Gregory Son of Robert & Elizᵃ Durham born Novʳ 12th. Bap⁴ Decemʳ 7th. 1746.
James Son of George & Mary Bristow born Novemʳ 11th. Bap⁴ Decemʳ 7th 1746.
Nanny Daughter of John & Mary Gutherie born Novʳ 8th. Bap⁴ Decemʳ 7th 1746.
Roger Son of Churchhill & Millecent Jones born Noʳ yᵉ 11th Bap⁴ 1746.
James Son of James & Judith Campbell born Decemʳ 29th 1746.
James Son of John & Martha Brooks born Novʳ yᵉ 1st 1746.
Oliver Son of William & Mary Moulson born Decemʳ 5th. Bap⁴ 1746.
Lucy Daughter of Edward & Martha Dillard born Octoʳ 20th. Bap⁴ Novʳ 16th 1746.
Salle Daughter of William & Elizᵃ Hackney born Decemʳ 3d 1746.
Dorrothy Daughter of John & Susanna Daniel born Decʳ 11th. Bap⁴ Janʳʸ 22d. 1746.
Thomas & Elizabeth son & Daughter of Wᵐ & Elizabeth Healy born Febʳʸ 12th. 1746.

A Child of Robert & Eliz⁂ Chiles born Febry 16th 1744/5.
Agatha Daughter of Robert & Eliz⁂ Daniel born Jan'y 6th 1744/5.
Elizabeth Daughter of George & Jane Blackley born Jan'y 3d. Bap⁂
    Feb'y 8th 1746.
Rachel Daughter of W⁂ & Elizabeth Chowning born Jan'y 24. Bap⁂
    Feb'y 8th 1746.
William Son of W⁂ & Elizabeth Buford born Feb'y 10th 1746.
Mary Daughter of John & Ann Meacham born Feb'y 1st. Bap⁂ April
    12th 1747.
Hannah Daughter of Daniel & Hannah Stringer born Jan'y 20th 1744/5.
Philemon Son of Harry & Jane Sears born March 10th 1744/5.
Sukey Daughter of W⁂ & Elizabeth Kidd born Feb'y 17th. Bap⁂
    April 12th 1747.
Mary Daughter of Edward & Eliz⁂ Whittekar born Feb'y 10th 1744/5.
George Son of Edward &   Blackbourn born Jan'y 16th 1744/5.
Elizabeth Daughter of John & Judith Wortham born April 5th. Bap⁂
    April 17th 1747.
Sarah Daughter of John & Jane Beaman born April 8th. Bap⁂ May
    3d 1747.
Elizabeth Daughter of Barth° & Eliz⁂ Yates born June y⁂ 10th Bap⁂
    June 1747.

Colo James Kidd & M⁂ Anna Fisher were married January 16th 1817
    an he ran away from her on the 17th day of May following.
James Steptoe and Jane Syphax were married on the 29th day of
    May 1819. and had a child on the 23d day of March 1821 (mu-
    lattoe Child Something like his father.)

Robert Son of Spencer Clarke & Anne * * * 25th 1789.
Chichester Son of D° born April 15th 1793.
Spencer Son of D° born October 16th 1795.
Margaret Yarrington Daughter of D° born December 15th 1797.
Ann & W⁂ Clark Son & Daughter of the above parents born March
    23rd 1800 baptized 27th of October 1800.
Polly Meacham daughter of William & Penelope Segar was born
    April 22nd 1803. Baptized March 29th 1804.
Mary Grymes Sayre was born May 19th 1805.

Births of Slaves for the Year of our Lord 1769.

John Saunders a Slave belonging to Anne Jones was born April 28th
    1769 & was baptized July 9th.
Jenny a Slave belonging to William Jackson was born May the 18th
    1769. & baptized July 9th.
Charles Nelson a Slave belonging to Anne Jones was born Oct'r 22d.
    1769. & baptized March 18th 1770.
Ambrose a Slave belonging to William Jackson was born June 11th.
    1773.
Tanna, a Slave belonging to John Seward Se'r was born May 30th
    1774.
Winney a Slave belonging to William Pryor was born December
    16th 1774.
Lucy a Slave belonging to John Seward was born Sep'r 16th 1776.

MARRIAGES.

Dudley Jolly & Martha Gardner Married May ye 14th 1716.
Richins Brame & Hannah Cheedle Married May ye 15th 1716.
Thomas Cardwell & Mary Blackly Married June ye 22 1716.
Thomas Brumwell & Dianah Underwood Married July ye 8. 1716.
Christopher Kelshaw & Mary Easter Married August ye 10. 1716.
Robert Deshago & Elizabeth Nicholls Married August ye 13. 1716.
John Fearn & Sarah Wortham Married November ye 1. 1716.
William Wood & Susanna Dinely Married November ye 9. 1716.
Thomas Mountague & Grace Nicholson Married December ye 21. 1716.
Robert Williamson & Elizabeth Minor Married December ye 21. 1716.
John Batchelder & Elizabeth Davis Married Jan'ry ye 2. 1716.
John Nichols & Elizabeth Osborn Married Jan'ry ye 3. 1716.
William Guttery & Lettice Burk Married Jan'ry ye 24. 1716.
Richard Smother & Mary Davis Married June ye 6 1717.
Nicholas Bristow & Mary Gardner Married June ye 27 1717.
David Murray & Jane Clark Married July ye 18. 1717.
William Stanard & Elizabeth Beverley Married August ye 1st 1717.
John Williams & Michall Curles Married August ye 22 1717.
James Janison & Rebecca Hackney Married Septem^r ye 5. 1717.
Nicholas Lewis & Michall Burk Married Septem^r ye 19. 1717.
John Miller & Sarah Hadley Married Septem^r ye 26. 1717.
John Moseley & Mary Nichols Married October ye 10. 1717.
John Johnson & Anne Ingram Married October ye 13. 1717.
John Carter & Mary Rice Married October ye 24 1717.
John Pace & Elizabeth Mountague Married October ye 24 1717.
James Bristow & Anne Jones Married Novem^r ye 7. 1717.
John Conner & Anne Sittern Married Decem^r ye 19. 1717.
William Mountague & Elizabeth Minor Married Decem^r ye 24. 1717.
William Rice & Catherine Caniff Married Decem^r ye 26 1717.
Thomas Vivion & Frances Thacker Married Jan'ry ye 2. 1717.
William Ogilvie & Anne Riske Married Jan'ry ye 9. 1717.
Stephen Feild & Susanna Jones Married Jan'ry ye 16. 1717.
John Ingam & Charity Waite Feb'ry ye 20. 1717.
John Blake & Johannah Ball Married Feb'ry ye 24. 1717.
Arthur Nash & Anne Allen Married Feb'ry ye 25. 1717.
George Freestone & Sarah Atwood married Feb'ry ye 25. 1717.
George Guest & Elizabeth Basket married Feb'ry ye 25 1717.
Patrick Marion & Betty Baker Married April ye 13 1718.
Richard Eastree & Mary Gaffield Married April ye 15 1718.
William Tomson & Mary Sibley Married April ye 24 1718.
William Hunt & Sarah Brock Married May ye 1 1718.
John Mullinax & Bridgett Hearn Married May ye 1. 1718.
   Bar Yates Min^r.

MARRIAGES.

William Davis & Sarah Pace Married June y^c 16. 1718.
Charles Cooper & Alice Nichols Married June y^c 26. 1718.
Robert George & Anne Nash Married July y^c 28 1718.
Thomas Stapleton & Mary Williamson Married Augst y^c 7. 1718.

Robert Gallbarth & Penelope Parrott Married Octo: y⁰ 2. 1718.
Isaac Allin & Elizabeth Symes Married Octo. y⁰ 7. 1718.
William Anderson & Sarah Goar Married Novr y⁰ 19 1718.
William Pepper & Honor Finney Married Nov'm^r y⁰ 27 1718.
Joseph Timberlake & Joanna Hackney Married Decem^r y⁰ 9. 1718.
Christopher Kilbee & Catherine Lewis Married Jan'y y⁰ 1 1718.
Benjamine Row & Mary Jervis Married Feb'y y⁰ 5. 1718.
John Pace & Mary Murry Married Feb'y y⁰ 10 1718.
Joseph Hall & Catherine Ranson Married Ap: y⁰ 23 1719.
James Ingram & Margrett Hardee Married July y⁰ 24 1719.
Henry Burk & Judith Trigg Married August y⁰ 13. 1719.
Thomas Gilly & Elizabeth Makerty Married August y⁰ 13 1719.
Charles Gresham & Mary Arven Married August y⁰ 15 1719.
Richard Taylor & Honor Pepper Married Octo. y⁰ 9. 1719.
Edmund Mickleburrough & Eliz^a George Married November y⁰ 19. 1719.
Thomas Tilley & Phebe Syddern Married Novem^r y⁰ 22 1719.
John Marston & Elizabeth Reades Married Decem^r y⁰ 18 1719.
Robert Holderness & Abigal Chelton Married Feb'y y⁰ 11 1719.
Oliver Segar & Jane Daniell Married May y⁰ 12. 1720.
Dennis O'Brian & Honor Bushnell Married May y⁰ 19. 1720.
Henry Blunt & Elizabeth Biggs Married June y⁰ 26. 1720.
John Dudley & Anne Hill Married June y⁰ 26 1720.
Robert Mash & Sarah Mazey Married July y⁰ 21 1720.
William Johnson & Mary Goodloe Married July y⁰ 21 1720.
Humphrey Jones & Sarah Hamerton Married July y⁰ 21 1720.
William Gardner & Elizabeth Crank Married August y⁰ 3. 1720.
Andrew Murrah & Sarah Perry Married Augst y⁰ 16. 1720.
Massey Yarrington & Anne Chowning Married Septem^r y⁰ 13. 1720.
Hezekiah Roads & Anne Hill Married Decem^r y⁰ 8. 1720.
John Larke & Elizabeth Blake Married Decem^r y⁰ 11. 1720.
George Barwick & Mary Edmonds married Decem^r y⁰ 14. 1720.
Patrick Knight & Mary Pendergrass Married Jan'y y⁰ 12. 1720.
Richard Moulson & Anne Shurley Married Jan^{ry} y⁰ 19. 1720.
Joseph Smith & Elizabeth Ball Married Feb'y y⁰ 7. 1720.
James Bristow & Mary Twyman Married Feb'y y⁰ 9. 1720.
John Southern & Margrett Kidd Married Feb'y y⁰ 17. 1720.
Zebulun Chelton & Mary Goar Married Feb'y y⁰ 20. 1720.
John Fearne & Anne Machen Married Feb^r y⁰ 20. 1720.
John Kidd & Rebecca Godbee Married Feb'y y⁰ 21. 1720.
William Batchelder & Elizabeth Watts Married April y⁰ 11 1720.
John Tomson & Catherine Twyman Married April y⁰ 13. 1727.
      Bar. Yates Mins^r.

MARRIAGES.

Joseph Pace & Ann Basford Married April y⁰ 18 1721.
William Dudley & Judith Johnson Married April y⁰ 27. 1721.
Tomson Betts & Anne Russell Married May y⁰ 12 1721.
John Southworth & Anne Syms Married May y⁰ 18 1721.
George Walker & Amey Lyall Married July y⁰ 4. 1721.
Thomas Kidd & Elizabeth Laurance Married July y⁰ 27 1721.
Robert Brown & Hannah owen Married August y⁰ 3 1721.
William Southworth & Anne Jordan Married August y⁰ 10 1721.

Richard Greenwood & Anne Baskitt Married August ye 10 1721.
William Johnson & Margrett Pace Married Septem^r ye 22 1721.
Alexander How & Mary Pace Married Septem^r ye 26. 1721.
Jonathan Johnson & Priscilla Tignor Married Septem^r ye 28 1721.
George Chowning & Martha Tugwell Married Octo. ye 19 1721.
Thomas Gilinwater & Elizabeth Marcum Married Novem^r ye 12 1721.
Thomas Norman & Jane Stapleton Married Novem^r ye 23 1721.
William Daniel & Anne Watts Married Decem^r y^o 7 1721.
Lewis Neal & Sarah Micham Married Decem^r y^o 26 1721.
William Chowning & Jannett Jacobus Married Decem^r ye 29 1721.
Henry Tugle & Mary Godbee Married March ye 30 1722.
Richard Callahan & Eliz^a Nutter Married March ye 31 1722.
Robert Walker & Elizabeth Alford Married March ye 31 1722.
Chichester Curtis & Mary Hargrove Married March ye 31 1722.
David Williams & Mary Ingram Married Augst ye 21 1722.
Henry Ball & Elizabeth Tugle Married Augst ye 23 1722.
William Roads & Hannah Miller Married Sept. ye 13 1722.
John Guttery & Mary Shay Married Sept y^o 23. 1722.
Alexander Graves & Mary How Married Octo ye 9. 1722.
Patrick Miller & Elizabeth Hill Married Octo. ye 11. 1722.
Patrick Kelly & Catherine Nicholls Married Octo. ye 26 1722.
Edward Clarke & Mary Hunt Married Octo. y^o 26 1722.
Thomas Amis & Rachel Daniel Married Novem^r ye 14 1722.
John Shorter & Elizabeth Underwood Married Decem^r ye 23 1722.
Paul Thilman & Jane George Married April ye 17 1723.
Robert Mash & Jane Roades Married April ye 23 1723.
Charles Thomas & Susanna Davis Married May ye 9 1723.
William Tomson & Mary Symes Married May ye 9 1723.
Thomas Faulkner & Ellis Ellis Married May ye 23 1723.
William Gray & Mary McCauley Married May ye 28 1723.
Richard Jones & Anne Davis Married August ye 1 1723.
John Ridgway & Anne Crank Married Septem^r ye 19 1723.
James Russell & Anne Hatton Married October ye 3 1723.
David Gutherie & Susanna Thruston Married October ye 11 1723.
John Chowning & Catherine Gardner Married October ye 24 1723.
John Burk & Lettice Dannolly Married Novem^r ye 6 1723.
John Robinson & Mary Storey Married Novem^r ye 8 1723.
Theophilus Branch & Frances Sandiford Married Decem^r ye 8 1723.
Rice Curtis & Martha Thacker Married Decem^r ye 26 1723.
n Marston & Phebe Tilley Married Jan^{ry} ye 2 1723.

Bar. Yates min^r

MARRIAGES.

Paulin Anderson & Judith Jones Married Jan^{ry} ye 9 1723.
William Bennit & Mary Humpherys Married April ye 9 1724.
George Twyman & Agatha Buford Married July ye 16 1724.
Richard Curtis & Susannah Curtis Married July ye 23 1724.
Thomas Wennan & Jane Porterfield Married August ye 14 1724.
Thomas Whitaker & Rebecca Hues Married August y^o 20 1724.
John Smith & Elizabeth Alding Married Octo. ye 27 1724.
William Owen & Ruth Mayo Married Novem^r ye 12 1724.
Randolph Roads & Sarah Davies Married Novem^r ye 27 1724.

Joseph Carey & Anne Sargent Married Decem'r y'e 3 1724.
Abraham Wharton & Mary Humpheries Married Jan'ry y'e 7 1724.
James Jones & Agatha Crank Married Jan'ry y'e 14 1724.
William Mansfeild & Frances Tuggle Married Jan'ry y'e 21 1724.
John Scanland & Keziah Ball Married Jan'ry y'e 27 1724.
Edward Ball & Sarah Owen Married Feb'ry y'e 4 1724.
John Blake & Anne Johnson Married Feb'ry y'e 9 1724.
John Evans & Catherine Nixon Married April y'e 15 1725.
John Goar & Mary Madras Married May y'e 13 1725.
Caleb Brooks & Elizabeth South Married June y'e 17 1725.
George Neavill & Anna Symes Married June y'e 22 1725.
John George & Michal Meacham Married July y'e 29 1725.
Peter Mountague & Elizabeth Merry Married Aug'rt y'e 19 1725.
Thomas Allen & Margrett Haines Married Sept. y'e 2 1725.
Joshua Lewis & Martha Marston Married Octo. y'e 7 1725.
John Tugle & Catharine Kelly Married Octo. y'e 8 1725.
James Daniel & Jenny Hicks Married Novem'r y'e 11 1725.
John Soanes & Sarah Thilman Married Novem'r y'e 25 1725.
John Gregory & Jane Kidd Married Decem'r y'e 3 1725.
John Weston & Elizabeth Wright Married Decem'r y'e 30 1725.
Thomas Lee & Anne Probart Married Jan'y y'e 6 1725.
W'm Chessells & Sarah Cole Married Feb'y y'e 10 1725.
Edward Whitaker & Elizabeth Hill Married Feb'y y'e 13 1725.
John How & Avarilla Hardee Married Feb'y y'e 22 1725.
Elias Burt & Anne Finney Married April y'e 11 1726.
W'm Wallis & Betty Davies Married April y'e 11 1726.
Robert Williamson & Elizabeth Mickleburrough Married Feb'y y'e 13 1726.
Anthony Ridway & Eliz'a Beaman Married April y'e 3 1727.
Richard Steevens & Mabell Dodson Married April y'e 14 1727.
John Good & Anne Gardner Married April y'e 27 1727.
John Bently & Mary Ellis Married May y'e 26 1727.
Joseph Hardee & Mary Mullins Married June y'e 20 1727.
William Anderson & Anne Humpheries Married June y'e 23 1727.
Henry Mickleburrough & Frances Alding Married July y'e 20 1727.
Thomas Oneby & Mary Stamper Jun'r Married July y'e 27 1727.
Henry Knight & Mary Tomson Married August y'e 3 1727.
Paul Philpotts & Clement Owen Married August y'e 10 1727.
James Dudley & Jane Stanton Married August y'e 24 1727.
Thomas Mountague & Penelope Warwick Married August 31 1727.
William Southworth & Catherine Allen Married September y'e 6 1727.

Bar. Yates Min'r.

MARRIAGES.

William Baker & Rachel Dodson Married September y'e 15 1727.
John Eberson & Elizabeth Brooks Married September y'e 22 1727.
Frances Porter & Elizabeth Hughs Married September y'e 28 1727.
James Heptinstall & Rebecca Bohame Married October y'e 24 1727.
John Glen & Mary Brayerly Married Jan'ry y'e 2 1727.
John Tomson & Susanna George Married Jan'y y'e 9 1727.
James Stiff & Edy Dudley Married Feb'y y'e 23 1727.
Thomas Brumell & Judith Ball Married April y'e 25 1728.

John Mackneel & Catherine Hammett Married May ye 6 1728.
Robert Crawford & Joyce Fletcher Married June ye 3 1728.
William Saunders & Susanna Thomas Married June ye 5 1728.
Thomas Todd & Lettice Thacker Married June ye 7 1728.
John Williams & Catherine Perrott Married July ye 17 1728.
Joshua Allford & Anne Blackburne Married July ye 21 1728.
John Allstone & Catherine Oneal married August ye 12 1728.
Henry Jolley & Anne Ellis Married August ye 15 1728.
John Bradley & Rebecca Jemson Married August ye 24 1728.
John Goodwin & Jane Gressett Married Septem^r ye 13 1728
William Davis & Elizabeth Shelton Married October ye 9 1728.
Jeremiah Earley & Elizabeth Buford Married October ye 16 1728.
John Barnett & Marran Gibbs Married Novem^r ye 13 1728.
William Kidd & Elizabeth Thurston Married Novem^r ye 13 1728.
William Thurston & Frances Kidd Married Novem^r ye 13 1728.
John Crockford & Lucretia Goar Married Novem^r ye 22 1728.
William Guttery & Frances Willbourn Married Novem^r ye 29 1728.
William Crutchfield & Jane Norman Married Decem^r ye 9 1728.
Joseph Meacham & Elizabeth Crutchfield Married Jan'y ye 9 1728.
Andrew Davis & Elizabeth Barbee Married Jan'y ye 10 1728.
George Godloe & Diana Minor Married Jan'y ye 13 1728.
John Ridgway & Anne Batchelder Married Feb'y ye 6 1728.
Henry Daniel & Mary Johnson Married Feb'y ye 11 1728.
Patrick Boswell & Elioner Commings Married Feb'y ye 18 1728.
William Balding & Judith Tugell Married April ye 8 1729.
John Bohannan & Agnes Newberry Married April ye 10 1729.
William Wood & Elizabeth Brown Married April ye 10 1729.
Robert Beverley & Anne Stanard Married April ye 10 1729.
Marvel Moseley & Mary Davis Married April ye 24 1729.
Henry Nash & Jochebed Moseley Married April ye 24 1729.
William Hill & Bridgett Mullinax Married April ye 24 1729.
William Thurston & Elizabeth Franks Married April ye 29 1729.
William Buford & Elizabeth Owen Married May ye 15 1729.
John Jones & Isabell Hill Married May ye 20 1729.
Hugh Roach & Anne Marston Married May ye 22 1729.
Thomas Saunders & Christian Davis Married June ye 4 1729.
Jacob Faulkner & Mary Crockford married June ye 19 1729.
George Nevill & Mary Gibbs Married June ye 20 1729.
Richard Waight & Sarah Blake Married July ye 16 1729.
Thomas Marston & Elizabeth Roach Married July ye 17 1729.
    Bar. Yates Min^r.

MARRIAGES.

Roger Lin & Frances Hughes Married August ye 5th 1729.
George Goodwin & Jane Haselwood Married August Y^e 14th 1729.
John Humphries & Elizabeth Hackney Married August Y^e 28th 1729.
Charles Curtis Johannah Gordon Married September Y^o 11th 1729.
Thomas Walker & Elizabeth Shorter Married Novem^r Y^e 21 1729.
John Marshall & Mary Gilpin Married Novem^r Y^e 24. 1729.
William Mountague & Jane Price Married Decem^r Y^o 3 1729.
Peter Lee & Catherine Tuke Married Decem^r Y^e 15 1729.
Thomas French & Mary Callahan Married Jan'y Y^e 20 1729.
William Bassett & Elizabeth Churchhill Married Jan'y Y^e 29 1729.

James Edwards & Joice Crawford Married March Y⁰ 6 1729.
John Philips & Margret Cronan Married March Y⁰ 31 1730.
Christopher Owen & Elizabeth Davis Married April Y⁰ 9th 1730.
Eustace Howard & Ruth Davis Married April Y⁰ 28th. 1730.
Patrick Welch & Catherine Redman Married May y⁰ 14th 1730.
Aquilla Snelling & Margret Allen Married May y⁰ 14th 1730.
William Chaver & Rebecca Gillet Married July y⁰ 8th 1730.
William Southern & Mary Saunders Married August y⁰ 3rd 1730.
John Crowdas & Mary Parsons Married August y⁰ 6th 1730.
Paul Philpots & Susanna Baxter Married October y⁰ 27th 1730.
Sampson Darrell & Elizabeth Smith Married Novem' y⁰ 17th 1730.
Robert Wilkins & Elizabeth Miller Married Novem' y⁰ 19th 1730.
Henry Nixon & Sarah Daniel Married Decem' y⁰ 10th 1730.
John Brand & Martha Ambler Married Decem' y⁰ 10th 1730.
Paul Thilman & Elizabeth Vivion Married Decem' y⁰ 16th 1730.
Thomas Skelton & Mary Probert Married Jan'y y⁰ 14th 1730.
Hugh Stuart & Judith Machen Married Jan'y y⁰ 29th 1730.
Robert Dudley & Jane Moulson Married Feb'y y⁰ 5th 1730.
John Davis & Sarah Chaften Married Feb'y y⁰ 11th 1730.
George Best & Margret Cooper Married Feb'y y⁰ 11th 1730.
Matthias Allen & Anne Herrin Married April y⁰ 19th 1731.
Robert Daniel & Elizabeth Carter Married April y⁰ 29th 1731.
Ignatius Tureman & Mary Pace Married June y⁰ 3th 1731.
Ralph Skelton & Mary Daniel Married June y⁰ 10th 1731.
Richard Hearn & Mary Hackney Married August y⁰ 13th 1731.
Bartholomew Scot & Elizabeth Northcoat Married Augs' y⁰ 18th 1731.
David Davis & Barker Jones Married September y⁰ 2th 1731.
James Gibson & Anne Stiff Married Septem' y⁰ 10th 1731.
Robert Smether & Constant Davies Married Septem' y⁰ 24 1731.
Thomas Cheney & Dorothy Lee Married Septem' y⁰ 30 1731.
Thomas Wakefield & Betty Gardiner Married October y⁰ 7 1731.
Robert Daniel & Mary Meacham Married October y⁰ 8 1731.
Joseph Carter & Catherine Ammon Married December y⁰ 1 1731.
Robert Johnson & Elizabeth Sutton Married December y⁰ 31 1731.
John Wily & Elizabeth Clark Married Jan'y y⁰ 21 1731.
Joseph Row & Mary Sandiford Married Jan'y y⁰ 26 1731.
James Edmundson & Christian Gregory Married Feb'y y⁰ 2 1731.
Robert Perrott & Sarah Mactyre Married April y⁰ 17 1732.

 Bar Yates Min'

MARRIAGES.

James Pressnall & Anne Daniel Married May y⁰ 14th 1732.
Richard Greenwood & Catharine Seares Married May y⁰ 18th 1732.
William Goar & Lucy Crockford Married May y⁰ 19th 1732.
James George & Agatha Watts Married May y⁰ 24th 1732.
John Lee & Anne Spyers Married June y⁰ 8th 1732.
Henry Perrott & Rachell Bayn Married June y⁰ 16th 1732.
Thomas Faulkner & Mary Owen Married June y⁰ 18th 1732.
John Owen & Sarah Chaftin Married July y⁰ 20th 1732.
John Bird & Alice Burnet Married August y⁰ 31st 1732.
James Stuart & Dianah Davies Married August y⁰ 31st 1732.

Charles Daniel & Jane Mickleburrough Married Septemr yᵉ 20th 1732.
Mathew Crank & Mary Basket Married October yᵉ 26th 1732.
Charles Wood & Mary Baldwin Married October yᵉ 29th 1732.
John Wortham & Judith Stewart Married Novemr yᵉ 2th 1732.
Patrick Knight & Anne Conner Married Novemr yᵉ 2th 1732.
Landon Carter & Elizabeth Wormeley Married Novemr yᵉ 16th 1732.
Michael Rudd & Anne Ball Married Movemr yᵉ 18th 1732.
Caleb Brookes & Margret Fox Married Novemr yᵉ 24th 1732.
John Berry & Mary Miller Married Novemr yᵉ 30th 1732.
Francis Samson & Margret Elliot Married Novemr yᵉ 30th 1732.
Nicholas Mealer & Anne Burnes Married Decemr yᵉ 26th 1732.
William Gardner & Mary Basket Married Jan'y yᵉ 12th 1732.
William Cheney & Elizabeth Cheney Married Jan'y yᵉ 22th 1732.
John Johnston & Anne Bennet Married Jan'y yᵉ 29th 1732.
Charles Maceras & Mary Eeles Married Feb'y yᵉ 4th 1732.
Anthony Collings & Mary ann Yates Married Feb'y yᵉ 24th 1732.
John Stamper & Sarah Perrot Married March yᵉ 25th 1733.
John Davis & Elizabeth Rhoeds Married April yᵉ 5th 1733.
Edward Dillard & Martha Alding Married April yᵉ 6th 1733.
Edward Bristow & Elizabeth Daniel Married April yᵉ 13th 1733.
John Walker & Catherine Yates Married (by Revᵈ Em. Jones) May yᵉ 10th 1733.
George Blackley & Jane Pace Married May yᵉ 16th 1733.
Peter Lee & Susanna Williams Married May yᵉ 16th 1733.
William Owen & Judith Daniel Married June yᵉ 1 1733.
Richard Carter & Mary Hill Married June yᵉ 4 1733.
John Williams & Catherine Davis Married June yᵉ 24 1733.
Patrick Purcell & Sarah Davis Married Septemr yᵉ 7 1733.
William Stapleton & Lucy Hardin Married September yᵉ 21 1733.
John Chowning & Rachel Tuggle Married Octo. yᵉ 3th 1733.
Richard Perrot & Elizabeth Greenwood Married Octo. yᵉ 9th 1733.
James Broun & Catherine Wood Married Octor yᵉ 17th 1733.
Henry Brooks & Sarah Cuffley Married Octor yᵉ 19th 1733.
John O'neal & Jane Mactyre Married Decemr yᵉ 7th 1733.
John Curtis & Susanna Saunders Married Decemr yᵉ 7th 1733.
   Bar Yates Minr.

MARRIAGES.

William Pace & Hannah Booten Married Decemr yᵉ 26th 1733.
Arthur Ware & Jane Daniel Married Jan'y yᵉ 26th 1733.
Valentine Ball & Susannah Lewis Married Jan'y yᵉ 31th 1733.
Charles Dougherty & Sarah Parrot Married Feb'y yᵉ 26th 1733.
Edmund Day & Mary Yarrow Married April yᵉ 14th 1734.
Charles Gunter & Judith Gutterie Married April yᵉ 15th 1734.
Richard George & Elizabeth Mayo Married April yᵉ 20th 1734.
John Connor & Mary Crosle Married May yᶜ 2th 1734.
Benjamine Davis & Judith Packett Married May yᵉ 28th 1734.
David Barwick & Dianah Hill Married May yᵉ 30th 1734.
John Greenwood & Lucretia Mactyre Married (by C. Thacker) July 25th 1734.
Alexander Frazier & Ann Wood Married (by C. Thacker) 7ber 8th 1734.

John Hardee & Agathe Gardiner Married January 5th (Banns) 1734.
Andrew Hardee & Constant Sears Married January 5th (Banns) 1734.
Daniell Moor & Mary Hollan Married January 31st (Banns) 1734.
Thos: Dawson & Margrett Cain Married April 10th (Banns) 1735.
William Hackney & Elizth Wilkins Married April 10th (Banns) 1735.
Willm Phillips & Hannah Graves Married April 7th (Licence) 1735.
Dennis Obryant & Jane Floyd Married April 19th (Banns) 1735.
Jno Dobbs & Mary Stamper Married May 11th (Banns) 1735.
Jno Doss & Sarah Herring Married June 17th (Banns) 1735.
Sam^{ll} Major & Elizabeth Jones Married June 22d (Banns) 1735.
James Dunbery & Elizabeth Owen Married June 26th (Banns) 1735.
Grigg Yarborough & Elizabeth Lewis Married June 27th (Banns) 1735.
James Porter & Mary Mason Married July 31th. (Banns) 1735.
Phillip Warwick & Cassandra Cheaney Married August 3d. (Banns) 1735.
Roger Kain & Ann Johnson Married August 10th (Bann) 1735.
Jno Vivion & Jane Smith Married August 12th (Banns) 1735.
Wm Mullens & Mary Greenwood Married Augst 27 (Banns) 1735.
Jno White & Elizth Pace Married Sept. 15 (Banns) 1735.
Jno Towles & Margarett Daniel Married Octr 9th (Banns) 1735.
Jno Humpris & Ann Jones Married Octr 14th (Banns) 1735.
Curtis Hardee & Elizth Tillman Married Novr 13th (Licence) 1735.
Robert Chowning & Betty Guttery Married Decr 24th (Banns) 1735.
Christopher Ammon & Mary Bristow Married January 29th (Banns) 1735.
John Warwick & Agathee Twyman Married March 8th (Banns) 1735.
Richard Ham & Diana Gibbs Married May 9th (Banns) 1736.
Jno Williams & Susanna Brookes Married May 30th (Banns) 1736.
Duel Kidd & Mary Sorrow Married July 13th (Banns) 1736.
James Gibson & Elizth Crosby Married July 22nd (Banns) 1736.
James Brown & Mary Swepson Married July 26th (Banns) 1736.
John Blake & Elizth King Married Sept 29 (Banns) 1736.
Thos Duckworth & Ann Buford Married Octr 4th (Banns) 1736.
Richd Jowel & Michal Miller Married Oct^o 20th (Banns) 1736.

Jno Reade Min^r.

MARRIAGES.

Alexander Roane & Mary Hipkins Married 9^{ber} 8th 1736.
Benjamin Kidd & Judith Chowning Married 10^{ber} 10th. 1736.
William Jones & Mary Langdon Married 10^{ber} 13th. 1736.
Thomas Betts & Elizabeth Burnet Married February 4th 1736.
Henry Mickleburrough & Susannah Daniel Married February 17th. 1736.
John Stevens & Mary Hughes Married February 18th 1736.
Alexander Snelling & Anna Humphreys Married April 4th. 1737.
John Matthews & Mary Herring Married April 4th. 1737.
William Anderson & Constance Alphin Married April 23th. 1737.
Robert Williams & Mary Brookes Married May 6th. 1737.
Randal Rhodes & Mary Bristow Married May 15th. 1737.
Benjamin Ball & Ann Owen Married May 20th 1737.

John Taliaferro & Frances Robinson Married Jun^e 30th 1737.
John Price & Ann Younger were Married June 17th 1737.
William Colley & Patience Bryant were Married July 4th. 1737.
James Amiss & Jane Seager Nichols were Married March 17th. 173⅜.
Nicholas Dillard & Mary Alldin Married Septem^r ye 16th 1737.
Richard Allin & Elizabeth Thurston Married Octo^r ye 23d 1737.
Thomas Tignor & Sarah Stiff Married Octo^r ye 27th 1737.
Daniel Stringer & Hannah Batchelder Married Decem^r ye 1st 1737.
George Lee & Mary Buford Married Decem^r ye 4th. 1737.
John Dunston & Mary Tyley Married Decem^r ye 20th 1737.
Robert Stureman & Mary Rice Married Decem^r ye 23d 1737.
Carter Burwel & Lucy Grymes Married Jany ye 5th 173⅜.
John Deagle & Mary Wharton Married Jany ye 16th 173⅜.
Charles Lee & Penelope Cheany Married Jany ye 24th 173⅜.
David Snodgrass & Elizabeth Banting Married Jany ye 22d. 173⅜.
William Boughtoun & Judith Hill Married Jany ye 22d. 173⅜.
John Reade & Frances Yates Married Feb^{ry} ye 2d. 173⅜.
Augustine Owen & Mary Clark Married Feb^{ry} ye 13th. 173⅜.
James Compton & Ann Steevens Married April ye 3d. 1738.
Russell Hill & Anne Towles Married April ye 11th 1738.
William Griffin & Rachel Smith Married April ye 13th 1738.
Thomas Maxwell & Kezia Blake Married May ye 2d 1738.

MARRIAGES.

George Goodwin & Elizabeth Warwick Married June ye 15th 1738.
John Rhodes & Mary Davis Married June ye 16th 1738.
Robert Dudley & Jane Segar Married Augst ye 10th 1738.
William Collins & Elizabeth Macktyer Married 1738.
George Lee & Judith Wormeley Married Sep^{ber} ye 30th 1738.
William Bond & Constant Smithey Married Octo^r ye 24th 1738.
Thomas Chainey & Cathrine Bristow Married Octo^r ye 26th 1738.
Thomas Tyre & Catherine Jones Married Novr ye 28th 1738.
Henry Sears & Jane Watts Married Decr ye 7th 1738.
Paul Phillpotts & Margret Wilburn Married Decm^r ye 27th 1738.

MARRIAGES.

Stanton Dudley & Judith Jackson Saturday March 12. 1790.
James Stiffe & Susanna Wood March 17th 1796.
James Stamper & Catharine Jackson March 20th 1796.
John Boss & Anne Jackson May 4th 1796.
Daniel Ball Siblee & Nancy Davis Miller June 2d 1796.
Nicholas Sebre & Betsa Baines June 15. 1796.
Thos Fauntleroy & Isabella Loussier Sep^t 1. 1796.
Christopher Harwood & Elinor Craine Sepr 1st 1796.
John Jarvis & Mary Dame Novr 11th 1796.

Henry Heffernan Rector.

The above List was given to the Clerk of the County.

John Montague of Essex County Married Mary   of Spotsylvania Novr 14th 1778.
James Burton & Sarah Currey of King & Queen County married Decr 3rd 1778.

William Garton & Judith Jackson married Dec' 15th 1778.
Thomas Dillard & Mary Dillard of King & Queen County married Dec' 30th 1778.
James Cardwell & Ann Eubank of King & Queen County married January 28th 1779.
Griffin Tuggle & Frances Berry married January 10th 1779.
John Bristow & Frances Brooks married January 31st 1779.
Benjamin Minor & Betsy Ross married May 1st 1779.
    Samuel Klug, Minis.

MARRIAGES.

William Peters & Henrietta Ridgway married Nov' 12th 1780.
Jacob Stiff Sanders & Lucy Humphris married November 16th 1780.
Alexander Anderson & Nancy Wilcox married Nov 26th 1780.
Johnston Wake & Nancy Jackson married January 6th 1781.
James Meggs & Mary Wilson married January 13th 1781.
Josiah Bristow & Elizabeth Wilkins married Feb'y 4th.
George Williams & Ann Chowning married February 24 1781.
Reuben Alderson & Mary Taff married February 19th 1781.
Thomas Roane & Sally Murray married March 4th 178 .
Samuel Thurston & Sarah Stamper Coats married March 9th 1 .
Benjamin Falkner & Anna Nichols married March 22nd 178 .
George Blake & Chrisse Saunders married March 22d 1781.
    Samuel Klug. Minister.

Isaac Wilcox Son of —— —— Ann Wilcox was born 1776.
Richard Son of John & Clara Daniel was born February 6 1776.
John Son of Robert & Susanna Groom was born April 1st 1776.
Philip Son of Philip & Frances Mountague was born June 19th 1776.
William Jones Son of William & Ann Jones was born Sep.
Thomas Mitcham Son of Joseph & Judith Brooks was born Jan'y 31st.
Elizabeth Daughter of of Lawrance & Frances Meacham was born—
Mary Daughter of John & Sukey Minter was born Oct'
Jack Fearn Son of William & Sarah Stiff was born Nov' 19th 1776.
Josias Son of John Parrish was born Oct' 3d 1777.
Benjamin Son of Benjamin & Elizabeth Bristow was born March 19th 1772.
Jack Phips Son of Benjamin & Sarah Bristow was born Sept' 4th 1775.
Randolph Son of Thomas & Mary Segar was born January 19th 1778.
John Son of Thomas & Sarah Ann Harrow was born February 22d 1778.
Thomas Son of James & Sarah Patterson was born February 17th 1762.
John Son of James & Ann Patterson was born December 2d 1766.
Richard Son of James & Ann Patterson was born April 17th 1768.
James Son of James & Ann Patterson was born March 10th 1771.
James Son of Benjamin & Jane Kidd was born January 9th 1771.
Ruth Thurston Daughter of Edmund & Ruth Kid was born May 8th 1771.

(Fragment)

Moll the Daughter of my negro woman Beas Dyed the thirtith of may laste.

Given under my hand this Seavententh of June 1739.

John Segar.

BURIALS.

John Mickleburrough dyed Octo^r ye 9 & was buried Octo^r ye 12. 1716.
Sarah Moscleey dyed Octo^r ye 9 & was buried October ye 11. 1716.
John Bristow dyed October ye 10 & was buried October ye 13. 1716.
Elizabeth Ray dyed October ye 22 & was buried October ye 25. 1716.
John Nash dyed October ye 10 & was buried October ye 12. 1716.
Thomas Winn dyed October ye 10. & was buried October ye 11. 1716.
Thomas Steel dyed October ye 21. & was buried October ye 22. 1716.
Agatha Curtis dyed October ye 22. & was buried October ye 24. 1716.
Elizabeth Ray dyed October ye 22 & was buried October ye 25. 1716.
John Clark dyed Novem^r ye 6 & was buried Novem^r ye 7. 1716.
William Gaffeild dyed October ye 25. & was buried October ye 28. 1716.
John Davis dyed October ye 23 & was buried October ye 25. 1716.
William Sandiford dyed October ye 22 & was buried October ye 24. 1716.
Thomas Elliot dyed Novem^r ye 19. & was buried Novem^r ye 22. 1716.
William Elliot dyed Novem^r ye 22. & was buried Novem^r ye 27. 1716.
Elizabeth Churchhill dyed Novem^r ye 11 & was buried Novem^r ye 16. 1716.
Matthew Kemp dyed November ye 16 & was buried Novem^r ye 23. 1716.
Edmund Hamerton dyed Novem^r ye 27 & was buried Novem^r ye 30 1716.
Minor Minor dyed Novem^r ye 30 & was buried Decem^r ye 3. 1716.
Sarah Mayo dyed Novem^r ye 29 & was buried Novem^r ye 30. 1716.
Frances Ingram dyed Novem^r ye 30 & was buried Decem^r ye 2. 1716.
Sarah Adcock dyed Decem^r ye 1 & was buried Decem^r ye 2. 1716.
Mary Powell dyed Decem^r ye 2d & was buried Decem^r ye 4. 1716.
Thomas Bewford Senr dyed Decem^r ye 9. & was buried Decem^r ye 11. 1716.
John Ingram dyed December ye 17 & was buried December ye 19. 1716.
William Lewis dyed December ye 8 & was buried December ye 10. 1716.
Benjamine Baldin dyed December ye 8 & was buried December ye 10. 1716.
Elizabeth Southworth dyed December ye 21 & was buried December ye 22. 1716.
Morrice Griffin dyed December y^e & was buried December ye 1716.
Anne Ball dyed December ye 14 & was buried December ye 16 1716.
Tabitha Nichols dyed December ye 18 & was buried December ye 21 1716.
Richard Atwood dyed Jan'y ye 1 & was buried Jan'y ye 3. 1716.
Lucy Bartlett dyed December 16 & was buried December 24. 1716.
Hezekiah Roades dyed Jan'y. ye 2 & was buried Jan'y. ye 7. 1716.
Mary Sandiford dyed Jan'y ye 3 & was buried Jan'y. ye 5. 1716.

William Turnett dyed Jan'y. y⁰ 10. & was buried Jan'y y⁰ 12. 1716.
Elizabeth Chelton dyed Jan'y y⁰ 10 & was buried Jan'y. y⁰ 12. 1716.
James Roades dyed Jan'y. y⁰ 11 & was buried Jan'y. y⁰ 13. 1716.
Catherine Southern dyed December y⁰ 31 & was buried Jan'y. y⁰ 3. 1716.
John Mullins dyed Jan'y y⁰ 20 & was buried January y⁰ 21. 1716.
Hannah Cheedle dyed January y⁰ 22 & was buried January y⁰ 24 1716.
Elizabeth Dudley dyed January y⁰ 11 & was buried January y⁰ 13 1716.
Mary Sandiford dyed January y⁰ 8. & was buried January y⁰ 11. 1716.
Elizabeth Timberlake dyed January y⁰ 8 & was buried January y⁰ 11 1716.
Thomas Davis dyed January y⁰ 10 & was buried January y⁰ 13. 1716.
Mary Trigg dyed Jan'y y⁰ 29 & was buried January y⁰ 31. 1716.
John Williams dyed Feb'y y⁰ 26 & was buried February y⁰ 27. 1716.
Jacob Presenall dyed March y⁰ 4 & was buried March y⁰ 6. 1716.
Robert James dyed Feb'y y⁰ 9 & was buried Febr'y y⁰ 10 1716.

    Bar. Yates. Minister.

BURIALS.

Sarah Perrott dyed March y⁰ 13 & was buried March y⁰ 15. 1716.
Sarah Bolton dyed Feb'y y⁰ 3 & was buried Feb'y y⁰ 6. 1716.
Jacob Blake dyed March y⁰ 10. & was buried March y⁰ 12. 1716.
Robert Couch dyed August y⁰ 30. & was buried August y⁰ 31. 1716.
Elizabeth Barwick dyed February y⁰ 3. & was buried February y⁰ 6. 1716.
Mathew Parry dyed April y⁰ 2. & was buried April y⁰ 4. 1717.
Anne Williams dyed April y⁰ 4. & was buried April y⁰ 6. 1717.
John Price dyed April y⁰ 19. & was buried April y⁰ 21. 1717.
James Mactire dyed April y⁰ 26. & was buried April y⁰ 27 1717.
Mary Allin dyed May y⁰ 6. & was buried May y⁰ 8. 1717.
James Riske dyed May y⁰ 7 & was buried May y⁰ 10. 1717.
Robert Murray dyed May y⁰ 16 & was buried May y⁰ 17. 1717.
Richard Reynolds dyed Ap: y⁰ 30 & was buried May y⁰ 1. 1717.
Hannah Guest dyed May y⁰ 10 & was buried May y⁰ 13. 1717.
Anne Austain dyed May y⁰ 17 & was buried May y⁰ 19 1717.
John Nash dyed June y⁰ 30. & was buried July y⁰ 1st 1717.
Elizabeth Pendergrass dyed July y⁰ 27. & was buried July y⁰ 29. 1717.
Thomas Cheedle dyed Sept y⁰ 1. & was buried Septem' y⁰ 3. 1717.
Elizabeth Whiteacre dyed August y⁰ 26. & was buried August y⁰ 29. 1717.
Mary Hughs dyed September y⁰ 9. & was buried Septem' y⁰ 11. 1717.
James Ball dyed September y⁰ 24. & was buried Septem' y⁰ 25. 1717.
Paul Durham dyed September y⁰ 28. & was buried Septem' y⁰ 29. 1717.
Sarah Ingram dyed September y⁰ 29. & was buried October y⁰ 1. 1717.
George Jennings dyed September y⁰ 4. & was buried Septem' y⁰ 5. 1717.
John Sparkes dyed September y⁰ 28. & was buried Septem' y⁰ 30. 1717.
Ruth Moxam dyed Octo. y⁰ 11. & was buried Octo. y⁰ 13. 1717.

Elizabeth Vivion dyed Octo. y⁰ 23. & was buried Octo: y⁰ 26. 1717.
Henry Anderson dyed Octo. y⁰ 24 & was buried Octo. y⁰ 26. 1717.
Thomas Underwood dyed Septemʳ y⁰ 9. & was buried Septemʳ y⁰ 11. 1717.
Henry Barnes dyed October y⁰ 23. & was buried October y⁰ 25. 1717.
Mary Wilson dyed October y⁰ 23. & was buried October y⁰ 24. 1717.
John Smith Junʳ dyed Novemʳ y⁰ 15. & was buried Novemʳ y" 18. 1717.
Elizabeth Davies dyed Decemʳ y⁰ 1. & was buried Decemʳ y⁰ 2. 1717.
Joseph Goar senʳ dyed Decemʳ y⁰ 7. & was buried Decemʳ y⁰ 8 1717.
Uriah Bolton dyed Novemʳ y" 19. & was buried Novemʳ y⁰ 21. 1717.
Peter Chelton dyed Decemʳ y⁰ 17. & was buried Decemʳ y⁰ 19. 1717.
William Marcum dyed Decemʳ y⁰ 17. & was buried Decemʳ y⁰ 19. 1717.
Thomas Warwick dyed Decemʳ y⁰ 31. & was buried Jan'y y⁰ 3. 1717.
Elizabeth Pace dyed Decmʳ y⁰ 30. & was buried Jan'y y⁰ 1. 1717.
Henry Chelton dyed Decemʳ y⁰ 28. & was buried Jan'y y⁰ 2. 1717.
Mary Couch dyed Novemʳ y⁰ 4. & was buried Novemʳ y⁰ 6. 1717.
Edmund Saunders dyed Jan'y y" 16. & was buried Jan'y y⁰ 19. 1717.
John Stiff dyed Jan'y y⁰ 23. & was buried Jan'y y⁰ 25. 1717.
Sarah Hadley dyed Decemʳ y⁰ 6. was buried Decemʳ y⁰ 9. 1717.
Mary Cooper dyed Jan'y y⁰ 18. & was buried Jan'y y⁰ 19. 1717.
Mabell Dodson dyed Feb'y y⁰ 8. & was buried Feb'y y⁰ 12. 1717.
William Hughes dyed March y⁰ 10. & was buried March y⁰ 12. 1717.

Bar. Yates. Minister.

BURIALS.

Bridgett Gordon dyed March y⁰ 5. & was buried March y⁰ 7. 1717.
Winnifred Nicholls dyed March y⁰ 10. & was buried March y⁰ 12. 1717.
Anne Gardner dyed March y⁰ 10 & was buried March y⁰ 13. 1717.
Winnifred Purvis dyed March y⁰ 15. & was buried March y⁰ 16. 1717.
Henry Nicholls dyed March y⁰ 18. & was buried March y⁰ 20. 1717.
John Burrow dyed October y⁰ 28. & was buried October y⁰ 30. 1717.
John Hughes dyed April y⁰ 5. & was buried April y⁰ 7. 1718.
Abigall Marston dyed March y⁰ 17. & was buried March y⁰ 20 1717.
Mary Roberts dyed March y⁰ 31. & was buried April y⁰ 2. 1718.
Anna Hughes dyed April y⁰ 28. & was buried April y⁰ 30. 1718.
Mary Marston dyed April y⁰ 4. & was buried April y⁰ 7. 1718.
Jane Ballard dyed April y⁰ 5. & was buried April y⁰ 6. 1718.
John Conner dyed April y⁰ 3. & was buried April y⁰ 4. 1718.
William Jones dyed April y⁰ 10. & was buried April y⁰ 12. 1718.
Willet Roberts dyed April y⁰ 11. & was buried April y⁰ 13. 1718.
Thomas Stiff dyed April y⁰ 11. & was buried April y⁰ 13. 1718.
Mary Middleton dyed April y⁰ 12. & was buried April y⁰ 14. 1718.
Diana Minor dyed April y⁰ 16. & was buried April y⁰ 18. 1718.
Elizabeth Pemberton dyed April y⁰ 20. & was buried April y⁰ 22. 1718.
Thomas Gates dyed May y⁰ 9. & was buried May y⁰ 11 1718.
Robert Purvis dyed May y⁰ 24. & was buried May y⁰ 25. 1718.
Rebecca Pearce dyed May 30. & was buried June y⁰ 1. 1718.

Arthur Nash dyed May ye 16. & was buried May ye 17. 1718.
John Sandiford dyed May ye 25. & was buried May y^n 27. 1718.
Sarah Betts dyed June ye 15. & was buried June ye 17. 1718.
Catherine George dyed Septem^r ye 26. & was buried Septem^r ye 28. 1718.
Peter Chilton dyed October ye 1. & was buried Octo. ye 4. 1718.
Anne Downey dyed October ye 14. & was buried Octo. ye 17. 1718.
Elizabeth Crank dyed October ye 26. & was buried Octo. ye 27. 1718.
Henry Month dyed Novem^r ye 14. & was buried Novem^r ye 14. 1718.
William Finney dyed Aprill ye 26. & was buried Aprill ye 30. 1718.
Priscilla Miller dyed Novem^r ye 6. & was buried Novem^r ye 7. 1718.
William Baker dyed Novem^r ye 19. & was buried Novem^r ye 20. 1718.
Elizabeth Vivion dyed Decem^r ye 6. & was buried Decem^r ye 8. 1718.
Jeptha Edmunds dyed Novem^r ye 23. & was buried Novem^r ye 25. 1718.
Solomon Crank dyed Novem^r ye 24. & was buried Novem^r ye 25. 1718.
Mathew Crank dyed Decem^r ye 3. & was buried Decem^r ye 5. 1718.
Elizabeth Stiff dyed Decem^r ye 3. & was buried Decem^r ye 6. 1718.
Catherine Row dyed Decem^r ye 14. & was buried Decem^r ye 16. 1718.
Elizabeth Elliott dyed Decem^r ye 23. & was buried Decem^r ye 27. 1718.
Edmond Bartlett dyed Decem^r ye 15. & was buried Decem^r ye 22. 1718.
Joanna Humpheries dyed Decem^r ye 19. & was buried Decem^r ye 23 1718.
Joanna Diggs dyed Jan'y ye 17. & was buried Jan'y ye 22. 1718.
Andrew Foulk dyed Jan'y ye 27. & was buried Jan'y ye 29. 1718.
Alexander Murry dyed Feb'y ye 19. & was buried Feb'y ye 23. 1718.
John Pendergrass dyed Jan'y ye 29. & was buried Jan'y ye 31. 1718.
Mary Gilley dyed Feb'y ye 6. & was buried Feb'y ye 8. 1718.
Charles Bishop dyed March ye 9. & was buried March ye 12 1718.
Bar. Yates. Minister.

BURIALS.

Abraham Trigg dyed Feb'y ye 25 & was buried Feb'y. ye 27. 1718.
Patrick Owen dyed March ye 10 & was buried March ye 11. 1718.
Edward Syddern dyed March ye 12 & was buried March ye 14. 1718.
Charity Ingram dyed Feb'y ye 28. & was buried March ye 2 1718.
Arthur Johnson dyed March ye 21. & was buried March ye 22 1718.
Ralph Broster dyed April ye 6 & was buried April ye 7 1719.
Anne George dyed April ye 7. & was buried April ye 9 1719.
Mary Daniel dyed March ye 26. & was buried march ye 27 1719.
Elizabeth Reynolds dyed March ye 14. & was buried march ye 16. 1718.
Philip Warwick dyed April ye 17. & was buried Aprill ye 20. 1719.
Robert Biggs dyed March ye 27. & was buried March ye 29 1719.
John Lucas dyed May ye 4 & was buried May ye 6. 1719.
Sarah Crank dyed July ye 12 & was buried July ye 14 1719.
Mary Shelton dyed July ye 18 & was buried July ye 19 1719.

Pearse Edward dyed August yʳ 2. & was buried Augsᵗ yⁿ 3 1719.
John Watts was killed September yᵉ 4. & was buried September yᵉ 9. 1719.
Joan Molloney dyed Septemʳ yᵉ 26. & was buried Septemʳ yᵉ 27. 1719.
Anne Bristow dyed Septemʳ yʳ 23 & was buried Septemʳ yᵉ 24. 1719.
Elizabeth Jones dyed Octo. yⁿ 10. & was buried October yᵉ 13. 1719.
Daniel Hues dyed Octo. yʳ 14. & was buried October yᵉ 15. 1719.
David Morgan alias Henry Smith dyed Octo. 28. was buried October yᵉ 31. 1719.
Alexander Graves dyed Novemʳ yᵉ 5. & was buried Novemʳ yᵉ 8. 1719.
Mildred Ryley dyed Novemʳ yᵉ 9. & was buried Novemʳ yᵉ 10. 1719.
John Dudley dyed Novemʳ yᵉ 25. & was buried Novemʳ yʳ 27 1719.
William Stanard dyed Decemʳ yᵉ 27. & was buried Decemʳ yᵉ 29 1719.
Anne Brooks dyed Decemʳ yʳ 21. & was buried Decemʳ yᵉ 23 1719.
Thomas Cheedle dyed Jan'y. yᵉ 10. & was buried Jann'y. yᵉ 11. 1719.
Edwin Thacker dyed Feb'y. yᵉ 16. & was buried Feb'y. yᵉ 17. 1719.
Penelope Cheney dyed March yᵉ 22. & was buried March yᵉ 24. 1719.
William Hearn dyed Decemʳ yⁿ 12. & was buried Decemʳ yᵉ 14. 1719.
Samuel Shakpurr dyed Ap. yᵉ 1 & was buried Ap: yᵉ 2 1720.
Catherine Mountague dyed April yⁿ 19. & was buried Ap: yᵉ 21 1720.
Richard Finney dyed March yᵉ 20. & was buried March yᵉ 23. 1719.
Elizabeth Jennings dyed Ap: yᵉ 15. & was buried Ap. yᵉ 17. 1720.
Hezekiah Roades dyed Ap: yᵉ 14. & was buried Ap: yᵉ 16. 1720.
Thomas Tilley dyed Ap: yᵉ 17. & was buried Ap. yᵉ 19. 1720.
Edward Siddean dyed Ap: yʳ 22. & was buried Ap: yᵉ 23 1720.
Sarah Fearn dyed Ap: yᵉ 15. & was buried April yᵉ 16 1720.
Jane Hardee dyed April yᵉ 10. & was buried April yᵉ 13 1720.
Elizabeth Berry dyed April yʳ 17. & was buried April yᵉ 19. 1720.
Elizabeth Mactyre dyed March yⁿ 26. & was buried March yᵉ 28 1720.
John Johnson dyed April yⁿ 5. & was buried April yʳ 7 1720.
Joseph Timberlake dyed March yᵘ 14 & was buried March yᵉ 17 1719.
Thomas Blunt dyed April yʳ 1. & was buried April yᵉ 3 1720.
William Hill dyed May yᵘ 6 & was buried May yᵉ 8 1720.
James Lewis dyed May yᵉ 10. & was buried May yᵉ 12 1720.
Faith Ducksworth dyed June yʳ 23. & was buried June yᵉ 24 1720.
Thomas Hill dyed August yᵉ 3. & was buried August yᵉ 4 1720.

Bar. Yates. Minister.

BURIALS.

Elizabeth Beverley dyed August yᵉ 6 & was buried August yᵉ 11. 1720.
John Curlett dyed August yⁿ 13 & was buried August yᵉ 14. 1720.
John Wignall dyed August yᵉ 9 & was buried August yᵉ 11. 1720.
Henry Ball dyed August yᵉ 27 & was buried August yᵉ 29. 1720.
Anne Wood dyed August yᵉ 18 & was buried August yᵉ 20. 1720.
Mary Lewis dyed August yᵉ 24 & was buried August yᵉ 25. 1720,
Agatha Wormeley dyed Sept. yʳ 10 & was buried Septeʳ yᵉ 11. 1720.
Mary Ranstead dyed Sept. yᵉ 10 & was buried Septemʳ yᵉ 12. 1720.
Cary Stamper dyed Sept. yᵉ 2 & was buried Septemʳ yᵉ 4. 1720.
Robert Aldin dyed Sept. yᵉ 4 & was buried Septemʳ yᵉ 5. 1720.

William Beamon dyed August ye 24 & was buried Angust ye 26. 1720.
James Rowe dyed October ye 9 & was buried October ye 11. 1720.
James Curtis j^r dyed Novem^r ye 4 & was buried Novem^r ye 7. 1720.
William Gordon dyed Novem^r ye 14 & was buried Novem^r ye 17. 1720.
Roger Jones jun^r dyed October ye 26 & was buried October ye 29. 1720.
Judith Robinson dyed Novem^r ye 18 & was buried Novem^r ye 22. 1720.
James Curtis dyed Novem^r ye 18 & was buried Novem^r y^o 23. 1720.
John Batchelder dyed Novem^r ye 26 & was buried Novem^r ye 29. 1720.
John Davis died Novem^r ye 27 & was buried Novem^r ye 29. 1720.
Avarilla Davis dyed Decem^r ye 2 & was buried Decem^r ye 4. 1720.
William Webb dyed Novem^r ye 28 & was buried Novem^r y^o 30. 1720.
Sarah Batchelder dyed Decem^r ye 3 & was buried Decem^r ye 7. 1720.
Elizabeth Batchelder dyed Decem^r ye 6 & was buried Decem^r y^e — 1720.
Rals Lyall dyed Decem^r ye 5 & was buried Decem^r ye 7. 1720.
John Baskett dyed Novem^r ye 28 & was buried Novem^r ye 30. 1720.
Easter Moxham dyed Novem^r ye 28 & was buried Novem^r ye 30. 1720.
Henry Baskett dyed Decem^r y^o 5 & was buried Decem^r y^o 7. 1720.
Sarah Baskett dyed Decem^r ye 8 & was buried Decem^r ye 9. 1720.
Onnor Baskett dyed Decem^r ye 14 & was buried Decem^r ye 15. 1720.
Susanna Wood dyed Decem^r ye 12 & was buried Decem^r ye 14. 1720.
George Johnson died Decem^r ye 10 & was buried Decem^r y^o 11. 1720.
Alice Kidd died Decem^r ye 14 & was buried Decem^r ye 15. 1720.
Elizabeth Chowing died Decem^r ye 10 & was buried Decem^r y^o 11. 1720.
Judith Shurley died Decem^r y^o 8 & was buried Decem^r ye 9. 1720.
Simon Probart died Decem^r ye 16 & was buried Decem^r ye 17. 1720.
Frances Thacker jun^r died Decem^r ye 23 & was buried Decem^r y^o 24. 1720.
John Bird died December ye 19 & was buried Decem^r ye 20. 1720.
Thomas Cary died December ye 21 & was buried Decem^r ye 23. 1720.
Margret Southworth died Decem^r y^c 16 & was buried Debem^r ye 18. 1720.
Mary Purvis died December ye 14 & was buried Decem^r y^o 16. 1720.
Mary Whistler died December ye 19 & was buried Decem^r ye 19. 1720.
Robert Daniell died December ye 27 & was buried Decem^r ye 29. 1720.
William Gilley died December ye 15 & was buried Decem^r ye 17. 1720.
Thomas Moor died December y^o 16 & was buried Decem^r ye 17. 1720.
John Camell died December ye 15 & was buried Decem^r ye 17. 1720.
John Micou died December ye 20 & was buried Decem^r ye 21. 1720.
Mary Pateman died December ye 15 & was buried Decem^r ye 16. 1720.
James Devolve died December ye 26 & was buried Decem^r ye 27. 1720.
Frances Williams died December ye 26 & was buried Decem^r ye 28. 1720.
Sarah Couch dyed October ye 19 & was buried October ye 22 1720.

    Bar. Yates Minister.

BURIALS.

James Meacham dyed Decemr. y[e] 12 & was buried Decem[r] y[e] 13. 1720.
Mary Buford dyed Decemr. y[e] 29 & was buried Decem[r] y[e] 30. 1720.
Samuel Kidd dyed Decem[r] y[e] 26 & was buried Decem[r] y[e] 27. 1720.
Elizabeth Williams dyed Decem[r] y[e] 26 & was buried Decem[r] y[e] 27. 1720.
Frances Daniell dyed Decem[r] y[e] 28 & was buried Decem[r] y[e] 29. 1720.
William Curlis dyed Jan'y y[e] 1 & was buried Jan'y: y[e] 3. 1720.
William Brooks dyed Jan'y. y[e] 4 & was buried Jan'y y[e] 6. 1720.
Penelope Gilbreath dyed Jan'y. y[e] 2 & was buried Jan'y. y[e] 4. 1720.
Hugh Watts dyed Jan'y. y[e] 2 & was buried Jan'y: y[e] 4. 1720.
Timothy Callahan dyed Jan'y: y[e] 3 & was buried Jan'y y[e] 5. 1720.
William Ingram dyed Decem[r] y[e] 10 & was buried Decem[r] y[e] 12. 1720.
James Walker dyed Jan'y. y[e] 12 & was buried Jan'y y[e] 17. 1720.
Benjamine Goare dyed Jan'y. y[e] 15 & was buried Jan'y y[e] 17. 1720.
Betty Cooper dyed Decem[r] y[e] 29 & was buried Decem[r] y[e] 31. 1720.
Henry Nicholls dyed Jan'y. y[e] 3. & was buried Jan'y. y[e] 5. 1720.
Charles Cooper dyed Jan'y. y[e] 15 & was buried Jan'y. y[e] 17. 1720.
George Howard dyed Jan'y. y[e] 23 & was buried Jan'y. y[e] 25. 1720.
Catherine Perrott dyed Decem[r] y[e] 28 & was buried Decem[r] y[e] 30. 1720.
Margret Kidd dyed Jan'y y[e] 4 & was buried Jan'y. y[e] 6. 1720.
George Stapleton dyed Jan'y. y[e] 8 & was buried Jan'y. y[e] 10. 1720.
Henry Buford dyed Jan'y. y[e] 16 & was buried Jan'y. y[e] 18. 1720.
Joseph Seares jun[r] dyed Jan'y. y[e] 17 & was buried Jan'y. y[e] 19. 1720.
Edward Cambridge dyed Jan'y. y[e] 18 & was buried Jan'y. y[e] 20. 1720.
Henry Freeman dyed Jan'y. y[e] 26 & was buried Jan'y. y[e] 28. 1720.
John Pace dyed Jan'y y[e] 20 & was buried Jan'y. y[e] 23. 1720.
Alice Norman dyed Decem[r] y[e] 20 & was buried Decem[r] y[e] 22. 1720.
John Owen dyed Jan'y y[e] 23 & was buried Jan'y y[e] 26. 1720.
Anne Deagle dyed Jan'y y[e] 30 & was buried Jan'y y[e] 31. 1720.
Joseph Marcum dyed Jan'y y[e] 11 & was buried Jan'y. y[e] 12. 1720.
Garritt Minor dyed Feb'ry y[e] 2 & was buried Feb'y y[e] 4. 1720.
Mary Graves dyed Feb'ry y[e] 2 & was buried Feb'y. y[o] 4. 1720.
Mary Warwick dyed Jan'y y[e] 8 & was buried Jan'y. y[e] 11. 1720.
Charles Lee dyed Jan'y y[e] 6 & was buried Jan'y. y[e] 9. 1720.
William Tignor dyed Feb'ry y[e] 5 & was buried Feb'y y[e] 8. 1720.
Aquilla Snelling jun[r] dyed Feb'y. y[e] 10 & was buried Feb'y y[e] 11. 1720.
Avarilla Hardee dyed Feb'y. y[e] 7 & was buried Feb'y. y[o] 9. 1720.
Sarah Freestone dyed Jan'y y[e] 7 & was buried Jan'y. y[o] 9. 1720.
Thomas Russell dyed Jan'y y[e] 21 & was buried Jan'y y[e] 23. 1720.
James Jameson dyed Jan'y y[e] 17 & was buried Jan'y. y[e] 19. 1720.
Benjamin Beamon dyed Jan'y. y[e] 25 & was buried Jan'y y[e] 27. 1720.
Mary Maderas dyed Feb'y. y[e] 5 & was buried Feb'y. y[e] 7. 1720.
Thomas Mountague Sen[r] dyed Feb'y. y[e] 9 & was buried Feb'y. y[e] 14. 1720.
Charles Macarty dyed Feb'y. y[e] 14 & was buried Feb'y. y[e] 16. 1720.
Peter Bromwell dyed Feb'y: y[e] 28 & was buried March y[e] 3. 1720.
Sarah Tomson dyed Feb'y y[e] 28 & was buried March y[e] 1. 1720.
Thomas Walker dyed March y[e] 1 & was buried March y[e] 4. 1720.

Mary Robinson dyed March ye 5 & was buried March ye 9. 1720.
Mary George dyed Feb'y: ye 22 & was buried Feb'y. ye 24. 1720.
Phillip Carter dyed Feb'y ye 27 & was buried Feb'y ye 28. 1720.
Susanna Midleton dyed Feb'y ye 28 & was buried March ye 1 1720.
William Probart dyed Feb'y ye 13 & was buried Feb'y ye 15 1720.

Bar Yates. Minister.

BURIALS.

Margrett Brooks dyed March ye 13 & was buried March ye 15 1720.
James Machen dyed March ye 22 & was buried 1720.
Sarah Mash dyed April ye 12 & was buried April ye 13 1721.
Edmund Mickelburrough jun^r dyed Ap: ye 15. & was buried April ye 17 1721.
Thomas Still dyed April ye 13 & was buried April ye 15 1721.
Anne Haselwood dyed April ye 28. & was buried April ye 30 1721.
Eloner Still dyed May ye 2d & was buried May ye 4 1721.
Joseph Jacobus dyed May ye 15. & was buried May ye 17 1721.
Dudley Jolly dyed May ye 9. & was buried May ye 11 1721.
John Guess dyed May ye 30. & was buried May ye 31 1721.
Sarah Ball dyed June ye 27 & was buried June ye 29 1721.
Lucy Beverley dyed July ye 6 & was buried July ye 8 1721.
John Dobs jun^r dyed July ye 13 & was buried July ye 14 1721.
Thomas Gresham dyed July ye 13 & was buried July ye 14 1721.
Eloner Williams dyed July ye 14. & was buried July ye 15. 1721.
Thomas Stiff dyed July ye 4. & was buried July ye 5 1721.
James Gilbert dyed August ye 14. & was buried August ye 15 1721.
James Gordon dyed August ye 19 & was buried August ye 20 1721.
Joseph Kidd dyed August ye 23. & was buried August ye 24 1721.
Grace Tomson dyed August ye 20. & was buried August ye 21 1721.
William Cottel dyed Sept. ye 4. & was buried Septem^r ye 5 1721.
William Ball dyed Septem^r ye 2. & was buried Septem^r ye 3. 1721.
Hannah Mactire dyed Septem^r ye 25 & was buried Septem^r ye 27 1721.
James Robbeck dyed Septem^r ye 28 & was buried Septem^r ye 30 1721.
Agatha Mosely dyed August ye 22. & was buried August ye 24 1721.
Mary Wormley dyed Octo: ye 14 & was buried Octo: ye 16. 1721.
Elizabeth Ingram dyed Octo. ye 7 & was buried Octo. ye 9. 1721.
Thomas Crank dyed Octo. ye 8. & was buried Octo. ye 10 1721.
Minor Williamson dyed Septem^r ye 27 & was buried Septem^r ye 29. 1721.
John Barnett dyed Octo: ye 31 & was buried Novem^r ye 2 1721.
Sarah Chowning dyed Novem^r ye 9. & was buried Novem^r ye 11 1721.
Thomas Chowning dyed Novem. ye 15. & was buried Novem^r ye 17 1721.
James Nutter dyed Novem^r ye 18. & was buried Novem^r ye 19 1721.
Thomas Diatt dyed Novem^r ye 5. & was buried Novem^r ye 7 1721.
Anne Nash dyed Decem^r ye 5. & was buried Decem^r ye 7 1721.
Catharine Canaday dyed Decem^r ye 1 & was buried Decem^r ye 3 1721.
Anne Moulson dyed Decem^r ye 8 & was buried Decem^r ye 10 1721.
John Purton dyed Novem^r ye 14. & was buried Novem^r ye 16 1721.
John Anderson dyed Novem^r ye 29. & was buried Decem^r ye 2 1721.
John Roads dyed Decem^r ye 25. & was buried Decem ye 27 1721.

Edward Canody dyed Jan'y ye 2 & was buried Jan'y ye 4 1721.
Alexander How dyed Jan'y. ye 7 & was buried Jan'y ye 9 1721.
Thomas Gibson dyed Jan'y. ye 18 & was buried Jan'y ye 19 1721.
John Vivion dyed Feb'y ye 12 & was buried Feb'y ye 16 1721.
Marvell Mosely sen^r dyed Feb'y ye 13 & was buried Feb'y ye 15 1721.
John Mickleburrough dyed Feb'y ye 13 & was buried Feb'y ye 15 1721.
William Lewis dyed Feb'y ye 28 & was buried March ye 2 1721.
John Smith Senr dyed Feb'y ye 19. & was buried Feb'y ye 23 1721.
Jacob Williamson dyed Feb'y ye 27 & was buried March ye 1 1721.
    Bar Yates Minisster.

BURIALS.

William Sadler dyed Ap: ye 10 & was buried Ap. ye 12 1722.
John Blewford dyed Ap: ye 18 & was buried Ap: ye 20. 1722.
Owin Winn dyed Ap: ye 17 & was buried Ap. ye 19. 1722.
Thomas Williams dyed Ap: ye 20. & was buried Ap. ye 22. 1722.
Jane Guttery dyed Ap. ye 22 & was buried Ap. ye 24. 1722.
James Bowman died April ye 10. & was buried Ap. ye 12. 1722.
George Bonner was drowned July ye 15 & was buried July ye 17 1722.
Henry Diamond was drowned July ye 15 & was buried July ye 18. 1722.
Bridgett Gordon dyed July ye 17 & was buried July ye 19. 1722.
John Johnson dyed July ye 11 & was buried July ye 12. 1722.
William Roach dyed July ye 31 & was buried August ye 2 1722.
John Maderas dyed August ye 1 & was buried August ye 3 1722.
Brown Gordon dyed August ye 15 & was buried August ye 16. 1722.
Mary Tomson dyed August ye 19 & was buried August ye 21 1722.
William Hendring dyed August ye 17 & was buried August ye 18 1722.
Mary Foy dyed August ye 23 & was buried August ye 24 1722.
Mary Wisdale dyed August ye 22 & was buried August ye 23 1722.
Elizabeth Southworth dyed Septem^r ye 15 & was buried Septem^r ye 16. 1722.
Margrett Baldwin dyed Octo: ye 7 & was buried Octo: ye 9 1722.
Elizabeth Summers dyed May ye 29 & was buried May ye 30 1722.
Anne Goodloe dyed Septem^r ye 7 & was buried Septem^r ye 8 1722.
James Greenwood dyed Octo: ye 16. & was buried Octo: ye 17 1722.
Elizabeth Emmerson dyed Octo. ye 1 & was buried Octo. ye 2 1722.
Robert Walker dyed Octo. ye 21 & was buried Octo. ye 22 1722.
Elizabeth Curtis dyed Novem^r ye 8. & was buried Novem. ye 9 1722.
James Mackmullen dyed Novem^r ye 14 & was buried Novem^r ye 15 1722.
James Brame dyed Septem^r ye 12. & was buried Septem^r ye 14 1722.
Dorothy Best dyed Jan'y ye 17 & was buried Jan'y ye 18 1722.
Jane Carnew dyed Decem^r ye 18 & was buried Decem^r ye 20 1722.
Thomas Langley dyed Feb'y ye 2. & was buried Feb'y ye 4 1722.
Anne Dudley dyed Feb'y ye 1 & was buried Feb'y ye 3 1722.
John Thilman dyed Feb'y ye 16. & was buried Feb'y ye 18 1722.
Elizabeth Pudduck dyed Feb'y ye 6 & was buried Feb'y ye 8 1722.
Edward Pearse dyed Feb'y ye 12 & was buried Feb'y ye 14 1722.
John Watts dyed Decem^r ye 17 & was buried Decem^r ye 19 1722.
Grace Southworth dyed Feb'y ye 24 & was buried Feb'y ye 25 1722.
Thomas Smith dyed March ye 11. & was buried March ye 14 1722.

William Anderson dyed April ye 7 & was buried April ye 9. 1722.
Arthur Donnolly dyed April ye 18 & was buried April y^o 20 1723.
Alice Benson dyed April ye 17 & was buried April ye 19 1723.
William Guttery dyed April ye 27 & was buried April ye 29 1723.
Benjamin Taylor dyed June ye 5 & was buried June ye 7 1723.
William Daniel dyed May ye 29 & was buried May ye 31 1723.
Sarah Portwood dyed July ye 7 & was buried July ye 9 1723.
Catherine Lomax dyed August ye 12 & was buried August ye 15 1723.
Malcolme Towerd dyed July ye 31 & was buried August ye 2 1723.
Robert Perrott dyed August ye 9 & was buried August ye 11 1723.
Benjamine Robinson dyed August ye 23. & was buried August ye 26 1723.
Grace Clay dyed Septem^r ye 20 & was buried September ye 22 1723.
James Cole dyed Septem^r ye 23 & was buried September ye 25 1723.
William Daniell dyed Octo ye 11. & was buried October ye 13 1723.

  Bar Yates. Minister.

BURIALS.

Thomas Smith dyed Octo. ye 16. & was buried Octo. ye 18 1723.
William Huskett dyed Novem^r ye 11. & was buried Novem^r ye 13 1723.
Elizabeth Newberry dyed Novem^r ye 5. & was buried Novem^r ye 8 1723.
Richard Warren dyed Novem^r ye 12. & was buried Novem^r ye 14 1723.
Elizabeth Banger dyed Novem^r ye 10. & was buried Novem^r ye 12 1723.
Hezekiah Roades dyed Decem^r ye 10 & was buried Decem^r ye 12 1723.
Samuel Worner dyed Decem^r ye 31 & was buried Jan'y ye 1 1723.
William Newberry dyed Jan'y ye 14 & was buried Jan'y y^n 19 1723.
John Davis died Jan'y ye 27 & was buried Jan'y ye 30 1723.
Chichester Curtis dyed Feb'y ye 1 & was buried Feb'y ye 5 1723.
John Miller dyed Jan'y ye 28 & was buried Jan'y ye 30 1723.
John Hickey dyed Feb'y. ye 6 & was buried Feb'y. ye 8 1723.
Frances Williams dyed Jan'y. ye 21. & was buried Jan'y ye 23 1723.
William Clark dyed Jan'y ye 30. & was buried Feb'y. ye 1 1723.
William Davis dyed Feb'y. ye 18 & was buried Feb'y. ye 20 1723.
John Mayo dyed March ye 5. & was buried March ye 10 1723.
Elizabeth Sadler dyed Feb'y ye 16. & was buried Feb'y ye 19 1723.
Sarah Watts dyed March ye 1. & was buried March ye 3 1723.
Jemima Batchelder dyed March ye 18. & was buried March ye 20. 1723.
Thomas Cheedle dyed March ye 31. & was buried April ye 1 1724.
Patrick Kelly dyed May ye 6. & was buried May ye 8. 1724.
Christopher Kelshaw dyed May ye 2. & was buried May ye 4. 1724.
Anne Anderson dyed May ye 7. & was buried May ye 9. 1724.
John Roe dyed May ye 19. & was buried May ye 21. 1724.
John South dyed May ye 21. & was buried May ye 23 1724.
Aaron Williams dyed July ye 10. & was buried July ye 12. 1724.
Frances Vivion dyed August ye 16. & was buried August ye 21 1724.
Esther Kelshaw dyed August ye 20. & was buried August ye 22 1724.

Anne Mactire dyed Septem^r ye 15. & was buried Septem^r ye 17. 1724.
Pinchback Hamerton dyed Septem^r ye 23. & was buried Septem^r ye 26. 1724.
John Rice dyed October 17 & was buried October ye 20. 1724.
Daniell Cain dyed Novem^r ye 7. & was buried Novem^r ye 9. 1724.
Nathan Sutton dyed Novem^r ye 25. & was buried Novem^r ye 27. 1724.
Richard Waight dyed Dec. ye 10. & was buried Decem^r ye 12 1724.
John Thomas dyed Dec. ye 4. & was buried Decem^r ye 6 1724.
Anne Smith dyed Decem^r ye 20. & was buried Decem^r ye 23 1724.
Mary Goodrich dyed Jan'y ye 17. & was buried Jan'y. ye 19 1724.
Jane Price dyed March ye 5. & was buried March ye 8. 1724.
Elizabeth Tugle dyed March ye 7. & was buried March ye 9. 1724.
Elizabeth Skipwith dyed May ye 11. & was buried May ye 13. 1725.
Rebecca Roach dyed June ye 18. & was buried June ye 19. 1725.
Arthur Davis dyed July ye 10. & was buried July ye 12. 1725.
Margrett Wood dyed July ye 17. & was buried July ye 19. 1725.
Lewis Baldwin dyed August ye 8. & was buried August ye 10. 1725.
Garrett Berry dyed Octo. ye 1. & was buried October ye 2. 1725.
John Foster dyed Septem^r ye 6. & was buried Septem^r ye 7. 1725.
Agnes Cummins dyed Septem^r ye 26. & was buried Septem^r ye 28 1725.
Jane Miller dyed october ye 6. & was buried October ye 7. 1725.
Jemimah Bristow dyed Octo: ye 13. & was buried october ye 15. 1725.
George Pace dyed Septem^r ye 10. & was buried Septem^r ye 12. 1725.
John Miller jun^r dyed Octo. ye 19. — was buried Octo: ye 23 1725.
Isaack Oliver dyed Octo. ye 16. & was buried Octo: ye 17 1725.
Robert Blackley dyed octo. ye 31. & was buried Novem^r ye 2 1725.

Bar. Yates. Minister.

BURIALS.

Angello Cummins dyed November ye 4 & was buried November ye 6 1725.
Henry Segar dyed November ye 28. & was buried November ye 30 1725.
Anne Hackney dyed Feb'y ye 8. & was buried Feb'y. ye 11. 1725.
Elizabeth. Batchelder dyed Jan'y ye 17. & was buried Jan'y. ye 19. 1725.
John Gibbs dyed Jan'y. ye 31. & was buried Feb'y ye 3. 1725.
Phillip Warwick dyed March ye 7. & was buried March ye 9 1725.
Sarah Steevens dyed March ye 11. & was buried March ye 13. 1725.
Robert Wharry dyed April ye 7. & was buried April ye 8. 1726.
Catherine Tomson dyed March ye 31. & was buried April ye 3. 1726.
Frances Kidd dyed April ye 2d. & was buried April ye 4. 1726.
John Merry dyed April ye 12. & was buried April ye 13. 1726.
Mary Gray dyed March ye 23 1725 & was buried March ye 25. 1726.
Robert Williamson dyed April ye 15. & was buried April ye 18. 1726.
Catherine Williamson dyed April ye 22. & was buried April ye 23. 1726.
Elizabeth Jones dyed March ye 29. & was buried March ye 31. 1726.
Elizabeth Mullens dyed April ye 2. & was buried April ye 4. 1726.
Benjamine Williamson dyed April ye 26. & was buried April ye 28. 1726.

Elizabeth Lee dyed June ye 2d. & was buried June ye 4. 1726.
Catherine Morgan dyed June ye 18. & was buried June ye 20. 1726.
Elizabeth Curtis dyed June ye 29. & was buried July y^c 1 1726.
John Hackney Dodson dyed May ye 8. & was buried May ye 10 1726.
Anne Wingo dyed June ye 15. & was buried June ye 16 1726.
Mary Holland dyed July ye 28 & was buried July ye 29 1726.
Jane Tompson dyed Septem^r ye 2 & was buried Septem^r ye 4 1726.
James Baskett dyed August ye 29 & was buried August ye 31 1726.
Elizabeth Daniell dyed July ye 27. & was buried July ye 29. 1726.
Sarah Kemp dyed Septem^r ye 17. & was buried Septem^r ye 20. 1726.
Mary Gibson dyed Septem^r ye 27. & was buried Septem^r ye 29. 1726.
John Hackney dyed Septem^r ye 25. & was buried Septem^r y^c 27. 1726.
John Degge dyed August ye 28. & was buried August y^c 31. 1726.
John Penniell dyed Septem^r ye 3. & was buried Septem^r ye 5. 1726.
Anne Greenwood dyed Septem^r ye 26. & was buried Septem^r ye 28 1726.
Humphery Jones dyed Novem^r ye 11. & was buried Novem^r ye 14. 1726.
John Price dyed Novem^r ye 16. & was buried Novem^r ye 19. 1726.
Bathsheba Horn dyed Novem^r ye 23. & was buried Novem^r ye 25 1726.
David George dyed Decem^r ye 19. & was buried Decem^r y^c 21. 1726.
Thomas Causer dyed Novem^r ye 10. & was buried Novem^r ye 12 1726.
Joseph Goar dyed Decem^r ye 8. & was buried Decem^r ye 10 1726.
Anne Goar dyed Decem^r ye 14, & was buried Decem^r ye 16. 1726.
Joseph Holland dyed Decem^r ye 11. & was buried Decem^r ye 13. 1726.
Wm Cain jun^r dyed Decem^r ye 29. & was buried Jan'y. ye 2 1726.
John Cain dyed Decem^r ye 30. & was buried Jan'y ye 2 1726.
Hezekiah Ellis dyed Decem^r ye 23. & was buried Decem^r ye 26. 1726.
Anne Ball dyed Decem^r ye 22 & was buried Decem^r ye 23 1726.
Augustine Owen dyed Decem^r ye 31. & was buried Jan'y ye 2 1726.
Anne Barwick dyed Jan'y ye 12. & was buried Jan'y. ye 14 1726.
Elizabeth Humpheries dyed Jan'y ye 15. & was buried Jan'y. ye 17 1726.
Anne Hill dyed Jan'y ye 15. & was buried Jan'y ye 17 1726.
Dorothy Blackburne dyed Jan'y y^e & was buried Jan'y. ye 7 1726.
Catherine Robinson dyed July 21 & was buried July ye 22 1726.
George Read dyed May ye 3. & was buried May ye 5. 1726.
Martha Moor dyed July ye 8. & was buried July ye 10 1726.
George Bohannon dyed August ye 23 & was buried August ye 24 1726.
Susanna Knight dyed August ye 21. & was buried Augs^t ye 23 1726.
Edward Ball dyed Septem^r ye 4. & was buried Septem^r ye 6 1726.
Martha Micurday dyed July ye 23. & was buried July ye 25 1726.
Anne Farrell dyed Septem^r ye 29. & was buried Octo ye 1. 1726.
Benjamine Clark dyed Octo. ye 8. & was buried Octo ye 10. 1726.
Alexander Smith dyed Octo: ye 9. & was buried Octo ye 11. 1726.
Joane Owen dyed Decem^r ye 12. & was buried Decem^r ye 14. 1726.
John Timberlake dyed Jan'y ye 12 & was buried Jan'y ye 14. 1726.
George Chowning dyed Jan'y ye 8. & was buried Jan'y ye 10. 1726.
John Merry dyed Jan'y ye 15. & was buried Jan'y ye 17 1726.
Agatha Smith dyed Jan'y ye 19. & was buried Jan'y ye 21. 1726.

William Chaffin dyed Jan'y y^r 3. & was buried Jan'y ye 5. 1726.
Thomas Norman dyed Jan'y ye 12. & was buried Jan'y ye 15. 1726.
John Wormley dyed Feb'y y^r 7. & was buried Feb'y ye 11 1726.
Anne Freeman dyed Feb'y ye 2 & was buried Feb'y ye 5 1726.
Mary Tompson dyed Jan'y ye 13 & was buried Jan'y y^o 16 1726.
Christopher Robinson dyed Feb'y ye 20 & was buried Feb'y ye 23. 1726.
Francis Timberlake dyed Jan'y ye 20 & was buried Jan'y ye 23. 1726.
Mary Smith dyed Jan'y y^r 28. & was buried Jan'y ye 31 1726.
John Micham dyed Feb'y ye 19. & was buried Feb'y ye 22 1726.
William Tompson dyed Feb'y ye 28. & was buried March ye 2 1726.
Elizabeth Maxsom dyed Jan^{ry} ye 29. & was buried Jan^{ry} ye 31. 1726.
Thomas Mahaffee dyed Feb'y ye 6. & was buried Feb'y. ye 8. 1726.
Robert Mahaffee dyed Feb'y y^r 10. & was buried Feb'y. y^o 12. 1726.
Peter Bennett dyed Feb^{ry} ye 12. & was buried Feb'y ye 14. 1726.
Elizabeth Marston dyed Feb^{ry} ye 25. & was buried Feb'y ye 27 1726.
John Sibley dyed Feb'y y^r 28. & was buried March ye 2 1726.
Sarah Dozier dyed March ye 5. & was buried March ye 7. 1726.
Margrett Scanderett dyed March ye 1. & was buried March ye 2. 1726.
Avarilla Davis dyed Jan^{ry} ye 14. & was buried Jan'y ye 16 1726.
Thomas Curtis dyed March ye 7. & was buried March ye 9. 1726.
Wm Heath dyed Feb'y y^r 28. & was buried March ye 1. 1726.
Sarah Davis dyed March ye 9. & was buried March ye 11. 1726.
Richard Walker dyed March ye 11. & was buried March ye 13. 1726.
Wm Ball dyed Feb'y ye 20. & was buried Feb'y ye 23 1726.
Grace Mountague dyed March ye 20. & was buried March ye 23 1726.
James Edmunston dyed March ye 23. & was buried March ye 24 1726.
John Hardee dyed March ye 13. & was buried March ye 15. 1726.
Mary Fenwick dyed Decem^r ye 29. & was buried Decem^r 31 1726.
John Alding dyed April ye 1. & was buried April ye 3. 1727.
Ellis Faulkner dyed March ye 20. & was buried March ye 22. 1726.
Dorothy Tignor dyed April ye 5. & was buried April ye 7. 1727.
Sarah Chessells dyed March ye 17. & was buried March ye 19. 1726.
Moses Norman dyed March ye 21. & was buried March ye 23 1726.
Elizabeth Read dyed April ye 6. & was buried April ye 7. 1727.
James Smith jun^r dyed April ye 13. & was buried April ye 15. 1727.
William White dyed April ye 16. & was buried April ye 17 1727.

Bar Yates Minister.

William Savage dyed April ye 17 & was buried April ye 19 1727.
Frances Berry dyed April ye 18 & was buried April ye 19 1727.
William Hunt dyed April ye 20. & was buried April ye 22. 1727.
Anne Crank dyed April ye 24. & was buried April ye 25. 1727.
William Hammelt jun^r dyed Feb'y ye 14. & was buried Feb'y ye 16. 1726.
Isaac Burton dyed April ye 21 & was buried April ye 23 1727.
Charles Whitaker dyed April ye 26. & was buried April ye 28. 1727.
Margrett Kidd dyed March ye 24. & was buried March ye 25 1727.
William Kidd dyed April ye 29. & was buried April ye 30. 1727.
Ruth Thurston dyed April ye 4. & was buried April ye 6. 1727.
Isaac Hardee dyed April ye 16. & was buried April ye 18. 1729.
William Batchelder dyed April ye 30. & was buried May ye 1. 1727.

Tobias Mickleburrough dyed April ye 18. & was buried April y^o 20 1727.
William Cummins dyed April y^o 25. & was buried April y^o 27. 1727.
Anne Cummins dyed May y^o 10. & was buried May ye 12. 1727.
Thomas Kidd dyed May ye 11 & was buried May y^o 13. 1727.
James Douglas dyed Feb^ry ye 4. & was buried Feb^ry ye 6. 1726.
George Sanders jun^r dyed May y^o 13 & was buried May y^o 15. 1727.
John Stuart jun^r dyed May y^o 27 & was buried May y^o 28. 1727.
Robert Waite dyed May ye 28 & was buried May ye 30 1727.
Margrett Daniel jun^r dyed May ye 5 & was buried May y^o 8. 1727.
Mary Cufley dyed May y^o 29 & was buried May y^o 31. 1727.
Sarah Anderson dyed Decem^r 17. & was buried Decem^r ye 19. 1726.
Richard Estree dyed May y^o 6. & was buried May ye 8. 1727.
Thomas Crank dyed May y^o 6: & was buried May ye 7. 1727.
Powel Stamper dyed May ye 22. & was buried May ye 23. 1727.
Moseley Daniel dyed May y^o 24. & was buried May ye 25. 1727.
Elizabeth Saunders dyed June ye 16. & was buried June ye 18. 1727.
Elizabeth Roads dyed July ye 18. & was buried July ye 20. 1727.
Robert Baker dyed July y^o 30. & was buried July y^o 31. 1727.
Lettice Cheney dyed August ye 5. & was buried August ye 6. 1727.
William Cheney dyed August ye 9. & was buried August y^o 10. 1727.
Edward Clark jun^r dyed August y^o 25. & was buried August ye 26. 1727.
Christopher Chaffin jun^r dyed August y^o 22. & was buried August y^o 23. 1727.
Patrick Miller jun^r dyed August ye 23 & was buried August y^o 24. 1727.
Thomas Mason dyed September ye 6. & was buried September ye 7. 1727.
Elizabeth Twyman dyed August y^o 29. & was buried August y^o 30. 1727.
Anne Weston dyed August ye 16. & was buried August ye 17. 1727.
Thomas Blackburne dyed Septem^r y^o 25. & was buried September ye 27. 1727.
Mary Wormeley dyed September y^o 27. & was buried September y^o 29. 1727.
Lettice Guttery dyed September ye 26. & was buried September ye 28. 1727.
Anne Ridgway dyed October ye 13. & was buried October ye 15. 1727.
Robert George jun^r dyed Novem^r ye 19. & was buried ye Same day 1727.
Elizabeth Green dyed Decem^r ye 21 & was buried Decem^r ye 23. 1727.
Thomas Shurley dyed Decem^r ye 22. & was buried Decem^r ye 23. 1727.
Lady Sarah Skipwith dyed Decem^r ye 26. & was buried Decem^r ye 30. 1727.
Charles Grymes dyed Decem^r ye 27 & was buried Decem^r y^o 30. 1727.
Elizabeth Thacker dyed Decem^r y^o 21. & was buried Decem^r ye 28. 1727.
John Smith dyed Novem^r ye 10. & was buried Novem^r ye 13. 1727.
John Johnson dyed Jan'y ye 16. & was buried Jan'y: ye 17. 1727.

William Humphcries dyed Jan'y y° 11. & was buried Jan'y. y' 13. 1727.
Anne Lewis dyed Jan'y y° 22. & was buried Jan'y y" 23. 1727.
Thomas Sears dyed Jan'y y° 9. & was buried Jan'y y° 11. 1727.
John Sears dyed Jan'y y° & was buried Jan'y y° 20. 1727.

Bar Yates Min^{tl}

Catherine Evans dyed Jan'y y° 14 1727.
Elizabeth Murrah dyed Feb'y y° 14 1727.
Laurence orrill jun' dyed Feb'y y° 27 1727.
Mathew Hunt dyed March y° 4 1727.
Thomas Haslewood dyed March y° 5 1727.
John Horton dyed March y° 25 1728.
Mary Bradley dyed March y° 15. 1727.
Benjamin Barbee dyed April y" 21. 1728.
Patrick Miller dyed April y" 29. 1728.
Sarah Baldwin ju' dyed June y° 3. 1728.
Sarah Baldwin dyed June y° 17. 1728.
Maurice Dempsie dyed July y' 8 1728.
John Shorter dyed July y° 15. 1728.
James Smith dyed August y° 26. 1728.
Elizabeth daughter of Daniel Hues dyed August y° 15. 1728.
Elizabeth Thurston dyed September y° 3 1728.
George Wortham son of George Wortham jun' dyed September y° 6. 1728.
Mary Gibbs dyed September y° 13. 1728.
Susannah daughter of Hezekiah Rhoades dyed September 24. 1728.
George Blake dyed Septem' y° 21 1728.
Alice Canser dyed Septem' y° 26 1728.
Agnes Newberry Sen' dyed October y° 6. 1728.
John Mullines dyed October y° 19. 1728.
Mary Saunders dyed Novem' y° 13. 1728.
John Ingram dyed Novem' y° 21. 1728.
Adam Corkburne dyed Decem' y° 14 1728.
Mary Kemp dyed Decem' y° 9th. 1728.
Betty Nevill dyed Decem' y° 23 1728.
Daniel Hues dyed Octo: y° 17. 1728.
Hannah Nevill dyed Decem' y° 31. 1728.
Henry Gilpin dyed September y° 8. 1728.
Joseph Hardee Sen' dyed March y° 28 1729.
John Southern Sen' dyed October y° 1st. 1728.
John Son of Thomas Lee dyed March y° 28. 1729.
Robert Johnston dyed March y° 27. 1729.
Joanna Cain dyed July y° 1. 1729.
James M°tire dyed July y° 20. 1729.
James Roan dyed July y° 24. 1729.
John Marston dyed August y° 20. 1729.
Lilly Mahaffee dyed September y° 1. 1729.
Thomas Son of John & Ann Fearn dyed September y° 2nd 1729.
Anne daughter of John Weston dyed September y° 6. 1729.
Daniel Hepunstall dyed Octo y° 3. 1729.
Thomas Take dyed October y° 7. 1729.

Mary Branch dyed September y⁶ 27. 1729.
Roger Hogg dyed Octo. yᵉ 7. 1729.
Bridgett Wilkings dyed September yᵉ 15 1729.
Thomas Marston dyed Octo. yᵉ 7 1729.
William Gardner dyed September yᵉ 1 1729.
Rebecca Dodson dyed October yᵉ 10 1729.
Hugh Ridley dyed October yᵉ 5 1729.
Mary Hatfeild dyed October yᵉ 14 1729.
Abigall Holderness dyed October yᵉ 17 1729.

   Bar Yates Minister.

John Steward dyed November yᵉ 15 1729.
William Ferrell dyed November yᵉ 30. 1729.
Abraham Glenn dyed November yᵉ 19. 1729.
Benjamine Sutton dyed October yᵉ 27 1729.
Clemence Philpotts dyed Novemʳ yᵉ 17 1729.
Anne yᵉ Wife of John Blake dyeed Decemʳ yᵉ 10 1729.
Margret yᵉ Wife of John Davis dyed Novemʳ yᵉ 28. 1729.
Mary yᵉ Wife of Aquilla Snelling dyed Decemʳ yᵘ 20 1729.
Robert Crawford dyed Janʳy yᵉ 7 1729.
Jane Thilman dyed Janʳy yᵉ 18 1729.
Daniel Johnson dyed Janʳy yᵉ 21 1729.
Edwin Thacker junʳ dyed Febʳy yᵉ 12 1729.
Mary Kelshaw dyed Febʳy yᵉ 1st 1729.
Mary Daniell dyed Febʳy yᵉ 12. 1729.
Thomas Greenwood dyed Febʳy yᵉ 10 1729.
Frances Thacker dyed March yᵉ 21 1729.
Richard Moulson dyed April yᵉ 7 1730.
Margret daughter of Henry Daniel dyed March yᵉ 22 1729.
William Nancut drowned April yᵉ 29 1730.
Thomas yᵉ son of Peter Mountague dyed March yᵉ 30 1730.
Mary daughter of William Guthrie dyed May yᵉ 5. 1730.
John son of John Miller junʳ dyed April yᵉ 8. 1730.
Jane daughter of Richard Allen dyed May yᵉ 7. 1730.
Elizabeth daughter of William Bristow dyed May yᵉ 26. 1730.
Ellis Faulkner dyed Seytember yᵉ 6. 1730.
Daniel Son of Joseph Page dyed September yᵉ 21. 1730.
Benjamine Son of Thomas Saunders dyed Octo yᵘ 4. 1730.
Thomas Machen dyed October yᵉ 12. 1730.
Robert Goodwin dyed September yᵉ 26. 1730.
James Harvie dyed October yᵉ 13. 1730.
Elizabeth daughter of Aquilla Snelling dyed Novemʳ yᵉ 11. 1730.
William Gray dyed Novemʳ yᵉ 14. was buried November yᵉ 18. 1730.
Dorothy Roach dyed Octo. yᵉ 20. 1730.
Hugh Huchison dyed Octo yᵉ 3. 1730.
Nathaniel Churchhill dyed Decemʳ yᵉ 21 was buried Dec. yʳ 22. 1730.
Lucretia Crockford dyed Decemʳ yᵘ 16. 1730.
Thomas Chusick dyed Janʳy yᵉ 17. 1730.
Mary Moseley dyed Janʳy yᵉ 17. 1730.
Paul Thilman dyed Febʳy yᵉ 4 1730.
Elizabeth the Wife of Robert Daniel dyed March yʳ 3 1730.
Jane yᵉ Wife of Thomas Cheney dyed March yᵘ 10. 1730.
Elizabeth Austin dyed march yʳ 13. 1730.

Mary Austin dyed march y̆ 20. 1730.
Hugh Mactire dyed april y° 12. 1731.
Chicheley Corbin Thacker dyed August y° 14. 1731.
Ruth y° daughter of Jacob Stiff dyed October y° 2. 1731.
Sarah daughter of John Grymes dyed October y° 25 was buried October y° 29. 1731.
Anne y° Wife of Richard Greenwood dyed October y° 30. 1731.
Thomas Greenwood dyed Novem' y° 1. 1731.
William son of William Guthery dyed Jan'y. y° 1. 1731.
Richard Hill dyed Jan'y y° 18. was buried Jan'y. y° 22 1731.
Elizabeth y° wife of Caleb Brooks dyed Jan'y: y° 19. 1731.
Catherine Lee dyed Jan'y: y° 11. 1731.

Bar Yates Min'.

A child of Henry Emerson's dyed Decem' y° 18 1731.
Frances Mansfield dyed Feb'y y° 21 1731.
Jane daughter of William Wood dyed March y° 9 1731.
Lucy Lister dyed Jan'y y° 18 & was buried Jan'y y° 26. 1731.
Charles y° Son of Sampson Darrell dyed Octo. y° 6 1731.
Anne y° Wife of John Johnston dyed Aprill y° 21 1732.
Thomas Blakey dyed May y° 17 1732.
Hugh Stewart dyed May y° 12 1732.
Hannah daughter of William Robinson dyed April y° 19 1732.
John Larke dyed July y° 9th. 1732.
Susanna Curtis dyed July y° 21. buried July y° 23 1732.
Lettice Wife of Jn° Burk dyed August y° 27 1732.
Charles Grymes dyed Septem' y° 19. was buried Septem' 22 1732.
William Bohannan dyed Septem' y° 20 1732.
Priscilla Johnson dyed Octo. y° 11. 1732.
Elizabeth y° Wife of Robert Johnson dyed October y° 17. 1732.
Elizabeth daughter of Henry Jolly dyed October y° 26 1732.
John Pollard dyed Novem' y° 28 was buried Novem' y° 30 1732.
William y° Son of John Johnson dyed Novem' y° 28 1732.
William Stanard dyed Decem' y° 3. was buried Decem' y° 7. 1732.
John Davis dyed Decem' y° 3 1732.
Elizabeth Larke dyed Novem' y° 26. 1732.
William Gayer dyed Decem' y° 14 1732.
John Gayer dyed Decem' y° 16. 1732.
Elizabeth Vivion dyed Jan'y y° 12 was buried Jan'y y° 16 1732.
Matthew Son of Eusebius Lewis dyed Decem' y° 16 1732.
Sarah Maccoy dyed Decem' y° 25. 1732.
Thomas y° Son of Richard Greenwood dyed Jan'y. y° 30 1732.
Jacob Cole dyed Feb'y y° 24 1732.
Avarilla Curtis dyed March y° 2 was buried March y° 5 1732.
William Chessells dyed March y° 4 1732.
Richard Allen dyed March y° 8 1732.
Jane Stewart dyed March y° 12, was buried March y° 14. 1732.
Susanna Chelton dyed April y° 29 1733.
Sarah Ross dyed May y° 23 1733.
James Walker alias Weekes dyed June y° 21. 1733.
William Wood dyed July y° 25. was buried July y° 28 1733.
Elizabeth Philpotts dyed July y° 22 1733.
William Sanders dyed July y° 23 1733.

John Son of Caleb Brookes dyed August ye 1 1733.
John Son of Joseph Alphin dyed August ye 24 1733.
Susannah daughter of Christopher Owen dyed Septem^r ye 9. 1733.
George Collett dyed Septem^r ye 30. was buried October ye 1. 1733.
Susam Pace dyed October ye 6 1733.
Alice Cooper dyed Septem^r ye 29 1733.
Thomas Smith dyed Septem^r ye 1st 1733.
Frances Gardner dyed Septem^r ye 16 1733.
Williamson Bryant dyed September ye 9. 1733.
John Guttery dyed October ye 24 1733.
Alexander Lister dyed Novem^r ye 11. was buried Novem^r ye 13. 1733.
James Meacham dyed October ye 27. buried October ye 28. 1733.

Bar Yates Min^r.

Alice Nichols dyed Novem^r ye 12 1733.
Mary daughter of John Tugle dyed Novem^r ye 16 1733.
John Sadler dyed Novem^r ye 11 1733.
Sarah daughter of Eusebius Lewis dyed Novem^r ye 4 1733.
Mary Barwick dyed Decem^r ye 8 1733.
Sarah Crank dyed Decem^r ye 24 1733.
Robert George Senr dyed January ye 21 & was buried January ye 23 1733.
Betty Wakefield dyed January ye 5 1733.
Ann Chowning dyed January ye 2 1733.
Thomas Wakefield dyed Feb'y ye 4 1733.
Thomas Cheney dyed Feb'y ye 14 1733.
Mary ye Wife of Henry Daniel dyed Feb'y ye 21. 1733.
William Wood dyed March ye 7. 1733.
Thomas Wood dyed March ye 3 1733.
Elizabeth ye Wife of Ralph Watts dyed Feb'y ye 15 1733.
Thomas Godding dyed Feb'y ye 25 1733.
Susannah ye Wife of Thomas Clark dyed Feb'y ye 19. 1733.
Elizabeth Dobbs dyed March ye 9. buried March ye 11. 1733.
Margrett Segar dyed March ye 13. buried March ye 15. 1733.
Stephen Ryley dyed March ye 19. 1733.
John Bryant dyed March ye 24. 1733. buried March ye 26 1734.
Sarah Crowdoss dyed March ye 16 1733.
Oliver Segar dyed March ye 26 buried March ye 28. 1734.
George Walker dyed March ye 27. buried March ye 29. 1734.
Ralph Shelton dyed March ye 13. 1733.
Henry Tugle jun^r dyed March ye 14 1733.
George Wortham Senr dyed April ye 5. buried April ye 7. 1734.
John Williams dyed April ye 12 1734.
Margret Daniel dyed March ye 17 1734.
Margret Blackey dyed Ap: ye 15 1734.
Joseph Southern dyed February ye 7 1733.
Edward Bodenham dyed March ye 17 1733.
William Owen dyed May ye 2 1734.
Sarah Acree dyed May ye 24 1734.
Sarah George dyed April ye 14 1734.
Frances daughter of Philip Brooks dyed June ye 13.

The Rev⁴ Mʳ Bartholomew Yates dyed the 26th. day of July 1734. buried the 2d. day Augᵗ 1734.
Ann daughter of John & Ann Smith died the 6 day September 1734.
Jeremiah Clowder dyed August 12th 1734.
Margaret Daniel Dyed August 11th 1734.
Penelopy Breame Dyed October 19th 1734.
Lettice Guttery Dyed November 15th 1734.
Catharine Montague Dyed October 20th 1734.
Mary Beauford Dyed November 27th 1734.
John Pace Dyed November 25th 1734.
Abraham Pace Dyed November 27th 1734.
Thomas Dudley Dyed October 13th 1734.

    Jnº Reade Minʳ.

Robᵗ Wilkins Dyed October 1st. 1734.
Phebe Marston Dyed October 16th 1734.
John Thurston Dyed December 27th 1734.
Joseph Hardee Dyed December 2d. 1734.
Mary Goodwin Dyed November 24th 1734.
Willᵐ Gayre Dyed January 10th 1734.
Richᵈ Parrott Dyed January 11th 1734.
Jnº Burk Dyed February 11th 1734.
Ruth yᵉ Wife of James Mayo Dyed February 6th 1734.
Elizᵗʰ Robertson Dyed January 26th 1734.
Lucy Daughter of Christopher & Mary Robinson Dyed March 7th 1734.
Nickols Bristow Dyed January 27th 1734.
Willᵐ Watts Dyed March 15th 1734.
Ann Wife of Jnº Gresham Dyed April 7th 1735.
Given unto y" { William Thurston Senʳ Dyed March 30th 1735.
Secretary's office { Michal Williams Dyed March 25th 1735.
  Ap. 1735. { Lucy Wife of Thoˢ Nash dyed June 2. 1735.
Amy Nickols Dy'd September 13th 1735.
Mary Brooks Dyed September 25th 1735.
Charged—Mary Wife of James Brown Dyed Novʳ 10th 1735.
Henry Ball Dyed Novʳ 21st (Elizᵗʰ Ball) 1735.
William Seagur Dyed Octoʳ 10th (Jane Seagur) 1735.
Eusebius Lewis Dyed Novʳ 21st (Mary Lewis) 1735.
Elizabeth Smith Dyed Novʳ 19th.
Jane Watts Decʳ 17th (Wᵐ Gardiner Senʳ) 1735.
Easter Moulson Dyed Decʳ 29th (Robᵗ Dudley) 1735.
Martha Daughter of George Chowning Dyed January 16th 1735.
William Son of Thoˢ & Ann Lee Dyed January 13th 1735.
Millicent Daughter of of Robert Daniel Dyed January 26th 1735.
Henry Parrott Dyed January 22nd (Rachel Parrott) 1735.
John Carrell Dyed January 3d (Jnº Williams) 1735.
Thomas Son of Hen: & Frances Bueford Dyed January 5th 1735.
Ann Ryley Dyed Feb'y 6th (Jnº Ryly) 1735.
Catherine Williams Dyed Feb'y 16th (Jnº Williams) 1735.
Richard Patman Dyed Janʳʸ 25th 1735.
Jane Wife of Robᵗ Dudley Dyed March 2d 1735.
John Hughes Dyed March 12. 1735.

Given to the S: O:
Ap: 1736.
{ Benjamin Greenwood Dyed Feb'y 15th (Eliz'h Perrot) 1735.
George Gest Dyed March 22 (Geo. Gest. Sen') 1735.

Abraham Wharton Dyed March 25th 1736.
George Berwick Dyed April 13th 1736.
John Hipkins Dyed January 8th 1736.
James Hipkins Dyed March 27th 1736.
William Crooker Dyed May 23d 1736.
Joseph Alphin Dyed May 20th 1736.
Mary Hardee Dyed June 14th (Andrew Hardee) 1736.
Joseph Pace Dyed June 18th (Benjn Pace) 1736.
Wm Brown Dyed July 10th (James Brown) 1736.
Keziah Ball Dyed July 9th 1736.
Edmund Mickleburrough Dyed June 26th (Jane Mickleburrough) 1736.
Sarah Rhodes Dyed June 30th (Randal Rhodes) 1736.
William Baldwin Dyed July 26th (Judith Baldwin) 1736.
      Jn° Reade Min^r.
Torn.   (Geo. Barbee) 1736.
Torn.   Best Dyed July 23d 1736.
Torn.   Registers omitted in ye year 1735.
Torn.   Octob^r 9th   (Tup. Tuggle) 1735.
Torn.   Octr 27th (Charles Wood) 1735.
Samuel Johnson Dyed Octr 19th (Wm Johnson) 1735.
Henry Allin Dyed Novr 1st (Mary Allin) 1735.
Thomas Mellican a Servt to Edwin Thacker Dyed Octr 4th 1736.
Sarah Perrott Daughter of Rachell Perrott Dyed Septr 12 1736.
Jane   a foundling Dyed Octr 3d 2736.

Given into y^e
Secret: Off.
Otc° 1736.
{ Jane Mickleburrough Dyed Augst 10th (Charles Daniel) 1736.
Frances Smith Dyed Octr 2d 1736.
Susanna Daughter of Jn° & Susanna Curtis Dyed Sept 24th 1736.

Jane Thurston Dyed Octr 14th (Willm Thurston) 1736.
Nichols Tuggle Dyed Octr 12th (Jn° Tuggle) 1736.
Thomas Corbin Dyed Novr 4th 1736.
Ann Betts dyed October 27th 1736.
John Mayo dyed 9^{ber} 24th 1736.
Jane Johnson dyed 10^{ber} 14th 1736.
Catherine Greenwood dyed March 13th 1736.
Ann Duckworth died March 19th 1736.
Thomas Warwick died Feb. 19th 1736.
Ann Clark dyed March 15th 1736.
John Shanks dyed January 21th 1736.
Sarah Owen dyed February 20th 1736.
Elizabeth ye daughter of William & Elizabeth Blackburne dyed 10^{ber} 13th 1736.
Anna ye daughter of William & Elizabeth Blackburn dyed 10^{ber} 21th 1736.
Elizabeth Stevens dyed January 18th 1736.
Sarah Blasedon dyed January 20th 1736.
Mary ye Wife of James Brown dyed 9^{br} 5th 1736.

Sarah ye Wife of Patrick Russel died January 19th 1736.
Martha daughter of Hugh & Ann Roach died May 22th 1737.
Mary ye daughter of John & Ann Johnson died January 4th 1736.
John ye Son of Elizabeth Humphries died June 21th 1737.
William ye Son of Thomas Sanders died June 9th 1737.
Sent to the Secret: Office October 1737. } Edward Hill died Feb. 20th 1736.
Sarah daughter of John & Martha Hardee died Sepr ye 28th 1737.
Ann Daughter of William Guthery died Sepr ye 8th 1737.
Christopher Sutton Senr died Octor ye 26th 1737.
Mary Gear died Novr ye 3d 1737.
Joseph Son of Joseph & Elizabeth Humphris died Decemr ye 12th 1737.
Henry Son of Joseph & Mary Tugle died Decemr ye 12th 1737.
Robert Perrott died Decemr ye 13th 37.
Marget ye Wife of Aquila Snelling Dyed Decemr ye 10th 37.
Ann Calahan dyed Febry ye 2d 1737/8.
Hannah Watts dyed Octr ye 5th 1737.
Jane ye Wife of George Goodwin dyed Janry ye 28th 1737/8.
James Son of William & Hannah Rhodes dyed April ye 11th 1738.
Curtis Parrott dyed May ye 14th 1738.
Churchhill Blakey dyed May ye 8th 1738.
Elizabeth Terry dyed May ye 26th 1738.
Bettey Daughter of John & Sarah Carrell dyed April ye 8th 1738.
Hannah Jenkins daughter of John Jenkins dyed Sepr ye 27. 1738.
John Losson dyed Octor ye 14th 1738.
Benjamin Thurston dyed Novr ye 30th 1738.
Catharine Walker dyed Octor ye 5th 1738.
Cuffley Son of Henry & Sarah Brooks dyed Decemr ye 2d 1738.
Francis Kelshaw dyed Janry: ye 15th 1738/9.
John Son of John & Sarah Stamper dyed febry: ye 16th 1738/9
Garret Son of Robert & Elizabeth Daniel dyed Febry: ye 19th 1738/9.
Elizabeth Yarbrough dyed March ye 4th 1738/9.
Frances Daughter of Russel & Anne Hill dyed March ye 12th 1738/9.
Elizabeth Daughter of Charles & Penelope Lee dyed March ye 23d 1738/9.
Mary Daughter of Andrew & Elizabeth Davis dyed March ye 14th 1738/9.
Patrick Pussil died April ye 23d 1739.
Edward Son of John & Judith Wortham died May ye 25th 1739.
Ann Daughter of John & Mary Matthews died Augst ye 2d 1739.
Edward Guthrie died Sepr 28th 1739.
Mary Daughter of Elizabeth Porter died Septr ye 19th. 1739.
Thomas Trench died Septr ye 23d. 1739.
Avirilla Waldin died Septr ye 28th. 1739.
William Owen died Novr ye 1st. 1739.
Hannah Brown died Novr ye 6th 1739.
Joyce Edwards died Novr ye 5 1739.
Isaac Rhodes Son of John & Ann Rhodes died Novr ye 18th. 1739.
Ann Parrott died Novr ye 16th 1739.
Charles Cooper died Decr ye 14th 1739.
William Fares died Janry ye 4th. 1739/40.

Agnes Southern died Feb'y y⁰ 11th. 1739/40.
y⁰ 15th ⎫ Sons of Samuel Batchelder
elder Died Nov' y⁰ 23rd ⎭   1739.
William Fluewelling Died March y⁰ 1st 1739/40.
Elias Williams Died March y⁰ 2d. 1739/40.
Peter Daniel Died March y⁰ 8th 1739/40.
Roger Jones died April 13th 1739.
John Tylor Died November y⁰ 21th 1740.
George Harrod Died March y⁰ 19th 173 9/10.
Absolom Hackney Son of William & Elizabeth Hackney Died October y⁰ 13th 1740.
Henry Bohannan died July 28th 1740.
Jane Daniel Died March y⁰ 10th. 1739.
Elizabeth Dudley died March y⁰ 18. 1739/40.
William Kid died April y⁰ 4th. 1740.
Jonathan Brooks died May y⁰ 17th 1740.
Elizabeth Pace died April y⁰ 6th 1740.
Thomas Hill Son William & Frances Hill died April 13th 1740.
Alexander Graves died June y⁰ 21th 1740.
Joseph Sears departed this Life June y⁰ 12th. 1740.
Ambrose Son of Paul Philpotts died August y⁰ 9th 1740.
John Son of Paul Philpotts died August y⁰ 9th 1740.
Edmund Fary died August y⁰ 20th. 1740.
Judith Daughter of Richard & Sarah Wait died September 24th 1740.
Elizabeth Davis Died September 19th. 1740.
John Martin Son of Hugh & Elizabeth Martin died October y⁰ 10th 1739.
William Segar died October y⁰ 6 1740.
Sarah Laughlin Died November y⁰ 25 1740.
Edward Smith died January the 7th 1739/40.
Elizabeth Lewis died January y⁰ 18th. 1739/40.
Cufflee Brooks died January y⁰ 2d 1739/40.
Sarah Williams died January y⁰ 13th 1739/40.
John Greenwood Died January y⁰ 26th 1739/40.
Diana Crowdas died January the 10th 1739/40.
Robert Son of Robert & Jane Dudley Died January y⁰ 4th 1740.
George Wortham Son of John & Judith Wortham Died January y⁰ 28th 1740.
Catharine Wood died January y⁰ 30th 1740.
Elias Williams died March y⁰ 2th 1739.
Peter Daniel died March y⁰ 8th 1739.
John Segar died December 19th 1740.
Ann Smith died March 15th 1740.
Benjamine Reader died March 21st 174 0/1.
William Dobbs died February y⁰ 8th 1740.
Mary Wife of Robert Daniel died March y⁰ 9th 174 0/1.
Katherine Daughter of Robert & Mary Daniel died March 24th 174 0/1.
Robert Brown died March 31st 1741.
Elizabeth Daughter of Philip & Eliz. Brook died April y⁰ 13th 1741.
Dorothy wife of Tho⁸ Chilton died April y⁰ 25 1741.
Benjamine Meacham died April y⁰ 8th 1741.
Elizabeth Daughter of William & Jane Mountague Died May y⁰ 16. 1741.

Sarah Daughter of James & Ann Campton died June y" 4th 1741.
George Son of James & Ann Compton died Sep' y" 6th 1741.
James Wood died Sep' y" 28th 1741.
Susanna Wood died Sep' y" 28th 1741.
Catherine Bristow died Decem' y" 16th 1741.
John Carter died Jan'y. 24th 174½.
Anthony Collins died Jan'y y" 27th 174½.
Lucy Stapleton died April y" 23d 1742.
Constant Anderson Wife of Wm Anderson died May y" 30th 1742.
Ann Daughter of George & Ann Wortham died April 6th 1742.
Sarah Daughter of John & Judith Wortham died April 6th 1742.
Ann Wife of James Compton died Octo' y" 1st 1742.
John Pace died Septem' y" 6th 1742.
Ann Wife of John Rhodes Sen' died Septem' y" 20th 1742.
William Bristow died Nov' y" 15th 1742.
Ruth Wife of William Owen died Novem' y" 6th 1742.
William Paret died Octo' y" 15th 1742.
Agatha Daughter of Ave Daniel died Sep' 15th 1742.
Mary Wortham died May y" 26th 1742.
Rebecca Kidd died June y" 20th 1742.
Mary Daughter of Tho" & Mary Shelton died August y" 5th 1742.
Sarah Chowning died August y" 18th 1742.
Mary Daughter of John & Susanna Williams died Octo' y" 1st 1742.
William Southern died Nov' y" 17th 1742.
Samuel Batcheler died Decem' y" 12th 1742.
Samuel Sheepherd Son of Henry Sheepherd Died Jan'y 18 1742.
Elinor Morton Died October 30th 1742.
Robert Daniel Died July y" 8th 1742.
Mary Turman Died March 12th 174⅔.
Elizabeth Humphris Died March y" 7 174⅔.
Thomas Shelton died March y" 24th 174⅔.
Milicent Daughter of John & Ann Croffield died Jan'y 23d 174⅔.
    Torn.   of Jacob Stiff died April 16th 1743.
    Torn.   iff Died May 1st 1743.
Benjamin Hackney died May 9th 1743.
John Fearn Died May y" 1st 1743.
Jane Lee Died September 5th 1743.
Catherine Daughter of Henry & Betty Daniel Died August 21st 1743.
Elizabeth Gest Died September 11th 1743.
Henry Daniel Died September 7th 1743.
Betty Wallace Died October 25th 1743.
Mary Guttrey Died Jan'y 2 1743.
Priscilla Stevens Died Jan'y 29th 1743.
Henry Tugle Died Jan'y 3d 1743.
Ann Croffield died Jan'y 24th 1743.
Sarah Wood Died Feb'y 27th 1743.
Jacob Rhodes Son of John Rhodes Sen' Died Feb'y 26 1743.
Frances Sears Died Feb'y 16th 1743.
Robert Rodes Died Feb'y 23d 1743.
Richard Lewis Died Feb'y 29th 1743.
John Dose Died March 17th 1743.
John Henesey Died March 4th 1743.

Ann Chowning Died March 12th 1743.
John Chowning Died March 19th 1743.
John Walker died March 174¾.
Mary Daughter of James & Eliz⁕ Meachan died March y⁰ 17th 1743.
Mary Rhodes died March y⁰ 26th 1744.
Phillip Warwick died March y⁰ 27th 1744.
Mary Wood died April y⁰ 9th 1744.
William Ryley died April y⁰ 6th 1744.
William Carrell died April y⁰ 4th 1744.
Patrick Night died March y⁰ 17th 174¾.
Eustace Howard died Feb'y y⁰ 28th 174¾.
George Chowning died April y⁰ 1st 1744.
Eliz⁕ Johnson died April y⁰ 23d 1744.
Martha Chowning died April y⁰ 6th 1744.
Mary Daughter of James & Eliz⁕ Dunlevy died Octo'   44.
Robert Alldin died June y⁰ 21st 1744.
Mary Bristow died Sep' y⁰ 5th 1744.
John Wortham died Jan'⁷ y⁰ 21st 1744.
Mary Wife of Jacob Stiff died Decem' 21st 1744.
Mary Wife of Wm Owen died April 24th 1744.
Elizabeth Wife of James Dunlevy died Sep' y⁰ 13th 1744.
Machen Son of John & Judith Wortham died Decem' y⁰ 30th 1744.
Elizabeth Wife of Curtis Hardee died Decem' y⁰ 26th 1744.
John Warwick died April y⁰ 4th 1744.
Rachel wife of Harry George died Feb'y y⁰ 10th 1744.
Elizabeth Clowdas died Aug^st y⁰ 7th 1744.
Mactyer Cornelius died Sep' y⁰ 28th 1744.
Elizabeth Gardner died July y⁰ 13th 1744.
Sarah Wife of Henry Emberson died Feb'y y⁰ 4th 1744.
Nathaniel son of Tho⁰ & Christian Sanders died Sep' 24th 1744.
Thomas Cheney died Feb'y y⁰ 10th 1744.
Jemima Daughter of Randolph & Sarah Rhodes died March y" 2nd 174⅘.
Ocany Santo died March y⁰ 17th 174⅘.
Thomas Son of Joseph Tugle died Jan'y y⁰ 26th 174⅘.
Elizabeth Daughter of Tho⁰ Mountague died Feb'y y⁰ 5th 1744.
Garret Daniel died Jan'y y⁰ 28th 174⅘.
William Johnson Sen' died March y⁰ 10th 174⅘
Arthur Thomas died April y⁰ 28th 1745.
Elizabeth Brooks died March y⁰ 9th } 174⅘
Philip Brooks died March y⁰ 24
William Cardwell died Decem' y⁰ 19th 1744.
Mary Sanders died Jan'y y⁰ 24th 1744.
James Jones died May y⁰ 4th 1745.
Winnie Morris a Mulatto died Aprill y⁰ 18th 1745.
Samuell Son of Edward & Mary Clark died June y⁰ 19th 1745.
Mary Overstreet died May y⁰ 25th 1745.
Mary Meacham died May y⁰ 27th 1745.
Elizabeth Wife of Wm Jones died June y⁰ 18th 1745.
Anne the Wife of Thomas Sovlt died Sep' 19th 1745.
Elizabeth Daughter of Wm Jones died Sep' 19th 1745.
William Pace Jun' died Octo' y⁰ 10th 1745.
William Son of Joseph Smith died Decem' y⁰ 2d 1745.

Mary Blakey died Jan'y y° 16th 1745.
Jane Daughter of Henry Mickleburrough died Jan'y y° 26th 174⅝.
Frances Daughter of Henry Mickleburrough died Jan'y y° 30th 174⅝.
John Son of George Wortham died y° 9th day of Jan'y 174⅝.
William Son of Wm Hill died April y° 25th 1746.
Elizabeth Brook died Novr y° 14th 1746.
Robert Norman died Decem^r 23d 1746.
Thomas Clarke died Sep^t 18th 1746.
Catharine Dobbs died Octo^r y° 31st 1746.
Rachel Daughter of Charles Wood died Septr y° 10th 1746.
Frances Daughter of Wm Hill died May y° 30th 1746.
Ann Daughter of Wm Daniel died Novem^r y° 25th 1746.
William Daniel died Novr y^r 28th 1746.
Josiah Daniel died Decem^r ye 21st 1746.
Agatha Daniel died Decem^r y° 29th. 1746.
John Son of John & Frances Ranes died May 15th. 1746.
Martha Dillion died April y° 26th. 1746.
Garett Son of Edmun Dillion died Sepr y° 11th. 1746.
Elizabeth Daughter of James Cole died Septr 29th. 1746.
Clare Marks died May y° 16th. 1746.
Anthony Smith Died Decem^r y° 1st 1745.
Blackley Son of John & Mary Gardner died Decem^r 12th 1746.
Elliner Devall Died Decem^r 7th 1746.
Rachel Chowning Junr Died Feb^ry 23d 174⅞.
Rachel Chowning Senr Died March y° 27th. 1747.
Hannah Bristow died March y° 10th. 174⅞.
Ruban Allin died April y° 15th 1747.

Register of Births & Christen   for the Year of our Lord 1768.

Jane Daughter of Nathaniel & Mary Burwell was born Septem the 7th. 1768 & baptized January y° 15th. 1769.
William Son of John & Dorothy Berry was born December the 21st. 1768. & baptized January 22d. 1769.
Charles Son of John & Anne Hodges was born * * the 12th 1768 & baptized the 28th. D°.
Randolph, Son of William & Mary Segar was bo * * the 22d. 1768 & baptized December 26th. 176*.
the 23th 1769.
William, Son of Abraham & Anne Clowdas was born the 19th Day of March 1769. & baptized in April D°.
Leonard Son of Robert & Mildred Stamper was born * * * born December 14th 1769.
William Chadwick Son of John & Sarah * * was born October 8th. 1769.

Register of Births & Christenings for the Year of our Lord 1769.

William Son of Thomas & Mary Segar was born February the 20. 1769. & baptized the 7th. of March.
William Son of George & Mary Davis was born February * *
ances Daughter of Lewis & Frances Dudley was born September 19th 1769 & baptized October 21st.

* * Son of Joseph & Elizabeth Tuggle was born * the 6th 1769, & Baptized Decr 29th.
* * of James & Mary Kidd was born December 26th. 1769 * * January 15th. 1770.
* * orn Son of Benson & Susannah Siblie was born the 5th 1769.
Robert, Son of John Long & Sarah his Wife was born August 12th 1769.
Nelson, Son of John Humphries & was born September 24th 1769.
Naney & Betsey Daughters of William & Ann Gardener were born February 22d 1769.
Henry, Son of John & Sarah Hutson was born April 2d 1769.
Catherine Daughter of John & Elizabeth Seward was born May 23d 1769.
James Son of Edward & Margaret Crouch was born June 2d 1769.
Frances, Daughter of William & Rachel Taylor was born June 17th 1769.
Henry Son of Henry & Elizabeth Thurston * * *

Births & Christenings for the year of or 1771.

William Brookes son of John & Anne Hodges born January 11. 1771.
John Son of Thomas & Mary Segar was born the 13 of March 1771 & baptized March 24th 1771.
William Harrow, Son of Thomas & Sarah Anne Harrow was born January 20th 1771.
Burwell Laton, Son of Thomas & Elizabeth Laton March 30th 1771.
James Morris, Son of John & Elizabeth Morris was March 11th 1771.
Edward Jones Bristow, Son of Benj^m & Elizabeth B was born June 16th 1770.
Benjamin Batchelder, Son of Joseph & Michal Batchelder was born may the 4th 1771.
Hamstead & Ranson, Sons of John & Judith Wake were born august the 4th 1771 & Baptized the 6th of Octr following.
Jane Daughter of Lewis & Frances Dudley was born Septr the 25th 1771 & baptised Octr 12th.
Mary, Daughter of William & Susanna Jackson was born Sep^{tr} 10th 1771.
Elizabeth, Daughter of John & Elizabeth Daniel was born Decr 20th 1771, & baptized the 18th Jany following.
John, Son of John & Anne Crowdas born September 27th 1771.
John, Son of John & Mildred Layton born Novr 12. 1771.
Daniel Ball, Son of Benson & Susanna Sibley was born Decr 14th 1771.
     Daughter of Humphrey & Elizabeth Wattkins s born September 16th 1771.
Catherine, Daughter of William & Rachel Taylor was born December 8th 1771.

John, Son of Abraham & Anne Crowdas was born the September 1771.

Stevens, Son of John & Sarah Mariah Craine born March 23rd 1772.

Registry of Funerals Commencing May 19th 1795.

Henry Heffernan Rector.

Colonel Smith was interred on Friday June 26 1795.
John Jackson was interred on Thursday July 2nd.
Cap Tuning on Saturday July 11th 1795.
Sarah Berkeley on Sunday Augt 16th 1795.
———— Dennison on Sunday Sep^t 20th 1795.
———— Curtis on Tuesday Sep^t 22nd 1795.
———— Peachey on Monday October 5th 1795.
———— Muse on Saturday Decr 12th 1795.
———— Adkins on Sunday January 24th 1795.
Benjamin Churchill April 6th 1796.
Sarah Letitia Heffernan died July 12th 1796 at 5 oclock in the morning, was buried on Thursday July 14th 1796. by the Revd Mr Smith.

Mrs. Hannah Kemp this 27th of april 1802 made oath before the Court sitting in Urbanna Coart House that Mrs. Sarah Letitia Heffernan died on the day & hour above recorded, she being present when Mrs. Heffernan died.

Ralph Wormeley.

Elizabeth Burwell Churchill died May 17th 1802.
Edmund Berkeley died July 8th 1802, 5^m past 7: p. m.
Mary Grymes died April 14th 1805.
Philip Ludwell Grymes died 18th of May 1805.
Jane Sayre died January 1st 1806.
Lucy Nelson Heffernan March 21st 1813.

Register of Marriages for the year of our Lord 1768.

John Dunlavy & Elizabeth Healey married nov^r 17th 1768.
Thomas Robinson & Mary Robinson Married December 10th 1768.
John Craine & Sarah Mariah Butterworth married Decr 10th 1768.
John Brown & Mary Acrey married Decr 10th 1768.
Steward Williams & Sarah Roan married Decr 11th 1768.
Robert Daniel jr. & Pene Lee married Decr 29th 1768.
William Acra & Elizabeth Blackley married Decr 30th 1768.

Marriages for the Year of Our Lord 1769.

Samuel Wood & Sarah Durham married Jany 19th 1769.
John Keys & Margaret Smith married Feby 4th 1769.
James Dunlavy & Elizabeth Falkner married Feby 17th 1769.
Henry Thurston & Elizabeth Brame married Feby 23rd 1769.
Alexander Rumage & Mary McDaniel married March 23rd 1769.
Howard Williams & Elizabeth Montague married March 23rd 1769.
John Layton & Mildred Sibley married March 25th 1769.
Bartholomew Yates & Anne Daniel married May 11th 1769.

Samuel Klug & Elizabeth Yates married. by the Rev⁴ Mr. Dunlap May 13th 1769.
Peter Kemp & Betty Daniel married May 18th 1769.
John Jackson & Elizabeth Boss married July 9th 1769.
William Degge & Mary Sutton married February 23rd 1770.
Edward Bristow Jr. & Mary Beaman married March 18th 177 .
Alexander Ramage & Hannah Chiles married april 10th 1770.
John Kidd & Elizabeth Jones married april 14th 1770.
Benjamin Williamson & Mildred Hutton Married april 26th 1770.
John Barrack sʳ & Mary Sanders married April 30th 1770.
John Chapman & Elizabeth Elliott married May 12th 1770.
John Barrack Jr. & Mary Sanders married June 2nd 1770.
William Daniel & Lucy Guttery married July 26th 1770.
Lyne Rowe & Martha Clark married Septʳ 26th 1770.
Isaac Palmer & Elizabeth Taff married Sepᵗʳ 28th 1770.
John Harwood & Mary Curtis married Novʳ 17th 1770.
William Smith & Nelly Livingston married Decʳ 1st 1770.
Humphrey Watkins & Elizabeth Thurston married Decʳ 2nd 1770.
James Bristow & Mary Brooks married Decʳ 9th 1770.
Roger Blackburn & Elizabeth Owen married Decʳ 15th 1770.
John Blake & Susannah Blake married Decʳ 24th 1770.
John Deagle & Hannah Sanders married Decʳ 25th 1770.
Thomas Brooks & Margaret Beaman January 29th 177–.
Edward Bristow jr. & Anne Brooks Married January 31st 177–.
Isaac Ware & Clara Stringer married March 16th 177–.
John Kemp & Sarah Batchelder married April 13th 1771.
Corbin Griffin (of York County) & Mary Berkeley married April 20th 1771.
Churchhill Gibson   M. Daniel married July 1771.
        son of ——— ——— August 17th 1773.
Lucy Blake, Daughter of Benjamin Seward was born January 1st 1773.
George, Son of Benjamin Kidd & Jane his Wife was born June 20th 1773.
Ann Chowning, Daughter of William & Rachel Taylor was born December 11th 1773.
John Thurston, Son of Benjamin & Frances Williams was born April 24th 1774.
William Son of Thomas & Mary Burton was born Novʳ 25th 17—.
William, Son of Henry & Elizabeth Thurston was born Sepᵗʳ 11th 177–.
William, Son of John & Frances Dean was born January 16th 1775.
Thomas Mitcham, Son of Joseph & Judith Brooks was born January 31st 1775.
William, Son of William & Mildred Pryor was born December 10th 1774.
Nancy Vevel Parriott was born the 5th of January 1775.
William Chowning, Son of Churchhill & Ann Blakey was born January 30th 1775.
Nancy, Daughter of Benjamin & Ann Seward was born the 15th day of September 1775.
Samuel, Son of Robert & Mildred Stamper was born the 6th of october 1775.

Elizabeth, Daughter of John & Frances Dean was born February 14th 1776.
Fanny, Daughter of Philip & Elizabeth Brooke was born February 5th 1776.
James, Son of James & Betty Stiff was born April 3rd 1775.
John Blake, Son of James & Betty Stiff was born September 23rd 1776.
Elizabeth, Daughter of Lewis & Judith Steevens was born January 24th 1777.
Ann, Daughter of John & Ann Hodges was born March 12th 1777.
William, Son of William & Dorothy Hutson of the Parish of Stratton Major in King & Queen County was born October 26th 1776.
Elizabeth, Daughter of Daniel & Mary Jefferson was born February 5th 1775.
David, Son of Daniel & Mary Jefferson was born March 30th 1777.
Sally, Daughter of James & Mary Kidd was born March 12th 1776.
James Jones, Son of James & Elizabeth Dunlevy was born Jan' 31st 1776.
George, Son of Robert & Mildred Stamper was born July 22nd 1777.
Edmond Abbott, Son of John & Mary Stevens was born Sep" 13th 1777.
Elizabeth Stannard, Daughter of John & Catherine Montague of the County of Essex was born October 30th 1777 & baptized Nov' 11th at the House of M' John Chinn of Lancaster County.
Simon Laughlin & Anne Scrosby married September y° 3rd 1772.
Robert Spratt & Anne Yates married Sep' 19th 1772.
James Crossfield & Anne Williams married October 27th 1772.
Churchhill Blakey & Anne Chowning married Oct' 24th 1772.
Nathaniel Burwell & Susanna Grymes married Nov' 28th 1772.
William Boldin & Mary Dunlevy married Dec' 21st 1772.
John Seward & Rebekah Groom married Dec' 27th 1772.
John Cornelius & Sarah Acra married Dec' 27th 1772.
Abner Crowdas & Sally Haily married Dec' 31st 1772.
William Keeling & Judith Hipkinstall married February 4th 1773.
Laurence Meacham & Frances Batchelder married February 4th 1773.
John Bryant & Mary Sears married March 6th 1773.
Michael Payne & Mary Elliott married March 26th 1773.
William Young & Jane Mickelburrough married April 8th 1773.
Philip Ludwell Grymes & Judith Wormeley married May 30th 1773.
Siah Cornelius & Jane Bray married May 30th 1773.
James Ware & Jane Machan married July 22nd 1773.
Robert Ware & Catherine Machan married July 22nd 1773.
John Askins & Anne Burton married Sep' 4th 1773.
John Dean & Frances Smith married Sep' 16th 1773.
Chowning Kidd & Catherine French married Sep' 23rd 1773.
John Chowning & Precilla Whitters married Sep' 24th 1773.
Thomas Wills & Sarah Dean married Sep' 25th 1773.
Benjamin Grymes & Sarah Robinson married October 9th 1773.
Joseph Brooks & Judith Hill married October 30th 1773.
William Pace & Cressy Sanders married November 4th 1773.
William Blake & Rachel Williams married Nov' 4th 1773.

—— —— Franky Garrett (King & Queen) married Nov' 4th 1773.
Thomas Tenoe & Judith Belfare married May 21th 1774.
George Hauks & Mary Tuggle married July 2nd 1774.
John Chowning & Catharine Chowning married July 16th 1774.
Joseph Martin & Ann Deagle married August 15th 1774.
George Lorimer & Hannah Thacker Timberlake married October 8th 1774.
Melchizedeck Brame & Catharine Gibson married November 11th 1774.
William Jones & Betty Churchhill married Nov' 24th 1774.
William Wood & Fanny Blake married Dec' 4th 1774.
John Miller & Hester Christian married Dec' 10th 1774.
John Boss & Judith Faulkner married Dec' 12th 1774.
James Stiff & Betty Blake married Dec' 17th 1774.
Thomas Blake & Ann Blake married Dec' 24th 1774.
Benjamin Stevens & Joannah Barrick married Dec' 25th 1774.
Benjamin Barrack & Frankey Clare married Dec' 31st 1774.
Zebulum Hearing & Johannah Jackson married January 3d 1775.
William Deagle & Martha Boss married January 15th 1775.
George Warwick & Elizabeth Chowning married January 30th 1775.
Richard Layton & Elizabeth Stodix married February 4th 1775.
Daniel Dejarnatt & May Davis married February 12th 1775.
William Hutson & Jane Falkner married April 17th 1775.
Lodowick Jones & Lucy Tarpley married May 6th 1775.
William Taylor & Priscilla Segar married May 13th 1775.
John Wiat & Sarah Charles married June 3d 1775.
Charles Dudley & Nanny Sutton married Sep'r 4th 1775.
James Turner & Martha Rowe married Sept' 29th 1775.
John Montague & Catharine Yates married Dec' 14th 1776.
Benj.ª Rhodes & Patience Kelly married Dec' 18th 1776.
Charles Whitticor & Mary Herrin married Dec' 21st 1776.
William Shackelford & Catharine Daniel married Dec' 21st 1776.
William Ware & Mary Bolden married Feb'y 15. 1777.
Thomas Crittendon & Catharine Shephard married Feby. 13th 1777.
Nicholas Tuggle & Susanna Abbot married Feb'y 16th 1777.
John Healey & Jane Warwick married March 30th 1777.
Thomas Willis & Mary Blake married May 3d 1777.
Richard Bird & Mary Pamplin married June 12th 1777.
Lunsford Daniel & Lydia Daniel married July 10th 1777.
John Owen & Mary Hill married Octr. 30th 1777.
Charles Howerton & Catharine Montague married Nov' 3d 1777.
Charles Grymes & Mary Hubard married Dec' 20th 1777.
Jonathan Eyre & Judith Kidd married Dec' 28th. 1777.
Joseph Barwick & Ann Sanders married January 3d. 1778.
James Maury Fontaine & Betty Carter Churchhill married Jan'y 3d. 1778.
James Wortham & Franky Smith married Jan'y 4th 1778.
Michael Osborn & Ann Bowers married January 10th, 1778.
Jeremiah Powell & Agnes Dudley married Jan'y 17th 1778.
William Owen & Jane Batchelder married Jan'y 13th 1778.
George Lee & Peggy Hardy married Jan'y 22d 1778.
William Robinson & Ann Dunlevy married February 10th 1778.
Benjamin Williams & Esther Smith married Feb'y 25th 1778.

Thomas Gaines & Katy Wortham married April 19th 1778.
Abraham Currell Blade & Elizabeth Davis married August 18th 1778.
Thomas Harwood & Lucy Meacham married Sep^t 27. 1778.
Samuel Brooks & Priscilla Piper married October 31st 1778.
John Brooks & Anne Mickelburrough married May 13th.
John Carter & Hannah Baylor of King & Queen County married May 15th 1779.
Harry Beverley Yates & Lucy Murray married May 23d 1779.
John Groom & Catharine Ware married May 30th 1779.
Delphos Scott & Sarah Faulkner married May 30th 1779.
John Fenning & Mary Humphreys married May 31st 1779.
Daniel Jefferson & Priscilla Barrick married August 1st. 1779.
George West & Winney Shelton married August 28th 1779.
Joseph Sylvester & Fanny Hayton married Decr 1st. 1779.
William Murray & Ann Kemp married Decr 18th 1779.
Isaac Mitchell & Mary Johnson, of Essex County, married Decr 19th. 1779.
George Brushwood & Sarah Garrett, of King & Queen County, married Decr 24th 1779.
William Bowden & Sarah Owen married Decr 26th 1779.
Edward Brook & Catharine Holleway married Decr 2 1779.
Roger Blackburn & Jane Hackney married Decr 30th 1779.
Oliver Daniel & Mary Stevens married January 1st 1780.
John Kidd & Lucy Collier married February 23d 1780.
William Moore & Elizabeth Swords married March 2d 1780.
Thomas Mountague & Ann Batchelder married March 23d. 1780.
William Elliot & Rebecca Deagle married May 18th 1780.
John Dance & Ann Ross married June 2d 1780.
Benjamin Kidd & Frances Dillard married June 3d 1780.
Matthew Elliot & Anne Hearing married Sep^{br} 17th 1780.
Robert Heughen & Joanna Hearing married Sep^{br} 17th 1780.
Isham Tatum & Rachel Garrett married Octr 19th. 1780.
Richard Cauthon & Anne Seward married Novr 9th 1780.
Samuel More & Martha Davis married March 28th 1781.
Sanders Bristow & Sarah Smith married March 29th. 1781.
William George & Ann Batchelder married April 8th 1781.
Reuben Lee & Sarah Williams married May 10th 1781.
Robinson Shackelford & Ann Bushrod Carpenter married May 12th 1781.
John George & Susanna George married May 22d 1781.
Warner Dunstan & Susanna Brooking of Gloucester married May 30th. 1781.
William Brown & Rhoda Callahan married August 18th. 1781.
George Rudolph & Elizabeth Hughes married in Kingston Parish Gloucester, September 13th. 1781.
John Flippen & Elizabeth Carney of Kingston Parish Gloucester married September 14th 1781.
Thomas Hayes & Mary Buckner Walker of Gloucester married Novr 3d. 1781.
Jonathan Denison & Jane Morgan married Decr 17th 1781.
Mordecai Cook & Elizabeth Scrosby married Decr 20th 1781.
Richard Crittendon & Frances Sykes, of King & Queen, married Decr 22d. 1781.

Robert Townley & Jane Anderson of King & Queen, married Dec' 29th. 1781.
John Coleman & Dorothy Wyatt, of Gloucester, married January 12th. 1782.
John Stephens & Elizabeth Collier, of King & Queen, married January 17th 1782.
Thomas Pierce & Milly Webb, of King & Queen, married January 19th 1782.
James Guthrie & Nancy Garrett, of King & Queen, married March 28th 1782.
John Dunn & Anne Cauthon, of Essex, married September 30th 1782.
William Bristow & Jane Chowning married October 5th 1782.
Thomas Patterson & Elizabeth Batchelder married Oct' 24th 1782.
Robert Coats & Mary Spann (of Gloucester) married Nov' 16th 1782.
Sydner Belfield (of Richmond) & Ann Young (of Essex) married November the 28th 1782.
John Pryor & Delphia Dilliard (of King & Queen) married Dec' 5th 1782.
William Hundley & Elizabeth Goode (of Essex) married Dec' 5th 1782.
William Moulson & Ann Guthrie (of King & Queen) married Dec' 6th 1782.
Benjamin Moore & Susanna Milbey (of King & Queen) married Dec' 19th 1782.
Christopher Brooke & Elizabeth Saunders married Dec' 24th 1782.
Thomas Bennet & Mary Hardy married Dec' 25. 1782.
James Hart & Milly Gest (of King & Queen) married Dec' 25th 1782.
Reubin Broadass & Elizabeth Garland (of Gloucester) married Dec' 26th 1782.
Francis Thornton & Elizabeth Hackney married Dec' 26th 1782.
James Cammiel & Heany Peters married January 2d 1783.
Michael Dixon & Catharine Didlake (King & Queen) married Jany 16th 1783.
Joseph Wyatt & Elizabeth Turner married January 23. 1783.
William Meredith & Ann Rootes married February 8th 1783.
Edward Trice & Ann Jeffries (King & Queen) married February 13th 1783.
John Groom & Elizabeth Curry (King & Queen) married February 14th 1783.
John Shackelford & Mary Drummond (King & Queen) married February 14th 1783.
John Mackendree & Ruthey Milby (King & Queen) married Sep' 28th 1783.
James Burton & Frances Yarrington (King & Queen) married October 23d 1783.
Miles Brown & Rachel Jordan (King & Queen) married Nov' 6th 1783.
James Clayton & Jane Dillard (King & Queen) married Nov' 13th 1783.
John Sadler & Mildred Corr (King & Queen) married Nov' 20th 1783.

John Dudley & Elizabeth Moulson married Nov' 21st 1783.
Philip Gulley & Mary Sutton married November 27th 1783.
Gregory Perry & Mary Mills (Gloucester) married Nov' 27. 1783.
Johnson Wake & Lucy Harvey married Dec' 4th 1783.
Job. Stone & Elizabeth Oakes (King & Queen) married Dec' 9th 1783.
Edmond Garret & Nancy Didlake (King & Queen) married Dec' 18th 1783.
George Dejarnet & Anne Walker (Essex) married Dec' 18th 1783.
John Downey & Rachel Sadler (Essex) married Jan'y 8th 1784.
Benjamin Kidd & Mary Guthrie (King & Queen) married Jan'y 8th 1784.
Reuben Layton & Martha Wilcox married February 19th 1784.
Benjamin Jacobs & Frances Blackley married March 27th 1784.
Richard Stalker & Elizabeth Emmerson married April 4th 1784.
John Robinson & Debby Dunlap married April 17th 1784.
John Good & Elizabeth Stevens married April 27th 1784.
Ralph Watts & Hanna Dunn married May 12th 1784.
Linzey Clark & Caroline Segar Brim married May 22d 1784.
Thomas Chowning & Elizabeth George married May 29th 1784.
Rlchard Gwathmey & Charlotte Spratt married June 3d 1784.
Thomas Cook & Kitty Meredith (King & Queen) married June 5th 1784.
George Fernald & Frances Madiex married June 26th 1784.
James Henderson & Elizabeth Milby married August
William Robinson & Ursule Robin
John Mickelburrough & Caty Allen married March 27th 1785.
Henry Batchelder & Elizabeth Dillard married March 31st 1785.
Benjamin Herring & Nancy Fleming married April 10th 1785.
George Sykes & Alice Mourning Livingston (King & Queen) married May 12th 1785.
Thomas Brooks & Anne Johnson married May 15th 1785.
Reubin Davenport & Jane Crump (King William) married May 28th 1785.
Benjamin Hackney & Jane George married June 2d 1785.
Lewis Boss & Sarah Boss married June 11th 1785.
Charles Whitaker & Elizabeth Stevens married June 30th 1785.
John Mitchell & Sally Gatewood (King & Queen) married June 30th 1785.
Thomas Wiatt & Catharine Robinson (Gloucester) married July 2d
George Blake & Betty Saunders married July 14th 1785.
Oliver Yarrington & Elizabeth Ware married July 15 1785.
Henry Chowning & Margaret Allen married Sept' 11th 1785.
William Edwards & Nancy Robinson (Gloucester) married October 15th 1785.
Stubberfield Bowls & Sally Collier (King & Queen) married October 20th 1785.
John Cloudas & Elizabeth Cloudas (Essex) married Oct' 27th 1785.
Thomas Healy & Sarah Mitchell married Oct' 29th 1785.
John Buckner & Dorothy Scrosby married November 24th 1785.
Beverley Deane & Tilley Webb (King & Queen) married Dec' 3d 1785.
John Hodges & Elizabeth Blackburn married December 3d 1785.

* * Woods & Elizabeth Brooks married December 17th 1785.
* * * & Catherine George married Feb'ʸ 14th 1790.
* * * & Dolly Coleman (K. & Q.) married Feb'ʸ 20th 1790.
George Haynes & Susanna Waller (K. & Q.) married March 20th 1790.
Thomas Hundley & Elizabeth McTyre (Essex) married April 1st 1790.
James Milby & Frances Ross married April 11th 1790.
Robert Didlick & Mary Baker (K. & Q.) married May 20th 1790.
William Curtis & Mary Robinson Whiting married June 5. 1790.
James Hall & Mary Walden (King & Q.) married June 24. 1790.

The above drawn off & sent to the Clks. of the several Counties wherein the marriages were solemnized.
Samuel Klug. Minister.

Lewis Hening & Jane Chapman married * *
Robert Mickleburrough & Elizabeth Dean married * *
Braxton Dunlevy & Mary Hibble married Dec'ʳ 22d 1791.
Robert Lumpkin jr. & Lucy Roane (K. & Q.) married Dec'ʳ 22d 1791.
William Healy & Elizabeth Bristow married Dec'ʳ 24th 1791.
Charles Walden & Mary Ison (K. & Q.) married Dec'ʳ 29th 1791.
Coleman Lumpkin & Sarah Calaun (Glos.) marieᵈ Jan'ʸ 7th 1792.
William Bland j'ʳ & Mary Ann Corr (K. & Q.) married Feb'ʸ 20th 1791.
Staige Davis & Elizabeth Gardner (K. & Q.) married Feb'ʸ 28th 17—.
James Batchelder & Mary Jackson married March
Thomas Sears & Anne Street (Essex) married February 11th 1786.
Thomas Brooke & Anne Taff. (Essex) married February 26th 1786.
Drury Bagwell & Catharine Ware (King & Queen) married Feb'ʸ 28th 1786.
Batchelder Thurston & Peggy Daniel married March 16th 1786.
George Gardner & Elizabeth Dunn married March 16th 1786.
Richard Mountague & Charlotte Mountague married March 19th 1786.
Bartholomew Bristow & Ann Saunders married April 15th 1786.
Samuel Brooking & Mary Baker married July 8th 1786.
William Kidd & Rachel Chowning married August 3d 1786.
Robert Wilson & Betty Payne married October 8th 1786.
William Craine & Sarah Major Dillard married October 14th 1786.
Thomas Lambeth & Lucy Kidd (King & Queen) married October 18th 1786.
John Corr & Frances Campbell (King & Queen) married October 24th 1786.
Thomas Royston & Elizabeth Royston (Gloucester) married October 26th 1786.
Reuben Layton & Elizabeth Burton married October 29th 1786.
Henry Kidd & Catharine Swords were married by the Revᵈ Mʳ Needler Robinson Nov'ʳ 26. 1786.

The above drawn off for the Clerks of those County's wherein the above Marriages were solemnized.

Josiah Bristow & Fanny Bristow married December 24th 1786.
Richard Hopkins & Frances Blake married December 26th 1786.
William Didlake & Lucy Boyd (King & Queen) married January 7th 1787.
John McWilliams & Elizabeth Green (King & Queen) married January 20th 1787.
Charles Roane & Maretia Garrett (King & Queen) married Jany 26th 1787.
Thomas Spencer & Nancy Foster (King & Queen) married Feby 17th 1787.
Thomas Burk & Elizabeth Sutton married March 8th 1787.
James Taylor Horseley & Johannah Dudley (Glouster) married March 14th 1787.
Ralph Bland & Frances Corr (King & Queen) married April 15th 1787.
Christian Ryner & Rhoda Dudley (Gloucester) married March 14 1787.
Smith Horsley & Elizabeth Rilee Glou married 20th Decr 1787.
Edward Watts & Ann Garrett K. & Q. married Decr 21st 1787.
John Norris & Agatha Garrett, K & Q, married Decr 22d 1787.
Thomas Montague & Catharine Vass married Decr 22d 1787.
James Didlake and Mary Gardner, K. & Q. married Decr 22d 1787.
William James & Elzabeth Major married Decr 22d 1787.
Charles Curtis & Ann Murray married Decr 22d 1787.
David O'Dear & Nancy Shepherd K. & Q. Decr 23d 1787.
Niels Winning & Ann Miller married Decr 24th 1787.
John Whitely & Sally Saunders married Decr 25th 1787.
William Halyard & Frances Stedman (King & Queen married Decr 26th 1787.
Thacker Campbell & Hannah Montague (Essex) married Decr 27th 1787.

Drawn off for the Clks. of those Counties wherein the above Marriages were Solemnized.

James Davis & Elizabeth Humphris married Jany 28th 1788.
Robert Wake & Ann Elliott married February 1st 1788.
Thomas Robinson & Elizabeth Dillard (King & Queen) married February 9th 1788.
John Curry Montague & Charlotte Montague married March 23d 1788.
John Wood & Nancy Longest married April 2d 1788.
James Baker & Johanna Bray married May 3d 1788.
George West & Frances Barrick married July 20th 1788.
Saunders Bristow & Nancy Crossfield married August 17th. 1788.
Thomas Jones & Elizabeth Didlake (K. &. Q.) married Augst 23. 1788.
John Wilkines & Lucy Gibson married Augst 31st 1788.
James Boss & Susan Powell married Sep^{br} 4th. 1788.
Lewis Walden & Judith Kidd married Septr 6th 1788.
Thomas Fargueson & Ann Didlak (K. & Q.) married Septr 7th 1788.
Robert Chowning & Fanny Abbott married January 1st. 1789.
William Kidd & Nancy Kidd married January 1st. 1789.
John Hebble & Elizabeth Haynes married January 17th 1789.

John Woodley & Mary Jefferson married January 19th 1789.
George Daniel & Lucy Clare married February 12th 1789.
Thomas Bray & Polly Bristow married February 21st. 1789.
Richard Bland & Mary Bowden K & Queen married March 14th 1789.
Beverley Carlton & Caty Drummond (K. & Q.) married March 19th 1789.
Robert Dudley & Ann Blake married April 19th 1789.
Zachariah Groom & Elizabeth Wyett married May 28. 1789.
Henry Chapman & Ann Bland (King & Queen) married June 11th 1789.
Philip Nelson & Sarah Nelson Burwell married June 27th 1789.
William Crittenden Webb & Fanny Wortham married July 11th 1789.
William Muire & Catharine Seward (K. & Q.) married Augst 20th. 1789.
John Hibble & Mary French married August 25th 1789.
Lewis Walden & Lucy Wallace (K. & Queen) married August 29th 1789.
John Crittenden & Polly Ware (King & Queen) married Decr 17th 1789.
Thomas Dudley & Betsey Shepard Crittenden (King & Queen) Decr 19 1789.
Henry Daniel Shepherd & Mary Daniel married December 19th 1789.
Philip Didlake & Lucy Falkner (King & Queen) married Decr 26th 1789.
Christopher Wake & Sarah Sommers married Decr 28. 1789.
Leonard George & Susanna George Daniel married Decr 31. 1789.
James Lee & Frances Thurston married January 5th 1790.
William Montague & Elizabeth Valentine married Jany 14th 1790.
Nathan Hall & Catharine Crossfield married January 28th 179 .
Nelson Daniel & Jean Blackburn married Februa— — ——.
Peter Wyatt & Josie Shepherd (King & Queen) married Octr 2d 1790.
Isaac Kidd & Polly Kidd married December 18th 1790.
George Davis Saunders & Charlotte Merchant married Decr 30th 1790.
Hudson Muse & Agnes Neilson married December 30th 1790.
William Jackson & Martha Vaughan married Jany 22nd 1791.
Simon Burton & Nancy Robinson married Jan'y 23rd 1791.
Benjamin Walden & Mary Dudley (K. & Q.) married Jan'y 29th 1791.
Benjamin Kidd & Ann Spencer married Feb'y 5th 1791.
William Wood & Fanny Jones married Feb'y 10th 1791.
Thomas Bland Jr. & Sarah Waller (K. & Q.) married Feby 19th 1791.
Henry Goinge & Betsey Paggot (K. & Q.) married March 5th 1791.
Samuel Drummond & Isbell Gibson (King & Queen) married March 179 .
Benjamin Heningham & Rose Berryman Shackelford (K. & Q.) married March 9th 1791.
Benjamin Collier & Rachel Ware (K. & Q.) married March 26th 1791.

Robert Jackman & Salley Hillen (Gloucester) married April 11th 1791.
William Shaw & Fanny Williams (K. & Q.) married April 26th 1791.
Richard Groom & Catharine Webb (K. & Q.) married April 21st 1791.
Thomas Siblee & Mary Layton married May 4th 1791.
John Gayle Sutton & Ann Wake married June 9th 1791.
William Holt & Polly Tisher married July 30th 1791.
James Groom & Frances Finley married Augst 6th 1791.
William Segar & Nancy Roane married Septr 24th 1791.
William Matthews & Elen Hunt married Octr 9th 1791.
Benjamin Dabney & Sarah Smith (K. & Q.) married Octr 8th —
Fragment.
William Reningham & Caty Kelligrew of Gloucester married March 29. 1782.
Bowden Newcomb & Rachel Currie, of King & Queen married April 3d 1782.
Abner Cloudas & Sarah Daniel married April 4th 1782.
Benjamin Hackney & Mary Stiff married April 6th 1782.
Charles Colly & Elizabeth Hudson, of King & Queen married April 14th 1782.
John Bennet & Elizabeth Richeson married April 21st 1782.
William Meredith & Judith Edmondson of King & Queen married April 30th 1782.
William Steptoe & Elizabeth Robinson married May 19th 1782.
Thomas Daniel & Judith Tool married May 24th 1782.
William Steward & Zena Medley (of Essex County) married May 24th 1782.
Pitman Wiatt & Martha Fuller (of King & Queen) married June 1st 1782.
Zachariah Crittenden & Eliz^a Ware (of King & Queen) married June 20th 1782.
John Tucker & Frances Pigg, King & Queen, married July 18th 1782.
Henry Lyn & Anne Parrott married July 30th 1782.
John Jesse & Catharine Beamon married August 4th 1782.
Jonathan Lewis & Sarah Gale Morgan married August 10th 1782.
William Booth & Mary Jones (Gloucester) married August 22d 1782.
John Sears & Lucy Medley married September 1st 1782.
John Clark & Frances Beamon married Septr 19th 1782.
Archibald Mullins & Susanna Beamon married Septr 19th 17

Samuel Klug, Minist.

John Cardwell & Elizabeth Stamper married February 27th 1783.
John Thurston & Sarah Sanders married February 27th 1783.
Harry Beverley Yates & Jane Montague married February 27th 1783.
Thomas Burk & Susanna Blake married March 2d 1783.
William Bristow & Jemima Blakemore married March 12th 1783.
John Jackson jr. & Mary Smith married March 22d 1783.
Major Odear & Rebecca Hooker (King & Queen) married March 27th 1783.

Adam Aldridge & Catharine Jackson married March 27th 1783.
William Wright & Mary Bowers (King & Queen) married March 30th 1783.
Gowen Jefferies & Ann Clark married April 14th 1783.
John Holderby & Ann Jordon married April 17th 1783.
George Sims & Susanna Dulany (Culpeper) married June 5th 1783.
Thomas Gord & Afia Lee married July 4th 1783.
James Healy & Ruth Bristoo married July 13th 1783.
William Kidd & Frances Tuggle married August 17th.
Thomas Griffin Peachy & Elizabeth Mills married September 22d 1783.
Peter Boles & Avery Hardy (of King & Queen) married September 25th, 1783.

   Samuel Klug, Minister.

Lucy daughter of Anne a Mulatto in ye Service of Sr Wm Skipwith born Feb'y ye 25 1722.
Nanny daughter of Kate a Slave belonging to John Gibbs born April ye 8 1722.
Rose daughter of Eve a Slave belonging to Hezekiah Ellis born April ye 30 1722.
Jon Son of Judy a Slave belonging to Robert Williamson jun^r May ye 12. 1722.
Phillis daughter of ——— a Slave belonging to Robert George Senr born May ye 31. 1722.
Ned Son of Jenney a Slave belonging to Rice Curtis born June ye 14. 1722.
Hylace daughter of Dinah a Slave belonging to Oliver Segar born June ye 27. 1722.
Bucker Son of Moll a Slave belonging to Thomas Smith born June ye 24. 1722.
Letty daughter of Jone a Slave belonging to John Bryan born June ye 1. 1722.
Jenny daughter of Betty a Slave belonging to John Smith Senr born July 25 1722.
Sam Son of Dinah a Slave belonging to Joseph Hardee born August ye 21. 1722.
Venus daughter of Kate a Slave belonging to John Shorter born August ye 20. 1722.
Monmouth Son of Sharlott a Slave belonging to Henry Thacker born Septem^r ye 11. 1722.
Will Son of Dido a Slave belonging to Capt John Smith born Septem^r ye 9 1722.
Charles Son of Beck a Slave belonging to Joseph Gour born August ye 18. 1722.
Nanny daughter of ——— a Slave belonging to Thomas Dudley born Sept. 16 1722.
Charles Son of Delah a Slave belonging to Humphrey Jones born Sept^{mr} 15. 1722.
Seberina daughter of Nell a Slave belonging to Humphrey Jones born Octo^{br} ye 5. 1722.

Pen daughter of Winney a Slave belonging to Edwin Thacker born Septmʳ yᵉ 20. 1722.

Gawin Son of Dinah a Slave belonging to William Segar born Octo. yᵉ 10. 1722.

Tom Son of Nanny a Slave belonging to Richard Hill born Novemʳ yᵉ 28 1722.

Newman Son of Lucy a Slave belonging to Gawin Corbin born Decemʳ yᵉ 14. 1722.

Toby Son of Kate a Slave belonging to Margrett Daniel born Decemʳ yᵉ 22. 1722.

Peter Son of Letty a Slave belonging to Richard Taylor born novemʳ yᵉ 18. 1722.

Letty daughter of Hannah a Slave belonging to Maurice Smith born Jan'y. yᵉ 28 1722.

Thomas & William Sons of Penelope a Slave belonging to yᵉ Estate of James Walker dec'd born March yᵉ 4 baptized March 22 1722.

Frank daughter of Jenny a Slave belonging to Mathew Hunt March yᵉ 21. 1722.

Nanny daughter of Jone a Slave belonging to Collᵒ John Robinson born March 16. 1722.

Hannah daughter of Clary a Slave belonging to Collᵒ John Robinson born March 22. 1722.

Sprigg Son of Hannah a Slave belonging to George Harding born March yᵉ 20. 1722.

Charles Son of Dinah a Slave belonging to Henry Armistead born March yᵉ 20. 1722.

Moll daughter of Sarah a Slave belonging to Robᵗ Williamson born April 1. 1723.

Judy daughter of Sarah a Slave belonging to John Digge born March 27. 1723.

Letty daughter of Sarah a Slave belonging to Richard Taylor born Feb'y. yᵉ 15. 1722.

Toby Son of Frank a Slave belonging to Oliver Segar born Feb'y yᵉ 20. 1722.

Robin Son of Hannah a Slave belonging to Gawin Corbin born March yᵉ 15. 1722.

Diana daughter of Frank a Slave belonging to Gawin Corbin born March yᵉ 20. 1722.

George Son of Judy a Slave belonging to Thomas Mountague born April yᵉ 18. 1722.

Jeffery Son of Margrett a Slave belonging to John Wormeley born April yᵉ 19. 1722.

Jack Son of Doll a Slave belonging to William Blackburne born April yᵉ 12. 1723.

Tom Son of Venus a Slave belonging to William Blackburne born April yᵉ 15. 1723.

Jack Son of Nell a Slave belonging to yᵉ estate of Edmund Berkley born April yᵉ 28. 1723.

Harry Son of Monday a Slave belonging to Samuel Batchelder born May 17. 1723.

Percilla daughter of Sue a Slave belonging to Gawin Corbin born May yᵉ 1. 1723.

Bristow Son of Beck a Slave belonging to Gawin Corbin born May y⁰ 5. 1723.
Peter Son of Rachel a Slave belonging to y⁰ Estate of Edm⁴ Berkeley dec'd born May 18. 1723.
Harry Son of Phillis a Slave belonging to Stockley Towles born May y⁰ 22. 1723.
Walley Son of Dellow a Slave belonging to Thomas Haselwood born May y⁰ 27. 1723.
Frank daughter of Judy a Slave belonging to Rice Curtis born June y⁰ 5. 1723.
Beck daughter of Venus a Slave belonging to Frances Timberlake born May y⁰ 29. 1723.
Frank daughter of Dye a Slave belonging to John Moseley born June y⁰ 17. 1723.
Jack Son of Alice a Slave belonging to Margarett Daniel born June y⁰ 12 1723.
Verina daughter of Lucy a Slave belonging to y⁰ estate of John Vivian dec'd born June 22 1723.
Sawney Son of Phillis a Slave belonging to John Grymes born Ap. y⁰ 1. 1723.
Del a Daughter of Margery a Slave belonging to John Grymes born April y⁰ 9. 1723.
* Son of Kate a Slave belonging to John Grymes born June y⁰ 11. 1723.
* daughter of Abigail a Slave belonging to John Grymes born June 25. 1723.
* daughter of Hannah a Slave belonging to y⁰ estate of Wᵐ Gordon dec'd. born April y⁰ 15. 1723.
Antony Son of ―― a Slave belonging to Armistead Churchhill born July y⁰ 3. 1723.
Peg daughter of ―― a Slave belonging to Armistead Churchhill born July y⁰ 10. 1723.
Tony Son of Sarah a Slave belonging to John Cheadle born July y⁰ 11. 1723.
Frank Son of Kate a Slave belonging to John Daniel born July y⁰ 4. 1723.
Doll daughter of Jenny a Slave belonging to y⁰ estate of Hobby Weeks born June 29. 1723.
Lena daughter of Sharlott a Slave belonging to Henry Thacker born July y⁰ 16. 1723.
Rebecca daughter of Phillis a Slave belonging to Tho', Machen born July 20. 1723.
Isaac Son of Phillis a Slave belonging to Tho' Machen born July 31. 1723.
Nan daughter of Poll a Slave belonging to y⁰ estate of Garritt Minor born July 27. 1723.
Eleanor daughter of Jenny a Slave belonging to y⁰ estate of John Vivion born Augsᵗ 27. 1723.
Lyddee daughter of Kate a Slave belonging to John Smith junʳ born August 26. 1723.
Will Son of Frank a Slave belonging to Edmond Mickelborough born Septemʳ y⁰ 5. 1723.

Lucy daughter of Carter a Slave belonging to Thomas Norman born Septem' y° 1. 1723.
Tom Son of Jenny a Slave belonging to William Chowning born Septem' 15. 1723.
Jack Son of Mary a Slave belonging to John Wormeley born Septem' y° 4. 1723.
Violett daughter of Kate a Slave belonging to John Gibbs born Septem' y° 21. 1723.
Hannah daughter of Sue a Slave belonging to John Price born August y° 23. 1723.
George Son of Moll a Slave belonging to Eliz^a Smith born Septem' y° 29. 1723.
Moll daughter of Judy a Slave belonging to John Price born October y° 29. 1723.
Betty daughter of Moll a Slave belonging to Anne Thacker born Sept. y° 15. 1723.
Jenny daughter of Kate a Slave belonging to John Wormeley born Novem' y° 5. 1723.
Kate daughter of Jenny a Slave belonging to y° estate of Wm Gordon born Nov. y° 15. 1723.
Billy Son of Jenny a Slave belonging to John Murry born octo. 18. 1723.
Phillis daughter of Judy a Slave belonging to Wm Stanard born Novem' y° 24. 1723.
Antony Son of Hannah a Slave belonging to William Gray born Octo. y° 16. 1723.
Peter Son of Judy a Slave belonging to William Blackbourne born Nov. 15. 1723.
Dick Son of Lucy a Slave belonging to John Wormeley born Decem' y° 5. 1723.
Judy daughter of Kate a Slave belonging to John Shorter born Decem' y° 17. 1723.
George Son of Kate a Slave belonging to Margrett Daniel born Decem' y° 21. 1723.
Dick Son of Nell a Slave belonging to Armistead Churchhill born Jan'" 2. 1723.
Margery daughter of Bess a Slave belonging to Henry Armistead born Jan'^{y} y° 23. 1723.
Margery daughter of Betty a Slave belonging to Augustine Owen born Jan'y y° 23. 1723.
Letty daughter of Judy a Slave belonging to John Hipkings born Feb'y y° 11. 1723.
Sampson Son of Beck a Slave belonging to Joseph Goar born Feb'y y° 15. 1723.
Sampson Son of Bess a Slave belonging to Mathew Kemp born March y° 4. 1723.
Frank Son of Judy a Slave belonging to John Smith Sen' born March y° 4. 1723.
Jemmy Son of Sarah a Slave belonging to Alexander Graves born Feb'y y° 12. 1723.
Titan Son of Sarah a Slave belonging to William Stanard born Feb'y ye 17. 1723.

Margret daughter of —— a Slave belonging to John Wormeley born March 12. 1723.
Rebecca daughter of Penelope a Slave belonging to James Walker decd. born. baptized Ap: 5. 1724.
Nell daughter of Judy a Slave belonging to John Degge born March ye 30. 1724.
Harry Son of Frank a Slave belonging to Mathew Kemp born April ye 7. 1724.
Charles Son of Pegg a Slave belonging to Henry Armistead born April ye 8. 1724.
Phillis daughter of Judy a Slave belonging to John Alding born March ye 24. 1723.
Tom Son of Megg a Slave belonging to Humphrey Jones born March 23. 1723.
Hanaball Son of Dinah a Slave belonging to Oliver Segar born April ye 1. 1724.
Sary daughter of Judy a Slave belonging to ye estate of Wm Daniel jun^r born Ap. ye 6. 1724.
Kate daughter of Nanny a Slave belonging to Bar. Yates born March ye 24. 1723.
Alice daughter of Phillis a Slave belonging to Thomas Churchhill born April ye 15. 1724.
Phillis daughter of Lucy a Slave belonging to ye estate of John Mayo born April 19. 1724.
Moll daughter of Flora a Slave belonging to John Wormeley born Ap. y^o 10. 1724.
Nan daughter of Bridgett a Slave belonging to John Wormeley born May ye 1. 1724.
White Son of Nan a Slave belonging to John Wormeley born May ye 20. 1724.
Judy & Jenny daughters of a —— Slave belonging to ye estate of James Curtis jun^r decd. born May 25. 1724.
Charles daughter of Dinah a Slave belonging to Joseph Hardee born May ye 17. 1724.
Will Son of Peg a Slave belonging to ye estate of John Owen born May ye 25. 1724.
Winney daughter of Jenny a Slave belonging to John Alding born May ye 28. 1724.
Robin Son of a —— Slave belonging to Christopher Robinson born May 26. 1724.
Hannah daughter of a —— Slave belonging to Christopher Robinson born June 3. 1724.
Alice daughter of Sabrina a Slave belonging to Edwin Thacker born Ap. 22 1724.
Frank daughter of Moll a Slave belonging to Wm Mountague born June ye 3. 1724.
Frank Daughter of Sarah a Slave belonging to Jno Cheedle born June ye 3. 1724.
Silas Son of Dinah a Slave belonging to William Segar born June ye 8. 1724.
Kezia daughter of Winny a Slave belonging to ye estate of Henry Thacker born June 25. 1724.

Letty daughter of Frank a Slave belonging to Anne Thacker born June 20. 1724.
Nan daughter of Hannah a Slave belonging to y⁵ estate of Wᵐ Gordon decd. born June 24. 1724.
Sam Son of Avey a Slave belonging to Humphrey Jones born May 26. 1724.
Nan daughter of Judy a Slave belonging to Robert Williamson junʳ born␣yᵉ 9. 1724.
Harry Son of Alice a Slave belonging to John Wormeley born July yᵉ 28. 1724.
Jane daughter of Beck a Slave belonging to Robert George junʳ born May 24. 1724.
Kendall Son of —— a Slave belonging to Henry Gilpin born Septemʳ yᵉ 5. 1724.
George Son of Bess a Slave belonging to Catherine Warwick born Septemʳ yᵉ 3. 1724.
Sarah daughter of Alice a Slave belonging to yᵉ estate of Edmund Berkeley born Septemʳ 8. 1724.
Will Son of Frank a Slave belonging to yᵉ estate of Edmund Berkeley born Septemʳ 14. 1724.
Robin Son of —— a Slave belonging to Mathew Kemp born Septemʳ 19. 1724.
Will Son of Kate a Slave belonging to Robert George Senʳ born Septemʳ 24. 1724.
Peter Son of Munday a Slave belonging to Samuel Batchelder born Septemʳ yᵉ 17. 1724.
Harry Son of Betty a Slave belonging to John Smith Senʳ born October yᵉ 7. 1724.
Scipio Son of Arminto a Slave belonging to John Grymes born Sept. yᵉ 19. 1724.
Simon Son of Ciss a Slave belonging to John Grymes born Sept. yᵉ 30. 1724.
Jeptha Son of Phebe a Slave belonging to John Grymes born Octo. yᵉ 8. 1724.
Enos Son of Phillis a Slave belonging to Rice Curtis born Octo. yᵉ 21. 1724.
Dinah daughter of Hannah a Slave belonging to yᵉ estate of Garritt Minor born Octo. yᵉ 5. 1724.
Jenny daughter of Eve a Slave belonging to Hezekiah Ellis born Octo. yᵉ 15. 1724.
Kate daughter of —— a Slave belonging to Robert Holderness born Octo. yᵉ 7. 1724.
Minter Son of Jone a Slave belonging to Rice Curtis born Novemʳ yᵉ 9. 1724.
Mingo Son of Frank a Slave belonging to David George born Octo: yᵉ 27. 1724.
Amy daughter of Hannah a Slave belonging to Maurice Smith born Novemʳ 29. 1724.
Mary & Rachel daughters of Rebecca a Mollatto belonging to Sʳ Wᵐ Skipwith born Nov. 30. 1724.
Nanny daughter of —— a Slave belonging to Francis Timberlake born Dec. 3. 1724.

Abigall daughter of Mary a Slave belonging to John Robinson born Dec. 11. 1724.
Jack Son of Christain a Slave belonging to Thomas Causer born Dec. 24. 1724.
Judy daughter of Jenny a Slave belonging to Matthew Hunt born Novem^r 29. 1724.
Letty daughter of Judy a Slave belonging to John Price born Decem^r ye 17 1724.
Billy Son of Sue a Slave belonging to Richard Taylor born Jan'y ye 1. 1724.
Rose daughter of Dye a Slave belonging to John Marston Senr born Jan'y ye 13. 1724.
Moll daughter of Doll a Slave belonging to William Blackborne Feb'y 5. 1724.
Judith daughter of Sharlott a Slave belonging to Henry Thacker born Feb'y ye 13. 1724.
Jack Son of Frank a Slave belonging to Francis Porter born Decem^r 10. 1724.
Davy Son of Winny a Slave belonging to Edwin Thacker born Jan'y ye 10. 1724.
Joe Son of Kate a Slave belonging to Roger Jones born Feb'y ye 28. 1724.
Matt Son of Nell a Slave belonging to Humphry Jones born Feb'y 2 1724.
Jeffrey Son of Winny a Slave belonging to Thomas Hackett born March 10. 1724.
Nanny daughter of Moll a Slave belonging to Anne Thacker born Feb'y 23 1724.
Austin Son of Hannah a Slave belonging to Robert Williamson born March 17 1724.
Hampton Son of Judy a Slave belonging to Tho. Mountague born April ye 1. 1725.
Nanny daughter of Sue a Slave belonging to Francis Porter born April ye 16. 1725.
Nan daughter of Letty a Slave belonging to Richd Taylor born Ap. 25 1725.
George Son of Moll a Slave belonging to John Segar born Ap. 23 1725.
Jemmy Son of Betty a Slave belonging to John Robinson Esqr born Ap. 6 1725.
Tamar daughter of Kate a Slave belonging to John Shorter born Ap. 26 1725.
Irene daughter of Judy a Slave belonging to William Stanard born May ye 9 1725.
Jerrell Son of Moll a Slave belonging to William Stanard born May ye 23 1725.
Driner daughter of Rosse a Slave belonging to Gawin Corbin born May ye 16 1725.
Major Son of Winey a Slave belonging to Gawin Corbin born May ye 25 1725.
Billy Son of Betty a Slave belonging to Armistead Churchhill born May ye 16 1725.

Hannah daughter of Flounder a Slave belonging to Armistead Churchhill born May yᵉ 12 1725.
Manuel son of Phillis a Slave belonging to Robert Holderness. born May yᵉ 14 1725.
Joan daughter of Dellah a Slave belonging to Humphry Jones born May yᵉ 23 1725.
Lettissha daughter of Judith a Slave belonging to Oliver Segar born May yᵉ 31 1725.
Jamey Son of ——— a Slave belonging to Mathew Kemp born June yᵉ 21 1725.
Phillis Daughter of Dinah a Slave belonging to William Segar born June yᵉ 6 1725.
Betty daughter of Dido a Slave belonging to John Smith senʳ born July ye 8.
Jack Son of Judy a Slave belonging to Rice Curtis born July yᵉ 10 1725.
Jack Son of Dy a Slave belonging to John Mosely born July yᵉ 9 1725.
Esther daughter of Abigal a Slave belonging to John Grymes born June yᵉ 29 1725.
Peg daughter of Rachel a Slave belonging to John Grymes born July yᵉ 11 1725.
Rose daughter of ——— a Slave belonging to Mathew Kemp born Augsᵗ yᵉ 18 1725.
Judy daughter of Margrett a Slave belonging to John Wormley born Augsᵗ 25. 1725.
Judy daughter of Kate a Slave belonging to John Wormley born August 29. 1725.
Peter Son of   a Slave belonging to John Murray born August 10. 1725.
Wonah daughter of Hannah a Slave belonging to George Hardine- born born July yᵉ 23. 1725.
Dan Son of   a Slave belonging to Matthew Kemp born Septemʳ yᵉ 19. 1725.
Betty daughter of Sarah a Slave belonging to Richᵈ Taylor born Augst yᵉ 18 1725.
Jemmy Son of Hannah a Slave belonging to Elizabeth Smith born Septemʳ yᵉ 17. 1725.
Oriel Son of Lucy a Slave belonging to yᵉ estate of John Vivion born Septemʳ 28 1725.
Betty daughter of Moll a Slave belonging to Elizᵃ Smith born October yᵉ 21. 1725.
Billy Son of Kate a Slave belonging to John Gibbs born October yᵉ 27 1725.
Winne daughter of Jenny a Slave belonging to Rice Curtis born Novemʳ yᵉ 12 1725.
Winne daughter of Kate a Slave belonging Margrett Daniell born Novemʳ 9 1725.
Silla daughter of Margery a Slave belonging to Oliver Segar born Novemʳ yᵉ 28 1725.
Phillis daughter of Nell a Slave belonging to John Wormeley born Novemʳ yᵉ 28 1725.

Jenny daughter of Megg a Slave belonging to Humphrey Jones born Novem' y° 26 1725.
Alce daughter of ——— a Slave belonging to John Wormley born Decem' y° 19 1725.
Silvia daughter of Judy a Slave belonging to Wm Blackbourn born Octo. y° 14 1725.
Sara daughter of Nan a Slave belonging to Wm Blackbourn born Octo y° 20. 1725.
Rose daughter of Betty a Slave belonging to Wm Blackbourn born Decem. 12 1725.
Penelope daughter of ——— a Slave belonging to John Wormley born Feb'y 9 1725.
Joan daughter of Kate a Slave belonging to Edwin Thacker born Feb'y 19 1725.
Mingo Son of Judy a Slave belonging to John Price born April 3d 1726.
Jemima daughter of Judy a Slave belonging to ye estate of John Vivion born March 16. 1725.
Hannah daughter of Judy a Slave belonging to Christopher Sutton born August 20 1725.
Sampson Son of Judy a Slave belonging to John Hipkins born April ye 1st 1726.
Judy daughter of Frank a Slave belonging to Edmund Mickleburrough born Ap. 22 1726.
Jemny Son of Kate a Slave belonging to Armistead Churchhill born March 16. 1725.
Rosegill Son of Wouna a Slave belonging to Armistead Churchhill born March 16 1725.
Phillis daughter of Carter a Slave belonging to Tho: Norman born April y° 26 1726.
Hampton Son of Hannah a Slave belonging to Martha Williamson born May ye 19 1726.
Dick Son of Dellah a Slave belonging to Thomas Haslewood born May y° 25 1726.
Agy daughter of Sabina a Slave belonging to Edwin Thacker born June ye 21 1726.
Alice daughter of Rachel a Slave belonging to Edmund Berkley born June y° 8 1726.
Davy Son of Phillis a Slave belonging to Thomas Machen born June y° 28 1726.
Jemmy Son of Hannah a Slave belonging to John Minor born June ye 25 1726.
Jenny daughter of Sarah a Slave belonging to Alexander Graves born July y° 2 1726.
Ned son of Lucy a Slave belonging to John Tugle born July ye 13 1726.
Margery daughter of Dinah a Slave belonging to Jacob Stiff born July y° 28 1726.
Abraham Son of Lucy a Slave belonging to Edwin Thacker born July y° 30 1726.
Winny daughter of Poll a Slave belonging to William Mountague born July 26 1726.

Moll daughter of Dinah a Slave belonging to Joseph Hardee born Septemʳ yᵉ 10. 1726.
Jack Son of Kate a Slave belonging to Robert George born Octo. 16. 1726.
Dinah daughter of Sarah a Slave belonging to Hezekiah Rhodes born Octo. yᵉ 18. 1726.
Betty daughter of Letty a Slave belonging to Elizabeth Weekes born Novemʳ yᵉ 10. 1726.
Ned Son of Frank a Slave belonging to Anne Thacker born Decemʳ yᵘ 6. 1726.
Sam Son of Poll a Slave belonging to John Minor born Decemʳ yᵉ 22. 1726.
Abraham Son of —— a Slave belonging to Matthew Kemp born July yᵉ 28. 1726.
Charlote daughter of —— a Slave belonging Matthew Kemp born Octo. yᵉ 12. 1726.
Charles Son of Rachell a Slave belonging to John Grymes born Jan'y yᵉ 2. 1726.
Frances daughter of Frank a Slave belonging to John Wormeley born Ap. yᵉ 11. 1726.
Jemima daughter of Rose a Slave belonging to Edwin Thacker born Octo: yᵉ 6. 1726.
Beck daughter of Nan a Slave belonging to John Wormley born April 19. 1726.
Phillis daughter of Kate a Slave belonging to Edward Clark born July 7. 1726.
Judy daughter of Jenny a Slave belonging to Samuel Batchelder born Augᵗ 1. 1726.
Charles Son of Jenny a slave belonging to Matthew Hunt born Augᵗ 7 1726.
Moll daughter of Kate a slave belonging to John Smith born Decemʳ yᵉ 2 1726.
Nan daughter of Phillis a slave belonging to Stockly Towles born Decemʳ 8 1726.
Will Son of Phillis a slave belonging to Rice Curtis born Jan'y yᵉ 17 1726.
Moll daughter of Moll a slave belonging to Elizabeth Smith born Feb'y 25 1726.
Charles Son of Venus a slave belonging to Francis Timberlake born Decemʳ 22 1726.
London Son of Sarah a slave belonging to William Stanard born May yᵉ 10. 1726.
London Son of Frank a slave belonging to Gawen Corbin born Feb'y yᵉ 28. 1726.
Ned Son of Rose a slave belonging to Gawen Corbin born March yᵉ 15. 1726.
Sarah daughter of —— a slave belonging to Armstead Churchhill born Feb'y yᵉ 27. 1726.
Winney daughter of Sarah a slave belonging to Robert Williamson born March yᵉ 6 1726.
Charles Son of Winny a slave belonging to Edwin Thacker born March yᵉ 8 1726.

Nimrod Son of Alice a slave belonging to Wm Stanard born April ye 8 1727.
George Son of Nathan a slave belonging to Marvil Moseley born March 1 1726.
Bristow Son of Jenny a slave belonging to Henry Tuggle born May ye 12. 1727.
Pat daughter of Juno a slave belonging to Matthew Kemp born May ye 17. 1727.
Phil Son of Rose a Slave belonging to George Harding born May ye 13 1727.
Jenny daughter of Dinah a slave belonging to ye estate of Tho. Smith born June ye 3 1727.
Sauney son of —— a slave belonging to ye estate of Jno. Wormley born May 13. 1727.
Abraham Son of Sue a slave belonging to Bar Yates born April ye 8 1727.
Judy & Winney daughters of Judy a Slave belonging to ye estate of Wm Daniell jun^r born May 24 1727.
Tom son of Winny a slave belonging to ye estate of Hen Thacker born May 24 1727.
Rose daughter of Hannah a Slave belonging to Eliz^a Smith born June ye 14 1727.
Jemmy Son of Jenny a slave belonging to John Murrah born June ye 11. 1727.
Sarah daughter of Dey a Slave belonging to John Roads born June ye 17. 1727.
Peter son of Bess a Slave belonging to Henry Armistead born July ye 2. 1727.
Jenny daughter of —— a Slave belonging to William Wood born July ye 10. 1727.
Harry son of a Slave belonging to Richard Perrott born July y" 12 1727.
Nell daughter of Jenny a Slave belonging to Armistead Churchhill born July ye 19. 1727.
Harry son of Dy a slave belonging to John Moseley born August ye 15. 1727.
Will son of Mundy a Slave belonging to Samuel Batchelder born August ye 17. 1727.
Harry son of a Slave belonging to Clement Owen born July ye 23 1727.
Catherine daughter of Penelope a Slave belonging to ye estate of James Walker dec'd born Augst 19 baptized August 29 1727.
Lucy daughter of Lettice a Slave belonging to ye estate of Hobs Weeks dec'd born Augst ye 8 1727.
Will Son of Jane a Slave belonging to ye estate of Hobs Weeks decd born Augst ye 8 1727.
Peter son of Jone a Slave belonging to ye estate of John Wormley born August ye 27. 1727.
Frances daughter of Sue a Slave belonging to ye estate of John Wormley dec'd born Septem^r ye 5. 1727.
Jack Son of Kate a Slave belonging to John Shorter born August ye 27. 1727.

Frank daughter of Hannah a Slave belonging to Sr Wm Skipwith born Augst ye 27 1727.
Maria daughter of Kate a Slave belonging to Robert George born August ye 29. 1727.
Moll daughter of Pegg a Slave belonging to Thomas Cheney born Septem^r ye 7. 1727.
Ishmael Son of Frank a Slave belonging to Oliver Segar born Septem^r ye 8 1727.
Nanny daughter of Sharlot a Slave belonging to Henry Thacker born Septem^r ye 23 1727.
Phillis daughter of Beck a slave belonging to Robert George jun^r born August 27 1727.
Jenny daughter of Moll a slave belonging to Anne Thacker born June 16. 1727.
Dinah daughter of Abigail a slave belonging to John Grymes born September 25 1727.
Winny daughter of Judy a slave belonging to William Stanard born Octo. ye 6 1727.
Flora daughter of Cate a slave belonging to ye estate of John Wormeley born October 17 1727.
Bridgett daughter of a Slave belonging to Armistead Churchhill born Novem^r ye 6 1727.
Sawney Son of a Slave belonging to Roger Jones born Novem^r 14. 1727.
Harry Son of Kate a Slave belonging to William Channing born Octo^r 23 1727.
Ben Son of Cato a slave belonging to John Moseley born Novem^r ye 18 1727.
Juno daughter of Sarah a slave belonging to William Stanard born Decem^r ye 8 1727.
Ben Son of Judy a slave belonging to ye estate of Jno Alding dec'd born Novem^r 12 1727.
Bess ye daughter of Nell a slave belonging to Humphrey Jones born Novem^r 18 1727.
Dick Son of Jenny a slave belonging to Wm Chowning born Decem^r ye 4 1727.
Maud daughter of Judy a slave belonging to John Smith born Decem^r 26 1727.
Dinah daughter of Nan a slave belonging to ye estate of John Smith born Jan'y 14 1727.
Phillis daughter of Jenny a slave belonging to Mathew Kemp born Feb'y ye 2 1727.
Hannah daughter of Moll a slave belonging to William Mountague born Jan'y 21 1727.
Nan daughter of Frank a slave belonging to Edmund Mickleburrough born Jan'y 29 1727.
Bess daughter of Kate a slave belonging to Mary Gibbs born Feb'y ye 1 1727.
Joan daughter of Joan a slave belonging to Jno Grymes born Feb'y ye 8. 1727.
Mingo son of Moll a slave belonging to Jno Grymes born Feb'y ye 9. 1727.

Nan daughter of Dillah a slave belonging to Henry Daniel born Feb'y y⁰ 8 1727.
Dick Son of Letty a slave belonging to Richard Tyler born Jan'y y⁰ 16. 1727.
Betty daughter of Jenny a slave belonging to Matthew Hunt born Feb'y 20 1727.
Sam & Crispin sons of Hannah a slave belonging to Laurence Orrell born y⁰ 20th of Feb'y 1727.
Phillis daughter of Jenny a slave belonging to y⁰ estate of Jn⁰ Wormley born Feb'y 17. 1727.
Tom Son of Margrett a slave belonging to y⁰ estate of John Wormley born March 8. 1727.
Betty daughter of Alice a slave belonging to y⁰ estate of John Wormley born March 12. 1727.
Nell daughter of Bridgett a slave belonging to y⁰ estate of John Wormley born March 27. 1728.
Amy daughter of Alice a slave belonging to Margrett Daniell born March 28. 1728.
Beck daughter of Jenny a slave belonging to John Smith born April y⁰ 1 1728.
Sarah daughter of Venus a slave belonging to Wᵐ Southworth born March 31. 1728.
Crozier & Daphny son & daughter of Kate a slave belonging to Margrett Daniel born April 26. 1728.
Harry Son of Nanny a slave belonging to y⁰ estate of Jn⁰ Wormley dec'd born April 24. 1728.
Lucy daughter of Sarah a free negro born at James Meacham's April y⁰ 8. 1728.
Charles Son of Doll a slave belonging to John Rhoads born April y⁰ 18. 1728.
Judith daughter of Phillis a slave belonging to Tho: Machen born April y⁰ 30 1728.
Amy daughter of a slave belonging to Armistead Churchhill born Feb'y y⁰ 20 1727.
Minter daughter of a slave belonging to John Grymes born April y⁰ 27 1728.
Toney Son of a slave belonging to Alice Causer born April y⁰ 24. 1728.
Betty daughter of Sue a slave belonging to Francis Porter born April y⁰ 21 1728.
Jenny daughter of Nanney a slave belonging to Lettice Thacker born June y⁰ 4. 1728.
Priscilla daughter of Alice a slave belonging to Edwin Thacker born June y⁰ 3 1728.
Nan daughter of Lucy a slave belonging to Edwin Thacker born May y⁰ 26. 1728.
Arabella daughter of a slave belonging to Gawin Corbin born Feb'y y⁰ 2. 1728.
Goy daughter of a slave belonging to Gawin Corbin born April y⁰ 13. 1728.
Sarah daughter of a slave belonging to Gawin Corbin born May y⁰ 21 1728.

Moll daughter of a slave belonging to Gawin Corbin born May ye 28 1728.
Frank daughter of a slave belonging to Gawin Corbin June ye 12 1728.
Grasheir son of a slave belonging to Gawin Corbin born June ye 14. 1728.
Lucy daughter of Phillis a slave belonging to Tho: Price born June ye 15. 1728.
Pompy son of Hannah a slave belonging to William Gray born April ye 22. 1728.
Caesar son of Judy a slave belonging to John Hipkins born June ye 26. 1728.
Cate daughter of a slave belonging to Gawin Corbin born June ye 24. 1728.
Cate daughter of Nell a slave belonging to ye estate of Jno Wormley born July ye 3. 1728.
Mingo son of a slave belonging to John Grymes born July ye 13. 1728.
Edward son of Jenney a slave belonging to John Grymes born April 21. baptized July ye 14. 1728.
Bess daughter of Bess a slave belonging to Henry Armistead born July ye 25 1728.
Juno daughter of a Slave belonging to Henry Gilpen born July ye 10. 1728.
Betty daughter of Winne a Slave belonging to Elizabeth Weekes born July ye 22. 1728.
Charles Son of Daphney a Slave belonging to Frances Smith born August ye 15. 1728.
Joice daughter of a Slave belonging to Henry Armistead born August ye 11. 1728.
Oliver Son of Rachell a Slave belonging to Edmund Berkley born August ye 20 1728.
Robin Son of Dey a Slave belonging to John Roades born August ye 9 1728.
Jack Son of a Slave belonging to Armistead Churchhill born August ye 20, 1728.
Betty daughter of Jenny a Slave belonging to Armistead Churchhill born Septem^r 11. 1728.
Antony Son of Betty a Slave belonging to ye estate of Capt. Jno Smith dec'd born Septem^r ye 8. 1728.
Ruth daughter of Sarah a Slave belonging to Anne daughter of James Smith born Septem^r ye 11. 1728.
Ben Son of Judy a Slave belonging to ye estate of John Vivion born Septem^r 21. 1728.
Peter Son of Pegg a Slave belonging to Robert Holderness born August ye 10. 1728.
Billey Son of Ben & Nan Slaves belonging to Wm Blackburne born Octo. 10. 1728.
Jeney daughter of Judy a Slave belonging to Eliz^a Smith born August ye 6. 1728.
Robin Son of Brinah a Slave belonging to Jonathan Brooks born Novem^r ye 4 1728.

Harry Son of Flora a Slave belonging to y" estate of Jn° Wormley dec'd born October y" 24. 1728.
Peter Son of a Slave belonging to Richard Hill born August y" 28. 1728.
Mary daughter of a Slave belonging to Richard Hill born August y" 29. 1728.
Betty daughter of Queen a Slave belonging to Gawin Corbin born Novem" y" 17. 1728.
Tony Son of Sarah a Slave belonging to Hezekiah Roads born Novem" y° 19. 1728.
Jenny daughter of Sharlott a Slave belonging to Henry Thacker born Novem" 10. 1728.
Hannah daughter of   a Slave belonging to Ralph Shelton born Decem" y° 6. 1728.
Gawin Son of Hannah a Slave belonging to Henry Mickleburrough born Decem" y" 16. 1728.
Will Son of Kate a Slave belonging to Edwin Thacker born July y° 6. 1728.
Tony Son of Eve a Slave belonging to Edwin Thacker born Decem" y" 3. 1728.
Robert Son of   a Slave belonging to Tho. Faulkner Sen" born Novem" y° 8 1728.
Neeton daughter of Hanah a Slave belonging to George Hardin born Decem" y" 27. 1728.
Judy   a Slave belonging to John Crockford born Jan'y y° 5. 1728.
Dianah daughter of Sarah a Slave belonging to William Stanard born Decem" y" 19. 1728.
Phil Son of   a Slave belonging to Roger Jones born Janua'y y° 9. 1728.
Judy daughter of Jenny a Slave belonging to Henry Tugel born Jan'y y° 21. 1728.
Thom Son of a Slave belonging to y° Estate Thomas Smith decd born Jan'y y" 26. 1728.
Judy daughter of Dillah a Slave belonging to Henry Daniell born Jan'y y" 31. 1728.
Benjamine Son of Hagar a Mulatto belonging to Rob' Johnson Sen" born Feb'y 2. 1728.
Molly daughter of a Slave belonging to John Crockford born Feb'y y" 14. 1728.
Mary daughter of Jenny a Slave belonging to Armistead Churchhill born Feb'y y" 21 1728.
Margery daughter of Jenny a Slave belonging to Francis Cheedle born Feb'y y° 23. 1728.
Davy Son of   a Slave belonging to Sarah Jones born March y° 1 1728.
Amy daughter of Winney a Slave belonging to Edwin Thacker born March y" 15. 1728.
Rose daughter of Maria a Slave belonging to Edmund Berkley born April y° 16. 1729.
Doll daughter of Sabina a Slave belonging to Edwin Thacker born April y° 2. 1729.

Robin Son of Cate a Slave belonging to William Chowning born April yᵉ 29. 1729.
Will Son of Cate a Slave belonging to John Burk born May yᵉ 23. 1729.
Hannah daughter of Venus a Slave belonging to Sarah Timberlake born May yᵉ 24. 1729.
Billy Son of Moll a Slave belonging to Elizabeth Smith born May yᵉ 28. 1729.
Odo daughter of Peru a Slave belonging to John Bryant born May yᵉ 11. 1729.
Tom Son of a Slave belonging to yᵉ estate of James Smith dec'd born June yᵉ 6. 1729.
Wonder Son of Rose a Slave belonging to George Hardin born May yᵉ 27 1729.
Kate daughter of Doll a Slave belonging to William Blackburne born 30th June 1729.
Judy daughter of Judy a Slave belonging to William Blackburn born June yᵉ 29 1729.
Frank daughter of Betty a Slave belonging to Gawin Corbin born June yᵉ 26 1729.
Jemmy Son of Frank a Slave belonging to Anne Thacker born July yᵉ 12 1729.
Ben Son of Sarah a Slave belonging to Alexander Graves born July yᵉ 15. 1729.
Sukey daughter of Dinah a Slave belonging to William Segar born July yᵉ 22 1729.
Edenburrough Son of Kate a Slave belonging to William Wood born Agust yᵉ 6. 1729.
Peter Son of Judy a Slave belonging to James Dudley born June yᵉ 14 1729.
Sampson Son of old Phillis a Slave belonging to Thos: Machen born July yᵉ 19. 1729.
Charles Son of young Phillis a Slave belonging Tho: Machen born August yᵉ 12. 1729.
Lucy daughter of Hannah a Slave belonging to Elizᵃ Smith born August yᵉ 12 1729.
Doll daughter of Sue a Slave belonging to Bar. Yates born September yᵉ 6. 1729.
Essex Son of Judy a Slave belonging to Thoˢ Mountague born September yᵉ 20. 1729.
Abigal daughter of Judy a Slave belonging to William Stanard born September yᵉ 12. 1729.
Mingo Son of Dye a Slave belonging to John Moseley born September yᵉ 20 1729.
Randolph Son of Dido a Slave belonging to yᵉ estate of Jnᵒ Smith decd. born Septemʳ yᵉ 14 1729.
Hamaton Son of Kate a Slave belonging to Robert George Senʳ born October yᵉ 15. 1729.
Della daughter of Peg a Slave belonging to Thomas Cheney born Novemʳ yᵉ 2. 1729.
George Son of Lucy a Slave belonging to Oliver Segar born Novemʳ yᵉ 7. 1729.

Gumbee Son of Phillis a Slave belonging to Jacob Stiff born Novem' y° 25. 1729.
Guy Son of Anakey a Slave belonging to Edwin Thacker born Novem' y° 30. 1729.
Gloster Son of Wilmuth a Slave belonging to Lawrance Orrill born Decem' 27. 1729.
Mertilda daughter of Winney a Slave belonging to Chicheley Thacker born Dec. 13. 1729.
Bristow Son of Jenny a Slave belonging to y° estate of Hobs Weeks born Decem' y° 19. 1729.
Tom Son of Letty a Slave belonging to y° estate of Hobs Weeks born Decem' y° 22. 1729.
Murreah daughter of Nell a Slave belonging to Humphrey Jones born Decem' y° 15. 1729.
Frank daughter of Kate a Slave belonging to Humphrey Jones born Decem' y° 30. 1729.
Hampton Son of Jenny a Slave belonging to Henry Tugel Sen: born Jan'y y° 25. 1729.
Billy Son of Jenny a Slave belonging to y° estate of Mathew Hunt born Jan'y. y° 29. 1729.
Alice daughter of Sary a Slave belonging to Edmund Michelborough born Jan'y 28, 1729.
Jenny daughter of Lucy a Slave belonging to Thomas Buford born Jan'y y° 26. 1729.
Lucy daughter of Nattor a Slave belonging to Marvill Moseley born Jan'y y° 9. 1729.
Numan Son of Frank a Slave belonging to Edmund Michelborough born Feb'y. y° 9. 1729.
Cateena daughter of Lucy a Slave belonging to y° estate of John Vivion born Feb'y 12. 1729.
Criss daughter of Lucy a Slave belonging to Edwin Thacker born Feb'y 12. 1729.
Dick Son of Moll a Slave belonging to Bar. Yates born Decem' 22. 1729.
Ned Son of Beck a Slave belonging to John Grymes born Novem' y° 25. 1729.
Ben Son of Cris a Slave belonging to John Grymes born Feb'y y° 5. 1729.
Joe Son of Alice a Slave belonging to Edwin Thacker born Feb'y y° 22. 1729.
Moll daughter of Hanah a Slave belonging to Lawrance Orrill born March y° 8. 1729.
Joice daughter of a Slave belonging to Hen: Armistead born March y° 9. 1729.
Daniel & Isaack Sons of Mary a Slave belonging to Armistead Churchhill born March 21. 1729.
Hannah daughter of Judy a Slave belonging to Tho' Mountague born March y° 25. 1730.
Hannah daughter of Kate a Slave belonging to Rich⁴ Tyler born March y° 28. 1730.
Frank daughter of Sarah a Slave belonging to Ralph Shelton born March 4. 1729.

Margery daughter of Alice a Slave belonging to Margret Daniel born Ap. 1 1730.
Frank daughter of ____ a Slave belonging to Armistead Churchhill born March 27. 1730.
Peter Son of Lucy a Slave belonging to Christopher Sutton born March y^e 31. 1730.
Cupid Son of Rose a Slave belonging to George Hardin born April y^e 15. 1730.
Kate daughter of Dido a Slave belonging to Mathew Kemp born April y^e 24. 1730.
Phillis daughter of Rose a Slave belonging to Edwin Thacker born May ye 2. 1730.
Isaac Son of Mary a Slave belonging to Armistead Churchhill born April ye 25. 1730.
Beck daughter of Daffine a Slave belonging to John Grymes born April y^e 28. 1730.
Frank Son of Judy a Slave belonging to John Smith jun^r born May y^e 17. 1730.
Kate daughter of Bett a Slave belonging to James Reid born April y^r 24. 1730.
Frank Son of Sue a Slave belonging to y^e estate of John Wormeley born May y^e 13. 1730.
Boson Son of ____ a Slave belonging to Paul Philpotts born March y^e 13. 1729.
Amey daughter of Frank a Slave belonging to Robert Daniel born May y^e 23. 1730.
Tom Son of Nanny a Slave belonging to y^e estate of Jno Smith decd born June y^e 20. 1730.
Jack Son of Jenny a Slave belonging to Frances Cheedle born June y^e 13. 1730.
Gabriel Son of a Slave belonging to Zacarias Gibbs born July y^e 2. 1730.
Frank daughter of Jenny a Slave belonging to Henry Tugel born June y^e 28. 1730.
Jemmy Son of Daphne a Slave belonging to Frances Smith born June y^e 25. 1730.
Patt Son of ____ a Slave belonging to Roger Jones born July y^e 16. 1730.
Harry Son of Venus a Slave belonging to Wm Southworth born June y^o 20. 1730.
Betty daughter of Dinah a Slave belonging to y^e estate of Tho. Smith decd. born Augst y^e 4. 1730.
Charles Son of Dinah a Slave belonging to y^e estate of Tho. Smith decd. born Augs^t 4. 1730.
Phillis daughter of Kate a Slave belonging to Wm Chowning born August y^r 19. 1730.
Robin Son of Munday a Slave belonging to Samuel Batchelder born Septem^r ye 2. 1730.
Jack Son of Murrea a Slave belonging to Edmund Berkeley born Augst ye 31. 1730.
Winney daughter of Moll a Slave belonging to Wm Mountague jun^r. born July ye 20. 1730.

Matt Son of Nancy a Slave belonging to ye estate of J^no Wormeley decd. born Sept. 4. 1730.
Hampshire Son of Beck a Slave belonging to John Lewis born September ye 21. 1730.
Bob Son of Beck a Slave belonging to John Crockford born September ye 20. 1730.
Letty daughter of Jude a Slave belonging to Mary Bristow born September ye 28. 1730.
Laurance Son of Jone a Slave belonging to ye estate of J^no Wormeley born Octo. ye 6. 1730.
Judy daughter of Hannah a Slave belonging to Sr Wm Skipwith born Octo. ye 20. 1730.
Peter Son of Sue a Slave belonging to Gawin Corbin born October ye 18. 1730.
Jenny Son of Bett a Slave belonging to John Moseley born Novem^r ye 7. 1730.
Sambo Son of Kate a Slave belonging to John Smith sen^r born Novem^r ye 18. 1730.
Tom Son of Jenny a Slave belonging to Coll^o Gawin Corbin born Novem^r ye 29. 1730.
Kate daughter of Winney belonging to Gawin Corbin born Novem^r ye 30. 1730.
Hannah daughter of Verena a Slave belonging to Jonathan Brooks born Decem^r ye 3. 1730.
Jack Son of Hannah a Slave belonging to Eliz^a Smith Senr born Decm^r ye 23. 1730.
Criss daughter of Nell a Slave belonging to ye estate of J^no Wormeley decd born Jan'ry 3. 1730.
Mingo Son of Beck a Slave belonging to John Grymes born Jan^ry ye 7. 1730.
Ben Son of Jenny a Slave belonging to Samuel Batchelder born Jan'ry ye 13. 1730.
Hannah daughter of Megg a Slave belonging to Humphrey Jones born Jan'ry ye 22. 1730.
Agie daughter of Judy a Slave belonging to William Stanard born Jan'ry ye 23. 1730.
Charles son of Nan a Slave belonging to Wm Blackbourne born July ye 31. 1730.
Moll daughter of Kate a Slave belonging to John Burk born Feb'y ye 10. 1730.
Simon Son of Judy a Slave belonging to John Hipkins born Decem^r ye 18. 1730.
Lucy daughter of Hannah a Slave belonging to Laurence Orrill born March ye 3. 1730.
Judy daughter of Moll a Slave belonging to ye estate of J^no Wormeley decd. born Feb'y ye 20. 1730.
Polly daughter of Alice a Slave belonging to ye estate of J^no Wormeley decd. born March 5. 1730.
Lettice daughter of Bridget a Slave belonging to ye estate of J^no Wormeley decd. born March 6 1730.
Billy Son of Dinah a Slave belonging to Christopher Robinson born March ye 11. 1730.

Letty daughter of Betty a Slave belonging to Christopher Robinson born March ye 16. 1730.
James Son of Peg a Slave belonging to William Owen born March ye 5. 1730.
Robin Son of Jenny a Slave belonging to William Hill born April ye 2. 1731.
Jemmy Son of Sarah a Slave belonging to Hezekiah Rhoads born April ye 8. 1731.
Chance daughter of Bess a Slave belonging to the estate of Wm Gordon born March ye 14. 1730.
Kate daughter of Judy a Slave belonging to Frances Alding born April ye 13. 1731.
Nat Son of Moll a Slave belonging to Andrew Davis born April ye 20. 1731.
Ben Son of Sarah a Slave belonging to Edmund Michelborough born April ye 15. 1731.
Letty daughter of Winny a Slave belonging to Edwin Thacker born April ye 9. 1731.
Ned Son of Jenny a Slave belonging to Henry Tugell Junr born May ye 5. 1731.
Phil Son of —— a Slave belonging to Christopher Sutton born April ye 27. 1731.
Jack Son of Hannah a Slave belonging to Henry Mickelborough born April ye 6. 1731.
Dinah daughter of Ruth a Slave belonging to Edwin Thacker born May ye 8. 1731.
Sarah daughter of Willmut a Slave belonging to Lawrence orrill born May 7. 1731.
Hannah daughter of —— a Slave belonging to John Murrah born May ye 17. 1731.
Betty daughter of Sue a Slave belonging to Bar. Yates born April ye 24. 1731.
Phillis daughter of Phillis a Slave belonging to Mary Machen born May ye 18. 1731.
Judy daughter of —— a Slave belonging to Wm Anderson born May ye 4. 1731.
Beck daughter of Kate a Slave belonging to Edwin Thacker born May ye 22d 1731.
Bat Son of Betty a Slave belonging to Henry Armistead born May ye 20. 1731.
Nanny daughter of Sharlott a Slave belonging to Henry Thacker born May 28. 1731.
Davy & Jenny Son & daughter of Jenny a Slave belonging to ye estate of John Wormeley decd. born June 13. 1731.
Judy daughter of a Slave belonging to Alexander Graves born June ye 10. 1731.
Rose daughter of Carter a Slave belonging to Wm Crutchfeild born June ye 20. 1731.
Jemmy Son of —— a Slave belonging to Sampson Darrill born June ye 28. 1731.
Ruth daughter of —— a Slave belonging to Roger Jones born July ye 15. 1731.

Cate daughter of Dillah a Slave belonging to Henry Daniel born June y⁰ 15. 1731.
Daphney daughter of Beck a Slave belonging to John Grymes born June y⁰ 29. 1731.
Rosa daughter of Marjory a Slave belonging to Hugh Stewart born July y⁰ 14. 1731.
Miny Son of —— a Slave belonging to James Dudley born July y⁰ 24. 1731.
Frank Son of Moll a Slave belonging to Eliz" Smith Senʳ born July y⁰ 19. 1731.
Winney daughter of Alice a Slave beloning to John Segar born July y⁰ 31. 1731.
Sary daughter of Flora a Slave belonging to yᵉ estate of Jnᵒ Wormeley decd. born August y⁰ 13. 1731.
Sue daughter of —— a Slave belonging to William Wood born August yᵉ 10. 1731.
Ben Son of Margary a Slave belonging to Oliver Segar born June yᵉ 25. 1731.
Mil daughter of Lucy a Slave belonging to Oliver Segar born July yᵉ 10. 1731.
Sue daughter of Betty a Slave belonging to yᵉ estate of Jnᵒ Smith ded. born August yᵉ 26. 1731.
Abram Son of Nanne a Slave belonging to yᵉ estate of Jnᵒ Smith decd. born Septemʳ yᵉ 1. 1731.
Frank Son of Phillis a Slave belonging to yᵉ estate of James Smith decd. born Septemʳ yᵉ 3. 1731.
Edy daughter of Alice a Slave belonging to Edwin Thacker born August yᵉ 18. 1731.
Alice daughter of Moll a Slave belonging to Armistead Churchhill born August yᵉ 23. 1731.
Margery & Lucy daughters of Judy belonging to yᵉ estate of Wᵐ Daniel junʳ born August yᵉ 24. 1731.
Peter Son of —— a Slave belonging to Rice Jones born August yᵉ 28. 1731.
Cromwell Son of Flora a Slave belonglng to John Grymes born August yᵉ 31. 1731.
Ben Son of Dinah a Slave belonging to Margrett Daniel born Septemʳ yᵉ 15. 1731.
George Son of Kate a Slave belonging to Robert George Senʳ born Septemʳ yᵉ 21. 1731.
Hannah daughter of Nan a Slave belonging to Wᵐ Hackney born Septemʳ yᵉ 24. 1731.
Numan Son of Sabina a Slave belonging to Edwin Thacker born october yᵉ 30. 1731.
Hannah daughter of Rose a Slave belonging to Wᵐ Bristow born october yᵉ 24. 1731.
Jack Son of Moll a Slave belonging to Henry Thacker born Novemʳ yᵉ 12. 1731.
Phil Son of Betty a Slave belonging to Sʳ Wᵐ Skipwith born August yᵉ 26. 1731.
James Son of Kate a Slave belonging to Jnᵒ Marshall born Decemʳ yᵉ 3. 1731.

Thamar daughter of Doll a Slave belonging to John Rhoads born Jan'y. ye 15. 1731.
Ned Son of Chris a Slave belonging to John Grymes born Jan'y ye 14. 1731.
Betty daughter of Eve a Slave belonging to Edwin Thacker born Jan'y ye 18. 1731.
Deinah Son of Lucy a Slave belonging to Thomas Buford born Jan'y ye 20. 1731.
Lucy daughter of Frank a Slave belonging to Edmund Mickelborough born Jan'y. ye 16. 1731.
Nancey daughter of Judith a Slave belonging to Thomas Mountague born Decem' ye 30. 1731.
Sango Son of Bellah a Slave belonging to ye estate of Thos Smith decd. born Jan'y. ye 24. 1731.
Sam Son of Phillis a Slave belonging to Jno Segar born Jan'y. ye 16. 1731.
Abram Son of Hannah a Slave belonging to Eliz^a Smith Senr born Feb'y. ye 20. 1731.
Frank daughter of Beck a Slave belonging to James Ried born Feb'y. ye 18. 1731.
Robin Son of Lucy a Slave belonging to Edwin Thacker born Feb'y. ye 16. 1731.
Billy Son of Dido a Slave belonging to Christopher Robinson born Feb'y. ye 22. 1731.
Phillis daughter of Jane a Slave belonging to Hugh Stewart born March ye 15. 1731.
Mingo Son of Kate a Slave belonging to John Smith Senr born April ye 9th 1732.
Billy Son of Alice a Slave belonging to Margrett Daniel born April ye 18. 1732.
Frank daughter of Kate a Slave belonging to Richard Tylor born April ye 28. 1732.
Phillis daughter of Moll a Slave belonging to Geo Wortham jun: born April ye 28. 1732.
Lucy daughter of Juno a Slave belonging to Mathew Kemp born May ye 21. 1732.
Bob Son of Winny a Slave belonging to Edwin Thacker born May ye 15. 1732.
Gilbert Son of Dinah a Slave belonging to ye estate of Thos Smith decd born May ye 15. 1732.
Tony Son of Peg a Slave belonging to Henry Armistead born May ye 20. 1732.
Sango Son of —— a Slave belonging to Anne Smith daughter of James Smith born June ye 2. 1732.
George Son of Sue a Slave belonging to ye estate of Jno Wormeley decd. born June ye 5. 1732.
Middlesex Son of Jenny a Slave belonging to Francis Cheadle born June ye 7. 1732.
Will Son of Cate a Slave belonging to John Moseley born June ye 18. 1732.
Cate daughter of Hannah a Slave belonging to Garrett Daniel born June ye 28. 1732.

Joe Son of Bess a Slave belonging to Paul Philpots born June ye 22 1732.

Phillis daughter of Letty a Slave belonging to John Davis born June ye 14. 1732.

Queen daughter of Bradford a Slave belonging to Gawin Corbin born July ye 25. 1732.

Cate daughter of Alice a Slave belonging to Gawin Corbin born July ye 28. 1732.

Hampton Son of Cate a Slave belonging to William Chowning born July ye 4. 1732.

Jenny daughter of Rose a Slave belonging to Edwin Thacker born July ye 30. 1732.

Abigal daughter of Clara a Slave belonging to Christopher Robinson born July ye 25. 1732.

Harry Son of Phillis a Slave belonging to ye estate of Jno Wormeley ded. born July ye 20. 1732.

Patt. daughter of Dye a Slave belonging to John Rhoads born July ye 24 1732.

Joe Son of Eve a Slave belonging to John Grymes born May ye 13. 1732.

Mar Son of Grace a Slave belonging to John Grymes born July ye 20. 1732.

Jenny daughter of Sara a Slave belonging to Ralph Shelton born Augus^t ye 10. 1732.

Pattey daughter of Annakey a Slave belonging to Edwin Thacker born Augs^t 14 1732.

Nan daughter of Peg. a Slave belonging to Thomas Cheney born Septem^r ye 10. 1732.

Betty daughter of —— a Slave belonging to Gawin Corbin born August 30. 1732.

Nell daughter of Hannah a Slave belonging to George Hardin born June ye 22 1732.

Ben Son of Kate a Slave belonging to John Burk born October y^o 1 1732.

Sarah daughter of Nanny a Slave belonging to ye estate of Jno Wormley dec'd born Sept. 21 1732.

Caesar Son of Kate a Slave belonging to John Marshall born Septem^r ye 27. 1732.

Sawney Son of Beck a Slave belonging to William Goar born October ye 30. 1732.

Edy daughter of Cate a Slave belonging to Humphry Jones born Septem^r ye 12. 1732.

Ralph Son of Lucy a Slave belonging to Humphry Jones born Septem^r ye 27. 1732.

Winney daughter of Alice a Slave belonging to Robert George born Octo. ye 27. 1732.

Sampson Son of Moll a Slave belonging Wm Mountague born Novem^r ye 23. 1732.

Daniel Son of Betty a Slave belonging to Wm Blackburn born Novem^r ye 16. 1731.

Nan daughter of Nan a Slave belonging to Wm Blackburn born July ye 15. 1732.

Hannah daughter of Doll a Slave belonging to Wm Blackburn born Septemr 14. 1732.
Peter Son of Hannah a Slave belonging to John Marshall born November 12 1732.
Daphne daughter of Judy a Slave belonging to Thos Mountague born Decemr 28. 1732.
Scipio Son of Judy a Slave belonging to ye estate of Wm Stanard decd. born Jan{r}y ye 31. 1732.
Dick Son of Alice a Slave belonging to Edwin Thacker born Jan{r}y ye 31. 1732.
Sue daughter of Lucy a Slave belonging to Christopher Sutton born Jan{r}y y{o} 12. 1732.
Juno daughter of Nan a Slave belonging to William Hackney born Jan{r}y ye 26. 1732.
Billy Son of Moll a Slave belonging to William Wood born Feb{r}y ye 3d. 1732.
Yangar Son of Dido a Slave belonging to William Owen born Octo. ye 14 1732.
Jenney daughter of Jenney a Slave belonging to Mary Hunt born Decemr 20. 1732.
Hannah daughter of Beck a Slave belonging to Jno Grymes born Feb{r}y ye 10. 1732.
Jenny daughter of Dinah a Slave belonging to Wm Saunders born Feb{r}y ye 7. 1732.
Winney daughter of Frank a Slave belonging to Robt Daniel born Feb{r}y ye 1. 1732.
Mingo Son of Bess a Slave belonging to ye estate of Wm Gordon dec'd born March ye 4 1732.
Caesar & Dick Sons of Jenny a Slave belonging to Armistead Churchhill born March ye 17. 1732.
Maud daughter of Judy a Slave belonging to Jno Smith junr born Octo. y{u} 2. 1732.
Rose daughter of Dy a Slave belonging to John Moseley born March ye 1. 1732.
Venus daughter of Phillis a Slave belonging to James Daniel born March ye 19. 1732.
Peter Son of Eve a Slave belonging to Edwin Thacker born March ye 31. 1733.
Flora daughter of   a Slave belonging to John Grymes born Ap. ye 1. 1733.
Beck daughter of Betty a Slave belonging to Christopher Robinson born March 22. 1733.
Sam Son of Dinah a Slave belonging to Christopher Robinson born April 20. 1733.
Frank daughter of Wonnah a Slave belonging to Henry Armistead born April 25. 1733.
Peter Son of Sarah a slave belonging to Hezekiah Rhoads born April ye 30. 1733.
Pheebe daughter of Beck a Slave belonging to John Lewis born April ye 29. 1733.
Cate daughter of Margrett a Slave belonging to ye estate of Jno Wormeley dec'd born April 22 1733.

Blade Son of Rose a Slave belonging to George Hardin born May y° 12. 1733.
Isaac Son of Dido a Slave belonging to Augustine Smith born June y° 3. 1733.
Dum Son of Frank a Slave belonging to Roger Jones born May y° 30 1733.
Dick Son of ——— a Slave belonging to Thomas Corbin born May y° 1. 1733.
Alice daughter of Judy a Slave belonging to y° estate of Wm Daniel dec'd born May y° 15 1733.
Nanny daughter of Kate a Slave belonging to William Wood born June y° 11. 1733.
Robin Son of Sue a Slave belonging to Bar. Yates born June y° 9. 1733.
Neator daughter of Alice a Slave belonging to Christopher Robinson born May y° 29 1733.
Cela daughter of Molly a Slave belonging to Christopher Robinson born May y° 20. 1733.
Hannah daughter of Kate a Slave belonging to Edwin Thacker born June y° 30. 1733.
Jack Son of Sarah a Slave belonging to Edwin Thacker born July y° 18. 1733.
Crumwell Son of Moll a Slave belonging to Elizabeth Smith born July y° 10. 1733.
Cate daughter of Judy a Slave belonging to Mathew Kemp born May y° 20. 1733.
Nanny daughter of Bess a Slave belonging to Mathew Kemp born June y° 27. 1733.
Jenny daughter of Venus a Slave belonging to Aquilla Snelling born July y° 29. 1733.
Phillis daughter of Jenny a Slave belonging to Henry Tugle jun^r born August y° 5. 1733.
Abraham & Jacob Sons of Jenny a Slave belonging to y° estate of Jn° Wormeley decd. born July y° 18. 1733.
Esther daughter of Winny a Slave belonging to John Grymes born August y° 1st 1733.
Sue daughter of Hannah a Slave belonging to Elizabeth Smith born July y° 30. 1733.
Letty daughter of Bess a Slave belonging to John Segar born August y° 9. 1733.
Roger Son of ——— a Slave belonging to John Grymes born August y° 20. 1733.
Isaac Son of Margery a Slave belonging to Oliver Segar born July y° 13. 1733.
Marlebrough Son of Moll a Slave belonging to Wm Montague born Augst 15. 1733.
Jeffery Son of Bradford a Slave belonging to Gawin Corbin born Augst y° 22. 1733.
York Son of Willmott a Slave belonging to Laurance Orrill born August y° 31. 1733.
Sangro Son of Jude a Slave belonging to John Hipkins born Septem^r y° 15. 1733.

Gabriel Son of Phillis a Slave belonging to Mary Machen born Septem͏ʳ yᵉ 24. 1733.
Lucy daughter of Nan a Slave belonging to William Hill born August yᵉ 26. 1733.
Hagar daughter of Phillis a Slave belonging to Jacob Stiff born Septem͏ʳ yᵉ 22. 1733.
Jemmy Son of Margery a Slave belonging to Frances Alding born August yᵉ 31. 1733.
Johny Son of Hannah a Slave belonging to Laurance Orrill born October yᵉ 2. 1733.
Priscilla daughter of Moll a Slave belonging to Christopher Robinson born May yᵉ 31. baptized Aug͏ˢᵗ 19. 1733.
Toby Son of Kate a Slave belonging to Augustine Smith born October yᵉ 10. 1733.
Ned Son of Sharlote a Slave belonging to Henry Thacker born October yᵉ 25. 1733.
Sue daughter of Jenny a Slave belonging to John Murrah born October yᵉ 30. 1733.
Toby Son of Dillah a Slave belonging to Henry Daniel born October yᵉ 5. 1733.
Laurance Son of Flora a Slave belonging to yᵉ estate of Jn͏° Wormeley ded. born Octoʳ yᵉ 12. 1733.
Margery daughter of Nell a Slave belonging to yᵉ estate of Jn° Wormeley decd. born Novem͏ʳ 15. 1733.
Jack Son of Jone a Slave belonging to Catherine Warwick born Novem͏ʳ yᵉ 30. 1733.
Sancho Son of Grace a Slave belonging to John Grymes born Novem͏ʳ yᵉ 9. 1733.
Jemmy Son of Billah a Slave belonging to yᵉ estate of Tho͏ˢ Smith born Decem͏ʳ yᵉ 23. 1733.
Dye daughter of Lucy a Slave belonging to Edwin Thacker born Novem͏ʳ yᵉ 25. 1733.
Sarah daughter of Sarah a Slave belonging to Edm͏ᵈ Mickleburrough born Decem͏ʳ yᵉ 3. 1733.
Harry Son of Cress a Slave belonging to Jn° Grymes born Decem͏ʳ yᵉ 29. 1733.
Jenny daughter of Lett a Slave belonging to Anne Smith born Jan͏ʳy yᵉ 14. 1733.
Nelly daughter of Molly a Slave belonging to Anne Wood born Feb͏ʳy yᵉ 3. 1733.
Phillis daughter of —— a Slave belonging to Mary Bristow born Feb͏ʳy yᵉ 9. 1733.
Susan daughter of —— a Slave belonging to Thomas Corbin born Jan͏ʳy yᵉ 29. 1733.
Mack Son of —— a Slave belonging to Thomas Corbin born Feb͏ʳy yᵉ 13. 1733.
Sarah daughter of —— a Slave belonging to Edmund Berkeley born March yᵉ 1. 1733.
Adam Son of Dinah a Slave belonging to yᵉ estate of Tho͏ˢ Smith decd. born March yᵉ 18. 1733.
Joe Son of Lucy a Slave belonging to Thomas Buford born March yᵉ 19. 1733.

Ben Son of Pegg a Slave belonging to William Owen born March y̎ 12. 1733.
Humphrey Son of Frank a Slave belonging to Christopher Robinson born Feb'y y̎ 4. 1733.
Andrew Son of Jenny a Slave belonging to Christopher Robinson born March y̎ 12. 1733.
Bristow Son of Judy a Slave belonging to John Vivion born April y̎ 1. 1734.
Gawen Son of Sabrina a Slave belonging to Edwin Thacker born March y̎ 26. 1734.
Rose daughter of Rose a Slave belonging to Gawin Corbin born March y̎ 9. 1733.
Moll daughter of Kate a Slave belonging to Gawin Corbin born March y̎ 22. 1733.
Alice daughter of Sarah a Slave belonging to Charles Grymes born April y⁰ 10. 1734.
Nan daughter of Munday, a Slave belonging to Samuel Batchelder born April y̎ 27. 1734.
Jack Son of Jenny, a Slave belonging to Armistead Churchhill born April y̎ 18. 1734.
Robin Son of Beck, a Slave belonging to James Reid born May y̎ 3. 1734.
Windsor Son of Nanny, a Slave belonging to y̎ estate of Jn° Wormeley decd. born April y̎ 28. 1734.
Sary daughter of Nan, a Slave belonging to y̎ estate of Jn° Smith Sen' decd. born May y̎ 11. 1734.
Will Son of Rose, a Slave belonging to William Bristow born May y̎ 23. 1734.
Bristol Son of Sarah, a Slave belonging to Alexander Graves born June y̎ 1. 1734.
Gawin Son of Phillis, a Slave belonging to James Daniel Jun' born May y̎ 22, 1734.
James Son of Nell, a Slave belonging to Humphrey Jones born April y̎ 15. 1734.
Mill daughter of Lucy, a Slave belonging to Humphrey Jones born March y̎ 2. 1733.
Antoney Son of Lucy, a Slave belonging to y̎ estate of oliver Segar born April y̎ 29. 1734.
Phil & Emanuel Sons of Hannah, a Slave belonging to Chris'⁰ Robinson born June 16. 1734.
Dick Son of Betty, a Slave belonging to Xtopher Robinson born June y̎ 27. 1734.
Judee daughter of Betty, a Slave belonging to y̎ estate of Jn° Smith ded. born June y̎ 7. 1734.
Moll daughter of Nany, a Slave belonging to James Crosbie born July 3. 1734.
Frank daughter of Judy, a Slave belonging to Eliza Annard born Oct. 20. 1734.
Phill Son of Mary, a Slave belonging to Co" Churchill born October 8th 1734.
Rose Daughter of Moll, a Slave belonging to George Worther born December 4th 1734.

Simon Son of Doll, a Slave belonging to Jn° Rhodes born June 29. 1734.
Peter Son of Dinah, a Slave belonging to Coll. Armistead born May 7. 1734.
Ben Son of Sue, a Slave belonging to Coll. Armistead born Augus 17. 1734.
Roger Son of Else, a Slave belonging to Jn° Blake born July 22d 1734.
Ben a Slave belonging to Coll. Churchill born October 24th 1734.
Dinah Daughter of Wonah, a Slave belonging to Coll. Armistead born Dec'r 2d 1734.
Dinah Daughter of Letty, a Slave belonging to W'm Daniel born June 24th 1734.
Sam Son of Kate, a Slave belonging to Churchhill Blacky born July 23rd 1734.
Europe Son of Jenny, a Slave belonging to Frances Cheedle born July 18th 1734.
Bristow Son of Kate, a Slave belonging to Jn° Moseley born October 12th 1734.
Sue Daughter of Hannah, a Slave belonging to Jn° Moseley born October 21st 1734.
Mintis Son of Alice, a Slave belonging to Jane Seager born Dec'r 7th 1734.
Jack Son of Hannah, a Slave belonging to Garrett Daniel born Nov'r 30th 1734.
Nanny Daughter of Sarah, a Slave belonging to Crispin Shelton born Nov'r 19th 1734.
Dick Son of Jone, a Slave belonging to Catherine Warwick born Dec'r 20th 1734.
Tom Son of ——, a Slave belonging to Thomas Corbin born Dec'r 19th 1734.
Ben Son of ——, a Slave belonging to Tho' Corbin born Dec'r 20th 1734.
Jack Son of Flora, a Slave belonging to Jn° Grymes born Dec. 16th 1734.
Sam Son of Judee, a Slave belonging to Jn° Smith Jun'r born Dec. 19th 1734.
Judee Daughter of Kate, a Slave belonging to Jn° Burk born Jan'y 2d 1734.
Johnny Son of ——, a Slave belonging to Matth: Kemp born March 17th 1733.
Jemmy Son of ——, a Slave belonging to Matth. Kemp born July 25th 1733.
Sam Son of —— a Slave belonging to Matth: Kemp born Jan'y 8th 1734.
Dinah Daughter of Nan, a Slave belonging to Will'm Hacknay born Dec'r 30th 1734.
Jenny Daughter of Virena, a Slave belonging to Jonathan Brooks born Feb'y 24th 1734.
Doll Daughter of ——, a Slave belonging to Thomas Corbin born Feb. 14th 1734.
Siller Daughter of Frank, a Slave belonging to Roger Jones born March 24th 1734.

Dinah Daughter of Hannah, a Slave belonging to Eliz. Smith born March 30th 1735.
Harry Son of Jenny, a Slave belonging to Wm Hill born Ap. 3rd 1735.
Mille Daughter of Sue, a Slave belonging to Tho* Price born March 3rd 1734.

Jn° Reade Min^r.

Judee, daughter of Winny, a Slave belonging to Edwin Thacker born Ap. 20th 1735.
Letty, Daughter of Rose, a Slave belonging to Edwin Thacker, born Ap. 6th 1735.
Wingo, Son of Dinah, a Slave belonging to Henry Daniel, born Ap: 24th 1735.
Dick, Son of Alice, a Slave belonging to Edwin Thacker, born May 31st 1735.
Jenny, Daughter of Rose, a Slave belonging to Geo. Hardin, born June 12th 1735.
Caesar, Son of Judy, a Slave belonging to Armistead Churchhill, born Ap: 10th 1735.
Phill, Son of Hannah, a Slave belonging to Armistead Churchhill, born Ap. 19th 1735.
Oliver, Son of Daffany, a Slave belonging to Jn° Grymes, born May 30th 1735.
Hannah, Daughter of Eve, a Slave belonging to Edwin Thacker, born Ap: 22nd 1735.
Phillis, Daughter of Bradford, a Slave belonging to Gawin Corbin, born May 13th 1735.
Jenny, Son of Cress, a Slave belonging to Jn° Grymes, born June 8th 1735.
Phill, Son of Phillis, a Slave belonging to Mary Machen, born June 12th 1735.
Jack, Son of Kate, a Slave belonging to Alexander Frazier, born June 22d 1735.
Hannah, Daughter of Sarah, a Slave belonging to Alexander Graves, born July 11th 1735.
Mille, Daughter of —— a Slave belonging to Gawin Corbin born June 29th 1735.
Lucy, Daughter of Jean, a Slave belonging to Mary Tugell born July 27th 1735.
Jemmy, Son of Kate, a Slave belonging to Alexander Frazeir, born June 23. 1735.
Sue, Daughter of Bess, a Slave belonging to Mathew Gale, born Augst 2. 1735.
Aaron, —— —— a Slave belonging to Gawin Corbin, born Augst 2. 1735.
Kate, Daughter of Jenny, a Slave belonging to Henry Tugle, born Sep^t 17th 1735.
Lucy, —— —— a Slave belonging to Gawin Corbin, born Sept. 10. 1735.
Buchan, Son of Molly, a Slave belonging to Alexander Frazier, born Sep. 29. 1735.
Anthony, Son of Sharlot, a Slave belonging to Henry Thacker, born Sep^t 28th 1735.

Matt, —— —— a Slave belonging to Armistead Churchhill, born Sep^t 10 1735.

Given into ye Secretary's office Decr 6th 1735 Charged. { Annacle Daughter of Judee, a Slave belonging to Jno Vivion, born Novr 4th 1735.
Rose, Daughter of Sue, a Slave belonging to Coll. Armistead born Octr 29th 1735.

Letty, Daughter of Margery, a Slave belonging to Jean Seager born Novr 2d 1735.

Phebe daughter of Sarah Oct^t 10th 1735. Sandy Son of Kate Decr 13th 1735. Slaves belonging to Gawin Corbin.

Will, Son of Sarah, a Slave belonging to Jno Goodwin, Novr 27th 1735.

Nell, Daughter of Moll, a Slave belonging to Armistead Churchhill, born Decr 3d 1735.

Bristow Son of Dillah, a Slave belonging to Henry Daniel born Dec: 17 1735.

Sary, Daughter of Hannah, a Slave belonging to Hen. Mickelburrough, born Jan. 2. 1735.

Nan, Daughter of Frank, a Slave belonging to Henry Armistead born Decr 3d 1735.

Hannah, Daughter of Judy, a Slave belonging to James Daniel born Jan'y 27. 1735.

Pompey, Son of Venus, a Slave belonging to Elizth Thurston, born Jan'y 28th 1735.

Dick, Son of Sarah, a Slave belonging to Edm^d Mickelburrough, born Jan'y 20th 1735.

Adam, Son of Judy, a Slave belonging to Ch. Robinson, born Feb: 4th 1735.

Frank, Daughter of Jenny, a Slave belonging to Jno Wortham, born Feb. 3d 1735.

Nanny, Daughter of Beck, a Slave belonging to James Reid born Feb: 12th 1735.

Duncan, Son of Sary, a Slave belonging to Elizth Stannard, born Feb: 13. 1735.

Frank, Daughter of Lucy, a Slave belonging to Thos Buford, born Feb: 19 1735.

Lucy, Daughter of Judy, a Slave belonging to Thos Mountague born Jany 28 1735.

Phill. Son of —— a Slave belonging to Humphrey Jones, born Decr 29 1735.

Nan, Daughter of —— a Slave belonging to Humphrey Jones, born Feb: 23 1735.

Three Negro Women named belonging to Christopher Robinson bap: Mar: 7 1735.

Tom, Son of Nanny, a Slave belonging to Ann Clarke, born Mar. 3d 1735.

Davy, —— —— a Slave belonging to Thomas Corbin, born Feb: 23 1735.

Frank, Daughter of —— a Slave belonging to Mathew Kemp born Feb: 28. 1735.

Will Son of —— a Slave belonging to Thos Laughlin born Mar: 12th 1735.

Peter Son of Judy, a Slave belonging to Mathew Kemp born Sep^t 4th 1735.
Ursly Daughter of Lucy, a Slave belonging to Jane Seager Feb: 21st 1735.

Given into ye S. O. Ap. 1736. } Dick Son of Jenny, a Slave belonging to Armistead Churchhill born March 31st 1736.

Jno Reade, Min^r

Rose Daughter of Frank a slave belonging to Christ^r Robinson born Ap 24. 1736.
Nicholas Son of Alice a slave belonging to Chris^r Robinson born May 2d 1736.
Sam Son of Judith a slave belonging to Thos Montague born Ap^l 24 1736.
Ave daughter of Sarah a slave belonging to Edwin Thacker born Novr 10th 1735.
Simon Son of Phillis a slave belonging to Jacob Stiff born May 9th 1736.
Dye Daughter of Judy a slave belonging to ye Estate of J^{no} Hipkins dec'd born April 8th 1736.
Doctor Son of Bess a slave belonging to Alex Frazier born June 17th 1736.
Harry Son of Letty a Slave belonging to ye Estate of Wm Stannard deceas'd born July 6. 1736.
Sam Son of Bess a slave belonging to Math^w Kemp. born May 19th 1736.
Annaca Daughter of Grace a Slave belonging to Armistead Churchill born June 17th 1736.
——— ——— ——— a slave belonging to Wm Gore born 17th June 1736.
Affrica Son of Winny a slave belonging to Edwin Thacker born July 19th 1736.
Chales Son of Jenny a slave belonging to Mary Murry, Seign^r born July 28th 1736.

The 3 following Registers omitted in 1735.

Mingo Son of Unity a slave belonging to Edward Dillard, born Septr 26th 1735.
Cupid Son of Beck a Slave belonging to Jno Lewis, born Octr 17th 1735.
Frank Daughter of Phillis a Slave belonging to Jno Seager, born Octr 20th 1735.
Gowin Son of Lucy a Slave belonging to Edwin Thacker born Octr 4th 1736.
Lemuel Son of Judith a Slave belonging to Eliz. Stannard born Augst 31st 1736.
Hannah Daughter of Judy a Slave belonging to Jedediah Bristow, born March 18th 1735.
Harry Son of Hannah a slave belonging to ye Estate of Jno Smith Dec^d born Augst 25th 1736.

Given unto ye Secret off Octr 1736. { Tom Son of Lett a slave belonging to Ann Smith, born Octr 14th 1736.
Jane Daughter of Moll a slave belonging to Alex. Frazier, born Sep^t 30th 1736.
Eve Daughter of Winney a Slave belonging to Jno Grymes, born July 18th 1736.

Tom Son of Nan a Slave belonging to James Scrossby, born Octr 18th 1736.
Alce daughter of Pegg a slave belonging to William Owen was born 10^{ber} 15th 1736.
Doll daughter of Hannah a slave belonging to Matthias Gale was born Jan 25th 1736.
Jemmy Son of Hannah a slave belonging to Garret Daniel was born Jan 27th 1736.
Tamar daughter of Judy a slave belonging to Mr. John Smith (Aldin) born Jan. 25th 1736.
Pegg daughter of Cress a slave belonging to John Grymes Esq: born Jan. 30th 1736.
Isaac Son of Dinah a slave belonging to John Grymes Esq. born Feb 17th 1736.
Annica daughter of Cate a slave belonging to ye estate of John Burk deceased born Feb. 5th 1736.
Philip —— a slav^e belonging to ye estate of Collo Tho. Corbin deceased, born Feb. 15th 1736.
Sampson Son of Joan a Slav^e belonging to Philip Warwick born March 2d 1736.
Dick Son of Kate, a slav^e belonging to Thomas Salt, born March 15th 1736.
Ben Son of Kate, a slav^e belonging to Churchhill Blakey born March 16th 1736.
Letitia daughter of Alse a Slav^e belonging to Mrs. Jan^e Segar born April 4th 1737.
Catena daughter of Rose a Slave, belonging to Coll Edwin Thacker born May 4th 1737.
Caesar Son of Kate a Slave, belonging to Mr. Alexander Frazier born May 21th 1737.
Betty daughter of Molly a Slav^e belonging to Mrs Page born Jan. 21st 1736.
Jack Son of Betty a Slave belonging to William Lawson born March 6th 1736.
Beck daughter of Judy a Slave, belonging to Mr. Alexander Frazier born March 6th 1736.
Frank —— a Slav^e belonging to William Lawson born January 10th 1736.
Jenny daughter of Moll a Slave, belonging to George Wortham born March 17th 1736.
Moll daughter of Jenny a Slav^e belonging to Hannah Watts born July 10th 1735.
Hannah a negro-child belonging to Roger Jones born Jan. 16th 1737.
Peter a negro boy of Doll belong^{ng} to John Rhodes was born 10^{ber} 10th 1736.
Avith a negro girl of Nan belonging to William Hackney was Jan. 10th 1736.
—— a negro boy of Jenny belonging to Major Matt Kemp. born July 14th 1736.
Mingo a negro-boy of Coll Churchhill was born Feb. 25th 1736.
Sarah a negro girl of Major Berkeley was born June 7th 1737.
Sam a negro boy of Major Berkeley was born July 1737.

Molly a negro girl of Major Berkeley was born July 20th 1737.
Rose a negro girl of Major Berkeley was born July 24th 1737.
Charles a negro boy of Coll John Grymes was born July 12th 1737.
Frank a negro boy of Coll Churchhill was born April 1st 1737.
Billy a negro boy of Coll Churchhill was born April 18th 1737.
Luce daughter of Sharlot a Slav* belonging to Mr Henry Thacker was born Aug 17th 1737.
Roger a slave belonging to ye Estate of Mr Thomas Corbin deceas'd born June 2d 1737.

Given to the Secr^et Offic^e 8ber. 1737.
{ Primus ye son of Kate a slav^e belonging to Coll Gawen Corbin born May 30th 1737.
Winny a slav^e belonging to Mr Humphrey Jones born July 9th 1737.
Billy a slav^e belonging to Coll. Gawen Corbin born July 14th 1737. }

A Negro child of Frank's belonging to Coll. Henry Armistead born Ausst ye 15th 1737.
Peter son of Jeney a Slave belonging to Henry Tugel born Octo^r ye 5th 1737.
Jemme Son of Dinner a slave belonging to Coll Henry Armstead born Sepr ye 18th 1737.
Margree a Negro child belonging to Edward Dillard born Octo^r ye 28th 1737.
Ealce Daughter of Letty a Slave belonging to Mrs Stanard born Novr ye 23 1737.
Robin Son of Jane a slave belonging to Mrs Hannah Watts born Sepr ye 17th 1737.
Ben Son of Janne a Slave belonging to Mary Hunt born July ye 3d 1737.
Tony child of Dido a Slave belonging to Maj^r Kemp born April 17th 1737.
Betty Daughter of Alice a Slave belonging to Christopher Robinson born Decem^r y^e 26. 1737.
Tamar daughter of Nan a Slave belonging to William Hill Senr born Decem^r y^e 27th 1737
Sprig Son of Juno a Slave belonging to George Hardin born Jan^r y^e 8th 173$\frac{7}{8}$.
Lucy daughter of Beck a slave belonging to James Reid born Jany y^e 14th 173$\frac{7}{8}$.
Billey Son of Phillis a Slave belonging to John Segar born Jany y^e 27th 173$\frac{7}{8}$.
Davey Son of Cate a Slave belonging to John Segar born Feby y^e 2d 173$\frac{7}{8}$.
Orson Son of Beck a Slave belonging to John Lewis born Feb^{ry} y^e 14th 173$\frac{7}{8}$.
Jack Son of Letey a Slave belonging to Henry Tugel born March y^e 21st 173$\frac{7}{8}$.
Mary Daughter of Penelope a Slave belong to John Walker born Novr 21st 1737.
Penalope Daughter of Jane a Slave belonging to John Walker born Novr 22d 1737.
―― Son of Kate a Slave belonging to Edward Thacker born Septem^r y^e 10th 1737.

Ben belonging to William Bristow born Feb^ry 1737.
Simon Son of Venis a Slave belonging to Aquila Snelling born March y^u 25th 1738.
Cloye Daughter of Cloye a Slave belonging to Co^ll Grymes born May ye 3d 1738.
Hannah Daughter of Hannah a Slave belonging to Co^ll Grymes born May ye 1st 1738.
Bowker Son of Kate a Slave belonging to Charles Daniel born May 24th 1738.
Nan daughter of Beck a Slave belonging James Mayo born March 25th 1738.
Charles Son of Judy a Slave belonging to George Hardin born April ye 1st 1738.
Harry Son of Bess a Slave belonging to James Crosby born May ye 15th 1738.
Frank daughter of Jude a Slave belonging to Jidediah Bristow born April ye 12th 1738.
Ann Daughter of Silvia a Slave belonging to Co^ll Grymes born May ye 7th 1738.
Jeny Daughter of Bess a Slave belonging to Alex^dr Frazier born May ye 13th 1738.
Jack Son of Judith a Slave belonging to Thos Mountague born June ye 11th 1738.
Nero Son of Jenny a Slave belonging to John Wortham born June ye 30th 1738.
Bess Daughter of Bess a slave belonging to Matthew Kemp born June ye 3rd 1738.
Oliver . . . . . belonging to John Smith born June ye 20th 1738.
Jene . . . . a Slave belonging to John Blake Senr born June ye 28th 1738.
Moll Daughter of Bess a Slave belonging to John Segar born June ye 29th 1738.
Peter Son of Hannah a Slave belonging to Co^ll Henry Armistead born June ye 19th 1738.
Simon Son of Hannah a Slave belonging to Geo. Hardin born June ye 20th 1738.
Lucy daughter of Beck a Slave born June ye 6th
Mary daughter of Beck a Slave born June ye 26th
} belonging to Chris^r Robinson 1738.
Jane daughter of Alice a Slave belonging to Co^ll Gawin Corbin born June ye 1st 1738.
Hampton Son of Phillis a Slave belonging to John Thompson born June ye 10th 1738.
Gloster Son of Judy a Slave belonging to Robt Daniel born July ye 8th 1738.
Will Son of Cres a Slave belonging to Co^ll John Grymes born July ye 10th 1738.
George Caine Son of Judy a Slave belonging to James Dunlevy born July ye 30th 1738.
James Son of Mortilly a Slave belonging to Co^ll Grymes born Aug^st 31st 1738.

Abygall daughter of Nell a Slave belonging to Humphrey Jones born Augst 29th 1738.
Sam Son of Hanna a Slave belonging to Henry Tugel born Augst ye 13th 1738.
Frank daughter of Rose a Slave belonging to Co^{ll} Thacker born Augst ye 19th 1738.
Mille daughter of Hannah a Slave belonging to John Smith Junr born Sepr ye 3rd 1738.
Ambrose & Sarah born of Murreah a Slave belonging to Edmund Berkeley Sepr 16th 1738.
Mille daughter of Nan a Slave belonging to Mary Jackson born Octo^r 22nd 1738.
Harrow daughter of Dorender a Slave belonging to Richard Corbin born Oct 7 1738.
Jemima daughter of Verena a Slave belonging to Curtis Hardee born Novr ye 1. 1738.
Sarah daughter of Kate a Slave belonging to Eliz: Burk born Novr 18 1738.
Susannah Daughter of Alice a Slave born Augst 30th belonging to Co^{ll} Thacker 1737.
Harry Son of Kate a Slave born Septr 10th belonging to Coll Edwin Thacker 1737.
Hezekiah Son of Annaka a Slave belonging to Co^{ll} Edwin Thacker born Octr 6th 1737.
Kate Daughter of Kate a Slave belonging to Co^{ll} Edwin Thacker born Novr 7th 1738.
Newman Son of Sue a Slave belonging to Thos Price born Octr 27th 1737.
Lucy Daughter of Phillis a Slave belonging to Thos Price born April 4th 1738.
Winney Daughter of Daphne a Slave belonging to Thos Price born Novr 3rd 1738.
Simon Son of Venus a Slave belonging to Aquilla Snelling born April 9th 1738.
Sarah Daughter of Judy a Slave belonging to Hope Sutton born Augst ye 27th 1738.
Joe Son of Filles a Slave belonging to William Owen born Decm^r 25th 1738.
Rose Daughter of Judy a Slave belonging to Matthew Kemp born Novr 16th 1738.
Tom Son of Bradford a Slave belonging to Co^l Gawin Corbin born Novr 26th 1738.
Benjamin Son of Grace a Slave belonging to Co^{ll} John Grymes born Decem^r 2d 1738.
Jenny Daughter of Nan a Slave belonging to James Scrosby born Decr 14th 1738.
Motley Son of Kate a Slave belonging to Edmund Berkeley born Decr 31st 1738.
Phil —— a Slave belonging to Thomas Laughlin born Jan^{ry} 8th 173$\frac{8}{9}$.
Pryscillia a Slave born June 1st.
Jeremy a Slave born June 16th.
Bridget a Slave born
} these belonging to Ralph Wormley—1738.

Simon Son of Jenny a Slave belonging to Matthew Kemp born Jan⁷⁷ 19th 173⁸/₉.

Sary Daughter of Jenny a Slave born Jan⁷⁷ 20th. ⎫ belonging to
Phebe Daughter of Tamar a Slave born Feb⁷⁷ 14. ⎬ Richard Corbin
　　　　　　　　　　　　　　　　　　　　　　　　⎭ 173⁸/₉.

Rachel Daughter of Moll a Slave belonging to Co¹¹ Armistead Churchhill born Feb. 15th 173⁸/₉.
Lewis Son of Sabina a Slave belonging to Co¹¹ Edwin Thacker born Feb⁷⁷ 20th 173⁸/₉.
Hagar a Slave belonging to Roger Jones born Feb⁷⁷ y⁸ 18th 173⁸/₉.
Lucy a Slave belonging to Co¹¹ Armistead Churchhill born Feb⁷⁷ y⁸ 14th 173⁸/₉.
Frank a Slave belonging to Alexander Frazier born Feb⁷⁷ y⁸ 3d 173⁸/₉.
Charles Son of Judy a Slave belonging to Chris⁷ Robinson born Feb⁷⁷ 24th 173⁸/₉
Dick a Slave belonging to Alex⁷ Graves born Feb⁷⁷ y⁸ 28th 173⁸/₉.
William Son of Winney a Slave belonging to Co¹¹ Edwin Thacker born March 1th 173⁸/₉.
Parker a Slave belonging to John Smith born March y⁸ 5th 173⁸/₉.
Harry Son of Judy a Slave belonging to Tho⁸ Mountague born Feb⁷⁷ 2d 173⁸/₉.
Letty Daughter of Corinder a Slave belonging to Wm Mountague born March 5th 173⁸/₉.
George Son of Doll a Slave belonging to John Rhodes born April 6th 1739.
Billey a Slave belonging to Richard Corbin born April y⁸ 14th 1739.
Harry Son of Hannah a Slave belonging to Mathias Gaille born April 19th 1739.
Lucy Daughter of Nan a Slave belonging to Wm Hackney born April 9th 1739.
Robin Son of Kate a Slave belonging to Alexander Frazier born April 27th 1739.
Betty Daughter of Jany a Slave belonging to Mary Murry born April 16th 1739.
Ned Son of Dido a Slave belonging to Matthew Kemp born April 15th 1739.
Frank Son of Lucy a Slave belonging to Tho⁸ Buford Sen⁷ born April 23d 1739.
Lucy Daughter of Judy a Slave belonging to Wm Gardiner Sen⁷ born May 20th 1739.
Judy Daughter of Judy a Slave belonging to John Smith born April 23d 1739.
Judy Daughter of Lucy a Slave belonging to Humphrey Jones born June 24th 1739.
Daphney Daughter of Pat a Slave belonging to Co¹¹ John Grymes born June 28th 1739.
Mingo —— —— a Slave belonging to Alexander Graves born July y⁸ 1st 1739.
Kate Daughter of Beck a Slave belonging to Co¹¹ Armistead born July 5th 1739.
Grace Daughter of Juner a Slave belonging to Matthew Kemp born Sep⁷ 2d 1739.

Grabril Son of Bess a Slave born May 28th } belonging to Co[ll]
Micall Son of Bettey a Slave born June 12th } Armistead 1739.
Sambo Son of Margery a Slave born July 7th }
Judy Daughter of Rose a Slave belonging to Tho[s] Chilton born Aug[st] y[e] 8th 1739.
Amis Daughter of Betty a slave belonging to Edmund Berkeley born Nov[r] 10th 1739.
Simon Son of Hannah a Slave belonging to Edmund Berkeley born Nov[r] 15th 1739.
Morear —— —— a Slave belonging to William Jones born Aug[st] y[e] 23. 1739.
Annaca —— —— a Slave belonging to Henry Mickelburrough born Oct[r] y[e] 24th 1739.
Bess Daughter of Phillis a Slave belonging to John Fearn Sen[r] born June 12th 1739.
Criss —— —— a Slave belonging to Rich[d] Tyler born Nov[r] y[e] 8th 1739.
Margret Daughter of Phillis a Slave belonging to John Segar born Dec[r] y[e] 17th 1739.
Dick Son of Beck a Slave belonging to James Mayo born Decem[r] y[e] 7th 1739.
Hare Son of Cate a Slave belonging to John Carter born Jan[y] y[e] 2d 1739.
Ampey Son of Margrey a Slave belonging to y[e] Estate of Oliver Segar born Jan[y] 28th 173$\frac{9}{10}$.
Peter Son of Frank a Slave belonging to y[e] estate Rog[r] Jones born y[e] 30th of Jan[y] 173$\frac{9}{10}$.
Rachel daughter of Alice a Slave born Jan[y] 4th. } these belonging to Co[ll]
Betty daughter of Sarah a Slave born Jan[y] 22d. } Thacker 173$\frac{9}{10}$.
Harry Son Cate a Slave belonging to Constant Daniel born Feb[y] y[e] 1st 173$\frac{9}{10}$.
Sarah daughter of Verena a Slave belonging to Jonathan Brooks born Feb[y] 7th 173$\frac{9}{10}$.
Lemuel Son of Judith born 31st of Aug[st] belonging to Eliz: Stanard 1736.
Alice Daughter of Letty a Slave belonging to Eliz: Stanard born Nov[r] y[e] 27th 1737.
Billy Son of Judith a Slave belonging to Eliz: Stanard born May 7th 1739.
Joe Son of Judith a Slave belonging to Eliz: Stanard born March 23d 1740.
Judith Daughter of Sarah a Slave belonging to Eliz. Stanard born April 18th 1740.
Margret Daughter of Letty a Slave belonging to Eliz: Stanard born July 27th 1740.
George Son Winefred Morris a free Mullatto was born December 19th 1740.
Letty Daughter of Sarah a Slave belonging to Richard Corbin was born May 2d 1740.
Bristow Son of Sarah belonging to Edwin Thacker was born March y[e] 7th 1740.

Muria of Peg belonging to John Smith born October 15th 1740.
Newman a Slave belonging to Richard Corbin was born Jan'y 8th 1739/40.
Charles Son of Hannah a Slave belonging to Wm Armistead born Febry 1st 1739/40.
Dinah daughter of Jenny born 25 of April belonging died the 6 Day of May 1739/40.
Peter Son of Jenny a Slave belonging to Daniel Stringer born November ye 7th 1740.
Sam a Slave belonging to Nicholas Dillard was born April ye 18th 1740.
Hannah Daughter of Sharlot a Slave belonging to Henry Thacker born April 15th 1740.
Dinah Daughter of Sue a Slave belonging to Wm Davis was born April 10th 1740.
Jubia Son of Rose a Slave belonging to Edwin Thacker born April 18th 1740.
Bess Daughter of Bess a Slave belonging to Alexander Frazier born May 1st 1740.
Diner Daughter of Diner a Slave belonging to William Armstead born May 21th 1740.
Emanuel & Daniel twin Sons of Sue belonging to William Armstead born May 12th 1740.
Wouna Daughter of Cate a Slave belonging to John Smith born May 20th 1740.
Guy Son of Phillis a Slave belonging to John Aldik born May 3d 1740.
Harry Son of Phillis a Slave belonging to John Thomson born July ye 21st 1740.
Dick A Slave belonging to John White born May ye 1st 1740.
Peter Son of Judy A Slave belonging to Robert Daniel born June 8th 1740.
Alice Daughter of Beck a Slave belonging to John Lewis born June 15th 1740.
Grace Daughter of Kate a Slave belonging to Edmund Berkley born May 20th 1740.
Febe a Slave belonging to John Blake born June the 17th 1740.
Buzbe Son of Judy a Slave belonging to Geo: Hardin born June 12th 1740.
Guy a Slave belonging to Armstead Churchill born June 11th 1740.
Nan Daughter of Hannah a Slave belonging to John Smith born June 11th 1740.
Cæsar Son of Judy a Slave belonging to Lawrence Orrill born July 25th 1740.
Eliza Daughter of Phillis belonging to John Smith born July 27th 1740.
Venus Daughter of Jude A Slave belonging to Thomas Mountague born Dec^{mb} 6. 1740.
Tom Son of Jude A Slave belonging to Jedidiah Bristow born Aug. 25th 1740.
Jack A Slave belonging to Charles Daniel born September 17th 1740.
Cate Daughter of Letty a Slave belonging to Henry Tugle born Sep^{ber} 13th 1740.

Jude Daughter of Dinah a Slave belonging to John Grymes born Sep^{ber} 21. 1740.
Lewis a Slave belonging to Ann Smith born December 25th 1739.
Charles a Slave belonging to Ann Smith born February 17th 173$\frac{?}{?}$.
Will Son of Nan a Slave belonging to Mary Jackson born Decem^{ber} 1. 1740.
Harry a Slave belonging to the Estate of John Segar born No^{ber} & died Decem^{ber} 19. 1740.
William Son of Beck a Slave belonging to James Reid was born Jan^{ry} 22. 1740.
Joyce a Slave belonging to Mary Marshall born Jan^{ry} 11th 1740.
Phillip Son of Sarah a Slave belonging to Chris^r Robinson born June y^e 23d 1740.
Beck Daughter of Frank a Slave belonging to Mary Lewis born Jan^{ry} 28. 1740.
Betty Daughter of Lina a Slave belonging to Henry Thacker born Feb^{ry} 17th 174$\frac{?}{?}$.
Glasco a Slave belonging to Henery Mickelburrough born Feb^{ry} 12. 1740.
Jack a Slave belonging to John Blakey born July 19th 1740.
Dina Daughter of Jenny a Slave belonging to Wm Fretwell born May 6th 174.
Averilla a Slave belonging to Peter Hudson born July 31st 1740.
Jamey Son of Jane a Slave belonging to Thomas Mountague born Dec^{mb} 6th 1740.
Frank Daughter of Jone a Slave belonging to Henry Daniel born Feb^{ry} 25th 1740.
Randol Son of Nan a Slave belonging to Wm Hackney born March 9th 1740.
Joe Son of Clarinda a Slave belonging to Wm Mountague born March 29th 174$\frac{?}{?}$.
Phil Son of Judy a Slave to Ch^r Robinson born March y^e 1st. 1740.
Lucy Daughter of Moll a Slave belonging to Alex. Frazier born April 1st 1741.
George Son of Kate a Slave belonging to Alex Frazier born April 8th 1741.
Sarah Daughter of Sarah a Slave belonging to Robert Mickleburrough born March ye 2d. 1741.
Sampson Son of Nan a Slave belonging to Matthias Gale born May ye 1st. 1741.
Jenny Daughter of Kate a Slave belonging to Co^{ll} Edwin Thacker born April 29th 1741.
Robin Son of Daffiny a Slave belonging to the Honble John Grymes Esqr born April 27th 1741.
Frank Son of Fortune a Slave belonging to Thos Laughlin born May ye 9th. 1741.
Mole Daughter of Hannah a Slave belonging to Thos Laughlin born May ye 23d 1741.
Ester Daughter of Bryner a Slave belonging to ye Estate of Oliver Segar born March 29th 1741.
Peter Son of Margry a Slave belonging to ye Estate of Oliver Segar born May ye 18th 1741.

Nat Son of Judeth a Slave belonging to Thoˢ Mountague born May
y ͤ 24th 1741.
Hampton Son of Verena a Slave belonging to John Hardee born
May y ͤ 10th 1741.
Jeney Daughter of —— a Slave belonging to Robert Truman born
June y ͤ 15th 1741.
Diana Daughter of Letty a Slave belonging to y ͤ Estate of M ͬ Stanard born July y ͤ 12th 1741.
Glascow Son of   a Slave belonging to y ͤ Estate of John Shorter
dec'd born July 15th 1741.
Richard Son of Alice a Slave belonging to Co ⁿ Thacker born July
y ͤ 3d 1741.
David Son of Doll a Slave belonging to John Rhodes born July y ͤ
24th 1741.
Nan Daughter of Jane a Slave belonging to Henry Mickelburrough
born Augˢ ͭ 19th 1741.
Dick Son of Sharlot a Slave belonging to Henry Thacker born Sep ͬ
y ͤ 16th 1741.
Ben Son of —— a Slave belonging to Mary Murry born Auguˢ ͭ y ͤ
20th 1741.
Grace Daughter Cresce a Slave belonging to Co ⁿ John Grymes born
Augˢ ͭ 10th 1741.
Frank a Slave belonging to Richard Corbin born Sep ͬ y ͤ 22d 1741.
Jack Son of   a Slave belonging to Rich ᵈ Corbin born Sep ͬ 26th 1741.
Sukey daughter of Phillis a Slave belonging to y ͤ Estate of M ͬ Stanard born Nov ͬ y ͤ 18th 1741.
Pressilla daughter of Jenny a Slave belonging to M ͬˢ Kemp born
April y ͤ 15th 1741.
Daniel Son of Judy a Slave belonging to M ͬˢ Kemp born Octo ͬ y ͤ
28th 1741.
Ann Daughter of Judy a Slave belonging to Lawrance Orril born
Sep ͬ y ͤ 3d. 1741.
Sarah Daughter of Rose a Slave belonging to William Bristow born
Decem ͬ y ͤ 14th 1741.
Tom Son of   a Slave belonging to William Gardiner Sen ͬ born
Sep ͬ y ͤ 12th 1741.
Dick Son of hannah a Slave belonging to M ͬ Gaile born Octo ͬ y ͤ
16th 1741.
Mary daughter of Frank a Slave belonging to Edm ᵈ Berkeley born
July y ͤ 2d 1741.
Anthony & Nelly children of Sabina a Slave belonging to Co ⁿ Edwin
Thacker born Sep ͬ y ͤ 6th 1741.
Harry Son of   a Slave belonging to Co ⁿ Edwin Thacker born
Nov ͬ y ͤ 4th 1741.
Scipio Son of Rose a Slave belonging to Thoˢ Chilton born March
y ͤ 6th 174½.
Daniel Son of Betty a Slave belonging to Edm ᵈ Berkeley born Decem ͬ y ͤ 8th 1741.
Patty daughter of Kate a Slave belonging to Edm ᵈ Berkeley born
Jan ͬʸ y ͤ 8th 174½.
Peter Son of —— —— a Slave belonging to Rich ᵈ Allen born Jan ͬʸ
y ͤ 17th 174½.

Rose Daughter of Lettis a Slave belonging to Tho⁸ Saunders born Jan⁷ y⁸ 2d 174½.
Alce Daughter of Alce a Slave belonging to Co¹¹ Gawin Corbin born Jan⁷ y⁸ 1st 174½.
Dinah Daughter of —— a Slave belonging to William Jones born Feb⁷ y⁸ 14th 174½.
Cate Daughter of Judah a Slave belonging to William Hackney born March 27th 1742.
Anthoney Son of Frank a Slave belonging to Samuel Batcheler born March 18th 174½.
Jane Daughter of Betty a Slave belonging to Cary Smith born March y⁸ 25th 1742.
Amy Son of   a Slave belonging to Ja⁸ Campbell born March y⁸ 28th 1744.
Sarah Daughter of Letty a Slave belonging to Jam⁸ Scrosby born March y⁸ 8th 174½.
Easter daughter of Bess a Slave belonging to Alexd' Frazier born April y⁸ 19th 1742.
Jemmey Son of Kate a Slave belonging to y⁸ estate of John Burk dec'd born April 22d 1742.
Peter Son of —— a Slave belonging to John White born April y⁸ 25th 1742.
Anthony Son of Kate a Slave belonging to Charles Daniel born March 18th 174½.
Adam Son of Pegg a Slave belonging to John Robinson born May 10th 1742.
Sampson Son of Juda a Slave belonging to Robert Daniel born May 13th 1742.
Taylor Son of Phillis a Slave belonging to James Amis born May 28th 1742.
Anthony Son of Moll a Slave belonging to Geo. Wortham born Aug⁸ᵗ 2d 1742.
Jack Son of   a Slave belonging to Ralph Wormeley born April 26th 1742.
Pegg Daughter of   a slave belonging to Ralph Wormeley born June 22nd 1742.
Judy Daughter of Letty a Slave belonging to Henry Tugle born Sep' 14th 1742.
Nanny Daughter of Jenny a slave belonging to Henry Tugle born Sep' y⁸ 6th 1742.
Jack Son of Judy a slave belonging to John Smith ald. born July y⁰ 6th 1742.
Billey Williamson Son of —— a slave belonging to Edward Clark born Octo' y⁸ 6th 1742.
Mille Daughter of —— a slave belonging to Ralph Wormeley born Oct' 2d 1742.
Phillis Daughter of —— a slave belonging to Ralph Wormeley born Oct' 14th 1742.
Godfry Son of Lucy a Slave belonging to Wᵐ Armistead born Sep' 15th 1742.
Doromb of Wounah a Slave belonging to Wᵐ Armistead born Oct' 10th 1742.

Tony Son of Hannah a Slave belonging to Coll Henry Armistead born Sepr 29th 1742.

Sam Son of —— a Slave belonging to Mary Roane born May ye 20th 1742.

Abram Son of —— a Slave belonging to Mary Roane born June 22th 1742.

Letty Daughter of Cate a Slave belonging to William Mountague born June 12th 1742.

Meriah Daughter of —— a Slave belonging to John Jones born born June 28th 1742.

Jeny Daughter of Cate a slave belonging to Matthias Gale born July 17th 1742.

Jack Son of Judy a Slave belonging to John Smith born July 6th 1742.

George Son of —— a Slave belonging to Churchhill Jones born July 7th 1742.

Neton Daughter of —— a slave belonging to Churchhill Jones born July 15th 1742.

Simon son of —— a slave belonging to Hugh Spotswood born July 18th 1732.

Peter Son of Jone a Slave belonging to Henry Daniel born Novr 24th 1742.

Dido Daughter of Fortin a Slave belonging to Thos Laughlin born Novr 28th 1742.

Jenny Daughter of —— a Slave belonging to John Smith born Novr 3d 1742.

Mirah Daughter of Sue a Slave belonging to Colo John Grymes born Decber 28. 1742.

Kezia Dughter of —— a Slave belonging to Curtis Hardee born Janry 22.

Cate Daughter of —— a Slave belonging to Nicholas Dillard born Febry 4th 1742.

Ben Son of Unity a Slave belonging to Edward Dillard born Feb. 26th 174$\frac{2}{3}$.

Jemme Son of Cloe a Slave belonging to John Willcox Febry ye 14th 174$\frac{2}{3}$.

Sue Daughter of —— a Slave belonging to Hope Sutton born Febry 6th.

Agatha Daughter of —— a Slave belonging to Ralph Wormeley born March 15. 174$\frac{2}{3}$.

Newman Son of Beck a Slave belonging to John Lewis born March 20 174$\frac{2}{3}$.

Lewis Son of Wonna a Slave belonging to George Hardin born Janry 2d 1743.

Judith Daughter of —— a Slave belonging to Thomas Laughlin born Janry 10. 1743.

Will Son of Kate a Slave belonging to Charles Daniel born Febry 27 1743.

Robin Son of Nan a Slave belonging to Charles Daniel born March 7. 1743.

Molly Daughter of Beck a Slave belonging to James Reid born April 9th 1743.

Booker Son of —— a Slave belonging to John Smith ju[nr] born April 14. 1743.
Judy Daughter of —— a Slave belonging to John Smith born Feb[ry] 28th 174¾.
Dick Son of Dy a Slave belonging to W[m] Hill jun[r] born May 29th 1743.
Phillis Daughter of Judy a Slave belonging to Law[r] Orrill born May 29th 1743.
Jemmy Son of Frank a Slave belonging to Mary Lewis born May 1th 1743.
Billy Son of —— a Slave belonging to Robert Dudley born May 20th 1743.
George Son of Letty a Slave belonging to Ann Smith born May 29th 1743.
Kate Daughter of —— a Slave belonging to Churchill Jones born June 4th 1743.
Massey Daughter of Dolly a Slave belonging to John Rhodes born June 19th 1743.
Dinah Daughter of Nan a Slave belonging to —— Gail born July 8th 1743.
Jenny Daughter of Nan a Slave belonging to William Hackney Sen[r] born July 4th 1743.
Hannah Daughter of Judy a Slave belonging to Henry Thacker born July 24th 1743.
Mary Daughter of Lena a Slave belonging to Henry Thacker born August 3d 1743.
Tom Son of Judy a Slave belonging to Thomas Marston born August 29. 1743.
Harry Son of —— a Slave belonging to Ralph Wormeley born July 8th 1743.
Cupit Son of —— a Slave belonging to Ralph Wormeley born July 27. 1743.
George Son of —— a Slave belonging to Ralph Wormeley born August 5th 1743.
Eve Daughter of —— a Slave belonging to Col[o] Edwin Thacker born August 21. 1743.
Sabina Daughter of Sabina a Slave belonging to Col[o] Edwin Thacker born Sep[ber] 9th 1743.
Annekin Daughter of a Slave belonging to Ralph Wormeley born September 7. 1743.
Lucretia Daughter of Phillis a Slave belonging to W[m] Mountague born September 7. 1743.
Mary Daughter of Frank a Slave belonging to Charles Lee born October 22. 1743.
Tom Son of Sharlot a Slave belonging to Henry Thacker born Oc[ber] 5. 1743.
Edee Daughter of Judith a Slave belonging to Thomas Mountague born Oc[ber] 16. 1743.
James Son of —— a Slave belonging to Mary Jackson born November 30th 1743.
Cupid Son of Venus a Slave belonging to Richard Alleen born Nov[ber] 20th 1743.

Nassan Son of —— a slave belonging to Ralph Wormeley born December 5th 1743.
Phalmoth Son of Lucy a Slave belonging to Chicheley Thacker born December 28. 1743.
Simon Son of Letty a Slave belonging to Thomas Sanders born December 16th 1743.
Kate Daughter of —— a Slave belonging to Col° Gawin Corbin born Jan'y 14th 174¾.
Joe Son of —— a Slave belonging to Col° Gawin Corbin born Jan'y 1. 174¾.
Jack Son of Jenny a Slave belonging to Henry Mickleburrough born Jan'y 21. 174¾.
Ben Son of Jenny a Slave belonging to Thomas Buford Sen' born Jan'y 28 174¾.
Jenny Daughter of Daphney a Slave belonging to Ann Smith born July 17th 1743.
Hannah Daughter of Cate A Slave belonging to Moris Smith born September 10. 1742.
Lucy Daughter of Letty a Slave belonging to Eliz* Tugle born Feb'y 12. 1743.
Tom Son of Hannah a Slave belonging to —— Gale born Feb'y 22nd 1743.
Dinah Daughter of —— a Slave belonging to Hugh Spotswood born Feb'y 24th 174¾.
Irenah Daughter of Phillis a Slave belonging to Beverley Stanard born Feb'y 15th 174¾.
Frances Daughter of —— a Slave belonging to Ralph Wormely born March 10th 174¾.
Harry Son of Kate a Slave belonging to Eliz* Burk born June y° 4th 1744.
Samuel Son of Ebo Frank a Slave born Octo' y° 10th 1742, Alce Daughter of Betty a Slave born Nov' y° 10th. 1742, Harry Son of Frank a Slave born December y° 15th 1742, Mareah Daughter of —— a Slave born Octo' 14th 1742, Mingo Son of Cate a Slave born Octo' y° 11th 1743, Cupit Son of Betty a Slave born December y° 16th 1744, James Son of Cates a Slave born Feb'y y° 9th 174⅘, Isaac Son of Ebo Frank born March 20th 174⅘, these belong to Edmund Berkeley.
Susannah Daughter of —— a Slave belonging Mary Roane born March 19th 174¾.
Tom Son of Janey a Slave belonging to Tho* Mountague born April 5th 1744.
James Son of —— a Slave belonging to Churchhill Jones born Marc y° 11th 1744.
Sam Son of —— a Slave belonging to John Jones born June 23d 1744.
Peter Son of Great Alice a Slave born Sep' 1744, Mary Daughter of Winny a Slave born December 15th 1744, Ralph Son of Little Alice a Slave born Feb'y 23 1744, Ruben & Eliz* Twins of Anaca a Slave born April 3d. 1745, Will Son of Jone a Slave born April 13th 1745, belonging to Edwin Thacker.
Cate Daughter of —— a Slave belonging to John Boss born May y° 20th 1744.

George Son of Rose a Slave belonging to John Rhoades born Feb[ry] 26th 1744.
Mary Daughter of Rose a Slave belonging to Pat Cheops born Dec[r] 14th 1744.
Dick Son of Sharlot a Slave born Nov[r] 25, Billey Son of Jenney a Slave born Dec[r] 20 1744, belonging to Henry Thacker.
Rachel Daughter of —— a Slave belonging to Obediah Daniel born Octo[r] 26th 1744.
Patty Daughter of Phillis born Octo[r] 1st. 1744.
Venus Daughter of Corender a Slave born Sep[r] 20th, Creasey Daughter of Cate a Slave born Octo[r] 28th 1744, belonging to W[m] Mountague.
Annaka Daughter of Judy a Slave belonging to W[m] Daniel born Sep[r] 3d 1744.
Amee Daughter of —— a Slave belonging to Christian Miller born Sep[r] y[e] 1st 1744.
Aga Daughter of Cate a Slave belonging to Mary Carter born May 17th 1744.
Nanny Daughter of —— a Slave belonging to Mary Kemp born July 18th 1744.
Diner Daughter of betty a Slave belonging to Ann Smith born April 21st 1744.
Adam Son of Margerya a Slave born 1744, Peter Son of Moll a Slave born 1744, belonging to Coll Grymes.
Ned Son of Judy a Slave belonging to Mary Roane born June 13th 1744.
Mary Daughter of —— a Slave born Sep[r] 1st 1744, Edward Son of —— a slave born Nov[r] 15th 1744, Sarah Daughter of —— a slave born Jan[ry] 18th 174$, Thomas Son of —— a slave born Feb[ry] 3d 174$, belonging to Ralph Wormley.
Francis Son of Betty a Slave born Sep[r] 27th belonging to Beverley Stanard.
Anne Daughter of —— a Slave belonging to y[e] Estate of John Smith born April 28th 1744.
Anthoney son of Betty a Slave belonging to John Smith jun[r] born April y[e] 9th 1745.
Ben son of Beck a Slave belonging to Charles Roan born Jan[ry] 14th 174$.
Tom Son of Jone a Slave belonging to James Machan born April 1st 1745.
Robin Son of —— a Slave belonging to y[e] Estate of Gawin Corbin April 22d 1745.
Toney Son of —— a Slave belonging to Thomas Sanders born April 25th 1745.
George Son of —— a Slave belonging to John Mackneele born Feb[ry] 21st 1744.
Will Son of —— a Slave belonging to Nicholas Dillard born May 2d 1745.
Sarah Daughter of Jeney a Slave belonging to John Wortham born June 22d 1744.
Susannah Daughter of Letty a Slave belonging to Bar: Yates born April 1745.

Jean Daughter of Diner a Slave belonging to Ann Wortham born Feb^{ry} ye 15th 1744.
Lucy Daughter of Beck a Slave belonging to George Wortham born May 6th 1745.
Jane Daughter of —— a Slave belonging to Edward Dillard born May 29th 1745.
Bristow son of Jeney a Slave belonging to John Kidd born July ye 1st 1745.
Lewis Son of Beck a Slave belonging to Chris^r Robinson born July 19th 1744.
Tamer Daughter of Moll a Slave belonging to George Wortham born July 13th 1745.
Judy Daughter of Mole a Slave belonging to Alexander Frazier born July 17th 1745.
Sara Daughter of Nan a Slave belonging to William Hackney sen^r born June 3d 1745.
Ben Son of Frank a Slave belonging to Eusebius Lewis born June 17th 1745.
Peter Son of Fillis a Slave belonging to William Hackney Junr born July 12th 1745.
Newman Son of Ruth a Slave belonging to Margaret Johnson born Augst 25th 1745.
Phebe Daughter of Helas a Slave belonging to Judith Segar born Decem^r 28th 1745.
Ralph Son of —— a Slave belonging to Elizabeth Hardin born Octo^r 16th 1745.
Plymouth Son of Lena a Slave belonging to Henry Thacker born Decem^r 17th 1745.
Kate Daughter of Dole a Slave belonging to John Rhodes born Sepr 26th 1745.
Gowin Son of Frank a Slave belonging to Eliz^a Tugle born Decem^r 23d 1745.
Sarah Daughter of Nana a Slave belonging to Charles Daniel born Octo^r 17th 1745.
Robin Son of Hannah a Slave belonging to Hugh Spotswood born Novr 5th 1745.
Robing Son of —— a Slave belonging to Richard Corbin born Feb^{ry} 20th 1745.
Adam Son of Rose a Slave belonging to John Smith born Jan^{ry} 5th ——.
Rachel Daughter of Fortin a Slave belonging to Thos Laughlin born April 23d 1745.
Chaney Daughter of —— a Slave belonging to John Berry born March 2d 1745.
Anth^o Son of —— a Slave belonging to Churchhill Jones born Jan^{ry} 1st 1745.
Jane Daughter of Rose a Slave belonging to Thos Chilton born Decem^r 12th 1745.
Peter son of —— a Slave belonging to Robert Elliot born Novr 16th 1745.
Milley Daughter of —— a Slave belonging to Robert Elliot born Decem^r 26th 1745.

Isaac Son of —— a Slave belonging to Richard Corbin born Sepr 3d 1745.
Beck Daughter of —— a Slave belonging to Eliz^a Hardin born March 14th 1745.
Tom Son of Jone a Slave belonging to Thos Buford Senr born Octo^r 19th 1745.
Jane Daughter of Margre a Slave belonging to Nicholas Dillard born Sepr 28th
Sampson Son of Hannah a Slave belonging to George Lee born March 4th 174⅝.
Simon Son of Judy a Slave belonging to Hope Sutton born Decem^r 1745.
Susaner Daughter of Phillis a Slave belonging to Rand^h Segar born Feb^ry 27th 1745.
Jemmy Son of Jude a Slave belonging to Wm Gardner Senr born March 18th 1745.
Tom & Samson Son of Mareah a Slave belonging to Edmund Berkeley born in July or Augst 1745.
Harry Son of Jenney a Slave belonging to Thos Laughlin born Augst 5th 1746.
Lewey Son of Moll a Slave belonging to Thos Laughlin born Augst 22d 1746.
Grace Daughter of Pate a Slave belonging to Wm Armistead born Feb^ry 6th 174⅝.
Cella Daughter of Frank a Slave belonging to Wm Armistead born March 2d 174⅝.
Mingo Son of Rose a Slave belonging to Robert Trueman born July 15th 1746.
Jack Son of —— a Slave belonging to John Murry born Augst 29th 1746.
Faney Daughter of —— a Slave belonging to Joseph Small born Decem^r 11th 1746.
Thos Goselen Son of Ann a Slave belonging to Phillip Grymes born Octo^r 28th 1745.
Lucana Daughter of Nan a Slave belonging to Mary Jackson born June 3d. 1746.
George Son of Hannah a Slave belonging to John Smith jun^r born July 20th 1746.
Tom Son of Bess a Slave belonging to Alex^{or} Frazier born July 18th 1746.
Simon Son of —— a Slave belonging to John Berry born July 8th 1746.
Sary Daughter of —— a Slave belonging to John Jones born July 18th 1746.
Clara Daughter of Kate a Slave belonging to Alex^{or} Frazier born March 30th 1746.
Charles Son of —— a Slave belonging to Mary Kemp born July 2d. 1746.
Tamer Daughter of —— a Slave belonging to Churchhill Jones born Novr 22d. 1746.
Jeney Son of Kate a Slave belonging to Charles Daniel born April 1st 1746.

Lewis Son of Moll a Slave belonging to Mary Rone born April 15th 1746.
Phillis & Frank Daughters a Slave belonging to Mary Rone born May 7th 1746.
Lucy Daughter of Judy a Slave belonging to Charles Daniel born May 27th 1746.
Dolly White Daughter of Dina a Slave belonging to Ann Smith born May 16th 1746.
Milla Daughter of Daphine a Slave belonging to Ann Smith born Nov' 11th 1746.
Sue Daughter of Phillis a Slave belonging to Tho' Price born April 26th 1746.
Daniel Son of Sabrina a Slave belonging to Jane Dudly born Octo' 29th 1746.
Jacob Son of Frank a Slave belonging to W'' Mountague born Octo' 25th 1746.
Isaac Son of Cate a Slave belonging to W'' Mountague born Nov' 25th 1746.
Simon Son of —— a Slave belonging to Francis Bryant born Aug'' 14th 1746.
Esther Daughter of Margery a Slave belonging to John Smith Jun' born Decem' 26th 1746.
Mill Daughter of Jane a Slave belonging to Thos. Mountague born Nov' 26th 1746.
Will Son of Letty a Slave belonging to Eliz' Tugle born Nov' 15th 1746.
Mille Daughter of —— a Slave belonging to George Blakey born Nov' 1st 1746.
Lette Daughter of —— a Slave belonging to John Jones born Feb'' 4th 1746.
Leaner Daughter of —— a Slave belonging to Massey Yarrington born Octo' 10th 1746.
Abbie Daughter of —— a Slave belonging to Armistead Churchhill born December 12th 1746.
Anthony Son of —— a Slave belonging to Armistead Churchhill born Jan'' 8th 1746.
Samson Son of Frank a Slave belonging to Catherine Batchelder born Sep' 17th 1746.
Lewis Son of Jeny a Slave belonging to Henry Mickleburrough born Jan'' 28th 174⁶.
Rachel & Esther Daughter of a Slave belonging to Armistead Churchhill born in 1746.
—— Daughter of Dey a Slave belonging to W'' Hill Sen' born April y' 25th 1746.
Betty Daughter of Jeny a Slave belonging to Tho' Beuford born March 6th 174⁶.
Abram Son of Hannah a Slave belonging to W'' Mountague born Jan'' 6th 174⁶.
Bess Daughter of Chance a Slave belonging to Matthias Gale born March 28th 1747.
Daffery Daughter of —— a Slave belonging to y' Estate of W'' Daniel born April 27th 1747.

Births of Negroes belonging to Samuel Klug.

Kate, Daughter of Nanny a Slave born April 1769.
George, Son of Nancy born 1773.
Randolph, Son of Nancy born 1775.
Matt, Son of Nancy born —— 1777.
Billy, Son of Nancy born September 1778.
Billy, Son of Peggy born —— 1773.
Dolly, Daughter of Peggy born 1775.
Tom, Son of Peggy born October 1779.
James, Son of Nancy born Novr 9th 1780.
Ned, Son of Mary born August 1st 1781.
Jack son of Peggy born January 21st 1782.
Abram, Son of Mary born May —— 1784.
Jesse son of Peggy born —— 1785.

Births of Negroes belonging to Mary Yates.

Jack, son of Cilla born 1769.
Beck, Daughter of Peny born April 1st 1770.
Billy, son of Pene born August 1772.
Sukey, Daughter of Pene born June 1775.
Nancy Daughter of Pene born Novr 13th 1777.
Sarah, Daughter of Alice born February 1779.
Anthony son of Pene, born March 1781.
Robin, Son of Pene, born Novr 13th 1783.
Eveline Ann Graica Daughter of Kate born August 25th 1794.
Fanny Daughter of Nancy a Slave belon^g to S. Klug was born Novr 7th 1785.
Frank, son of Peggy born July 1787.
Levie, son of Mary, born August 1787.
Peter son of Mary born March 1792.

Fragment 115 and 116.

John Walden & Frances Crittenden (K. & Q.) married March 24th 1792.
James Hopkins & Mary Brooks married April 15th 1792.
Nelson Humphris & Lucy Jones married April 15. 1792.
Thomas Hugget & Frances Ware (K. & Q.) married April 22d. 1792.
Francis Collier & Susannah Dillard (K. & Q.) married
William Jack   Martha Vass
The above * *
Richard Minie & Francis Leigh (K. & Q.) married June 29th 1793.
Burgess Kidd & Sarah Daniel married July 27th 1793.
Robert Watson & Mary Hibble married August 11th 1793.
* * Keith & Mary Holden Taliaferao (K & Q.) married August 22nd 1793.
* * * * Elizabeth Adams (K. & Q.) mar: Septr 12 1793.

Here begins ye Regester for ye death of Slaves from Septem^r in ye year 1715 w'ch before were Sett down together wth ye christian burrialls.

Apollo a negro belonging to Wm Stanard dyed Septem^r ye 3 was buried Septem^r 4 1715.

Hester a negro belonging to Wm Stanard dyed Septem^r ye 24 was buried Septem^r 25 1715.

Toney a negro belonging to John Davies dyed Novem: ye 26 was buried Novem 27. 1715.

Bob a negro belonging to John Robinson dyed Octo: 20 was burid Octo: 21 1715.

Nanny a negro belonging to Frances Thacker dyed March 25 was buried March 26 1716.

Kitt a negro belonging to ye estate of Edwin Thacker dec'd dyed May ye 19 buried 20th 1716.

Hagar a negro belonging to Wm Sandiford dyed June ye 16. buried June ye 17 1716.

Sindab a negro belonging to Gawin Corbin dyed ye 2 of August buried August ye 3 1715.

Ned a negro belonging to ye estate of Hen: Thacker dec'd dyed Sept^{mb} 8 buried ye 9 1716.

Betty a negro belonging to Tho: Machen dyed March ye 17 buried ye 18 1715.

Grasheir a negro belonging to Tho: Machen dyed March ye 23 buried ye 24 1715.

Ben a negro belonging to Hen: Tugell dyed October ye 23 buried ye same day 1716.

Sarah a negro belonging to Thomas Warwick dyed Jan'y ye 10 buried ye 11 1716.

Bess a negro belonging to Bar Yates dyed Feb'y ye 4 buried ye same day 1716.

Dinah a negro belonging to Nicholas Bristow dyed Feb'y 10 buried Feb'y 11 1716.

Betty a negro belonging to Sarah Hadley dyed Feb'y ye 4 buried ye same day 1716.

Jenny a negro belonging to John Robinson dyed Feb'y ye 22 buried Feb'y ye 23 1716.

Billy a negro belonging to ye estate of Henry Thacker dec'd dyed March ye 17. buried ye 18 1716.

Jack a negro belonging to Charles Lee dyed March ye 7. buried March ye 8 1716.

Rose a negro belonging to ye estate of Wm Churchhill dec'd dyed Feb'y 10 buried ye 11 1716.

Jacob a negro belonging to ye estate of Wm Churchhill dec'd dyed Feb'y ye 14 buried ye 15 1716.

Moll a negro belonging to ye estate of Wm Churchhill dec'd dyed March 5 buried ye 10 1716.

Rose a negro belonging to Wm Barbee dyed March ye 28 buried ye same day 1717.

Hannah a negro belonging to ye estate of Edwin Thacker dyed May ye 6 buried May ye 1717.

Will a negro belonging to Henry Armistead dyed June ye 4 buried June ye 5th 1717.

Emanuell a negro belonging to Henry Armistead dyed June ye 8. buried June 9 1717.

Burrows a negro belonging to Henry Armistead dyed June ye 10. buried June 11. 1717.

Tom a negro belonging to ye estate of Eliz^a Churchhill dyed May ye 10 buried May 11 1717.

Corey a negro belonging to John Murry dyed July ye 5 buried July ye 6 1717.

Jack a negro belonging to John Murry dyed July ye 13 buried July ye 14 1717.

Ben a Negro belonging to Matthew Hunt dyed Septem^r ye 7. buried ye same day 1717.

Alice a negro belonging to John Grymes dyed Feb'y ye 1 buried Feb'y ye 2 1716.

Judy a Negro belonging to John Smith Senr dyed Novem^r ye 15. buried Novem^r 16 1717.

George a Negro belonging to John Smith Senr dyed Novem^r ye 18. buried Novem^r 19 1717.

Harry a Negro belonging to Wm Barbee dyed Decem^r ye 2 buried Decem^r 3 1717.

Ned a negro belonging to Anne Thacker dyed Decem^r ye 6 buried Decem^r 8 1717.

Toney a Negro belonging to John Wormeley dyed Decem. ye 13 buried Dec. 15 1717.

Jack a Negro belonging to Jacob Stiff dyed Jan'y ye 12 buried Jan'y 13 1717.

Jack a Slave belonging to Wm Daniel jun^r dyed Feb'y 26. buried Feb'y 27 1717.

Poll a slave belonging to Phillip Warwick dyed March y^n 11. buried March 12. 1717.

Dick a slave belonging to Christopher Sutton dyed Ap: 15: buried Ap: 16 1718.

Moll a Slave belonging to Gawin Corbin dyed March ye 10. buried March 11. 1717.

Kitt a slave belonging to John Robinson dyed June 30. buried July 1. 1718.

George a slave belonging to Jacob Stiff dyed August ye 28. buried August 29. 1718.

Billy a slave belonging to John Smith Junr dyed Septem^r 25. buried ye same day 1718.

Will a Slave belonging to John Vivion dyed August 30. buried August 31 1718.

Ibbo a slave belonging to John Smith dyed Octo: ye 16. buried Octo: 17 1718.

Captain a Slave belonging to Robert Daniel dyed Novem^r ye 20. buried Novem^r 21 1718.

Betty a slave belonging to William Ogilvie dyed Decem^r ye 20 buried Decem^r 21 1718.

Sue a slave belonging to Robert Dudley dyed Jan'y ye 12. buried Jan^r ye 13. 1718.

Tony a slave belonging to ye estate of Wm Churchhill dec'd dyed Jan'y 17. buried Jan'y 18. 1718.

Bar Yates minister.

Sarah a slave belonging to Robᵗ George junʳ dyed Decemʳ 22 buried yᵉ 23. 1718.
Betty a slave belonging to Edwin Thacker dyed Febʳʸ 2. buried Feb'y yᵉ 3. 1718.
Toney a Slave belonging to John Aldin dyed March yᵉ 23. buried yᵉ same day 1718.
Ben a slave belonging to William Segar dyed Feb. 2. buried Feb. yᵉ 3. 1718.
Dick a Slave belonging to John Vivion dyed May yᵉ 7. buried May yᵉ 8. 1719.
Megg a slave belonging to John Segar dyed May yᵉ 26. buried May yʳ 26.
Jenny a slave belonging to James Smith dyed June yᵉ 1. buried June yᵉ 2. 1719.
Lucy a slave belonging to John Vivion dyed June yᵉ 3. buried June yᵉ 4 1719.
Jack a Slave belonging to Sam Loe dyed May yᵉ 23. buried May yᵉ 24 1719.
Tom a slave belonging to John Roades dyed July yᵉ 20. buried July yᵉ 21 1719.
Phill a slave belonging to Matthew Kemp dyed August yᵉ 5. buried Augsᵗ yᵉ 6 1719.
Harry a slave belonging to Thomas Cheney dyed Sept. yᵉ 15 buried Sept. yᵉ 16. 1719.
Margery a Slave belonging to Robert Dudley dyed Sept. yᵉ 24. buried Sept. 24 1719.
Sam a slave belonging to William Segar dyed Octo yᵉ 10. buried Octo. 11. 1719.
Thomas a slave belonging to Bartho: Yates dyed Jan'y yᵉ 10. buried yᵉ 11. 1719.
Caesar a slave belonging to Mathew Kemp dyed Feb'y yᵉ 7. buried Feb'y yᵉ 8. 1719.
Toney a slave belonging to John Vivion dyed Jan'y yᵉ 20. buried Jan'y yᵉ 21. 1719.
Billey a slave belonging to Edwin Thacker dyed Feb'y yᵉ 29. buried yᵉ same day 1719.
Catherine Lee a Slave belonging to Isaack Burton dyed Feb'y 29. buried yᵉ same day 1719.
Kate a slave belonging to Charles Cooper dyed Jan'y 22. buried Jan'y yᵉ 23. 1719.
Dick an Indian Slave belonging to John Grymes dyed Ap: 2d buried Ap: 3. 1720.
Jack a slave belonging to John Grymes dyed Ap: yᵉ 14. buried Ap. 15 1720.
Dinah a slave belonging to Henry Armistead dyed Ap: yᵉ 8. buried Ap. 9 1720.
Sampson a slave belonging to Matthew Kemp dyed Ap: yᵉ 26. buried Ap: 27 1720.
Jenny a slave belonging to John Smith Junʳ dyed May yᵉ 1. buried May 2 1720.
Jenney a slave belonging to George Wortham dyed May yᵉ 28. buried May 29. 1720.

Frank a slave belonging to Bar. Yates dyed June 25. buried June 26 1720.
Will a slave belonging to Henry Armistead dyed June y° 3. buried June 4. 1720.
Toby a slave belonging to John Smith jun' dyed June 22. buried June 23 1720.
Frank a slave belonging to John Robinson dyed August 1. buried y° Same day 1720.
Frank a slave belonging to Armistead Churchhill dyed Augst. 3. buried y° same day 172
Doll a slave belonging to John Lewis dyed Septem' y° 1. buried y° same day 172
Harry a Slave belonging to Mathew Kemp dyed Septem' y° 7th 172
Nanny a slave belonging to James Curtis dyed Novem' 15. buried Nov. 16 1720.
Aleck a slave belonging to James Curtis dyed Novem' 16. buried Nov. 17 1720.
Will a Slave belonging to y° estate of y° abovesd James Curtis dyed Novem' 21. buried 22. 1720.
Nan a Slave belonging to Anne Mayo dyed Novem' y° 20. buried Novem' 21 1720.
Cæsar a Slave belonging to Henry Tugle dyed Novem' y° 27. buried y° same day 1720.
Graysheir a Slave belonging to Bar Yates dyed Decem' 16. buried Decem' 17 1720.
Harry a Slave belonging to William Davies dyed Decem' 16. buried Decem' 17. 172
Peter a Slave belonging to James Meacham dyed Novem' 27. buried Nov. 28 172
Jupiter a Slave belonging to Edwin Thacker dyed Novem' 22. buried Novem' 23 1720.
Dick a Slave belonging to Frances Thacker dyed Decem' y° 2. buried Decem' y° 5 1720.
Jemmy a Slave belonging to Edwin Thacker dyed Decem' y° 4. buried Decem' y° 5 1720.
Sarah a Slave belonging to Edwin Thacker dyed Decem' y° 9. buried Decem' 10 1720.
Charles a Slave belonging to Matthew Hunt dyed Decem' y° 28. buried Decem' 29 1720.
Ralph a Slave belonging to Roger Jones dyed Decem' y° 11. buried Decem' 12 172
Jemmy a Slave belonging to C: C: Thacker dyed Decem' y° 30. buried Decem' 31 1720.
Cornbonora a Slave belonging to Harry Beverley dyed Decem' y° 31. buried y° Same day 1720.
Old Jack a Slave belonging to Bar. Yates dyed Jan'y y° 3. buried Jan'y y° 4 1720.
Jack a Slave belonging to Marvil Moseley dyed Decem' y° 12 buried Dec. 13. 1720.
Kate a Slave belonging to Matthew Hunt dyed Jan'y y° 11. buried Jan'y 12. 1720.

Sawny a Slave belonging to John Grymes dyed Decem' y° 22. buried Decem' 23. 1720.
Absolom a Slave belonging to John Grymes dyed Jan'y y° 4. buried Jan'y y° 5 1720.
Harry a Slave belonging to John Grymes dyed Jan'y y° 18. buried Jan'y y° 19 1720.

Bar. Yates Minister.

Yoto a Slave belonging to Mess™ Bell & Dee dyed Jan'y y° 22 & buried y° 23 1720.
Jenny a Slave belonging to William Daniel Sen' dyed Jan'y y° 10. buried y° 11 1720.
Jack a Slave belonging to James Meacham dyed Jan'y y° 17. & was buried 18 1720.
John a Slave belonging to Henry Thacker dyed Jan'y y° 31. & was buried Feb. 1 1720.
Mingo a Slave belonging to James Curtis jun' Estate dyed Feb'y y° 2. buried Feb. 3 1720.
Della a Slave belonging to Humphery Jones dyed Jan'y y° 23. buried y° 24 1720.
Roger a Slave belonging to Humphery Jones dyed Jan'y y° 23. buried y° 24 1720.
Della a Slave belonging to Rob' George Sen' dyed Jan'y y° 27. buried y° 28 1720.
Jemmy a Slave belonging to Robert George Sen' dyed Jan'y y° 29. buried y° 30 1720.
Hannaball a Slave belonging to Tho. Mountague Sen' dyed Jan'y y° 10. buried y° 11 1720.
Dina a Slave belonging to Frances Ransone dyed Feb'y y° 18. buried Feb'y y° 19. 1720.
Phillis a Slave belonging to William Segar dyed Feb'y y° 13. buried Feb'y y° 14 1720.
Guy a Slave belonging to Henry Goodloe dyed Feb'y y° 18. buried Feb'y y° 19 1720.
Adam a Slave belonging to Thomas Haselwood dyed Feb'y y° 22. buried Feb'y 23 1720.
Dublin a Slave belonging to Alexander Graves dyed March y° 7 1720.
Jenny a Slave belonging to Rob' Williamson Sen' dyed March 6 1720.
Sampson a Slave belonging to John Segar dyed March y° 20 1720.
Charles a Slave belonging to John Smith Jun' dyed March y° 28 1721.
Cate a Slave belonging to Jacob Stiff dyed April 13 1721.
Peter a Slave belonging to Hen: Armistead dyed May y° 6 1721.
Peter a Slave belonging to Patrick Kelley dyed May y° 9 1721.
Judy a Slave belonging to Edwin Thacker dyed May y° 21 1721.
Joice a Slave belonging to Mathew Kemp dyed June y° 13 1721.
Billy a Slave belonging to John Robinson dyed July y° 7 1721.
Daniel a Slave belonging to y° estate of Edm⁴ Berkley dyed May y° 24 1721.
Bess a Slave belonging to George Harding dyed June y° 28 1721.

Degar a Slave belonging to yᵉ estate of Garritt Minor dyed July yᵒ 4 1721.
George a Slave belonging to yᵉ estate of Garritt Minor dyed July yᵉ 14 1721.
Cress a Slave belonging to yᵉ estate of Collᵒ Churchhill dyed 1721.
Frank a Slave belonging to yᵉ estate of Collᵒ Churchhill dyed 1721.
Winney a Slave belonging to Rice Curtis dyed July yᵉ 24 1721.
Tom a slave belonging to Roger Jones dyed March yᵒ 7. 1721.
Sarah a slave belonging to yᵉ estate of Garritt Minor dyed Augsᵗ yᵉ 6 1721.
Jemmy a Slave belonging to yᵉ estate of Garritt Minor dyed Augsᵗ yᵒ 15: 1721.
Tom a slave belonging to James Daniel dyed August 30. 1720.
Jeffry a slave belonging to Christopher Robinson dyed Septemʳ yᵉ 10. 1721.
Sarah a Slave belonging to Robert George Senʳ dyed August yᵉ 22. 1721.
Mary a slave belonging to Christopher Robinson dyed Septemʳ yᵉ 9 1721.
Harry a Slave belonging to John Berry dyed Septemʳ yᵉ 20. 1721.
Phillis a Slave belonging to Thomas Mountague dyed Novemʳ yⁿ 10. 1721.
Venus a slave belonging to Robᵗ George Senʳ dyed Novemʳ yᵉ 11. 1721.
Letty a Slave belonging to Bar Yates dyed Novemʳ 19. 1721.
Sarah a slave belonging to yᵉ estate of Hen. Thacker dec'd dyed Decemʳ yᵉ 1. 1721.
Toby a slave belonging to Mathew Kemp dyed Decemʳ yᵒ 16 1721.
Sarah a slave belonging to Bar Yates dyed Decemʳ yᵒ 21. 1721.
Bristow a Slave belonging to Henry Tugle dyed Decemʳ yᵒ 16. 1721.
Roger a slave belonging to Mathew Kemp dyed Decemʳ yᵉ 29. 1721.
James a Slave belonging to Hen. Armistead dyed Jan'y yᵉ 6. 1721.
Harry a slave belonging to Mathew Hunt dyed Jan'y yᵉ 5. 1721.
Cæsar a slave belonging to yᵉ estate of Hen. Thacker dec'd dyed Feb'y yᵉ 1. 1721.
Penn a Slave belonging to Tho: Mountague dyed Jan'y yᵒ 24. 1721.
York a slave belonging to yᵉ estate of Hen: Thacker dec'd dyed Feb'y yᵉ 1. 1721.
Jack a slave belonging to Stockly Towles dyed Jan'y yᵒ 31 1721.
Sarah a Slave belonging to Stockly Towles dyed Feb'y yᵉ 2 1721.
Robin a Slave belonging to Stockley Towles dyed Feb'y yᵉ 18 1721.
Jack an Indian Slave belonging to John Smith dyed Feb'y yᵒ 17. 1721.

    Bar Yates—Minister.

Fragment—Dolly Daughter of John & Jane Bray was born January 2rd 1765.

    By Henry Heffernan Rector.

Lura a Slave belonging to John Smith junʳ dyed Feb'y yᵒ 22 1721.
Antony a slave belonging to Bar Yates dyed March yᵉ 5 1721.
Bess a slave belonging to Rice Jones dyed March yᵒ 12 1721.
Jack a Slave belonging to John Segar dyed April yᵉ 11 1722.
Abram a slave belonging to Hobs Weeks dyed April yᵉ 18 1722.

Joe a slave belonging to John Smith dyed April ye 26 1722.
Robert a Slave belonging to James Batchelder dyed May ye 4 1722.
Alice a slave belonging to Eliz^a Vivion dyed May ye 3 1722.
Jenny a slave belonging to Bartho: Yates dyed May ye 22 1722.
Bob a Slave belonging to John Robinson dyed May ye 25 1722.
Sawney a slave belonging to Robert Williamson Senr dyed May ye 7. 1722.
Jack a slave belonging to Jonathan Johnson dyed August ye 21 1722.
Monmouth a Slave belonging to Henry Thacker dyed Septem^r ye 20 1722.
Charlott a slave belonging to ye estate of John Vivion dec'd dyed August 15. 1722.
Sarah a slave belonging to Augustine Smith dyed Octo ye 13 1722.
Letty a Slave belonging to John Moseley dyed Octo. ye 16 1722.
Tom a slave belonging to Alexander Graves dyed Novem^r ye 16 1722.
Paul a slave belonging to Matthew Kemp dyed Decem^r ye 20 1722.
Tom a Slave belonging to Richard Hill dyed Decem^r ye 4 1722.
Toby a slave belonging to Margrett Daniel dyed Decem^r ye 29 1722.
Nanny a slave belonging to ye estate of Garritt Minor dec'd dyed Octo ye 20 1722.
George a slave belonging to Matthew Kemp dyed Jan'y ye 24 1722.
Charles a slave belonging to Joseph Goar dyed Feb'y ye 1 1722.
Betty a slave belonging to Paul Thilman dyed Jan'y ye 29 1722.
Billy a slave belonging to John Segar dyed Jan'y ye 29 1722.
Merenry a slave belonging to William Stanard dyed Feb'y ye 28 1722.
Nanny a slave belonging to John Robinson Esqr dyed March ye 23 1722.
Sarah a slave belonging to John Degge dyed April y^o 19. 1723.
Ned a slave belonging to John Cheadle dyed April y^o 15 1723.
Joe a slave belonging to Robert Williamson jun^r dyed April ye 28 1723.
Anne a slave belonging to John Gibbs dyed May ye 26 1723.
Harry a slave belonging to Willlm Hackney dyed June ye 15 1723.
Frank a slave belonging to Thomas Norman dyed June ye 14 1723.
Nell a slave belonging to ye estate of Edmund Berkley dec'd dyed June y^o 8 1723.
Harry a slave belonging to Samuel Batchelder dyed June ye 30. 1723.
Tom a slave belonging to John Price dyed July ye 9 1723.
Kate a slave belonging to ye estate of Wm Gordon dec'd April ye 28 1723.
Collonell a Slave belonging to Armistead Churchhill dyed July ye 10 1723.
Old Alice a slave belonging to Bar Yates dyed August ye 17 1723.
Jack a slave belonging to James Daniel dyed July ye 28 1723.
Sam a slave belonging to Wm Mountague jun^r dyed August y^o 13. 1723.
Toney a slave belonging to John Cheadle dyed August ye 19 1723.
Toby a slave belonging to Armistead Churchhill dyed Septem^r ye 8 1723.
Frank a slave belonging to Gawin Corbin dyed Novem^r ye 16 1723.
Bristow a slave belonging to Gawin Corbin dyed Novem^r ye 18 1723.

Beck a slave belonging to Francis Timberlake dyed Novem' y° 22. 1723.
Tom a slave belonging to Mathew Kemp dyed Novem' y° 19 1723.
Frank a slave belonging to Mathew Kemp dyed Novem' y° 25 1723.
Kate a slave belonging to Frances Thacker dyed Decem' y° 2. 1723.
Hannah a slave belonging to Frances Thacker dyed Decem' y° 20 1723.
Jo a slave belonging to John Wormeley dyed Decem' y° 6. 1723.
Sarah a slave belonging to John Dodson dyed Decem' y° 20 1723.
Tom a slave belonging to Stockly Towles dyed Decem' y° 27 1723.
Nell a slave belonging to Armistead Churchhill dyed Jan'y y° 2 1723.
Dick a slave belonging to Armistead Churchhill dyed Jan'y y° 5. 1723.

   Bar Yates Minister.

Brownstown a Slave belonging to William Blackbourn dyed Jan'y y° 14. 1723.
Pen a slave belonging to Edwin Thacker dyed Jan'y y° 27 1723.
Will a slave belonging to Edmund Mickleburrough dyed Feb'y y° 4 1723.
Peter a slave belonging to Thomas Cheney dyed Feb'y y° 4 1723.
Betty a slave belonging to Anne Thacker dyed Feb'y y° 22 1723.
Jack a slave belonging to Catharine Warwick dyed March y° 2 1723.
Will a slave belonging to y° estate of Thomas Smith, dec'd dyed March y° 4 1723.
Peter a slave belonging to William Kidd dyed April y° 13 1724.
Kate a slave belonging to Charles Cooper dyed April y° 15 1724.
Joe a slave belonging to John Wormley dyed Septem' y° 15 1723.
Tom a slave belonging to John Wormley dyed March y° 5 1723.
Nan a slave belonging to John Wormley dyed May y° 2 1724.
White a Slave belonging to John Wormley dyed May y° 21 1724.
Silas a slave belonging to William Segar dyed June y° 15 1724.
Bess a slave belonging to Roger Jones dyed June y° 16 1724.
Hannah a Slave belonging to John Wormley dyed July y° 15 1724.
Jack a slave belonging to John Alding dyed June y° 30 1724.
Jack a slave belonging to John Robinson dyed August y° 19 1724.
Simon a Slave belonging to John Grymes dyed Octo: y° 16 1724.
Jenny a slave belonging to y° estate of John Vivion dec'd was drowned Sept. 15. 1724.
Jack a slave belonging to John Crockford hanged himself Octo: y° 30 1724.
Lucy a Slave belonging to Thomas Norman dyed Novem' y° 25 1724.
Mary daughter of Rebecca a Molatto belonging to S' W'" Skipwith dyed Decem' y° 3 1724.
Rachel daughter of Rebecca a Molatto belonging to S' W'" Skipwith dyed Decem' 17 1724.
Dick a Slave belonging to S' W'" Skipwith dyed Decem' y° 17. 1724.
Amey a slave belonging to Maurice Smith dyed Decem' y° 26 1724.
Rachel a slave belonging to John Robinson dyed Jan'y 15 1724.
George a slave belonging to Bar: Yates dyed Jan'y y° 19 1724.
Will a Slave belonging to Edmund Bartletts estate dyed Jan'y y° 4 1724.
Harry a slave belonging to Robert Daniel dyed Jan'y y° 20 1724.

Jack a slave belonging to Bar. Yates dyed April y° 21 1725.
Beck a slave belonging to Colo John Robinson dyed May y° 2 1725.
Robin a Slave belonging to Mathew Kemp dyed May y° 19 1725.
Winney a slave belonging to John Alding dyed May y° 22 1725.
Jenny a slave belonging to John Wormley dyed June y° 8 1725.
Seymor a slave belonging to Christopher Robinson dyed July y⁺ 5 1725.
Charles a slave belonging to Joseph Hardee dyed October y° 18 1725.
Betty a Slave belonging to Elizabeth Smith dyed Novem' y° 9 1725.
Hannah a slave belonging to Armistead Churchhill dyed Novem' y° 15 1725.
Dimond a slave belonging to John Wormley dyed Decem' y° 20 1725.
Letitia a Slave belonging to Oliver Segar dyed Jan'y y° 12 1725.
Sambo a slave belonging to Henry Tugle dyed Jan'y y° 30 1725.
Rosegill a slave belonging to John Wormley dyed Jan'y y° 20 1725.
Margrett a slave belonging to John Wormley dyed Feb'y y° 9 1725.
Anthony a Slave belonging to John Smith Sen' dyed March y° 1 1725.
Moll a slave belonging to Thomas Cheney dyed March y° 5 1725.
Jenny a slave belonging to James Bristow dyed March y° 16 1725.
Cæsar a slave belonging to John Price dyed March y° 26 1726.
Bungy a Slave belonging to John Grymes dyed April y° 4 1726.
Sue a slave belonging to John Robinson dyed April y° 13 1726.
Hannah a slave belonging to John Robinson dyed April y° 14 1726.
Jemima a slave belonging to y° Estate of John Vivion dyed March y° 26 1726.
Irene a Slave belonging to Wm Stanard dyed August y° 24 1725.
Will a slave belonging to James Smith dyed April y° 8 1726.
Will a slave belonging to y° estate of John Owen dyed April y° 11 1726.
Sambo a slave belonging to Humphry Jones dyed April y° 30 1726.
Austin a Slave belonging to Martha Williamson dyed June y° 5 1726.

    Bar Yates Min'.

Robin a Slave belonging to John Segar dyed June y° 7 1726.
Ben a Slave belonging to John Price dyed July y° 1st 1726.
Dick a Slave belonging to Rice Curtis dyed July y° 29 1726.
Tony a Slave belonging to John Price dyed August y° 7 1726.
Cromwell a slave belonging to John Price dyed August y° 14 1726.
Jack a Slave belonging to Robt. George dyed October y° 18 1726.
Jack a Slave belonging to Nicholas Bristow dyed Novem' y° 15 1726.
Dinah a Slave belonging to Mark Bannerman dyed Decem' y° 3 1726.
Mintar a Slave belonging to Rice Curtis dyed Decem' y° 10 1726.
Tom a Slave belonging to Rice Curtis dyed Decem' y° 12 1726.
Jenny a Slave belonging to Joseph Goar dyed Decem' y° 8 1726.
Charles a Slave belonging to Wm Blackburne dyed Decem' y° 15 1726.
Venus a Slave belonging to Wm Blackburne dyed Decem' y° 18 1726.
Corridon a Slave belonging to Wm Blackburn dyed Jan'y y° 5 1726.
Silvia a Slave belonging to Wm Blackburn dyed Jan'y y° 9 1726.
Sharp a Slave belonging to y° estate of Augustine Owen dyed Jan'y 1. 1726.
Lucy a Slave belonging to Wm Owen dyed Jan'y y° 19 1726.

Sarah a Slave belonging to Christopher Robinson dyed August y° 7 1726.
Mingo a Slave belonging to y° estate of John Price dyed Decemʳ y° 17 1726.
Cate a Slave belonging to Edward Clark dyed Feb'y y° 7 1726.
Tom a Slave belonging to Edward Clark dyed Febry y° 8 1726.
Matt a Slave belonging to Mark Bannerman dyed Febry y° 8 1726.
Commins a Slave belonging to y° estate of Francis Timberlake dyed Jan'y y° 23 1726.
Lettice a Slave belonging to Thomas Machen dyed Jan'y y° 28 1726.
Bridgett a Slave belonging to y° estate of Christopher Robinson dec'd dyed Febry 25 1726.
Sarah a Slave belonging to y° estate of William Daniel jʳ dyed Febry y° 9 1726.
Toby a Slave belonging to Frances Smith dyed March y° 6 1726.
Dinah a Slave belonging to Jacob Stiff dyed Febry y° 2 1726.
Sampson a Slave belonging to y° estate of Wᵐ Gordon dyed March y° 17 1726.
Robin a Slave belonging to y° estate of Wᵐ Gordon dyed March y° 17 1726.
Dinah a Slave belonging to Rice Curtis dyed March y° 26 1726.
Isaak a Slave belonging to Gawen Corbin dyed Febry y° 26 1726.
George a Slave belonging to Gawen Corbin dyed Febry y° 28 1726.
Robin a slave belonging to Gawen Corbin dyed Febry y° 28 1726.
Ned a Slave belonging to Gawen Corbin dyed March y° 1 1726.
Joan a Slave belonging to Gawen Corbin dyed March y° 8 1726.
Hampshire a slave belonging to Gawen Corbin dyed March y° 10 1726.
Devonshire a slave belonging to Gawen Corbin dyed March y° 15 1726.
Aberry a Slave belonging to Gawen Corbin dyed March y° 23 1726.
Winny a slave belonging to William Mountague dyed March yʳ 5 1726.
Beck a slave belonging to John Grymes dyed Febry y° 16 1726.
Ruth a slave belonging to John Grymes dyed Feb'y y° 18 1726.
Betty a slave belonging to John Grymes dyed Feb'y y° 20 1726.
Hector a slave belonging to John Grymes dyed Feb'y y° 26 1726.
Mars a slave belonging to John Grymes dyed March y° 10 1726.
Rose a slave belonging to John Grymes dyed March y° 10 1726.
Ralph a slave belonging to John Grymes dyed March y° 29 1726.
Sarah a slave belonging to John Smith dyed March y° 29 1726.
Hager a slave belonging to Armistead Churchhill dyed Feb'y 25 1726.
Peter a slave belonging to Armistead Churchhill dyed Feb'y 27 1726.
Sam a slave belonging to Armistead Churchhill dyed Feb'y 16 1726.
Daniel a Slave belonging to Armistead Churchhill dyed Febʳʸ 19. 1726.
Hagar a slave belonging to Armistead Churchhill dyed Febʳʸ 23. 1726.
Arrow a slave belonging to y° estate of John Wormley dec'd dyed Feb'y 10 1726.
Beck a slave belonging to y° estate of John Wormley dec'd dyed March y° 20 1726.

Sawney a Slave belonging to y⁰ estate of John Wormley dec'd dyed March y⁰ 12 1726.
Cæsar a slave belonging to William Gray dyed Jan'y y⁰ 28. 1726.
Greshear a slave belonging to y⁰ estate of John Wormley dec'd dyed April 15 1727.
Tom a slave belonging to John George dyed April y⁰ 22 1727.
Moll a Slave belonging to y⁰ estate of Thomas Smith dyed May y⁰ 5 1727.
Charles a slave belonging to Matthew Hunt dyed April y⁰ 23 1727.
Nan a slave belonging to John Segar dyed May y⁰ 12 1727.
Rachel a slave belonging to y⁰ estate of John Wormley dyed May 13. 1727.
Hannah a Slave belonging to y⁰ estate of Garritt Minor dyed May y⁰ 24 1727.
Judy a slave belonging to y⁰ estate of John Price dyed April 30 1727.
Bess a slave belonging to y⁰ estate of John Gibbs dyed June y⁰ 17 1727.
Petro a slave belonging to John Murrah dyed June y⁰ 30 1727.
Peter a Slave belonging to Henry Armistead dyed July y⁰ 9 1727.
Nell a slave belonging to Armistead Churchhill dyed July y⁰ 24 1727.
Nanny a Slave belonging to Bar Yates dyed August y⁰ 10 1727.
Sarah a slave belonging to John Rhodes dyed August y⁰ 26 1727.
Nanny a slave belonging to Henry Thacker dyed october y⁰ 1 1727.
Winny a Slave belonging to Thomas Cheney dyed Septem'r y⁰ 14 1727.
Tom Brideman a slave belonging to y⁰ estate of John Wormley dec'd dyed October y⁰ 5 1727.
Cromwell a slave belonging to Armistead Churchhill dyed August y⁰ 4 1727.
Venus a Slave belonging to Daniel Listney dyed September y⁰ 20 1727.
Bridgett a slave belonging to Armistead Churchhill dyed Decem'r y⁰ 15 1727.
Toney a slave belonging to Frances Alding dyed Decem'r y⁰ 14 1727.
Jane a Slave belonging to William Stanard dyed Jan'y y⁰ 1 1727.
Harry a slave belonging to y⁰ estate of John Wormley dec'd dyed Jan'y y'' 2 1727.
Pompey a slave belonging to Armistead Churchhill dyed Jan'y y⁰ 18 1727.
Tom a slave belonging to Sarah Murrah dyed Feb'y y⁰ 5 1727.
Toby a Slave belonging to John Fearn dyed Jan'y y⁰ 20th 1727.
Natt a slave belonging to y⁰ estate of Jno. Wormley dyed Feb'y y⁰ 17. 1727.
Hampton a slave belonging to Laurance Orrill dyed Feb'y y⁰ 8th 1727.
Nan a Slave belonging to Henry Daniel dyed Feb'y y⁰ 10 1727.
Oliver a slave belonging to Edmund Bartlett dyed Feb'y y⁰ 3 1727.
Robin a Slave belonging to Alexander Graves dyed Feb'y y⁰ 28 1727.
Jack a Slave belonging to Mary Hunt dyed March y⁰ 15 1727.
Peter a slave belonging to Stockley Towles dyed March y⁰ 17 1727.
James a slave belonging to Edmund Bartlett dyed March y⁰ 4 1727.
Bacchus a slave belonging to Wᵐ Stanard dyed Ap: y⁰ 4 1728.
Nell a slave belonging to y⁰ estate of Jnᵒ Wormley dec'd dyed April y⁰ 19 1728.

Frank a Slave belonging to John Smith dyed April ye 20 1728.
Crosier a slave belonging to Oliver Segar dyed April ye 17. 1728.
Crispin a slave belonging to Laurance Orrill dyed April ye 13 1728.
Sam a slave belonging to Laurance Orrill dyed May ye 1 1728.
Dick a Slave belonging to Richd Taylor dyed May y^d 18 1728.
Beck a slave belonging to ye estate of Jno. Wormley dyed June ye 19 1728.
Simon a slave belonging to ye estate of Jno Wormley dyed June ye 21 1728.
Peter a slave belonging to ye estate of Jno Wormeley dyed August ye 1 1728.
Scipio a slave belonging to Matthew Kemp dyed August ye 11. 1728.
Dick a slave belonging to Henry Armistead dyed August ye 29. 1728.
Sam a Slave belonging to William Thurston dyed August ye 25. 1728.
William a slave belonging to Bar Yates dyed September ye 29 1728.
George a slave belonging to Marvell Moseley dyed September ye 14 1728.

Bar Yates Min^r.

Dinah a slave belonging to Oliver Segar dyed ye 15. of September 1728.
Winney a slave belonging to Christopher Robinson dyed Octo. y^o 5 1728.
Toney a slave belonging to Matthew Kemp dyed Octo: ye 20 1728.
Peter a slave belonging to William Segar dyed Octo: ye 12 1728.
Tom (son of Beck) a slave belonging to John Grymes Dyed Novem^r ye 3d 1728.
Cate (Daughter of Cate) a slave belonging to John Grymes dyed Novem^r ye 3d 1728.
Mingo a slave belonging to John Grymes dyed Novem^r ye 28 1728.
Lucy a slave belonging to John Tugell dyed Decem^r ye 10 1728.
Nan a slave belonging to Edwin Thacker dyed Decem^r ye 8 1728.
Robert a slave belonging to Tho: Faulkner Senr dyed Novem^r ye 13 1728.
Ben a slave belonging to ye estate of John Vivion dyed Decem^r ye 16 1728.
Judy a slave belonging to George Hardin dyed Decem^r ye 17 1728.
Judy a slave belonging to John Crockford dyed Jan'y ye 10 1728.
Harry a slave belonging to ye estate of Tho: Smith dyed Jan'y ye 1 1728.
Gawen a slave belonging to Henry Mickleburrough dyed Jan'y ye 3 1728.
Judy a slave belonging to Henry Tugel jun^r dyed Feb'y ye 16 1728.
Mary a slave belonging to Richd Hill dyed Feb'y ye 23 1728.
Harry a Negro boy belonging to William Chowning dyed Feb'y ye 21 1728.
Jack a Slave belonging to ye estate of Wm Daniel jun^r dyed March ye 13 1728.
Thom a slave belonging to Thomas Smith dec'd dyed March ye 12 1728.

Maggy a slave belongin to Curtis Perrott dyed Feb'ry y' 26 1728.
Betty daughter of Winny a molatto belonging to Elizabeth Weeks dyed April y⁰ 10 1729.
Isaac Son of Jenny a slave belonging to y⁰ estate of Jn⁰ Wormley decd dyed April y⁰ 5. 1729.
Primas a slave belonging to Wm Owen dyed April y⁰ 26 1729.
Wooser a Slave belonging to Humphrey Jones dyed May y⁰ 1 1729.
Hannah a slave belonging to Ralph Shelton dyed May y⁰ 27 1729.
Wonder a slave belonging to George Hardin dyed June y⁰ 11. 1729.
Mingo a slave belonging to John Grymes dyed May y⁰ 29 1729.
Will a slave belonging to Elizabeth Weeks dyed May y⁰ 27 1729.
Dick a slave belonging to William Chowning dyed August y⁰ 10. 1729.
Charles a slave belonging to Thomas Machen dyed August y⁰ 26. 1729.
Jenny a slave belonging to Thomas Dudley dyed August y⁰ 28 1729.
Abigall a slave belonging to John Grymes dyed August y⁰ 30 1729.
Pancha a slave belonging to John Grymes dyed September y⁰ 10 1729.
Jenny a slave belonging to William Wood dyed September y⁰ 20 1729.
Della a slave belonging to Thomas Cheney dyed Novem^r y⁰ 4 1729.
Jack a slave belonging to William Segar dyed Decem^r y⁰ 5 1729.
Boson a slave belonging to Paul Philpott dyed Novem^r y⁰ 10 1729.
Tom a slave belonging to y⁰ estate of Hobs Weekes dyed Jan'ry y⁰ 24 1729.
Toney a slave belonging to Edmund Mickleburrough dyed Feb'ry y⁰ 2 1729.
Frank a slave belonging to Francis Porter dyed Feb'ry y⁰ 14 1729.
Betty a slave belonging to Francis Porter dyed Feb'ry y⁰ 14 1729.
Oliver a Slave belonging to Edmund Berkley dyed Jan'ry y⁰ 18 1729.
Rose a slave belonging to Edmund Berkley dyed Jan'ry y⁰ 18 1729.
Cashus a slave belonging to Armistead Churchhill dyed Feb'ry y⁰ 14 1729.
Alice a Slave belonging to Edmund Mickleburrough dyed Feb'ry y⁰ 20 1729.
Ben a Slave belonging to Robert Daniell dyed Feb'ry 25 1729.
Ned a Slave belonging to John Tugell dyed Feb'ry y⁰ 11 1729.
Lander a Slave belonging to y⁰ estate of Wm Gordon dyed Feb'ry y⁰ 2 1729.
Maulkam a Slave belonging to Alexander Frazier dyed Feb'ry y⁰ 15 1729.
Syfax a Slave belonging to Armistead Churchhill dyed March y⁰ 11 1729.
Robin a slave belonging to Armistead Churchhill dyed March y⁰ 14 1729.
Moll a Slave belonging to Laurance Orrell dyed March y⁰ 8 1729.
Alice a Slave belonging to William Stanard dyed Jan'ry y⁰ 16 1729.
Samson a slave belonging to James Dudley dyed March y⁰ 20 1729.
Harry a Slave belonging to Frances Alding dyed Jan'ry y⁰ 16 1729.

   Bar Yates. Min^r

York a Slave belonging to Matthew Kemp dyed April y⁰ 10 1730.

Sarah a slave belonging to George Harding dyed April y⁶ 25 1730.
Tom a slave belonging to Gawin Corbin dyed April y⁰ 26 1730.
Diamond a slave belonging to Gawin Corbin dyed April yʳ 16 1730.
Ruth a Slave belonging to Anne Smith junʳ dyed April yᵉ 21 1730.
Sampson a slave belonging to Thomas Machen dyed April yᵉ 20 1730.
Bob a slave belonging to William Chowning dyed May yᵉ 12 1730.
Jenny a Slave belonging to yᵉ estate of Thomas Smith dec'd dyed May y⁰ 25 1730.
Amey a slave belonging to Edwin Thacker dyed May y⁰ 28 1730.
Judy a Slave belonging to yᵉ estate of Wᵐ Daniel junʳ dyed June yʳ 18 1730.
Winny a Slave belonging to yᵉ estate of Wᵐ Daniel junʳ dyed June yᵉ 18 1730.
Charles a slave belonging to yᵉ estate of Wᵐ Daniel junʳ dyed June yᵉ 20 1730.
Beck a Slave belonging to John Curtis dyed July yᵉ 8 1730.
Mary a slave belonging to Thomas Cheney dyed July yᵉ 4 1730.
Sawney a slave belonging to Oliver Segar dyed June yᵉ 24 1730.
George a Slave belonging to Oliver Segar dyed June yʳ 27 1730.
Pat a slave belonging to Roger Jones dyed July yʳ 21 1730.
Frank a Slave belonging to John Smith Senʳ dyed March y⁰ 30 1730.
Jenny a slave belonging to John Smith Senʳ dyed August yʳ 6 1730.
Tom Son of Nan a slave belonging to the estate of Jnᵒ Smith dec'd dyed Augsᵗ y⁰ 24 1730.
Sarah a slave belonging to Edmund Berkley dyed August yᵉ 27 1730.
Jemmy a slave belonging to Frances Smith dyed Septemʳ yᵉ 25 1730.
Daphney a slave belonging to Frances Smith dyed Septemʳ yᵉ 27 1730.
Charles a slave belonging to yᵉ estate of Tho. Smith dyed October yᵉ 9 1730.
Bob a slave belonging to John Crockford dyed Novemʳ yʳ 6 1730.
Jacob a slave belonging to George Harding dyed Novemʳ yʳ 30 1730.
Harry a slave belonging to John Hipkings dyed Decemʳ yʳ 14 1730.
Tom a Slave belonging to Gawin Corbin dyed Decemʳ yʳ 24 1730.
Daniel a Slave belonging to Armistead Churchhill dyed Feb'y yᵉ 1 1730.
Jeney a slave belonging to John Moseley dyed Feb'y yʳ 1 1730.
Moll a slave belonging to John Burk dyed Feb'y yᵉ 16 1730.
Betty a slave belonging to yᵉ estate of Thoˢ Smith dec'd dyed Feb'y. yᵉ 11 1730.
Liddey a slave belonging to Jnᵒ Smith Senʳ dyed Feb'y yᵉ 10 1730.
Criss a Slave belonging to Edwin Thacker dyed March yᵉ 26 1731.
Jack a slave belonging to Henry Mickleburrough dyed April yʳ 25 1731.
Jupiter a slave belonging to Hugh Stuart dyed April yᵉ 21 1731.
Amy a slave belonging to Margret Daniel dyed May yᵉ 15 1731.
Letty a slave belonging to Collᵒ Edwin Thacker dyed June yʳ 25 1731.
Jack a slave belonging to Jacob Stiff dyed June y⁰ 30 1731.
Cate a Slave belonging to yᵉ estate of John Wormley dec'd dyed August y⁰ 20 1731.
Antony a slave belonging to yᵉ estate of Jnᵒ Smith dec'd dyed August yᵉ 27 1731.

Tom a slave belonging to ye estate of James Smith dec'd dyed August ye 28 1731.
Lettey a Slave belonging to John Hipkings dyed Septem^r ye 6 1731.
Margery a slave belonging to ye estate of Wm Daniel jun^r dyed Septem^r ye 27 1731.
Phillis a slave belonging to Mary Machen dyed October ye 22 1731.
Jenny a slave belonging to Henry Thacker dyed October ye 18 1731.
Moll a Slave belonging to Henry Thacker dyed Novem^r ye 19 1731.
Jenny a slave belonging to Stokley Towles dyed Novem^r ye 21 1731.
Phil a slave belonging to Sr Wm Skipwith dyed Decem^r ye 26 1731.
Hannaball a Slave belonging to Mathew Kemp dyed Feb'y ye 3 1731.
Cate a slave belonging to Margrett Daniel dyed Feb'y ye 3 1731.
Rosa a slave belonging to Hugh Stewart dyed Jan'y ye 27 1731.
Richmond a slave belonging to Armistead Churchhill dyed March ye 20 1731.
Ned a slave belonging to John Grymes dyed May ye 4 1732.

Bar Yates—Min'.

Betty a Slave belonging to Edwin Thacker dyed May ye 28 1732.
Beck a slave belonging to Thos Corbin dyed May y^r 15 1732.
Frank a slave belonging to ye estate of James Smith dyed June y^r 10th 1732.
Sawney a slave belonging to Henry Armistead dyed April y^r 20 1732.
Tom a slave belonging to ye estate of Jno Wormeley dyed June ye 18 1732.
Gunner a Slave belonging to ye estate of Jno Wormeley dyed July ye 6 1732.
Robin a slave belonging to Edwin Thacker dyed July ye 12 1732.
Harry a slave belonging to Edwin Thacker dyed August ye 3 1732.
Joe a slave belonging to John Grymes dyed August ye 5 1732.
Will a slave belonging to Margret Daniel dyed Septem^r ye 3 1732.
Old Frank a Slave belonging to ye estate of Jno Wormeley dec'd dyed Septem^r ye 1 1732.
Lucy a slave belonging to Matthew Kemp dyed Octo ye 8 1732.
Nan a slave belonging to John Crockford dyed Octo ye 20 1732.
Gilbert a slave belonging to ye estate of Tho: Smith dec'd dyed Novem^r 26 1732.
Kate a Slave belonging to John Marshall dyed Novem^r ye 15 1732.
Billey a slave belonging to William Wood dyed Feb'y ye 11 1732.
Winney a slave belonging to Robt Daniel dyed Feb'y ye 24 1732.
Frank a Slave belonging to Augustine Smith dyed March ye 11 1732.
Marlburrough a Slave belonging to Wm Mountague dyed March ye 12 1732.
Abraham a slave belonging to ye estate of John Smith dec'd dyed March ye 9. 1732.
Kate a slave belonging to Samuel Batchelder dyed April ye 27 1733.
Peter a Slave belonging to Hen: Armistead dyed April ye 10 1733.
Toney a slave belonging to Hen: Armistead dyed April ye 20. 1733.
Lucy a slave belonging to Thomas Price dyed May ye 20. 1733.
Phillis a slave belonging to Anne Smith dyed April ye 17. 1733.
Dinah a Slave belonging to ye estate of Hugh Steward dec'd dyed April ye 27 1733.

Toney a slave belonging to John Crockford dyed May y° 25. 1733.
Frank a slave belonging to Tho' Corbin dyed May y° 26. 1733.
Flora a slave belonging to John Grymes dyed May y° 12. 1733.
Cæsar a slave belonging to Armistead Churchhill dyed March y° 18. 1732.
Dick a slave belonging to Armistead Churchhill dyed March y° 18. 1732.
Ralph a slave belonging to John Segar dyed June y° 16. 1733.
Ambrose a slave belonging to John Grymes dyed July y° 3 1733.
Yango a slave belonging to William Owen dyed July y° 13 1733.
Venus a slave belonging to James Daniel jun' dyed August y° 14. 1733.
Mingo a slave belonging to y° estate of W'" Gordon dyed October y° 2. 1733.
Jemmy a slave belonging to Frances Aldin dyed Septem' y° 25 1733.
Jemmy a slave belonging to Stokly Towles dyed Decem' y° 8. 1733.
Bess a Slave belonging to Stokly Towles dyed Decem' y° 12. 1733.
Joe a slave belonging to Edwin Thacker dyed Novem' y° 13. 1733.
Cyrus a Slave belonging to Edwin Thacker dyed Decem' y° 8. 1733.
Dorinda a slave belonging to Edwin Thacker dyed Decem' y° 15. 1733.
Robin a slave belonging to Jn° Curtis dyed Novem' y° 10. 1733.
Cyphax a slave belonging to Edwin Thacker dyed Novem' y° 29 1733.
Scipio a slave belonging to y° estate of W'" Stanard dec'd dyed Jan'y y° 1. 1733.
Jack a slave belonging to Catherine Warwick dyed January y° 13. 1733.
Jack a slave belonging to Matthias Gale dyed Jan'y y° 26. 1733.
Sam a slave belonging to Frances Alding dyed Decem' y° 15. 1733.
Judy a slave belonging to Frances Alding dyed Jan'y y° 6 1733.
Gabriel a slave belonging to Mary Machen dyed Feb'y y° 7. 1733.
Bess a Slave belonging to John Williams dyed Feb'y y° 21. 1733.
Judy a slave belonging to Thomas Saunders dyed March y° 2d 1733.
Sarah a slave belonging to Edmund Berkeley dyed March y° 24. 1733.

Bar Yates Min'.

Ralph a Slave belonging to Christopher Robinson dyed Decem' y° 18 1733.
Simon a slave belonging to Christopher Robinson dyed Jan'y y° 3d 1733.
Phil a slave belonging to Christopher Robinson dyed Jan'y y° 20. 1733.
Harry a slave belonging to Christopher Robinson dyed Jan'y y° 10. 1733.
Diana a slave belonging to Christopher Robinson dyed Jan'y y° 10 1733.
Betty a slave belonging to Christopher Robinson dyed Jan'y y° 29 1733.
Phillip a slave belonging to Christopher Robinson dyed Feb'y y° 2 1733.
Joan a slave belonging to Christopher Robinson dyed Feb'y y° 16 1733.

George a slave belonging to Wm Buford dyed April ye 6 1734.
Bess a slave belonging to Wm Buford dyed March ye 23 1733.
Bluff a slave belonging to John Grymes dyed April ye 16 1734.
Gunner a slave belonging to ye estate of Thos Smith dec'd dyed May ye 2 1734.
Jenny a Slave belonging to ye estate of Jno Wormeley dec'd dyed April ye 15 1734.
Ben a Slave belonging to ye estate of Jno Wormeley dec'd dyed Aprill ye 22d 1734.
Toby a Slave belonging to ye estate of Jno Wormeley dec'd dyed May ye 7 1734.
Nocco a Slave belonging to John Grymes dyed May ye 20 1734.
Cromwell a Slave belonging to John Grymes dyed May ye 25 1734.
Bacchus a Slave belonging to John Grymes dyed June ye 2 1734.
Tom a Slave belonging to Mary Sadler dyed May ye 21 1734.
Peter a Slave belonging to Edwin Thacker dyed June ye 2d 1734.
George a Slave belonging to Frances Alding dyed May ye 30 1734.
Esther a Slave belonging to John Grymes dyed June ye 13 1734.
Sam a Slave belonging to Bar Yates dyed June ye 11 1734.
London a Slave belonging to ye Estate of Jeremiah Chouder dyed 7^{ber} 1734.
Rose a Slave belonging to Honble Jno Grymes Dyed Decr 5th 1734.
Ben a Slave belonging to Coll: Armstead Dyed August 18th 1734.
Ben a Slave belonging to Coll. Churchhill Dyed October 30th 1734.
Jemmy a Slave belonging to Wm Mountague Dyed June 23d 1734.
Nal a Slave belonging to Frances Bryant Dyed Augst 12th 1734.
Exeter a Slave belonging to Henry Thacker Dyed July 31st 1734.
Bristow a Slave belonging to Alexander Graves Dyed July 24th 1734.
Harry a Slave belonging to ye Honble Jno Grymes Dyed Augst 27 1734.
Hanah a Slave belonging to Matthias Gale Dyed October 28th 1734.
Sam a Slave belonging to Henry Tugle Dyed November 4th 1734.
Jack a Slave belonging to ye estate of Jno Short Dec^d Dyed November 6th 1734.
Jupiter a Slave belonging to Coll. Armstead Dyed Feb. 25 1734.
Peter a Slave belonging to Jno Curtis Dyed March 18 1734.
Dinah a Slave belonging to Jno Curtis Dyed March 25 1735.
Sam a Slave belonging to Robt Daniel Dyed March 26th 1735.
Judee a Slave belonging to Edwin Thacker Dyed June 21st 1735.
Will a Slave belonging to Mary Meacham Dyed July 8th 1735.
Buchan a Slave belonging to Alexander Frazier Dyed Octr 3d 1735.
Doll a Slave belonging to Thomas Corbin Dyed Sep^t 27th 1735.
Mille, Daughter of Lucy a Slave belonging to Jean Seager Dyed Octr 8th 1735.
Ben a Slave belonging to Coll. Armistead Churchhill Dyed Decr 11. 1735.
Frank a Slave belonging to Robt Daniel Dyed January 17th 1735.
Fergus a Slave belonging to James Reed Dyed Feb. 3d 1735.
Aaron a Slave belonging to Gawen Corbin Dyed Jan^{ry} 26 1735.

    Jno Reade Min^r

Hannah a Slave belonging to Lawrence Orrell Dyed Feb 21st.
Ishmael a Slave belonging to ye estate of Thos Smith Dec'd Dyed March 2d 1735.

Nan a Slave belonging to Humphry Jones Dyed March 5. 1735.
Jenny a Slave belonging to John Ridgeway Dyed Feby 19. 1735.
Bookry a Slave belonging to Gawin Corbin Dyed March 19 1735.
Simon a Slave belonging to ye estate of Jno Hipkins dec'd Dyed May 4th 1736.
Kate a Slave belonging to Matthias Gale Dyed Decr 8th 1735.
Kate a Slave belonging to Henry Tuggle Dyed Septr 29th 1735.
Sampson a Slave belonging to Henry Thacker Dyed Octob^r 13th 1735.
Judee a slave belonging to ye Estate of Jno Shorter Deceas'd Dyed Octob^r 26th 1735.
York a slave belonging to Laurence Orrill Dyed Octob. 6th 1735.
Azor a Slave belonging to Gowen Corbin Dyed July 20th 1736.
——— a slave belonging to Wm Goare Dyed 1736.
Harry a slave belonging to ye Estate of Wm Stannard Deceas'd Dyed July 19th 1736.
Annaca a Slave belonging to Armstead Churchill Dyed Sep^t 29th 1736.
Jenny a slave belonging to Jno Curtis Dyed Octr 15th 1736.
Roger a slave belonging to Jno Ryly Dyed Octr 13th 1736.
Simon a slave belonging to Jno Rhodes Dyed Octr 28th 1736.
Guy a Slav^e belonging to William Blackburn dyed 10ber 10th 1736.
Ben a Slav^e belonging to William Blackburn dyed Jan. 2d 1736.
Peter a slav^e belonging to William Blackburn dyed Jan. 10th 1736.
Old-Will a slav^e belonging to William Blackburn dyed May 8th 1737.
Little-Nan a Slav^e belonging to William Blackburn dyed May 13th 1737.
Sarah a slave belonging to William Blackburn dyed May 17th 1737.
Phebe a slave belonging to Gowin Corbin dyed 10^{ber} 25th 1736.
Doll a Slav^e belonging to Matthias Gale dyed Feb. 1st 1736.
Joe a slav^e belonging to Thomas Burford dyed March 23th 1736.
Ben a slave belonging to Gowin Corbin dyed April 24th 1737.
Phillis a slave belonging to Mary Machen dyed 10^{ber} 20th 1735.
Judy a Slave belonging to Alexander Frazier dyed March 16th 1735.
Harris a slav^e belonging to Mr Ralph Wormley died January 173.
Lawrence a slave belonging to Mr Ralph Wormley died January 173.
Abram a Slav^e belonging to Mr Ralph Wormley died January 1736.
Alice a slav^e belonging to Mr Ralph Wormley died January 1736.
Sancho a slave belonging to Mr Ralph Wormley died January 173.
Sangro a slav^e belonging to Mr Ralph Wormley died Feb. 173.
Jack a Slave belonging to Coll Churchhill died Feb. 18th 1736.
Mingo a slave belonging to Coll Churchhill died Feb. 25th 1736.
Frank a slave belonging to Coll Churchhill died March 4th 1736.
Punch a slave belonging to Coll Churchhill died March 28th 1737.
Harry a Slave belonging to Coll Churchhill died April 7th 1737.
Brutus a slav^e belonging to Coll. Churchhill died April 9th 1737.
Dick a slave belonging to Coll Churchhill died April 9th 1737.
Rose-Gill a slave belonging to Coll Churchhill died April 10th 1737.
Hannah a Slav^e belonging to Coll Churchhill died April 18th 1737.
Will a slave belonging to Coll Churchhill died April 25th 1737.
Kate a slave belonging to Coll Churchhill died May 8th 1737.
Mingo a slave belonging to Coll Churchhill died May 10th 1737.

Em^l Jones, Minister.

Antony a Slave belonging to Coll. Churchhill died May 13th 1737.
Tony a slave belonging to Coll. Churchhill died May 1737.
York a slave belonging to Coll. Churchhill died Jun° 1737.
Sango a Slave belonging to Coll. Churchhill died Jun° 1737.
Robin a slave belonging to Coll. Churchhill died Jun° 1737.
Bluff a slave belonging to Coll. Churchhill died June 1737.
Cæsar a Slave belonging to Coll Churchhill died June 1737.
Jenny a Slave belonging to Coll Churchill died June 23th 1737.
Scipio a Slave belonging to Coll Churchhill died July 10th 1737.
Betty a Slave belonging to Coll Churchhill died July 16th 1737.
Maria a Slave belonging to Major Berkeley died Jun° 20th 1737.
Abraham a Slave belonging to Coll. John Grymes died April 29th 1737.
Easter a Slave belonging to Capt. William Blackburn died Jun° 1737.
George a Slave belonging to Capt. William Blackburn died Jun° 1737.
Billy a Slave belonging to Coll Churchhill died April 18th 1737.
Juno a Slave belonging to Coll Churchhill died June 5th 1737.
Beck a negro girl belonging to Coll Churchhill died June 23th 1737.
Jenny a Slave belonging to Coll Churchhill died June 23th 1737.
Betty a Slave belonging to Coll Churchhill died July 12th 1737.
Tony a Slave belonging to Coll Churchhill died May 6th 1737.
Nell a Slave belonging to Coll Churchhill died May 22th 1737.
Grace a Slave belonging to Coll Churchhill died May 25th 1737.
Venus a slave belonging to Coll Churchhill died June 2d 1737.
Daniel a Slave belonging to Mr Christopher Robinson died 10^{ber} 14th 1736.
Peter a slave belonging to Mr Christopher Robinson died Jan 3d 1736.
Kate a slave belonging to Mr Christopher Robinson died Jan 4th 1736.
Lucy a Slave belonging to Mr Christopher Robinson died Jan. 6th 1736.
Hannah a slave belonging to Mr Christopher Robinson died Feb. 4th 1736.
Betty a Slave belonging to Mr Christopher Robinson died Feb. 6th 1736.
Tony a slave belonging to Mr Christopher Robinson died Feb. 10th 1736.
Jenny a slave belonging to Mr Chick^{e}ly Thacker died May 23th 1737.
Middlesex a slave belonging to Mr Alexander Frazier died August 14th 1737.
Jack a Negro belonging to William Owen dyed Novr ye 22nd 1737.
Frank a Negro child belonging to Armistead Churchhill dyed Novr ye 28th 1737.
Laurence a Slave belonging to Armistead Churchhill dyed Decem^r ye 16th 1737.
Mat a Negro Child belonging to Armistead Churchhill dyed Decem^r ye 20th 1737.
Middlesex a Slave belonging to Alexander Frazar dyed Augst ye 14th 1737.
Yassum a Slave belonging to Mary Hunt dyed Octo^r 3th 1737.
Letty a slave belonging to William Mountague dyed Decem^r ye 2d 1737.

a slave belonging to William Owen dyed Decem^r ye 20th 1737.
Harry a Slave belonging to Edwin Thacker dyed Febry. ye 6th 1738.
Minter a slave belonging to Co^{ll} Grymes dyed April ye 29th 1738.
Judith a slave belonging to Roger Jones dyed May ye 20th 1738.
Tony Son of Dido a slave belonging to Maj^r Kemp. dyed 1738.
Annica daughter of Kate a Slave belonging to Eliz^a Burk dyed June ye 11th 1738.
Nanny a slave belonging to Alexander Frazier dyed July ye 7th 1738.
Toney a slave belonging to William Lawson dyed July ye 3d 1738.
Cenes a slave belonging to Co^{ll} Armistead Churchhill dyed June ye 28th 1738.
Titus a slave belonging to Co^{ll} Armistead Churchill dyed July ye 18th 1738.
Rachel a Slave belonging to Co^{ll} Grymes dyed Augst ye 31th 1738.
Charles a Slave belonging to Co^{ll} Grymes dyed Sepr ye 6th 1738.
Jack a Slave belonging to Robt Daniel dyed Octr ye 19th 1738.
Jack a slave dyed June ye 12th, Will a slave dyed July ye 12th, Kate a slave dyed July ye 20th, Peter a slave dyed July ye 30th, Joe a slave dyed Augt ye 8th, these belonging to Matthew Kemp 1737.
Dianah a slave died belonging to Ralph Wormley 1738.
Jane a slave belonging to Ralph Wormley Feb^{ry} 23d 1738.
Robin a slave belonging to Henry Tugle Died Novr ye 19th 1738.
Dick a slave belonging to Co^{ll} Armistead Churchhill died Decem^r ye 20th 1738.
Will a slave belonging to Thos Shelton died Decr ye 14th 1738.
Jeney a slave belonging to John Blake Senr died Feb^{ry} ye 29th 1738.
Charles a slave belonging to   died Feb^{ry} ye 17th 1738.
Dick Son of Judey a slave belonging to ye Estate of Oliver Segar died Feb^{ry} 10th 1738.
Gloster son of Judy a slave belonging to Robert Daniel died March ye 11th 1738.
Sam a Slave belonging to ye Estate of Oliver Segar died March ye 23th 1739.
Moll, Ails, & Rachel three Slaves belonging to Co^{ll} Armstead Churchhill died May ye 5th 1739.
Moll Daughter of Bess a Slave belonging to John Segar died May ye 13th 1739.
Sarah Daughter of Mareah a Slave belonging to Edmund Berkeley died June 4th 1739.
Judy a slave belonging to Humphrey Jones died Augst ye 18th 1739.
Sue a slave belonging to Gawin Corbin died Jan^{ry} ye 19th 173
Ambrus Son of Mareah died Octo^r ye 10th belonging to Edmund Berkeley 1739.
Toney a slave belonging to ye Estate of Olliver Segar died Novr ye 30th 1739.
Isaac Son of Margery a slave belonging to ye Estate of Oliver Segar died Jan^{ry} 7th 1739/40.
Judith Daughter of Frank a slave belonging to ye Estate of Oliver Segar died Jany ye 19th 1739/40.
Margret Daughter of Letty a slave belonging to Eliz: Stanard died Augst 9th 1740.

Simon Son of Jenny belonging to the Estate of Matthew Kemp died March 20th 1740.
Betty daughter of Bess belonging to the Estate of Mathew Kemp died March 21st 1740.
Nanny belonging to the Estate of Richard Hill Died Feby 8th 173$\frac{9}{10}$.
George belonging to Mathias Gaile died Feby 2d 173$\frac{9}{10}$.
Letty belonging to Richard Corbin died January y^e 4th 1740.
Peter belonging to Churchill Jones died Feby 28th 173$\frac{9}{10}$.
Ned Belonging to Matthew Kemp died Feb'y 28th 173$\frac{9}{10}$.
Sambo belonging to Checkeley Thacker died Feby 5th 173$\frac{9}{10}$.
Deal belonging to Henry Thacker died Feby 6th 173$\frac{9}{10}$.
Malbrough belonging to Henry Thacker died Feby 13th 173$\frac{9}{10}$.
Grace belonging to Matthew Kemp died June y^e 15 173$\frac{9}{10}$.
Letty belonging to William Mountague died May 27 1740.
Cate belonging to Henry Tugle died September y^e 20th 1740.
Jude belonging to Henry Daniel died October y^e 16th 1740.
Stafford belonging to Richard Corbin died December 26th 1740.
Busbee Son of Judy a Slave belonging to Geo: Hardin died January 28 174$\frac{0}{1}$.
Frank son of Fortune a slave belonging to Thos Laughlin died July y^e 19th 1741.
Betty a slave belonging to Cary Smith died July y^e 14th 1741.
Hannah Daughter of Sharlot a slave belonging to Henry Thacker died Sepr 22nd 1741.
Hannah a Slave belonging to Mary Murrah died April y^e 1st 1741.
Diego a free negro died Sep^t 3 1741.
Dick Son of Sharlot a slave belonging to Henry Thacker died Decem^r ye 17th 1741.
Will a Slave belonging to William Bristow died Augst ye 20th 1741.
Phillis Daughter of Juno born in King Wm County and died in Middlesex June y^e 8th (belonging to Edm^d Berkeley) 1741.
Simon Son of Juno born in y^e same County & died in Middlesex April 7th 1741.
Daniel Son of Betty a slave belonging to Edm^d Berkeley died Decem^r y^e 10th 1741.
Jenny a slave belonging to Robert Fureman died Jany y^e 17th 174$\frac{1}{2}$.
Sarah a Slave belonging to Mary Graves died Jany y^e 18th 174$\frac{1}{2}$.
Natt son of Judith a slave belonging to Thos Mountague died Novem^r y^e 15th 1741.
Phebe a slave belonging to John Blake died y^e 6th of April 1742.
Charles a slave belonging to Co^{ll} Armistead died June 1742.
Harry, Dick, Judy, Tamar & Chance, slaves belonging to George Hardin died in Feby March 174$\frac{1}{2}$, & April 1742.
Sampson belonging to Phillip Warwick died July y^e 15th 1742.
Phillis a slave belonging to Thos Chilton died Novr y^e 11th 1742.
Susanna a slave belonging to Mary Roane died March y^e 15th 174$\frac{1}{2}$.
Will a slave belonging to Mary Roane died May 19th 1742.
Catherine a slave belonging to Mary Roane died May 13th 1742.
Sampson a slave belonging to Matthias Gale died June 15th 1742.
Sampson a slave belonging to Robert Daniel died Feby y^e 8th 1742.
Nassau a slave belonging to Jacob Stiff died April 26th 1743.

Ben a slave belonging to Mary Murrey died April 1743.
Simon a slave belonging to Hugh Spotswood Died May 1th 1743.
Tony Son of Willmott a slave belonging to Law^r Orrill Died June 12 1743.
Tony a slave belonging to John Rhodes died September 27th 1743.
Jack son of Rose a slave belonging to John Rhodes Senr died Sep^{ber} 27. 1743.
Scipio a slave belonging to Thomas Chelton died October 6th 1743.
John a slave belonging to Mary Graves died March 17th 1743.
Jenny Daughter of Daphny a slave belonging to Ann Smith died Sep^{ber} 28 1743.
Robin a Slave belonging to John Smith jun^r died December 16th 174–.
Sacco a slave belonging to Coll^o Gawin Corbin died Decem^{ber} 16th 174
Ann a slave belonging to Laurance Orrel died March 26th 1743.
Bob a slave belonging to Anthony Smith died March 17th 174$\frac{3}{4}$.
George a slave belonging to Ann Smith died April 13th 1744.
Sampson a negroe child belonging to Bev. Stanard Died 174
Joe a slave belonging to Thos Laughlin died Feb^{ry} 19th 1743.
Moll Daughter of Hannah a slave belonging to Thos Laughlin died March 3d 1743.
Jeane a slave belonging to William Hill died Novr 29th 1743.
Hannah a slave belonging to y^e Estate of Richard Hill died Jan^{ry} y^e 3d 174$\frac{3}{4}$.
Little Alice a slave belonging to Edwin Thacker died March 19th 1744.
Jeny a slave belonging to John Lewis died Octo^r y^e 16th 1744.
Jeny a slave belonging to Eliz^a Tugle died Feb^{ry} 15 1744.
Phillis a Slave belonging to Jedediah Bristow died Decem^r y^e 30th 1744.
Hannah a slave belonging to Jedediah Bristow died Jan^{ry} 7th 1744.
Willmuth a slave belonging to Law. Orrill died March 20th 1744.
Fillis a Slave belonging to John Alldin died July ye 2d 1744.
Judy a slave belonging to John Alldin died July ye 22d 1744.
Margret Daughter of Letty a slave belonging to B. Stanard Augst 14th 174.
Margere a Slave belonging to Jacob Stiff died 1744.
Gumbe a slave belonging to Jacob Stiff died 1744.
Cate a slave belonging to Robert Chowning died Novr 16th 1744.
Moll a Slave belonging to Mary Roane died April 30th 1744.
Bob a slave belonging to Charles Daniel died June ye 27th 1744.
Hannah a slave belonging to Thos Laughlin died Decem^r 23d 1744.
Jack Wilshire a Slave belong to Coll John Grymes died 1743.
Dick a slave belonging to Chicheley Thacker died April 17th 1745.
Kate a slave belonging to Eliz^a Burk died May y^e 1st 1745.
Sam a Slave belonging to y^e Estate of John Smith died Feb^{ry} y^e 9th 174$\frac{5}{6}$.
Glasgow a slave belonging to Matthew Gale Died July y^e 9th 1745.
Alce a slave belonging to Clary Daniel Died Augst 2d 1745.
Tom a Slave belonging to Ann Smith Died Augst y^e 16th 1745.
Daphina a slave belonging to Ann Smith Died Decem^r y^e 22d 1745.
Mille a slave belonging to Ann Smith Died Jan^{ry} y^e 11th 174$\frac{5}{6}$.

Isaac a Slave belonging to Richard Corbin died Feb'y y^e 28th 1748.
Robin a slave belonging to Richard Corbin died June y^e 3d 1746.
Samson a slave belonging to Edmund Berkeley died Octo^r 1746.
Adam son of Rose a Slave belonging to John Smith Junr died Novr 3d. 1746.
George Son of Hannah a slave belonging to John Smith Junr died Novr 13th 1746.
Will a Slave belonging to Eliz^a Tugle died Decem^r ye 28th 1746.
Dinah a slave belonging to Edmund Dillion died March 31st 1746.
Daphne a slave belonging to John Grymes Esqr died April ye 30th 1746.
Sampson a slave belonging to George Lee died April 12th 1746.
Harington a Slave belonging to Alexander Frazier Died May 22d 1746.
Rachel a slave belonging to Armistead Churchhill died 1744.
Tom a Slave belonging to George Wortham died Jan'y 21st 1744.

A Fragment.

John Son of John & Sarah Sanders born Feby 18th, baptized March 13th 1757.

The above extracted from the Register of Christ Church Parish by

April 2d 1774.   Samuel Klug

MARRIAGES.

Drawn off & sent to the Clerks of Counties wherein the marriages * solemnized.

Samuel Klug, Minister.

  * liam Corrie Beale & Anne Corbin (King & Queen) mar. May 26th 1792.
  * er Minter & Mary Matthews married June 17th 1792.
Thomas Saunders & Mary Stiff married July 29 1792.
John Southern & Elizabeth Bowers (K & Q.) married Sept 1 17 * *
George Dillard & Molly Batchelder married Septr 6th 1792.
George Humphris & Nancy Foudry married Septr 9th 1792.
William Brooking & Betty Daniel married Septr 22d 1792.
John Miller & Avarilla Saunders married October 25th 1792.
Richard Walden & Hannah Dudley (K. & Q.) married October 25th 1792.
Gabriel Jones & Elizabeth Healy married Decr 13th 1792.
Joseph Boss & Elizabeth Barrick married Decr 27th 1792.
Robert Bowden & Mary Garret (K. & Q.) married Decr 27th 1792.
Thomas Spann & Patsey Hall (Gloucester) married Decr 29 1792.
Francis Anderson & Frances Spencer (K. & Q.) married Jan'y 10th 1793.
William Palmer & Ursula Robinson married February 10th 1793.
Benjamin Walden & Mildred Didlake (K & Q.) married Feby 21st 1793.
Francis Shackelford & Mary Corr (K. & Q) married April 27th 1793.
John Darby & Lucy Harrison Churchhill married April 30th 1793.
William Kidd & Sally Stamper married May 18th 1793.

Tunstall Banks & Polly Murray Curtis married May 23d 1793.
Laurence Muse & Jane Southall married June 1st 1793.

A Fr*gment.

* iam C. Humphris & Elizabeth * * *
* liam Wake & Lucy Billups Powel Decr 21st 1799.
Augustine Blake & Sarah Robinson Decr 22nd 1799.
William Humphries & Elizabeth Davis March 2nd 1800.
Elliott Muse & Betty Tayloe Corbin May 3rd 1800.
Edwin Upshaw & Lucy Roane May 25th 1800.
Henry Hefferman & Lucy N. Berkeley Sep^t 28 1800.

by the Reverend Mr Smith.

Josiah Burns & Mary Garland Novr 29 1800.
John Mountain & Elizabeth Jones Decr 26 1800.

The above List given to the Clerk of the Court.

Henry Hefferman Rector.

* Do.

William George & Elizabeth Greenwood July 19.
Samuel William Sayre & Jane Grymes July 23.
James Healy Junr & Elizabeth M: Jones Octr 18.
Zachariah Crittenden & Catharine Jackson Octr 25th.
John Chowning & Catharine Blakey Decr 4th 1804.
Ralph Wormeley & Elizabeth Boswell May 7th 1805.
William Robinson & Martha Haines Stubbs August 22nd 1805.

The above List made out & Sent to the Clerk.

Thomas Cooke & Catharine B. Didlake Jan: 16th 1806.
Alexander Bristow & Nancy Brown August 9th 1806.
Benjamin Wiltshire & Nancy Kidd September 5th 1806.
Samuel William Sayre & Virginia Bassett Sepr 20 1806.

Henry Hefferman Rector.

Peter Son of John & Jane Bray was   June 10th 1767.
Betsy, Daughter of Jonn & Margaret Callaham born April ye 11. 1768.
Benjamin Son of James & Mary Kidd was born October 23d 1761.
Nancy, Daughter of James & Mary Kidd was born September 1763.
Jane, Daughter of James & Mary Kidd was born February 11th 1765.

From another book.

Robert Norman, Son of John & Alice Blake, Born May 29th 1775.
Samuel, Son of John & Alice Blake, Born February 17th 1777.
John, Son of William & Rachel Bristow, was born July 16th. 1777.
Thomas, Son of James & Mary Kidd was born June 15th 1778.
John Blake, Son of James & Betty Stiff was born September 23d 1776.
Elizabeth Baker, Daughter of James & Betty Stiff was born September 10th 1778.
Betty Daughter of John & Frances Thurston was born February 21st 1776.

Levi, Son of James & Elizabeth Dunlevy was born September 16th 1778.
Charles, Son of Benjamin & Franka Blake was born Nov' 21st 1778.
Alfred, Son of Joseph & Sarah Boss was born Dec' 26th 1778.
John Son of William & Sarah Boss was born Nov' 18th 1778.
Elizabeth, Daughter of Philip & Frances Montague was born February 2d. 1779.
William Newcomb, Son of William & Anne Newcomb was born February 4th 1779.
Elizabeth, Daughter of Charles & Ann Reade was born September 24th 1779. & baptized Oct' 27th.
Rachel Murray Beverley, Daughter of Harry Beverley & Lucy Yates was born February 24th & baptized March 3d. 1780.
Reuben Laten Son of John Parish & ――― his wife was born Dec' 8th 1779.
William Lewis illegitimate Son of Elizabeth Lewis was born October 10th 1777.
Anthony Son of Thomas Harrow was born April 19th 1780.
Ann, Daughter of Francis & Mary Bland was born June 28th 1780.
Daniel, Son of Daniel & Priscilla Jefferson was born September 14th 1780.
John Archibald, Son of William & Ann Murray was born October 9th 1780.
James Son of George & Sarah Brushwood was born Oct' 7th 1780.
Robert Beverley, Son of Beverley & Milly Daniel was born August 21st 1776.
Lucy Daughter of Beverley & Milly Daniel was born August 23d 1778.
Frances Ann Travers Daughter of Beverley & Milly Daniel was born January 2d 1780.
Mary Daughter of John & Ann Hibble was born June 19th 1773.
Elizabeth Stanard, Daughter of Harry Beverley & Lucy Yates was born August 7th 1781. and Baptized August 26th.
William Sourd Son of   Sourd in King & Queen was born Oct' 8th 1781.
William Latané Son of Philip & Frances Mountague was born Nov' 27th 1781.
John Son of Daniel & Priscilla Jefferson was born Jan' 14th 1782.
Laban son of William Corr of King & Queen born Jan' 3d 1782.
John son of W⁜ & Mary Bland born, Jan' 21st 1782.
Robert Son of Josiah & Elizabeth Bristow was born 22d Day of October 1781.
Laban son of William Corr born 3d of January 1782.
John, son of Daniel & Priscilla Jefferson born January 14th 1782.
John son of William & Mary Bland born January 21st 1782.
Valentine Son of Robert & Susanna Groom born February 14 1782.
John Batchelder Son of William & Ann George born August 3d 1782.
Susanna Daughter of Lewis & Judith Stevens born Oct' 27th 1782.
Mary Reeves, Daughter of Richard & Mary Bird was born November the 6th 1782.
Susanna Daughter of Lewis & Judith Stephens born Oct' 27th 1782.
Richard Miller, Son of Thomas & Mary Segar was born December 16th 1782.

William Chowning son of Churchhill & Ann Blakey was born January 30th 1775.
* * * * ter of Churchhill & Ann Blakey was born   *   2d 1778.
* * * * * * Churchhill, Ann Blakey was born * * * 1779.
* * * * lld Ann Blakey was born
William Son of John & Clara Daniel was born November 19th 1781.
William, Son of James & Betty Stiff was born March 19th 1783.
Thomas Meacham, Son of James & Betty Stiff was born June 7th 1785.
Kitty Taylor, Daughter of Mary Taylor was born December 14th 1776.
Patty Brooks, Daughter of John & Ann Brooks was born July 2d 1783.
Catherine George, Daughter of James & Mary Smith was born June 20th 1784.
John Richerson, Son of James & Mary Smith was born January 28th 1787.
Lewis Dudley, Son of William & Ann George was born the 16th of July 1785.
James Meacham, Son of William & Ann George was born the 27th September 1787.
Sarah, Daughter of Harry Beverly & James Yates was born January 13th 1788.
William Son of William George and Ann his Wife was born the 15th day of May. 1790.
John, Son of John & Lickey Minter, born January 30th 1783.
John son of Thomas & Judith Daniel born February 12th 1783.
Martin, son of Thomas & Sarah Ann O'Harrow was born April 16th 1783.
Lucy Daughter of Joseph Milbey was born May 23d 1783.
Thomas, son of Thomas Clark was born July 5th 1783.
Catharine, Daughter of Richard & Ann Cauthorn was born August 28th 1783.
Isaac Holloway, son of Edward & Catherine Brooks was born December 7th 1783.
Catharine Klug, Daughter of Harry Beverley & Jane Yates was born March the 1st 1784 & baptized March 14th.
John Draper, Son of John & Milly Parish was born March 12th 1784.
Martha, Daughter of Philip & Frances Montague was born April 30th 1784.
Frances Shackelford Daughter of William & Mildred Pryor was born June 22d 1783.
George, Son of George Dame & Mary his Wife was born March 8th 1784.
Thadeus, Son of George & Elizabeth Daniel was born the 18th July 1784.
Alice Berry, Daughter of John & Mildred Sadler was born July 25th 1784.
Lucy, Daughter of W^m & Mary Bland was born Sep' 16th 1784.

Lucy, Daughter of Daniel & Priscilla Jefferson was born October 7th 1784.
James, Son of Thomas Harrow was born March 30th —aptised May 1st 1785.
John, Son of Richard & Anne Cauthorn was born February 15th 178.
Betsey, Daughter of Major & Phebe Guthree was born November 24th 1785.
Elizabeth, Daughter of James & Elizabeth Dunlevy was born April 1st 1782.
Nancy, Daughter of James & Elizabeth Dunlevy was born December 22d. 1785.
William Foster, Son of Cuthbert & Elizabeth Snow was born June the 2d. 1786.
Robert, Son of James & Elizabeth Wilkines was born August 30th 1786.
Thomas Hill, Son of Daniel & Priscilla Jefferson was born August 10th 1787.
Elizabeth Averilla, Daughter of John Parish was born May 22d 1787.
James Son of William & Mary Hall was born February 11th 1788.
Ambrose, Son of Robert & Ann Wake was born April 8th 1788.
James Son of Benjamin & —— Dudley was born June 8th 1788.
George Meacham Son of James & Mary Smith was born Feby 8th 1789 & Baptized June 7th 1789.
Caty Price, Daughter of Henry D. Shepherd & Mary his Wife was born 13th of November 1790.
Matthew French Son of John & Mary Hibble was born July 22d 1790.
John, Son of John & Lucy Wilkins was born January 26th 1791.
Lewis Dudly, Son of William George & Ann his Wife was born the 16th Day of July 1785.
James Meacham, Son of William George & Ann his Wife was born the 27th Septr 1787.
Susanna Brooking, Daughter of James Batchelder & Mary his Wife was born Septr 3d 1792.
* * * * * * & Sarah Tugle was born January 7th.
* * Son of William & Mary Bristow was born Sepr 1st.
* * ty Daughter of Kilman & Mary Calehan was born Sepr 12th.
Robert Son of —— —— Wilkins was born September 9th.
Clara Daught^r of William & Mary Williamson was born Novr 13th.
James Son of John & Joanna Dunlevy was born Septr 27th
Hannah Daughter of Samuel & Ann Wood was born Decem^r 10th.
Sarah Daughter of John & Eliz^a Batchelder was born June 7th.
Elizabeth Daughter of William & Elizabeth Owen was born.
John Son of Edward & Mary Kidd born Octr 15th & Bapt^d Octob^r 23d 17.
Ann Daughter of Jacob & Susanna Blake born Novr 13th 17.
Thomas Son of Stephen & Ann Tenoe was born Febry 23d 175.
Frances Daughter of John & Mary Yarrington was born May 29th 17.
Curtis Son of William & Eliz^a Daniel was born Augt 14th.
James Son of Charles & Mary Hodges was born April 28th 17 *

Fanny Bowles Daughter of John & Mary Bowles was born March 27th 17 *
Josiah Son of Henry & Micah Blan was born July 5th 17 *
A Child was born (Daughter) of Daniel & Hannah Stringer Sepr 11th 17 *
Robert Son of John & Jane Chowning was born Decr 3d Bapt^d Janry 13th: 1754: 17 *
Mary Daughter of John & Eliz^a Lewis was born Janry 6th & Bapt^d 21st Do. 17 *
William Son of William & Jane Meacham was born June 12th 17 *
Philamon the Son of George & Mary Bristow was born Decr 31st 17 *
Ann Daughter of Robert & Ann Lenn was born Novr 20th 17 *
Elizabeth Daughter of William & Jane Mountague was born the 26th Day Augt 17 *
William Son of James & Sarah Deagle was born April 26th 17 *
Elizabeth Daughter of Cornelius & Eliz^a Deforeest was born Decr 10th Bap^d January 11 (1754) 175 *
David Son of Christopher & Ann Miller was born July 10th 175 *
John son of James and Jane Dunlevy was born Febry 15th 1754.
Joseph son of Joseph & Judith Eggleston was born Novr 25th & Bapt^d Decr 1st follg 1754.
James the son of William & Sarah Stiff was born March 4th 1754.
Mary Daughter of Philip & Mary Grymes was born Febry 12th 1754.
Gabriel son of Eusebius & Martha Lewis was born April 1st & Bapt^d 28th 1754.
Thomas son of Samuel & Eliz^a Batchelder was born Jan^{ry} 19th Bapt^d Febry 1754.
Nelson Son of George & Mary Daniel was born Febry 8th 1754.
William Son to Henry & Elizabeth Johnson was born June 10th 175 *
John Son of John & Mary Bowles was born Decr 24th 175 *
Benjamin Son of John & Martha born April 30th 175 *
Sarah Daughter of Benj^a & Dorothy Rhodes was born Augt 25th 175 *
George Son of Thomas & Rose Blake was born Febry 17th 17 *
John the son of John & Eliz^a Bryant was born Janry 18th.
Charles Mechen Son of John & Judith Wortham born July 18th.
John Son of Meacham & Eliz^a George was born Sep^t 19th.
Ann Daughter of James & Mary Berry born Novr 25th.
      & Rebecah Dudley born Febru 26 & Bapt
     Daught^r of John & Jane Beaman born July 1st
*   *   the Daughter of Edward & Rebecker Saunders born Febry 5th 1754.
*   *   Son of Edwd & Eliz^a Bristow born May 6th Bapt^d 26th 1754.
*   *   ley Daughter of Henry & Tabbitha Shepherd born March 7th 1754.
*   achel & Esther, Daughter of George & Mary Lee born May 24th 1754.
*   *   nnah, Daughter of John & Betty Cornelius Born May 21st 1754.
*   rances Daughter of John & Lucresey Greenwood, Born June 3d 1754.
Mary, Daughter of John & Eliz^a Howard, born July 17th 1754.

Anne Davis's Son John Born Janry 15th 1754.
Catherine Daughter of William & Elizᵃ Chowning March 13th 1755.
Mary Daughter of James & Frances Smith born Febry 16th 1755.
William Son of James & —— Green born Janry 18th 1755.
Samuel Son of Joseph & Mikel Batchelder born Janry 1st 1755.
Elizabeth Daughter of William & Sarah Robinson born May 18th 1755.
Richard Son of George & Jane Blackley, born Janry 25th 1755.
Mary Daughter of John & Frances Taylor born Febry 5th 1755.
Leonard Son of Robert & Lucy Daniel born March 10th Baptᵈ March 16th 1755.
Judith Daughter of Edward & Mary Southern born Jan'y 24th 1755.
Ann Daughter of George & Mary Blake born Febry 11th 1755.
John son of John & Elizᵃ Lewis born Feby 17th Baptized March 30th 1755.
Ann Daughter of Lewis & Bettey Mountague born March 30th 1755.
Elizabeth Daughter of Richard and Ann Daniel born Ditº 1st 1755.
Nelson son of Jacob and Winifred Rice born Ditº 21st 1755.
Judith Heptinstall daughter of James & Judith Heptinstall born March 27th 1755.
Humphrey son of Needels & Jane Hill born April 7th 1755.
Stephen Son of Stephen & Ann Tenoe Born April 26th Bapᵗ May 4th 1755.
Mary Daughter of Henry & Jane Sears, Born March 24th 1755.
Francis Daughter of William & Sarah Roan Born April 3d 1755.
Josiah Son of Josiah & Elizᵃ Brame born April 12th 1755.
Hannah Daughter of David & —— Snodgrass born Decʳ 3d Baptᵈ Janry 17th 1747.
John son of John & Lucretia Greenwood born Augᵗ 6th Baptᵈ Sepʳ 6th 1747.
Mary Daughter of George & Mary Lee born April 22nd Baptᵈ May 3d 1747.
* es son of Joseph & Eliza Collins born May 8th 1747.
ces son of Wᵐ & Ruth Bristow born Sepᵗ 25th & Baptᵈ Octʳ 2nd 1747.
  * * * born August 18th
  * * * Daughter was born March 4th
  * · * beth Lenn the Daughter of Robert Lenn & Ann his Wife was born Janry 28.
Margaret Beaman Daughter of John Beaman & Jane his Wife was born Novʳ 30th.
Frances Pain Daughter of Mary Guthery was born March 18th.
Elizabeth Thurston Daughter of John Thurston & Catherine his Wife was born March 3d.
Benjamin Pace Son of William Pace & Hannah his Wife was born January 28th.
William Bristow the son of John Bristow & Mary his Wife born Octobʳ 6th.
Elizᵃ Southren the Daughter of Edward Southren & Mary his Wife was born Sepᵗ 20th
John Mulins the Son of William Mulins & Mary his Wife was born August 23d.

Samuel Brooks the son of John Brooks & Martha his Wife born October 20th.
A Child of Tho' Berry & Catharine his Wife born Oct' 22nd.
Ann Deagle Daughter of William Deagle and Maryan his Wife was born July 6th.
Ann Daniel Daughter of Robert and Lucy Daniel was born 23d Aug^t.
Elizabeth Baker the Daughter of Benjamin Baker and Frances his wife was born.
Jerusha Bowls —— of John Bowls and Mary his Wife was born Sepr 20th.
Catey Horseley Daughter of Tho' Horseley and Rhoda his wife born Octr 1st.
Anne Williams the Daughter of John & Susannah Williams was born Decr 10th.
John Son of Major & Ann Pryor his Wife born Augt 24th.
Samuel Greenwood Son of Samuel Greenwood dec'd & Francis his Wife born Febry 26th.
Thomas son of Thomas Dudley & Joice his Wife was born April 21st.
Elizabeth Daughter of Lewis & Betty Mountague his Wife was born Augt 28th.
William son of Amey Mylls born January 4th.
Mary the Daughter of Samuel Thompson & Mary his Wife was born Octr 26th.
William Son of William & Betty born April 14th.
Mary Daughter of John & Joanna Dunlevy born July 8th.
Josiah son of William & Eliza Daniel born Decr 30th.
William Son of Charles & Ruth Moulson born May 7th Bapt^d 20th.
Alse Wilkin Daughter of James & Judith Heptinstall was born Sepr 7th.
Isham Son of Christopher & Ann Miller born Sepr 20th.
Jacob Urie Son of John & Constant Urie was born Decr 3d.
Rhoda Boss the Daughter of John Boss Senr & —— —— was born Sep^t 27th.
William Son of Churchhill & Millicent Jones was born Novr 17th.
Andrew Son of Andrew & Eliz^a South was born Novr 1st.
Frances Daughter of John & Eliz^a Batchelder born March 23d.
Agatha Daughter of James & Judith Campbell born Octr 8th.
Mary Daughter of Wm Brooks & Catherine his Wife was born Augt 5th Bap^d 25th.
John Son of Henry & Ann Washington born May 27th Bap^d the 29th & died 30th.
Jacob Son of John & Mary Rhodes was born May 6. Bap^t 17th D^o.
Elizabeth Daughter of William & Mary Williamson was born May 12th.
Mary Daughter of W^m & Jane Meacham was born July 18th: 1751.
John Son of Joseph & Mary Sinah born Octr 12.
Thomas Son of Thomas & Roase Blake was born Novr 8th.
Judith Daughter of Peter & Sarah Robinson was born Sepr 5th. Bapt^d 21st. Do.
Churchhill Son of James & Isabel Gibson was born April 15th.
Sarah Daughter of John & Eliz^a Cornelius was born April 22nd.

Molly Jones the Daugh' of William & Sarah Jones was born April 20th 1751.
* * * of John & Martha Brooks was born Dec' 29 * * *
* * * * * Betty Dean Born 1752.
* of W^m & Sarah Stiff was born Dec' 3d 1752.
* Daughter of William & Marg^t Rountree born April 26th 1752.
* Son of William & Eliz^a Chowning was born Dec' 11th 1752.
* Daughter of Ed^{wd} & Mary Southren was born October 23d 1752.
  Daugh of William & Ruth Bristow born Janry 12th Bap^t 28th 1752.
* iam Son of John & Catharine Thurston born Janry 3d 1752.
* Son of Rich^d & Ann Daniel born Novr 18th Bap^t 26th 1752.
* rles Son of John & Martha Shecard was born Octr 2nd 1752.
* Son of Jacob & Winney Rice was born Sep^t 28th 1752.
  rh Son of David & Dinah Barrick was born Augt 18th 1752.
  Daughter of Benjamin & Doritha Rhodes born July 13th 1752.
* s Son of Edward & Martha Dillard born Augt 25th 1752.
* * ma Daughter of John & Mary Patterson was born Decr 22nd 1752.
* * les Son of Charles & Ann Roane was born Octr 3d. 1752.
* * Son of William & Anne Sadler was born Decr 17th 1752.
  Daught^r of Henry & Susanna Mickelburrough was born Jan^ry 15th 1752.
* * jamin Son of William & Mary Mullins was born Febry 8th 1752.
* * y Daughter of James & Jane Dunlevy was born March 26th 1752.
* * uel Son of George & Ruth Chowning was born June 15th 1752.
* uel Son of William & Frances Guthery was born July 8th 1752.
* * hel Daughter of John & Jane Beaman was born June 12th 1752.
* nnah Daughter of Philip & Mary Grymes was born March 4th 1752.
* nces Daughter of Needels & Jane Hill born Dit^o 22nd 1752.
* y Daughter of Meacham & Eliz^a George born Febry 20th 1752.
* iam Son of Samuel & Eliz^a Batchelder born Janry 7th Bapt^d 19th 1752.
* am Son of William & Eliz^a Owen born Dit^o 12th 1752.
* ery Goar Daughter of John & Mary Herring born May 22nd 1752.
* mas Son of Thomas & Sarah Tugle born March 29th 1752.
* m Daughter of John & Eliz^a Anderson born April 7th 1752.
* hn Son of Samuel & Mary Bristow born June 7th.
* hn Son of Alex. & Eliz^a Reade born Febry 5th Bap^t 15th Idem 1752.
* Son of Charles & Ruth Moulson born March 21st 1752.
* nry Son of Ric^d & Jane Overstreet born Febry 20th 1752.
* ncy Daughter of John & Judith Wortham born Janry 20th 1752.
* verley Son of Robert & Lucy Daniel born June 8th 1752.
* braham Son of Lewis & Betty Mountague born Janry 6th 1753.
* nhey Daughter of John & Ann Bird born March 27th 1753.

* argaret Goar Daughter of Harry & Mary Anderson born Febry 20th 1753.
* shsha Daughter of John and Mary Brooks born Dit° 5th 1753.
* lizabeth Daughter of Robert Clemons & Jane Warren born March 16th 1753.
* mas Son of Richard & Phebe Burk born Dit° 29th 1753.
* Daughter of James & Martha Green born March 27th 1753.

From another book.

Registry of Births & Christenings.

Henry Hefferman Rector.

Churchhill Anderson Son of John Hodges & Mary his Wife born August 12th 1795 baptized Jan. 31st 1796.
George Son of John & Lucy Croffield born Decr 30th 1795. and baptized on Sunday the 9th of May 1796.
Wm Son of Daniel & priscilla Jefferson born November 17th 1791.
Diana Daughter of Daniel & priscilla Jefferson born Jan: 29. 1795.
   Registered this 4th of May 1796 at the request of Said Daniel Jefferson.
Eliza Churchill Daughter of John Darby and Lucy his Wife born on the 7th of November 1795. privately baptized & publickly received in Church on Sunday the 30th of October 1796.
Jacob & Elizabeth Blake Twins of Thomas Blake, and Inecy his Wife born the 11th of September 1791.
William Blake born 6th of January 1794. of the Same.
Anne Blake born the 15th of January 1796. D°
All baptized Sunday June 4th 1797.
Jefferson born Feb: 1798. baptized May 20th 1798 of Daniel & Priscilla Jefferson.
William Clark Son of Josiah Bristow & Fanny his wife born October 25th 1787.
Mariah Daniel Daughter of Said Parents born March 11th 1789.
Elizabeth Daniel born 24th of October 1793.
Frances Clark born July 10th 1796.
Robert Blakey Kidd Son of Thomas & Nancy Kidd born June 23d 1800. baptized Janu^y 1st 1805.
Mary Anne Kidd Daughter of the same parents born Decr 10th 1806 baptized January 1st 1808.

A Negro boy belonging to George Lee was born Octr 20th.
Negro boy belonging to Latané Mountague an Orphan was born Sepr 7th.
Negro Girl belonging to Christ^r Miller born Octr 19th.
Lucy the Daughter of Negro Maud belonging to ——— born Sepr 20th.
Patt a Negro Girl belonging to Edwd Blackburn born July 13th.
Will a Negro boy belonging to Gales Estate born Sep^t 12th.
Frank Daughter of Negro Jane belonging to George Fearn was born Novr 10.
Winney the Daughter of Daphne belonging to Thos Mountague was born Octr 14th.
Moll Rachel Serinah three Negro Girls belonging to Churchhill Jones born (at one birth) Augt 26th.

Winney a negro Girl belonging to John Jones was born Nov' 15th.
Lucy the Daughter of Chloe belonging to Cap' Wilcox was born Nov' 16th.
Thomas a negro boy belonging to the Orphans of Hump'y Jones dec'd was born Feb.
James the Son of Rose belonging to John Rhodes was born April 11th.
William Jackson the son of Phillis a slave belonging to Alex' Reade born Aug' 20th.
Mill a Negro Girl belonging to W'm Hackney jun' was born March 20th.
Poll Daughter of Jenny belonging to Tho' Buford was Born Janry 7th.
Judy the Daughter of Moll belonging to Mary Roane was born 9th Day of June.
Anna Daughter of Judy a slave belonging to Henry Thacker born Dec'.
John Son of Lena a slave belonging to Henry Thacker, born Sep' 7th.
Kate Daughter of Judy a slave belonging to Eliz* Burk born Oct' 21st.
Clara a Negro Girl belonging to Ann Daniel born August 1st.
Phill a slave belonging to Robert Daniel born August 10th.
Sarah a slave belonging to Henry Johnson born July 23d.
James a slave belonging to Gales Estate born July 12th.
Benjamin Son of Phillis a slave belonging to John Wortham born Dec' 24th.
Abram son of Bess a slave belonging to Alexd' Frazier born Nov' 22nd.
Billey son of Phillis a slave belonging to Beverley Stanard born June 11th.
Margaret Daught' of Betty a slave belonging to D° born Febry 10th.
Jacob a slave belonging to the Estate of Hump'y Jones dec'd born April 15th.
Nell a slave belonging to James Scrosby born May 2d.
Milly a slave belonging to George Wortham born Aug' 18th.
Sarah a slave belonging to Judith Gunter was born June 28th.
Beck Daughter of Frank a slave belonging to James Reid born May 8th.
Juda Daughter of Dinah a slave belonging to John Blake Sen' born May 5th.
Sampson a slave belonging to George Wortham born May 16th.
Agga Daughter of Jane a slave belonging to Tho* Mountague born May 4th.
John Son of Ebo Frank a slave belonging to Edm'd Berkeley born Sep' 10th.
Pompey Son of Rose a Slave belonging to John Smith born Dec' 23d.
—— —— Slave belonging to W'm Mountague Born April 17th.
—— —— Slave belonging to Do. born July 19th.
—— —— Henry Mickelburrough.
—— Do. born Do. 25th.
——ghter of Lettice a slave belonging to Thomas Sanders.
  * * a Male child belonging to the Estate of George Wortham dec'd born 175 *

Slave belonging to George Wortham born Febry 23d 175*.
Son of Daphne a Slave belonging to Thomas Mountague born Sep‘ 23d 1752.
Daughter of Sue a Slave belonging to John Wilcox born Aug‘ 6th 1752.
   the Son of Chloe a Slave belonging to Do. born Do. 12th 1752.
   Slave belonging to Joseph Sinath born 1752.
* ard a Slave belonging to William Meacham born April 17th 1752.
Daughter of Oder a Slave belonging to Frances Bryant born April 11th 1752.
a Slave belonging to Do. born June 4th 1752.
Daughter of Daphne a Slave belonging to Daniel Stringer born May 23d: 1752.
* aim a Slave belonging to Frances Bryant born Oct' 9th 1752.
* as a slave belonging to Charles Lee born September 22d 1752.
* braham Son of Frank a slave belonging to Richard Tyler born April 10th 1752.
* ll a slave belonging to Henry Johnson born 16th July 1752.
* Son of Doll a Slave belonging to John Rhodes born June 28th 1752.
a Son of —— belonging to John Berry born July 4th 1752.
* ah Daughter of Juda a slave belonging to C. Henry Thacker born Aug. 28. 1752.
* arry son of Jenny a slave belong'g to Dit° born Nov' 27th 1752.
* e Daughter of Ebo Frank a Slave belonging to Edmond Berkeley born Oct' 1753.
* chard a slave belonging to James Scrosby born Sep' 1st 1753.
* arah Daughter of Jenny a slave belonging to Edm⁴ Berkeley born April 24th 1753.
* wis Son of Hannah, a Slave Dit° born May 15th 1753.
* umwell Son of Dudley Betty a slave Dit° 24th 1753.
* dia Daughter of Beck a slave Dit° born June 13th 1753.
* emmy a slave belonging to Mary Clark born April 3d 1753.
Ben a Slave belonging to Eliz* Blake born Nov' 30th 1753.
Sarah Daughter of Mary a Slave belonging to the Est° of George Wortham dec'd born Oct' 10th 1753.
Harry a slave belonging to Christopher Robinson born Febry 24th 1753.
Sarah a slave Dit° born June 2d 1753.
Beck the Daughter of Nanna a slave belonging to James Reid born Nov' 1st 1753.
   ccas Son of Sarah a Slave belonging to Lewis Mt'gue born July 19th 1753.
* Rey Daughter of Nancey a Slave belong* to Tho* Mt'gue born June 8th 1753.
Bess a slave belonging to Christ' Robinson born June 24th 1753.
   a Slave Dit° born July 22nd 1753.
   a Slave belonging to George Lee, born April 25th 1753.
* ert Son of Dinah a slave belonging to Ann Wortham jun' born Dec' 11th 1753.
* binah Daughter of Phillis a slave belonging to John * *
   *   * of a Mulato Wench belonging to J.

Slave belonging Dit° born Oct' 7th.
a slave Dit° born Dec' 2nd.
* * ice a Slave belonging to John Smith jun' born June 15th.
Phillis a slave belonging to Ralph Wormeley born April 16th.
Abram a Male Slave belonging to D° born Sep' 10th.
Sam Do belonging to Dit° born Nov' 1st.
William Dit° born Janry 22rd.
Catherine a Female Dit° born May 24th.
Mille Dit° born July 24th.
Cate Dit° born Dit° 26th.
Beller Daughter of Jilson a Slave belong' to Rich⁴ Corbin born April 1st.
Aaron Son of Nona slave Dit° born July 12th.
Felicia Daughter of Judy a slave belonging to Henry Thacker born Aug' 2nd.
Nan a Slave belonging to William Hackney born Oc'' 12th.
Adam a Slave belonging to George Wortham born June 28th.
Jane Daughter of Beck a slave belong' to —— Daniel born March 18th.
Judy Daughter of Hannah a Slave belonging to George Lee born June 16th.
James Son of Chaney a Slave belong' to Mary Jones born Dec' 1st.
Sarah Daughter of Beck a Slave belonging to John Lewis born Aug' 23d.
Davie Son of Moll a slave belong' to Alex' Frazier born Sep' 16th.
Will son of Rose a Slave belonging to John Smith Jun' born Oct' 7th.
Simon son of Janna a slave belonging to W'' Buford, born Dec' 1st.
Dolly Daughter   a slave belonging to Edw⁴ Clark born June 26th.
Ann Daughter of Unity a slave belonging to Edw⁴ Dillard born March 16th.
Daphne Daughter of Nanna a Slave belonging to John Jones, born Febry 10th.
Peter Son of Frank a Slave belonging to Samuel Wood, born Janry 19th.
Jack Son of —— a slave belonging James Machan born Febry 16th.
Davy & Frank Son & Daught' of Frank a slave belong' to Eusebius Lewis born Dec' 23 17 .
Sampson Son of Isbell a slave belonging to Rich⁴ Corbin born Janry 19th 17 .
Dick Son of Grace a slave Dit°   born D° 23d 17
Judy Daughter of Letty a Slave belong' to Tho' Sanders, born June 20th 17 .
Charles Son of —— a slave belonging to Churchhill Jones, born Dec' 24th 17 .
Ambrus Son of —— a slave Dit°   born Janry 2d 17 .
Jane Daught' of Daphne a Slave belong' to the Estate of Rich⁴ Sheet decd born Janry 9th 17 .
Susanna Daughter of Mary a slave belonging to Tho' Clark born Janry 23d 17 .
Dey the Daughter of Rose a Slave belonging to John Rhodes Sen' born Nov' 6th 17 .
Isaac Son of Dinah a slave belonging to Ann Smith born Febry 4 17 .

Frank son of —— a slave belong⁵ to George Wortham born March 5th 17 .
Winne Son of —— a Slave belonging to John Boss born April 10th.
Nanny Daughter of ——a slave belonging to Armistead Churchhill born Jan'ʸ 24th 17 .
Joe Son of Cate a Slave belon⁵ to Matthias Gale born March 7th.
—— slave belon⁵ Ditº born Do 19th.
—— —— Ralph Wormeley born May 24th.
Do.
—— Son of —— a slave belong. to Armistead Churchhill born July.
—— Son of Moll a Slave belong. to George Wortham born Sepᵗ 14th.
—— Daughter of Maud a slave belong to John Smith dec'd born May 20th 1748.
—— Son of Rose a slave belong to Thomas Chilton born July 4th 1748.
—— Daughter of Phillis a slave belonging to Wᵐ Hackney junʳ born Aprˡ 3d 1748.
—— Daughter of Hannah a Slave belong to George Lee born Octʳ 17th 1748.
—— D. of a slave belong to John Berry born April 19th 1748.
—llir Daughter of —— a Slave belong to Ditº born July. 1st 1748.
—lle Daugᵗ of Nann a slave belong to Charles Daniel born April 21st 1748.
—llick Son of Kate a slave belong to Ditº born May 12th 1748.
—— Son of—— a Slave belonging to William Meacham born Janry 30th 1748.
—ll Son of Phillis a Slave belonging to John Wortham born Novʳ 3d 1748.
—ry Son of Moll a Slave belong to Alexʳ Frazier born March 18th 174⅘.
—ris Son of —— a Slave belonging to Armistead Churchhill born Sepᵗ 25th.
—ry Daughtʳ of Ruth a Slave belonging to Margaret Johnson born June 29th 1748.
—— Son of —— Margery a Slave belonging to Nicholas Dillard born April 22nd 1748.
—— Daughtʳ of —— a slave belonging to Edwᵈ Blackburn, born April 24th 1748.
—ck Son of Dick & Judy a slave belonging to Mary Roane born April 26th 1748.
—— Son of Jonay a slave belon⁵ to Thomas Buford Senʳₜborn Febʳʸ 16th 1748.
—— son of Margery a slave belong to Nicholas Dillard born April 9th 1748.
—my Daughʳ of —— a slave belong to Mary Clark born March 7th 174⅘.
—ewman Son of Frank a Slave belong to George Chowning born March 25th 1748.
—ter Daughtʳ of Oder a Slave belong to Frances Bryant born April 10th 1748.
—— Daughtʳ of Moll a Slave belong to Mary Roane born Augᵗ 20th 1748.

Peter Son of Ann a Slave belong to James Scrosby born Augt 28th 1748.
Billy By a Malato Wench Named Letty born Sep^t 16th belong to D^o 1748.
—loa the Daughter of Prudence a Slave belonging to Frances Bryant born Janry 30th 174$\frac{8}{9}$.
Dick son of Sue a Slave belong to John Wilcox born March 12th 174$\frac{8}{9}$.
—ane Daughter of Ann a Slave belonging to Mary Jackson born Janry 31st 174$\frac{8}{9}$.
Harry son of Chloe a slave belonging to John Wilcox born March 28th 174$\frac{8}{9}$.
Moses Son of Penelope a slave belong^g to Beverley Stanard born Febry 10th 174$\frac{8}{9}$
Penelopy Daughter of Phillis a Slave belong to Dit^o born March 26th 1749.
Kate Daughter of Lucy a slave belonging to D^o born March 26th 1749.
Ben son of —— a slave belonging to Churchhill Jones born April 16th 1749.
——— Daughter of Lucy a slave belonging to Humphrey Jones born June 24th 1749.
Nell Daughter of Lucia a Slave belonging to Henry Mickelburrough born Sep^t 18th 1749.
Beck Daughter of a slave belon^g to Nicholas Dillard born Octr 15th 1749.
Peter son of Betty a slave belonging to John Smith jun^r born Octr 30th 1749.
Anna Daught^r of Judy a slave belonging to Henry Thacker born Decr 28th 1749.
—— Daught^r of Sue a Slave belonging to Alex^r Frazier born
—— Daughter of Nelley a Slave belonging to
—— Slave belonging to W^m
—— —gh^r of Phillis a slave bel:g to Judith Wortham born Apri
Harry Son of Moll a slave bel:g to Lewis Mountague born Jun
James Son of Jenny a slave belonging Henry Thacker born May 29th 17 .
Will Son of Nanne a slave belong^g to Sarah Jones born June 25th 17 .
George Son of Lucy a slave bel:g to John Seward born Octr 5th 17 .
Kate Daught^r of Jane a slave bel:g to George Fearn born Decr 25 17 .
Christopher Junkins, Son of Lena slave bel:g to Henry Thacker born January 28th 17 .
Brimer Daugh^r of —— a slave bel:g to Jam^s Brown born March 1st 1760.
Frank Daughter of Lucy a slave bel:g to James Reid born March 7th 1760.
Rachel Daught^r of Sarah a slave bel:g to Lewis Mountague born March 18 1760.
William Son of Nanny a slave bel:g to James Reid born April 23d 1760.
Cilla Daug^r of Jenny, a slave belong^g to Edm^d Berkeley born March 1760.

Peg, Daugh' of Kate a Slave blong to Dit° born April 1760.
Unity, Daughter of Moll Carter bel:g to Wm Meacham born Augt 28th 1760.
Will, Son of Jane, a slave bel:g to Penelope Mountague born July 7th 1760.
George, Son of Hannah a slave bel:g to Philip Mountague born Novr 11 1760.
Jack a slave belonging to the Est^e of George Wortham dec'd born Sep^t 15. 1760.
Kitt son of —— a slave bel:g to Nicholas Dillard born April 15th 176 .
Toney Son of —— a slave bel:^g to Anne Jones born Janry 3d 17
Lede Daught^r of Render a slave belong:^g to Thos Sanders born Janry 24th 17
Lucy Daug^r of Nanny a slave —— born April 17th 17
Lewis, son of Jane, a slave bel:^g to George Fearn born July 7th 17.
Tom son of —— a slave belonging to John Seward born Novr 5th 1760.
James Son of —— a slave belong:^g to John Humphris born Decr 20th 1760.

Births of Negro Children.

Lewis Son of —— a slave belonging to Ralph Wormeley born April 24th.
David son of —— a slave belonging to Dit° born Septr 17th.
Izbel Daught^r of —— Dit° belonging to Dit° born Octr 22nd.
Laurence son of —— Dit° belonging to Dit° born Janry 18th.
Betty Daughter of —— Dito belonging to Dit° born Febry 23d.
Jenny Daughter of —— Dit° belonging to Dit° born March 7th.
Mason son of —— Dit° belonging to Dit° born Febry 14.
Nicholas son of —— Dit° belonging to Dit° born Dit° 19. 17 .
Minne Son of —— Dito belonging to Dit° born March 7.
Dick Son of Rose belonging to Edmund Berkley born July 17.
Abram son of —— Dit° belonging to Dit° born May.
Penny Daught^r of —— Dit° belonging to Dit° born July 5.
Joshua son of —— a slave belonging to George Wortham born Novr 12th.
Stephen Son of —— a slave belonging to Massey Yarrington born Septr 30th 1751.
Nell Daughter of Beck a slave belonging to Edmond Berkeley born June 1751.
Johnny son of Ebo Frank Dit° belonging to Dit° born Oct^r, Thomas son of Mariah Dit° belonging to Dit° born Novr 30 1751.
Sarah Daught^r of —— a Dit° belonging to Nicholas Dillard, born Augt 1751.
A Negro child a slave belonging to Thomas Boothe born Augt 13th 1751.
Judy Daughter of Hannah a slave belon^g to Frances Meacham Daniel born Nov. 20. 1751.
George son of —— a slave belonging to Churchhill Jones born Augt 2nd 1751.
Judy Daughter of —— a slave belonging to Dit° born Decr 19th 1751.

Dinah Daught' of —— Dit° belonging to Dit° born Oct' 3rd 17
Hary Son of Hannah Dit° belonging to Thomas Mountague born March 14th
Daniel son of —— Dit° belonging to Mary Jackson born Febry 8th
Moll Daughter of —— Dit° belonging to John Gardner born March 8th.
Jemmy son of —— a slave belonging to Churchhill Jones born March
James son of Great Nan a slave belonging to Lewis Mountague born Januy 11th 175 .
Lucy Daught' of Jenny a slave belonging to Thomas Buford born March 22 1755.
Jack son of Jane a slave belonging to Thomas Mountague born April 27th 7
William Smith son of Lena a slave belon:⁵ to Henry Thacker born Mar 14th.
Sarah Daugh' of Frank, a slave belonging to Henry Daniel born Feb'.
George son of —— a slave belong:⁵ to Gales Est⁰ born March 17th 1756.
Phill son of —— a slave bel:⁵ to Wm Meacham born April 12th 1756.
Moll Daugh' of —— a slave bel:⁵ to Wm Roane born May 26th 1756.
Easter Daugh' of a slave bel:⁵ to Dit° born June 26th 1756.
—— Daught' of —— a slave bel:⁵ to the Est⁰ of Geo. Wortham dec'd born Ap' 1756.
—— a slave bel⁵ to Gales Est⁰ Born.
—— Daugh' of a Slave belong⁵ to Wm Jone.
—bin Son of —— a slave belong⁵ to Nicho⁵ Dillard born May 5 1756.
—bin Son of —— a slave belong⁵ to the Estate of John Alldin dec'd born July 15 1756.
Fill Son of —— a Slave belonging to Edwd Ware born Sep' 6th 1756.
Sally Daug' of Letty a slave belong⁵ to Tho⁵ Saunders born Nov' 20th 1756.
—nny Daug' of Phebe a slave belong⁵ to John Bryant born Dec' 26th 1756.
Cloe Daughter of —— a slave belong⁵ to Mary Clark Ma^{ch} 25th 1757.
Easter Daugh' of Hannah a slave bel⁵ to Philip Mountague born Ap' 11th 1757.
—h Daugh' of Moll a Slave bel⁵ to Lewis Mountague born May 7th. 1757.
—ler Daughter of Jane a Slave bel⁵ to Geo. Fearn born June 5th 1757.
Sally Daugh' of Hannah a Slave bel⁵ to James Daniel, born Aug 20th 1757.
Cate Daugh' of Juday a slave bel⁵ to Dit° born Aug' 26th 1757.
Ben Son of Lucy a slave belong⁵ to Martha Orril born Sep' 2rd 1757.
Jane Daugh' of Jane a Slave bel⁵ to Penelope Mountague born Oct' 15th 1757.
Bristow Son of Nanny a slave bel⁵ to Philip Mountague born Oct' 19th 1757.
Sue Daug' of Jane a slave bel⁵ to John Meacham born Oct' 20th 1757.

Harry Son of Nanny a slave bel^g to James Reid born Octr 26th 1757.
Antony Son of Jenny a slave bel^g to Henry Thacker born Novr 6th 1757.
—— Son of Sue, a slave belong^g to Alex^r Frazier born Novr 23rd 1757.
—y Daug^r of a Slave belong^g to Dit^o born Novr 24th 1757.
—— Son of Lucy a slave bel^g to James Reid born January 10th 1758.
—z Son of Lena a Slave bel^g to Henry Thacker, born Janry 18th 1758.
Newman, Son of Odour, a slave bel^g to John Yarrington born Jany 6. 1758.
Moses, Son of Hannah a Slave bel^g to Nicholas Dillard born Feby 1st 1758.
Hope, Daug^r of Kate a slave bel^g to Gale's Est^e born Febry 27th 1758.
—ses son of —— a slave bel^g to the Est^e of George Wortham dec'd born May 19. 1758.
—te Daug^r of —— a slave belonging to Dit^o born May 27th 1758.
Milly, Daug^r of —— a slave bel^g to James Brown born July 6th 1758.
Nelson, Son of a slave bel^g to Willm Roane born July 12th, 1758.
Mansor, and James Son of Alice a Slave bel^g to Wm Chowning born Augt 27. 1758.
Betty, Daug^r of —— a slave bel^g to the Est^e of Gale born Sep^t 23d 1758.
Joanna Daughter of Nanny a Slave bel^g to Henry Thacker born Novr 20th 1758.
—— a slave belong^g to Henry Thacker born.
—— slave belonging to Betty .

—— born Sep^t 7th Bapt^d 27th Do.
—— Daughter of —— & —— South born Janry 16th.
—— Son of John & Ann Meacham, was born Febry 5th.
Lucy Daughter of Robert & Lucy Daniel born Decr 4th Bapt^d 26th Do.
Lucy Daughter of John & Mary Bowles born April 4.
William Son of John & Agathy Hardee born Novr 19th & Bapt^d Janry 10.
James Son of James & Jane Dunlevy born June 6th Bapt^d 7th Do.
James Son of John & Tabitha Fox born Octr 21st.
Ann Daughter of William & Hannah Pace born Novr 18th Bapt^d Decr 20th.
George son of Smith & Rachel South born Jan 11th & Bap^d Jan. 31st.
Judith Daughter of John & Christian Boss Febry 7.
Mary Daughter of Jacob & Ann Acree born June 9th.
Richard Son of Eusaleus & Martha Lewis born Novr 1st.
George Son of John & Martha Hudson born Janry 10th.
Frances Williams Daughter of John & Susanna Williams born Janry 31st.
Elizabeth Daughter of W^m & Rachel Brooks born June 17th.

Jane Daughter of James & Frances Smith born Sep^t 12th & Bapt^d Octr 18th.
Vivion Son of Henry & Susanna Mickelburrough born Novr 6th.
Thomas Son of James & Cassandra Machan born Febry 14th & Bapt^d March 3d.
Richard Son of Charles & Ruth Moulson born Octr 9th & Bapt^d Novr 8th.
Thomas the Son of Thomas & Ann Waid born Octr 26th.
Peter Son of W^m & Jane Mountague born May 13th.
Mary Daughter of William & Mary Blackburn born July 23d & Bapt^d Augt 9th.
Hannah Daughter of Jacob & Barshebe Rice born Febry 9th.
George Son of Charles & Penelopa Lee born May 17th.
Henry Son of Henry & Betty Daniel born June 6th.
Jane Daughter of George & Mary Fearn born July 5th & Bapt^d 17th.
William Son of Edward & Mary Southern born Augt 5th.
James Son of Richard & Phebe Jones was born Sepr 14th.
William Son of Edward & Ann Blackburne born Octr 18 & Bapt^d 23d Do.
Josiah Son of James & Averiler Cole born May 5th.
John Son of Jacob & Sarah Vallentine born July 11th.
Churchhill Son of W^m & Sarah Jones born Decr 30th.
Mary Daughter of John & Judith Faulkner born Novr 23d.
Christopher Son of W^m & Sarah Morgain born May 18th.
Ann Daughter of John & Eliz^a Lewis born Augt 3d Bapt^d 28 Do. 17 .
Lucy Daughter of John & Jane Chowning born Sep^t 1st 17 .
Elizabeth Daughter of John & Mary Rhodes born March 14 17 .
—— Son of Robert & Mary Bonds born April 4th & Bapt^d 11th Do. 17 .
—hn Son of John & Martha Brooks born Augt 28th 17 .
—hn & James Sons of Humphrey & Amy Garret born Augt 23d 17.
—ge Sons of Charles & Penelopy Lee born Augt 19th Bap^t 17 .
—— —— —— Tugle born Augt 25th.
—les Wood & Margaret Elegitimate son & Daughter of C.
—hanne Daughter of Charles & Mary Medeiras born May 26th & Bap^t June.
—lliam son of John & Anne Wormeley born June 26th.
—ah Daughter of Armistead & Hannah Churchhill born Sepr 4th Bapt^d 11. Do. 1748.
—mes son of John & Mary Bream born Octr 18th & Bapt^d Novr 20th 1748.
—lliam son of William & Elizabeth Healy born July 29th 1748.
Agatha Daughter of Rich^d & Ann Daniel born March 29th 1748.
—ess son of John & Constant Urie born July 8th 1748.
—— Daughter of W^m & Mary Williamson born Sep^t 7th Bapt^d 18th Do. 1748.
Mary Daughter of John & Catharine Smith born Sep^t 2nd 1748.
Elizabeth Daughter of John & Frances Taylor born Sep^t 17th 1748.
Churchhill son of Churchhill & Millicent Jones born Sep^t 27th 1748.
Mary Daughter of John & Mary Bowles born Sep^t 21st Bapt^d Octr 9th 1748.
—— son of Charles & Ann Roan born Novr 14th Bapt^d Decr 11th 1748.

John son of George & Mary Bristow born Novr 7th 1748.
—uel son of Samuel & Ann Wood born Novr 2nd & Bapt^d 20th Do. 1748.
—abeth Daughter of W^m & Ann Summers born Decr 6th 1748.
—— Daughter of Edwd & Eliz^a Bristow born Decr 8th 1748.
—— Daughter of William & Mary Greenwood born April —th Bapt^d 24 Do. 1748.
—— Daughter of W^m & Mary Mullins born April 4th Bapt^d 24 Do. 1748.
John son of George & Mary Blake born March 30th 1748.
Benjamin son of John & Susanna Seward born May 29th Bapt^d June 26th 1748.
—— Daughter of Robert & Mary Gibson born June 14th 1748.
Thomas son of John & Mary Norman born March 4th 1748.
—— Daughter of John & Jane Beaman born Decr 17th 1748. Bapt^d Janry 22. 174$\frac{8}{9}$.
—— son of George & Jane Blakey born Janry 18th Bapt^d Feb^{r}y 12th 174$\frac{8}{9}$.
George son of Robert & Ann Trueman born Febry 17 174$\frac{8}{9}$.
—atha Daughter of Henry & Tabatha Shepherd born — th 174$\frac{8}{9}$.
Mildred Daughter of John & Jane Hutton born Janry 13th 174$\frac{8}{9}$.
Mary Daughter of Lewis & Betty Mountague born Febry 24th 1748 Bapt^d Mar^h 26th 1749.
—— son of John & Frances Robinson born April 11 1749.
—— Daughter of John & Agatha Hardee born April 9th 1749.
Martha Daughter of John & Martha Steward born March 24th 1749.
Elizabeth Daughter of James & Dorrithy Davis born April 2nd 1749.
Doroth Daughter of George & Mary Lee born March 31st 1749.
John son of John & Betty Cornelius born Janry 10th Bapt^d Febry 12th 174$\frac{8}{9}$.
Ransom son of Robert & Eliz^a Durram born Janry 18th 1750.
—anna Daughter of John & Susanna Sords born May 20th 1750.
—jamin son of Thomas & Sarah Tugle born June 11th
—rah Daughter of Henry & Susanna Mickelburrough born May 22nd
—atherine Daughter of Samuel & Eliz^a Batchelder born April 29th
Mary Daughter of Joseph & Elen Beard born Sep^t 23d
William son of William & Eliz^a Dean born April 15th
—bert son of John & Frances Robinson born Augt 29th
—alph son of Harry & Mary Anderson born April 15th
—— —— —— Henry Gardner born Augt 11th 17 .
—— ——ghter of John & Mary Gardner born Augt 17th 17 .
——ions Son of Cornelius & Sarah Deforces born Sepr 27th 17 .
Judith Daughter of William & Eliz^a Haley born May 18th 17 .
William Son of John & Elizabeth Lewis born July 31st & Bapt^d Septr 2nd 1750.
Richard Son of Rich: & Ann Daniel, born April 16th. 1750.
Ignatious & Ann Son & Daugh^r of Robert & Ann Turman born Decr 4th. 1750.
William Son of William & Elizabeth Owen, born Febry 10th 175 .
Robert Son of Robert & Elizabeth Elliot, born July 14th 175 .
Thomas Son of Jacob & Ann Acree, born June 5th 175 .
Anne Daughter of George & Jane Blackley, born June 2d 175 .
Ann Daughter of Parrott & Eliz^a Prindle born June 25th 175 .

Ann Daughter of Tobias & Margaret Allen, born April 2nd 175 .
George Son of George & Mary Bristow, born March 27th.
Thomas Son of William & Mary Bristow born March 27.
Charles Son of Edward & Eliz^a Bristow born April 27.
Persilah Daughter of Edward & Eliz^a Whittecar born Augt 16th 1 .
Josiah Son of John & Agatha Hardee born, June 19th 1751.
Mary Daughter of Samuel & Ann Wood born, Dit^o 19 175 .
William Son of Daniel & Hannah Stringer born Sep^t 20th 175 .
Mary Daughter of James & Dorothy Davis, born Octr 18 175 .
John Son of John & Jane Chowning born Oct^{or} 4th 17   .
William Son of Henry & Tabitha Shepherd born Novr 24th 175 .
Elizabeth Daughter of Ambrus & Kezia Dudley, born Decr 27th 175.

Births of Negroes.

Dinah Daughter of Peg a Slave belonging to the Est^e of Charles Gunter decd, born Febry 7th 1754.
Esther Daught^r of Cate a slave belonging to Edmon Berkeley, born Febry. 1754.
Johnny Son of Jenney a slave belonging to Dit^o born January 175 .
Edward Skinner Son of Nanny a Slave belonging to Henry Thacker, born June 26th 175 .
Phil Son of —— a slave belong.g to Churchhill Jone, born June 27th 175 .
Phillis Daughter of —— a slave belong.g to Dit^o born July 2nd 175.
Cate Daughter of —— a slave belon—g to Wm Meacham born Febry 21st 17 .
Rose Daughter of —— a slave belon.g to William Jones decd, born May 4th –7 .
Charlot Daughter of Jenny a Slave belonging to Henry Thacker, born Febry 7th 175 .
—— Johnson son of Hagar a slave belonging to Jacob Stiff born March 18th 175 .
—— Daught^r of —— a slave belonging to Martha Orriell born April 8th 1754.
—— Daught^r of —— a slave belonging to Christ^r Robinson born April 15th 175 .
—m Son of Hannah a Slave belonging to Nicholas Dillard born May 5th –75 .
—n Son of —— a slave belonging to William Bristow born June 4th –7 .
                              Mary Clark born Decr 26th.
—upe Son of —— a Slave belonging to Gale's Estate born Sep.
—ster Daught^r of Jeany a slave belonging to Alex^r Frazier born Dec^r.
Joyce Daughter of Ebo Frank a slave belonging to Edmon Berkeley born Dec.
Hannah Daught^r of Tamer a slave belon:g to John Rhodes born Sep^t 5th 1754.
Betty Daught^r of Nanny a Slave belonging to James Reid born Decr 27th 1754.
Betty Daughter of Sue a Slave belonging to John Meacham born Sep^t 9th 1754.
Sam Son of Moll a Slave belonging to Lewis Mountague born Octr 1. 1754.

Ailce Daught' of —— a slave belonging to the Est⁰ of George Wortham Decd born Nov' 21st 1754.
Nann Daught' of —— a slave belonging to Christ' Robinson born June 14th 17 .
Grace Daught' of —— a slave belonging to Dit⁰ born Nov' 28. 175 .
Penny Daughter of —— belonging to Henry Mickelborough born Apr¹ 10th 175 .
James Son of Prudence a Slave belonging to Frances Bryant born March 14th 1755.
Wall Son of Daphne a Slave belonging to Thomas Mountague, born Febry 6th 1755.
Peg Daught' of —— a slave belonging to Christ' Robinson, born Janry 11th 1755.
Will Son of —— a slave belonging to Dit⁰ born February 21st 1755.
Ned & Tom Sons of —— belonging to Dit⁰ born Dit⁰ 27th 1755.
Booker Son of Frank a slave belonging to John Wortham born Janry 4th 1755.
Meney Son of —— a slave belonging to Thomas Sanders born Janry 15th 1755.
Nathaniel Wilson, Son of Phillis, a slave belonging to John Wortham born July 27th 1755.
Tom Son —— belonging to John Berry born Feby 4th 1755.
John Son of a Slave belonging to Frances Orril, born May 12th 1755.
Peter, Son of Jane a slave belonging to Tho⁵ Mountague born May 17th 1755.
Margery, Daugh' of a Slave belonging to Nicholas Dillard born May 25th 1755.
Henry, Son of Lena a Slave belonging to Henry Thacker born June 10th 1755.
Peter Son of a slave belonging to Joseph Batchelder born July 9th 1755.
Sam, Son of Bess belonging to Wͫ Jones's orphans born July 25th 1755.
Criss Daughter of Nann a slave belonging to Sarah Jones born June 20th 1755.
Lettey Daughter of Phebe a slave belonging to John Bryan born Sep' 7th 1755.
Daphney, Daug' of Frank a slave belonging to Rich⁴ Taylor born Oct' 3. 1755.
William & Harry sons of Moll a slave belonging to Jane Whan, born Oct' 20th 175 .
Robert, Son of Kate a slave belonging to Charles Lee born Oct' 18th 17 .
Dilce Daug' of Betty a slave belonging to Beverley Stanard born Nov' 23d 175 .
Thomas Son of Jenny a slave belonging to Henry Thacker born Dec' 8th.
Frances, Daughter of Nanny a slave a slave belonging to Dit⁰ born Dec.
Isan Daughter of Lucy a a slave belong⁵ to Dit⁰ born Aug¹
Elizabeth, Daughter of a slave belonging to James Green born Dec' 14th.

* ank Daughter of a slave belonging to the Estate of George Wortham dec'd born Decr 17th.
Beck Daugh^r of Rose a slave belong^g to John Rhodes born
* amuel, son of a slave belg to Chr^r Robinson born Janry 16th
* A Female Negro * *

From another book.
Registry of Marriages Commencing May 19th 1795.

Henry Hefferman Rector.

Leonard George & Margaret Vance married by Licence August 6th 1795.
James Kidd & Caty Meckelborough married by License August 15 1795.
Richard Cooke & Eliza Blueford married by Licence September 6th 1795.
Vincint Yarrington & Elizabeth B. Stiffe married by Licence November 5th 1795.
Meacham Wortham & Joana Wake married by Licence November 14th 1795.
George Shepherd & Unice Tuning married by Licence November 21st 1795.
Francis Corbin & Ann Munford Beverley of Essex C° married by Licence at Blandfield December 3rd 1795.

The above List made off & sent to the Clerk of the County.

Marriages commencing January 1st 1796.

William Nelson Stiffe & Sarah Healy married by Licence Thursday January 28th 1796.
Peter Robinson & Nancy Stiffe Thursday Feb: 18th 1796.
Tom Stiffe & Elizabeth Davis Saturday Feb. 20th 1796.
John Layton Junr & Lucy Wilkins Novr 17th 1796.
Paulin Anderson Blackburn & Sally Hodges Jan: 10th 1797.
John Seward & Mary Shepherd February 2nd 1797.
Richard Henry Corbin & Betty Taylor Corbin Feb: 10th 1797.
John Trigg & Susanna Collier of Gloucester March 30th 1797.
William Layton & Mary Atkins April 1st 1797.
Thomas Healy & Frances Montague May 6th 1797.
Charles Brown & Catharine Hackney July 8th 1797.
Archibald Richie & Patsey Hepkins Roane July 25th 1797.
John Quarles & Elizabeth S. Yates October 12th 1797.
Stapleton Davis & Alice Blake Novr 23rd 1797.
Zachariah Collins & Ann Burton Decr 1st 1797.

Henry Heffernan Rector.

The above List was given to the Clerk of the County.

Matthew Glen & Elizabeth Garland Decr 26th 1797.
James Owen & Winny Bennett January 27th 1798.
Augustine Blake & Peggy Marshall June 23rd 1798.
Robert Long & Johanna Blake July 5th 1798.
Samuel Blake & Sarah Wood Sepr 20th 1798.
James Wiatt & Fanny Curtis October 10th 1798.

Robert U. Blake & Letetia Baldry November 20th 1798.
John Murray & Lucy Sutton December 25th 1798.
John Blake Long & Sarah Blake Dec' 30th 1798.
                                    Henry Heffernan Rector.
   The above List was given to the Clerk of the County.
Thomas Cooke & Rachel Murray Beverley Yeates married Jan: 15th 1799.
John Tayloe Corbin & Juliet Muse married January 31st 1799.
John Spencer & Molly Cooke of King & Queen February 7th
William Robinson & Frances Healy February 28th.
John Waller & Nancy Sears of Gloucester March 7th 1799.
Eli Taylor & Elizabeth Dudley May 4th 1799.
Samuel Montague & Elizabeth Stannard Montague July 11th 1799.
Thomas Sears & Catey Collier August 1st 1799.
—— —— Harriet Murray September 16th 1799.
—— —— Wiatt Nov' 14th 1799.
John B. Stiffe & Lucy Siblee January 3rd 1801.
Thomas Kidd & Anne Blakey February 5th 1801.
Samuel Stamper & Sally Kidd April 4th 1801.
Robert Barrick & Lucinda L. Jackson April 23rd 1801.
Matthew Kemp & Lucy Daniel May 21st 1801.
Thomas L. Churchill & Elizabeth B. Berkeley May 28th
Berrin Abbot & Nancy Dejarnett June 18th 1801.
Thomas R. Corr & Mary Anne Bland August 27th 1801.
William C. Humphrees & Sarah McGeehee Sep' 15th 1801.
Edward McGehee & Caroline C. Jones Dec' 7th 1801.
Benjamin Marable Jun' & Mary Lyell Dec' 10th 1801.
Staige Humphries & Diana Barrick December 12th 1801.
Thomas T. Montague & Elizabeth Montague Dec' 19th 1801.
Meacham Wortham & Lucy Bristow January 6th 1802.
William C. Blakey & Jane Healy January 28th 1802.
John Major & Mary Murray February 6th 1802.
William Curtis & Ariana Maria Grymes February 6th 1802.
Charles Robinson & Elizabeth Wood February 18th 1802.
Henry Blakey & Frances O. George August 29th 1802.
Isaac Reveer & Sarah Barrick Dec' 30th 1802.
John Siblee & Ann Barrick Nov' 4th 1802.
   The above List made out & given to the Clerk.
Nelson Stamper & Elizabeth Meacham Jan: 13th 1803.
Ransone Wake & Mary Elliot February 10th 1803.
Henry Gaines & Mira Muse March 10th 1803.
Edmund Read & Lucy Cloudas June 30th 1803.
William St. John & Nancy Harwood Sep' 1st 1803.
James Hopkins & Susanna Davis Nov' 10th 1803.
John Robinson & Susanna Blake Jan. 1 1804.
Charles Gibson & Nancy Mickleborough   13th 1804.
Tayloe Braxton & Anna Frances Maria Corbin Mar: 6th 1804.
John George & Jane Meacham March 29th 1804.
William George & Patty Jacobs married April 12th.
Philip Grymes & Sarah R. Steptoe May 20th.
George Layton & Catharine Adkinson May 20th 1807.
Beverley A. Blake & Nancy Reed July 15th 1807.

John Battaile & Mary Willis Dangerfield Nov' 18. 1807.
John Darby & Lucy B. Churchill Dec' 15. 1807.
James Baytop & Catharine K. Yates Dec' 31. 1807.
Matthew Major & Elizabeth Blakey Jan'' 30. 1808.
John Bristow & Mary Watson Jan. 31. 1808.
   The above List sent to the Clerk Middlesex.
Robert Blakey & Frances D. Roane Oct' 12. 1808.
Thomas Street & Nancy Owen Dec' 14. 1809.
George Henly & Harriet Roane Dec' 21st 1809.
Thomas Evans & Sarah S. Montague Jan 22. 1810.
James Chowning & Maria Sutton June 7th 1810.
Isaac Kidd & Lucy Lee Sep' 3rd 1811.
George D. Nicolson & S. T. Wormeley Dec' 4. 1811.
Rich'd M. Segar & P. Roane January 16. 1812.
John Bristow & Nancy Walden Feb. 1st 1812.
Isaac Jones & Betsey Owen June 5th 1811.
Southey Derby & Agnes Powell married July 7.
Jeremiah Spencer & Mary Blackburn married July 15th 1769.
Thomas Roberts & Mildred Goslin married August 20th 1769.
Daniel Jefferson & Mary Dunlavy married October 19th 1769.
Thomas Layton & Elizabeth Rhodes married October 27th 1769.
John South & Sarah Sears married November 2d 1769.
Churchhill Jones & Judith Churchhill married November 11th 1769.
George Blake & Judith Healy married December 23d 1769.
William Matthews & Lucy Hudgings married Dec' 24th 1769.
John Hibble & Anne Robinson married December 24th 1769.
   Marriages for the Year of our Lord 1770.
John Clare & Susanna Davis married January 14th 1770.
Hugh Walker & Catherine Morgan married January 20th 1770.
Philip Sears & Frances Bryan married January 23d 1770.
William Jeffries & Esther Lee married February 10th 1770.
Daniel Turner & Catharine Montague married February 17th 1770.
            Samuel Klug, Minister.
David Ker of King & Queen County & Frances Tucker married
   August 8th 1771.
Lewis Boss & Anne Deagle married August 14th 1771.
John Mactyer & Susanna Clark married Oct' 16th 1771.
Anderson Miller & Dorothy Berry married Oct' 17. 1771.
Asher Bray & Sally Tuggle married Nov' 3d 1771.
James Dunlevy & Anne Belfore married Nov' 30th 1771.
Benjamin Seward & Anne Blake married Dec' 12th 1771.
John Sanders & Anne Clare married Dec' 14th 1771.
Isaac Stephens & Elizabeth Wroe married Dec' 17 1771.
Robert M°Tyer & Fanny Lee married Dec' 24 1771.
William Patterson & Elizabeth Southern married Dec' 28 1771.
John Bagot & Mary Wortham married January 8th. 1772.
Moses Matthews & Alice Hiptinstall married Jan'' 9th 1772.
John Richeson & Mary George married March 29th 1772.
Robert Longest & Betty Dudley married July 5th 1772.
John Daniel & Clara Williamson married August 2d 1772.
            Samuel Klug, Minister.

Births & Christenings for the Year of our Lord. 1770.

Felicia Daughter of Gawin Corbin & Johanna his Wife was born February 1st 1770 & baptized Feb'y 11th.
Len Son of Richard & Mary Bristow was born January 18th 1770. & baptized Feb'y 13th.
William Nelson Son of William & Sarah Stiff was born Jan 30th 1770. & baptized Feb'y 28th.
Sally Willcocks Daughter of Mary Willcocks was   *   January 1st 1770 & baptized March 18th.
Bartholomew Son of Bartholomew & Anne Yates   *   January 17th 1770 & baptized March 25th.
William Blake, the Son of Jacob & Susanna Blake was born September 2d. 1770.
William Robinson Son of Charles & Anne Robinson was born June 10th 1770.
Edward Jones Bristow Son of Benj^a & Elizabeth Bristow was born June 16th 1770.
William Son of John & Margaret Callaham was born January 1st 1770.
Polly, Daughter of Daniel & Mary Jefferson was born Novr 7th 1770.
Dorothy Daughter of Joseph & Ann Parrott was born February 25th 1770.

Johnny Son of Jenney a Slave belonging to Harry Beverley born Feb'y 1.
Hannah daughter of Kate a slave belonging to Henry Tugell born March 2.
Lucy daughter of Frank a slave belonging to Matthew Kemp born March ye 30.
Hannah daughter of Dye a Slave belonging to John Mosely born Ap: ye 6.
Dinah daughter of Alice a slave belonging to Robt Daniel sen^r born May 17.
James Son of Sarah a Slave belonging to ye estate of Tho: Warwick born Sept. 21.
Frank daughter of Jenney a slave belonging to Hobbs Weeks born Feb^ry ye 17.
Jefferey Son of Jenney a slave belonging to Humphery Jones born May 12 17 .
Betty daughter of Poll a Slave belonging to Garritt Minor born June 20 17 .
Ben Son of Phillis a slave belonging to William Segar born June 28 17 .
Peter Son of Moll a slave belonging to Roger Jones born July ye 7th 17 .
Billy Son of Sarah a Slave belonging to John Smith jun^r born July 25 17 .
Phillip Son of Mary a slave belonging to Edm^d Bartlett baptized July 13. & about 1 year old.
Frank daughter of Jane a slave belonging to Frances Ransom born July 12.
Letty daughter of Judy a Slave belonging to John Aldin born July 20.

Frank daughter of Judy a slave belonging to Rob⁺ Williamson jun⁺ born Augs⁺ 1.
Robin Son of Phillis a Slave belonging to Anne Mayo born July 25.
Robin Son of Moll a slave belonging to John Smith Sen⁺ born August 26.
Dinah daughter of Sarah a slave belonging to George Harding born Novem⁺ 19.
Rose daughter of Phillis a Slave belonging to Tho: Meacham born Decem⁺ 20.
Roger Son of Nell a Slave belonging to Humphery Jones born July 25.
Peter Son of Bess a slave belonging to Philip Warwick born Feb⁺y 14.
Osman Son of Kate a Slave belonging to Frances Thacker born 25 June.
Billy Son of Lettey a slave belonging to Edwin Thacker born Novem⁺ 22.
Eve daughter of Venus a slave belonging to Hezekiah Ellis born Jan⁺y y⁺ 30.
Kate daughter of Dina a slave belonging to Jacob Stiff born March y⁺ 15 171 .
Simon Son of Rebecca a Slave belonging to S⁺ W⁺ Skipwith born Jan⁺y 11. 171 .
Frank daughter of Sarah a slave belonging to Alexander Graves born Decem 15. 171 .
Sarah daughter of Sarah a slave belonging to Gawin Corbin born March 25 17 .
Charles & Easter Son & daughter of Frank a Slave belonging to Gawin Corbin born April 1 171 .
Anthony Son of Lettice a slave belonging to Bar Yates born Ap: 2. baptized May 17. 171 .
Jack Son of Wan a slave belonging to James Daniell born May y⁺ 17. 171 .
Nanny daughter of Jeney a Slave belonging to Rice Curtis born May y⁺ 5. 171 .
Betty daughter of Sarah a slave belonging to Richard Hill born Ap: y⁺ 30. 171 .
Toby Son of Sue a Slave belonging to William Barbee born June y⁺ 18. 171 .
Essex Son of Rose a slave belonging to Gawin Corbin born June y⁺ 16. 1719.
Randall Son of Phillis a slave belonging to Gawin Corbin born June y⁺ 22. 171 .
Sarah daughter of Poll a Slave belonging to Garritt Minor born June y⁺ 30. 1719.
Lucy daughter of Jenny a slave belonging to John Vivion born May y⁺ 24 1719.
Jack Son of Flownder a slave belonging to y⁺ estate of M⁺ Churchhill born May 6. 1719.
Harry Son of Wonna a slave belonging to Mathew Kemp born July y⁺ 2d. 1719.
Cyrus Son of Judy a slave belonging to William Stanard born June y⁺ 24 1719.

Jemmy Son of —— a slave belonging to William Hackney born June y̐ 5 1719.
Tom son of —— a slave belonging to John Roads born July y̐ 15 1719.
Phill son of Juno a slave belonging to Matthew Kemp born July y̐ 18 1719.
Primus son of a slave belonging to Lewis Tomkies born August y̐ 12. 1719.
Harry son of Guinea a slave belonging to Thomas Dudley born Augst y̐ 6 1719.
Wonna daughter of Jeny a slave belonging to John Degge born July y̐ 1 1719.
Winney daughter of Pegg a slave belonging to Thomas Cheney born Sept. y̐ 9. 17
George Hooper son of Han a slave belonging to Garritt Minor born Sept y̐ 14. 17
Kate daughter   a slave belonging to Edmund Mickleburrough born Sept 26.
Ben negro Son of Soll belonging to R. Grymes.
Katy negro daughter of Kate belonging to Frances Thacker born May 25 17
—artin a negro son of Letty belonging to Wm Young born Feb. 10 1714.
Judith a Negro daughter of Sarah belonging to Thos. Warwick born May 6 1716.
Dick a negro Son of Sarah belonging to George Harding born May 14 1718.
Alice a negro Daughter of Alice belonging to Jno Grymes born baptized July 22 17
Betty a negro Daughter of Phillis belonging to Gawin Corbin born Feb^{ry} 20th 1715.
Pompey a negro son of Sue belonging to Gawin Corbin born Ap: 2 1715.
Syndab a negro son of Moll belonging to Gawin Corbin born June 25 1715.
Hannah a negro daughter of Sarah belonging to Gawin Corbin born March 27 1716.
Jack a negro Son of Frank belonging to Gawin Corbin born Ap: 19 17
Suke a negro Daughter of Rose belonging to Gawin Corbin born May 21 17
Natt a negro Son of Jeney belonging to Rice Curtis born Augt 24 1714.
Jack a negro son of Moll belonging to Peter Mountague born Augst 3 1716.
Poll a negro Daughter of Bess belonging to Phillip Warwick born Augst 13 1716.
Ben a negro son of Cate belonging to John Hord born Septem^r y̐ 5 1716.
Margery daughter of Judy a negro belonging to Robt Dudley born Septem 27 1716.
Dina negro daughter of Bess belonging to Nicholas Bristow born Dec. 16 1716.

Toney a negro Son of Jeney belonging to John Degge born Augst ye 5 1716.
Letty a negro daughter of Alice belonging to Wm Stanard born Octo: ye 22 1716.
Thomas a negro Son of Letty belonging to Bar Yates born Decem. 28. baptized Feb^{ry} 9.
Cummah Son of Betty a negro belonging to Thomas Smith born Jan'y 3 1716.
Letty daughter of Alice a negro belonging to Wm Stanard born Octo: 24 1716.
Molly daughter of Hannah a negro belonging to Wm Stanard born Ap: 30 1717.
Charles son of   a negro belonging to Thomas Dudley born May 24
Will son of Phebe a negro belonging to Thomas Mountague born June 17
Ben son of Jenney a negro belonging to Capt James Bristow born June 26
Frank daughter of Dido a negro belonging to Capt John Smith born June 14
Nimine daughter of Jenney belonging to Capt. John Smith born June 26
Sampson son of Phillis a negro belonging to Roger Jones born May 25
Harry son of Sue a negro belonging to Wm Barbee sen^r May 30
Sam Son of Moll a negro belonging to Gawin Corbin born Novem^r 13
Alice daughter of Kate a negro belonging to Gawin Corbin born Jan^r 12
Sanco son of Sue a negro belonging to Gawin Corbin born June 11
Harry Son of Della a negro belonging to Thomas Haselwood born May ye 14 1717.
Billy son of Moll a negro belonging to John Segar born June ye 14 1717.
Phillis son of Judy a negro belonging to Robert Daniell born June ye 23 1717.
Jenny daughter of Letty a slave belonging to William Young born June ye 18
Sam Son of Janey a slave belonging to Rice Curtis born July ye 30
James son of Jane a slave belonging to John Grymes born June 23 Baptized.
George Son of Peg a Slave belonging to Thomas Cheney born August ye 9.
Ned Son of Betty a Slave belonging to Capt John Smith born August ye 24.
Frank Son of Bess a Slave belonging to Henry Armistead born Sept.
Peter Son of Mentas a slave belonging to John Grymes born Jan^{r}y.
Sarah Daughter of Judy a Slave belonging to John Grymes born March 25.
Sue Daughter of Rose a slave belonging to John Grymes born Novem^r 6.
Robin Son of Flora a Slave belonging to John Grymes born Octo. 21.
John Son of Lucy a slave belonging to John Grymes born July 29 17

Hannah daughter of Judy a slave belonging to John Degge born Septemʳ 25. 17 .
Bob Son of Beck a slave belonging to William Davis born Novemʳ yᵉ 1717.
Clarinda daughter of Kate a slave belonging to William Stanard born Novem 3. 1717.
Toney Son of Mary a slave belonging to yᵉ estate beth Churchill born D. 14.
Phillis daughter of Phebe a slave belonging to Tho. Mountague born Jan'y yᵉ
Nan daughter of Judy a slave belonging to Wᵐ Daniel junʳ born Novemʳ yᵉ 6.
Bridgitt daughter of Sarah a slave belonging to Gawin Corbin born Jan'y yᵉ 4.
Cate daughter of Letty a slave belonging to Fran: Weekes born Jan'y yᵉ 6 1719.
Jenny Son of Letty a slave belonging to Catherine Young born Jan'y yᵉ 10 1719.
Dick Son of Frank a slave belonging to Matthew Kemp born Feb'y yᵉ 6 1719.
Moll daughter of Mary a slave belonging to yᵉ estate of Armistead Churchhill born Dec. 28. 1719.
Wonna daughter of   a slave belonging to yᵉ estate of Armistead Churchhill born Janʳ 4. 1719.
Charles Son of Sarah a slave belonging to John Smith junʳ born Feb'y yᵉ 11 1719.
Scipio Son of   a slave belonging to John Grymes born March yᵉ 13 1719.
Mary daughter of   a slave belonging to John Grymes born March yᵉ 13 1719.
Rose daughter of Rose a slave belonging to John Grymes born March yᵉ 17 1719.
Sue daughter of   a slave belonging to John Grymes born March yᵉ 27 172 .
Peg daughter of Dinah a slave belonging to Henry Armistead born March 20 17 .
Abram Son of Lucy a Slave belonging to Henry Armistead born March 23 1719.
Sampson Son of Dido a slave belonging to Matthew Kemp born April 21 1720.
Tom Son of Phillis a slave belonging to Stokely Towles born May yᵉ 4 1720.
Beck daughter of Kate a slave belonging to Augustine Smith born June yᵉ 18 1720.
Kate daughter of Munday a slave belonging to John Batchelder born July 4 1720.
Ben Son of Frank a slave belonging to David George born July 4 1720.
Frank daughter of Diana a slave belonging to Armistead Churchhill born June 5. 1720.
Letty daughter of Moll a slave belonging to Tho: Mountague born Octo. yᵉ 17. 1713.

Jack Son of Frank a slave belonging to Tho: Mountague born Jan'y 27. 1713.

Cæsar Son of Frank a slave belonging to Tho: Mountague born Ap: y° 30 1716.

Sampson Son of Frank a slave belonging to Tho: Mountague born Feb'y y° 28 1717.

Eugene Son of Moll a Slave belonging to Tho: Mountague born Octo: y° 25. 1719.

Dinah daughter of Kate a slave belonging to Charles Jones born July y° 25.

Nan daughter Felicia a salve belonging to Anne Mayo born Augst 30.

Clarinda daughter of a slave belonging to James Curtis jun^r born June 20 17 .

Gabrill Son of Nell a slave belonging to y° estate of Edm^d Berkley born Sept 4 17 .

Judy daughter of Alice a Slave belonging to Robert Daniell July y° 17 17 .

Ben son of Kate a slave belonging to William Daniel Senr born Sep^t y° 8 1720.

Hampton son of Judy a slave belonging to John Aldin born Sep^t y° 27 1720.

Juno daughter of Hannah a slave belonging to George Harden born Sept. 23. 1720.

Ned Son of   a slave belonging to John Smith jun^r born Sept. y° 10. 1720.

Penn daughter of Sarah a slave belonging to Robert Williamson born Sept. 29. 1720.

Will son of Dellow a slave belonging to Tho: Hazelwood born Octo: ye 10. 1720.

Lucy daughter of Judy a slave belonging to Robert Williamson jun^r Novem 1. 1720.

Sabrinah daughter of Frank a slave belonging to Oliver Segar born Sept. 18 1720.

Gawin son of Dinah a slave belonging to Oliver Segar born Sept. 22 1720.

Charlott daughter of Jeney a slave belonging to John Vivion born Novem^r 15. 1720.

Frank daughter of Alice a slave belonging to Edmond Bartlett's estate born 9^{ber} 28. 1720.

Betty daughter of Mary Whistler a mulatto in ye Service of John Price born May 2

Will son of Mary Whistler a mulatto in ye Service of John Price born April 26

Toney son of Judy a slave belonging to John Price born April y° 6

Alice daughter of Sue a slave belonging to John Price born Sept. y° 14

Mercury son of Judy a slave belonging to Wm Stanard born Novem^r y° 17

Beck daughter of Jenney a slave belonging to Matt: Hunt born Decem^r y° 10

Gawin son of Nell a slave belonging to Humphery Jones born Decem^r y° 9

Ben Son of Jeney a slave belonging to John Smith born Decem' y* 18

Phillis daughter of Eve a slave belonging to Hezekiah Ellis born Novem' y* 21

Jack son of Phillis a slave belonging to Roger Jones born Decem' y*

Kate daughter of Moll a slave belonging to John Segar born Decem' y* 10

Flora daughter of Judy a slave belonging to John Degge born Jan'y y* 3

Stephen Monday son of   a slave belonging to   born Decem' y* 21

Jude daughter of hannah a slave belonging to   born Jan'y

Jemmy Son of Hannah a slave belonging to Garritt Minor born Feb 20 1720.

Nero son of Phillis a slave belonging to Thomas Machen born March 27 1721.

Joice daughter of Dido a slave belonging to Matthew Kemp born April y* 13 1721.

Hannah daughter of Beck a slave belonging to Robt George jun^r born April 4 1721.

Peter son of Bess a slave belonging to Henry Armistead born April 21 1721.

Winney daughter of Jenny a slave belonging to Rice Curtis born April 27 1721.

Dego son of Poll a slave belonging to y* estate of Garritt Minor born April y* 28. 1721.

Ross son of Hannah a slave belonging to William Gray born April y* 18 1721.

Judy daughter of Winney a slave belonging to Edwin Thacker born Ap: y* 10. 1721.

Harry son of Sarah a slave belonging to Armistead Churchhill born Ap: y* 29 1721.

Sprigg son of   a slave belonging to Henry Gilpin born May y* 5. 1721.

Tamar daughter of Sarah a slave belonging to George Harding born May y* 30. 1721.

Johny son of Coss a slave belonging to Harry Beverly born May 25. 1721.

Billy son of Betty a slave belonging to John Robinson born July y* 2. 1721.

Cross son of Wonna a slave belonging to y* estate of Armistead Churchhill born June 6 1721.

Letty daughter of   a slave belonging to John Moseley born June 15. 1721.

Frank daughter of   a slave belonging to Thomas Norman born July 11 1721.

Jack son of Letty a slave belonging to Hobs Weeks born July y* 1 1721.

Tom Son of Wonne a slave belonging to Mathew Kemp born July y* 27 1721.

Moll Daughter of Frank a slave belonging to Edmund Mickleburrough born July 20. 1721.

Sue daughter of Jenny a slave belonging to Armistead Churchhill born May y⁶ 1, 1721.
Judey daughter of Pugg a Slave belonging to Armistead Churchhill born July 15. 1721.
Dinah daughter of Kate a slave belonging to Roger Jones born August y⁶ 6. 1721.
Pen daughter of Judy a slave belonging to Tho: Mountague born August 7. 1721.
Frank daughter of Jenny a Slave belonging to Samuell Batchelder born August 12. 1721.
Ned Son of Sarah a slave belonging to John Cheadle born Septem' y⁶ 1. 1721.
Robin Son of Sarah a slave belonging to Alexander Graves Septem' y⁶ 10. 1721.
Jack Son of Sarah a slave belonging to Henry Armistead born Septem' y⁶ 16. 1721.
Corridan Son of Judy a Slave belonging to William Blackburne born Sept. 10. 1721.
Roger Son of Juno a slave belonging to Mathew Kemp born Sept. 15. 1721.
Sarah daughter of Winny a slave belonging to y⁶ estate of Henry Thacker dec'd born Sept 24. 1721.
Frank daughter of Sarah a slave belonging to William Stanard born Sept. 17. 1721.
Kate daughter of Judy a Slave belonging to William Daniell jun' born Novem' 1. 1721.
Judy daughter of Kate a slave belonging to William Hackney born Nov. 6. 1721.
Bristow Son of Sue a slave belonging to John Price born Novem' 28. 1721.
Letty daughter of Sue a Slave belonging to Bar Yates born Jan'⁷ y⁶ 5. 1721.
Lura daughter of Sarah a slave belonging to John Smith jun' born Feb'⁷ y⁶ 5. 1721.
Ishmael Son of Moll a Slave belonging to John Smith Sen' born Jan'⁷ y⁶ 18. 1721.
Kate daughter of Frank a slave belonging to Anne Thacker born Octo. y⁶ 4 1721.
Toney Son of Dinah a slave belonging to John Marston born Jan'⁷ y⁶ 25. 1721.
Cæsar Son of Judy a Slave belonging to John Price born Feb'⁷ y⁶ 15. 1721.
Moll daughter of Moll a slave belonging to James Hipkings born Novem' y⁶ 4. 1721.
Sawney Son of Mary a slave belonging to Armistead Churchhill born March 10. 1721.
Frank Daughter of Dido a slave belonging to Matthew Kemp born April y⁶ 1. 1722.
Betty daughter of Jenny a Slave belonging to John Grymes born May 28. baptized August y⁶ 13. 1721.
Sarah daughter of Margery a slave belonging to John Grymes born Feb'⁷ y⁶ 16. 1721.

Margery daughter of Rose a Slave belonging to John Grymes born Feb'y y⁰ 27. 1721.
Daniel Son of Flora a slave belonging to John Grymes born March y⁰ 29. 1722.
Ben Son of Phillis a slave belonging to Anne Mayo born Feb'y y⁰ 14 1721.
Poll daughter of Frank a Slave belonging to David George born April y⁰ 4 1722.
Simon Son of Frank a slave belonging to Matthew Kemp born April 3d. 1722.
Judy Daughter of Dina a slave belonging to Jacob Stiff born Aprill y⁰ 9 1722.
Abram Son of Jeny a Slave belonging to Hobs Weeks born April y⁰ 11 1722.
Kate daughter of   a slave belonging to Wm Mountague born March y⁰ 30 1722.
Alice daughter of Jenny a slave belonging to Eliz° Vivion born May y⁰ 2 1722.
Lucy daughter of   a slave belonging to Garritt Minor born May y⁰ 11 1722.
Jenny daughter of   belonging to Thomas Mountague born May 19. 1722.

              Bar Yates Min^r.

INDEX.

Abbott, Berrin, 303, Ellinor 35, Fanny 206, Susanna 201.
Acree, Ann, 151, 153, 156, 160, 297, 299, Jacob 151, 153, 156, 160, 297, 299, Jno. 153, Mary 198, 297, Sarah 156, 189, 200, Thos. 299, Wm. 160, 198.
Acton, Honour, 39, 50, Richard 39, 50, Samuel 37, 39, 50.
Adams, Ely, 257, Hannah 81.
Adcock, Sarah, 172.
Adkins, 198.
Adkinson, Cath., 303.
Alden, Armistead, 118, Cath., 28, 63, Eliz. 67, 154, Ellianor 24, 28, Frances 67, 78, 86, 94, 105, 159, Jane 150, 154, 155, 159, Jno. 24, 67, 78, 86, 94, 105, 150, 154, 155, 159, 184, Marg't 118, Martha 86, Mary 105, 170, Robert 24, 28, 150, 176, 195, Thos. 118.
Alderson, Reubin, 171.
Aldridge, Adam, 209.
Alford, John, 38, Lettice 38, Mary 43, 83, 122, Rich'd 43, 122, Ruth 122, Sarah 38.
Allcock, John, 88, Sarah 88.
Allen, Ann, 14, 16, 24, 28, 31, 55, 89, 106, 150, 300, Barbara 9, Cath. 108, 204, Eliz. 55, 83, 96, 106, 147, 150, 155, 156, Erasmus 9, Henry 117, 147, 160, 191, Isaac 106, Jane 128, 187, John 9, Marg't 156, 160, 204, 300, Mary 89, 96, 102, 108, 113, 117. 128, 191, Richard 14, 16, 24, 28, 31, 55, 85, 89, 96, 108, 113, 117, 128, 147, 150, 155, 170, 187, 188, Ruban 155, 196, Thos. 23, Tobias 24, 102, 156, 160, 300, Wm. 7, 20.
Allinson, Ann, 10, 11, David 9, 10, 11, Joane 9, 10, 11, Mary 9.
Allison, Ann, 19, Kath. 35.
Almond, Mary, 47.
Alphin, Constance, 169, Constantine 108, John 189, Joseph 81, 108, 109, 191, Ransom 108.
Amiss, Jas., 170, John, Rachel, Thos. 115.
Ammon, Chr., 144, 169, Eliz. 148, Frances, Mary, 144.
Amris, Jane, 80.
Anderson, Alex., 171. Andrew 141, Anne 127, 137, 141, 181, Benj. 110, Constant 194, Eliz.

288, Fra. 280, Geo. 137, Henry 103, 156, 159, 174, 289, 299, Jane 203, John 179, 288, Joseph 127, Marg't 289, Mary 156, 159, 289, 299, Ralph 299, Sarah 103, 110, 119, 159, 185, Wm. 36, 103 110, 119, 127, 137, 141, 156, 169, 181.
Anderton, Ann, Geo. 14.
Andrews, Joseph, 79.
Archer, Eliz., Jno., Rebecca, 122.
Arle, Thos., 63.
Areley, Jas., 80.
Armistead, Eliz., 36, Mary 63.
Arrow, Rich'd, 18.
Arrowy, Anne, Jno., Michael, 124.
Ashton, Eliz., Thos., 46, Marg't 8.
Ashur, Diana, 69, Jno. Susanna 69, 73, Wm. 73.
Ashwin, Ann, 20.
Askail, Rich'd, 39.
Askew, Eliza, Margret, Rich'd, 14.
Askins, Jno., 200.
Aston, Ann, John, May, 44.
Athy, Mary, 36. 37.
Atkins, Mary, 302.
Attford, Rich., 80.
Atwood, Eliz., 39. Henry 91, Jas. 14, 16, 26, John, 14, 79, Mary 14, 16, 26, 80, Michall 62, Rich'd 16, 62, 77, 91, 172, Sarah 62, 79, 91.
Austin, Cath., 131, Christian 70, Eliz., 82, 131, 187, John 47, 70, 80, Mary 70, 131, 188, Thos. 131, Wm. 47.

Baden, Eliz., Henry, Wm., 153.
Bagot, Jno.. 304.
Bagwell, Drury, 205.
Baines, Betsa, 170, Chr., Rebecca 102.
Baily, Eliz., Henry, 80.
Baker, Benj., 122, 187, Chas. 47, Eliz. 48, 287, Francis 287, Isabella 22, Jas. 206, Jno. 48, Mary 205, Rachel 122, Rob't 185, Susannah 47, Thos. 48, Wm. 47, 122, 175.
Baldry, Letitia, 303.
Baldin, Benj., 95, 172, Eliz., 80, 88, Jno. 68, Martha 105, Mary 76, 80, Sarah 68, 88, 95, 99, 105, Wm. 68, 76, 88, 95, 99, 105.
Baldwin, Edwin, 45, Joseph 142, Judith 130, 138, 142, 191, Kath., Keziah 45, Lewis 116, 181, Marg't 111, 180, Mary 16, Sarah 111, 116,

138, 186, Thos. 16, Wm. 11, 16, 111, 116, 130, 138, 142, 191.
Ball, Ann, 36, 76, 90, 113, 172, 183, Arthur 48, Azrah 191, Benj. 103, 154, 169, 172, Dan'l 88, 159, David 154, Edw'd 48, 67, 71, 76, 88, 94, 103, 121, 127, 183, Eliz. 20, 22, 67, 85, 113, 130, 190, Henry 79, 90, 96, 100, 107, 113, 176, 190, Jas, 96, Johanna 48, Jno. 107, 127, Keziah 48, 67, 71, 76, 88, 94, 103, Mary 71, Phebe 76, Sarah 90, 96, 100, 107, 121, 127, 154, 159, 179, Wm. 94, 179, 184.
Ballard, Eliz., 87, Henry, 30, Jane, 174, John 10, 87, Thos. 30.
Banbry, Eliza, Daniel, Mary, 8.
Banks, Anthony, Eliz., Isabella, 42, Saul 30, Tunstall 281.
Banting, Eliz., 170.
Barbee, Ann, 76, Benj. 70, 186, Eliz. 34, 76, Geo. 191, Gray 88, Hannah 27, Jno. 76, 81, Mary 70, 76, 92, 98, Wm. 27, 34, 63, 70. 76, 92, 98.
Barber, Wm., 63.
Barlow, Jas., 66, John 7, 40, Mary 40, 66, Phebe 40, Wm. 66.
Barnatt, Ann, 64, 69, 72, 91, 101, 123, 130, Henry 123, 130, Jane 20, John 64, 69, 72, 91, 101, 123, 179, Mary 123, Rich'd 69, Sarah 72, Wm. 91, 130.
Barnes, Henry, 174, Johanna 85, Mary 21.
Barrick, Amy, 43, Anne 89, 160, 183, 303, Benj. 201, David 21, 145, Diana 145, 303, Eliz. 31, 33, 89, 93, 155, 280, Francis 206, Geo. 8, 31, 33, 43, 89, 95, 109, 118, 145, Jas. 93, 160, Joanna 201, John 199, 201, Jos. 201, Mary 31, 33, 109, 118, 155, 189, Prisc. 202, Rachel 109, Robt. 109, 303.
Bartlett, Edm'd, 175, Lucy 172.
Barton, Ann, 302.
Basford, Rich'd, Martha, Thos., 67.
Baskett, Abraham, 64, Dan'l, Edw'd, 144, Eliz. 15, 19, 25, 29, 33, 91, Henry 25, 87, 93, 177, Honor 64, 177, Jas. 64, 183, John 15, 19, 177, Martha 87, Mary 53, 93, 144, Sarah 87, 93, 177, Thos. 19, 91, Wm. 91.
Bassett, Henry, 80, Virginia 281.
Batchelder, 10, Anne 202, Benj. 197, Eliz. 98, 104, 109, 118, 123, 177, 182, 203, 284, 285, 288, 299, Francis 200, 287, Hannah 109, 170, Henry 118, 204, Jemima 104, 181, Jas. 98, 111, 205, 284, Jane 201, John 7, 8, 90, 98, 104, 114, 141, 162, 177, 284, 287, Jos. 123, 197,
286, Kath. 90, 96, 118, 123, 299, Mary 8, 90, 280, 284, Michal 197, 286, Rebecca 8, Sam'l 90, 96, 104, 111, 118, 123, 194, 285, 286, 288, 299, Sarah 8, 50, 118, 177, 199, 284, Susan 284, Thos. 288, Wm. 8, 50, 90, 96, 109, 114, 118.
Bateman, Ann, Edward, 11, Lettice, 78, 86, Mary 86, Thos. 11, 86.
Battaile, John, 304.
Batts, Cath., Mary, Thos., 90.
Baylor, Hannah, 202.
Baytop, Jas., 304.
Beall, Wm., 280.
Beamon, Benj., 104, 178, Cath. 208, Eliz. 83, 85, 104, 159, Francis 208, Jane, Jno., 159, 161, 285, 286, 299, Marg't, Mary 199, Sarah 161, Susan 208, Wm. 104, 177.
Beamont, Thos., 37, Wm. 35.
Beard, Elen, Joseph, Mary, 299.
Beauford, May, 190.
Begerley, Eliz., 82.
Begge, Mary, Robert, 43.
Belfare, Judith, 201.
Belfield, Sydner, 203.
Belfore, Anne, 304.
Bell, John, 82, Jonathan, Mary, Sarah, 94.
Bendall, Arthur, 27. Eliz. 24, 27, 34, Jas. 24. 27, 34, Sarah 63.
Bennett, Eliz., 69, 121, John 208, Jos. 131, Mary 37, 115, 121, 125, 131, 138, Peter 65, 115, 184, Rich'd 37, 72, 138, Sarah 60, 65, 69, Thos. 203, Wm. 23, 65, 69, 72, 115, 121, 125, 131, 138, 302.
Benson, Alice, 181, Dorothy 28. Robt. 28, Thos. 24, 28.
Bentley, Matthew, 7, Mary, Matthew, 8.
Berkeley, Edm'd, 89, 126, 130, 140, 146, 153, 198, Eliz. 303, Lewis 140, Lucy 89, 126, 281, Mary 126, 130, 146, 153, 199, Sarah 89, 153, 198.
Berrick, David, 23, 76, 150, 154, 158, 191, Diana 150, 154, 158, Eliz. 76. Geo. 76, 191, Jno. 158, Wm. 150.
Berry, Ann, 100, 122, 126, 131, 141, 285, Cath. 287, Dorothy 196, 304, Edw'd 38, Eliz. 60, 72, 75, 77, 176, Fra. 17, 60, 184, Garret 47, 60, 72, 75, 181, Geo. 77, Honor 37, Jas. 72, 141, 285, Jno. 82, 93, 100, 112, 126, 139, 196, Kath. 38, Mary 75, 93, 100, 112, 131, 139, 285, Sarah 38, Susan 112, 139, Thos. 47, 122, 126, 131, 141, 287, Wm. 93, 196.
Best, Dorothy, 180, Eliz. 23, Geo. 131, 138, Jno. 131, Marg't 131, 138, Mary 138.
Betson, Anthony, Mary, 138.
Betts, Ann, 191, Sarah 175, Thos. 169.

316

Beverley, Agatha, 94, Ann 129, 302, Chr. 31, 33, Eliz. 45, 48, 68, 77, 94, 105, 129, 176, Henry 45, 47, 48, 68, 77, 94, 105, Judith 63, 77, Kath. 7, 16, 31, 33, 35, 76, Lucy 105, 179, Marg't 76, Mary 47, Peter 77, Robt. 7, 16, 18, 31, 33, 48, 76, 129, Susan 68, 76, Thos. 7, 31, Wm. 16.

Bewford, Anne, 100, Eliz. 77, 86, 95, 100, 149, Henry 78, 80, 94, 101, 149, Jno. 77. 101, 180, Mary 78, 94, 95, 101, Sarah 86, Thos. 78, 86, 94, 95, 100, 172, Wm. 78, 149.

Biggs, Eliz., 70, 76, 87, 97, Jane 87, Jas. 97, Mary 70, Robt. 63, 70, 76, 87, 97, 175.

Bird, Ann, 288, Eliz. 60, 66, Henry 66, Jno. 60, 66, 177, 288, Mary, Rich'd 201, 282, Sarah 60.

Bishop, Chas., 175.

Black, Ann, 60, 78, 81, James 60, 78, Philemon 78.

Blackburn, Ann, 114, 191, 298, Dorothy 183, Edward 128, 161, 298, Eliz. 89, 97, 102, 108, 114, 122, 128, 191, 204, Geo. 161, Hannah 102, Jean 207, Jemima 208, Mary 298, 304, Millicent, 122, Paul 302, Roger 109, 202, Thos. 108, 185, Wm. 89, 97, 108, 114, 122, 128, 191, 298.

Blackford, Eliz., Hannah, Wm., 144.

Blackley, Agatha, 86, Ann 55, 62, 67, 78, 86, 88, 97, 104, 299, Eliz., 161, 198, Francis 97, 204, Geo. 78, 139, 152, 154, 157, 161, 286, 299, Jane 26, 34, 55, 139, 152, 154, 157, 161, 286, 299, Jno. 34, Mary 162, Reuben 154, Richard 286, Robt. 22, 26, 34, 55, 62, 67, 78, 86, 88, 97, 104, 182, Sarah 139, Thos. 29, 33, Wm. 104.

Blake, Abra., 202, Alice 281, 302, Ann 119, 123, 187, 201, 207, 284, 286, 289, 304, Augustine 281, 302, Benj. 282, Betty 201, Bev. 303, Chas. 282, Churchhill 42, Diana 9, 20, Eliz. 9, 20, 42, 46, 47, 59, 68, 69, 76, 87, 110, 119, 138, 143, 146, 159, 289, Frances 201, 206, 282, Geo. 9, 42, 44, 46, 59, 68, 69, 84, 87, 121, 171, 186, 204, 285, 286, 299, 304, Hannah 121, Jacob 68, 69, 123, 284, 289, Joane 9, 21, Joanna 110, 116, 127, 149, 302, Jno. 9, 42, 46, 110, 116, 119, 127, 138, 142, 143, 146, 149, 169, 187, 199, 281, 299, Joseph 76, Kezia 170, Lucy 7, 9, 23, 29, 149, Marg't 42, Mary 138, 201, 286, 299, Rose 159, 285, 287, Robt. 303, Sarah 9, 47, 142, 143, 303, Sam'l 281, 302, Susan 199, 208, 284, 303, Thos. 42, 87, 159, 201, 285, 287, 289, Wm. 200, 289.

Blakey, Ann, 199, 283, Betty 113, Cath. 147, 281, Churchhill 82, 86, 88, 94, 101, 107, 113, 119, 125, 140, 147, 192, 199, 200, 281, 283, Eliza. 304, Geo. 94, 143, 146, 299, Henry 303, Hester 143, Jacob 305, Jane 119, 143, 146, 150, 299, John 101, 103, 150, Johanna 103, Keziah 103, Marg't 84, 88, 189, Martha 150, Mary 196, Robt. 107, 146, 304, Sarah 86, 88, 94, 101, 107, 113, 119, 125, 140, 147, Susan 140, 304, Thos. 83, 86, 188, Wm. 199, 303, 305.

Bland, Ann, 207, 282, Fra. 282, Henry 285, Jno. 282, Josiah 285, Lucy 283, Mary 282, 283, 303, Micah. 285, Rich. Thos. 207, Wm. 205.

Blazedon, Marg't, 108, Mary 100, Sarah 100, 108, 191, Wm. 82, 100, 108.

Bloss, Jane, 38, Jno. 36, 38.

Blueford or Blewford, Eliza., 302, Henry 27, Jno. 11, Mary 19, 38, Thos. 19, 27, 38.

Blunt, Ann, 103, Eliz. 107, 114, Fra. 103, Henry 107, Mary 114, Susannah 107, Thos. 176.

Bocker, Jone, 63.

Bodenham, Edw'd, 189.

Bodgham, Hannah, 44, Jno. 23, 34, 44, Joyce 44, Mary 34, 36, 37, Wm. 34.

Bohannan, Agnes, 130, Ann 151, Eliz. 115, 121, 124, 130, Geo. 121, 183, Henry 151, 193, Jno. 130, 151, Jos. 115, 121, 124, 130, Nevill 115, Sarah 124, Wm. 130, 188.

Boles, Peter, 209.

Bolden, Mary, 201, Wm. 200.

Bolton, Anne, 80, Uriah, 174.

Bond, Wm., 170.

Bonds, Mary, Robt., 298.

Bonner, Geo., 180.

Boodle, Eliz., 52, Hannah 52, Jacob 52, 53, Jno. 39, 41, Martha 7, Mary 38, 41, Robt. 23, 38, 39, 41.

Booth, Wm., 208.

Bosely, Fra., 82, Hannah 81.

Boss, Alfred, 145, 282, Christian 155, 297, Eliz., 199, Jas. 206, Jno. 138, 145, 155, 201, 282, 287, 297, Jos. 280, 282, Judith 297, Lewis 204, 304, Martha 201, Prisc. 138, Rhoda 287, Sarah 145, 204, 282, Susannah 138, Wm. 155, 282.

Boulton, Ann, 44, 46, Dan'l, Eliz. 21, Jno. 44, 46, Sarah 46, Uriah 44, Wm. 170.

Bourk, Jno., Sarah, 40, Mary 31, 40.

Bowden, Geo., 85, 91, Jno., Sarah 91,

317

Mary 207, Newcomb 208, Robt. 280, Wm. 202.
Bowen, Math., 80.
Bowers, Ann, 201, Eliz. 280, Stubblefield 204.
Bowles, Fanny, 285, Jerusha 287, Jno. 157, 285, 287, 297, 298, Lucy 297, Mary 285, 287, 297, 298, Thos. 157.
Bowman, Benj., 50, Jas. 105, 180, Jno. 50, 52, 105, Marg't 105, Mary 50, 52.
Boyd, Lucy, 206.
Bradass, Reubin, 203.
Bradley, Anne, 118, Eliz. 91, Ezekiah 77, Jas. 128, Jno. 77, 82, 91, 100, 109, 118, 128, Mary 77, 91, 100, 109, 118, 186, Rebecca 128, Robt. 109, Wm. 77.
Braine, Eliz., 100, 111, 122, 142, 198, 286, Hannah 11, 107, 116, Jas. 180, Jno. 26, 83, 100, 111, 122, 142, 286, Kerenhappuch 107, Mary 26, 87, Mile. 116, Pen. 142, Richins 111, 116.
Brammount, Hope, 63.
Branch, Francis, 114, 122, Mary 60, 114, 187, Nich's 60, Theophilus 60, 114, 122.
Braxton, Tayloe, 303.
Bray, Asher, 304, Henry 20, Jane 200, 281, Johanna 206, Jno. 281, Peter 281, Thos. 207.
Breame, Ann, 27, Eliz. 109, Jedidah 109, Jemminah 157, Jno. 27, 109, 150, 155, 157, 160, 298, Josiah 155, Mary 26, 27, 150, 155, 157, 160, 298, Pen. 190, Sarah 150.
Bremont, Bebecca, 82.
Brent, Giles, 22, Jane, Jno., 16.
Bressell, Eliza, 20, Eusebias 39, Mary 35.
Brewer, Ann, 30, 58, Jno. 20, 54.
Brider, Ann, 63.
Bridge, Francis, Marg't 22.
Bridger, Margaret, 18.
Bridyforth, Henry, Jas. Mary 91.
Brine, Robt., 82.
Briscoe, Christian, 63.
Brim, Alice, 38, Eliz. 19, Joh. 19, 28, 38, 40, Mary 19, 28, 38, 40, Peter 55, Rich'd 40.
Bristow, Alex., 281, Ann 117, 120, 176, Bartho. 205, Benj. 171, 197, 305, Cath. 87, 92, 109, 127, 153, 170, 194, Chas. 99, 300, Edw'd 73, 79, 148, 156, 159, 197, 199, 305, Eliz. 19, 81, 40, 124, 128, 130, 139, 148, 156, 159, 171, 187, 197, 205, 281, 285, 289, 300, 305, Fanny 20, 62, 89, Geo. 114, 160, 285, 299, 300, Hannah 98, 196, Jas. 99, 109, 114, 120, 128, 143, 160, 199, Jane 143, Jedediah 87, 153, Jemima 114, Jere. 182, Joanna 15, 51, 88, John 15, 19, 27, 34, 40, 42, 50, 51, 55, 87, 92, 107, 130, 171, 172, 281, 286, 299, 304, 305, Jonah 281, Josiah 130, 171, 206, 289, Len 305, Lucy 303, Marg't 19, 73, 89, 99, 111, 117, 124, Mary 51, 55, 87, 92, 107, 109, 120, 128, 129, 143, 160, 169, 195, 284, 285, 286, 288, 299, 300, 305, Michall 15, 19, 27, 34, 40, 42, 50, 80, 111, Nich's 42, 107, 114, 120, 129, 190, Phil. 285, Polly 207, Rachel 281, Ralph 175, Rich'd 98, 148, 305, Robt. 281, Ruth 286, Sam'l 129, 288, Sarah 50, 156, 171, Saunders 202, 206, Thos. 34, 82, 87, 92, 300, Tomson 153, Wm. 19, 63, 73, 79, 89, 99, 111, 117, 120, 124, 139, 187, 194, 203, 208, 281, 284, 286, 289.
Broadbent, Mary, 20.
Brock Eliz., 81.
Bromley, Dorothy, Robt., Sarah, 154.
Brooke, Thos., 205.
Brooking, Sam'l, 205, Susan 202, Wm. 280.
Brooks, Alice, 79, Ann 40, 50, 52, 79, 157, 176, 199, 283, Caleb 141, 145, 188, 189, Cath. 139, 145, 149, 155, 287, Chas. 16, Chr. 203, Cuffly 148, 192, 193, Dorothy 151, Ed. 202, Eliz. 19, 28, 40, 79, 86, 97, 105, 127, 138, 141, 154, 155, 157, 158, 188, 193, 195, 196, 200, 205, 297, Frances 122, 138, 171, 189, 200, Hannah, 192, Henry 86, 139, 143, 148, 154, 192, Humphry 105, Jacob 60, Jas. 139, 145, 155, 160, 200, John 16, 20, 77, 31, 34, 40, 50, 60, 80, 81, 86, 89, 93, 97, 102, 105, 110, 112, 113, 122, 131, 137, 145, 148, 152, 155, 157, 160, 189, 193, 199, 202, 283, 289, 298, Joseph 171, 199, Judith 171, Lettice 154, Mary 34, 81, 86, 93, 102, 110, 112, 113, 122, 131, 139, 145, 148, 152, 155, 157, 160, 169, 190, 199, 257, 287, 289, 298, Marg't 102, 141, 179, Martha 160, 287, 298, Mayo 137, Patty 283, Paul 143, Phil. 28, 89, 97, 102, 112, 127, 138, 141, 158, 189, 193, 195, 200, Priscilla 89, 97, 105, 112, Prudence 158, Rachel 141, 154, 157, 297, Rich'd 19, 28, 40, Robt. 151, Ruth 209, Sam'l 202, 287, Susan 93, Sarah 27, 34, 60, 81, 139, 143, 148, 154, 157, 169, 192, Thos. 19, 105, 171, 199, Wm. 35, 40, 50, 52, 60, 79, 80, 86, 89, 97, 105, 113, 139, 148, 152, 178, 287, 297
Brown, Cath., 158, Chas. 302, Ed. 93, Eliz. 68, 70, 73, 77, 82, 98, Gaf-

field 73, Henry 70, 73, 77, 98, Jas. 68, 80, 149, 158, 169, 190, 191, 198, Jno. 198, Martha 93, Mary 30, 35, 68, 158, 190, 191, Miles 203, Nancy 281, Robt. 193, Sam'l 149, Thos. 31, Wm. 70, 93, 191, 202.
Brumwell, Eliza., 19, 27, Ellinor 15, 42, Judith 150, Marg't 27, 80, Peter 15, 18, 19, 27, 42, Sarah 15, Thos. 42, 150, 162.
Brushword, Geo., 202, 282, Jas., Sarah, 282.
Bryant, Eliz., 285, Fra. 129, 304, Jno. 129, 189, 200. 285, Patience 170, Williamson 129, 189.
Bucher, Mary, Rich., 25.
Buford, Agatha, 68, Ambros 42, Ann 157, 169, Eliz. 42, 68, 131, 142, 157, 161, Fra. 142, Henry 142, 178, Jno. 131, Mary 170, 178, Thos. 68, Wm. 131, 157, 161.
Buckner, John, 204.
Buck, Ann, 63, Amy 141, Eliz. 124, Fra. 190, Henry 107, 112, 163, 190, Jane 14, Jeffery 95, John, 14, 25, 31, 51, 76, 84, 91, 107, 124, 141, 188, 190, Josiah 281, Judith 107, 112, Lettice 51, 124, 162, 188, Mary 25, 51, 78, 95, 100, Michal 71, 76, Nicholas 78, Phebe, Rich. 289, Sarah 100, Thos. 76, 78, 95, 100, 141, 190, 206, 208.
Buford, Susan, 37.
Burnet, Ann, 87, Eliz. 169, Jane 16, Jone 45, Loretta 15, 16, 19, 24, Sarah 19, 24, 87, Wm. 16, 18, 19.
Burnham, John, 22.
Burrow, Jno., 174.
Burton, Ann, 200, Eliz. 18, 205, Isaac 184, Jas. 170, 203, Mary 199, Nath. 200, Simon 207, Thos., Wm. 199.
Burwell, Carter, 70, Jane, Mary, Nat. 196, Sarah 207.
Bushnell, Wm., 81, 84.
Butcher, Eliz., 25, Rich., 28.
Buttler, Mary, 28, Richard 28.
Buttersby, Johannah, 21.
Butterworth, Sarah M., 198.

Cain, Dan'l, 112, 182, Hannah 99, 106, 112, 117, 126, 131, 186, Jas. 117, Joanna 186, Jno. 183, Marg't 169, Wm. 82, 99, 106, 112, 117, 126, 131, 183.
Callahan, Ann, 147, 192, Betsy 281, Eliz. 142, 147, 152, 156, Jas. 152, Jayne 82, Jno. 142, 281, 305, Kelman 284, Marg't 281, 305, Mary 284, Pat. 142, 147, 152, 156, Rhoda 202, Sarah 205, Tim. 178, Wm. 156, 305.
Calloway, Eliz., 18.
Calvert, Philip, 84.

Cammiel, James, 203.
Campbell, Agatha, 287, Fra. 205, Jas., Judith 160, 270, Jno. 177, Thacker 206, Cambridge, Ed. 81, 178.
Campton, Ann, Geo., Sarah, Jas., 194.
Canady, Ann, 65, 73, Cath. 179, Edw'd 29, 33, 180, Eliz. 55, 65, 73, Lacklin 65, 73, Mary 55, 82, Wm. 65.
Cane, John, Hannah, Wm., 77, Walter 39.
Cap, Ann, Eliz., Math., 78.
Carbett, John, 63.
Carder, Ann, 70, Sarah, Uriah 65, 70.
Cardis, Judith, Uriah, 46, Jno., Uriah 59.
Care, Mary, 50.
Cardwell, Agatha, 160, Anne 35, 103, Eliz. 80, Jas. 171, Jane 109, 115, 120, 125, Jno. 208, Lewis 160, Mary 29, 33, 97, 103, 109, Thos. 11, 97, 103, 120, 162, Wm. 97, 109, 115, 120, 125, 195.
Caree, Mary, 63.
Carlton, Bev., 207.
Carney, Eliz., 202, Jane 180.
Carpenter, Ann, 202.
Carrell, Cath., 126, Eliz. 138, Jno. 126, 131, 138, 190, Sarah 126, 131, 138, Wm. 195.
Carryer, Marg't, Jno., Ellianer, 12.
Carter, Ann, 54, 105, Eliz. 30, 82, 93, 99, 105, 112, 139, Fra., 93, Geo., 93, 99, 105, 115, Henry 99, Joseph 35, 40, 62, Landon 139, Mary, 40, 52, 54, 62, 68, 78, Pen 25, 34, 53, 87, Phil. 52, Robt. 68, 139, Susan 87, Thos, 25, 87, 177, Wm. 20, 23, 25, 30, 34, 40, 52, 53, 54, 62.
Carvenoth, Honnor, 63.
Cary, Ann, 38, Oswald 20, 39, Thos. 177.
Causer, Alice, 186, Thos. 183.
Cauthorn, Ann, 203, 283, 284, Cath. 283, Jno. 284, Rich. 202, 283, 284.
Chadwick, Jno., Sarah, Wm., 196.
Chaffin, Chr., 94, 100, 108, 115, 120, 185, John 94, 120, Mary 108, 120, Sarah 94, 100, 108, 115, Wm. 115, 184.
Chainey, Thos., 170.
Chambers, Ann, 29.
Chancellor, May, Wm., 103.
Chapman, Henry, 207, Jane 205, Jno. 199.
Charles, Sarah, 201.
Chaseman, Sarah, 22.
Chayney, Edw'd, 38, Eliz. 50, Pen 26, 38, Thos. 26, Wm 26, 54.
Cheyney, Cath., Thos., 158.
Cheedle, Anne, 106, Hannah 52, 162, Jno. 37, 38, 50, 52, 96, 104, 106, 113, Lettice 96, 104, 106, 113, Mil-

licent 38, 50, 52, Thos. 81, 104, 113, 120, 176, 181.
Chelton, Abigail, 41, 42, 47, 114, Ann 72, Dorothy, 152, 193, Eliz. 43, 93, Marg't 65, Mary 47, 72, 76, 82, 108, 114, 152, Peter 23, 41, 42, 47, 63, 81, 174, 175, Sarah 108, Susan 188, Thos. 42, 65, 72, 76, 93, 152, 193, Zebulon, 47, 108, 114.
Cheseld, Sarah, Wm., 120.
Cheshire, Anne, 85, 93, Ellonar, 93, Wm. 93.
Cheney, Cassandra, 102, 169, Cath. 149, 154, Eliz. 96, 149, Jane 87, 90, 96, 102, 108, 117, 187, Lettice 185, Pen 170, 176, Thos. 82, 87, 90, 96, 102, 108, 117, 149, 154, 187, 189, 195, Wm. 87, 185.
Childe, Ann, 11, Hannah 199, Henry 7, Marg't 82.
Chills, Mary, 80.
Chinn, Jno., 200.
Chisman, Cath., Geo., Peter, 62.
Chissells, Wm., 188.
Chowning, Robert, 9, Absalom, 85, 89, Ann 26, 38, 40, 51, 111, 128, 144, 155, 171, 195, 200, Betty, 143, 149, 152, 155, Cath. 116, 121, 128, 201, Chas. 149, Easter 155, Eliz. 93, 103, 129, 153, 155, 157, 161, 177, 201, 286, Fra. 137, Geo. 93, 103, 111, 129, 137, 145, Henry 153, 183, 204, Geo. 38, 93, 103, 111, 118, 123, 129, 137, 142, 183, Jane 104, 203, 298, Jas. 304, Jennett 112, 114, 119, 127, John 78, 112, 116, 121, 123, 127, 128, 139, 144, 145, 149, 156, 160, 201, 281, 286, 298, 300, Joseph 127, Jone 10, Judith 93, 169, Lucy 298, Martha 111, 118, 123, 129, 137, 142, 145, 190, Rachel 116, 139, 144, 145, 149, 153, 160, 161, 205, Robt. 10, 26, 38, 40, 51, 87, 143, 149, 152, 155, 169, 206, 285, Ruth 143, Sam'l 40, 112, 114, Sarah 78, 85, 87, 89, 92, 97, 104, 153, 156, 174, 194, Thos. 26, 78, 80, 87, 89, 92, 97, 139, 179, 204, Wm. 103, 112, 114, 119, 123, 127, 153, 155, 157, 286.
Christian, Hester, 201.
Churchhill, Alice, 77, Armistead 64, 77, 121, 125, 129, 137, 146, 148, 156, 298, Benj. 198, Betty 201, Eliz. 64, 69, 172, 198, Hannah, 79, 121, 125, 129, 137, 146, 148, 156, 298, Jno. 77, 81, 125, Judith 156, 304, Lucy 148, 280, 304, Nath. 129, 187, Prisc. 69, Thos. 303, Wm. 63, 64, 69, 121.
Churchyard, Eliz., Herman, Sarah, 60.
Chusick, Thos., 187.

Clare, Anne, 304, Frankey, 201, Jno. 304, Lucy 207.
Clabor, Eliz., 18.
Clark, ——, 24, Abraham 70, Ann 34, 70, 72, 75, 88, 94, 99, 161, 191, 209, Bartho. 88. Benj. 116, 183, Cath. 22, Chichester 161, Edw'd 19, 70, 72, 75, 88, 94, 99, 114, 116, 122, 124, 130, 141, 147, 151, 154, 158, 160, 183, 185, 195, Eliz. 81, 141, Fra. 289, Geo. 35, 154, Jane 156, Jas. 99, Jno. 70, 110, 151, 172, 208, Judith 35, 82, 147, Lizzy 204, Marg. 161, Martha 199, May 75, 114, 116, 122, 124, 130, 141, 147, 151, 154, 158, 160, 161, 170, 195, 199, Robt. 35, 40, 101, 161, Ruth 72, 124, Sam'l 158, 195, Sarah 35, 40, 107, 156, 160, 170, Spencer 161, Susannah 101, 110, 113, 304, Thos. 40, 81, 101, 110, 113, 196, 283, Wm. 94, 114, 161, 181.
Clay, Anne, 24, 80, Geo. 14, 24, 63, Grace 181, Jas. 203, Mary 85, Sarah 14, 24.
Clever, Ann, 36.
Clemons, Eliz., Jane, Robt., 289.
Clincker, Thos., 24.
Cloudas, Alner, 208, Abra. 146, 159, Ann 142, 146, Cath. 158, Eliz. 158, 195, 204, Jno. 152, 204, Lucy 303, Mary 152, 159, Wm. 146, 158, 159.
Clowder, Jer., 190.
Coats, Robert, 203, Sarah 171.
Cocke, Anne, 82, Hannah 31, Jane 18, Math. 81, Nich's 36, 37.
Cockborn, Adam, 186, Aaron, Dorothea, Susanna 117.
Cocking, Hannah, Sarah 30, Jno. 22.
Coffly, Francis, 70, 73, 77, 80, Mary 73, 77, Sarah 73.
Colbee, Nich's, 33, 36, 37, Rose, Wm., 33.
Cole, Ave, 157, 160, 298, Eliz. 160, 196, Jacob 112, 188, Jas. 102, 107, 112, 157, 160, 181, 196, 298, John 102, Josiah 298, Ralph 23, Sarah 102, 107, 112, 157.
Coleman, Dolly, 205, Geo. 80, Jno. 203.
Collett, Geo., 189, Wm. 179.
Colley, Chas., 151, 208, Patience 147, 151, Wm. 147, 170.
Collins, Ann, 98, Anthony 194, Cath. 27, Eliz. 286, Jno. 22, 27, 98, Joseph 286, Lawrence 98, Marg't 27, Rich. 22, Sally 204, Wm. 170, Zach. 302.
Collis, Ambros, 14, 18, Eliz. 14, Mary 14.
Collier. Benj., 207, Cath. 303, Eliz. 11, 203, Fra. 257, Lucy 202.

Comby, Jno. 22.
Comings, Agnes, 116, Angelo 88, 116, Elinor 88, 116, Wm. 88.
Compton, Ann, Geo., 153, Jas. 153, 170.
Condon, Ann, John, David, 152.
Conner, Anne, Mary, 100, Jno. 100, 174.
Conaway, Ann, 9, Mary 63.
Cooke, Eliza, 79, Marg't 11, Molly 303, Mordecai 202, Rich. 302, Thos. 204, 281, 303.
Cooper, Alice, 104, 189, Ann 41, 46, Betty 178, Chas. 91, 104, 192, Eliz. 19, 37, Jas. 41, 46, 47, Jno. 157, Lucretia 155, 157, Marg't 47, Mary 21, 79, 91, 174, Martha 79, Parti 79, Rebecca 41, 82, Wm. 104.
Copeland, Grace, Wm., John, 12.
Corbin, Alice, 9, 10, 18, Ann 9, 10, 280, 303, Betty 281, Fra. 302, Felicia 303, Gawin 303, Johanna 303, Lettice 9, 10, Rich. 302, Thos. 191, Winifrid 9, 10.
Cornelius, Billy, 285, 295, Eliz. 159, 287, Hannah 159, Jno. 159, 200, 285, 287, 299, Mactyer 195, Sarah 287.
Corr, John, 205, Laban 282, Mary 205, 280, Thos. 303.
Coster, Mary, 37.
Cotterell, Wm., 18.
Couch, Aventa, 69, Averilla 65, 76, Dorothy 76, Ed. 65, 69, 82, 93, 99, Eliz. 69, Mary 93, Robt. 65, 76, Sarah 93, 99, 177.
Courlles, Mary, 174, Mercy, Michael, Wm. 61.
Craine, Ellinor, 170, Jno., Sarah, Stevens 198, Wm. 53, 205.
Crank, Agatha, 77, Ann 60, 77, 78, 91, 184, Eliz. 60, 62, 63, 77, 78, 90, 100, 175, Math. 60, 62, 77, 90, 100, 137, 175, Mary 91, 137, Sarah 175, 189, Solomon 100, 175, Thos. 63, 78, 179, 185.
Crosswell, Jas., 83, Peter 178.
Crooker, Wm., 191.
Cranford, Robt., 187.
Creyke, Henry, 8, 25.
Crisp, Thos., 35.
Crittenden, Betsy, 207, Fra. 257, Jno. 10, 207, Rich. 202, Thos. 203, Zach. 208, 281.
Crockford, Lucretia, 187.
Croffield, Ann, 150, 155, 194, Geo., Lucy 287, Jas. 150, Jno. 150, 194, 287, Millicent 155, 194.
Crosby, Eliz'th, 169.
Crossfield, Cath., 207, Jas, 200, Nancy 206.
Crouch, Ed., Jas., Margaret, 197.

Croucher, Marg't, Thos., 88.
Crowdas, Abra., 198, 200, Ann 197, 198, Diana 146, 193, Eliz., 122, 127, Jno. 146, 198, Mary 127, 138, 146, Sarah 189, Wm. 122.
Crutchfield, Edm'd, Eleaner, 119, Stapleton 128, Wm. 119, 128.
Cuffley, Mary, 185.
Cummins, Agnes, 181, Angelo 83, 109, 182, Anne 103, 185, Christian 109, Elinor 103, 109, Jno., Geo. 52, Wm. 185.
Curlett, John, 176.
Currell, Betty, Jno., Sarah, 192.
Curry, Elizabeth, 203, Rachel, 208, Sarah, 170.
Curtis, ——, 10, 198, Agatha 81, 88, 172, Averilla 34, 41, 80, 188, Chas. 28, 34, 36, 129, 206, Chichester 181, Chr. 88, 150, Eliz. 31, 33, 51, 55, 61, 62, 85, 115, 129, 145, 180, 183, Fra. 119, 150, 302, Geo. 52, Giles 34, Jane 34, Jas. 31, 33, 34, 51, 81, 88, 150, 177, Jno. 63, 72, 84, 145, 191, Johanna 129, Mary 34, 52, 61, 119, 199, Martha 115, 119, 127, Mercy 52, 55, Michael 55, Polly 281, Rebecca 72, Rice 62, 115, 127, Rich'd 72, 119, 122, 130, Rose 28, 34, 36, 122, Susan 145, 188, 191, Thos 41, 61, 184, Wm. 52, 178, 205, 303.
Cutter, John, 39.
Cutton, Chr., Hope, Mary, 72.
Custin, John, 80.

Dabney, Benj., 208.
Dagnell, Margret, Sarah, 91, Sam'l 82, 91.
Dainly, Susanna, Wm., 92.
Dalley, Frances, 20.
Dame, Geo., 283, Mary 170, 283.
Dangerfield, Jno., 63, Mary 304, Sarah 29.
Daniel, Abra., 140, Agatha, 25, 63, 101, 127, 148, 161, 194, 196, 298, Ann 72, 95, 112, 118, 127, 139, 145, 152, 155, 156, 160, 196, 199, 286, 287, 298, 299, Ave. 148, 194, Bealy 152, Benj. 144, Betty 150, 155, 157, 194, 199, 280, 288, Bev. 282, Cath. 80, 152, 155, 193, 194, 201, Chas. 72, 137, 140, 144, 149, 150, 191, Chicheley 130, Chr. 143, Clara 155, 171, 283, Constance 40, 50, Constant 152, Curtis 284, Dorothy 160, Eliz., 55, 72, 75, 95, 103, 107, 110, 112, 117, 122, 128, 138, 143, 148, 150, 155, 161, 183, 187, 192, 197, 283, 284, 286, 287, 297, Fra. 91, 152, 158, 178, 282, Garret, 65, 148, 155, 192, 195, Geo. 122, 131, 207, 283, 285, Henry 55, 131, 150, 152, 155, 157, 187, 189, 194, 298, Jas. 64, 72,

321

78, 91, 96, 109, 114, 120, 124, 130, 140, 149, Jane 124, 130, 137, 140, 144, 149, 150, 193, Jochebed 14, 21, 25, 103, Jno. 31, 50, 63, 78, 109, 138, 160, 171, 197, 202, 283, 304, Josiah 118, 196, 287, Judith 75, 283, Leonard 286, Lucy 112, 158, 282, 286, 287, 288, 298, 303, Lunsford 201, Lydia 201, Maria 289, Marg't 50, 55, 64, 65, 72, 78, 82, 96, 109, 112, 114, 120, 124, 169, 187, 189, 190, Mary 21, 55, 62, 78, 88, 95, 101, 117, 131, 139, 144, 152, 153, 155, 157, 187, 189, 193, 207, 285, Milly 139, 190, 282, Mosely 157, 185, Nelson 207, 285, Obediah 153, 157, Oliver 202, Peter 140, 150, 193, 196, Phebe 114, Rachel 64, Reuben 107, Robt. 36, 50, 55, 65, 78, 95, 107, 112, 122, 128, 138, 139, 143, 144, 148, 150, 152, 155, 157, 158, 161, 178, 187, 190, 192, 193, 194, 198, 282, 286, 287, 288, 297, Rich. 14, 72, 75, 95, 103, 110, 156, 160, 171, 286, 298, 299, Sam'l 128, Sarah 62, 153, 157, 208, 257, Susanna 160, 169, 207, Thad. 283, Thos. 150, 208, 283, Vivion 120, Wm. 21, 25, 29, 33, 40, 51, 55, 62, 78, 82, 88, 91, 95, 101, 112, 118, 127, 139, 145, 152, 156, 181, 196, 199, 283, 284, 287.
Darbby, Eliz., Lucy, 289, Jno. 280, 304.
Darrell, Chas., 131, 188, Eliz., Sampson 131.
Davenport, Reubin, 204.
Davids, David, Jonathan, Mary, 77.
Davidson, Kath., Mary, 50, Rich. 38, 50.
Davis, Alice, 13, 17, 50, 95, Andrew 128, 140, 146, 148, 151, 192, Ann 17, 30, 70, 72, 286, Arthur 182, Ave. 95, 177, 184, Barbee 140, Benj. 16, 70, 72, 77, 80, 138, 140, 142, 145, 148, Christian 72, Constant 93, 99, David 37, 50, 51, 62, 66, Dianar 86, Dorothy 159, 300, Elisha 59, Eliz. 59, 92, 98, 103, 127, 128, 138, 140, 142, 143, 146, 148, 150, 152, 155, 157, 159, 162, 174, 192, 202, 299, 302, Fra. 99, Geo. 14, 16, 146, 196, Henry 17, 18, 30, 170, Jas. 106, 159, 299, 300, Jno. 13, 18, 25, 31, 33, 63, 67, 71, 76, 77, 84, 86, 88, 92, 93, 99, 106, 110, 138, 143, 145, 148, 152, 155, 157, 172, 177, 181, 187, 188, 206, 286, Judith 142, 145, 148, Lewis 157, Marg't 67, 71, 77, 93, 106, 148, 187, Martha 50, 51, 88, 202, Mary 62, 66, 70, 84, 92, 99, 148, 152, 170, 175, 192, 196, 201, 300,
Rachel 92, Rich. 92, 151, Robt. 59, Sarah 13, 25, 27, 70, 80, 92, 110, 184, Staige 205, Stapleton 302, Susan 14, 16, 70, 71, 143, 303, 304, Thos. 70, 76, 92, Wm. 67, 80, 83, 99, 103, 110, 127, 128, 152, 155, 159, 181, 186.
Dawd, John, 7.
Dawson, Leon, Marg't, 142, Thos. 142, 169.
Day, Ann, 145, Ed. 141, 145, 148, Jane 127, Jno. 127, 141, Judith 127, Mary 141, 145, 148.
Dayly, John, Mary, Sarah, 77.
Dazier, Jas., Jno., Sarah, 121.
Deacon, Patrick, 82.
Dearelone, John, 22, 25, Kath., Marg't 25.
Deagle, Ann, 87, 178, 201, 287, 304, Jas. 117, 285, Jno. 95, 155, 170, 196, 199, Mary 155, Moryan 287, Pat. 87, 95, 106, 110, 117, Rebecca 87, 95, 106, 110, 117, 202, Sam'l 106, Sarah 285, Wm. 201, 289.
Deam, Beverly, 204.
Dean, Eliz., 200, 205, 299, Fra. 199, 200, Jno. 199, 200, 299, Wm. 199, 299.
Deforces, Cornelius, Sarah, 299.
Deforest, Eliz., Cornelius, 285.
Degge, Anthony, 89, Jas. 100, Johanna, John 78, 80, 88, 89, 100, Wm. 199.
Dejarnatt, Dan'l, 201, Geo. 204, Nancy 303.
Dempsie, Maurice, 186.
Denison, ——, 198, Cath. 80, Jno. 202.
Dennis, Cath., Jno., Rebecca, 46.
Depree, Abraham, 35.
Deputy, Mary, Thos., 90, Robt. 18, 80.
Derby, Southey, 304.
Deshago, Robt., 162.
Dess, Wm., 81.
Devall, Elliner, 196.
Deverdall, John, 21.
Devolve, Jas., 177.
Dewd, Rachel, Rich., 7.
Dewton, Penelope, 82, Rich. 31.
Dews, Augustine, Jone, Rich., 29, Wm. 48.
Diamond, Henry, 180.
Diatt, Thos., 179.
Didlake, Ann, 206, Cath. 203, 281, Eliz. 206, Fra. 202, Jas. 206, Mildred 280, Nancy 204, Phil. 207, Robt. 205, Wm. 206.
Diggs, Joanna, 175.
Dillard, Delphia, 203, Ed. 139, 143, 149, 150, 156, 160, 196, Eliz. 156, 204, 206, Fra. 139, Garret 196, Geo. 280, Jno. 149, Jane 203, Lucy 160, Martha 139, 143, 149, 150, 156, 160, 196, Mary 143, Nichs.

170, Phil. 207, Sarah 205, 257, Thos. 171.
Dinely, Susannah, 162.
Ditton. Edm'd, Martha, 147, 154, Jno. 154, Ruth 147.
Dixon, Michael, 203.
Dobbs, Cath., 120, 196, Eliz., Jno. 102, 107, 114, 120, 125, Jno. 169, 179, Sam'l 125, Wm. 107, 193.
Docker, Ann, 19, Edward 19, 20, Fra. 19, 54.
Dodson, Eliza, 14, Fra. 14, 18, 44, 47, 60, 69, 71, 85, Jane 69, Mabel 44, 60, 69, 71, 85, 174, Rachel 44, Rebecca 71, 187.
Donnelly, Arthur, 82, 181.
Doss, 16, 30, 33, 37, Jno. 16, 18, 30, 33, 150, 169, 194, Elliner 16, 63, Mary, Sarah 150, Thos. 30, 33, Wm. 16.
Douglas, Jas., 185.
Dowrey, Eliz., 33.
Dowlin, Ann, 28, Anthony 28, 40, 51, Eliz. 40, 51.
Downe, Kath., 38.
Downey, Anne, 175, Jno. 204.
Downing, Wm., 11, 68, Dan. 81, Eliz. 11, 68, 81, Lettice 82.
Douton, Anthony, Eliza, 19, 38, Thos. 38.
Dozier, Sarah, 184.
Drue, Mary, 20.
Drummond, Caty, Sam'l, 207, Mary 203.
Dudding, Humphrey, 26, 28, Mary 28, Sarah 26.
Dudenfield, Ann, 21.
Duckworth, Abel, Faith, 88. 97, 105, Ann 191, Faith 176, John 105, Mary 88, Thos. 169.
Dudley, Agnes, 201, Ambros 46, 104, 119, 300, Ann 42. 45, 111, 113, 119, 127, 139, 145, 180, Averilla 68, Benj. 284, Betty 304, Chas. 201, Chichester 91, Dorothy 44, 69, 72, Edith 43, 69, 72, Eliz. 16, 18, 34, 43, 44, 68, 69, 73, 82, 91, 95, 97, 100, 104, 111, 113, 193, 300, 303, Francis 30, 33, 41, 44, 46, 80, 196, 197, Geo. 43, Hannah 280, Jas. 16, 18, 34, 38, 43, 45, 69, 71, 124, 131, 141, 190, 193, 197, 284, Jane 124, 131, 148, 152, 190, 193, 197, Jno. 22, 43, 44, 69, 72, 110, 113, 119, 127, 139, 145, 176, 204, Joyce 155, 287, Judith 111, 120, Keziah 300, Marlow 148, Mary 24, 38, 39, 42, 76, 82, 145, 207, Rebecca 285, Rich. 72, Robt. 43, 55, 68, 69, 71, 91, 95, 100, 104, 120, 148, 152, 170, 190, 193, Sarah 16, 28, Staunton 131, 170, Thos. 30, 33, 38, 39, 41, 44, 73, 80, 97, 110, 155, 190, 217, 287, Wm. 24, 45, 111, 120, 124.
Duff, Geo., 51, 53, Jno. 51, 54, Rebecca 51, 53.
Dues, Rich., 20.
Duggin, Alice, John, Thomas, 89.
Duglas, Ann, 45, 80, James 45, Johannah 46.
Dulany, Susanna, 209.
Dunberry, Jas., 169.
Dunkington, Ann, Eliz., 56.
Dunn, Hanna, 204, Jno. 203.
Dunlevy, Ann, 201, Braxton 205, Deb. 204, Eliz. 149, 153, 195, 200, 282, 284, Jas. 149, 153, 195, 198, 200, 282, 284, 285, 287, 297, 304, Jane 285, 297, Joanna 284, 287, Jno. 198, 285, 287, Levy 282, Mary 153, 195, 200, 284, 287, 304, Wm., 149.
Dunlin, Eliza, 28.
Dunn, Elsy, 205.
Dunston, Eliz., Thos., Wm., 46, Jno. 170, Warner 202.
Durham, Sarah, 198, Eliz. 160, 299, Gregory 160, Ransom 299, Robt. 160, 299.
Dye, Ann, Arthur, 157, Jane, Rich'd 146, Sarah 157.
Dyer, James, 20.

Early, Eliz., 85, 67, 126, Jeremiah 67, 126, Jno. 126, Thos. 67.
Easter, Mary, 162.
Eddington, Dorothy, 21, Eliz. 35.
Edey, Sarah, 29.
Edmondson, Jas., 184, Judith 208.
Edmunds, Mary, Nicholas, 72.
Edmunds, Jeptha, 63, 72, 80, 175.
Edwards, Ellianor, 18, Joyce 192, Wm. 204.
Edw'd, Pearse, 176.
Eggleston, Judith, Joseph, 285.
Elee, Jno., 20, 54.
Ellerson, Eliz., Jno., Mary, 124.
Ellis, Edw'd, 17, Hezekiah 98, 183, Mary, Sarah 98.
Elliott, Ann, 148, 206, Eliz. 79, 86, 90, 148, 155, 157, 160, 175, 199, 299, Jno. 160, Math. 157, 202, Mary 31, 33, 79, 90, 200, 303, Marg't 86, Robt. 155, 157, 160, 299, Sarah 31, 33, 35, Thos. 31, 82, 86, 90, 148, 172, Wm., 81, 90, 172, 202.
Elwood, Grace, 20.
Emmerson, Ann, 113, Eliz. 50, 100, 107, Geo. 113, Henry 35, 50, 62, 68, 78, 107, 118, 123, 129, 188, 196, Jas. 118, Jane 123, Joanna 68, Jno. 78, Marg't 129, Mary 62, 68, 78, Sarah 107, 118, 123, 129, 196, Thos. 62, Wm. 113.
English, Geo., Rich., Sarah, 151, Mary 20.

Erixon, Hance, 19, 20, Judith 19, 20.
Estree, Rich'd, 185.
Eubank, Ann, 171.
Eyre, Jon., 201.

Fares, Wm., 192.
Fargueson, Thos., 206.
Farrell, Anne, 183, Cath. 27, Edw'd 97, 104, Judith 97, Marg't 97, 104, Rich'd 23, 27, 30, 33, Sarah 30, 33, Winifrid 17, 30, 33.
Fary, Edm'd, 193.
Faulkner, Anne, 110, Benj. 171, Eliz. 137, 198, Ellis 115, 121, 126, 184, 187, Henry 110, Jacob, 137, Jane 201, Jno. 298, Judith 201, 298, Lucy 107, Mary 115, 137, Mildred 137, Thos. 115, 121, 126, Wm. 81.
Fearman, John, 34, 35, 38, Sarah 50, Ursula 34, 38, 50, Wm. 38.
Fearn, Ann, 80, 109, 115, 121, 130, 142, 149, 186, Dorothy 121, Geo. 104, 298, Jane 298 Jno. 35, 98, 104, 109, 115, 121, 127, 130, 149, 162, 186, 194, Judith 130, Machen 115, Mary 34, 80, 109, 298, Sarah 98, 104, 142, 176, Thos. 34, 127, 149, 186.
Fenning, John, 202.
Fenwick, Mary, 184.
Fernald, Geo., 204.
Ferrell, Cath., Martin, 128. Wm. 128, 187.
Finley, Fanny, 208, Hugh 63.
Finney, Honour, 86, Jno. 57, 79, Marg't 57, Rich'd 176, Wm. 80, 175.
Fitz, Jeffries, Ann, Thos., 30, Wm. 20, 30.
Fisher, Anne, 161, Chr. 39.
Fleet, Ann, Henry, Wm., 104.
Fleming, Frances, 214, Jno., Sarah, Susan, 124.
Fletcher, Edward, Hannah, Mary, 27.
Flippen, John, 202.
Floyd, Humphry, 23, Jane, 169.
Fluewelling, Wm., 193.
Foster, Eliz., 75, 83, Grace 20, Jno. 75, 80, 81, Nancy, 206.
Follwell, Henry, 82.
Fontaine, Jas., 201.
Foudry, Nancy, 280.
Fourget, Chas., Eliz., 139.
Foulk, Andrew, 175.
Fox, Jas., Jno., Tabitha, 297.
Fowle, Nicholas, 35.
Free, Eliza., 35.
Freeman, Ann, 25, 184, Barnett, 25, Henry, 53, 178.
Freeston, Geo., 41, 113, Mary 41, 103, Sarah 103, 178, Wm. 41.
Fretwell, Jno., 148, Mary, Wm., 144, 148, 153, Rebecca 153.
Frygore, Francis, 20.

French, Anne, 131, Esther 79, Mary 22, 131, 137, 142, 207, Thos. 131, 137, 142, Wm. 137.
Fuller, Martha, 208.
Fulsher, Anne, Jno., Sarah, 118.
Furnett, Alice, 42, 46, Joan 46, Jno., Wm., 42.

Gabriell, Anne, 26, 82, Jno. 26, Rich'd 21, 23, 26.
Gaffield, Wm., 172.
Gaines, Dorothy, Rich., Wm., 146, Henry 303, Thos. 202.
Gale, Henry, 54.
Gallifor, John, 63.
Gardiner, Agatha, 97, 169, Ann 52, 55, 66, 77, 92, 97, 124, 141, 174, 197, Betsey 197, Blackly 158, 196, Cath. 66, 137, Diana 16, 85, 92, Eliz. 110, 165, 205, Fra. 137, 189, Geo. 205, Henry 299, Jno. 110, 158, 196, Jas. 137, 147, 299, Judith 124, Martha, 159, 162, Martin 85, Mary 16, 47, 52, 141, 147, 151, 155, 159, 196, 206, 299, Rinning 81, 84, Solomon 155, Thos. 16, 20, Wm. 47, 52, 66, 92, 97, 110, 124, 141, 147, 151, 155, 159, 187, 197.
Garland, Eliz., 203, 302, Mary 281.
Garrett, Agatha, 206, Amy 159, 298, Ann 206, Edm'd 209, Franky 201, Humphry 159, 208, Martha 206, Mary 280, Nancy 203, Rachel, Sarah 202.
Gasking, Lewis, 29.
Gaston, Wm., 171.
Gates, Peter, 16, Rose 16, 25, 30, 38, Stokely 81, Thos. 16, 18, 25, 30, 38, 174.
Gatewood, Sally, 204.
Gayer, Jno., 188, Lucy, Mary 123, Wm. 123, 188, 190.
Gear, Mary, 192.
Gellett, Ann, Eliz., Tho., 31.
George, Alice, 12, 37, Ann 111, 117, 122, 128, 141, 175, 282, 283, 284, Betty 111, Cath. 40, 60, 68, 81, 78, 88, 96, 120, 175, Dan'l 88, David 12, 60, 68, 78, 96, 98, 183, Eliz. 141, 144, 146, 285, 288, Fra. 303, Hally 78, Henry 146, 195, 207, Jane 55, Jas. 283, Joanna 68, Jno. 12, 60, 62, 117, 120, 123, 139, 145, 150, 202, 282, 284, 285, 303, Judith 88, Leon 150, 207, 302, Lewis 283, 284, Mary 12, 96, 123, 179, 304, Meacham 123, 285, 288, Michall 120, 123, 139, 145, 150, Rachel 146, 196, Rich. 79, 141, 144, Robt. 35, 40, 51, 55, 62, 79, 111, 117, 122, 123, 128, 185, 189, Sarah 40, 51, 55, 62, 79, 82, 122, 189, Smith 62, Susannah 139, 144, 202, Wm. 281, 282, 284.

Gerrard, Anne, Jane, 90.
Gess or Gest, Eliz., 15, 142, 151, Geo. 142, 151, 191, Milly 203, Susan 15, Wm. 142.
Gibbs, Anne, 111, Diana 89, 169, Eliz. 44, 46, 87, Gregory 16, John 16, 43, 46, 47, 59, 64, 72, 75, 82, 99, 128, Jane 44, Mary 16, 43, 47, 59, 64, 70, 72, 75, 94, 111, 117, 128, 186, Marrin 46, 70, Sarah 117, Pen. 87, 89, Rich. 82, 87, 89, Thos. 44, 115.
Gibson, Cath., 201, Chas. 26, 303, Churchhill 199, 287, Gregory 26, Henry 154, Isabel 149, 154, 207, 289, John 10, Jas. 149, 154, 169, 287, Jno. 81, 149, Lucy 206, Marke 11, Mary 26, 183, 299, Math. 11, Robt. 299, Thos. 180.
Gilbert, Jas., 179.
Gilbreath, Pen., 178.
Gilliam, Ann, 38, 41, 42, Eliz. 38, 44, Jane 44, Jno. 42, Lucas 41, Robt. 38, 41.
Gilley, Eliz., Jane, 44, 48, Mary 175, Thos. 44, 48, 57, 81, Wm. 57, 177.
Gilliams, Ann, 25, Fra., Robt. 25.
Gilpin, Henry, 186.
Ginkins, Ann, Charles, John, 146.
Goar or Gore, Ann, 76, 183, Benj. 59, 178, Eliz. 81, Henry 102, 143, Jno. 119, 130, 143, Joseph 42, 43, 76, 81, 90, 98, 102, 109, 115, 174, 183, Joshua 45, 59, Lucretia 76, 90, 98, 102, 109, 115, Lucy 144, Marg't 42, 43, Mary 42, 45, 46, 119, 130, 143, 144, Rachel 119, Sarah 45, Susan 140, Wm. 90, 140.
Goddin, Mary, 65, Thos. 65, 82, 189.
Godby, Edw'd, 48, 60, 66, Frances 48, 60, 66, 81, Jno. 66, Mary 48, Rebecca 60.
Godwin, Ann, Thos., Wm., 76.
Golden, Thos., 81.
Golder, Eliz., Mary, Thos., 75.
Good, Ann, 124, 129, Cath. 129, Eliz. 203, Jno. 124, 129, 204, Michael 124, Thos. 209.
Goodloe or Goodlow, Ann, 63, 88, 180, Ave. 94, Cath. 105, Eliz. 54, 62, 68, 79, 88, 94, 105, Geo. 54, Henry 54, 62, 68, 79, 85, 88, 94, 105, Jane 79.
Goodridge or Goodrich, Eliz. 34, 79, Marg't 34, Mary 182, Pat 34, Rebecca 53.
Goodwin, Geo., 129, 139, 170, 192, Jane 129, 138, 139, 142, 170, 192, Jno. 68, 79, 138, 142, Mary 190, Robt. 129, 138, 187.
Gordon, Bridg't, 94, 99, 100, 174, 180, Brown 180, Jas. 179, Jno. 23, 94, Marg't 99, Wm. 94, 99, 177.
Goslin, Mildred, 304.

Gough, Mary, Edw'd, Susannah, 43, Wm. 37.
Grant, Mary, 35.
Grasson, Charles, Mary, Tho., 34.
Graves, Alex., 78, 88, 101, 176, 193, Ann 45, 101, Benj. 45, Hannah 88, 169, Mary 78, 88, 101, 178, Sam'l 45.
Gray, Ann, 43, 44, Eliz. 82, Geo. 44, Mary 63, 182, Sam'l 44, Wm. 187.
Green, Ann, 13, Eliz., 185, 206, Jno., Mary, 13, 126, Rich., 126.
Greenstead, Richard, 29, 33.
Greenwood, Ann, 112, 119, 124, Benj. 120, 155, 192, Betty 138, Cath. 138, 141, 191, Eliz. 111, 115, 120, 126, 149, 159, 281, Henry 141, Jas. 111, 115, 180, 289, Jno. 142, 149, 151, 155, 158, 193, 285, 286, Lucretia 142, 151, 155, 158, 285, 286, Lodowick 158, Martha 289, Mary 124, 155, 159, 169, 299, Mildred 112, Rhodes 149, Rich. 112, 119, 124, 138, 141, 188, Rob't 155, Sam'l 126, 287, Thos. 111, 115, 120, 126, 142, 187, 188, Wm. 151, 159, 299.
Gresham, Amy, 45, 48, Anne 92, 102, 190, Chas. 48, 103, Eliz. 44, Fra. 44, 48, 82, Gardiner 48, Jno. 48, 92, 102, 190, Mary 45, 103, Thos. 44, 45, 92, 179, Wm. 103.
Greene, May, 33.
Gresson, Corbin, 199, Mary, Rachel, Wm. 148, Morris 172, Wm. 170.
Grindee, Jane, Thos., 99.
Groom, Jas., 208, Jno. 171, 202, 203, Rebecca 200, Rob't 171, 282, Rich. 208, Susan 171, 282, Val. 282, Zach. 207.
Grymes, Alice, 115, Ariana 303, Benj. 200, Chas. 112, 188, Eliz. 119, 131, 138, 185, 201, 202, Fra. 138, Jane 281, Jno. 43, 101, 105, 110, 112, 115, 119, 128, 131, 138, 160, 188, Lucy 101, 105, 110, 112, 115, 128, 131, 138, 160, 170, Ludwell 198, Mary 119, 160, 198, 285.
Guess, or Guest, Eliz., 26, 28, 80, 101, 107, 117, 124, 129, Geo. 20, 26, 52, 78, 87, 96, 101, 107, 110, 117, 124, 129, Hannah 78, 87, 96, Jane 96, John 107, 179, Judith 129, Mary 26, 52, 78, 96, 110, Michael 124, Nath. 28, 117, Wm. 28.
Guillams, Ann, Peter, Rob't, 31.
Gunter, Chas., Judith, Wm., 143.
Guthrie, or Guttery, Ann, 54, 111, 116, 149, 158, 192, 203, Betty 102, 169, 284, Dan'l 149, Ed. 192, Eliz. 34, 40, 50, 51, 92, 116, Fra. 129, 141, 145, 150, 155, 158, 286, Jas. 126, 303, Jane 94, 157, 180, Henry 121, Jno. 29, 33, 34, 40, 50, 51, 54, 81,

82, 94, 101, 112, 114, 121, 126, 141, 157, 189, Lettice 102, 111, 116, 185, 190, 199, Marg't 155, Mary 51, 54, 112, 114, 121, 126, 129, 157, 188, 194, 284, 286, Major 284, Nanny 101, 160, Phebe 116, 284, Phil. 204, Rachel 116, Rich'd 50, Sarah 149, Wm. 102, 111, 112, 116, 126, 129, 141, 145, 150, 155, 158, 162, 181, 188, 192.
Guthridge, John, 25, Fra., Geo., Mary 147, Henry 25, Rebecca 25.
Guy, John, 26, 53, Mary 26, 53, Thos. 26, 37.
Gwathney, Reich., 204.

Hackett, Chichely, 117, Jno. 98, Martin 91, Mary, Thos. 91, 98, 103, 109, 117, Wm. 103, 181.
Hackney, Absalom, 151, 193, Alice 90, 97, 104, 109, 114, 120, Ann 114, 183, Benj. 109, 159, 194, 204, 208, Cath. 302, Eliz. 46, 145, 151, 153, 155, 156, 159, 160, 203, Jacob 155, Jane 202, Johanna 46, Jno. 95, 120, 183, Lewis 145, 153, Mary 35, 44, 90, Priscilla 156, Rebecca 44, 95, Sarah 104, 160, Wm. 41, 44, 46, 82, 90, 97, 104, 109, 114, 120, 145, 151, 153, 155, 156, 159, 160, 169.
Haddley, John, Jas., 28, Sarah 174.
Haily, Sally, 200.
Haines or Haynes, Alice 71, Ann 43, 71, Chas. 43, 45, 64, 71, Eliz. 43, 45, 48, 51, 64, 206, Geo. 205, Hannah 51, Joseph 29, Mabel 29, Marg't 48, 64, Sarah 45, 86, Thos. 51.
Halcomb, Geo., Sarah, Wm., 149.
Haley, Eliz., Judith, Wm., 299.
Hall, Eliz., 18, Jas. 205, 284, Martin 60, Mary 60, 284, Nathan 207, Patsey 280, Wm. 284.
Halyard, Wm., 206.
Ham, Rich'd, 169.
Hamat, Cath., 69, Eliz. 69, 87, Wm. 69, 87, 184.
Hamerton, Edm'd, 93, 172, Lydia 85, 93, Pinchback 182, Sarah 93.
Hamilton, Jas., Mary, 126.
Hancock, Eliz., 19, 27, 41, Fra. 19, Thos. 19, 27, Wm. 41, 63.
Hanks, Geo., 20, 201.
Harbinson, Eleonar, Wm., 127.
Hardee, Abra., 110, Agatha 145, 148, 153, 155, 160, 297, 299, 300, Andrew 140, 145, 149, 153, 158, 169, Ave. 66, 77, 79, 81, 91, 99, 106, 119, 125, 178, Cath. 155, Chas. 91, Constance 140, 145, 148, 149, 153, 158, Curtis 169, 195, Eliz. 155, 195, Isaac 184, Jane 176, Jno. 77, 79, 88, 110, 119, 124, 145, 148, 153, 155, 160, 169, 184, 297, 299, 300, Joanna 77, Joseph 66, 77, 79, 86, 91, 99, 106, 145, 186, 190, 300, Marg't 77, 88, 94, 110, 158, Martha 94, 192, Mary 86, 119, 124, 140, 191, 203, Mildred 125, Peggy 201, Perrott 99, Rhoda 149, Robert 77, Sarah 88, 106, 148, 192, Wm. 160, 297.
Hardin, Ann, 96, Eliz., Geo., 77, 96, Thos. 77.
Hardy, Sarah, 88.
Haren, Jonathan, Mary, 159.
Harfoot, Wm., 54, 63, 80.
Hargrow, Augustine, Mary, 110.
Harkins, Bryan, Hannah, Cornelius, 9.
Harrell, Edw'd, 80.
Harrelson, Eliza, 18.
Harrison, Jos., 53, Sarah, 37.
Harrod, Geo., 193.
Harrow, Anthony, 282, Jas. 284, Jno. 171, Sarah 171, 197, Thos. 171, 197, 282, 284, Wm. 197.
Hart, James, 203.
Hartley, Ann, 35.
Harvie, Ann, 115, Eliz. 115, Jas. 187, Jno. 115, Joseph 21, 31, Lucy 204, Mabel 31, Nicholas 63.
Harwood, Chr., 170, Jno. 199, Nancy 303, Thos. 202.
Haslewood, Ann, 40, 81, 96, 107, 179, Fra. 53, Geo. 10, 23, 40, 53, Jane 79, 96, 107, 112, Jno. 81, Mary 28, 112, Thos. 28, 96, 107, 112, 186.
Hatfield, Mary, 187.
Hatton, Anne, John, Roger, 96.
Hayes, Thos., 202.
Haynes (See Haines).
Hayton, Fanny, 202.
Haywood, Conquest, Josh., Mary, 119.
Hazlewood (See Haslewood).
Healy, Eliz., 158, 160, 198, 280, 298, Fra. 303, Geo. 304, Jane 303, Jas. 209, 281, Joanna 158, Jno. 201, 160, 204, 302, Wm. 158, 205, 298.
Heath, Anne, 116, Fra. 116, 121, 124, 129, Henry 129, Jas. 130, Jno. 121, 124, 129, 161, Mary, Thos., 130, Wm., 121, 184.
Hearn, Jno., Mary, 152, Wm., 176.
Hebble, John, 206.
Hedgcock, Thos., 18.
Hefferman, Henry, 170, 198, 263, 281, 289, 302, Letitia, Lucy, 198.
Hendring, Wm., 180.
Henderson, James, 204.
Hendson, Eliz., Isaac, Peter, 145.
Henesey, Jno., 194, John, Mary, 138, 143, 149, 153, 154, 194, Thos. 143, Wm. 154.
Henning, Ann, Jno., Mary, 77.
Heningham, Benj., 207.

Hening, or Hearny, Ann, 69, 73, 95, 101, 109, 116, 157, 202, Benj., 101, Geo. 116, Henry 204, Joanna 202, Jno. 69, 73, 95, 101, 109, 116, 157, 288, Lewis 205, Mary 157, 169, 201, 288, Sarah 73, 164, Wm. 69, Zeb. 201.
Heptenstall, Alice, 287, 304, Dan'l 127, 186, Eliz. 140, Jas. 123, 127, 130, 140, 286, 287, Judith 200, 286, 287, Rebecca 123, 127, 130, 140, Wm. 130.
Herbert, Frances, 20.
Heughen, Robt., 202.
Heyward, Thos., 39.
Hibble, Ann, 282, Jno. 207, 282, 284, 304, Math. 284, Mary 205, 257, 282, 284.
Hickey, Chas., 79, Eliz. 66, 79, 82, Jno. 66, 79, 181.
Hickman, Thos., 22.
Hill, Ann, 14, 19, 26, 30, 33, 46, 48, 69, 76, 87, 92. 129, 149, 183, 192, Diana 92, Dorothy 20, Edw'd 192, Eliz. 69, Ellen 21, Fra. 86, 88, 89, 96, 103, 110, 118, 123, 129, 149, 192, 196, Humphrey 286, Isaac 81, Isabella 46, Jane 286, Jno. 26, Joseph 21, Judith 103, 170, 200, Mary 14, 87, 201, Needles 118, 286, Rebecca 19, 30, 33, 79, Rich. 84, 89, 188, Russell 96, 149, 192, Susannah 17, Thos. 14, 19, 26, 30, 33, 86, 110, 176, Wm. 10, 26, 46, 48, 69, 76, 82, 86, 87, 89, 92, 96, 103, 110, 118, 123, 129, 176, 196.
Hillen, Sally, 208.
Hipkins, Andrew, 40, Jas. 83, Jno. 34, 191, Mary 169, Patsey 302, Sarah 34, 40, Winifrid 80.
Hoard, Jane, Jno., 78, 88, Jas. 88.
Hobbs, Wm., 37.
Hodges, Ann, 196, 197, 200, Chas. 158, 196, 284, Churchhill 289, John 158, 196, 197, 200, 209, 286, 289, 302, Mary 286, 289, Sally 302, Thos. 158, Wm. 197.
Hodgekings, Ann, 20.
Hogans, Rich'd, 18.
Hogg, Roger, 187.
Holderby, Jno., 209.
Holderness, Abigail, 187,
Holland, Dan'l, Jane, 68, Eliz. 81, 118, 183, Mary 118, 169, 183.
Holleway, Cath., 202.
Holley, Wm., 22.
Hollinsworth, Hannah, 22.
Holt, Wm., 208.
Holly, Alice, 63.
Hollyday, Rose, 18.
Homes, Anne, Joseph, Rob't, 78.
Hone, Kath., 18, Theophilus 29, 31.
Hooker, Rebecca, 208.

Hopkins, Eliz., 23, Jas. 8, 31, 257, 303, Mary 8, 31, Rich. 206, Sarah 8.
Hore, Bathsheba, 183, Eliz. 61, Jane, Jno. 61, 68, Susanna 68.
Horne, Jonathan, 80.
Hornsby, May, Thos., 142.
Horseley, Catey, Rhoda, Thos., 287, Jas. 206.
Horton, Jno., 186.
House, Eliza, 16, Nicholas, 16, 18.
How, Alex., 180.
Howard, Ann, 71, 152, Eliz. 155, 285, Eustace 130, 142, 152, 155, 195, John 130, 285, Mary 285, Ruth 130, 142, 152, 155, Wm. 71.
Howell, Rich'd, 11.
Howerton, Chas., 201.
Howes, Sarah, 81.
Hoyl, Ann, 69, 81, Eliz. 69, Sam'l 69, 79.
Hoyt, Eliz., Mary, Sam'l, 71.
Hubard, Mary, 201.
Huchison, Hugh, 187.
Hucklescot, Thos., 30.
Huddle, Mary, 80.
Hudging, Aaron, Johanna, Mary, 156, Lucy 304.
Hudson, Ann, 153, 157, 160, Eliz. 156, 208, Geo. 153, Jno. 153, 297, Mary 160, Martha 297, Peter 156, 160, Sarah 156, Wm. 157.
Hughs, Ann, 55, 106, 174, Dan'l 82, 88, 92, 96, 101, 109, 115, 121, 176, Eliz. 15, 19, 35, 70, 121, 186, 202, Fra. 88, 92, 96, 101, 106, 109, 115, 121, Jno. 65, 79, 82, 89, 92, 98, 174, 190, Mary 63, 88, 89, 98, 169, Millicent 37, Rebecca 65, 70, 89, 98, Rich. 55, Robena 15, Sarah 13, Thos. 115, 257, Wm. 19, 20, 174.
Hummings, Philip, 20.
Humphries, ——, 281, Ann, 15, 20, 69, 95, 146, 153, 169, Ave. 129, Cath. 37, Eliz. 41, 47, 64, 69, 72, 76, 95, 102, 118, 130, 137, 143, 183, 192, 194, 206, Geo. 153, 280, Joanna 72, 85, 175, Jno. 15, 72, 76, 130, 137, 143, 146, 153, 169, 192, 197, Joice 97, Joseph 15, 41, 64, 69, 72, 76, 95, 102, 105, 118, 192, Lucy 171, Mary 64, 202, Nelson 197, 257, Rebecca 47, 72, 76, 97, 105, Robt. 41, 47, 72, 76, 97, 105, Sarah 118, Staige 303, Wm. 29, 130, 186, 303.
Hundley, Thos., 205, Wm. 202.
Hunt, Dorothy, 53, Elen 208, Mary 67, Math. 67, 80, 186, Wm. 81, 184.
Hunter, Dan'l, Mary, Seth, 147, Jno. 8.
Hutchings, Mary, 20.
Hutchinson, Henry 76, Jno., 69, 76, 80, Jos., Mary 69, 72, 76, 80, Wm. 72.

Hutson, Ann, 147, Dorothy 200, Ed. 51, Henry 147, 197, Jno. 197, Rebecca 51, Wm. 51, 200.
Hutton, Jane, Jno., 299, Mildred 199, 299.

Ingram, Ann, 27, 35, 44, Ave. 120, Charity 101, 175, Eliz. 40, 82, 179, Fra. 90, 172, Harding 128, Jas. 27, 40, 105, 109, 114, 120, 124, 128, Jno. 90, 101, 105, 109, 114, 120, 124, 128, 172, 186, Marg't 105, 109, 114, 120, 124, 128, Prisc. 109, Sam'l 35, 44, 101, Sarah 29, 35, 40, Solomon 108, Wm. 178.
Ison, Mary, 205.

Jackman, Rob't, 208.
Jackson, or Jaxson, 13, Ann, 20, 170, Cath. 209, 281, Elianor 80, Joanna 201, Jno. 198, 199, 208, Judith 170, 171, Lucinda 303, Mary 147, 205, Nancy 171, Susan 23, 197, Wm. 207.
Jacobs, Benj., 204, Patty 303.
Jacobus, Ann, 106, Angel 53, Jennett 106, Jos. 106, 179.
James, Dorothy 28, 38, 50, 52, Ed. 28, Eliz. 38, Jane 32, John 120, Mary 50, Priscilla 120, Rob't 28, 38, 52, 120, Wm. 206.
Jameson, James, 178.
Jarvis, Jno., 170, Sarah, West, 95.
Joy, Ely, 25.
Jefferson, Dan'l, 200, 304, 305, David 200, Eliz. 200, Mary 200, 207, 305, Polly 305.
Jeffries, Anne, 203, Dan'l 159, 202, 282, 284, 289. David 159, Diana 289, Gowen 209, Jno. 282, Jochebid 159, Lucy 284, Prisc. 282, 289, Thos. 284, Wm. 30, 304.
Jellett, Ann, Eliz., Thos., 33.
Jenkins, Eliz., 80, Hannah, Jno., 192, Marg't 81.
Jenkinson, Mary, 37.
Jenison, Eliz., Jas., Rebecca, 100.
Jenning, Eliz., 176.
Jesse, Jno., 208.
Jolly, Ann, 128, Dudley 79, 162, 179, Eliz., Henry, 128, 188.
Jones, Agatha, 119, 126, 139, 152, Ann 41, 53, 109, 118, 154, 169, 171, 209, Barker 79, Benj. 87, 106, 139, Caroline 303, Cath. 94, 156, 170, Churchhill 45, 160, 287, 298, 304, Chas. 106, Dorothy 106, 154, Ellianor 21, 87, Eliz. 15, 18, 19, 87, 90, 96, 152, 154, 158, 169, 176, 182, 195, 199, 281, Gabriel 281, Henry 41, Hannah 54, 66, Humphrey 8, 21, 24, 67, 79, 87, 90, 96, 156, 183, Isaac 204, Isabel 129, Jane 27, 36, 118, Jas. 66, 109, 126, 152, 195, Jno. 54, 66, 71, 80, 87, 90, 106, 109, 129, Joseph 87, Joshua 154, Judah 59, Lodowick 90, 201, Lucy 257, Marg't 29, 33, Mary 14, 15, 19, 20, 44, 45, 47, 56, 59, 66, 69, 73, 78, 82, 94, 154, 159, 208, 288, Millicent 287, 298, Nich's 27, 81, Parnell 71, 90, 106, Peggy 156, Phebe 154, 298, Rebecca 71, Rich. 118, 154, 298, Rice 18, 27, Roger 44, 45, 47, 56, 59, 69, 73, 94, 160, 177, 193, Sarah 119, 288, 298, Sissely 21, Susan 44, 47, Thos. 14, 15, 56, 126, 158, 206, Wm. 29, 66, 78, 119, 154, 159, 169, 171, 174, 195, 201, 287, 288, 298.
Johnson, Ann, 99, 110, 115, 120, 145, 149, 169, 188, 192, 204. Arthur 175, Aquilla 115, Benj. 149, Cath. 140, Dan'l 128, 187, Eliz. 63, 75, 120, 188, 195, 285, Esther 75, Geo. 99, 177, Henry 75, 123, 285, Jno. 20, 29, 44, 76, 82, 110, 115, 120, 138, 140, 145, 149, 176, 177, 180, 181, 185, 188, 192, Joice 70, Judith 65, 70, 76, 115, Lucy 44, Marg't 111, 120, 123, 128, 148, 155, 158, May 109, 192, 202, Priscilla 110, 115, 120, 125, 138, 188, Rob't 65, 70, 76, 188, Rebecca 84, Sam'l 155, 191, Sarah 149, Stephen 109, 152, Wm. 37, 109, 111, 120, 123, 128, 149, 152, 155, 188, 195, 285.
Johnston, Eliz., 33, 40, 51, 60, Geo. 29, 33, 40, 51, 60, Henry 60, John 33, Jane 146, Marg't 146, Rebecca 40, Rob't 186.
Jordan, Ann, 64, 79, 82, Jane 63, Jas. 64, 79, Jno. 79, Rachel 203.
Jowel, Michal, Ratlif, 145, Rich. 145, 169.

Kain, Roger, 169.
Keeling, Cath., Thos., 92, 96, 101, 106, Lydia 92, Osborn 101, Wm. 200.
Keith, ——, 257.
Kelly, Patience, 201, Pat. 181.
Kelshaw, Ann, 97, Chr. 97, 101, 106, 110, 162, 181, Esther 110, Fra. 106, 110, 192, Jno. 110, Mary 97, 101, 106, 110, 187.
Kemp, Ann, 47, 61, 117, 202, Eliz. 110, Ellinor 61, Hannah 198, Jno. 199, Judith 130, Math. Mary 47, 104, 110, 117, 125, 130, 172, 186, 303, Peter 199, Rachel 61, Sarah 183.
Ker, David, 304.
Kersey, Eliz., Elianor, 51, Jno. 51, 53.
Key, Alice, 81, Jno. 148, Mary 82.

Kidd, Aaron, 88, Agatha 66, Alice 60, 66, 78, 94, 100, 102, 177, Ann 102, 137, 149, Benj. 144, 147, 156, 158, 169, 171, 199, 204, 202, 281, Betty 143, Burgess 257, Cath. 109, Chowning 158, 200, Duel 86, 144, 149, 169, Ed. 158, 171, Eliz. 13, 23, 128, 137, 143, 161, Fra. 66, 119, 122, 182, Geo. 111, 144, 199, Henry 78, 156, 205, Isaac 202, 304, Jemima 129, Jane 13, 22, 79, 102, 171, 281, Jas. 19, 94, 105, 144, 147, 161, 169, 197, 281, 302, Joan 199, Jno. 19, 79, 105, 119, 122, 137, 139, 147, 151, 202, 284, Jos. 179, Judith 111, 144, 149, 156, 158, 201, 202, 205, Lucy 149, 205, Marg't 55, 61, 66, 77, 79, 86, 88, 94, 99, 100, 105, 109, 149, 178, Mary 13, 118, 137, 144, 281, 285, 289, Moses 77, Nancy 208, 281, 289, Pat. 118, 137, 149, Polly 207, Rebecca 111, 119, 122, 129, 139, 149, 151, 194, Robt. 61, 86, 289, Ruth 171, Sam'l 178, 179, Sarah 19, 151, 200, 303, Sukey 161, Thos. 13, 53, 60, 66, 78, 94, 100, 102, 185, 281, Wm. 13, 55, 60, 61, 66, 77, 94, 99, 109, 128, 137, 143, 161, 184, 199, 206, 280, Winifrid 60.

Kilbee, Cath., 59, 103, 108, 114, Chr. 103, 108, 114, Joanna 44, 45, 59, 80, 103, Hannah 65, Mary 20, Wm. 20, 54, 59, 65, 114.

Killigrew, Caty, 208.

Kilpin, Wm., 85.

King, Ann, 13, Eliz. 169, John 75, 81, Julian 75, 81, Hannah 82, Marg't 23, Martha 27, 34, 37, Rebecca 13, 63, Sarah 81, Wm. 18, 27, 34.

Kingsley, Thos., 63.

Klug, ——, 171, 199, 205, 208, 209, 280, 304.

Knight, Susan, 183.

Lambeth, Thos., 205.

Lane, Eliz., Jno., 38.

Langdon, Mary, 169.

Langhee, Isabella, 80.

Langley, Thos., 180.

Lantor, Isabella, 60, 64, 67, 72, Jno. 52, Marg't 60, Mary 67, 72, Peter 52, Thos. 52, 60, 64, 67, 72.

Larke, Jno., Eliz., 188.

Larking, John, 27.

Laughlin, Ed., Thos., 141, 151, Sarah 141, 151, 193, Simon 151, 200.

Lauright, Eliza., 11.

Laundress, Math., 80.

Lawrence, Eliz., 18, Rich'd 22.

Lawson, Ann, 45, Efferydytus 26, Hannah 145, Isabella 170, James 157, Jane 85, 90, Jno. 20, 26, 141, 144, 153, 157, 192, Joshua 20, Mary 26, 141, 144, 153, 157, Rowland, Sarah 45, Thos. 145, Wm. 141, 145.

Layton, Burwell, Eliz., 197, Geo. 303, Jno. 197, 198, 302, Mary 208, Mildred 197, Reuben 204, 205, Rich. 201, Thos. 197, 304.

Ledford, Math., 43, 53.

Lee, Afia, 209, Alice, 29, Anne 86, 122, 127, 141, 148, 154, 158, 190, Cath. 151, 188, Chas. 14, 25, 75, 85, 86, 91, 101, 151, 154, 158, 170, 178, 192, 298, Dorothy 78, 86, 91, 101, 299, Eliz. 14, 25, 38, 85, 148, 158, 183, 192, Esther 285, 304, Fanny 304, Geo. 154, 158, 170, 201, 285, 286, 299, Hannah 126, Isaac 158, Jane 155, 194, Jas. 154, 155, 202, Jno. 14, 87, 126, 186, Lettice 14, 38, Lucy 304, Marvell 86, Mary 35, 154, 285, 286, 299, Nich's 38, Pen. 148, 151, 155, 158, 192, 198, 298, Reuben 202, Rich. 14, Sam. 86, Sarah 148, Thos. 14, 25, 122, 126, 127, 148, 154, 158, 186, 190, Wm. 122, 154, 190.

Leigh, Francis, 257.

Lenn, Ann, Robt., 285, 286.

Lestridge, Cath., 24.

Lewis, ——, 91, Ann 105, 123, 186, 298, Edm'd 125, Eliz. 50, 52, 53, 75, 88, 97, 102, 106, 112, 116, 125, 169, 193, 282, 285, 286, Eusebias 52, 83, 95, 98, 105, 111, 124, 130, 188, 189, 190, 285, 297, Gabriel 285, Griffin 53, Grace 29, 53, Jas. 41, 42, 46, 60, 120, 286, 176, Jno. 20, 50, 52, 53, 75, 88, 97, 98, 102, 106, 112, 116, 125, 208, 285, 286, 298, 299, Jone 41, 42, 46, 60, 120, Joshua 120, 123, Kath. 20, Marg't 37, 112, Martha 123, 125, 285, 297, Math. 188, Mary 23, 75, 95, 105, 111, 117, 124, 125, 130, 176, 285, Rich. 116, 194, 297, Sarah 80, 189, Susanna 97, Thos. 50, 106, 186, Walter 14, Wm. 172, 180, 282, 299, Zebulon 76.

Lightfoot, Philip, 18.

Linn, Frances, Marg't, Roger, 128.

Lister, Alex, 189, Lucy 188.

Littlefield, Jno., 35.

Livingston, Alice, 204, Nelly 199.

Lomax, Cath., 181, Jno. 63, Eliz. Lunsford, Mary, 131.

Lone, Eliz., 37, Nich. 23, 39.

Long, Dorothy, 15, 35, Dan'l 15, 31, Eliz. 125, Jno. 125, 197, 303, Rob't 197, 302, Sarah 197, Wm. 125.

Longest, Nancy, 206, Rob't 304.

Lorimer, Geo., 201.

Low, Anne, 57, 69, 72, 75, 97, Fra. 57, Jno. 97, Lettice 81, Marvel 75, Mary 69, Sam'l 57, 69, 72, 75, 97.
Loyall, Ann, 158, 181, Eliz. 11, 158, Jno. 36, 37, 158, Marg't 11, 21, Mary 38, 80, 83, Ralph 38, Wm. 17, 23, 34, 38, 80.
Lucas, Ave., 99, Etheldred, 93, 99, Jno. 99, 175, Judith 86, 93.
Lumpkin, Coleman, 205, Rob't 205.
Lyall, Amey, 91, 101, 106, Eliz. 156, Henry 208, Jno, 106, 156, Mary 303, Ralph 92, 101, 106, 177, Wm. 85, 92, 101.

Mabraine, Mary, 23.
Maccoy, Sarah, 188.
Mackendree, John, 203.
Mackmullen, Jas., 180.
Machen, Cath., 200, Cassandra 159, 298, Henry 98, Jas. 159, 179, 298, Mary 90, 98, Thos. 82, 90, 98, 187, 298.
Macky, David, Robt., Eliza., 76, Jas. 81.
Macrory, Frances, 38.
Madarius or Maderas, Chas. 77, 145, 298, Jno. 139, 145, 180, Mary 77, 139, 145, 178, 298.
Madcrions, Chas., Mary, 55.
Mahaffee, Lilly, 186, Thos. 184.
Major, Eliz., 143, 146, 152, 169, 206, 304, Geo. 143, Jno. 303, Math. 304, Rich. 146, Sam'l 143, 146, 169, Sarah 152.
Man, Dorothy, 30, 37, Eliza 20, Jane 58, 65, Jno. 30, 58, 65, Theophilus 30.
Mannuel, Ann, 62, 66, 77, Dorothy 85, Edm'd 62, Jno. 62, 85, Kath. 77, Pat. 66, 77.
Mansfield, Francis, 120, 125, 188, Mary 120, Wm. 120, 125.
Marable, Benj., 303.
Marcum or Markham, Eliz., 48, 72, 76, 84, 91, 98, Jno. 48, 98, Joseph 76, 178, Sam'l 72, Wm. 48, 72, 76, 91, 98.
Marion, Anne, 85, Bridget 93, Patrick 85, 93.
Marks, Ann, 159, Clare 155, 159, 196, Jno. 155, Wm. 155, 159.
Marston, Abiggail, 71, 174, Ann 46, 47, 59, 65, 70, 71, Eliz. 129, 184, Jno. 46, 47, 65, 71, 82, 116, 123, 129, 130, 186, Martha 59, Mary 174, Phebe 116, 123, 130, 190, Thos. 46, 54, 116, 129, 187.
Marsh, Benj., 35, Eliz., Wm. 51.
Marshall, Peggy, 302.
Martin, Cath, 130, Eleanor 82, Eliz. 47, 146, 148, 150, 193, Hugh 130, 146, 148, 150, 193, John 148, Jos.

130, 146, 201, Marg't 47, Oliver 150, Sarah 36, 37.
Marye, Johanna, 22.
Masey, or Massey, Alice, 55, 62, 86, 93, Ann 38, 93, Eliz. 50, 78, John 34, 38, 62, Marg't 34, 54, Martin 23, 50, Mary 23, Milliner 38, Ralph 34, 55, 62, 78, 85, 86, 93, Sarah 55.
Mash, Eliz., Jane, Rob't 117, Sarah 179.
Mason, Ann, Eliz , Josiah, 15, Joseph 18, Mary 169, Rebecca 81, Thos. 185.
Matthews, Ann, 56, 145, 192, Edw'd 21, Eliz. 160, John 56, 70, 82, 145, 149, 153, 157, 160, 192, Mary 280, Moses 304, Phebe 29, Sam'l 70, Wm. 56, 70, 153, 208, 304.
Maxum, Eliz., 57, 73, 75, 184, Ell. 73, Ruth 70, Thos. 70, 73, 75, 79.
Maxwell, Johanna, 147, John 151, Kezia 151, 154, Thos. 147, 151, 154, 170.
Maynell, Catharine, Dorothy, Robert, 16, 19.
Mayo, Anne, 93, Ellen 18, Jas. 140, 144, 147, 160, 190, Jno. 144, 150, 181, 191, Martha 144, 147, 150, Ruth 140, 190, Sarah 93, 172, Val. 82, 86, 140.
McCarty, Chas., 178.
McDaniel, Mary, 198.
McGee, Edward, 303.
McGuire, Eliz., Jno., 33, 88, Mary 38, Phebias 33.
MacNeal, Cath., Jno., 139, 158, Nell. 158, Wm. 139.
McTire, Ann, 112, 182, Betty 105, Cath. 87, 90, 97, 105, 112, 120, 126, Eliz. 96, 170, 176, 205, Fra., 204, Hannah 88, 96, 179, Henry 97, Hugh 87, 91, 105, 112, 120, 126, 188, Jas. 81, 88, 186, Jno. 304, Lucretia 97, Rob't 304, Sarah 91.
McWilliams, Jno., 206.
Meacham, Ann, 161, 297, Benj. 126, 193, Bernard 154, Eliz. 80, 128, 154, 155, 171, 195, 303, Fra. 171, Henry 79, Jane 61, 66, 78, 285, 287, Jas, 79, 80, 87, 93, 100, 126, 155, 178, 189, 195, Jno. 48, 52, 79, 80, 84, 161, 297, Joseph 61, 66, 78, 128, Laurence 171, 200, Lucy 202, Michall 27, Mary 48, 52, 60, 79, 80, 93, 100, 126, 128, 155, 161, 195, Michal 52, 79, Sarah 61, Susanna 48, Thos. 60, Wm. 52, 100, 154, 285, 287.
Medaris, Benj. 159, Chas., Mary 62, 154, 159, Eliz. 154, Jno. 62.
Medarst, Chas., Mary, 150.
Medley, Elianor, Jno., 88, 94, Jas. 88, Lucy, Robt. 94, Zena 208.

Meeres, Henry, 53.
Merry, Jno., 182, 183.
Meggs, Jas., 171.
Merchant, Charlotte, 207.
Meredith, William, 203, 208.
Meriwether, 291.
Mesan, Allexander, Eliz., 44.
Meuler, Ann, Nichs., 137, 142, Eliz. 137.
Michaell, Ed., 9, Jane, Marg't, Patrick 40.
Michener, Jno., 71, Mary 21, 71, 80.
Mickleberry, Ed., Jane, Henry, 65.
Mickelburrough, Ann, 202, Caty 302, Ed. 9, 39, 55, 61, 65, 78, 86, 106, 137, 179, 191, Eliz. 28, 38, 106, Fra. 124, 128, 137, 141, 200, Henry 124, 128, 137, 141, 146, 157, 195, 289, 298, Jas. 146, Jane 55, 61, 78, 86, 124, 191, 200, Jno. 55, 61, 172, 180, 204, Nancy 303, Robt. 61, 106, 205, Sarah 63, Susanna 146, 157, 298, Tobias 23, 28, 53, 78, 185, Vivion 298.
Micou, Jno., 177.
Micurday, Martha, 183.
Middleton, Mary, 27, 174, Prisc. 27, 179, Susanna 179.
Millener, John, Mary, 65.
Milby, Eliz., 204, Jas. 205, Jos., Lucy 283, Ruth 203, Susanna 203.
Miller, Anderson, 304, Ann 81, 105, 139, 145, 206, 285, 287, Chr. 139, 145, 285, 287, David 285, Eliz. 112, 118, Hannah 65, Jane 118, 126, 162, 182, Jno. 44, 46, 48, 65, 70, 92, 100, 105, 110, 112, 117, 121, 126, 145, 181, 187, 201, 280, Mary 92, 117, Mical 44, 46, 48, 65, 70, 139, 169, Pat. 46, 112, 118, 185, 186, 287, Prisc. 100, 175, Sarah 100, 105, 110, 117, 121, 126.
Mills, Eliz., 209, Mary 204.
Minie, Rich., 257.
Minor, ——, 82, 172, Benj. 171, Diana 77, 174, Doodis 11, 14, Eliz. 14, 23, 162, Garrett 14, 77, 80, 178, Jno. 77.
Mins, Ann, 14, 16, 21, Eliz. 14, 21, Thos. 14, 16, 21, 54.
Minter, ——, 280, Jno. 171, 283, Mary 171, Sukey 171, 283.
Mitcham, Ann, 108, Dan'l 55, Dorothy 68, Eliz. 53, 118, Henry 68, Jas. 27, 108, 118, Jane 82, Jno. 15, 24, 27, 51, 55, 82, 184, Jos. 15, Judith 89, Mary 68, 108, 118, Mical 15, 24, 51, 55, Pead 51, Thos. 89.
Mitchell, Isaac, 202, Jno., Sarah 204.
Molloney, Joan, 176.
Moore, Benjamin, 203.
Moor, Dan'l, 143, 169, Eliz., Mary 143,

Macham 85, Martha 183, Rich. 63, Thos., 177.
More, Sam'l, 202.
Moore, Wm. 202.
Month, Henry, 175.
Monnoughon, Jas., 82.
Morgan, Ann, 65, Chr. 298, Cath. 183, 304, David 178, Jane 202, John 65, Sarah 208, Wm, 298.
Morris, Eliz., Jas., Jno., 197, Macktyre, Prudence, Thos., 78.
Morton, Elinor, 194.
Moseley, Agatha, 66, 86, 90, 97, 108, 127, 179, Anne 131, Eliz. 117, Jenny 111, Jno. 90, 100, 111, 117, 123, Joshabee 86, Judith 97, Marvel 19, 63, 66, 86, 90, 97, 108, 127, 131, 180, Mary 100, 111, 117, 123, 127, 131, Sarah 19, 100, 172.
Moulson, Ann, 108, 179, Chas. 113, 287, 288, 298, Eliz. 207, Esther 125, 190, Geo. 119, Jane 113, 119, 125, 190, Mary, Oliver, 160, Rich. 108, 113, 119, 203, 298, Ruth 125, 287, 288, 299, Wm. 160, 203, 287.
Mountague, Abra., 54, Ann 286, Betty 286, 287, 288, 299, Cath. 55, 148, 149, 176, 190, 200, 201, 304, Charlotte 206, Clem. 114, Eliz. 124, 149, 193, 195, 198, 200, 282, 285, 287, 303, Fra. 302, Grace 99, 104, 109, 114, 184, Hannah 206, Island 31, Jane 138, 144, 149, 152, 158, 193, 208, 285, 288, Jas. 152, Jno. 19, 109, 138, 170, 200, 201, Lettice 54, Lewis 286, 287, 299, Mary 19, 21, 62, Martha 283, Mary 299, Pen. 124, 148, Peter 19, 99, 124, 127, 143, 187, 288, Phil. 171, 282, 283, Thos. 55, 99, 104, 109, 114, 124, 129, 143, 162, 178, 187, 195, 202, 303, Sam'l 158, 303, Sarah 304, Wm. 54, 62, 84, 86, 138, 144, 149, 152, 158, 193, 207, 282, 286, 288.
Mountain, Jno., 281.
Moxham, Easter, 177.
Mugguire, Eliza, 31, Jno., Habias, 31.
Muire, Wm., 207.
Mullins, Anne, 119, Arch. 208, Cath. 159, Chas. 30, Eliz. 40, 79, 82, 122, 147, 182, Jno. 186, 286, Mary 30, 40, 79, 115, 119, 122, 143, 147, 150, 159, 186, 286, 299, Rob't 115, Wm. 43, 79, 143, 147, 150, 159, 169, 286, 299, Zach. 23, 30, 40.
Munday, Jno., 80, Rob't, 20.
Mundin, Averila, Frances, Jno., 71.
Murry, Alex., 12, 14, 16, 24, 31, 108, 125, 175, Ann, 12, 14, 91, 99, 206, 282, Andrew 108, David 99, Eliz., 30, 121, 186, Harriet 303, Jane 99, 103, Jno. 14, 91, 97, 103, 108, 114,

121, 125, 282, 303, Lucy 202, Mary 12, 14, 24, 30, 91, 97, 103, 108, 114, 282, 303, Rebecca 14, Rob't 16, Sarah 81, 108, 171, Wm. 202, 282.
Murrow, Ann, Marg't, 55.
Musgrave, Eliz., 19, 24, 30, 42, Michael 19, 20, 24, 30, Thos. 30.
Mylls, Amey, Wm., 287.
Mynor, Doodis, 25, 30, Eliz. 25, 30, Jno. 25, Mary 31, Peter 30.
Muse, 198, Elliot, Juliet 303, Lawrence 281, Hudson 207, Mira 303.

Nancut, Wm., 187.
Nash, Ann, 66, 179, Arthur 46, 175, Eliz. 53, Henry 130, 144, Jochebed 130, 144, Jno. 41, 46, 58, 63, 66, 130, 172, Kath. 50, Lucy 190, Mary 41, 50, 85, Wm. 144, Rebecca 53.
Naylor, Thos., 39.
Needham, Prudence, 36.
Needles, Dorothy, 42, 44, Fra. 42, John 44, Mary 80, Wm. 31, 42, 44, 46.
Negro Children, Births of, 58, 59, 62, 73, 74, 75.
Neilson, Agnes, 207.
Nelson, Phil., 207.
Nevill, Betty, 125, 126, 186, Geo., Hannah 121, 125, Mary 121.
Newberry, Agnes, 71, 77, 186, Eliz. 181, Mary 77, Wm. 71, 77, 181.
Newton, Amey, Ann, 48, Dorothy 55, 80, Jno. 80, Nichs., Thos. 55, Wm. 44.
Newcomb, Ann, Wm., 282.
Nickingson, Michaell, 21.
Nicholls, Alice, 15, 29, 33, 92, 189, Ann 171, 190, Cath. 33, Eliz. 23, 162, Griffin 92, Henry 15, 53, 92, Jane 106, 170, Jno. 31, 54, 98, 162, Kath. 27, Tabitha 172, Winifrid 15, 174.
Nicholson, Geo., 304, Grace 53, 162, James 31, Wm. 29, 33, 39.
Night, Pat., 195.
Norman, Alice, 89, 178, Ann 14, Eliz. 14, 60, 112, Henry 14, Jane 112, 117, Jno. 299, Mary 25, 299, Moses 25, 89, 184, Robt. 60, 117, 196, Thos. 25, 112, 184, 299.
Norris, Jno., 206.
Norwood, Mary, 63.
Nunnam, Hannah, Ann, 13.
Nutter, Jas., 179.

Oakes, Elizabeth, 204.
Obryant, Dennis, 169.
Ockoldham, Mary, 63.
O'Dear, David, 206, Major 208.
Okendime, Patrick, 80.
Okill, Jno., 84.

O'Harrow, Sarah, Martin, Thos., 283
Older, Sarah, Thos., 124.
Oldner, Geo., Sarah, Thomas, 105.
Oliver, Isaac, 118, 182, Susanna, Thos., 81, 111, 118, 120, Wm. 111, 120.
Onely, Samuell, 20.
Orphan, Amey, 8, 24, Anne 16, Constance 77, Henry 24, Joseph 16, 73, 77, Jno. 77, Marg't 24.
Orrill, Lawrence, 186.
Osborn, Alice, Ann, 38, Eliz. 162, Henry 23, 37, 38, Mary 63, Michal 201.
Osbondistall, Mary, 20.
Overstreet, Jane, 288, Jas. 152, 157, John 152, Mary 157, 195, Rich. 288.
Owen, Ann, 73, 94, 169, 170, Augustine 47, 72, 75, 89, 94, 101, 114, 148, 154, 170, 183, Betsey 304, Chr. 47, 72, 137, 189, Clem. 47, Constant 114, Edw'd 21, Eliz. 91, 97, 137, 150, 169, 199, 284, 288, Emory 71, Hannah 76, 86, 91, Jacob 108, Jas. 101, 302, Jane 47, Joan 72, 75, 89, 101, 108, 114, 183, Jno. 71, 73, 75, 78, 80, 81, 86, 91, 93, 94, 97, 137, 140, 142, 148, 155, 178, 201, Judith 139, 142, 146, 150, Mary 89, 151, 148, 154, 155, 195, 199, Michal 73, 78, 86, 93, 97, Nancy 304, Pat. 71, 80, 175, Ruth 194, Susan 189, Sarah 139, 191, 202, Wm. 71, 76, 78, 86, 137, 139, 140, 146, 150, 154, 189, 192, 194, 195, 201, 284, 288, 299.

Pace, Abra., 190, Ann 110, 117, 122, 129, 145, 190, 297, Benj. 131, 140, 286, Dan'l 129, Eliz. 52, 68, 79, 93, 131, 141, 169, 193, Geo. 85, 117, 182, Hannah 141, 151, 154, 158, 297, Jane 68, Jno. 52, 54, 68, 79, 93, 110, 151, 178, 190, 194, Jos. 117, 122, 129, 191, Marg't 54, Mary 126, 131, 140, 145, Neusome 79, Sarah 52, 154, 158, 195, 200, 286, 297, Susan 189, Wm. 126, 141, 151, 154, 158, 195, 200, 286, 297.
Page, Dan'l, Jos., 187, Mann 82.
Pagett, Betsy, 201.
Palmer, Isaac, 199, Sarah 82, Wm. 280.
Pamplin, Mary, 201.
Pannell, Loretta, 18.
Pant, Wm., 194.
Parris, Eliza, 20.
Parish, Eliz., 284, Jno. 171, 282, 283, 284, Milly 283, Reuben 282.
Parke, Edw'd, 80, Fra. 81, Jane 20.
Parker, James, 18, 35.
Parr, Ralph, 29.

Parrott, Ann, 192, 208, 305, Cath. 144, 158, Curtis 192, Dorothy 153, 305, Eliz. 11, 153, Henry 142, 190, Jas. 158, Jos. 305, Lodowick 140, Nancy 199, Rachel 142, Robt. 140, 144, Rich. 190, Sarah 142, 144, Thos. 158, Wm. 153.
Parry, Betty, 89, Math. 88, 89, Rich'd 54, Wm. 88.
Parson, Johh, 63, Mary 80.
Pate, Eliza, 80, Jas. 35.
Pateman, Mary, 177, Rich. 190, Thos. 63.
Patris, ——, 18, Eliz., Matthew 15, 24, Jno. 1·, Thos. 24.
Patterson, Ann, 171, Jas. 160, Jno. 171, Mary 156, 160, Rich. 156, 171, Sarah 160, Susan 156, Thos. 208, Wm. 304.
Payne, Anne, 51, 52, 81, Bernard 52, Betty 205, Cath. 95, 102, 108, 114, 121, Eliz. 38, 52, Fra. 102, Jno. 20, 114, Lettice 95, Mabel 38, 51, Mary 31, 80, Michall 200, Nichs. 35, 51, Thos, 21, 95, 102, 108, 114, 121.
Peachy 198, 209.
Pead, Agatha, 39, Duell, Sarah, 31, 34, 39.
Pearse, Ed., 180, Eliz., Jno., Mary, 62, Robt. 174.
Peirce, Cath., 51, 93, Chas. 51, Ed. 37, 51, 93, Rebecca 93, Thos. 203.
Pemberton, Eleonour, John 97, Eliz. 97, 174.
Peniell, Eliz., John, 91, 107, 117, Thos. 107, Wm. 117.
Pendergrass, Edm'd, 101, Eliz. 91, Jno. 83, 91, 175, Mary 85, 99, 101, Robt. 101.
Percifull, Mary, 63.
Perkins, Eliza., 79.
Perrott, Agatha, 122, Ann 94, 101, 108, 114, 128, Ave. 42, 108, Betty 89, Chas. 128, Cath. 89, Clara 94, Curtis 42, 94, 101, 108, 114, 122, Frank 41, Cath. 79, 86, 106, 111, 178, Efforella 25, Eliz. 191, Henry 41, 68, Jas. 111, Jno. 106, Marg't 36, Mary 42, 80, Robt. 28, 42, 77, 79, 80, 86, 89, 106, 111, 192, Rachel 191, Rich. 11, 25, 28, 29, 31, 33, 36, 53, 68, 80, 87, Sarah 25, 28, 41, 42, 53, 68, 78, 79, 80, 86, 87.
Perry, Gregory, 204, Math. 81.
Peters Heany, 203, Wm. 171.
Petty, Ann, 15, Christian 12, 15, Max. 12, 15, 16, 36, 38.
Pew, Penelope, 20.
Phillips, Eliz., 25, 65, 144, Cath. 68, Jane, Jno., 68, Marg't 65, Paul 139, 144, 170, Philip 25, Susan 139, 144, Thos. 25, Wm. 169.

Philpots, Ambrose, 193, Benj. 149, Clem. 121, 187, Eliz. 188, Jane 25, Jno. 106, 193, Marg't 149, Paul 106, 124, 149, 193, Sarah 124, Susan 106.
Phiney, Ann, John, 48, Marg't 46, 48, Rich. 46.
Picket, Mary, 63.
Pickworth, Benjamine, 19, Jno. 22.
Pigg, Fra., 208.
Pinion, Eliz., Jno., 99.
Pinnell, Jno., 82.
Piper. Prisc., 202.
Pitts, Sarah, 80.
Poobert, Hannah, Simon, Wm., 52.
Poole, Alexander, Mary, Sarah, 12, Wm. 12, 29, 36, 37.
Porter, Ann, 53, Barbary 47, Eliz. 123, 127, 192, Fra. 9, 59, 123, 127, Jane 47, 59, 80, 123, Jas. 169, Jos. 48, Mary 47, 127, 192, Rob't 39, Thos. 47, Wm. 47, 54, 59.
Portword, Sarah, 181.
Pound, Margaret, 25, Jno. 22, 25.
Powell, Agnes, 304, Jer. 201, Lucy 281, Marg't 20, Mary 172, Pyth. 33, Susan 206.
Prendergast, Ed., 82.
Pressnall, Jacob, James, Mary, 78.
Preston, Jacob, Mary 60, 66, Sarah 60.
Price, Ann, 146, 150, Cath. 13, 25, 137, 142, 146, 150, Eliz. 13, Jane 13, 25, 29, 96, 102, 107, 112, 150, 182, Jas. 96, Jno. 79, 96, 102, 107, 112, 146, 150, 170, 183, Leon 142, Marg't 13, 36, 37, Mary 13, Rob't 25, 37, 39, Sam'l 107, Thos. 137, 142, 146, 150, Wm. 112.
Prichard, Eliz., 28, Rebecca, Roger 21, 28, 40, 51, Sarah 40.
Prill, Ann, Cath., Jno., 154.
Prindle, Ann, Parrott, 107, 299, Eliz., 299.
Priest, Cath., 42, 81, Eliz., Wm. 42.
Priestnall, Eliz., 53, Geo. 23, Jacob 90, Martha 80, Mary 90.
Prill, Ann, 107, 154, 299, Cath. 154, Eliz. 299, Jno. 154, Perrott 107.
Probert, Ann, 65, 67, Hannah 55, 65, 67, 79, 81, Mary 79, Simon 179, Wm. 55, 65, 67, 79, 177.
Pryor, Ann, 287, Fra. 283, Jno. 203, 287, Major 287, Mildred 199, 283, Wm. 199, 283.
Pudduck, Eliz., 180.
Pullen, Thos., 39.
Purcel, Henry, Mary, Wm., 153.
Purify, Thos., 36, 37.
Purton, Jno., 179.
Purvis, Alice, 85, 88, Geo. 92, Henry 99, John 31, 33, 82, 87, 88, 92, 99, Mary 177, Rob't 99, Winifred 88, 92, 99, 174.

333

Putman, Ann, 127, Jno. 112, Henry, Sarah, 112, 127.
Quarles, Jno., 302.
Quidley, Patrick, Thompson, 48.
Radford, Ann, Mary, 84, Edw'd 82, 84, Thos. 29, 31.
Rattenig, Sarah, Wm., 79.
Ramage, Alex., 199, Eliz. 35.
Ranes, Frances, John, 196.
Ranger, Eliz, 181.
Ranstead, Mary, 176.
Ratford, Jas., Mary, 149.
Rawlings, Jeremiah, Peter, Eliza., 40.
Ray, Eliz., 94, 172, Gabriel 94.
Reade, Alex., 288, Chas, 282, Ed. 303, Eliz., 184, 282, 288, Fra. 157, Geo. 183, Jno. 140, 142, 157, 169, 170, 183, 191, 237, 274.
Reader, Benj., 193.
Reagin, Cath., 103, Fra. 97, John, Prudence, 92, 97, 103.
Reardon, Honour, 80.
Reed, Ann, Edw'd, Michael 141, Nancy 303.
Reenes, Mary, Thos. 10.
Reeveer, Isaac, 303.
Reeves, 11.
Renand, Honor., Leonard, 149.
Reningham, Wm., 208.
Rennall, Honor, 64, Rich'd 64, 69.
Ress, Daniell, John, Susannah, 43.
Reymey, Ann, Barnard, Wm., 16.
Reynolds, Eliz., Honour, 77, Rich. 22, 77.
Reynor, Ann, 33.
Rhodes or Rodes, Alice, 34, 46, 82, Ann 76, 99, 104, 108, 112, 116, 118, 119, 123, 125, 155, 194, Benj. 104, 143, 201, 287, Dorothy 285, Chr. 130, Eliz. 27, 42, 44, 47, 59, 65, 112, 185, 278, 304, Geo. 94, Hannah 113, 116, 130, 192, Hezekiah 23, 27, 34, 43, 76, 108, 112, 113, 119, 152, 172, 176, 186, 298, Isaac 112, 192, Jemima 138, 195, Jacob 194, 287, Jas. 59, 140, Jno. 81, 99, 104, 108, 112, 118, 123, 152, 158, 170, 194, 195, 287, 298, Mary 27, 47, 82, 94, 152, 155, 158, 195, 287, 298, Randolph 118, 138, 143, 169, 195, Sarah 118, 138, 143, 191, 195, 285, Seth 65, Susan 119, 186, Wm. 46, 47, 113, 116, 123, 130, 140, 179, 197.
Rice, Ann, 51, 114, Archibald 202, Barsheba 298, Cath. 109, 114, Jacob 100, 108, 114, 116, 286, 298, Eliz. 100, 108, 116, 138, Hannah 100, 298, Jno. 109, 125, 138, 182, Mary 125, 138, 170, Nelson 286, Nichs. 29, 51, Wm. 116, Winifrid 286.
Richans, ———, 37.
Richardson, Chas., 77, 82, Jas., Eliza 77, Martha 18.
Richeson, Eliz., 208, Geo., Mary, Wm. 153, Jno. 304.
Right, Eliz., Thos., Rosamond, 125.
Ridley, Hugh, 187.
Ridgway, Agatha, 117, Ann 40, 50, 117, 122, 185, Eliz. 40, Henrietta 171, Jno. 50, 117, 122.
Riley, Ann, 88, 190, Eliz. 206, Jno. 88, 109, Mary 88, 109, Mildred 176, Stephen 190, Wm. 195.
Rily, Jno., Mary, 95, 116, Mildred 95, Stephen 116.
Riseing, John, Eliza, Wm., Elizabeth, 13.
Roach, ———, 129, 140, 145, 150, Ann 192, Dorothy 129, 187, Eliz. 76, Hugh 76, 82, 104, 129, 140, 145, 150, 192, Judith 145, Martha 192, Mary 104, Rebecca 76, 98, 104, 140, 182, Wm. 98.
Roan, Alex., 169, Ann 130, 156, 158, 159, 298, Chas. 156, 158, 159, 298, Fra. 286, 304, Harriet 304, Jas. 186, Lucy 205, 281, Nancy 208, Sarah 198, 286, P. 304, Thos. 171, Wm. 180, 286.
Robbeck, Jas., 179.
Rober, Thos., 35.
Roberts, Ann, 16, Eliz. 70, Gabriel 16, 63, 70, Griffith 16, Isabel 23, 26, 76, Jno. 65, 71, Mary 65, 70, 71, 73, 76, 80, 174, Robt. 22, 26, Sarah 70, Thos. 26, 54, 63, 65, 304, Ursula 35, Walter 63, Willett 71, 73, 174.
Robin, Ursule, 204.
Robinson, Agatha, 7, Ann 8, 13, 23, 39, 71, 124, 131, 138, 143, 147, 153, 304, 305, Benj. 143, 181, Bev. 112, Bridg't 23, Cath. 60, 64, 70, 71, 73, 76, 112, 138, 183, 204, Chas. 303, 305, Chr. 7, 35, 39, 40, 53, 60, 63, 70, 89, 93, 96, 101, 137, 138, 140, 143, 146, 147, 153, 184, 190, 305, Clara 41, 80, Eliz. 138, 190, 208, 286, Fra. 70, 89, 299, Hannah 131, 188, Henry 99, Jno. 60, 64, 73, 76, 93, 112, 143, 147, 159, 204, 299, 303, Joseph 76, Judith 89, 96, 101, 143, 177, 287, Lucy 140, 190, Mary 70, 140, 143, 147, 179, 190, 198, Nancy 207, Needles 204, 205, Peter 101, 287, Rich. 8, 13, 31, 43, 81, Sarah 147, 159, 200, 281, 286, 287, Thos. 71, 124, 198, 206, Theo. 40, 53, Ursula 280, Wm. 73, 96, 124, 131, 138, 143, 153, 188, 201, 204, 281, 286, 305.

Rogers, Jno., 140, Humphrey 146, Mary, Robt. 140, 146, Wm. 31.
Rootes, Anne, 203.
Ross, Andrew, 12, 25, Ann 202, Betsey 171, Fra. 205, Jas. 25, Jno. 20, Mary 12, 25, Sarah 188, Thos. 12.
Rowe, Anne, 115, Benj., 103, 108, Cath. 46, 93, 175, Dorothy 115, Eliz. 27, Jas. 103, 177, Jno. 93, 146, 181, Joseph 146, Lyne 199, Martha 201, Mary 27, 103, 108, 146, Ruth 108, Thos. 27, Wm. 46.
Royston, Thos., Eliz., 205.
Russell, Ann, 118, Eliz. 23, Jas. 118, 192.
Rudolph, Geo., 202.
Rumage, Alex., 198.
Ryder, Grace, 8, 26, Jno. 20, 26, Henry 8, Mary 26.
Ryell, Jennett, 80.
Ryon, Wm., 80.

Sackerman, Sarah, 20.
Sadler, Alice, 283, Anne 159, Eleanor 38, 50, Eliz. 26, 113, Jane 123, Jno. 84, 113, 117, 123, 129, 189, 203, 283, Mary 113, 117, 123, 129, 159, Mildred 283, Rachel 204, Rich'd 38, Sam'l 26, Sarah 26, Wm. 38, 50, 159, 180.
Salt, Jane, Humphrey, 40, Thos. 40, 82.
Salter, Joane, Jno., 26, Sarah 23, 26, Thos. 82.
Sanders or Saunders, Alex., 127, Ann 91, 94, 106, 113, 145, 205, Ave. 280, Benj. 187, Betty 204, Christain 127, 130, 145, 157, 159, 196, Chrissy 171, 200, Clem 8, Edw'd 13, 23, 35, 42, 72, 76, 81, 84, 85, 91, 96, 101, 103, 109, 155, 174, 285, Eliz. 13, 76, 92, 96, 101, 103, 109, 117 127, 157, 159, 185, 203, Geo. 42, 91, 94, 106, 113, 185, 199, 207, Hannah 199, Jacob 171, Jno. 76, 81, 92, 96, 101, 103, 107, 117, 127, 153, 157, 280, 304, Judith 106, Lucretia 141, Mary 8, 42, 72, 76, 82, 107, 127, 155, 186, 195, 199, Nath. 157, 196, Rebecca 285, Sarah 72, 96, 127, 157, 206, 208, 280, Susan 127, Thos. 72, 107, 127, 130, 141, 145, 157, 159, 187, 192, 196, 280, Wm. 107, 113, 117, 127, 141, 188, 192, 201.
Sandersee, John, 28.
Sandford, Eliz., 24, Fra. 76, John 24, 28, 174, Mary 76, Sarah 24, 28, Wm. 28, 76.
Sandeford, Ed., Geo., 42, Jno. 41, 42, 43, 44, 84, Mary 42, 43, 172, Sarah 41, 43, 44, Susan 35, Wm. 82.
Santo, Ocany, 195, Wm. 184.
Saserson, Isaac, 21.

Savage, Wm., 184.
Sayre, Jane, 198, Mary 161, Sam'l 281.
Scandent, Marg't, 184.
Scanland, John, Keziah, 119.
Scarbrough, Augustine, 21, 26, 28, Dorothy 26, 28, Fra. 43, 47, Mary 26, 28, Merora 43, Wm. 38, 47.
Scinco, Anne, 83.
Scott, Delphos, 202.
Scrosby, Ann, 200, Dorothy 204, Eliz. 149, 202, Jas. 149.
Seager or Seger, Ann, 95, 102, 107, 115, 121, 127, 147, 182, Cath. 17, 102, Henry 117, Jane 109, 112, 126, 130, 170, Jno. 28, 121, 130, 137, 172, 197, Josiah 109, Judith 126, Marg't 137, 189, Mary 15, 17, 25, 28, 40, 41, 53, 196, 197, 282, Oliver 25, 109, 112, 117, 121, 130, 137, 189, Pen, Polly 161, Prisc. 201, Randolph 15, 17, 25, 28, 38, 39, 41, 53, 191, 195, 196, Rich. 282, 304, Thos. 147, 171, 196, 197, 282, Wm. 40, 83, 95, 102, 107, 115, 121, 127, 147, 161, 190, 193, 196, 208, Winifred 15.
Sears, Betty, 121, Constant 169, Edw'd 178, Eliz. 148, Fra. 116, 194, Henry 97, 148, 150, 157, 161, 170, 286, Jane 148, 150, 157, 161, 286, Jno. 121, 208, Jos. 88, 93, 97, 103, 107, 116, 129, 193, Mary 18, 88, 93, 97, 103, 107, 112, 116, 121, 129, 148, 150, 157, 161, 200, 286, Nancy 303, Nichs. 170, Phil., Sarah 304, Thos. 103, 129, 303, Violetta 86, 93.
Selaman, Chas., Esther, Owen, 69.
Serd, Eliz., 153, John, Susanna, 149, 153.
Serdsborow, Frances, Wm., 54.
Seward, Ann, 199, 202, 299, Benj. 199, 304, Bernard 159, Cath. 187, 207, Eliz. 197, Jno. 159, 200, 299, 302, Lucy 199, Susan 159, 299.
Shackleford, Fra., 280, Jas. 35, Jno. 203, Robinson 202, Rose 207, Wm. 201.
Shakpurr, Sam'l, 176.
Shanks, Jno., 191.
Sharlott, Eliz., 84.
Sharpe, Mary 26, Samuel 22, Thos. 26.
Shaw, Ann, 146, Mary, Thos., 50, 138, 146, Wm. 138, 208.
Sheeres, Jno., 20.
Sheffield, Wm., 22.
Shelton, Benj, 115, Cath. 104, Crispin 87, 104, 140, Dan'l 126, Jas. 21, Jno. 110, Letitia 140, Mary 21, 87, 90, 96, 104, 110, 115, 126, 146, 150, 154, 175, 194, Micajah 154, Peter 34, Ralph 87, 90, 96, 104, 110, 115,

335

126, 189, Reuben 96, Susan 34, Thos. 146, 150, 154, 194, Wm. 140.
Shepherd, Ann, 57, Cath. 201, 284, Fra. 53, Geo. 302, Henry 160, 194, 207, 285, 299, 300, Jno. 8, 53, Josie 207, Mary 57, 81, 284, 302, Nancy 160, 206, Sam'l 194, Tabitha 160, 285, 299, 300. Wm. 29, 300.
Shibley, Herodias, 81.
Shiprel, Milecent, Tabitha, 155.
Shippey, Lettice, 24, 63, Mary 24, 33, Rich'd 24.
Shore, Eliz., 115, Grace 9, Henry 115, Joan 9, Jno. 115, 186, Mary 12, Thos. 9, 12.
Shorter, Eliz., Jno., Henry, 115.
Shurley, Aba., 61, Ann 61, 62, 81, Judith 77, 177, Marg't 62, Rich'd 61, Thos. 61, 185.
Sibley, Ann, 66, 68, Benson 159, 197, Dan'l 170, 197, Eleanor 68, Eliz. 81, 159, Grace 46, Jno. 46, 54, 184, Lucy 103, Mildred 198, Susanna 197, Thos. 68, 159, 208.
Siddean, Ed., 176.
Sidom, Ann, Edw'd, 60, 66, Sarah 60.
Silvester, Alice, 84.
Simons, Ann, Eliz., Tho., 48.
Sims, Geo., 209.
Simpson, John, 39, Mary 22, 23, Sam'l 31.
Sinah, John, Joseph, Wm., 287.
Sitterne, Edw'd, 36, Jane 37.
Skipwith, Ann, 29, 56, Eliz. 115, 182, Fuller 105, Henry 89, Robt. 77, Reuben 85, Sarah, 77, 96, 185, Wm. 56, 66, 89, 96, 105, 115.
Slauter, Eliza, 35, Jno. 8.
Slawter, Eliz., Jno., Margarett, 27.
Slaves, births of, and owners of, 161, 209, 257, 272, 280, 305, 313, deaths 272 et seq.
Smith, Abigail, 69, Agatha 183, Alex. 36, 108, 183, Allen 7, Amey 9, Ann 14, 20, 21, 56, 58, 69, 76, 87, 88, 92, 94, 97, 98, 103, 104, 108, 110, 112, 113, 116, 118, 123, 143, 151, 190, 193, Anthony 14, 21, 108, 196, Arthur 46, 69, Benj. 147, Cath. 20, 77, 122, 156, 159, 283, 298, Cary 94, 151, Clara 113, Col. 198, Diana 116, Ed. 193, Elinor 46, Eliz. 15, 17, 26, 45, 50, 56, 77, 112, 113, 119, 122, 126, 137, 143, 147, 151, 190, Esther 201, Fra. 97, 98, 126, 156, 181, 200, 201, 286, 290, Geo. 284, Gregory 87, Henry 77, 88, Jacob 55, Jas. 56, 58, 69, 94, 103, 110, 184, 186, 283, 284, 286, 298, Jane 40, 92, 107, 169, 298, Jno. 8, 10, 26, 56, 76, 88, 92, 97, 98, 103, 107, 108, 113, 116, 118, 119, 122, 123, 126, 151, 156, 159, 174, 180, 185, 190, Judith 151, Keziah 137, Marg't 9, 10, 22, 76, 198, Martha 123, Mary 23, 46, 69, 88, 151, 184, 208, 284, 286, 298, Maurice 123, Michael 81, 94, Oswald 110, Rachel 103, 120, 157, Ralph 9, Randolph 50, Rebecca 35, 88, Robt. 15, 36, 37, 45, 55, 159, Ruth 56, 122, Sam'l 36, 37, Sarah 69, 92, 94, 113, 157, 202, 208, South 157, Thos. 15, 17, 18, 26, 54, 56, 57, 84, 85, 87, 98, 104, 108, 112, 119, 181, 189, Unity 88, Wm. 21, 103, 182, 199.
Snelling, Alex., 95, 147, 169, Ann 145, 147, Aquilla 95, 106, 113, 119, 125, 130, 137, 145, 178, 187, 192, Benj. 137. Eliz. 130, 187, Henry 125, 141, 147, Jane 147, Joan 141, 147, Marg't 130, 137, 145, 192, Mary 95, 106, 113, 119, 125, 147, 187, Prisc. 81, 119, Sarah 81.
Snodgrass, David, 170, 286, Hannah 286, Nathan 147.
Snow, Eliz., Cuthbert, Wm., 284.
Sommers, Sarah, 207.
Sords, Jno., Susan, 299, Wm. 282.
Sorrow, Mary, 141, 169, Sam'l 141.
Souldier, Rich'd, Bishop, 21.
South, Andrew, 91, 160, Eliz. 91, 304, Geo. 297, Jane 281, Jno. 91, 160, 181, 304, Rachel 160, 297, Smith 297.
Southern, Agnes, 193, 304, Averilla 148, Ed. 158, 286, Benj. 130, Cath. 66, Eliz. 286, 298, Jane 158, Jno. 111, 118, 123, 130, 148, 186, 189, 280, 299, Jas. 123, 189, Marg't 111, 123, 130, Mary 140, 148, 151, 158, 286, 298, Sarah 151, Susan 118, Wm. 111, 140, 151, 298.
Southward, John, Mary, 40, Wm. 37, 40.
Southworth, Ann, 110, 111, 114, 115, 118, 121, Cath. 79, 125, Eliz. 125, 172, 180, Grace 180, Jas. 115, Jno. 110, 114, 118, 121, Marg't 79, 177, Thos. 114, Wm. 79, 85, 115, 125.
Sovlt, Ann, Thos., 195.
Sparkes, Benjamine, 86, Jno., Mary, Wm. 96.
Spann, Mary, 203, Thos. 280.
Spencer, Ann, 105, 207, Fra. 280, Jeremiah 304, Jno. 303, Judith 29, 33, 107, Mary, Sam'l 107, Thos. 53, 206.
Spratt, Charlotte, 204, Robt. 200.
Stacy, Eliza, 15, 27, Thos. 15, 27, 36.
Stake, Rose, 18.
Stalker, Richard, 204, Wm. 7.
Stamper, Cary, 86, 176, Dorcas 10, Eliz. 8, 12, 208, Geo. 200, Jas. 170, Jno. 8, 10, 12, 23, 89, 102, 140, 144,

148, 153, 156, 159, 192, Leon 196, Letitia 113, Mary 86, 89, 96, 102, 113, 159, 169, Mildred 196, 199, 200, Nelson 303, Powell 81, 86, 89, 96, 102, 113, 120, 140, 185, 192, Paul 96, Robt. 140, 196, 199, 303, Sam'l 199, 303, Sarah 140, 144, 148, 153, 156, 159, 192, Susan 96.
Stanard, Ann, 84, 86, Bev. 109, Eliz. 102, 106, 109, 113, Eltonhead 14, 39, Sarah 14, Wm. 14, 81, 84, 86, 106, 109, 176, 188.
Stanly, Jonathan, 18, Mary 30, Rebecca 30, 36, Thos. 30.
Stapleton, Ann, 52, Eliz. 116, 140, Fra. 25, 28, 40, 103, Geo. 28, 178, Jane 64, Jno. 25, Joyce 116, Lucy 140, 194, Marg't 63, Mary 64, 103, Thos. 25, 28, 40, 52, 64, 103, Wm. 140.
Staunton, Jane, Jno., 70, Theo. 63, 65, 70.
Stedman, Fra., 206.
Stevens, Absalom, 157, Ann 82, 146, 170, Benj. 201, Ed. 200, Eliz. 152, 157, 191, 200, 204, Fra. 146, Hugh 188, Isaac 304, Jno. 91, 146, 169, 200, 203, Judith 200, 282, Lewis 200, 282, Mabel 131, 142, Mary 28, 63, 146, 200, Morris 107, Nath. 152, Prisc. 194, Robt. 7, Rich. 54, 91, 96, 100, 107, 113, 131, 142, 146, 152, 157, Sarah 54, 182, Susan 282.
Steptoe, Jas., 161, Sarah 303, Wm. 208.
Stewart, Amy, 92, Cath. 107, Chas. 114, Jane 92, 99, 107, 188, John 92, 99, 107, 114, 158, 185, 187, 188, 299, Martha 158, 299, Wm. 208.
Stiff, Ann, 91, Betty 200, 281, 283, Constantine 81, Edy 125, Eliz. 42, 87, 91, 97, 101, 107, 111, 117, 122, 125, 128, 175, 281, 302, Jacob 30, 81, 87, 91, 97, 101, 107, 111, 117, 122, 128, 188, 194, 195, Jas. 59, 170, 200, 201, 281, 283, 285, Jno. 97, 125, 171, 174, 200, 283, 303, Mary 195, 208, 280, Nancy 302, Nich. 42, Ruth 122, 188, Sarah 30, 81, 101, 170, 171, 285, 305, Thos. 23, 30, 42, 59, 87, 107, 117, 174, 179, 283, 302, Wm. 128, 171, 282, 285, 302, 305.
Still, Eloner, 179, Eliz. 48, Thos. 48, 172, 179.
St. John, Wm., 303.
Stodix, Eliz., 201.
Stone, Job, 204, Jno. 35.
Stradford, Eliz., Mary, 13.
Straughan, Cath., 64, 66, 70, 88, 94, Crispin 94, 303, Ed. 88, Mary 70, Rich. 63, 64, 66, 70, 88, 94, Thos. 64.

Street, Cath., 146, 151, 157, Mary 157, Rich. 146, 151, 157, Thos. 304.
Stringer, Clara, 199, Hannah 151, 154, 158, 161, 170, 285, 300, Lucy 158.
Stubbs, Martha, 281.
Suckling, Ann, 18.
Summers, Eliz., 24, 30, 40, 55, 180, Fra. 55, Jno. 24, 30, 40, Marg't 18, 68, Wm. 68.
Sutton, Ann, 26, 299, Beamont 96, Benj. 120, 187, Cath., 61, Chr. 14, 61, 63, 65, 69, 77, 90, 96, 104, 111, 116, 120, 192, Dorothy 24, Ed. 61, Eliz. 14, 26, 43, 63, 65, 206, Hope 65, 69, 77, 86, 90, 96, 104, 111, 116, 120, 125, Jno. 14, 26, 61, 77, 208, Lucy 303, Mary 199, 204, Michal 125, Nancy 182, 201, Nathan 116, Wm. 104, 299.
Sturman, Robt., 170.
Swepstone, Jane, 82, Mary 169.
Swift, Eliz., 50, 53, Jno. 37, 50, Paul 50.
Swords, Eliz., 202, Henry 205.

Taff, Anne, 205, Eliz. 189, Mary 171.
Taliaferro, Mercy, 257, Jno. 170.
Tarpley, Lucy, 201.
Tarrell, Mary, Robt., 66.
Tatum, Isham, 202.
Taylor, Ann, 18, 23, 199, Benj. 181, Betty 302, Cath. 197, Chr. 109, Eli 303, Eliz. 298, Fra. 52, 286, Honor 105, Jane 52, 121, Jno. 286, 298, Kitty 283, Mary 283, 286, Rachel 197, 199, Rich. 105, 109, Robt. 11, Wm. 197, 199, 201.
Teel, Eliz., 23.
Tegnall, Thos., 84.
Tenoe, Ann, 159, 284, 286, Stephen 159, 284, 286, Thos. 201.
Terrill, Eliz., 79, Mary 82.
Terry, Eliz., 192, Wm. 27.
Thacker, ——, 10, Alice 11, 37, Ann 73, 85, 124, Chich. 12, 73, 131, 188, Ed. 11, 61, 101, 104, 108, 111, 115, 119, 124, 131, 138, 139, 176, 187, 188, 191, Eliz. 28, 61, 82, 84, 101, 104, 108, 111, 115, 119, 124, Eltonhead 11, 12, Fra. 45, 61, 101, 111, 117, 188, Henry 11, 12, 45, 73, 108, Jno. 61, Lettice, Martha 11, 22, 23, 73, Mary 108.
Thackston, Eliz., 23, Rich'd 28, 39.
Thilman, Eliz., 169, Fra. 64, Jane 114, 128, 187, Jno. 180, Paul 37, 62, 64, 84, 114, 128, 187, Rich. 128, Sarah 64, 114.
Thomas, Anne, 15, 92, Ancoretta 15, Arthur 82, 100, 108, 113, 120, 195, Chas. 110, 116, Eliz. 108, Jno. 10, 116, 182, Marg't 21, Mary 92, 100, 108, 113, 120, Robt. 15, 18, Susan 110, 116, Wm. 113.

Thompson, Cath., 109, 115, 187, Ed. 10, Eliz. 25, 63, Grace 33, 45, 101, 179, Jane 109, 130, 183, Jno. 109, 115, 124, 130, 142, 147, Marg't 17, Mary 22, 45, 53, 116, 180, 184, 287, Robt. 11, Rich. 147, Sam'l 45, 287, Sarah 45, 82, 106, 142, 178, Susan 124, 130, 142, 147, Thos. 21, 25, 43, 81, 116, Wm. 20, 31, 33, 45, 101, 104, 106, 116.
Thornton, Thos., 81.
Thruston, Ann, 141, 155, Batch. 205, Benj. 141, 192, Betty 281, Cath. 286, Duel 141, Eliz. 121, 124, 141, 158, 170, 186, 197, 199, 286, Fra. 127, 139, 145, 151, 155, 158, 203, 207, 281, Henry 139, 142, 197, 198, 199, Jane 142, 145, 197, Jno. 121, 124, 141, 145, 208, 281, 286, Jos. 190, Judith 141, Ruth 124, 184, Sam'l 171, Wm. 121, 127, 139, 142, 145, 151, 155, 158, 190, 197, 199.
Tidbury, Jno., 22.
Tight, Eliz., 63.
Tignor, Dorothy, 26, 34, 99, Mary 26, Prisc. 89, 99, Thos. 170, Wm. 20, 26, 34, 39, 89, 99, 147, 178.
Tilley, Anne, Phoebe 104, Thos. 104, 176.
Timberlake, Eliz., 104, Fra. 104, 113, 121, 184, Hannah 201, Joanna 103, Jos. 103, 176, Jno. 183, Rich. 121, Sarah 104, 121.
Timberlin, Eliz., Mary, 91, Jos. 87, 91.
Tindall, Cary, Rich'd, Peter, 52.
Tinny, John, Joice, 89, 113, Mary 89.
Tisher, Polly, 208.
Tool, Judith, 208.
Torksey, Eliz., 13, Philip 13, 22.
Tosely, Eliza, 16, 81, Tho. 16.
Towerd, Malcolme, 181.
Towles, Ann, 95, 102, 107, 113, 119, 123, 129, 141, 170, Cath. 107, Eliz. 95, Fra. 129, Hannah 75, Henry 75, Jno. 143, 169, Judith 141, Marg't, Oliver 143, Stokely 75, 95, 102, 107, 113, 119, 123, 129, 141.
Townley, Robt., 203.
Townsend, Cassandra, 42, Damaris 56, 70, Eliz. 70, Fra. 42, 82, Jas. 56, Jno. 56, 70, Thos. 42.
Toy, Mary, 44, 180, Phil., Sarah 44.
Tracy, Timothy, 53.
Trench, Cath., Mary, 147, Thos. 147, 192.
Trice, Edward, 203.
Trigg, ——, 26, Abra. 26, 68, 72, 80, 82, 86, 88, 94, 102, 175, Alice 53, Dan'l 26, 30, 33, 86, 88, Eliz. 68, 72, Judith 86, 88, 94, 102, Mary 68, Rich. 33, Sarah 30, 33, 80, Susan 30, 86.

Trueman, Ann, Geo., 299, Robt. 147, 299, Susan 147.
Tucker, Fra., 304, Jno. 208.
Tugwell, Alice, 9, Ann 12, 29, 105, Benj. 111, 158, 299, Cath. 120, 125, 140, 143, 145, 152, 156, 158, Eliz. 92, 98, 105, 110, 111, 117, 182, 197, Fra. 60, 209, Griffin 145, 171, Henry 12, 52, 53, 60, 64, 82, 92, 98, 105, 110, 111, 116, 117, 126, 144, 189, 192, 194, Jane 158, Jno. 64, 116, 120, 125, 140, 143, 145, 152, 158, 189, 191, Jos. 144, 149, 153, 192, 195, 197, Lodowick 153, Lucretia 81, Mary 9, 12, 52, 60, 64, 81, 110, 116, 120, 126, 144, 149, 153, 189, 192, 201, Nichs. 143, 191, 201, Rachel 12, Sarah 153, 284, 304, Tabitha 125, Thos. 9, 12, 98, 153, 156, 158, 195, 288, 299, Wm. 81, 117, 145.
Tuke, Thos., 186.
Tuydey, Eliz., 14.
Tuyman, Agatha, 117, 122, 126, 131, 169, Cath. 55, 79, 126, Eliz. 117, 185, Geo. 117, 122, 126, 131.
Tyler, Jno., 193, Mary 170.
Tyre, Jane, Rachel, 105, Thos. 170.
Twyman, Kath., Geo., 55.

Underwood, Diana, 54, 67, 71, 76, 87, 162, Eliz. 67, Jno. 54, 67, Nathan 54, 67, 71, 76, 87, Ruth 76, Thos. 87, 174.
Upshaw, Ed., 281.
Upton, Marg't, 79.
Uric, Ann, 159, Constant 156, 159, 287, Jacob 287, Jno. 156, 159, 287, 298, Wm. 156.
Uris, Agnes, Constance, John, 151.

Valentine, Eliz., 207, Jacob, Jno., Sarah 298.
Vallott, Ann, 40, 51, 53, 81, Cath. 40, Claud. 40, 51, 53.
Vance, Marg't, 302.
Vass, Cath., 206.
Vaughan, Martha, 207, Mary 27, 107, Thos. 22, 27, Wm. 27, 83, 107.
Vause, ——, 9, Agatha 39, 81, Constance 29, 33, Jno. 18, 22, 36, 39, Martha 257.
Vickars, Benoni, Jno., Ruth, 110.
Vivion, Diana, 80, Eliz. 90, 97, 100, 102, 174, 175, 188, Fra. 100, 181, Jno. 25, 63, 82, 90, 97, 100, 102, 169, Margaret 25, 63.
Volve, Thos., 85.
Vinte, Mary, 24.
Vynn, Jeremy, 36, 37.

Wacham, Jno., 84.

Wadding, Thos., 24.
Wait, Ann, 68, Charity 90, Eliz. 151, Geo. 155, Jndith 193, Robt. 185, Rich. 80, 90, 151, 155, 182, 185, 193, Sarah 151, 155, 193.
Wake, Ambrose, 284, Ann 208, 284, Chr. 207, Eliz. 155, Joanna 302, Jno. 87, 197, Johnson 171, 204, Judith 197, Hamstead 197, Mary 87, Michal 155, Ransom 197, Rich. 87, Robt. 155, 206, 284, Rosanna 303.
Wakefield, Betty, 189, Wm. 20.
Walcom, Jno., 21.
Waldin, Avirilla, 192. Benj. 207, Chas. 205, Jno. 257, Lewis 206, 207, 257, Nancy 304.
Walerton, Eliza, 22.
Wallford, Ed., 81.
Walkell, Mary, 80.
Walker, Amy, 113, 122, 129, Ann 113, 204, Caroline 129, Cath. 85, 86, 139, 192, Chas. 52, 113, Clara 86, 145, Eliz. 113, Geo. 113, 122, 129, 189, Hugh 304, Jas. 80, 105, 121, 178, 188, Jno. 138, 145, 195, Mary 52, 122, 202, Robt. 113, 180, Rich. 184, Sarah 139, Thos. 178, Wm. 86.
Waller, Eliz., 13, Jno. 13, 303, Sarah 207, Susan 205, Wm. 13.
Wallace, Ann, 35, 43, 46, 69, Betty 125, 131, 152, 156, 194, Cath. 24, Dorothy 43, Eliz. 147, 152, Jane 69, Jno. 131, Josiah 147, Lucy 156, 207, Mary 23, 47, 80, Sam'l 152, Val. 24, 46, Wm. 43, 46, 69, 131, 147, 156.
Walters, Cath., John, Wm., 28.
Walton, Geo., 37.
Ward, Ann, Thos., 298, Eliz. 30, Susan 98.
Ware, Cath., 202, 205, Eliz. 208, Fra. 257, Hen. 82, Isaac 199, Jas. 200, Polly 207, Wm. 201.
Warner, Mary, 83, Sam'l 181.
Warren, Rich'd, 181.
Warwick, Abra., 147, Agatha 147, 148, 150, 151, Cassandra 144, 156, Cath. 68, 84, 88, 95, Eliz. 77, 86, 151, 170, Geo. 148, 201, Jane 84, 201, Jno. 86, 95, 147, 151, 156, 169, 195, Mary 88, 95, 178, Pen. 66, Phil. 68, 79, 88, 95, 144, 148, 150, 156, 169, 175, 182, 195, Sarah 86, Thos. 68, 77, 79, 82, 95, 144, 191, Wm. 150.
Washington, Ann, Henry, John, 287.
Watkins, Eliz., 197, Humphrey 197, 199.
Watliss, Eliz., Wm., 56.
Watson, Presilla, William, 9, Geo. 36, Mary 304, Rich. 257, Wm. 7.

Watts, Agatha, 69, 98, Cath. 98, Ed. 206, Eliz. 42, 90, 98, 105, 107, 116, 189, Hannah 42, 69, 192, Hugh 22, 26, 34, 38, 42, 69, 178, Jane 8, 11, 90, 142, 170, 180, Johanna 26, 34, 38, Jno. 8, 39, 83, 84, 90, 98, 129, 140, 170, 176, 180, Mary 26, 39, 142, Ralph 11, 82, 98, 107, 116, 118, 204, Rich. 129, Sarah 8, 18, 129, 181, Wm. 34, 142, 190, Winifred 23.
Waycomb, John, Eliz., 53.
Weathers, Jno., 20.
Weatherby, Alice, Tho., Marg't, 8.
Weatherstone, Eliz., 15, Marg't 24, Thos. 15, 24.
Weaver, Kath., 20.
Webb, Anne, 82, Cath. 208, Fra. 26, 35, Isaac 82, Jas. 20, 26, Mary 104, Milly 203, Tilly 204, Wm. 177, 207.
Weekes, Abra., 10, 97, Cath. 10, Eliz. 25, 33, 36, 78, Fra. 25, 33, 58, Hobbs 33, 78, 80, 87, 91, 97, Lettice 53, Marg't 22, Mary 78, 81, 87, 91, 97, Millicent 10, 87, Thos. 25, 91.
Weight, Cath., Henry, 118.
Welch, ——, 9, Eliz., Marg't 11, Mary 18.
West, Geo., 202.
Weston, Ann, 18, 120, 185, 186, Eliz. 120, 123, 126, 129, Geo. 202, 206, Hannah 19, Jno. 19, 120, 123, 126, 129, 186, Mary 129, Nich. 19.
Weyanoke, ——, 288.
Weybole, Barbary, 18.
Wharton, Abra., 119, 125, 131, 139, 191, Eliz. 125, John 139, Mary 119, 125, 131, 139, 170, Rebecca 119, Wm. 131.
Wharry, Robt., 182.
Whately, Jno., 80.
Wheatherstone, Marg't, 63.
Wheeler, Ellinor, 27, 34, Mark 105, Prisc. 27, Sarah 105, Thos. 27, Wm. 82, 105.
Whelling, Caleb, Eliz., 53.
Whistler, Anne, 92, Mary 92, 177.
White, Eliz., 27, 29, 143, Fra. 155, Jas. 27, Jno. 143, 155, 169, Jos. 143, Thos., 27, 85, Wm. 184.
Whitely, John, 206.
Whiting, Mary, 205.
Whitlock, James, Jno., Marg't, 56.
Whittacre, Ann, 126, Chas. 42, 122, 184, 201, 204, 300, Ed. 42, 122, 126, 151, 156, 161, 184, 300, Eliz. 122, 126, 151, 156, 161, 184, 300, Marg't 42, Mary 161, Prisc. 300, Robt. 79, Thos. 151, 184, Wm. 39.
Whitters, Precilla, 200.
Wiatt, ——, 303, Jas. 302, Jno. 201, Pitman 208, Thos. 204.

Wignall, John, 176.
Wilburn, Marg't, 170.
Wilbuton, Ann, 11.
Wilcox, Ann, 146, 171, Eliz. 81, Fra. 146, Isaac 171, Jno. 146, Mary 305, Martha 204, Nancy 171, Sally 305.
Wilkerson, Ralph, 37, 53.
Wilkins, Bridg't, 120, 123, 187, Eliz. 140, 169, 284. Jas. 123, 284, Jere. 140, John 206, 284, Lucy 284, 302, Robt. 120, 123, 140, 190.
Williams, Aaron, 181, Anne 12, 27, 64, 80, 81, 89, 95, 146, 200, Benj. 127, 139, 200, 201, Billington 95, Brid't 8, 23, 127, Cath. 64, 69, 71, 127, 190, Chas. 54, 64, Ed. 9, 48, 64, 69, 71, Eliz. 23, 26, 65, 71, 77, 103, 118, 171, Elias 193, Eloner 179, Fra. 89, 177, 181, 199, 200, 297, Geo. 171, Howard 64, 198, Hugh 10, Jane 111, Jas. 15, Jno. 8, 15, 26, 29, 33, 81, 89, 95, 103, 104, 111, 118, 123, 127, 139, 150, 154, 156, 169, 189, 194, 199, 297, Jos. 95, 103, Judith 69, 71, 103, Marg't 8, 12, 79, Mary 8, 15, 104, 146, 154, 194, Micall 104, 111, 118, 123, 139, 190, Rachel 200, Rich. 8, 12, Robt. 77, 127, 146, 169, Sarah 8, 124, 144, 193, 202, Steward 198, Susan 150, 154, 156, 194, 297, Thos. 8, 9, 23, 26, 31, 48, 65, 180.
Williamson, ——, 25, Aaron, 22, Andrew 15, 42, Augustine 42, Benj. 57, 123, 182, 199, Cath. 19, 28, 38, 41, 44, 52, 57, 82, 182, Chas. 44, Clara 284, 304, Eliz. 42, 83, 101, 106, 111, 115, 123, 287, Fra. 19, 79, 101, Henry 25, Jacob 180, Marg't 15, 52, Martha 38, Mary 44, 284, 287, 298, Minor 106, 179, Owin 180, Robt. 19, 20, 41, 44, 52, 57, 111, 115, 123, 162, Wm. 29, 284, 287, 298, Winifred 25.
Willis, Bridget, 30, 52, Eliz. 53, 79, 141, Elbner 10, Isabel 30, Jno. 10, 39, 78, Martha 78, Mary 10, Oliver 141, Rich. 10, 78, 79, Thos. 201, Wm. 23, 30, 52, 141.
Wills, Ancoretta, 18, Thos. 200.
Wilson, Abra., 144, Andrew 51, Eliz. 90, 144, Isabel 51, Jno. 51, 171, Martha 144, Mary 16, 24, 171, Robt. 90, 205, Sarah 16, Thos. 16, 18, 24, 90, 205.
Willshire, Benj., 281.
Winger, Thos., 37.
Wingo, Ann, 183.
Winn, Anne, 93, Eliz. 61, Jane 78, Jno. 54, 67, Mary 46, Rich. 54, 61, 67, 78, 82, 93, Sarah 46, 54, 67, 78, Thos. 93, 172.
Winning, Niels, 206.

Wright, Ann, 18, Jno. 118, Lucy 106, Mary 112, Rose, Thos., 106, 112, 116, Wm. 121, 209.
Wisdale, Mary, 180.
Withers, Erasmus, Frances, 9.
Withnell, Chr., 10.
Wood, Ann, 17, 126, 154, 157, 166, 176, 284, 299, 300, Cath. 105, 144, 193, Chas. 140, 144, 152, 156, 190, 196, Ed. 126, Eliz. 8, 15, 17, 61, 126, 139, 144, 153, 154, 303, Hannah 284, Jane 105, 154, 159, 188, Jas. 153, 194, Jno. 61, 206, Marg't 182, Mary 15, 140, 144, 152, 156, 157, 195, 300, Rachel 156, 196, Rich., Ruth 144, Robt. 17, Sam'l 154, 157, 160, 170, 177, 194, 198, 284, 299, 300, Susan 152, 170, 177, Sarah 302, Thos. 61, 189, Wm. 8, 15, 105, 139, 144, 153, 159, 160, 162, 180, 201, 207.
Woodard, Wm. 23.
Woodgar, Martha, 20.
Woodyard, Kath., 81.
Woodley, Jno., 207.
Wooley, Ann, Geo., Sarah, 16.
Worsdell, Eliz., Mary, 87, Rich'd 20.
Workley, Cath., Benjamine, Eliz., 44.
Wortly, Cath., 82.
Wormeley, ——, 10, 82, 140, Agatha 105, 108, 176, Ann 298, Cath. 8, 15, Chr. 7, Eliz. 63, 89, 92, 99, 102, 105, 108, 114, 119, 145, Fra. 8, 22, 24, Jno. 89, 92, 99, 102, 105, 114, 119, 184, 298, Judith 24, 170, 200, Mary 102, 119, 179, 185, Ralph 8, 15, 36, 84, 92, 145, 198, Sarah 84, 89, 99, 145, 198, 304, Wm. 298.
Wortham, Ann, 89, 123, 128, 142, 144, 150, 155, Chas. 285, Constant 144, Ed. 66, 148, 192, Eliz. 12, 28, 33, 36, 37, 161, Fra. 207, Geo. 12, 42, 64, 66, 71, 89, 95, 123, 128, 142, 150, 155, 159, 186, 192, 194, 196, Jas, 95, 141, Jno. 12, 31, 33, 36, 39, 64, 128, 138, 141, 144, 148, 150, 153, 155, 159, 162, 193, 195, 196, 285, 302, Joseph 12, Judith 138, 141, 144, 148, 150, 153, 156, 159, 162, 192, 194, 195, 285, 288, Machen 144, 195, 302, 303, Marg't 12, Mary 12, 64, 66, 70, 71, 95, Oswald 12, Prudence 39, Robt. 42, Sarah 12, 64, 153, 162, 194, Thos. 150.
Wright, Rich., Sarah, 145.

Yarbrough, Eliz., 142, 146, 192, Griffin 146, Grigg 142, 169, Sarah 142.
Yarrington, Amy, 146, Ann 142, 146, Fra. 203, 284, John 142. 284, Mary 284, Olive 204, Vincent 302, Wm. 142, 146.

Yarrow, Mary, 75, 90, 99, Math. 90, Thos, 75, 90.
Yates, Anne, 200, 305, Bar. 63, 67, 69, 85, 87, 93, 94, 96, 98, 100, 106, 108, 109, 112, 114, 116, 118, 122, 124, 129, 131, 137, 139, 140, 154, 161, 175, 176, 179, 180, 181, 182, 184, 186, 187, 188, 189, 190, 198, 259, 262, 263, 265, 266, 269, 270, 272, 273, 305, Cath. 67, 69, 70, 201, 283, 304, Eliz. 161, 302, Fra. 100, 170, Harry 202, 208, 282, 283, Jane, Jas. 283, Lucy 282, Rachel 303, Robt. 93, Sarah 69, 67, 70, 87, 93, 100, 144, 154.
Yorkes, Mary, Philip, 26.

Young, Ann, 203, Dianah, Johan 14, Wm. 14, 200.
Younger, Ann, 170.
Zachary, David, 88, Eleanor, John 64, 88.

NOT CLASSIFIED.

Neale, Mary, 81.
Needles, Frances, 82.
Nicholls, Winifred, 82.
Nixson, Anne, 81.
Norman, Eliz., 82.

Shereefes, ——, 10.

www.ingramcontent.com/pod-product-compliance
Lightning Source LLC
Chambersburg PA
CBHW071153300426
44113CB00009B/1187